INTERNATIONAL RELATIONS

INTERNATIONAL RELATIONS

SECOND EDITION

ERIC B. SHIRAEV
GEORGE MASON UNIVERSITY

VLADISLAV M. ZUBOK
LONDON SCHOOL OF ECONOMICS

NEW YORK   OXFORD
OXFORD UNIVERSITY PRESS

Oxford University Press is a department of the University of Oxford.
It furthers the University's objective of excellence in research,
scholarship, and education by publishing worldwide.

Oxford   New York
Auckland   Cape Town   Dar es Salaam   Hong Kong   Karachi
Kuala Lumpur   Madrid   Melbourne   Mexico City   Nairobi
New Delhi   Shanghai   Taipei   Toronto

With offices in
Argentina   Austria   Brazil   Chile   Czech Republic   France   Greece
Guatemala   Hungary   Italy   Japan   Poland   Portugal   Singapore
South Korea   Switzerland   Thailand   Turkey   Ukraine   Vietnam

For titles covered by Section 112 of the US Higher Education
Opportunity Act, please visit www.oup.com/us/he for the
latest information about pricing and alternate formats.

Published by Oxford University Press
198 Madison Avenue, New York, New York 10016
http://www.oup.com

Oxford is a registered trademark of Oxford University Press

Library of Congress Cataloging-in-Publication Data
Shiraev, Eric, 1960-
International relations / Eric B. Shiraev, George Mason University, Vladislav M. Zubok,
London School of Economics. -- Second edition.
     pages cm
   ISBN 978-0-19-045435-7
  1. International relations. I. Title.
   JZ1242.S555   2016
   327--dc23

                                                                        2015023935

Printing number: 9 8 7 6 5 4 3 2 1

Printed in the United States of America
on acid-free paper

Brief Contents

Contents

3 The Liberal Perspective 77

4 Alternative Views 113

PART II. THREE FACETS OF INTERNATIONAL RELATIONS

CHAPTER 5 International Security 152

CHAPTER 6 International Law 185

CHAPTER 7 International Political Economy 219

8 International Terrorism 258

9 Environmental Problems and International Politics 295

CHAPTER 10 Humanitarian Challenges 332

Preface

W E WROTE THIS BOOK TO ADDRESS A NEW generation of students who have unprecedented access to global information yet need the background to fully understand and evaluate it. Statistics, video clips, tweets, maps, eyewitness reports, scholarly articles, and biographies—all are just a click away. But how can we effectively navigate through this wealth of data and opinions? We wanted to guide students through this information by paying special attention to the rigorous, critical evaluation of facts and by discussing several frameworks of analysis—at least two major tasks in teaching international relations today.

With that in mind, we designed this book to offer a consistent framework, one that helps students approach the field of international relations with an engaged, serious mindset and a critical eye. This second edition of *International Relations* builds on the success of the first and offers a more structured analysis of world events and a greater variety of pedagogical tools. We summarize major international events and developments, present contending approaches, discuss current problems and their potential solutions, and consider real-world applications of analysis. The educational tools we have built into this book will equip students not only with facts and concepts for a solid background but also with the skills for critical thinking. Students will learn to distinguish opinions from evidence-guided reasoning. We show students that the complexities of today's world are not likely to fit a single point of view. We encourage them, with the help of case studies and questions, to cross the boundaries of research traditions and think independently.

What's New in This Edition?

This thoroughly updated edition of *International Relations* reflects important discussions about today's rapidly changing world. Responding to feedback from the reviewers and users of the textbook, we have updated the discussion on main theoretical concepts, and we have added to the coverage of new security challenges, such as asymmetrical conflicts and cyberterrorism. We have also expanded the treatment of international political economy and humanitarian crises. In addition, we have offered various interpretations of more recent developments, such as the Russian-Ukrainian conflict, tensions related to China, chronic instability in the Middle East and North Africa, policies of the European Union, and the plight of refugees in many parts of the world. We are deeply thankful to all who made comments on the textbook, especially our colleagues from the field of international politics, history, foreign policy, and security studies, as well as many students who commented on this textbook's Facebook page (www.facebook.com/InternationalRelationsTextbook).

Revision highlights include:

- More advanced discussions of structural realism (Chapter 2);
- Reorganized analyses of neoliberal theories (Chapter 3);
- More thorough presentation of liberal views on war and the use of force (Chapter 3);
- Discussions of scenarios stemming from China's increasing impact on international relations (Chapters 4 and 7);
- Analyses of Russia's takeover of Crimea from Ukraine in the context of international law (Chapter 6);
- Discussions of Western sanctions on Russia (Chapter 6);
- Expanded analyses of the impact of liberal ideas on international political economy and economic development (Chapter 7);
- Discussions of the role of multinational corporations in international affairs (Chapter 7);
- Updates on "hybrid war" and asymmetrical conflicts (Chapter 8);
- Discussions of new sub-state structures such as ISIS (Chapter 8);
- Critical analyses of Islamic fundamentalism as a breeding ground for terrorism (Chapter 8).

A Consistent Learning Framework

The chapters follow a three-part framework—Ideas, Arguments, and Contexts and Applications—so that students know what to expect:

1. **Ideas.** In an engaging opening case in every chapter we introduce the chapter's main theme. Following this case, we present chapter learning objectives to focus students on the essential information to look for. Next we cover basic concepts and definitions, key facts and developments, and major international problems related to the chapter's theme.

2. **Arguments.** In the second section of each chapter we present the main frameworks and approaches used to analyze these facts, events, and problems. The book reflects a wealth of conceptual discussions, including the growing prominence of alternatives to realism and liberalism. Through real issues, case studies, and frequent questions, in this book we help students cut across research traditions to look for their own answers. In the process,

students will see that any single approach or model cannot in itself explain the complexities of today's world.

3. **Contexts and Applications.** In the third section of each chapter, we show students how to apply these approaches in individual, state, and global contexts.

In addition, each chapter closes with an extended application called **The Uses of History**, in which we consider a case in depth. These cases focus on real-life ramifications and pose new questions.

Approach

We introduce the critical thinking approach in Chapter 1 and then apply it in every chapter. Rather than merely presenting facts and theories of international relations, we show students how to explain and evaluate them critically. Emphasis on critical thinking helps students achieve at least two goals. First, it shows them how to extract more valuable, complex information from apparently simple facts or research data. Second, it teaches them to be informed skeptics.

In addition we know from experience that students need substantial context to fully understand contemporary issues and to see the relevance of an analytical framework. We therefore provide abundant examples throughout the book, many examining parallels between past and present yet considering the limits of historical analogies. This carefully integrated context not only gives students a way to frame information and make connections but also helps correct misconceptions.

Summary of Features

Chapter-opening cases provide vivid examples that set the stage for the chapter and pose framing questions.

Learning Objectives focus students on the key information to look for in each chapter. These are echoed in the Critical Thinking section of the Visual Review at the end of the chapter.

Learning Objectives	
	▶ Define the scope and aims of international relations as a discipline.
	▶ Identify major actors in international relations and the main areas in which they interact.
	▶ Recognize major challenges and problems the world is facing today.
	▶ Describe the methodology of international relations in analyzing information.
	▶ Critically analyze a case related to war and democracy.

Case in Point boxes present current or historical events and issues and contain Critical Thinking questions that can easily be used for class discussions or written assignments.

CASE IN POINT > *Fair Trade*

Fair trade (known also as *trade justice*) initiatives suggest that developed countries should agree that developing nations can sell their products, primarily agricultural goods and resources, at assured prices. Manufacturers and distributors must not use child labor, slavery, an unsafe workplace, or other forms of abuse and discrimination. *TransFair USA*, a nonprofit organization, certifies and labels products manufactured under fair trade principles. Thanks to fair trade, certified coffee, tea, cocoa, fresh fruit, rice, and sugar are all available at tens of thousands of

CRITICAL THINKING
❶ Would you support the mandatory application of fair trade principles to all food imports to the United States? Critics argue that you must then pay a higher price for food. Proponents of fair trade reply that in Norway and Germany, for example, higher food prices do not seem to devastate family budgets. ❷ Assignment: For a week, write down the price and country of origin of every food product you consume. If a product is foreign, add 10 percent to its price. (For example, if you buy a cup of Columbian coffee for $2.00, add $0.20.) Tally the total at the end of the week; this is how much you would

Yukiko Doi, head of the Fair Trade Nagoya Network, Japan, campaigns to have Nagoya win the status of a "Fair Trade Town," helping manufacturers in developing countries achieve better terms of trade.

 Read more about fair trade on the companion website.

In Debate boxes we ask students to consider their own views on a controversial question. In these boxes we also point to online resources for further research on the topic.

An icon in the margin and in Debate boxes indicates that relevant readings or links are available on the companion website, www.oup.com/us/shiraev.

DEBATE   WILL THE GLOBAL POWER STRUGGLE EVER END?

Realism is an evolving concept. Consider, for example, whether the United States should continue to strive for a unipolar order or move to a multipolar world. One group of experts argues that international stability and peace depend on many states acting together. For instance, in *Ethical Realism*, Anatol Lieven and John Hulsman (2006) write that the United States cannot act alone in a global world: It would quickly exhaust its resources and fail. America should therefore continue to play a leadership role but voluntarily restrain its power: Act more cautiously, pay greater respect to other states, and use the strengths of its allies.

Critics of ethical realism maintain that power still determines the international order, and that most other states are incapable of making a difference (Joffe 2009). This means that the United States is bound to be the leader for some time, whether other states want it or not. Moreover, as soon as the United States gives up its domination, the world will fall into chaos.

WHAT'S YOUR VIEW?
❶ Defend the view that the global power struggle should and will eventually end: As a starting point, the most powerful countries including the United States should

become less "selfish," thus making power politics more "ethical." If big powers start considering other countries' interests, the world will face significantly fewer conflicts. ❷ Defend the view that the power struggle will never end: States will exploit the weaknesses of other states. As soon as the United States shows signs of weakness, other states will assume leadership roles and start a new round of power struggles.

 Read more about ethical realism on the companion website.

Check Your Knowledge questions appear throughout, checking student comprehension at key points in the text.

CHECK YOUR KNOWLEDGE ▷ Name the three pillars of terrorism.
▷ Explain the Basque conflict from the position of the "three pillars."

Key Terms are boldfaced, listed at the end of each chapter, and defined in the glossary at the back of the text.

The extended analytical cases called The Uses of History at the end of every chapter feature detailed accounts of noteworthy developments from the past several decades (such as the Cuban Missile Crisis, "misperceptions and realities" in the War on Terror, and "celebrity interventions" in humanitarian issues).

THE USES OF HISTORY: The European Community

EU and local interests may clash. In front of the European Parliament in Brussels, Belgium, protestors speak out against the statutory German minimum wage act in 2015.

In Visual Reviews at the end of each chapter we map out the key concepts according to each chapter's consistent structure: (1) Ideas, (2) Arguments, and (3) Contexts and Applications, followed by Critical Thinking questions that reflect the chapter learning objectives.

In an appendix on IR careers we provide descriptions of the major career categories as well as resources for finding positions in the field of IR.

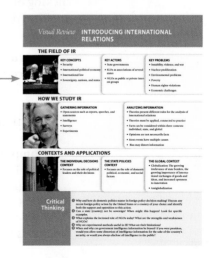

Organization and Coverage

The book contains ten chapters and is divided into three parts and a Conclusion:

• In **Part I, Studying International Relations** (Chapters 1–4), we introduce the field and describe how to think critically about international relations. In addition to an overview of the discipline, Part I includes three full chapters on major theories and approaches: realism, liberalism, and constructivism and other alternative views.

• In **Part II, Three Facets of International Relations** (Chapters 5–7), we cover international security, international law, and international political economy. We discuss issues including war, economic policy, free trade, territoriality, universal jurisdiction, and human rights, to name a few.

• In **Part III, Twenty-First Century Challenges** (Chapters 8–10), we explore current domestic and global challenges that are likely to continue into the future. These topics include terrorism and nonstate violent radicalism, global environmental problems, and humanitarian crises.

• A brief Conclusion serves as an extended exercise, guiding students in making predictions about the future of international relations.

Supplements

Oxford University Press offers instructors and students a comprehensive ancillary package for qualified adopters of *International Relations*.

Ancillary Resource Center

The Ancillary Resource Center at **www.oup-arc.com** is a convenient, instructor-focused single destination for resources to accompany this book. Accessed online through individual user accounts, the ARC provides instructors with up-to-date ancillaries while guaranteeing the security of grade-significant resources. In addition, it allows OUP to keep instructors informed when new content becomes available. Register for access and create your individual user account by clicking on the Instructor's Resource link at www.oup.com/us/shiraev.

The ARC for *International Relations* (**www.oup-arc.com/shiraev**) contains a variety of materials to aid in teaching:

- **Instructor's Resource Manual with Test Item File**—The Instructor's Resource Manual includes chapter objectives, detailed chapter outlines, lecture suggestions and activities, discussion questions, video resources, and Web resources. The Test Item File includes more than eight hundred test questions selected and approved by the authors, including multiple-choice, short-answer, and essay questions.
- **Computerized Test Bank**—Using the test authoring and management tool Diploma, the computerized test bank that accompanies this text is designed for both novice and advanced users. Diploma enables instructors to create and edit questions, create randomized quizzes and tests with an easy-to-use drag-and-drop tool, publish quizzes and tests to online courses, and print quizzes and tests for paper-based assessments.

- **PowerPoint–Based Slides**—Each chapter's slide set includes a succinct chapter outline and incorporates relevant chapter graphics.

CNN Video DVD

Offering recent clips on timely topics, this DVD provides videos tied to the chapter topics in the text. Each clip is approximately 5–10 minutes in length, offering a great way to launch your lectures.

Course Cartridges

For qualified adopters, OUP will supply the teaching resources in a course cartridges designed to work with your preferred Online Learning Platform. Please contact your Oxford University Press sales representative at (800) 280-0280.

E-Book

This text is also available as a CourseSmart eBook (978-0-19-045437-1) at www.coursesmart.com. CourseSmart's eTextbooks can be read on any browser-enabled computer or mobile device and come with the ability to transfer individual chapters or the entire book offline. Furthermore, CourseSmart was the first to introduce free eTextbook apps for the Android and Apple devices for an even better reading experience.

Companion Website

International Relations is also accompanied by an extensive companion website at **www.oup.com/us/shiraev**. This open-access website includes a number of learning tools to help students study and review key concepts presented in the text. For each chapter, you will find learning objectives, key-concept summaries, quizzes, essay questions, Web activities, and Web links. Facebook page: www .facebook.com/InternationalRelationsTextbook

NEW Interactive Media Activities

Five interactive media activities integrate learning across chapters. These simulations include *Negotiating a Climate Change Treaty, Keeping the Peace in Guinea-Bissau, Negotiating with China, Stopping an Epidemic,* and *Preventing World War.*

Packaging Options

Adopters of *International Relations* can package **ANY** Oxford University Press book with the text for a 20 percent savings off the total package price. See our many trade and scholarly offerings at **www.oup.com**, then contact your local OUP sales representative to request a package ISBN. **In addition, the following items can be packaged with the text for free:**

- *Oxford Pocket World Atlas*, **sixth edition**—This full-color atlas is a handy reference for international relations students (package ISBN 978-0-19-049447-6).
- *Very Short Introduction* **Series**—These very brief texts offer succinct introductions to a variety of topics. Titles include *Terrorism*, second edition, by Charles Townshend (package ISBN 978-0-19-049450-6), *Globalization*, third

edition, by Manfred Steger (package ISBN 978-0-19-049448-3), and *Global Warming*, second edition, by Mark Maslin (package ISBN 978-0-19-049451-3), among others.

- *Now Playing* **Video Guide**—Through documentaries, feature films, and YouTube videos, *Now Playing: Learning Global Politics Through Film* provides video examples of course concepts to demonstrate real-world relevance. Each video is accompanied by a brief summary and three to five discussion questions. Qualified adopters will also receive a Netflix subscription that enables them to show students the films discussed in the *Now Playing* guide. Please use package ISBN 978-0-19-049449-0 to order.
- *The Student Research and Writing Guide for Political Science*—This brief guide provides students with the information and tools necessary to conduct research and write a research paper. The guide explains how to get started writing a research paper, describes the parts of a research paper, and presents the citation formats found in academic writing. Please use package ISBN 978-0-19-046759-3 to order.
- *Current Debates in International Relations*—This volume presents forty-nine readings drawn from major scholarly journals, magazines, and newspapers including *Foreign Affairs*, *Foreign Policy*, *International Relations*, and *The Wall Street Journal*. It provides a broad selection of articles—both classical/theoretical and practical/applied—and steers students through major international issues, offering contending yet complementary approaches. Please use package ISBN 978-0-19-045855-3 to order.

Acknowledgments

Invaluable contributions, help, and support for this book came from many individuals. We are grateful for the insightful feedback and critical advice of colleagues and reviewers, the thorough efforts of research assistants, and the patience and understanding of family members. We also take this opportunity to acknowledge the tremendous support we received at virtually every stage of this project's development from the team at Oxford University Press. Executive Editor Jennifer Carpenter championed this project from the start; Assistant Editor Matt Rohal arranged reviews, saw to the details, and kept the project on schedule; Development Editor Lauren Mine provided constant support and good ideas during the writing stage; Christian Holdener, Senior Project Manager, coordinated and skillfully directed our work before it moved to the production stage; Senior Production Editor Marianne Paul guided the book through production. We appreciate the work of our Copyeditor, Elizabeth Bortka, and our Indexer, Robert Swanson. Thank you for your care and professionalism.

Special thanks to William Wohlforth from Dartmouth University; Mark Pollack, Richard Immerman, and Petra Goedde from Temple University; Mark Kramer and Mary Sarotte from USC; Norman Naimark, David Holloway, and Mikhail Bernstam from Stanford University; Thomas Blanton from the National Security Archive; William Taubman from Amherst College; Odd Arne Westad and Mike Cox from the London School of Economics; John Ikenberry from

Princeton University; Ted Hopf from the National University of Singapore; David Sears from UCLA; James Sidanius from Harvard University; David Levy from Pepperdine University; Bob Dudley, Colin Dueck, Eric McGlinchey, and Ming Wan from George Mason University; Cheryl Koopman from Stanford University; Philip Tetlock from the University of Pennsylvania; Christian Ostermann, Robert Litwak, and Blair Ruble from the Woodrow Wilson Center; Andrew Kuchins from the Center for Strategic and International Studies; Alan Whittaker from the National Defense University; and Scott Keeter from the Pew Research Center for inspiring us early and throughout our careers.

We received constant help, critical advice, and validation from our colleagues and friends in the United States and around the world. We express our gratitude to John Haber, Mark Katz, Dimitri Simes, Paul Saunders, Henry Hale, James Goldgeier, Eric John, Peter Mandaville, Jason Smart, Richard Sobel, Henry Nau, Martijn Icks, Stanislav Eremeev, Konstantin Khudoley, and Vitaly Kozyrev. A word of appreciation to Olga Chernyshev, Elena Vitenberg, Michael Zubok, John and Judy Ehle, Dmitry Shiraev, Dennis Shiraev, and Nicole Shiraev. We can never thank them enough.

We also thank the reviewers commissioned by Oxford University Press for this second edition:

Richard Aidoo, Coastal Carolina University
Juliann Emmons Allison, University of California–Riverside
Leslie Baker, Mississippi State University
Teh-Kuang Chang, Ball State University
David Claborn, Olivet Nazarene University
Mariam Dekanozishvili, Coastal Carolina University
Laura Dodge, George Mason University

Sean Ehrlich, Florida State University
Vaidyanatha Gundlupet, University of Texas at San Antonio
Marcus Holmes, College of William & Mary
Mir Zohair Husain, University of South Alabama
Colin D. Pearce, Clemson University
Marc Schwerdt, Lipscomb University
Daniel Tirone, Louisiana State University

We continue to be grateful to the reviewers of the first edition as well for their insightful and valuable comments:

Victor Asal, State University of New York at Albany
Abdalla Battah, Minnesota State University, Mankato
Dylan Bennett, University of Wisconsin–Washington County
Austin Carson, Ohio State University
Suheir Daoud, Coastal Carolina University

José de Arimatéia da Cruz, Armstrong Atlantic State University
Daniel Friedheim, Drexel University
Nathan Gonzalez, California State University, Long Beach
Gregory Granger, Northwestern State University of Louisiana

Eric A. Heinze, University of
 Oklahoma
Marcus Holmes, Fordham University
Lisa Kissopoulos, University of
 Cincinnati Clermont College
Tobias Lanz, University Of South
 Carolina–Columbia
Jeffrey Lewis, Cleveland State
 University

Patrice McMahon, University of
 Nebraska–Lincoln
Andrea Neal-Malji, University of
 Kentucky
James Rae, California State
 University–Sacramento
Christopher J. Saladino, Virginia
 Commonwealth University

We would be remiss if we did not express a word of gratitude to the administration, faculty, staff, and students at our academic institutions where we have consistently been provided with an abundance of encouragement, assistance, and validation.

The journey continues.

Eric Shiraev and Vladislav Zubok
WASHINGTON, DC—LONDON—PHILADELPHIA—ROME—MOSCOW

To the Student

Imagine that to study international relations you have obtained the power to travel back in time and space and witness the most extraordinary events that shaped the world. How far back and where would you go and which events would you choose? Would you pick a seat in a crowded room among revolutionary conspirators? Would you be a fly on the wall in the White House, listening to a president's top-secret discussion with a foreign leader? Would you like to be present at the peace conference in Yalta in 1945, watching how Franklin Roosevelt, Joseph Stalin, and Winston Churchill decided the future of the world? Or would you prefer to climb atop the Berlin Wall on November 9, 1989, to chip off a chunk of this monstrous barrier, the symbol of the Cold War? Would you rather be among the few physicians contemplating Doctors Without Borders in 1971? Maybe you would attend the 2011 NATO meeting about military intervention in Libya. Or maybe you would choose to witness the discussion between American and Iranian leaders debating the future of Iran's nuclear program.

Too many choices, too many people. . . . But even if you saw everything you wanted and met everybody you planned, what exactly could you learn from that experience? And what lessons could you draw when everything in the world is so rapidly changing? During just the last two decades, the world has witnessed the September 11 attacks, two wars launched by the United States, the birth of several new sovereign states, the rapid growth of economic superpowers in Asia and Latin America, the global financial crisis and the resulting economic slowdown, and the turbulent revolutions and violent conflicts in the Middle East and North Africa. As you are reading these pages, something highly important is likely to be happening in some part of the world. Is it feasible to draw any serious lessens from a kaleidoscope of rapidly unfolding events, let alone study something that happened ten years, twenty years, or even longer ago?

We believe such valuable lessons exist and that we need to study them and study carefully. Reliable knowledge of international relations takes more than observing things unfolding at this hour. Experts in international politics do more than register a perpetual chain of events. They *analyze* the inner logic of these events. Therefore, we will need serious analysis, or the breaking up of something complex into smaller parts, to comprehend their important features and interactions.

And even this is not enough. If you want to become a successful professional dealing with international relations—a politician or diplomat, researcher or military officer, blogger or college professor, lawyer or president—you cannot focus merely on analysis of events without understanding their context. How would you know which events to analyze and what their significance is? Which news stories deserve immediate action—and what action? To answer these questions, you will have to gain a broader knowledge about international relations. To make conclusions, you have to study, analyze, and generalize not only the headlines popping up on the screen of your mobile device but also the rich database of facts, opinions, and theories accumulated over the years. You will need to familiarize yourself with some general "rules" and patterns of international behavior as well as exceptions to these rules: for example, the ways countries, leaders, and international organizations like the United Nations are likely to act and the ways they almost never act.

The more you become educated about international relations, the more you will realize that there are many things you don't know. This awareness of the limitations of your knowledge will be a sign that you are mastering the science of international relations—that you are ready to patiently test your conclusions against the stubborn realities of this ever-changing, complex world.

Now back to your earlier choices: Did you pick the most outstanding events or individuals to meet? What questions will you ask? What lessons do you think you may learn by observing these events and conversing with these individuals? Consider your answers as your entry-level contribution to the studies of international relations. Welcome to the journey!

Maps of the World

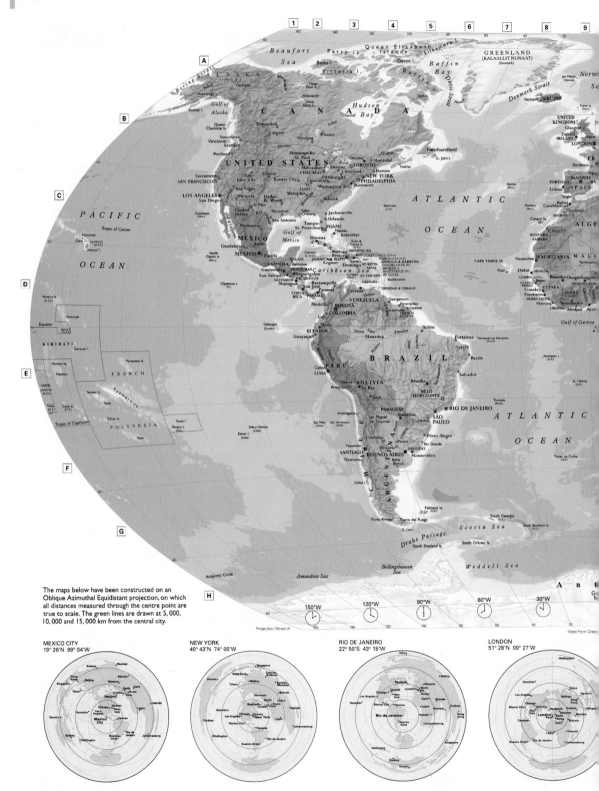

The maps below have been constructed on an Oblique Azimuthal Equidistant projection, on which all distances measured through the centre point are true to scale. The green lines are drawn at 5,000, 10,000 and 15,000 km from the central city.

Projection: Winkel III

West from Gree

MEXICO CITY
19° 26'N 99° 04'W

NEW YORK
40° 43'N 74° 00'W

RIO DE JANEIRO
22° 50'S 43° 15'W

LONDON
51° 28'N 00° 27'W

1:47 000 000

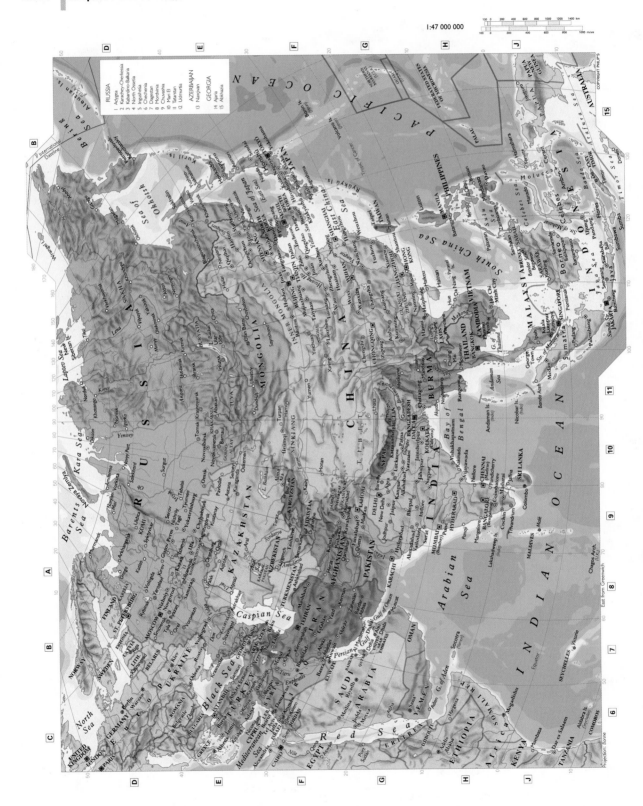

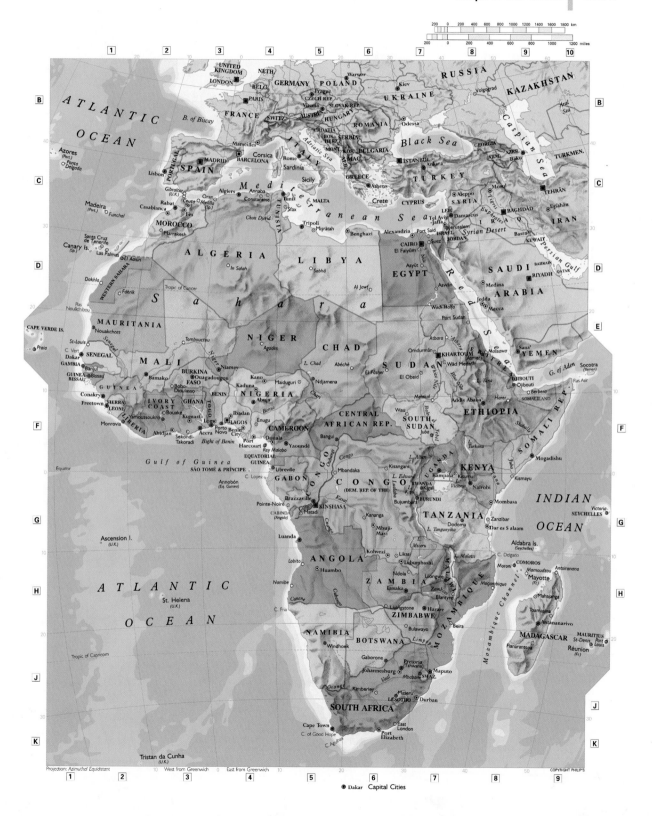

● Dakar   Capital Cities

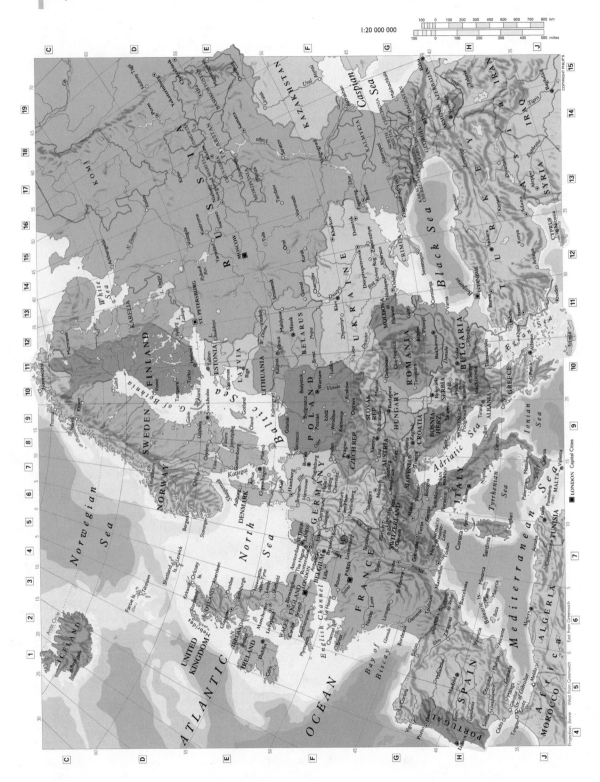

1:20 000 000

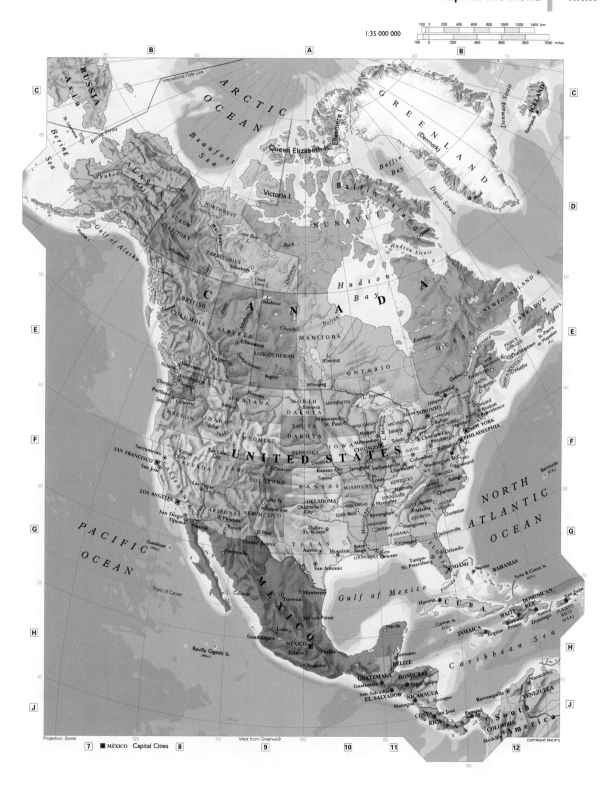

1:35 000 000

1:35 000 000

1 ■ LIMA Capital Cities

Projection: Lambert's Azimuthal Equal Area

COPYRIGHT PHILIP'S

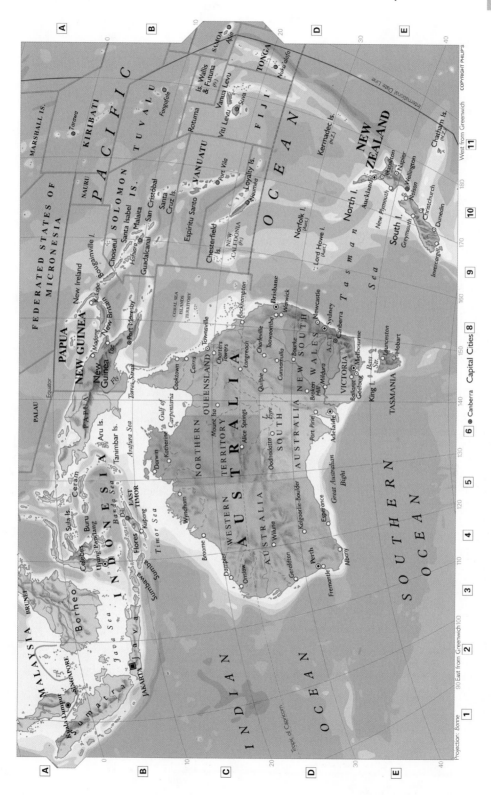

Introducing International Relations

1

It is possible to live in peace.
— MAHATMA GANDHI (1869–1948)

W E LIVE IN A FASCINATING AND RAPIDLY CHANGING WORLD. CONSIDER THE FOLLOWING:

- Not long ago, the European Union was the best example of an economically successful and stable regional organization. Today, many are asking if this union will survive the decade. Do you think the European Union will get weaker or stronger by 2020?

- In 2010, it seemed that North Africa was stable and that corrupt dictators would govern the Arab countries for many years to come. Yet the beginning of the Arab Spring one year later brought uncertainty to the entire region. In what direction is this region moving now?

- Twenty years ago, textbooks published in the United States no longer identified Russia's policies as the major challenge to international peace. Today many have reconsidered that view. What other major security challenges could appear in the near future?

Even the most permanent-seeming aspects of international relations cannot be taken for granted. Wars erupt in places that remained stable for decades, and new borders are drawn by violence. Other long-term conflicts end, and borders change peacefully. Change is the norm. Today, people travel and migrate on a scale previously unknown in human history. Meanwhile, Facebook and Twitter bring billions of people together across

Previous page: How much do borders matter in a global world? Some have essentially disappeared, yet others are being fortified. This recently constructed 109 mile fence runs along Hungary's border with Serbia. Why was this fence built, and how long will it remain?

national borders. Powerful social media platforms such as these can help bring down authoritarian governments but can also provoke hatred and violence. In this rapidly evolving world, how can we understand the international events of the day and confidently anticipate the world's future?

The first step is to look to history. Knowledge of events past helps us interpret the present. Some students approach the history of international relations as if taking a train past important landmarks. First comes the rise of European nation-states, then come the empires in the nineteenth century, then World Wars I and II, then the Cold War. Yet these developments are far more complicated and meaningful than they may appear to students who take this view. Almost every problem you witness today—injustice, border disputes, ethnic conflicts, violence, and more—have direct causes in history, which we should critically examine.

But where are these empires and feuding superpowers now? The world shaped by those early states, empires, and wars is seemingly gone. A new global world has emerged and is rapidly evolving. Most of the major international developments that we will discuss emerged after the late 1980s: the establishment of the European Union, the growth of NATO, the economic transformation of China, the globalization of information, and the rise of global terrorism.

In this book, we respect history as a key source of knowledge. At the same time, we realize the limitations of this knowledge in explaining the present and predicting the future. To explain and predict efficiently, we need to first develop an understanding of the main ideas and arguments of international relations. We will discuss and contrast traditional and novel ideas of international relations. For instance, some experts call today's world "flat," no longer divided into the superior West and "the rest." Others, on the contrary, warn about the deep divisions between the countries of the prosperous and arrogant "North" and the poor and desperate "South." Some believe that today's environmental problems are more important than the issues of borders, wars, and security. Their opponents insist that borders, wars, and nuclear weapons require constant and undivided attention. Who is right?

We want to include as many ideas and arguments as possible to show that the world is a diverse, dynamic place. We will see that international relations involves not only big countries like the United States and China but also, critically, nonstate or intergovernmental organizations like the European Community and the United Nations. We will see, too, how their roles are changing in an era of globalization. We feel the urgency of studying international relations in a world facing matters of war, the environment, poverty, human rights, and injustice. All these problems require not only critical understanding but also educated solutions. Welcome to the field of international relations.

Learning Objectives

▶ Define the scope and aims of international relations as a discipline.
▶ Identify major actors in international relations and the main areas in which they interact.
▶ Recognize major challenges and problems the world is facing today.
▶ Describe the methodology of international relations in analyzing information.
▶ Critically analyze a case related to war and democracy.

The Field of International Relations: Key Concepts, Actors, and Problems

international relations The study of interactions among states, as well as the international activities of nonstate organizations.

International relations (IR) studies interactions among states and the international activities of nonstate organizations. These interactions take many forms. They may be negotiations about territorial disputes, migration of people across borders, trade agreements, charitable activities, court decisions about an international criminal organization, economic sanctions against another country, or food deliveries to the population of a country suffering from a natural disaster. *International relations* is a field in social science. However, this term can also refer to the foreign affairs of states and of intergovernmental (IGOs) and nongovernmental (NGOs) organizations.

What Is International Relations?

International relations is a field of social science in which scholars discuss their ideas, arguments, and theories. It is also an applied field because it seeks to understand the realities of today's world as well as to suggest solutions to the world's many problems. Even an abridged list of the issues related to international relations can be overwhelming, but several topics remain prominent year after year. We can group these into three main areas: (1) international politics, (2) international political economy, and (3) international law.

International politics is how states interact and how they pursue and protect their interests. Countries naturally try to secure their borders and to reduce outside threats and aggressions, and one of the most important topics in relations among states is the issue of war and peace. War has been inseparable from international politics for centuries. In today's world, many countries try to avoid the use of military force and act through diplomacy. At the same time, however, military confrontations continue. Stop for a moment now and identify at least two significant military conflicts today. Who is fighting? Why are they fighting?

Countries buy and sell their natural resources and manufactured products, offer and accept financial assistance, and support or block certain economic transactions with other countries. The study of **international political economy** focuses on economic relations and how global markets affect the international system. For example, oil and gas as energy sources are significant factors in the world's politics: Countries regard these resources and their pipelines as both a source of profit and an element of security. Search for most recent stories about pipelines and disputes over oil and gas. Where are these disputes occurring?

International law, the third main area of study, is about mutually agreed formal rules and regulations concerning interactions among states, institutions, organizations, and individuals involved in international relations. As we will see later in this book, international law is effective only as long as countries recognize and follow it; there is no supreme power above countries to enforce it. Furthermore, powerful countries sometimes follow and enforce international law selectively.

The field of international relations differs from comparative politics, which focuses more on comparing political entities and systems rather than on how they interact. Yet the interests of both disciplines frequently overlap. The study of international relations has become increasingly multidisciplinary. A specialist in international relations nowadays should know the basics of fields such as government, economics, history, sociology, cultural studies, psychology, and military studies, to name a few. For instance, if you study the diplomacy and wars in the Middle East today, you have to know the history of the Arab Caliphates and of the Persian and Ottoman Empires. You have to understand Islam and its different strands. You should learn why international politics makes it difficult for Iran and Arab countries to cooperate against common threats. And you have to be familiar with the political economy of oil to understand international involvements in this region. In brief, we have to be ready to gather and analyze data and ideas from many fields. (See Figure 1-1.)

Let's now turn to a few simple questions. These only hint at the potential depth and scope of international relations as a discipline, but they may highlight a few educational or professional pursuits that interest you.

international politics The political aspects of international relations, focusing on power-related interests and policies.

international political economy The ways in which politics and economics interact in an international context.

international law Principles, rules, and regulations concerning the interactions between countries and other institutions and organizations in international relations.

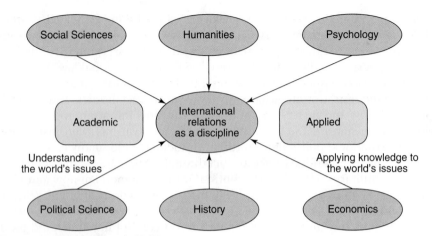

FIGURE 1-1 The field of international relations.

The UK and U.S. ambassadors to the United Nations speak to each other during a meeting of the UN Security Council in New York City in 2015. A permanent member of the Security Council may veto any UN resolution. Do you think this right of veto should be canceled? Should the UN be reformed to give more voting power to other countries?

WHO CREATED THE UNITED NATIONS SECURITY COUNCIL, AND WHY? In 1945, the United States, the Soviet Union, and the United Kingdom, the victors of World War II, created a global international organization called the United Nations. Together with their war allies China and France, they proposed a governing body of the United Nations—the Security Council. These five states became permanent members of this council, with the right to veto any decision voted by all other members of the United Nations. Ten temporary members out of almost two hundred countries also join the Security Council for two-year terms on a rotating basis, yet they have no veto power. Does this mean that the Security Council is a non-democratic institution ruled by the "big five" permanent members? Do you believe that the "big five" should eventually lose their permanent status and veto power? Or would you give other countries permanent membership on the Security Council? Which specific countries would you recommend and why?

When studying international relations, you will learn how the contemporary international system was built and that some countries have gained more power than others in various international organizations. You will also learn that it is desirable but often very difficult to conduct international affairs in a democratic way.

HOW MUCH DOES IT COST TO PROTECT THE UNITED STATES FROM FOREIGN THREATS? Exact numbers are difficult to come by. Some reports are classified, and others are always dated. In 2015, overall U.S. defense expenditures were estimated at close to $1 trillion. Out of this amount, more than $140 billion went to support veterans, and about $60 billion was spent to support foreign allies. About $60 billion was allocated to the Department of Homeland Security, and over $80 billion was spent on intelligence. The Defense Department received the biggest share, which is more than $600 billion. Keep in mind that military operations in Afghanistan and Iraq were funded through separate bills. In your view, does Washington spend too much, too little, or just the right amount on protecting America? Some experts argue that we should overspend on defense because it is better to be safe than sorry. Do you agree? Or maybe many foreign threats are simply exaggerated. Could you name which ones?

As you explore international relations, you will be able to form your own opinion about the costs of security and defense policies. You will also critically examine other factors and forces, different from defense and intelligence, that may contribute to peace and security in international relations.

The range of events and developments in international relations may appear too complicated and chaotic to understand. Yet there is logic in all these developments. To understand it, we have to examine some basic definitions.

WHAT PORTION OF THE U.S. FEDERAL BUDGET IS DESIGNATED FOR FOREIGN AID? Reports over the past several years suggest that approximately 1 percent of the federal budget is given to foreign aid, which is approximately $50 billion. No other country gives as much as the United States. Is this too much, too little, or the right amount?

You may say that this figure is too little and that the wealthiest nation in the world could and should do much more in terms of international aid to help nations in need. In relative terms, Sweden, Norway, and a dozen other countries spend a bigger share of their wealth on foreign aid. Besides, a substantial portion of this aid is spent on weapons. You may also maintain that no matter how much you help foreign countries, your help will be inefficient or ineffective unless these countries are ready to take responsibility for serious economic and social reforms.

When studying international relations you will learn that size and content of international aid is the subject of constant political, moral, and ideological debates. You will have to make your own decision about which side of the argument to support.

Key Concepts

State sovereignty is a central concept in the study of international relations. A **state** is commonly defined as a governed entity with a settled population occupying a permanent area with recognized borders. We will use the terms "state" and "country" interchangeably in this text. **Sovereignty** refers to the independent authority over a territory. Let's consider these terms in some detail.

SOVEREIGNTY

In the context of international relations states (countries) are sovereign when they have no authority above them, such as a government, a court, or an international organization telling them what to do within their territory such as

state   A governed entity with a settled population occupying a permanent area with recognized borders.

sovereignty   The supremacy of authority exercised by a state over its population and its territory.

Kurdish men sing independence songs at the funeral of two young men killed while fighting the Islamic State in Syria in 2014. Why don't some large ethnic groups, such as the Kurdish people, have a sovereign state?

collecting taxes, using resources, and so on. India and Pakistan, for example, became sovereign states in 1947, after the United Kingdom, their former colonial ruler, had partitioned India and transferred power to local authorities in the two newly formed sovereign countries.

Sovereignty refers to a territory and also to the allegiance of the people living on it. Territorial disputes, as history shows, frequently cause military confrontations. European states began to develop and protect sovereignty a few hundred years ago. In 1648, a handful of Christian kingdoms and principalities in Europe agreed that only they (and not the Roman Catholic Church) should determine the religious identity of their subjects. By the twentieth century, the most important marker of sovereignty was ethnic identity or nationality—a new and loose concept based on a combination of culture, territorial markers, and language. Disputes over territorial issues have always been common causes of international conflict. (See "Case in Point: *The End of a French-German Obsession: Alsace-Lorraine*.")

International treaties and economic and military capacities of countries support their sovereignty. Therefore, some states' sovereignty today may be strong, whereas others' remains weak. For instance, in Africa most state boundaries emerged as a result of colonization by Western powers within the last two hundred years. These boundaries ignored the ethnic and tribal divisions that had existed for centuries. Politicians guided cartographers and ethnographers, mostly from Britain, France, Belgium, Portugal, Germany, and Italy, who drew new countries' lines—often with a simple ruler. Some African governments, such as the Central African Republic and Somalia, are unable these days to control their own territory efficiently, battling numerous tribal warlords and rebel groups that challenge state power. Consider the case of Somaliland and Puntland. They declared independence from Somalia in the 1990s, but most other countries do not consider them independent states. Recognition by the strongest countries and a majority of other countries is an important factor that determines any new state's sovereignty. To illustrate, in 2013, various groups of Islamic fundamentalist rebels operating in Syria and Iraq proclaimed the Islamic State of Iraq and the Levant (currently known as ISIS). The United Nations, human rights organizations, and the members of the international community did not recognize ISIS and condemned its rampant violence.

According to the definition, sovereignty allows the state to claim that everything taking place inside its borders belongs to its **internal affairs**, and no outside authority may interfere in this state's activities. For centuries, sovereign states were expected to have armies, print their own money, collect taxes,

internal affairs
Matters that individual states consider beyond the reach of international law or the influence of other states.

CASE IN POINT > *The End of a French-German Obsession: Alsace-Lorraine*

If you travel by train or car, crossing the border between France and Germany today is hardly noticeable. It wasn't that way in the past. Consider the case of Alsace-Lorraine, a relatively small territory that Germany and France contested for centuries in several bloody wars (see Map 1-1). France consolidated its sovereignty over the territory during the revolution of the end of the eighteenth century. After the war of 1871, the newly formed German Reich annexed Alsace-Lorraine. In 1919, after Germany lost in World War I, France reclaimed its sovereignty over the territory. Not for long. After Germany attacked France in 1940, the residents of the region became citizens of Hitler's Third Reich. Only in 1944,

after the British-American troops defeated the Nazis, did Alsace-Lorraine join France one last time.

It is only appropriate that after many years of disputes and violence, Strasbourg, the principal city in this region, became the official seat of the European Parliament. There representatives from France, Germany, and other member-states discuss and resolve common issues of the united continent.

CRITICAL THINKING

Later in this book we will learn about territorial conflicts that continue to cause international tensions. India and Pakistan, Armenia and Azerbaijan, China and Japan, Argentina and the United Kingdom,

Israel and Syria, Russia and Ukraine, and many other countries are dealing with their unresolved territorial disputes. Why is there so much tension over territories? To some, the answer to this question is obvious: The disputed territories have natural resources, and this is what countries care about above all.

❶ What factors other than resources contribute to territorial conflicts? Explain. Consider issues such as the importance of a territory for a people's national and religious identity, pressures of domestic political forces, and the security concerns. ❷ Imagine for the sake of argument that Mexico asked the United States to return— as a sign of good will—some small territories within California and New Mexico that previously belonged to Mexico. How do you think the United States should react to this request?

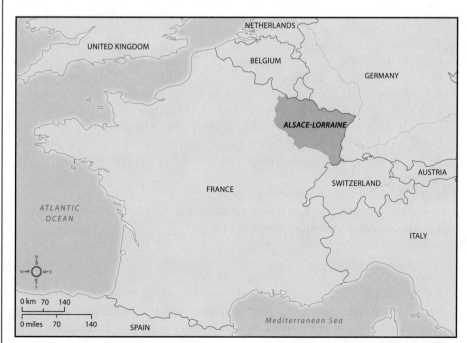

MAP 1-1 The region of Alsace-Lorraine.

and issue laws. This expectation is no longer accurate. States themselves can limit their own sovereignty and delegate authority to international organizations (such as the United Nations) or to international treaties that, for instance, refer to human rights, environmental protection, and so on. Many European countries, members of the European Union, voluntarily gave up on their currencies (such as marks, franks, liras, and pesos) to establish one common currency, the euro. In studying international relations, you will find that sovereignty can also be limited by other states or taken away forcefully. The ultimate violation of sovereignty is occupation by foreign powers. Could you give a few examples when a sovereign country lost its sovereignty as a result of military actions taken by other states? How did these countries restore their sovereignty?

NATIONS AND STATES

The terms *state*, *country*, and *nation* are often used interchangeably. In most cases, however, we prefer to speak about states, because the term *nation* has several meanings. We may think of a **nation** as a legal term or as a collective identity. In legal terms, about two hundred countries in existence today (and the number is changing) consider themselves nations, recognized by other states. The term has the clearest meaning when it applies to a homogeneous country, usually populated by one ethnic group with no large ethnic minorities. For example, it is common to say the "Finnish nation," referring to people who live on the territory of Finland, speak the Finnish language, and have ancestors of the Finnish origin. The meaning of "British nation" is more complicated and disputed, as there are people there with Scottish, Welsh, and English identities.

Ethnic minorities and their claims for their "nationhood" remain a constant challenge to many sovereign states. Many believe that nations can be "invented" or constructed even before they acquire a physical space and gain sovereignty over it. Kurdish nationalists in Turkey and Iraq often speak about the *Kurdish nation*, although there is no Kurdistan as a sovereign state. **Separatism** is advocacy of or attempts to establish a separate state within an existing sovereign state. States almost always resist national separatism, seeing it as a grave threat to state sovereignty. In Turkey, the pursuit of Kurdish national identity is outlawed. China fights against separatism in its predominantly Muslim area Xinjiang. Could you add to this list of examples?

nation   A large group of people sharing common cultural, religious, and linguistic features and distinguishing themselves from other large social groups. A nation may also refer to people who have established sovereignty over a territory and set up international borders recognized by other states.

separatism   The advocacy of or attempt to establish a separate nation within another sovereign state.

CHECK YOUR KNOWLEDGE

▶ Define and explain state sovereignty.
▶ What is separatism? Is separatism always dangerous for international peace?
▶ Give two interpretations of the term *nation*.

Key Actors

People today cannot act like the citizens of ancient Greek and Roman city-states: they do not gather on a central square to vote on international trade agreements or foreign wars. Instead, they have representatives who possess the authority to deal with international affairs. These officials are either elected or appointed to represent a **state government** (which we may also call a *national government* or simply a *government*)—an institution with the authority to formulate and enforce its decisions within a country's borders.

STATE GOVERNMENT AND FOREIGN POLICY

State governments conduct **foreign policy**—actions involving official decisions and communications, public and secret—with other state governments, nongovernmental organizations, corporations, international institutions, and individual decision makers. A country's foreign policy is usually directed by ministries of foreign affairs through embassies or other official offices in foreign countries. **Diplomacy** is the practice of managing international relations by means of negotiations. In cases when formal diplomatic relations do not exist between two states, there may be informal channels of communication involving third parties, special emissaries, and even personal contacts.

For example, for many years Iran and the United States did not have official diplomatic relations. The embassy of Pakistan to the United States for many years served as a mediator through a specially established "interests section." In addition, other mediators facilitated the discussions between Tehran and Washington. The content of foreign policy ranges from peace treaties to threats of force; from trade agreements to trade sanctions; from scientific, technical, and cultural exchange programs to visa and immigration policies. State governments usually prefer diplomatic means of interaction, but violence or a threat of it frequently backs diplomatic moves.

In today's developed democratic states, all three branches of government commonly participate in foreign policy, although their roles differ. Within the *executive branch*, government structures dealing with international relations include a ministry or department of foreign affairs. (In the United States, this is called the State Department; in India it is the Ministry of External Affairs; in the United Kingdom, it is the Foreign Office.) The *legislative branch* passes laws about the direction and handling of foreign policy. In democratic countries, parliaments commonly ratify (or approve) international agreements signed by state executive leaders. In the United States, every international treaty signed by the president must be "advised and consented to" by a two-thirds vote in the Senate. Congress also allocates money to conduct foreign policy according to the federal budget. Congress may also instantly finance specific policies or actions related to foreign policy.

The *judicial branch* is involved in foreign policy in several ways. For example, courts can make assessments about the applicability of certain international laws or agreements on the territory of the state. The courts also decide on claims submitted by foreign countries including businesses and private individuals. (In Chapter 6, we will discuss international law in more detail.) In some countries—in the United States and France, for example—their presidents have significantly more influence on foreign policy of their countries compared to the executive in the United Kingdom or the Netherlands. Differences between foreign policy executed by democratic and nondemocratic governments are also important, as we will discuss later. (See Figure 1-2.)

state government
An institution with the authority to formulate and enforce its decisions within a country's borders.

foreign policy
A complex system of actions involving official decisions or communications related to other nation states, international institutions, or international developments in general.

diplomacy   The practice of managing international relations by means of negotiations.

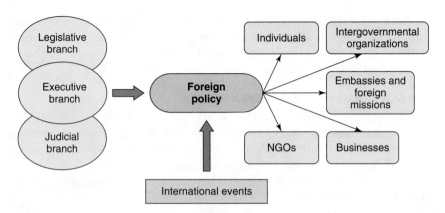

FIGURE 1-2 Foreign policy of a democratic state.

INTERGOVERNMENTAL ORGANIZATIONS

intergovernmental organizations (IGO)
Association of several nation-states or nongovernmental organizations for the purpose of international cooperation.

Besides sovereign states, another major player on the field of international relations is **intergovernmental organizations (IGOs)**. These are associations of several states such as the United Nations, formed in 1945 to increase the collective responsibility of its member states, keep peace through a voluntary collective effort, and serve as an authoritative mediator in international conflicts. (We will learn about its role in Chapters 3 and 6). Other IGOs are created for a combination of strategic economic, security, and political purposes. We will see later how the North Atlantic Treaty Organization (NATO) led a military action in Bosnia in the 1990s and against the Libyan government in 2011. Still other IGOs pursue primarily economic goals, like the Organization of Petroleum Exporting Countries (OPEC), which sets standards for how much oil member states should produce and sell on the global market. Of course, economic and political goals of IGOs are often interconnected and may interfere with one another. OPEC's power to set global prices, however, is severely limited by political and other differences among its members.

IGOs increase global accountability of individual states and, to some degree, limit their sovereignty. States receiving loans from international financial institutions, like the International Monetary Fund (IMF), must modify their financial and economic policies according to the Fund's standards. In theory, international institutions are not created to dictate policy to smaller or weaker states. Their mission is to promote mutual security, create a climate of trust, monitor international treaties, and encourage financial stability and economic development. Yet in reality IGOs can be dependent on powerful, rich countries, that provide a big share of these organizations' funding. IGOs can suffer from bureaucratic, political, and ideological biases, and internal political disagreements, as we will discuss in Chapter 3.

NONGOVERNMENTAL ORGANIZATIONS

nongovernmental organization (NGO)
Public or private group unaffiliated formally with a government and attempting to influence foreign policy, to raise international concerns about a domestic problem or domestic concerns about a global issue, and to offer solutions.

In recent years, a growing set of nongovernmental actors plays an increasingly important role in foreign policy of many countries. **Nongovernmental organizations (NGOs)** are public or private interest groups attempting to influence foreign policy, raise international concerns about a domestic problem or domestic concerns about a global issue, and offer help in the solution of these problems. The NGOs we will study deal mostly with international issues. (There are also NGOs dealing with domestic problems.) NGOs today support nuclear disarmament and environmental protection; relief programs in poor regions; and the distribution of medication, educational services, and other forms of international assistance and cooperation. NGOs are usually the product of individual volunteer efforts or civic movements. Some of them may receive government support in the form of grants.

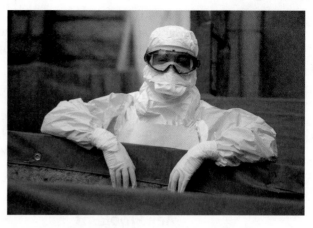

Dr. Julia Garcia wears a protective suit at an Ebola treatment center in Guinea in 2014. Garcia works for Doctors Without Borders, one of the most powerful NGOs, which gets the help of thousands of professionals from all continents. Under what circumstances could NGOs be more efficient than governments in solving international problems?

What explains the increased role of NGOs in today's world? At least three reasons exist. In many democracies, government bureaucracies and political appointees are held more accountable to the public and their actions become more transparent with the help of nongovernment groups and the media. NGOs also grow stronger because democracies improve access to information related to foreign policy. For instance, the U.S. Freedom of Information Act (FOIA), strengthened in the 1970s by the U.S. Congress, led to the establishment of the National Security Archive by a group of investigative journalists, a public group that urges and pressures the U.S. government to declassify and release foreign policy-related information. In 1996 to 1998 the National Security Archive's scholars consulted CNN in producing its twenty-four-part documentary *Cold War*, which is widely used in classrooms. Recently, the National Security Archive released transcripts of more than twenty interviews the FBI conducted with the former Iraqi president Saddam Hussein after his capture by the U.S. troops.

A second reason for the prominence of NGOs is globalization and growing attention to humanitarian problems and human rights. Even the most powerful government organizations cannot pay equal attention to every world problem. After the end of the Cold War, for example, when many Western powers were paying only limited attention to Africa, hundreds of NGOs filled the void. They began to raise funds to address the spread of AIDS, small arms and violence, corruption, and the collapse of health services in poor countries. While governments are often selective in their reaction to violations of human rights and political freedoms, many NGOs prioritize these issues and bring them to the media's attention.

Finally, NGOs have benefited from new communication and information technology. Because of the spread of technology and social media, most governments, government-controlled media, and business elites cannot keep their long-established monopoly on printed information. In 2014, almost 30 percent of Americans said they received their news (among other sources) through Facebook. Shares of other social networks grow (Pew 2014). This gives NGO activists more visibility; they can compete with corporate journalists as reliable sources and analysts. The Internet enables NGOs to raise funds, solicit volunteers, and organize complex projects without relying on governmental bureaucracies or big news organizations.

<table>
<tr><td>CHECK YOUR KNOWLEDGE</td><td>▶ What is diplomacy?
▶ In democracies, how do the branches of government commonly participate in foreign policy? How do their roles differ?
▶ What is the difference between NGOs and IGOs as international organizations?</td></tr>
</table>

Key Problems

Understanding international relations will provide you with analytical tools and confidence for explaining and addressing the significant problems of today and tomorrow. You will be better prepared to influence discussions about your country's foreign policy and build a more prosperous and stable world. Before we continue, stop for a second and list five or six of the most significant challenges and issues that you think the world is facing today. In your opinion, what can be done to address these challenges? What role would you choose for yourself?

Now compare your choices to the challenges discussed below. Here we will mention just a few issues to get going. (See Figure 1-3.) We will revisit these issues and many other challenges in the following chapters.

VIOLENCE AND WAR

Conflict and violence—internal as well as international—are major sources of instability. Violent conflicts take human lives, bring suffering, disrupt international trade, damage the environment, and require substantial material resources. Instability, in turn, serves as a source of new conflicts and wars. Each war has its own origin, history, and consequences. Nevertheless, several important trends have emerged. Military dictatorships conducting brutal policies against their own population are likely to act violently against their neighboring states. Unstable or failing governments unable to exercise their basic functions are often prone to use radical and violent measures to defend themselves. Unsettled ethnic conflicts frequently result in violence and threaten

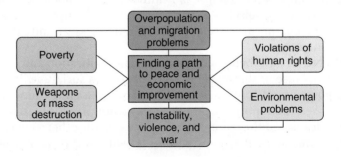

FIGURE 1-3 The interconnected challenges of international relations.

international peace. Small radical groups, not directly affiliated with any country, can also cause violence and international instability. They try to achieve their political goals by violence or threats of hostility against authorities or the civilian population. International terrorism has emerged as a threat to stability and a serious international problem as well, as we will see in Chapter 8.

What should be done to diminish violence and reduce instability? There is no single or simple policy to prevent violent conflicts or to end them quickly. At least two opposing view exist. Some argue that powerful countries have no other viable options except keeping international stability by force. Stronger, more powerful states, in this view, can best maintain regional and global stability themselves, without long debates. A range of policies, including preventive actions, economic sanctions, and military involvement, should reduce the threats of international instability and violence, including international terrorism.

On the other hand, there is the view that force only breeds more violence, because the causes of instability are mostly social and political. From this position, the international community should urgently invest in education, reduce poverty, address injustice, and thus diminish major causes of instability and violence. Which point of view do you support? What specific measures would you personally propose to reduce violence in international relations? We look in depth at security and instability in a global world in Chapter 5, and we address violence and injustice throughout.

WEAPONS OF MASS DESTRUCTION

Nuclear, chemical, and biological weapons can quickly and indiscriminately kill tens of millions of people. Therefore they are called **weapons of mass destruction (WMD)**. The fate of our planet rests in the hands—or, literally, at the fingertips—of a few government officials with access to nuclear arsenals. This is not an exaggeration. Even a fraction of the existing nuclear weapons could wipe out human life. The United States dropped two atomic bombs on Japanese cities Hiroshima and Nagasaki in 1945. The Soviet Union tested its first atomic bomb in 1949. The nuclear race between these two countries lasted until the end of the 1980s. Also, the Soviet Union, the United States, and the United Kingdom have worked on new types of chemical and bacteriological weapons. Today, the nuclear arms race has significantly slowed down, and the production of other WMD ceased. Only a few countries today openly possess nuclear weapons, including the United States, Russia, China, France, the United Kingdom, India, and Pakistan. North Korea and Israel, as many experts believe, have nuclear weapons without declaring it, and South Africa had them but later destroyed them. The Soviet Union continued to have bacteriological weapons until the very end, and we do not know if Russia still has them (Hoffman 2010).

However, a big concern remains today: **nuclear proliferation**—the spread of nuclear weapons, materials, information, and technologies. Why does it remain a serious challenge? For one thing, an unstable government could make frantic decisions costing millions of lives, or it could be too weak to protect its nuclear arsenals or prevent its scientists, in possession of secrets of WMD, from selling their knowledge to terrorist and criminal groups. The danger of such

weapons of mass destruction (WMD)
Nuclear, chemical, and biological weapons that can quickly and indiscriminately kill tens of millions of people.

nuclear proliferation
The spread of nuclear weapons, material, information, and technologies to create nuclear weapons.

proliferation was strong early in the 1990s after the collapse of the Soviet Union. The United States took considerable diplomatic and financial efforts to remove nuclear weapons and materials from newly independent countries such as Kazakhstan and Ukraine (Hoffman 2010). One of the United States' policy priorities in the Middle East and Asia today is to prevent new countries from acquiring nuclear weapons.

How can the world address the danger of WMD and the nuclear danger in particular? Two strategies exist. Most governments these days support the idea that the nuclear countries should gradually reduce their nuclear arsenals and no new countries should acquire these weapons. Others prefer universal nuclear disarmament, which would mean that every nuclear state gives up its nuclear weapons once and for all. Which strategy do you find more practical? How can further proliferation of nuclear weapons be stopped if some countries want to develop them? We will consider these questions and related arguments in Chapter 5.

ENVIRONMENTAL PROBLEMS

Environmental problems caused by human activities threaten human health and well-being. Industrial development, the rapid growth of urban areas, and increased consumption all play a role. We can think of two broad categories of environmental problems: *contamination* and *depletion*. The first includes pollution of the air, water, and soil. The second includes threats to forests, sources of fresh water, and many plants and animals. As a result, many governments have implemented programs to reduce pollution and conserve resources. They have opened national parks and restricted the use of land and water in their countries.

Government regulations, scientists, public opinion, NGOs, and international institutions are all important in restraining major polluters, such as corporations and addressing other causes of pollution such heating and certain agricultural practices. However, there is no universal agreement on how to address such international environmental problems as ocean pollution or global climate change. For instance, have you heard of the Great Pacific Garbage Patch? It is a huge area of exceptionally high concentrations of debris, plastics, chemical sludge trapped in the ocean by the currents. By the time you read this page, check what has been done to address this problem.

Strict rules regarding pollution and economic production can be effective, but they have limitations. And countries like China argue that their priority is not the environment but getting hundreds of millions of people out of poverty. How do we keep our environment safe and at the same time guarantee economic development? There are no easy answers. International relations teaches us that every decision about the environment is a trade-off, and we discuss how to evaluate the gains and losses in Chapter 9.

POVERTY

Over two centuries ago, British scholar Thomas Robert Malthus pointed to a disequilibrium that threatened world stability. Food supplies, he wrote, cannot keep up with a growing population. This, he warned, would result in wars and violence. Today our planet has enough resources to supply every human being with food, water, and basic medical care. In the 1950s and 1960s, spectacular progress in agriculture, often called the *green revolution*, seemed to remove the danger of mass famine. Why then does poverty and famine persist in some parts of the world? According to the United Nations, today close to one billion people live on less than $1.25 per day. More than a quarter of the world's population does not have access to running water. Preventable infectious diseases continue to kill hundreds of thousands of people, predominantly children, every year. In 2014 alone, malaria, a deadly infectious disease, killed close to one million people worldwide, mostly in Africa (WHO 2014).

Can we significantly reduce poverty? Several viewpoints exist, of which we highlight two. For example, many argue for the benefits of market economies, like those in Japan, the United States, and most Western countries. Here companies produce as much as they can, people can purchase the goods they need, and prices rise or fall with relatively little government planning or regulation. Almost every prosperous country in today's world has implemented market principles. Critics however argue that the market, if left to itself, creates huge income disparity and keeps millions in poverty. Some critics of market economy suggest a sustained global effort based on the redistribution of wealth through a massive investment into poor countries. What other solutions can you see as effective in solving world poverty? Would you, for example, support a global tax, for instance 1 percent of your annual income, to help the world's poor? If not, why? If yes, who should manage these funds? We will discuss the global economy and development in Chapters 4 and 7 and poverty in Chapter 10.

The Amazonian town of Açailândia, Brazil, produces pig iron. Brazil is fueled with charcoal from illegal felling of rainforest. The Brazilian Amazon, home to 60 percent of the world's rain forest (which produces 20 percent of the earth's oxygen), is threatened by rapid development. Is it possible to move people out of poverty while preserving the environment?

Afghan workers arrange copies of a morning newspaper at printing facility in Kabul, Afghanistan. Reporters Without Borders, a nonprofit group, ranked Afghanistan 128th out of 180 countries on its 2014 press freedom index. Afghanistan's leaders pledged to uphold constitutional protections for a free media. What is Afghanistan's ranking in the freedom index today?

VIOLATION OF HUMAN RIGHTS

International pressure grows on governments to protect their citizens threatened by the brutality of injustice, systematic violence, unlawful seizure of property, and physical abuse. However, for billions of people, access to justice, lawyers, or transparent courts is beyond their reach. In many parts of the world, property rights and civil rights are guaranteed only to small groups of people—commonly political, business, and government elites. Personal connections consistently replace the law.

In the past, some governments committed serious violations of human rights—all in the name of ideologies such as Communism, fascism, and Nazism, or because of ethnic, racial, and religious bias. Today, the Chinese and Iranian governments do not think twice before jailing and executing people for political dissent. Many governments conceal violations of human rights behind the arguments of "cultural specificity," "traditions," and "values." In some African and Asian countries, women but not men can be brutally punished for adultery. Another source of human rights violations is poverty, or extreme hardship. Hundreds of thousands of children every year are traded on the illegal slave market, forced into begging and drug trades, or become soldiers (U.S. Department of State 2014). The physical and sexual exploitation of children remains widespread. Many other rights are violated too. However, the world is far from agreeing on what rights should be considered universal that is applicable to every person and which are subject to cultural traditions.

Do you think the world should have a universal constitution that would clearly spell out the basic rights of people regardless of their nationality and religion? If you disagree, explain why. If you agree, which rights do you want to see as universal? Which international agency should enforce them? Do you support the idea that each country should have the right to reject guaranteeing certain rights to their citizens based on cultural traditions? Give an example if you think this idea is plausible. Chapters 6 and 10 explore the debates about international law and human rights.

OVERPOPULATION AND MIGRATION

Population growth presents significant challenges. The world's population is more than seven billion now and is projected to grow to eight billion by 2025. Overpopulation threatens the minimum conditions to sustain a reasonable quality of life. It can lead to serious health, environmental, and social problems including poverty and crime. At the same time, many affluent countries are actually experiencing a decline in population, including Western Europe and Japan, and the results here, too, will be felt in the years ahead. Birth rates are declining Europe, Latin America, and many Asian countries. At the same time life expectancy steadily increases, more people stay retired, thus bringing significant financial burden to many countries' social welfare programs.

Global migration is the movement of populations across state borders in search of better living conditions and jobs. By 2013, according to the United Nations, over 232 million people, or 3.2 percent of the world's population, were international migrants—an increase of 57 million since 2000 (UNIS 2013).

For millions of people, migration solves their economic and social problems. Many become citizens of other countries. At the same time, many immigrants continue to face significant problems. Immigration often causes resistance and polarizes domestic politics in many developed countries. Millions of people continue to be victims of involuntary migration: They are forced to move from their homes and often cross international borders for fear of their lives.

How do you think wealthy countries should assist other countries that struggle with overpopulation problems? Do you believe that states should agree on global quotas for immigration? Or perhaps you think that people should move across borders without restrictions? We will discuss the full range of these problems in Chapters 7 and 10.

A PATH TO PEACE AND ECONOMIC IMPROVEMENT

International relations as a discipline does not focus solely on threats and problems. One of the most important reasons we study international relations is to design policies and build a stable, healthy, and prosperous world. Informed opinion can be influenced by success stories, and there are many examples of conflict resolution and sound political management. We will study these examples in every chapter. Here we mention just two.

In 1992, the Czech and Slovak leaders of Czechoslovakia discussed and reached an agreement to split the country and establish two independent states. Most partitions of one country into two in the past were inseparable from war and destruction. But this case was a dramatic example of a peaceful separation. After the partition, both countries joined the European Union, and they remain close economic and political partners. What can we learn from this peaceful separation? Do you think that other countries could deal with ethnic separatist movements in a peaceful and civilized way, without resorting to violence? We explore these questions in Chapters 2, 3, and 8.

A second example is China. During the lifetime of one generation China evolved from an isolated and poor country into the biggest world economy. The government abandoned revolutionary slogans and encouraged entrepreneurship. Hundreds of millions of people have moved out of poverty and formed the middle class. China became an assertive player in international affairs. What we can learn from China's success? Can China's economic model become a standard for the rest of the world to follow? In Chapters 4 and 7 we will explore these questions in more detail.

Important political decisions lie ahead, with our future at stake. We will be returning to these and many other problems in every chapter. In the concluding section of the book, we will revisit them once more, as we ask you to consider what solutions your generation may find.

How We Study International Relations

The study of international relations includes three basic kinds of investigation. The first activity is informational: We gather facts to describe events and developments. The second is interpretive: We analyze the facts to explain why events take place. In this stage, we rely on concepts or schemes to organize and interpret what we know, and Chapters 2 to 4 take up some of the most important approaches, theories, and tools for studying international relations and applying the findings. The third activity is critical thinking: We look critically at the facts and their interpretations.

Gathering Information

Policy makers, their advisers, journalists, NGO activists, and researchers must all rely on information about international relations. How do we gather unbiased information?

GOVERNMENTAL AND NONGOVERNMENTAL REPORTS

The Federal Reserve—the central banking system of the United States—submits a semiannual report to the Congress about the country's economic growth, inflation, and international trade. Foreign governments, international financial organizations, and individual investors from all countries eagerly await such reports to formulate and correct economic, trade, and investment policies.

Other statistical reports, too, contain facts related to foreign policies, economic production, finances, accomplishments, conflicts, and other relevant issues. Governments and nongovernmental organizations release periodic publications about the economy, defense, commerce, tourism, employment, education, and other developments. For example, the Center for Global Development (www.cgdev.org), a nonprofit organization in Washington, D.C., conducts research and publishes informational analyses about how rich countries' policies and their foreign aid impact people in the developing world.

How reliable are these reports? To judge their accuracy, we have to consider three factors. The first is the *self-interest* of the organization publishing a report. Even statistical publications can be distorted and some facts overlooked for political or other purposes. A second factor is the *professional prestige* of the institution providing a report. A high reputation is earned by accurate past publications. The third factor is *competition* from other sources of information:

A competitive climate tends to lead to higher-quality reports. Because of the complexity of today's world and the differences in collecting data, statistical reports should be obtained from several sources. (Go online to read the most recent reports and review the initiatives of the Center for Global Development related to foreign aid, migration, education, and global environmental issues. Discuss the most important topics of the day.)

In developing democracies or nondemocratic countries, the quality of reports may be in doubt because it is difficult to confirm their accuracy. Some nondemocratic governments deliberately distort statistics on the spread of HIV and violence against women. In democratic countries, in contrast, citizens, political groups, the media, and NGOs can more easily question and challenge official reports—and often do.

EYEWITNESS SOURCES

Professionals frequently use their own observations, or **eyewitness accounts**. In some cases, they may be the only available source of information.

eyewitness accounts
Descriptions of events by individuals who observed them directly.

Investigative journalism has brought a new dimension to eyewitness reports. A journalist accredited by a news organization or working independently enters a foreign country or a zone of conflict (often without obtaining permission from local officials), conducts interviews, takes pictures, uploads them, and makes the information available to the world. Representatives of NGOs visit places where formally accredited journalists or diplomats are prohibited. Thanks to such reports, the world learned about violence in Chile in the 1970s; ethnic cleansing in Bosnia in the 1990s; human trafficking in contemporary Southeast Asia; and serious violations of human rights in Syria, Somalia, and many other countries. Providing eyewitness accounts, however, can be risky. Reporters Without Borders, an international NGO, regularly posts reports about journalists imprisoned, persecuted, or killed for doing their job (http://en.rsf.org).

content analysis
A research method that systematically organizes and summarizes both what was actually said or written and its hidden meanings (the manifest and latent content).

Government officials, especially when they retire, may provide information about their foreign-policy decisions, the reasoning behind their actions, and their interactions with foreign leaders. Political memoirs often include details previously unavailable even to experts. Beware, though: People do not write memoirs to emphasize their mistakes. They want to show off their achievements. Even when witnesses try to describe facts truthfully, they almost inevitably put their spin on what they saw and remembered.

COMMUNICATIONS

Official documents are often the best available sources on how states interact with each other. A *communiqué*, which is an official report about an international meeting, regularly provides clear and unambiguous information about the intentions, expectations, and actions of two or more states. Correspondence between state leaders is often helpful in understanding policy strategies. Letters exchanged between President Roosevelt and the Soviet leader Joseph Stalin during World War II reveal that these leaders carefully avoided ideological disagreements to defeat Germany and to establish a postwar peace.

One tool for examining texts like these is **content analysis**—a research method that systematically organizes and summarizes both the *manifest* content (what was actually said or written) and the *latent* content (the analysis of meaning) in speeches, interviews, television or radio programs, letters, newspaper articles, blogs, and other reports. For example, specialists have found that the more ideologically driven a U.S. president's speech is, the less sophisticated are the explanations of foreign policy (Tetlock 2011).

Speeches and press conferences of political leaders are valuable source of information. They articulate domestic political goals, such as public mobilization. Winston Churchill, for example, delivered one of his most famous speeches in Fulton, Missouri, on March 9, 1946. He hoped to convince the United States to be in alliance with Great Britain to contain the Soviet Union's power. Today U.S. presidents articulate their foreign policy objectives every year in an annual report known as the State of the Union. You can easily compare these reports, by conducting a content analysis of the parts related to international relations.

Secrecy is often necessary in certain diplomatic negotiations. Most government documents remain classified for years: states are interested in keeping their secrets away from the public. Journalists and researchers use the FOIA (see about it earlier) to declassify secret documents sometimes by the United States' government just a year or two after they were created. Some classified documents can be leaked to the press. The controversial group WikiLeaks in

CASE IN POINT > *Facts and Lies*

Sometimes governments or individuals spread deliberate lies and fabricate documents. By creating "fake" facts and news, political forces hope to manipulate public opinion, gather sympathy and support, justify their actions, or receive political and material gains. Consider the Katyn massacre.

In April 1940, Soviet authorities ordered the execution of more than 22,000 Polish officers after the Soviet Army had occupied a portion of Polish territory. The Nazis discovered the mass graves in 1943 and began to use them as a propaganda tool in hopes of splitting the anti-Nazi coalition of the Soviet Union, Great Britain, and the United States. Stalin's government resorted to denial, accusing the Nazis of committing the murders. The Western allies of the Soviet Union, willing to keep strategic relations with Moscow, accepted the Soviet government's version and downplayed reports of an international medical commission suggesting that the murders were committed by the Soviet secret police (Zaslavsky 2004). During the Nuremberg trials in 1945 and 1946, the Katyn massacre was, with connivance of Western powers, ascribed to the Nazi regime. Only in 2010 did the Russian government openly acknowledge the murders, calling the tragedy a "military crime."

CRITICAL THINKING

We learn from history that politicians have often lied to their people about significant international developments.

❶ In which ways have the technological opportunities for leaders to lie changed in today's world compared to the twentieth century? ❷ Can you think of important factors that may reduce a leader's incentive to mislead the domestic and international community? Consider, among other things, the technological changes of the past ten years as well as the growing influence of NGOs. ❸ Can you suggest other factors that may increase the leader's incentives to mislead the domestic and international community? For the sake of argument, are there instances when a leader's misleading the public about certain developments is justifiable?

2010 released to the Internet tens of thousands of stolen classified documents related to international communications among governments. The U.S. government argued that this was a criminal act. Many American diplomats and their colleagues in other countries were compromised. This case poses an important moral and legal dilemma. Should journalists and researchers use only legally obtained documents? As a researcher, would you personally use documents that have been obtained illegally?

INTELLIGENCE ●

Julian Assange, founder of the WikiLeaks website, which posted hundreds of thousands of classified documents.

Today, approximately 80 percent of intelligence information comes from published and open sources such as blogs, press briefings, or newspaper articles. Leaders and diplomats rely on open sources, but also on intelligence sources. **Intelligence** is any information about the interests, intentions, capabilities, and actions of foreign countries, including government officials, political parties, the functioning of their economies, activities of NGOs, or the behavior of private individuals. Intelligence can be open and covert, electronic or human (in professional lingo, "elint" and "humint"). The 2013 scandal involving former U.S. intelligence employee Edward Snowden not only revealed that governments had access to private communications of hundreds of millions of people but also raised important legal questions related to intelligence-gathering in today's global world.

Not all intelligence influences decision-making by state governments. First, to do so, the materials should have particular relevance for security and foreign policy. Second, the information needs to come from a reliable source or should be checked against other sources. Third, to become intelligence, the information needs to be trusted and accepted by political leaders, who often believe they are better judges of international relations than intelligence officials. For decades, the effective use of intelligence information by the Central Intelligence Agency (which is a major intelligence-gathering organization of the federal government) was often delayed by complicated bureaucratic rules. The changes that began in 2015 were aimed at removing such barriers and providing better communications among CIA divisions responsible for information gathering and intelligence analysis.

intelligence
Information about the interests, intentions, capabilities, and actions of foreign countries, including government officials, political parties, the functioning of their economies, the activities of nongovernmental organizations, and the behavior of private individuals.

Another big problem is the multiplicity of intelligence signals, none of which are conclusive enough alone. In the United States, United Kingdom, Russia, and China, several intelligence services report to different government agencies. They may be in competition and not always well coordinated. In retrospect, many intelligence failures are, in reality, the failures of leadership to recognize foreign threats (Goodman 2008). For instance, the U.S. government overlooked the impending attacks on the World Trade Center and the Pentagon in 2001 despite intelligence signals that indicated a possible criminal use of civilian aircrafts by foreign nationals.

SURVEYS

In **surveys**, groups of people answer questions on topics such as foreign policy. In the United States, presidential approval ratings are important indicators of popular support for U.S. foreign policy. Although public opinion does not set

survey Investigative method in which groups of people answer questions on a certain topic.

foreign policy directly, it does constrain it. Presidents and other decision makers are unlikely to go against overwhelming public opinion. To avoid an electoral defeat, a democratic government has to generate public support for its foreign actions and international programs (Shiraev and Sobel 2006).

Two types of surveys are most valuable for the study of international relations: *opinion polls* and *expert surveys*. Opinion polls gather information, usually on a national sample, about attitudes related to other countries, international events, or their own country's foreign policy. Expert surveys reflect professional opinions about a country, a country's foreign policy, or an international problem. For example, NGO Freedom House in Washington, D.C., publishes annual reports on the degree of democratic freedoms in most countries. Based on experts' evaluations, the *Freedom in the World* survey provides an annual evaluation of the state of global freedom. These ratings determine whether a country is later classified as free, partly free, or not free. Transparency International (TI) is another NGO that uses surveys. To create its Corruption Perceptions Index, TI compiles surveys that ask international entrepreneurs and business analysts to express their perceptions of how corrupt a country is (see Table 1-1).

focus group
A survey method involving small discussion groups used intensively in foreign policy planning, conflict resolution analysis, and academic research.

Focus groups are another survey method used intensively in foreign-policy planning, conflict resolution, or academic research. A typical **focus group** contains from seven to ten experts who discuss a particular situation and express their opinion about issues raised by the group's moderators. They are often given the opportunity to analyze issues in an informal atmosphere, relatively unconstrained by their government, military rank, or academic position.

EXPERIMENTAL METHODS

experiment
A research method that puts participants in controlled testing conditions. By varying these conditions, researchers can examine the behavior or responses of participants.

The study of international relations can also rely—surprising as it may sound—on experiments. In **experiments** (often called *laboratory experiments* or *simulations*), scholars put participants in controlled conditions as in a game. By varying these conditions, the researchers can examine behavior and learn about stereotypes, perceptions, and habits (Kydd 2005). Certainly nobody stages a small war to find out how countries would behave under extreme circumstances. Yet scholars have reconstructed "real-life" situations for decades.

TABLE 1-1 Corruption Perceptions Index, 2014, Selected Ranks and Countries (Updated February 21, 2015)

Rank	Country
Top 7 (least corrupt)	Denmark, New Zealand, Finland, Sweden, Norway, Switzerland, Singapore
21–25	Chile, Uruguay, Austria, Bahamas, UAE
94 (shared by several)	Armenia, Colombia, Egypt, Gabon, Liberia, Panama
Bottom 7 (most corrupt)	Turkmenistan, Iraq, South Sudan, Afghanistan, Sudan, North Korea, Somalia

The lower the rank of a country, the less corrupt the country is perceived to be. The United States is ranked 17 on the list.

One early contribution of experimental methods was related to group decision-making, such as within a government team or the president's cabinet. It was shown, for instance, that when people make decisions in groups, they often become less critical to proposals initiated by the leader. This phenomenon is *groupthink*—the tendency of groups to make rushed or illogical decisions because of a false sense of unity and support for the leader (Janis and Mann 1977).

Experiments can be used for educational goals to study conflict analysis and resolution. Participants in experimental situations play different roles and represent conflicting sides, such as Israeli and Palestinian authorities or the leaders of Iran, Syria, and the United States. The resulting discussions and decisions are carefully recorded and analyzed.

Analyzing Information

THE IMPORTANCE OF THEORY AND ITS APPLICATIONS

Knowledge of international affairs takes more than observation. **Analysis** is the breaking of something complex into smaller parts to understand their essential features and relations. This is difficult enough, but even more is needed. What makes countries' leaders to change their foreign-policy course? Are there specific policies that are likely to prevent war? Will the world benefit from having a strong global government elected by all world citizens? These and scores of other questions cannot be answered without looking into broader ideas about how international relations works. The ancient Greeks called this knowledge "from above" **theory** (θεωρια). Theorizing about international relations requires strong empirical knowledge and a measure of imagination.

analysis Breaking down a complex whole into smaller parts to understand its essential features and their relationships.

theory A general concept or scheme that one applies to facts in order to analyze them.

DEBATE > THE CORRUPTION PERCEPTIONS INDEX

This index has become valuable in international business and political decisions. It is based on several surveys from IGOs, NGOs, and research firms. Private companies and governments often consider it in their decisions about international investments, loans, and agreements. We shouldn't forget, however, that this index has its biases (Cobham 2013). Corruption is very difficult to measure directly. It is based mainly on experts' perceptions, which can be influenced by a score of factors possibly unrelated to corruption. Critical media reports about a country's political development may negatively affect expert views of corruption there. A traveling diplomat may give a country a low score partly because luggage was mishandled at a local airport, for example, or a businessperson making a substantial and easy profit in another country may overlook serious corruption there. What other subjective factors might influence experts' perceptions of other countries?

WHAT'S YOUR VIEW?

Visit the website for Transparency International at www.transparency. org to see the most recent Corruption Perceptions Index. ❶ Do you think that the Corruption Perceptions Index should be used as a serious indicator? Why or why not? ❷ What are some practical applications of the Corruption Perceptions Index? Suggest ways to improve the Index's validity.

Many foreign-policy debates ultimately rest on competing theoretical visions. The dominant theories in the last half a century were realism and liberalism. Most recently, a theory of constructivism began to win support among those who study international relations. There are other alternative theoretical approaches, including Marxism, feminism, world-systems theory, and others (Walt 2005a). Different theories present different rules for the analysis of international relations. It is becoming increasingly common these days to take into consideration several theoretical perspectives. In Chapters 2, 3, and 4 we consider main theories describing international relations, their commonalities, and their differences.

Critical Thinking in International Relations

Critical thinking is an active and systematic strategy for understanding international relations on the basis of sound reasoning and evidence (Levy 2009). It is not simply criticizing, disapproving, and passing skeptical judgments on your government or international developments. It is a set of skills that you can master. It is a process of inquiry, based on the important virtues of *curiosity, doubt,* and *intellectual honesty.* Curiosity helps you "dig below the surface," to distinguish facts from opinions. Doubt keeps us from being satisfied with overly simple explanations. And intellectual honesty helps in recognizing and addressing bias in our own opinions.

DISTINGUISHING FACTS FROM OPINIONS

Scientific knowledge is the systematic observation, measurement, and evaluation of facts. This knowledge is rooted in procedures designed to provide reliable and verifiable evidence. The study of international relations is not a "hard science." The behavior of states, NGOs, and international organizations is difficult to describe in terms of mathematical formulas and controlled experiments. We still, however, can learn to separate facts from opinions. Facts are verifiable events and developments. Opinions are speculations or intuitions about how and why such developments may or may not have taken place.

One of the most dramatic episodes in international relations was the Cuban Missile Crisis in 1962. The U.S. representative to the United Nations, Adlai Stevenson, presented photographs of Soviet nuclear missiles in Cuba taken by an American spy plane. Stevenson presented facts: The Soviet missiles had been placed on the island a few weeks earlier. Years later, in 2003, U.S. Secretary of State Colin Powell similarly sought to persuade a skeptical United Nations to authorize the American invasion of Iraq. He presented pictures of Iraqi facilities that allegedly produced WMD. However, these facilities have not been found, and most experts today are certain that the U.S. administration did not have evidence of factories producing nuclear weapons in Iraq. At best, it acted on convictions and lacked the facts.

Distinguishing facts and opinions is complicated. Some facts are deliberately hidden or distorted by state authorities or interest groups. Other facts are in dispute for many years. For example, Armenia and Turkey for many years now remain in disagreement on the nature and scale of the mass death of Armenians at the hands of Turks in 1915. The Armenian position is that the

Turkish state orchestrated the killings and that 1.5 million died. Turkey insists that the deaths were war casualties and the numbers were much smaller. The disagreements about the facts caused many years of tensions between Armenia and Turkey (Akçam 2007).

Anyone seeking information on the Internet must be especially cautious: Many seemingly reliable sites are full of speculations and statements presented as "facts." In reality, they are just unverified opinions. Even more often, facts are presented in a selective, one-sided way. Psychological studies show that people tend to embrace the facts that they like and events they approve of but ignore information that appears to challenge their views. A passionate supporter of democracy may argue in a blog that democracy always brings stability and peace. However, this person could easily overlook facts showing that a transition to democracy, especially in the countries with a history of ethnic and religious hostility, could contribute to even greater violence. Several powerful cases in point are Iraq, Afghanistan, Libya, and Egypt, and we will look at each of them in the course of this book.

Our desire to be objective is often constrained by the limits of language. Because people use language to communicate, they frequently "frame" facts, or put them into a convenient scheme. Most articles we read are framed so that contradictory and confusing information becomes simple. Often facts that challenge the article's view are omitted. Framing in the mass media works with remarkable effectiveness despite an often partial and imbalanced selection of facts (Graber and Dunaway 2014; Ward 1999).

One of the slides that U.S. Secretary of State Colin Powell displayed during his presentation to the UN Security Council in New York City in 2003. U.S. authorities mistakenly believed these Iraqi facilities were associated with biological or chemical weapons.

We also attach convenient verbal labels to the subjects we discuss. Labels such as *hawks, warmongers, aggressors, victims, doves, defeatists, hardliners,* and *softies,* to name just a few, frequently appear in the media. How accurately do these describe specific behaviors and particular events? International relations provides many examples showing that decision makers, like most people, often assume things when it is convenient to do so.

Separating facts from opinions should help you navigate the sea of information related to world events. It can start with looking for new and more reliable sources of facts. You can take the following steps:

- Whenever possible, try to establish as many facts as possible related to the issue you are studying.
- Check your sources for their reliability. Some supposed facts may also be more plausible on the surface than others.
- If there is a disagreement about the facts, try to find out why the differences exist. What are the interests and motivations behind these differences? The more facts you obtain, the more accurate your analysis will be.

LOOKING FOR MULTIPLE CAUSES

Virtually any international event has many underlying reasons or causes. As critical thinkers studying international relations, we need to consider a wide range of possible influences and factors, all of which could be involved to varying degrees in the shaping of international events.

As a historic example of multiple causes, many Americans tend to explain the collapse of Communism in Eastern Europe and the Soviet Union by Ronald Reagan's unrelenting military and economic pressure. Although this pressure was real, the Soviet Union's demise was caused by several intertwining factors, including disillusionment with Communist ideology, a growing economic and financial crisis, and the disastrous domestic policies of Soviet leadership. (See Figure 1-4.)

As another more contemporary example, look at the global decline in fertility rates—the average number of children a woman has. Why is this decline taking place? Is it just a reflection of increasing living standards in countries like India and Brazil? Or are women in countries like Turkey and Iran gaining more power within the family to decide how many children they have? Or maybe

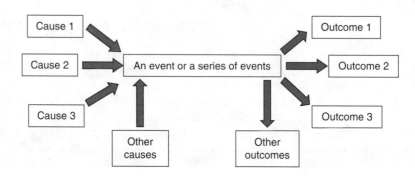

FIGURE 1-4 Multiple causes and outcomes of events.

more women choose career over family, like some do in South Korea and Japan? An answer should look for the many factors influencing fertility rates, including cultural practices, economic development, women's education, and government policies. (We will return to this topic in Chapters 4 and 10.)

BEING AWARE OF BIAS

We have to keep in mind that our opinions, as well as the opinions of people around us, may be inaccurate. Every interpretation of the facts is made from someone's point of view. And people tend to avoid information that challenges their assumptions and gravitate to information that supports their views (Graber 2010). Nobel Prize–winning studies show that people tend to bring emotional biases to simple logical judgments (Kahneman and Tversky 1972). When it comes to international relations, it is easy to support leaders we like and to oppose the policies of those we dislike. (Think of the Democrat-Republican divide in the United States). Our personal attachments, interests, preferences, and values have a tremendous impact on the facts we gather and judgments we make about international events. Ask your classmates which periodicals they read the most. Opinion polls show that people's party affiliations are correlated with their choices of certain news sources (Pew Research Center 2010). There are no completely unbiased newspapers or television networks. Be self-critical for a moment and answer these questions: Which printed and online publications do you like the most? To get world news do you prefer to watch CNN or Fox News? How do your choices correspond with your views of international relations?

Bias is often caused by different experiences and life circumstances. Personal emotions can deepen misunderstandings and disagreements, by causing us to refuse to learn new facts and accept new information. **Parochialism**, a worldview limited to the small piece of land on which we live, necessarily narrows the experiences we can have. It is a powerful roadblock in the study and practice of international relations.

An emphasis on critical thinking will help you as a student of international relations. You will learn to retrieve verifiable knowledge from apparently endless fountains of information, from media reports to statistical data banks. You will also learn to be an informed skeptic and decision maker.

parochialism
A worldview limited to the small piece of land on which we live or to the narrow experience we have.

▶ What is the Freedom of Information Act (FOIA)?
▶ Explain the method of content analysis.
▶ Briefly describe the three rules of critical thinking described in the chapter.

CHECK YOUR KNOWLEDGE

Contexts and Applications

Theories in international relations must be applied and tested. In this book, we will analyze together how different theories determine the way people look at the major issues in international relations, from war and terrorism to the environment and human rights. We will discover how tricky it is to apply theories to infinitely rich realities. Theories may bring different conclusions as we apply them to different contexts. In this book we consistently apply theories to three

Chinese president Xi Jinping, front, leads the members of the Politburo Standing Committee as they arrive for a plenary session of the National People's Congress in 2015. The Politburo of the Chinese Communist Party usually makes foreign policy decisions collectively.

contexts. The first one is decisions by individual actors, such as presidents, prime ministers, and other officials and leaders. Somebody has to make a decision, sign a treaty, stop a conflict, and initiate a policy. We will try to apply knowledge of international relations to see how and why leaders make those decisions. The second is policies of countries, with their complex political institutions, ideologies, political parties, customs, and traditions. The third is the dynamics of a complex global system of international relations as a whole.

Contexts that we discuss are not necessarily the same as "level of analysis" that theoretical-minded scholars of international relations sometimes use. Levels mean a hierarchy of growing importance and abstraction. We turn to contexts instead because they constantly interact and reflect realities that all of us see and understand. Now let's consider each briefly in turn.

The Individual Decisions Context

Focusing on the role of political leaders and studying their decisions is a rewarding tool for the study of international relations. Each decision maker is a unique individual with a personal history and educational background, with unique preferences, prejudices, and idiosyncrasies. Some are often cautious and indecisive. Others can be impatient and even reckless. Some listen to experts and change their views of foreign policy. Still others come to office with an agenda that they are reluctant to change despite the objections of their advisers (Fredrik 2008; Beschloss 2007).

Consider just two examples. In January 1950, thirty-eight-year-old Kim Il-sung, the ambitious and nationalistic Communist leader of North Korea, successfully lobbied Soviet leader Joseph Stalin to support his attack on South Korea. The Soviet and American military had divided Korea in 1945 during joint military actions against Japan. Such a division was seen as a matter of military and political convenience. Kim, with Stalin's help, decided to change this situation in his favor. Newly declassified sources from Soviet archives reveal that Stalin's decision to support Kim triggered the Korean War. At the same time, the road to war cannot be imagined without Kim's energetic and, as it turned out, misguided promises to win in a few weeks.

In March 2014, Russian president Vladimir Putin made a decision to seize the Crimean Peninsula, a part of Ukraine, and "return" it to Russia. This peninsula was conquered by the Russian Empire from the Ottoman Empire in the eighteenth century. Yet in the twentieth century, one of the Soviet leaders transferred this territory to Ukraine, which was one of fifteen republics comprising the Soviet Union. After the end of the Soviet Union, Crimea became a part of Ukraine, a new sovereign country. Russian nationalists as well as many ordinary Russians disagreed. However, Russian political leaders for many years respected Ukraine's territorial integrity. In 2014, president Putin, however, made the decision to appeal to Russian nationalism and seized the peninsula. This decision by one person (and probably a few of his close associates) significantly worsened Russia's relations with the vast majority of democratic countries around the world. It will have significant consequences for international relations for years to come.

Leaders rarely make decisions single-handedly. Usually, decisions are the outcome of complex domestic struggles, bargaining, coalition building, and compromises. Let's turn next, then, to the state context.

The State Policies Context

As an old expression has it, foreign policy begins at home. Domestic political, economic, and social factors all play a significant role (Putnam 1988). Domestic issues influence the daily interactions of governments, NGOs, and international institutions. In democracies, policies are more transparent than in authoritarian states. People in democratic countries, NGOs, and media have more influence on foreign-policy decisions. However, they may also dislike when their leaders focus mostly on foreign policy and neglect domestic issues.

In July 1945, British prime minister Winston Churchill came to an international conference in Berlin to negotiate with Stalin and President Truman. However, he had to leave the conference after just a few days because his Conservative party had lost elections to the rival Labor party. The leader who had led the country successfully through World War II could not get enough votes to keep his political power because of domestic politics. Conversely, international developments can influence domestic ratings of political leaders. During most military campaigns abroad—especially if they are short and successful—the approval ratings of U.S. presidents go up. However, if casualties continue to mount among American troops, national surveys show that public support declines little by little, and the rating of the president goes down accordingly (Holsti 2004). Often in this book, we will see how foreign-policy actions are designed, in part, for domestic purposes—to satisfy the voter.

Powerful domestic lobbies also play an important role in foreign policy. In the United States, lobbies represent lawyers, unionized workers, farmers, oil companies, and many other groups. There are also lobbies pushing for certain policies related to specific countries. Mass media—including newspapers, television, radio, and the Web—are also influential promoters or opponents of foreign policies. In some nondemocratic countries, powerful ethnic clans and religious authorities can play a vital role in foreign relations as well. In Iran today, an assortment of religious authorities (called ayatollahs) and government bureaucrats make calls on most foreign affairs issues. In China, the president, vice-president, and foreign minister are officially responsible for foreign policy. In reality, all important decisions regarding foreign policy and security are made by the Politburo Standing Committee of the Communist Party of China—a group of five to nine people, usually all men. In 2015, the median age of the Standing Committee's seven men was sixty-seven years and all of them had significant experience working in local and central government.

The Global Context

Individual decisions by state leaders and domestic political factors influence foreign policy and international relations. But it takes a global context to understand how international relations really work.

Two opposing tendencies are present in today's international developments. **Globalization** refers to the growing irrelevance of state borders, the importance of international exchanges of goods and ideas, and increased openness to innovation. It is a major shift in politics, communications, trade, and the economy at large. Cellular phones designed in Finland and manufactured in China now ring in African towns and villages. Millions of people have jobs and bring home a stable income because factories create products for sale in other countries. Communications, travel, and international commerce have eliminated many political, legal, ideological, and cultural barriers. Optimists believe that the world is abandoning old prejudices. It is destined to become more dynamic, flexible, and tolerant than ever before (Bhagwati 2004).

There is, however, resistance. **Antiglobalization** is an array of international movements that see globalization as aggravating old problems and creating new ones. One of the most obvious problems is the growing contrast between wealthy and poor regions—often labeled the global North and South. Advocates of antiglobalization offer a variety of responses, ranging from a more active role for the state in economic affairs to religious fundamentalism. Some believe that resisting globalization is the only way to oppose powerful international monopolies and corrupt governments. Others are afraid of losing their jobs to other countries, where pay is far lower. The global market may sound appealing, but not in the homes of the unemployed (Held 2007).

Studying international relations requires an understanding of the interaction of multiple factors, players, conditions, and contexts. Although events

globalization The growing interdependence of countries and their economies, the growing importance of international exchanges of goods and ideas, and increased openness to innovation.

antiglobalization Resistance to globalization, or an active return to traditional communities, customs, and religion.

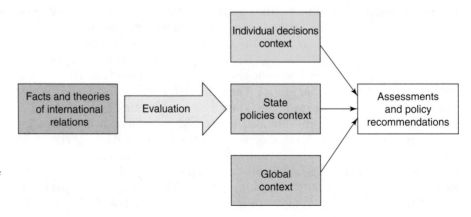

FIGURE 1-5 Analysis of international relations in three contexts

may appear chaotic, they can nonetheless be understood. Armed with the facts about what we study, the theories we use, and the contexts, we can recognize trends and avoid biased judgments. You will find exactly that as a consistent framework in each chapter. (See Figure 1-5.)

THE USES OF HISTORY: Can Democracy Be Exported?

Background

During a class discussion, we asked, "Can democracy be exported from one country to another?" Several students immediately said no. The United States, they reasoned, was trying to use military force to build democratic states in Afghanistan and Iraq. Washington committed significant human and material resources to achieve this goal. However, the students continued, this foreign policy experiment failed. They mentioned the casualties, the continuing political instability, and the violence that these countries have to face as a result of foreign occupation.

Other students disagreed. They turned to the examples of Japan and Germany more than sixty years ago. The governments of these two countries—both military dictatorships and both sworn enemies of the United States—had lost World War II, and the occupying powers established new political systems. Eventually, after years of transition, Japan and Germany became prosperous democracies and the United States' allies. In fact, a military occupation resulted in a peaceful democratic transition. "Democracy can be exported," these students concluded.

Whose arguments were more compelling? To have a productive discussion, it is often important to ask more specific, detailed questions that will require the use of supporting facts. We suggested these follow-up questions:

- Why was democracy successful in Germany and Japan, and why is it failing in Afghanistan and Iraq?
- What is the difference between the international situation and conditions in Germany and Japan in the 1940s and in Afghanistan and Iraq today?
- How can foreign policy of the United States favor or hinder the "export of democracy"?

To address these questions, we decided to review some basic facts from the past and then critically compare them with more recent developments. Our assessments and predictions should have practical applications: They will help us in making more informed judgments about democracy, military conflicts, international conditions, and the future of foreign policy.

Analysis

Japan lost more than three million people in the war and almost a quarter of its economy. Germany lost more than eight million people. In both countries, people were devastated by years of war. The threats of massive unemployment, lawlessness, and hunger were real.

In 1945, German and Japan officially capitulated. In May, the United States, Great Britain, France, and the Soviet Union occupied the entire territory of Germany. In September, the United States occupied Japan. From the beginning, the American strategy was to promote liberal capitalism and democracy. In Germany, the U.S. faced Soviet opposition in Germany's eastern parts, which were occupied by the Soviet Union. Great Britain and France, together with the United States, occupied Germany's western parts so that the Allies supported American strategies. In Japan the U.S. had no significant foreign opposition to implement its policies. War criminals were arrested, tried, and prosecuted. New labor unions began to function along with new political parties. Universal voting rights were granted and parliamentary elections took place. Courts began to adjudicate. Market economies grew. The United States drafted the first Japanese constitution, enacted in 1947. The Federal Republic of Germany, a new democratic state, was created in 1949. West Germans and Japanese were unhappy about the military occupation of their countries, but they strongly preferred American occupation and Western-style reforms to Soviet Communism (Dower 2000).

Unlike Germany and Japan, Iraq and Afghanistan did not fight in a major war against the United States and its allies (as we will see further in Chapter 8). Neither country signed a capitulation agreement. Most people in Iraq and Afghanistan saw the U.S. military presence as illegitimate. It was commonly perceived as part of a Western strategy directed at Islamic countries. Almost immediately, too, an organized armed opposition to foreign occupation emerged.

Also in contrast to Japan and Germany in the 1940s, Iraq and Afghanistan are culturally diverse communities with multiple ethnic, tribal, and religious groups. In Japan and Germany, the foreign occupational force successfully imposed its authority in provinces. In Iraq, and even more so in Afghanistan, local warlords, not the central government, established their power in many places (Crawford and Miscik 2010).

What, in summary, were the differences between the occupations of Germany and Japan, on one hand, and the occupations of Iraq and Afghanistan on the other? What were the differences in the United States' policies in these cases? What were the international context and international factors that affected the outcome?

History of Modern Institutions and Democratic Governance

In the twentieth century, before the war, both Germany and Japan had experience with modern bureaucratic and civil institutions and (in Germany's case) a constitutional democracy. Afghanistan and Iraq had very little experience with modern institutions, not to mention democratic governance.

International Economic Context

Before the occupation, Germany already was the most industrialized country in Europe, with advanced education and science. Japan held the same distinction in Asia. Both countries had educated professional classes. The United States helped German and Japanese exports and pulled these countries' economies into the U.S.-led international trade system. By contrast, Iraq and especially Afghanistan did not have advanced economies or sizable professional classes. Iraqi oil can stimulate the country's economy. Afghanistan, however, does not have easily available natural resources.

International Relations and Domestic Context

In Germany and Japan, there were no significant forces capable of or willing to organize an armed resistance against the occupying powers. In fact, political groups, which collaborated with the occupation authorities, mobilized people to accept change and to build democratic institutions. This was in part a reaction in Germany and Japan to the crushing military defeat and the dismantling of the older political system. The presence of the Soviet Union in eastern parts of Germany and near Japan created a clear choice for the Germans and the Japanese: to accept America's influence or to fall under the Soviet influence. They made up their minds in favor of Western models. In Afghanistan and Iraq, domestic and foreign opposition to the occupation worked to dismantle democratic reforms.

International Legitimacy of Occupation

Any foreign occupation may be viewed as illegitimate. A long occupation further erodes the legitimacy of local authorities. In Germany and Japan, the occupation had international legitimacy—most countries considered it necessary to occupy and reform the two countries that had been aggressors and caused significant destruction in Europe and Asia. Also the United States was using the perceived threat of the Soviet Union to prolong the occupation. In Iraq and Afghanistan, there was no such significant foreign threat. The population in these countries commonly viewed the governments in Baghdad and Kabul as "American puppets."

International Support

Both occupation and institution building require lasting domestic and international support. In the 1940s, the vast majority of Americans, according to Gallup polls, supported the war and occupation of Japan and Germany. They gave their troops full support at home. American allies, such as Great Britain, France, and South Korea, welcomed for their own reasons the presence of the

An Afghan girl begs for money as her mother sits in the middle of the road on the outskirts of Kabul in 2015. Despite years of occupation and international efforts, economic recovery in Afghanistan is slow, and democratic institutions are extremely weak.

TABLE 1-2 Building Democracy under Occupation: The Cases of Four Countries

Developments	Japan	Germany	Afghanistan	Iraq
Declaration of War by the United States	Declared	Declared	Not	Not
Military Occupation	By the United States	By the United States and allies	By the United States and allies	By the United States and allies
Ethnic Composition of the Occupied Countries	Relatively homogeneous	Relatively homogeneous	Ethnically and religiously diverse	Ethnically and religiously diverse
Infrastructure of the Occupied Territory	Relatively developed	Developed	Almost absent; difficult to administer	Underdeveloped; difficult to administer
Perception of Foreign Occupation	Perceived as a result of their own military defeat	Perceived as a result of their own military defeat	Perceived as foreign aggression and invasion	Perceived as foreign aggression and invasion
Experience with Democracy	Modest experience before the 1930s	Experience before 1933	Almost absent	Almost absent
Economic Factors	Developed economy	Developed economy	Underdeveloped economy	Underdeveloped economy
Accountability of New Officials	High	High	Low	Low
Political Mobilization Against the Occupation	None	None	Significant and persistent	Significant and persistent
Foreign Support of the Occupation	Strong	Strong	Mixed	Mixed

American forces in Germany and Japan. In contrast, the engagements in Afghanistan and particularly in Iraq divided the nation, created divisions among U.S. allies, and caused significant criticism globally. (See Table 1-2.)

We have briefly compared the conditions in four countries and linked them to the ability to conduct democratic reforms while under military occupation. As you can see, we have found ourselves drawing on history, political science, economics, sociology, and other disciplines as well. You may add your own assessments and use new facts to support them.

Questions

1. Consider the following position. Do you support it? Why or why not?
   Some foreign governments should be helped to govern only after they first establish order and stability; then they can be assisted with efforts in building democratic institutions.

2. Discuss why in some countries there was no significant resistance against foreign powers.

3. In 2014, Russia annexed the Crimean Peninsula—a territory of Ukraine, a sovereign state. Research and discuss why the people of Crimea did not resist the annexation. What was the reaction of the international community to the annexation?

4. Visit the websites for Gallup and Pew Research to find out how many Americans now consider the U.S.'s involvement in Iraq and Afghanistan a mistake. How many Americans supported and opposed the U.S. involvement back in 2003? Why did opinions evolve over the years?

CONCLUSION

It is possible to live in peace, Gandhi believed. But that possibility is not yet a reality. We need to find the inner logic in the kaleidoscope of decisions, mistakes, and success stories in today's tightly interconnected world. Do we need theory to understand international relations? Which theoretical visions are most helpful today, and in which situations? How can we apply those views to solve real-life problems and to build peace? We invite you to join us in considering such questions across time, borders, and disciplines. You will not be just a passive reader, we hope, but an active explorer. The better you understand the world today, the better you will be able to navigate it in the future.

KEY TERMS

analysis 25
antiglobalization 32
content analysis 21
critical thinking 26
diplomacy 11
experiment 24
eyewitness accounts 21
focus group 24
foreign policy 11
globalization 32
intelligence 23

intergovernmental organizations (IGO) 12
internal affairs 8
international law 5
international political economy 5
international politics 5
international relations (IR) 4
nation 10
nongovernmental organization (NGO) 12

nuclear proliferation 15
parochialism 29
separatism 10
sovereignty 7
state 7
state government 11
survey 23
theory 25
weapons of mass destruction (WMD) 15

INTRODUCING INTERNATIONAL RELATIONS

THE FIELD OF IR

KEY CONCEPTS
- Security
- International political economy
- International law
- Sovereignty, nations, and states

KEY ACTORS
- State governments
- IGOs as associations of several states
- NGOs as public or private interest groups

KEY PROBLEMS
- Instability, violence, and war
- Nuclear proliferation
- Environmental problems
- Poverty
- Human rights violations
- Economic challenges

HOW WE STUDY IR

GATHERING INFORMATION
- Open sources such as reports, speeches, and statements
- Intelligence
- Surveys
- Experiments

ANALYZING INFORMATION
- Theories present different rules for the analysis of international relations
- Theories must be connected to practice
- Facts can be considered within three contexts: individual, state, and global
- Opinions are different from facts
- Events have multiple causes
- Bias distorts information

CONTEXTS AND APPLICATIONS

THE INDIVIDUAL DECISIONS CONTEXT
- Focuses on the role of political leaders and their decisions

THE STATE POLICIES CONTEXT
- Focuses on the role of domestic political, economic, and social factors

THE GLOBAL CONTEXT
- Globalization: The growing irrelevance of state borders, the growing importance of international exchanges of goods and ideas, and increased openness to innovation
- Antiglobalization

Critical Thinking

❶ Why and how do domestic politics matter in foreign policy decision-making? Discuss any recent foreign-policy action and identify both the support and opposition to this action.

❷ Can a state (country) not be sovereign? When might this happen? Look for specific examples.

❸ What explains the increased role of NGOs today? What are the strengths and weaknesses of NGOs?

❹ Why are experimental methods useful in IR? What are their limitations?

❺ When and why can government intelligence information be biased? If you were president, would you allow some distortion of intelligence information for the sake of the country's security, or would you always disclose all intelligence to the public?

The Realist Perspective 2

The sad duty of politics is to establish justice in a sinful world.
—REINHOLD NIEBUHR

*L*ORD OF THE FLIES BEGINS DRAMATICALLY ENOUGH. IN FACT, IT BEGINS WITH THE BOYS BEING EVACUATED IN THE MIDST OF WAR. THEY HAVE GATHERED ON A DESERTED Pacific island after a plane crash, in which no adults survived. At first the boys attempt to maintain order. They elect a smart and physically fit leader, Ralph, and make arrangements for their rescue. Then, gradually, things fall apart. Hunger and fear undermine prudence, rationality, and authority. The boys become convinced that a mythical creature, the Lord of the Flies, lives in an island cave. A strong-willed boy, Jack, rebels against Ralph and starts his own "tribe," armed with spears and basing its strength on violence and obedience to the chieftain. They hunt wild pigs. In time most of the boys, attracted by food and driven by fear, desert to Jack. Ralph is left with a few staunch followers, and the tribe refuses a peaceful coexistence with them. The violence turns deadly. Only the appearance of a British ship, which has spotted the fires of the "tribal war," saves Ralph from imminent death. A British officer is stunned by what he sees—the wild looks and wilder, savage behavior. When he asks who is in charge, the boys burst into tears. They are suddenly reminded who they are.

Lord of the Flies, published in 1954, has become a classic, and its author, William Golding, was awarded the Nobel Prize for Literature. Released during the Cold War, it has also become a byword for brutal power struggle in a climate of insecurity. Here even boys degenerate into a murderous mob. As we will see in

Previous page: Dutch soccer fans clash with police in Rome ahead of a Europa League match in 2015. The threat of fan violence can necessitate strong police presence and may provoke a show of force. Is force the only means to prevent outbreaks of domestic as well as international violence?

this chapter, many theorists and politicians often hold out the same vision of human behavior, and they apply that vision to the behavior of countries. Their argument goes that countries pursue self-centered interests and tend to join forces against one another. Without an effective power to establish order, the world turns to violence. But if power is used judiciously and responsibly, the world may remain stable.

▶ Discuss the concepts of power and structure in international relations.
▶ Identify the key principles of realism in international relations, and explain how these principles evolved over time.
▶ Explain the meaning of states' interests, self-help, balance of power, polarity, and international order.
▶ Interpret realpolitik as a key application of realism.
▶ Critically apply realism within three contexts of international relations.

Learning Objectives

Ideas

Realism is an approach to international relations that focuses on states (sovereign countries) and their interests, balance of power, and the structure of international relations. According to realism, only states can be players in international relations. They defend their interests, protect their resources, create alliances, react to outside threats, and impose their will on others (Walt 1987). Their ability to do so is called **power**, which takes military, economic, political, and other forms.

Realists claim that states should have different interests, because they differ in size, geographical position, and economic and military strength. Great powers have more choices than weaker ones. According to realists, states try to build order in the situation of **anarchy**, without any authority or law above them. Because of this situation, states cannot rely on their allies to survive. Instead, they should primarily use their own strength and resources. The **international system** describes checks and balances among states as they exercise their power to promote their interests. The way states act depends on the structure of the international system—how many big states compete there, how power is distributed among them. Stronger states use their power to impose a particular order on weaker states. The weaker states may accept this protection or seek other options at their own risk. Their interests are limited and mostly local (Waltz 2010; Donnelly 2009).

States are constantly searching for the best position within the international system. Sometimes they try to change and even overthrow it. Realists do

realism   An approach to international relations that focuses on states and their interests, balance of power, and the structure of international relations.

power   A state's ability to protect its own security and impose its will on other states and actors.

anarchy   From a realist perspective, a condition of international relations that requires states to rely only on their own power.

international system   Checks and balances among states as they exercise their power to promote their interests.

not believe that intergovernmental organizations, not to mention NGOs, can decisively influence international affairs.

Realists argue that international relations can best be explained by looking at the *balance of power* among the most powerful states. To check each other and maintain order, states use violent and nonviolent means to keep or change the balance of power—or to prevent other states from doing the same. The ultimate violent policy is war. Common nonviolent policies include building alliances and coalitions, increasing economic and military strength, and engaging in diplomacy. This chapter will discuss **realpolitik** (a term borrowed from German)—a policy based on realist assumptions that the foundation of a nation's security is power and the threat of its use.

realpolitik A policy based on realist assumptions that the foundation of a nation's security is power and the threat of its use.

According to realism, no international order is perfect and lasts forever. Great powers rise and fall. And the danger of war is always present. This does not mean that politicians and diplomats should not reach agreements, strive for peace, and create international rules. This means, according to realists, that the real choice is between an imperfect order and something much worse (Jackson 2005).

This chapter critically examines realist assumptions about international relations, their transformation, and their applications from three points of view: individual, state, and global. We shall explore in the end how realist assumptions worked in the creation and development of the North Atlantic Treaty Organization (NATO).

Understanding Power in International Relations

What gives a state the ability to use power? Is it simply weapons or something less tangible, such as fear? For centuries, military force was the most important form of power. The size and strength of regular armies became key indicators

The Congress of Berlin, by Anton von Werner. This 1878 meeting led by German chancellor Otto von Bismarck marked the peak of an international system based on a balance of power among several of the most influential European states.

of power for sovereign European states. In the eighteenth and nineteenth centuries, some economic and financial indicators became just as important (Kaufman et al. 2007). Measurements of power were becoming more complex and in the twentieth century included men and women in reserve, tons of steel produced, battleships, submarines, tanks, aircrafts, and stockpiles of nuclear warheads and missiles, as well as quality of railroads and access to seaports.

As the Cold War continued, the significance of nonmilitary aspects of power in international relations grew. The economic competition between the capitalist and Communist systems brought forth the importance of **gross domestic product (GDP)**, or the value of all goods and services produced within the borders of a state. During the Cold War, the West demonstrated its growing strength in economic and financial power. As far as the realist logic goes, if states accumulate wealth, they can not only pay for their own defense, but also buy more security and influence by attracting allies and partners around the world. Aside from economic aspects of power, the West was also advancing in cultural battles: The American lifestyle proved often to be more attractive than Communist propaganda. This added to the power of the West in the Cold War (Jarausch 2008). We will learn more about these forms of power in Chapters 3, 4, and 10.

gross domestic product (GDP) The total market value of all the goods and services produced within the borders of a nation during a specified period.

Some states become dominant, while others play the roles of "middle" and "small" powers. The distribution of power in the world, realists argue, sometimes allows one state to dominate all the rest. This situation, called **hegemony**, has existed historically in some regions of the world. The decline of one great power and rise of another leads to war: whoever wins becomes a hegemon (Organski 1968; Gilpin 1981). In the nineteenth century, the United Kingdom was a world power, but its hegemony was challenged by Germany and the United States. The realist approach also recognizes regional powers, which are important second-rank players in international relations. Some of these states are former great powers, such as Germany, United Kingdom, and Russia today. Each has dominated in the past but has had to scale back at some point in history (Greer 2005). Why do great powers retreat and shrink? Usually this happens after a country loses in a military conflict or faces significant economic difficulties. Germany was defeated in World War I and World War II, but reemerged as the largest economic power of Europe. The United Kingdom won both wars, but exhausted itself militarily and economically, and had to disband its empire. Russia emerged as a regional power after the collapse of the Soviet Union, which had been a global power.

hegemony One state's overwhelming power in relation to other states.

The Development of Realism

An understanding of state power and state interests is essential to understanding how the realist view developed. We turn next to the intellectual roots of realism, its rise in Europe, and its evolution into neorealism.

INTELLECTUAL ROOTS

As one realist author notes, "Theories underlie contending policies in a real world" (Betts 2011). The earliest lessons of realism are drawn from ancient history. In his *History of the Peloponnesian War,* Athenian general Thucydides wrote of the struggle among Greek city-states in the fifth century BCE. He described in stark words the difference between powerful and weak states: "The strong do what they will and the weak suffer what they must." Philosopher Niccolò Machiavelli wrote his famous book *The Prince* in 1513 as a manual on how to survive in the rivalry among cities and principalities of Italy: "It is much safer to be feared than to be loved." Machiavelli thought that a ruler has only one real source of power: his army. He believed this army should consist of free citizens rather than paid mercenaries. Philosopher Thomas Hobbes in *Leviathan* (1651) wrote that without order imposed by the state, humans naturally struggle against one another, driven by competition and in search of glory. The idea that states pursuing their interests might act like people gained popularity among many intellectuals. Realists generally believe that human beings are not necessarily benevolent. They are, rather, inherently selfish, greedy, and competitive.

REALISM PREVAILS IN EUROPE

In the seventeenth century these realist assumptions became state policy. In Europe, after thirty years of devastating wars, the monarchs of the Holy Roman Empire, France, Sweden, and various German states realized that it was impossible for one ruler, even the most powerful one, to dominate the entire continent. In 1648, the monarchs of Europe convened at a diplomatic congress and reached the Peace of Westphalia. They recognized each other sovereignty and for the first time created an international system of sovereign states.

The *Westphalian system* lasted for the next two centuries, as Europe tested various combinations and rules of international relations. States practiced their diplomatic skills and the art of power balancing. The set of major players kept changing: It included England, Austria, then Russia, and, at last, Italy and Germany. All of them accepted the rules of realism. From 1805 to 1812, the French emperor Napoleon challenged the system and almost united continental Europe under his power (Caporaso 2000). Yet, after Napoleon's defeat in 1815, competition and power balancing among states returned and lasted until the outbreak of World War I in 1914. Klemens Metternich, Austria's chancellor from the 1820s through the 1840s, was the indisputable master of power games, which allowed the Austrian Empire to dominate central Europe. In the 1860s, Prussian chancellor Otto von Bismarck began to practice brilliant diplomacy, isolating Prussia's enemies one by one. With the help of this diplomacy and a series of quick, victorious wars, he managed to end Austria's supremacy and create the powerful German empire. Metternich's and Bismarck's effective realist strategies came to be called *realpolitik*. This German word is now often used in English and other languages as well (Williamson 1998).

Germany's rapid growth at the very center of Europe made the balancing of state interests increasingly difficult and dangerous, and ultimately Germany found itself surrounded by powerful countries that feared its rising strength. This contributed to the outbreak of World War I (1914–18). After that terrible war, which took the lives of tens of millions, France and Britain emerged victorious and Germany was defeated—with the United States joining the war

On the companion website (www.oup.com/us/shiraev), read excerpts from *History of the Peloponnesian War* and more about the Peace of Westphalia.

on the winning side in 1917. But the European order could not be restored. The collapse of Russia and the Habsburg (Austro-Hungarian) Empire led to revolutions, and several new weak and quarreling states replaced the defeated empires. Instead of Russia, the Communist Soviet Union emerged, self-isolated but feared by many. Germany, although defeated, retained its territory and industrial power, with a possibility of a quick comeback. Adolf Hitler, who came to power in Germany on the wave of ideology called Nazism, believed that Germans could be the "master race" of Europe. In 1939, the Nazis plunged Europe again into another world war.

In 1945, the powerful Soviet Union, the Communist successor to tsarist Russia, defeated Nazi Germany in the East but in the process established its own sphere of influence in Eastern Europe. The British Empire, weakened by the war, could not contain the expansion of the Soviet Union in Europe. As a result, the United States stepped in, and the **Cold War** emerged. This was the period of tensions and competition between the two international blocs: the one created and dominated by the Soviet Union and the other composed of the countries led by the United States. The Cold War created a new order, dividing Europe into two parts. Yet it was a very different kind of system compared with the Westphalian system. The art of balancing and realpolitik were not so important, because it was very difficult for small states to abandon one side of the system and move to the other. However, Europe did not plunge into hegemonic war because both sides feared that it could lead to a nuclear war.

Adolf Hitler before members of the German Reichstag in Berlin in September 1939, announcing that Germany was at war with Poland. Germany's aggression forced Britain and France to declare war on Germany, beginning World War II.

Cold War (1946–89)
The state of tensions and competition between the Soviet Union and its allies on one side, and on the other, the Western world, including the United States, Western Europe, and their allies.

REALISM BECOMES A THEORY

Although realism was often viewed as immoral and pessimistic, it influenced many politicians and scholars in Europe at the turn of the twentieth century. The most important ideas justifying realism appeared in the writings of Edward H. Carr (1892–1982), a British historian and analyst, and Hans J. Morgenthau (1904–1980), a Jewish émigré to the U.S. from Germany. Reinhold Niebuhr (1892–1971), an American theologian, also contributed valuable ideas. Carr harshly criticized European statesmen and diplomats who had failed to prevent two world wars. The politicians, he claimed, overestimated the role of moral values and misunderstood the role of power in international relations (Carr 1969). Both Morgenthau and Niebuhr witnessed the atrocities of World

Life magazine covers featuring the nuclear bomb and ways to protect oneself from its effects. In the early 1960s, fears of nuclear attack ran high in the United States. These fears fueled the arms race with the Soviet Union. What kind of fears may affect international relations today?

War II and believed that moral arguments and good intentions, if not backed by force, could not stop an aggressor.

Morgenthau's 1948 book *Politics among Nations* postulated several principles of realism. Most importantly, he defined the concept of state interests in terms of power. Power is the ultimate prize, and every state seeks more of it. In his definition, power could be measured by geographical location (the United Kingdom and the United States are better off compared to others because they are protected by seas), natural resources, industrial capacity, military force, population size and growth, national solidarity, the quality of diplomacy, and the ability of governments to rule and mobilize people and resources. Morgenthau further argued that ethical arguments should be excluded from the analysis of world politics. State leaders' attempts to stand by ethical principles would lead to costly mistakes. Moral values may play an important role in foreign policy, but in most cases states should pursue two connected goals: maximize their benefits and reduce their losses (Morgenthau 2006).

Niebuhr too discussed politics and moral values. In *Moral Man and Immoral Society: A Study of Ethics and Politics* (1934), he disagreed with American missionaries, such as Quakers, who believed in America's "goodness" and thought that its inspiring example to other nations could improve the world. He insisted that states, unlike individuals, could not act in a "Christian way." In an immoral society and immoral world, good and responsible people must learn to use power to impose their will on others. In this way, they could tame anarchical forces and save the world from self-destruction.

In the late 1940s, realism as a theoretical approach best explained the global conflict between the United States and the Soviet Union. From the realist position, the Cold War was a global struggle for power. The views of Morgenthau and Niebuhr gained support from many influential foreign policy strategists in the United States, such as George Kennan, Dean Acheson, George Marshall, Paul Nitze, and Walter Lippmann. The lessons of the war and the campaigns of the Soviet Union shaped the critical perceptions of an entire generation of diplomats and international scholars (Leffler 2007; Williams 2006). By the end of the 1940s, realism had become the cornerstone of the emerging academic discipline of international relations. For some time, realism triumphed over alternative viewpoints.

NEOREALISM (STRUCTURAL REALISM)

Morgenthau's principles did not amount to a concise theory of international relations. He wrote on many subjects, including human nature, diplomacy, geographic conditions, and the role of domestic politics and ideologies. All these and other factors, he wrote, influenced world politics and the way states acted. In the 1960s Kenneth Waltz, an American political scientist, set aside all these concepts and focused on two: anarchy and balance of power. He argued that no order is possible in international relations, only anarchy. No agreements among sovereign states can ensure the survival of those states. To put it simply, an international system is a self-help system: each state is ultimately on its own. Therefore, each state seeks a secure place in the international system according to the distribution of power (Waltz 2001).

Waltz's approach reduces the complexity of world politics to "structure," defined by anarchy and distribution of power among states. This theory is often called *structural realism*, or **neorealism**: seeking security, states function within the structure of the international system. Imagine the world as a pool table with many billiard balls, each representing a sovereign state. More powerful states are represented by balls that have freedom to move in any direction. Less powerful states are represented by balls that have very limited freedom of movement because they are near a side, for example. Configurations of the billiard balls on the table determine different structures of international relations.

Waltz's theory of structural realism helped explain international relations during the Cold War. If the world is divided between the United States and the Soviet Union, then all other states had to adapt to this bipolar structure. They might not switch sides. Their behavior would be different if the world had a multipolar structure (as in Europe two centuries before).

Yet how do domestic politics and the individual choices of state leaders affect international relations? Waltz acknowledged that the nature of political leadership and domestic politics affected states' foreign policy. He argued, however, that his theory does not explain why certain decisions were made. Neither does it predict foreign policy. Rather, it explains how states should adapt to the structure of international relations. This adaptation, Waltz argued, is the only *rational* way of acting. Such foreign policy, according to neorealism, is always defined by the international structure of power and not necessarily by domestic politics and views of individual leaders. But what if state leaders, instead of adapting to anarchy and seeking security for their country, start acting irrationally? Neorealism provides no explanation for such developments.

@ Read more about George Kennan, Dean Acheson, George Marshall, Paul Nitze, and Walter Lippmann, the practitioners of modern American realism, on the companion website.

neorealism (structural realism) The theory that each state seeks a secure place in the international system according to the distribution of power.

Soviet premier Aleksei Kosygin (at microphone) and U.S. president Lyndon B. Johnson at a Summit in Glassboro, New Jersey, in June 1967. During the Cold War, global power was mostly distributed between the two "poles"—the Soviet Union and the United States. In your view, how many poles does the world have today?

On the companion website, read more about the Camp David accords (1978–79), the balance of power that the accords intended to establish, and the impact of these agreements on the distribution of power in the Middle East.

Structural realists were poorly prepared to explain the sudden change of Soviet policies under Mikhail Gorbachev, for example, followed by a rapid reduction of international tensions and the end of the Cold War in the late 1980s. Facing new international realities and the surprising end of the global rivalry, some supporters of neorealism began to question its fundamental assumption—the centrality of anarchy and power balance among states (Walt 1998). However, many realists continued to argue that anarchy, security, and self-help are the core of international relations. As we will see later in this chapter, they still argue that states engage in power games and continue to treat other states as potential adversaries (Mearsheimer 2003). First, however, we must understand better what is meant by power, what defines and constrains the international order, and how states achieve security.

CHECK YOUR KNOWLEDGE

▶ What was the Westphalian system?
▶ Define *realpolitik*.
▶ Describe the concept of self-help.
▶ Why is Waltz's realism *structural*?

International Order

As the distribution of power among states changes, so does the structure of international order. According to the neorealist approach, power distribution among states can be of three types: *unipolar, bipolar,* or *multipolar.*

POLARITY AND INTERNATIONAL ORDER

In the nineteenth century the structure of international order was **multipolar**. A few European great powers, including France, Britain, and Russia, dominated the world with the exception of the Western Hemisphere, where the rising power of the United States was a decisive factor. Britain was the most powerful state financially. It had the largest navy to protect the largest colonial empire. Yet its dominance was not a complete hegemony. Britain had to balance its power with other strong states. By the end of the nineteenth century, the United States and Germany surpassed Britain as industrial powers and centers of education and scientific-technological innovation. During the first forty years of the twentieth century, the world remained largely multipolar. The defeat of Germany and Japan in World War II and the decline of Britain and France in the 1940s transformed the old multipolar order into a new **bipolar order**, dominated by the United States and the Soviet Union. During the 1970s and 1980s, the emergence of other regional centers of power (an integrated Western Europe, Japan, and the oil-producing countries of the Middle East) began to erode this bipolarity. The Nonaligned Movement, which included a number of countries (such as India, Yugoslavia, and Egypt) not belonging to any major power bloc, gained influence by exploiting the struggle between the two superpowers. And China split with the Soviet Union but did not accept the U.S. hegemony (Willets 1983).

When the Soviet Union collapsed in 1991, the international order became **unipolar** because no single state or coalition of states could seriously challenge the military might of the United States. The United States appeared to be the world's hegemonic power. Waltz and other neorealists expected this order would not last because other smaller states would regroup at the opposite side of the "pool table" to balance the power of the United States. For two decades after the Cold War this balancing did not take place. The European Union emerged in 1992, but it could not become a powerful political player. The Nonaligned Movement withered. In the past several years, signs have appeared of a possible return to a multipolar order. Among the causes of such a change is economic ascendancy of a number of countries (Zakaria 2008; Hiro 2010). India became a regional power and China grew to be the largest world economy. Together with Brazil and Russia, they account for nearly 30 percent of the world's land and are home to almost 45 percent of the world's population (Borah 2011). These countries may face serious economic challenges, yet they pursue their own interests and do not accept the predominance of the United States. (See Figure 2-1.)

Which type of order, from the realist perspective, is the most stable? Morgenthau believed that any multipolar order should contain more opportunities for balancing and, therefore, is the most stable. The advocates of bipolarity reasoned that it provided a predictable order and left little room for anarchy. In 1990, John Mearsheimer wrote an essay with a provocative title: "Why We Will Soon Miss the Cold War." He predicted that without global bipolarity, the world would plunge into a long period of power struggle (Mearsheimer 1990).

Other realist scholars, most of them Americans, came up with the *hegemonic stability theory*—they claimed that a unipolar world is supposed to be the most stable and peaceful international order. There are simply no states that

multipolar order
A world with multiple centers of power or influence.

bipolar order
A type of world organization based on two centers of power or influence.

unipolar order
A world with only one center of power or influence.

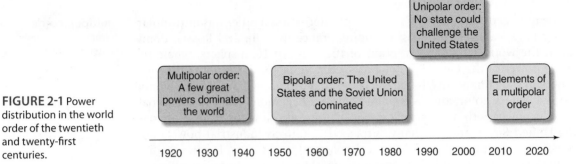

FIGURE 2-1 Power distribution in the world order of the twentieth and twenty-first centuries.

can dislodge the dominant great power (Webb and Krasner 1989). Also, it is better if one state provides a global leadership, thus diminishing international anarchy (Kindleberger 1973; Wohlforth 1999; Joffe 2009). Critics of this theory argued that the status of the United States tempted it to launch two wars (in Afghanistan and Iraq), stretched out its resources overseas, and did not help prevent most international conflicts of the past twenty years.

INTERNATIONAL ORDER AND POLITICS

From the neorealist viewpoint, stronger states occupy a place in an international order favorable to them by using a wide range of means—including negotiations, compromises, and economic aid—all according to their power. (See Figure 2-2.) Other states may join or be forced to join. As an example, the United States and a number of Western European countries formed an alliance to contain the power of the Soviet Union after 1945. The Soviet Union forced a number of Eastern European countries into a bloc on the opposite side. After the collapse of the Soviet Union, however, all former Soviet allies in Eastern Europe, and even some ex-republics of the Soviet Union, joined NATO, seeking security under Washington's protection.

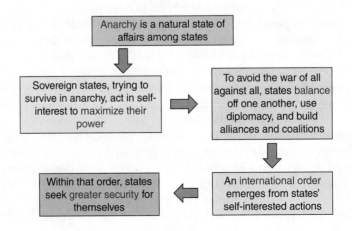

FIGURE 2-2 The logic of realism.

Cuban dictator Fidel Castro in 1967. In an example of a small ally influencing a big power, Castro was able to obtain Soviet support for Cuba's military engagement in the wars in Angola in 1975 and the Horn of Africa in 1977. Can any American ally today influence the policies of the United States in a similar way, and if so, how?

Smaller states, too, despite their economic and military weakness, can develop effective policies to protect their interests in an existing order (Maude 2004). For instance, Cuba under the rule of the Communist leader Fidel Castro in the 1960s was greatly dependent on Soviet economic aid. Yet Cuba was not impotent. It exercised significant influence on the Kremlin's foreign policy. For the Soviet leaders, the loss of Cuba as an ally in the Western Hemisphere would have been a painful blow to their global reputation and influence. Fidel Castro could even goad the Soviets into supporting Cuba's military engagement in the wars in Angola in 1975 and the Horn of Africa in 1977 (Gleijeses 2003). (See Map 2-1.) In a very different context, Afghanistan, Pakistan, and Iraq in recent years often acted to turn their dependence on the United States in their favor. Could you suggest any contemporary examples of small powers wielding a great deal of influence in their alliance relationships?

@ On the companion website, read more about the wars in Angola (1975) and the Horn of Africa (1977) and about the strategies of Cuba, the Soviet Union, and the United States in Africa.

> ▶ Explain bipolarity and multipolarity in international relations. Give examples.
> ▶ What is hegemonic stability?
> ▶ Why should we miss the Cold War, according to Mearsheimer?

CHECK YOUR KNOWLEDGE

The Rise and Fall of Great Powers: Realist Lessons

Now let's look at how realism explains the rise and fall of great empires in the past. These examples illustrate several realist and neorealist assumptions about power, its distribution, and the international order. We shall return to these

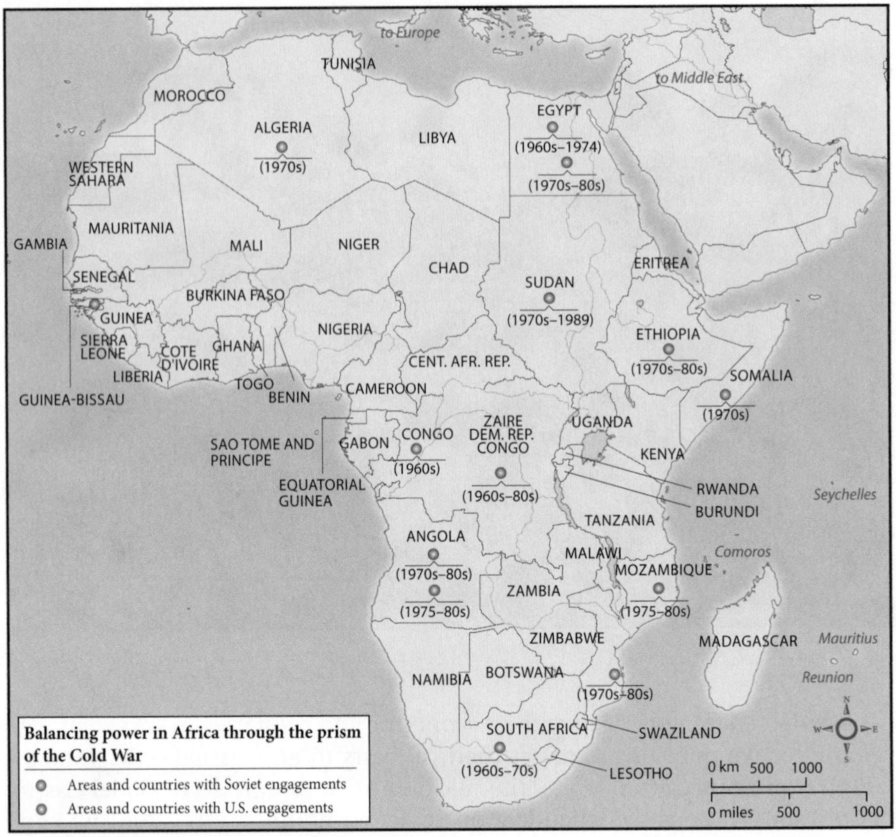

MAP 2-1 Africa and the bipolar order. Using anti-colonial rhetoric, the Soviet Union and its allies supported any political regime in Africa that would adopt anti-Western policies. Similarly, using anti-Communist rhetoric, the United States and its allies offered support to any government resisting the Soviet Union's engagements in Africa.

Balancing power in Africa through the prism of the Cold War

- Areas and countries with Soviet engagements
- Areas and countries with U.S. engagements

historical cases in later chapters as we compare realism with other approaches to international relations.

THE OTTOMAN EMPIRE

The Ottoman Empire had its roots in Anatolia (Asia Minor) but at its peak spread through the entire Middle East, parts of Europe, and North Africa. (See Map 2-2.) The Ottoman rulers maintained both *expansionist* and *protectionist* policies: The empire grew, while the ruling sultans offered the leaders of the conquered territories protection in exchange for their resources. The main goals of the sultans were to gain control over the Mediterranean Sea, Egypt, and Mesopotamia, and to obtain possession of the Balkans, a mountainous region of southeastern Europe. The Ottoman state combined Islam and efficient administration to rule over numerous peoples, extract large resources, and build a state-of-the-art military force.

For centuries, the empire could manage to prevail against its major rivals. As the power of the Ottomans grew, however, the resistance to its further expansion grew as well. European states formed coalitions to halt any further expansion of the Ottomans beyond the Balkans. In 1683, after the

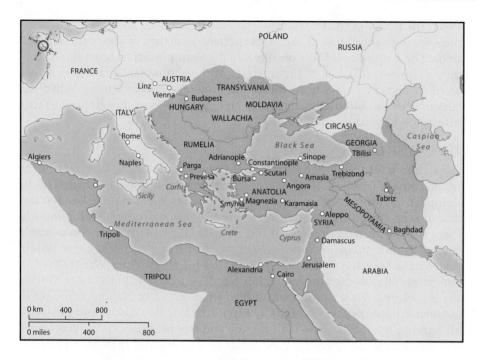

MAP 2-2 The Ottoman Empire in the sixteenth century.

decisive Battle of Vienna, the Ottoman expansion into Europe was stopped (Philippides 2007).

The positions of Ottoman Empire vis-à-vis European states deteriorated in the eighteenth and nineteenth centuries. A number of European states experienced economic growth and military-technological innovation, while the Ottomans appeared to be stuck in time. In the late eighteenth century, Russia was able to conquer the areas along the northern coasts of the Black Sea, Crimea, and Bessarabia (contemporary Moldova) and could set its eyes on Istanbul (Constantinople) and the Turkish Straits between the Black Sea and the Mediterranean Sea. Russia's success, however, was a threat to the regional power balance. Major European states, including France and the United Kingdom, now feared a stronger Russia, not the weakening Ottomans. From 1853 through 1856, these states, together with the Ottomans, defeated Russia in the Crimean War (Royle 2004; Figes 2012). During 1877 and 1878 they prevented Russia from taking Istanbul and establishing its hegemony in the Balkans.

Reformist political forces in the Ottoman Empire attempted to emulate the developed European states: The last sultan was overthrown by the group of Turkish nationalists who looked up to Germany as a model for reforms. In World War I (1914–18) they formed an alliance with Germany and Austria-Hungary. The defeat of Germany allowed the United Kingdom and France to break the Ottoman Empire into pieces and establish their domination in the Middle East for several decades.

In this example, realist arguments have been used to explain how the Ottoman Empire emerged but was later checked by a coalition of European states.

When the power of the Ottomans began to decline, and the power of its enemies grew, Istanbul had to adapt to the new structure of international relations. The Empire could rely on several European powers to resist Russia, but only as long as this was in the interests of those powers. Britain and France acted to prevent Russia from filling the growing power vacuum. When the structure of the international system changed, however, Britain and France dismembered the Ottoman Empire.

THE BRITISH EMPIRE

Great Britain (or the United Kingdom of Great Britain, or just Britain) was the island country that built the first true global empire. It also participated in the European balance of power, managing it skillfully for a long time. London was able to keep any European state from becoming strong enough to dominate in Europe and threaten British trade and security. In particular, London was able to keep France, its major continental European rival, in check. Great Britain seized most French colonial possessions after the Seven Years' War (1756–63), which was an offset for the loss of her North American colonies later. During the Napoleonic Wars in the early 1800s, when Emperor Napoleon sought to conquer Europe, Britain successfully supported Russia, Prussia, and Austria—all fighting against France—with money and troops. British money, soldiers, and diplomacy finally ensured the defeat of Napoleon in 1815 and the establishment of a new European balance of power.

For the rest of the century, Great Britain confirmed its role of an almost-hegemonic power. British industries, trade skills, governmental system, financial, and naval power were recognized as superior around the world. One of the oldest parliamentary governments, Great Britain also produced successful domestic reforms and skillful foreign policy. British statesmen, such as William Gladstone (1809–1898) and Benjamin Disraeli (1804–1881), despite ideological and political differences between them, combined the policy of balance among European powers with the construction of the largest colonial empire in the world (Aldous 2007).

During the nineteenth century London acted on the belief that the key to British greatness lay in its colonies. British colonial policies in India became a classic realist example of the strategic importance of military power. A relatively small British military with superior technology (navy, rifles, and machine guns) assumed control of the entire subcontinent that contained a population almost ten times greater than the population of its imperial metropolis (Hopkirk 1994).

Another vital interest of the British Empire was control over trade routes across the Mediterranean Sea and through the Suez Canal in Egypt. Not only did the British seize the canal's control (although the rights for the canal belonged to an international consortium) from the French, who opened it in 1869, they also established their control over Egypt and Palestine. Throughout most of the nineteenth century, the British Empire competed against France for the control of Africa and against Russia for domination in South Asia and Afghanistan. In Afghanistan, however, London suffered two military defeats (in 1842 and 1882). Finally, the British had to scale down, and they reached an

The British Royal Horse Artillery charges against unmounted Indians near Allahabad, India, during the Sepoy Rebellion, 1857.

agreement with Russia concerning the spheres of influence in Persia. Afghanistan was left alone for some time. Similarly, Britain and France reached agreements on the distribution of their colonies in Africa (Ferguson 2004).

Britain with its allies won the Crimean War against Russia and checked Russia's approaches to India. Yet a more serious challenge to Britain's hegemonic position was coming from Germany. The fast economic growth of Germany after its unification in 1871 marked the beginning of the end of the previously successful British policy of power balancing in Europe. By the beginning of the twentieth century, London had to join a formal alliance with France and Russia in order to curb the rising Germany's military and economic power. World War I became, from the neorealist perspective, a hegemonic war.

It was also a breaking point for the British Empire. Victory over Germany was too costly for London, and its power was in a steady decline. British policies of appeasing Nazi Germany from 1935 to 1939 led to Germany's strengthening and could not prevent another battle for hegemony (Clarke 2008). During World War II (1939 to 1945), Great Britain (now increasingly called the United Kingdom) won only because the United States and the Soviet Union joined it against Nazi Germany. The British Empire reached the limits of its economic and political resources. After the end of the war, London could no longer pay the costs of keeping colonies and could not contain the victorious Soviet Union. The British government decided to lean on the United States and granted independence to its imperial domains. In 1956, when Egypt's leader Gamal Nasser seized the Suez Canal, the United Kingdom (in alliance with France) tried to take it back by force. Yet under American pressure London had retreated. The United Kingdom accepted a lesser role in international affairs and never had serious foreign policy differences with the United States (Buchanan 2008).

As you can see, according to realist assumptions, a relatively small country turned into a great power by using its geography, political wisdom, skillful diplomacy, sea power, and international trade. During the nineteenth century, Britain developed additional sources of power, such as superior industries and finances, while retaining the old ones. All this allowed Britain to retain a hegemonic position in the changing international system for a long time. Yet when the distribution of power shifted decisively not in London's favor, the United Kingdom wisely adapted to the new structure. By doing so, it preserved its important international position, and today maintains good relations with many of its former colonies.

THE UNITED STATES: AN "EMPIRE OF FREEDOM AND THE DOLLAR"?

During the nineteenth century, the United States practiced territorial expansion in North America but noninvolvement in European affairs. Its economy grew fast. From the realist view, it was reasonable for the United States to establish its own sphere of influence while staying away from a power struggle in Europe. This foreign policy ensured that the United States never acted as a junior partner to any powerful European state. By the early twentieth century, the United States was the greatest power in the hemisphere and the second strongest naval power after Great Britain. Its unique location gave the United States the best possible vantage point to act as a major world player without provoking a hostile reaction of European powers.

By contrast to old European empires, the United States did not use its power to acquire colonies. Instead, it became a continental power. America even acted as an anticolonial power in the war against Spain in the end of the nineteenth century (although it toyed with the idea of acquiring its own colonies). When World War I broke out, the United States remained neutral and amassed wealth from trade with both warring sides, but primarily Great Britain. In 1916 and 1917, Washington chose to join an alliance of Great Britain, France, and Russia against Germany and its allies (Tomaszewski 2002). This made the United States a primary victor of the war, without being exhausted by it. Yet, because of its politics of isolationism, the U.S. chose not to play the role of a hegemon at that time. Only the Japanese attack on the American Pacific fleet at Pearl Harbor on December 7, 1941, ended the era of American isolationism and launched a new era of American global involvement. From that moment, the United States joined Great Britain and the Soviet Union against Japan and Germany and used its superior military and economic force to protect its interests and maintain the favorable balance of power in the world.

By 1945, the United States was about to build a new world order: It was by far the wealthiest country in the world, over half of global industrial production was American, and Washington had atomic bombs. Most of Europe and Japan were in ruins after the war. In terms of power, the United States was the only global actor after 1945, far superior to the Soviet Union, which was exhausted by the war. Washington moved to define the basic rules of post–World War II international finances and trade. The United States fought wars in Europe and in the Western hemisphere to establish its "empire." Yet, according to neorealism, it became a hegemon in 1945 by default as a result of its significant industrial and financial power, advanced military, and nuclear monopoly. Other great powers were either defeated or exhausted. The United States used its power to contain the Soviet Union (and later Communist China) and to maintain military superiority.

The United States continued to expand its influence and acquire military bases around the world, but it did so with the assistance of so-called *dollar*

CASE IN POINT > *The Monroe Doctrine*

On December 2, 1823, President James Monroe outlined a set of unilateralist principles of American foreign policy in the Western hemisphere. These principles or rules of behavior in the international arena are known today as the **Monroe Doctrine**. In this doctrine, the United States declared it had no interest in European conflicts. At the same time, the United States would resist any attempt of a European power to intervene in the Western hemisphere. Such attempts would be considered dangerous to the peace and safety of the United States (Monroe 1823).

As you read Monroe's words, pay particular attention to why the United States chose to act alone to resist the intrusions of European powers in the North, South, and Central Americas:

> In the wars of the European powers in matters relating to themselves we have never taken any part, nor does it comport with our policy to do so. It is only when our rights are invaded or seriously menaced that we resent injuries or make preparation for our defense. With the movements in this hemisphere we are of necessity more immediately connected, and by causes which must

be obvious to all enlightened and impartial observers. The political system of the allied powers is essentially different in this respect from that of America.... We owe it, therefore, to candor and to the amicable relations existing between the United States and those powers to declare that we should consider any attempt on their part to extend their system to any portion of this hemisphere as dangerous to our peace and safety. With the existing colonies or dependencies of any European power we have not interfered and shall not interfere. But with the Governments who have declared their independence and maintain it, and whose independence we have, on great consideration and on just principles, acknowledged, we could not view any interposition for the purpose of oppressing them, or controlling in any other manner their destiny, by any European power in any other light than as the manifestation of an unfriendly disposition toward the United States. (Source: James Monroe, *Seventh Annual Message to Congress*, December 2, 1823. Full text can be found at www.ourdocuments.gov)

Several U.S. presidents—among them Theodore Roosevelt (1901–

09), Dwight Eisenhower (1953–61), and Ronald Reagan (1981–89)—used the Monroe Doctrine to justify their unilateral actions in the Western hemisphere. U.S. armed forces intervened in Latin America whenever Washington saw a political, economic, or ideological threat to its interests in the Western hemisphere. Examples include interventions in Mexico (1911–12), Guatemala (1954), Cuba (1961), Chile (1973), Grenada (1983), and Panama (1989).

CRITICAL THINKING

❶ Which international events or issues might cause the United States to intervene in Latin America today? Suggest and discuss a few possibilities, such as the activities of an international drug cartel or massive violations of human rights. What type of intervention would it be? ❷ What would you do if a major country outside the Western hemisphere—Russia or China, as an example—would challenge the Monroe Doctrine in the near future by establishing a military base in Central America? Under what conditions could such a military base appear? Explain your position.

diplomacy, using the uniquely strong position of the U.S. economy and the dollar. Americans opened up their huge domestic market to their old and new allies, including the Germans and Japanese. Washington also made its international policies legitimate in the eyes of American allies as a struggle for freedom against Communism. This approach worked remarkably well: Most European states and some other countries agreed to accept the United States' protection. Japan continued to welcome American troops in its territory long after the formal end of the U.S. occupation, because of the threat of China and the Soviet Union, and also because the United States opened American markets to Japanese goods. Unlike the Soviet Union, the United States treated its allies not as satellites but as members of a voluntary alliance. Some historians argue that Americans created a special type of an empire—an "empire by invitation" (Lundestad 1986; Nelson 1992). When France in 1966 decided to leave the military structures of NATO to regain greater sovereignty in its defense policy, the United States grudgingly respected this decision. Close political and economic ties between the United States and France survived despite considerable tension.

When the Soviet Union and its empire in Eastern Europe collapsed in 1989–1991, Washington acted prudently, seeking to offer a new Russia and other post-Soviet states a place in the European and global order under U.S. hegemony. This time, however, the United States did not act as generously as it did immediately following 1945.

Read about the Chinese, Russian, and Spanish Empires on the companion website.

HOW GREAT POWERS EVOLVE

What should we learn from these three cases? Countries that had unusual advantages in accumulating power spread their influence far beyond their borders to establish an international order that favored them. They did it above all with their superior military power. But diplomacy and the ability to balance other states were also crucial factors. Our three examples also show that the usual cause of the decline of great powers is a change in the distribution of power due to the rise of other states. The Ottoman Empire declined steadily for centuries yet was stable as a part of an international order. The British Empire declined faster, because the international order the British had helped to create was ruined by two world wars, and by rapid growth of American and Soviet power. The weakening of these two empires had different outcomes as well. The Ottoman Empire finally collapsed in 1923, leaving its former possessions in the Middle East and North Africa unstable and ridden by ethnic strife. In contrast, the British Empire declined gracefully, and many of its former colonies became stable and prosperous countries. They have continued to maintain cultural, economic, and political links with one another.

What can realism suggest about the current status of the United States as a global power? Opinions vary. On the one hand, some politicians and scholars in the past several years have begun to speak about the decline of American power (Buchanan 2009; Lundestad 2012). Costly military engagements in Iraq and Afghanistan made America's allies and friends wonder if the United States could lead the international system. However, advocates of hegemonic stability theory maintain that the United States should and is likely to remain a predominant global power without any serious challengers or substitutes. The problems and questions from the realist perspective remain. For example: what will be the new sources of American power? How will the United States adapt to the changing structure of international relations? Will it maintain its financial power? Will it avoid a major confrontation with China? Regardless of what happens, the changes will affect the international order.

▶ Why did the Ottoman Empire fight the Crimean War? Give a realist explanation.

▶ Why did the United Kingdom accept a lesser role in international affairs after 1945? Give a realist explanation.

▶ What is dollar diplomacy?

▶ Explain the phrase "an empire by invitation."

CHECK YOUR KNOWLEDGE

Arguments

Realism is an impressive and influential theory. Yet how well does it explain the complexity of international relations ? We now examine several principles of power politics especially those related to the issues of security and war. We also study so-called predator states acting in violation of international rules. Finally, we turn to how, according to neorealism, states respond to threats to international stability.

DEBATE > WILL THE GLOBAL POWER STRUGGLE EVER END?

Realism is an evolving concept. Consider, for example, whether the United States should continue to strive for a unipolar order or move to a multipolar world. One group of experts argues that international stability and peace depend on many states acting together. For instance, in *Ethical Realism*, Anatol Lieven and John Hulsman (2006) write that the United States cannot act alone in a global world: It would quickly exhaust its resources and fail. America should therefore continue to play a leadership role but voluntarily restrain its power: Act more cautiously, pay greater respect to other states, and use the strengths of its allies.

Critics of ethical realism maintain that power still determines the international order, and that most other states are incapable of making a difference (Joffe 2009). This means that the United States is bound to be the leader for some time, whether other states want it or not. Moreover, as soon as the United States gives up its domination, the world will fall into chaos.

WHAT'S YOUR VIEW?

❶ Defend the view that the global power struggle should and will eventually end: As a starting point, the most powerful countries, including the United States, should become less "selfish," thus making power politics more "ethical." If big powers start considering other countries' interests, the world will face significantly fewer conflicts. ❷ Defend the view that the power struggle will never end: States will exploit the weaknesses of other states. As soon as the United States shows signs of weakness, other states will assume leadership roles and start a new round of power struggles.

 Read more about ethical realism on the companion website.

Realpolitik

Actions of states based on power-related considerations are often labeled *power politics* or, as we have seen, *realpolitik*. As you remember, the Ottoman Empire, the United Kingdom, and the United States applied their power in relatively similar ways by attempting to advance their vital interests and keeping their rivals in check. All of these countries were actively recruiting foreign states, even including their historic enemies, to advance their own interests and neutralize opponents. There are certain rules or principles of successful realpolitik.

RULES OF ENGAGEMENT

A state's geographical location, history, ideology, political regime, or economic conditions, as we have seen, affect its power politics. Supporters of realism outline several rules or principles that states must take into consideration when they are engaged in realpolitik. Consider two such rules.

First, the chances to succeed are significantly higher when the state has a substantial military and economic advantage over other countries. A strong economy and massive armed forces diminish other countries' capacities to impose their will or retaliate. There is a relative advantage, and an absolute advantage. The United States had a relative advantage over the Soviet Union during the Cold War, but in the 1990s, after the Soviet collapse, Washington achieved an absolute superiority (Mearsheimer 2003). The greater the power advantage, neorealists argue, the more freedom the country has to adapt to the anarchic structure of international relations.

Second, a state should not make too many commitments that constrain its freedom of action. Conducting foreign policy under moral considerations or out of solidarity may often hurt one's own state's interests (Nau 2002). For example, America's support of an independent Taiwan, on the grounds that this state is democratic and friendly toward the United States, can also be a strategic liability for Washington (Carpenter 2006). This support may drag the United States into a conflict with China, which rejects Taiwan's sovereignty. Neorealists also argued that the United States should not have helped Ukraine in its conflict with Russia, because Washington had more significant challenges coming from China and others resulting from the instability in the Middle East (Mearsheimer 2014).

PREDATOR STATES

predator state
A state conducting policies of systematic disregard for international rules and turning to belligerent actions in the international arena.

Supporters of realism believe that power politics, for the most part, tends to make war less likely and peace more stable. In reality, it is not always so. If a state perceives a weakness in an existing international order, it may challenge the power distribution by generating aggressive policies that disregard the rights and sovereignty of others. A **predator state** acts belligerently in regard to other states, in systematic disregard for international rules. For example, with Hitler in control of the government, Nazi Germany rapidly armed itself and began to act as a predator state in Europe. In 1990, Iraq acted in a similar way in the Persian Gulf.

Predator states act in ways that may dramatically shift the balance of power in a region or even globally. These rapid power shifts, however, can generate a backlash in the form of international coalitions and alliances. The Grand Alliance of the United Kingdom, the United States, and the Soviet Union emerged as a result of German and Japanese aggression. In 1991, a big coalition, including the United States and the Soviet Union, emerged against Iraq in response to its annexation of Kuwait. (See Figure 2-3.)

POWER SHIFTS

Not only do rapid shifts of power create international instability and disorder, they also cause counteractions that may affect any existing power balance. Two types of responses to instability are common. First, stronger states can form alliances against an emerging threat, as we have seen with the Grand Alliance. Second, weaker states can make deals with predator states, bargaining for a place in a new world order that the predator state may eventually create by conquest and aggression (Walt 1987). In rare cases, states have the option of staying neutral in an international conflict. Switzerland and Sweden did it during World War II. But even those states had to make tacit deals with Germany to avoid war and possible losses.

Vietnamese General Do Ba Ty (left) and U.S. General Martin Dempsey meet in Vietnam in 2014. Vietnam and the United States are engaged in security cooperation, prompted by China's military activities in the region.

International Order and War

Wars or armed conflicts are the ultimate application of force. Carl von Clausewitz (1780–1831), a prominent military thinker of the nineteenth century, coined the realist formula that war is *a continuation of politics by other means* (von Clausewitz 1982). For Clausewitz, war is necessary to validate state power, just as money is necessary for a business transaction.

It would be a mistake, however, to equate realism with war. Realism does not teach us that war is the only logical outcome of power struggle and anarchy. On the contrary, powerful states benefit from an international order that prevents large-scale wars. Great powers prefer to use the threat of force, rather

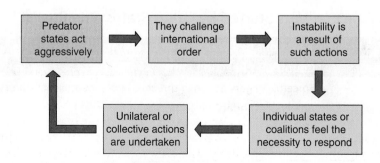

FIGURE 2-3 Predator states and international order. A predator state challenges international order, creating instability. Other states respond individually or collectively to restore the order. The predator state is defeated completely or changes its aggressive policies.

than actual force, to support their diplomacy, settle territorial disputes, establish political control, prevent attacks against themselves, and achieve economic goals. At the same time, realism admits that war cannot always be avoided and remains an effective instrument of realpolitik.

TYPES OF RESPONSES TO THE USE OF FORCE

If a military conflict occurs and affects the power distribution, states usually take action (Mearsheimer 2003). The nature of these actions depends on how states calculate their interests, threats to their interests, and a possible outcome of their inaction and counteraction.

One possible reaction is *forceful*: a threat to a balance of power is obvious, and it can be successfully removed. The 1990 occupation of Kuwait by Iraq caused the United States to organize a massive international military response against the aggressor. The U.S.-led troops quickly forced Iraq out of Kuwait in 1991.

A second possible reaction is *ambivalent*: a threat is serious, but an outcome of war is uncertain. After 2014, President Obama was concerned about Russia's gross violation of Ukraine's sovereignty: Russia annexed Crimea and provided military support for pro-Russian separatists in Ukraine's southeastern territories. Washington and its European allies imposed economic sanctions on Russia. At the same time, Russia consistently denied its use of force against Ukraine, and neither Washington nor NATO significantly escalated the conflict.

A third reaction is *indifferent*. In this case, a war does not affect directly the state's interests and stakes of involvement may be high. Bloody conflicts in Africa claimed millions of lives, yet in most cases strong powers did not take actions to intervene and stop them. During the Cold War, the United States and the Soviet Union often intervened only to prevent the defeat of the local group they supported with arms or ideologically (Westad 2007). After the Cold War ended, these interventions stopped (See Table 2-1.)

PROBABILITY OF WAR

When do power shifts lead to war? One view holds that the probability of war is high when two large states or two groups of states have a roughly equal measure of political, economic, and military capabilities. A state that is less satisfied with this distribution of power has reason to attack (Organski 1968).

TABLE 2-1 How States React to Wars Started by Other States: The Realist View

Country B's Possible Reactions to a War Started by Country A	
Effect on Country B's Interests	**Country B's Reaction**
Significant	Forceful: Military action or threats of violence against Country A
Moderate	Ambivalent: Indecisive and hesitant
Little to none	No action

In recent history, this view could not be tested: Even during the Cold War, the Soviet Union was much weaker militarily and economically than the United States. In the second decade of this century, China remains much weaker militarily and politically than the United States.

Neorealists link the probability of war to the structure of international relations and how states adapt to changes in power distribution. Yet they disagree on when this adaptation may lead to a war. They offer two kinds of arguments.

Visit the companion website to learn more about wars related to regional power shifts.

Defensive realists argue that anarchy breeds uncertainty, which encourages states to stay away from violence and to demonstrate self-restraint. Experts such as Kenneth Waltz (2001), Stephen Van Evera (2001), and Jack Snyder (2005) argue that historically, states consider war only as a last resort. The cost of war and the destruction it causes diminish any military or economic gains it could produce. At the same time, like most realists, these experts do not believe that wars can be prevented at all times. They view wars as a tragic result of major shifts of power. This happened in 1914, when World War I broke out in Europe.

Offensive realists suggest that the same situation of anarchy and uncertainty pushes stronger states to maximize their power at all times. This group includes Randall Schweller (2008), Peter Liberman (2006), and John Mearsheimer (2003). They argue that states tend to act ahead of serious threats to the international order. For instance, the best way to respond to a situation of instability is using force against predator states early, before they grow stronger. The failure of great Western powers to stop Hitler in the 1930s was a tragic mistake. Going to war against Germany earlier, rather than engaging in "appeasement acts," such as compromises and negotiations, would have been the correct policy. (See Table 2-2.)

Nonmilitary Responses

Most followers of the realist approach do not endorse war or threats of war as the only means of international relations. Realists also discuss peaceful, nonmilitary means of power balancing in foreign affairs.

Economic incentives, direct economic help, or sanctions are examples of nonmilitary responses of a country. These policies can be temporary or long-term. A relatively long-term policy was the Marshall Plan. In 1948, the Congress of

TABLE 2-2 Neorealist Arguments about War

Neorealist Views	Main Assumptions
Defensive realism	Wars are the result of the breakdown of international order. Great powers, in most occasions, seek to prevent open military conflicts. However, they can be drawn into wars by the anarchic dynamic of international relations.
Offensive realism	Wars and the use of force are more than accidents. They are tools that great powers use to build and protect international order, so as to prevent predator states from destroying the existing hierarchy of power.

A McDonald's restaurant in Yalta on the Crimean peninsula. It remained closed in 2015 due to U.S. and European sanctions imposed over Russia's involvement in the Ukrainian crisis.

the United States approved the first $5 billion of a special aid package to Europe, which had been devastated by World War II. As we will see further in Chapter 3, this plan helped Western European states, including Italy and West Germany, to restore economic and political stability and reduced the danger of a Communist takeover. The direct economic assistance to these countries continued until 1952. The United States also provided massive aid simultaneously to Israel and Egypt as an economic incentive to balance power and keep peace in the Middle East.

At the same time, states often use *economic sanctions* to punish other states that fail to cooperate, including limits on trade and financial operations. During the last three decades, the United States has imposed economic sanctions on Iraq, Iran, Libya, Cuba, North Korea, and Myanmar, and most recently on Russia, as we will discuss further in Chapter 7.

Neorealists recognize that states have a wide range of foreign policy options—including military and nonmilitary responses—to pursue their interests. Still, realism has difficulty adapting to many international developments, as we see next.

CHECK YOUR KNOWLEDGE

▶ Explain a key difference between realism and neorealism.
▶ Explain three types of responses to military threats.
▶ What are the main similarities and differences between offensive and defensive realism?

Contexts and Applications

How successful is realism in interpreting international relations? What are the strengths and weaknesses of this approach? How can realist ideas and arguments be applied to the world of international relations? As discussed in Chapter 1, we need to examine these questions in three contexts: individual, state, and global.

The Individual Decisions Context

Hans Morgenthau (1978), the classic theorist of realism, wrote about the role of morality, intuition, and emotion in the actions of state leaders, but the next generation of realists became less interested in the impact of individuals on power politics. To most of them, the course of international relations is shaped not so much by the personal choices of leaders, but rather by the international structure. Leaders of states adapt to this structure and cannot act otherwise.

This logic of neorealism, however, fails to explain the appearance of predator states and sudden threats to international order. If neorealists are correct, it did not matter that Hitler became chancellor of Germany in 1933. Germany, according to their logic, would have acted as a predator state anyway, because it was not satisfied with its place in the international order. Many historians and political scientists, however, reach different conclusions. Without Hitler's aggressive ideas and without the Nazi Party, Germany would not have amassed formidable military power so quickly and could not have conquered most of Europe (Tetlock et al. 2006).

We have already seen that the lack of attention to the individual context left neorealists unprepared for the peaceful end of the Cold War. In response, defenders of neorealism argue that Gorbachev was an exception that proves the rule. The Soviet leader reacted to waning Soviet power by trying to keep the power balance. He failed to adapt adequately to the changing distribution of power in the international order of the 1980s. He made too many mistakes. As a result, the Soviet Union disintegrated, and Gorbachev resigned from his post.

Still, the end of the Cold War obliged policy-oriented realists to take a closer look at individual leaders. Following the work of Alexander George (1969), they began to accumulate case studies that take into account the individual choices of state leaders (Goldgeier and Tetlock 2001). One test of realist theories comes with the death of a state leader. Can the loss of an individual produce important shifts in foreign policy or the distribution of power? Some facts provide supportive evidence. When Franklin D. Roosevelt died in April 1945 and Harry Truman became president, the United States began to act with less restraint toward the Soviet Union. The American use of two atomic bombs against Japan produced a dramatic power shift and contributed to the Cold War. If Roosevelt had been alive, it is possible that he might have decided not to use these bombs. The death of Egyptian president Gamal Abdel Nasser in 1970 brought to power Anwar Sadat, who abandoned the radical politics of his predecessor, restored Egypt's diplomatic relations with Israel, and brought Egypt closer to the United States.

The State Policies Context

While insisting on the importance of economic and military policies, realists in the past were often reluctant to consider other domestic political factors. Realists generally believed that states, democratic or not, tend to disregard ideological and political differences with other states if it suits their security interests. For years, despite its claim of support for freedom and democracy, the United States supported a wide range of dictatorships and non-democratic regimes in Latin America, Africa, and Asia.

Yet domestic political factors matter. In 1980, for example, Democratic U.S. president Jimmy Carter imposed a grain embargo on the Soviet Union to punish it for the invasion of Afghanistan. However, the embargo hurt the American farmers who exported grain to the Soviets. Immediately, Republican politicians put aside their anti-Communist rhetoric and spoke against the grain embargo. It was lifted when Reagan, a Republican, replaced Carter as president in 1981.

Robert Putnam (1988) argues that foreign policy is conducted on at least two levels: the domestic and the international. At home, domestic groups pursue their interests by pressuring the government to adopt favorable policies. Politicians respond to those groups' pressures. At the international level, governments play a balancing act between domestic interest groups and foreign policy goals. Leaders of sovereign states have to act simultaneously on both levels, like a game played on two chessboards. (That is why this model is called *two-level game theory*. We will return to it in Chapter 4.) Interest groups could be representatives of the military, corporations seeking defense contracts, the national security elite, foreign policy experts, or lobbying groups (Wittkopf and McCormick 2004).

To a certain degree, domestic political contexts determined the reactions of different states to the crisis in Ukraine that began in 2014. The United States and Canada, both with limited economic interests in Russia and Ukraine, had a strong Ukrainian community who demanded that both countries provide significant military aid to Ukraine to help it defend itself against Russia-backed separatists. Germany and France have significant business interests in Russia, and the public in these countries feared a larger military conflict. Poland and the three Baltic states (with still powerful memories of the Soviet occupation in 1940) wanted Washington to set up military bases there to contain Russia. And neutral Finland, which shares a long border with Russia, preferred caution and negotiations. In every case, domestic context influenced the way these states adapted to the threatening shifts in international order.

Domestic lobbies and social movements play a significant role in the foreign policy of democratic states. In peacetime, and in the absence of

CASE IN POINT > *Individual Leaders and Their Foreign Policy*

Does an assassination or the death of a country's leader change its foreign policy and international relations? As we see from Table 2-3, a leader's death may indeed be followed by dramatic change. Yet in some cases there is virtually no change, and the state continues with the same policies.

CRITICAL THINKING

❶ As a critical thinker, to draw an educated conclusion about the impact of political assassination on policy, you have to examine as much evidence as you can gather. Would other assassinations not listed in the table tell a different story?

❷ A leader's death is just one event among many domestic and international factors that affect state policies. Most probably, a combination of these multiple factors sways foreign policy from its course or keeps it in place. Which specific factors would you consider, and why?

❸ Do some online research to put together a more comprehensive database of state leaders' deaths and their states' subsequent foreign policies. Follow the format of Table 2-3. Study these cases and make your own conclusions.

TABLE 2-3   Foreign Policy Consequences of a Leader's Death

Leader's Death	Consequences for Foreign Policy and Power Balance
Joseph Stalin, Soviet Leader Date: 03/05/1953	Stalin's death led to crises in Eastern Europe and later produced the Sino-Soviet rivalry; these events resulted in a perceived dramatic shift in power between East and West.
John Kennedy, President of the United States Date: 11/22/1963	There were no significant changes in U.S. foreign policy; no changes in the power balance between the United States and the Soviet Union took place. Kennedy's successor, Lyndon Johnson, continued and escalated the Vietnam War started by Kennedy.
Gamal Abdel Nasser, President of Egypt Date: 09/28/1970	Although President Sadat, his successor, promised to continue Nasser's policies, an important policy shift followed; it ended in a peace treaty between Egypt and Israel and brought Egypt closer to the United States.
Hafizullah Amin, President of Democratic Republic of Afghanistan Date: 12/27/1979	Moscow suspected Amin of leaning toward the West. He was killed by the Soviet assault units that began a massive invasion that lasted until 1989 and had global consequences.
Anwar Sadat, President of Egypt Date: 10/6/1981	Sadat was assassinated for his reconciliatory policies toward Israel. There was no significant change in Egypt's foreign policy. Egypt under Sadat's successor, President Mubarak, relied on the United States and kept peace with Israel.
Indira Gandhi, Prime Minister of India Date: 10/31/1984	Gandhi was assassinated by her Sikh bodyguards. Her son Rajiv succeeded her. He continued the foreign course of nonalignment but leaned toward the Soviet Union.
Yitzhak Rabin, Prime Minister of Israel Date: 11/04/1995	Rabin was assassinated by a Jewish fundamentalist who attempted to torpedo the peace negotiations with the Palestinians. Israel, however, continued peace talks; they failed later for different reasons.
Lech Kaczyński, President of Poland Date: 04/10/2010	After Kaczyński died in a plane crash in Russia, his successor Donald Tusk abandoned harsh anti-German and anti-Russian rhetoric. Poland remains firmly tied to the EU and NATO.
Muammar Qaddafi, President of Libya Date: 10/20/2011	Anti-government fighters killed Qaddafi. Libyan insurgency received substantial Western military aid. The future of a new Libya remains uncertain.
Kim Jong-il, Supreme Leader of North Korea Date: 12/17/2011	After the sudden death of Kim Jong-il, his young son Kim Jong-un succeeded him. The North Korean regime shows no immediate signs of change in domestic or foreign policy.

immediate foreign threats, democratic states find it more difficult to conduct power politics. Any initiative in international relations requires compromises with bureaucracies and lobbies, which often pursue different agendas (Marrar 2008). A ruling political party, for example, may make concessions to the opposition party on domestic policy in exchange for support on foreign policy—a process known as *log rolling* (Laver 1997). During the early stages of the Cold

Palestinian youth hurl stones at the Israeli army during clashes in the Aida refugee camp north of Bethlehem in 2014. Domestic opposition from both sides for many years destroyed a chance for negotiations. Are there successful alternatives?

War, many U.S. congressmen and senators supported the containment of Communist threats, but only if new military bases would go to their constituents. These bases created jobs, brought additional revenues, and satisfied many voters. Similarly, the United Kingdom in the 1980s initially rejected President Reagan's Strategic Defense Initiative ("Star Wars")—until British leaders realized that sectors of their economy would benefit from multimillion-dollar defense contracts coming from the United States (McFarlane 1998).

Defensive realists acknowledge the importance of domestic political factors. Historically, governments initiate military conflicts in response to what they perceive as foreign security threats. Domestic political forces—including political parties and lobbies—may downplay or exaggerate such threats (Van Evera 1999). For decades, Israel and Palestinian political groups locked horns, trying to force each other to accept their plans. Israel wanted Palestinians to recognize Israel in its present borders. Palestinians wanted Israel to recognize their right to have a sovereign state. After the Oslo Accords of 1993 and 1995, the United States and the world community pushed both sides to the negotiating table.

However, domestic concerns that these accords would jeopardize security escalated. In Israel, supporters of the political right, especially settlers in the occupied territories, resisted the idea of Palestinian sovereignty. In 1995, a Jewish settler assassinated Israeli prime minister Yitzhak Rabin as retribution for his conciliatory polices toward the Palestinians. On the other side of the conflict, several groups of Palestinians in the early 2000s unleashed a violent uprising, the *intifada*, to intimidate and weaken Israel. The powerful Palestinian political group Hamas opposes the existence of Israel as a sovereign state. Most recently, the growing popularity of Islamic fundamentalism has significantly diminished any realistic chances for mutual recognition between Palestinians and Israelis. Domestic contexts and political pressures, neorealists would argue, reflect the state of anarchy and instability in the Middle East.

In sum, domestic political factors play a serious role in foreign policy and international relations, and supporters of realism explain these factors as reflecting the anarchical and unstable international system.

CHECK YOUR KNOWLEDGE
▶ What is the two-level game model of foreign policy?
▶ Explain log rolling.

The Global Context

The strength of social theories often lies in their ability to help formulate effective policies in the real world. The realist view of international relations had its greatest influence during the Cold War, a time of competition between two sets of leaders and two political systems. Supporters of realpolitik then brought up the entire experience of world history, from ancient Greece to European nation-states, to argue that preponderant power and containment of the Soviet Union was the best grand strategy to pursue. Yet now the Cold War is long over. How well does the realist view of international relations explain the complexity of today's world from a global perspective?

Realists take issue with the most prolific critics of realpolitik (Fukuyama 1993) and the assumption that, after the end of the Cold War, countries would turn to new principles of international relations based on the pursuit of mutual interests and common good. Instead, realists generally remain convinced that countries will not bargain away their security and are unlikely to maintain peaceful and mutually profitable cooperation without a consolidating force to keep global and regional developments in check (Betts 2011).

Realists argue that the end of a bipolar world could bring more rather than less instability, particularly on a regional level. Some regional balances are likely to show clear signs of strain. Most recent developments validate realist concerns. For instance, the runaway growth of China's power in the twenty-first century may generate tensions in Sino-Japanese and Sino-American relations. Japan, China's old-time regional rival, and the United States, which has become an Asia-Pacific power, oppose any rapid and forceful shifts in the balance of power in China's favor. India has also moved to offset China's growing power by improving ties with the United States. When Western countries backed Ukraine during the crisis that began in 2014, Russia sharply pivoted toward China, looking to compensate for Moscow's growing political and financial vulnerability. Returning to the pool table analogy, China appears to begin acting as a powerful ball on the table of international relations. Meanwhile, smaller countries must either accept its domination or look for protection elsewhere.

As realists believe, politics is always about distribution of power, and the time for superpowers has not passed. Current security threats include nuclear proliferation by countries such as North Korea and Iran and the actions of terrorist groups such as the Islamic State. Big countries have incentives to cooperate against these threats. At the same time, the traditional problem of domination in the international system has not disappeared. The debate continues among realists of how the United States can play a dominant role in world affairs (Joffe 2013; Booth and Wheeler 2008). Many smaller states in Eastern Europe, South Asia, and Southeast Asia, as the argument goes, will need a strong America. First, these states fear that without U.S. protection, powers like China or Russia might threaten their security. Second, America can help provide international stability that would benefit smaller states. The alternative could be worse: a state of global tensions with smaller states engaged in mutual threats and wars (Jervis 2003).

Others argue that Washington cannot play the role of a global policeman. They argue the United States ought to scale back the use of military force in international conflicts, foster greater cooperation with key allies, and rebuild its international image (Walt 2005b). Supporters of the realist view also believe

A nuclear power plant in Karachi, Pakistan, under construction in 2015. To meet chronic electricity shortages, Pakistan has been working with China to expand nuclear power generation capability. Will China's economic ascendancy make it a new superpower in Asia and globally?

that American domination can last only as long as its foreign policy and military power meet the security interests of other states. U.S. policies should satisfy national elites and address domestic public opinion in other countries as well (Joffe 2009). Conversely, without a "global cop," states will quickly create strong coalitions and pursue multipolar global arrangements.

Putting the Contexts Together

According to realism, the power and leadership of the United States will be the crucial factor in the future of the international order. First, if the United States finds ways to remain an indispensable global leader and manage the rise of other great powers, world stability will be strengthened. Occasional challenges to U.S. power will continue but will not last for long. For realists, especially realists of American origin, this is the best possible scenario.

Second, if America's power and leadership continue to erode, global instability might arise. Several centers of power can act with increasing autonomy, possibly including European Union, China, Russia, India, and Brazil. Economic competition will continue, but states will be less inclined to go to war owing to its devastating economic consequences. This scenario is most likely, if the current international trends continue unchecked.

One can imagine yet another scenario. The salience of military power and danger of instability and war will decline, because the United States and other states, big and small, will cooperate in international organizations. Traditional fears and the use of military power would dissolve in the new liberal networks of cooperation, trade, and economic interdependence. States will transfer

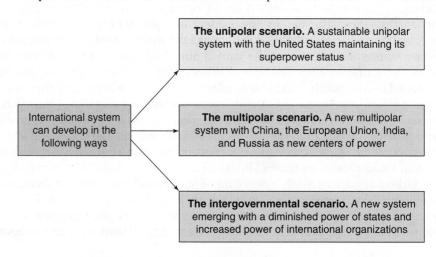

The unipolar scenario. A sustainable unipolar system with the United States maintaining its superpower status

International system can develop in the following ways

The multipolar scenario. A new multipolar system with China, the European Union, India, and Russia as new centers of power

The intergovernmental scenario. A new system emerging with a diminished power of states and increased power of international organizations

FIGURE 2-4 Realist view of the future of global polarity.

attention and resources to humanitarian issues, such as the global environment and mutual help during natural catastrophes. All realists, despite their mutual differences, reject this scenario as extremely unlikely—in fact, as a fairy tale. (See Figure 2-4.)

We will discuss the third scenario in the next chapter, where we turn to a leading challenger to realism—the liberal perspective.

THE USES OF HISTORY: The North Atlantic Treaty Organization

Background

The history of the North Atlantic Treaty Organization (NATO) illustrates how states behave in a time of uncertainty and fear. The alliance emerged in 1949 at the urging of the Netherlands, Belgium, and Denmark. They feared the power of the Soviet Union and a possible resurgence of Germany after World War II. Losing trust in Britain or France, these small countries appealed to the United States to provide protection to Western Europe. The United States, worried that an unstable Europe might fall into the orbit of the rival Soviet Union, immediately accepted the offer.

For the next four decades, NATO solved several problems that European balance of power could not. The dangerous rivalry between Germany and France, which led to several wars, was over. After a few years of French objections, in 1955, West Germany became a full-time member of NATO (Zelikow and Rice 1995). Lord Ismay, the first secretary general of NATO, noted that NATO's mission at that time was "to keep Americans in [Europe], to keep Russians out and to keep Germans down" (Ismay 1960).

Above all, NATO helped the United States to become a European power and then a global power. Although NATO claimed to be a defensive alliance, the huge military superiority of the United States allowed some strategists to entertain plans to "roll back" the Soviet sphere of influence in Eastern Europe. They hoped to throw off Soviet power from East Germany, Poland, Czechoslovakia, Hungary, and Romania and to drive it back to the borders of the Soviet Union. These offensive plans had to be dropped when the Soviet Union became a nuclear superpower. This new balance of power allowed the Kremlin to crush the anti-Communist revolution in Hungary in 1956 with impunity, while NATO states observed passively.

NATO was shaken as well by a serious crisis in relations among the United States, the United Kingdom, and France. Paris and London strove to remain strong regional and colonial powers. Washington, however, pressured them to scale back their actions. The crisis culminated in 1956, when Egypt nationalized the Suez Canal. In retaliation, the United Kingdom and France attacked Egypt without consulting with the United States. Furious, Washington essentially forced Paris and London to back off.

After France lost much of its influence in the Middle East as a result of the Suez incident, many expected a deepening rift in relations between

After twelve years of military operations in Afghanistan, NATO troops withdraw in 2014. Should NATO conduct military operations far away from the zone of Europe's and North America's immediate security concerns?

Read more on the companion website about the Suez crisis and the beginning of a shift in power relations in Western Europe.

Washington and Paris. Some predicted the end of the Western alliance. Soviet leaders advanced the idea of simultaneously disbanding NATO and the Warsaw Treaty Organization, which was the Moscow-dominated security bloc of Eastern and Central European Communist states. For several years, NATO faced contradictions and crises, its future uncertain, but it survived even after France decided in 1966 to leave NATO's military organization while remaining a political member. The organization's headquarters had to move from Paris to Brussels.

Facing a potentially costly and dangerous arms race, European members of NATO in 1967 proposed the new doctrine of *détente*, or peaceful coexistence between the West and the Communist bloc. The United States eventually decided to support the concept but adapt it to American interests. This led to a number of disagreements between Washington and the Western European countries, and a number of separate treaties between Moscow and West Germany. Yet the détente reached its limits, and dangerous accumulation of nuclear and conventional weapons continued (White 2007).

The nuclear issue remained a divisive problem. From the start, Washington promised to provide a "nuclear umbrella" to protect its European allies. It was understood that in case of any Soviet conventional attack in Europe, the United States would deliver a massive nuclear assault against the Soviet Union. However, facing the growing Soviet thermonuclear power, Europeans began to wonder: Would the United States risk incurring a Soviet nuclear retaliation by attacking? Would it put New York and Los Angeles at risk to defend Hamburg or Amsterdam? In response, President Eisenhower and his advisers decided to give a few nuclear-tipped missiles to the West German army. Their plan, however, produced furious opposition—not only in the Soviet Union, but also in West Germany. After the United Kingdom and France expressed their own concerns, Washington's plans to make Germany a nuclear power were dropped. London and Paris accelerated their own national atomic programs, and the United Kingdom and France became nuclear powers (Schmidt 2001).

Nuclear weapons continued to contribute to growing tensions between NATO and the Soviet Union. To boost its nuclear credibility, the United States placed American medium-range missiles in Italy and Turkey, both NATO members. The Soviet Union, of course, interpreted this action as an immediate threat. Moscow's response contributed, in part, to the most dangerous move of the Cold War, the sending of Soviet medium-range missiles to Cuba in 1962. The Cuban Missile Crisis ended peacefully, and most American nuclear systems stationed in Italy and Turkey were removed. A nuclear balance seemed achievable. From the realist view, such a balance should have brought stability, but mutual fears and mistrust continued. Why?

Analysis

Offensive realists argue that both sides feared the introduction of new nuclear systems, drastically shifting the balance of power. Even in the early 1970s, a period of gradual reduction of tensions between the West and the Soviet Union, the U.S. Navy brought nuclear weapons closer to the Soviet Union. This, in turn, made the Kremlin retaliate with the deployment of a new generation of medium-range missiles (called SS-20 in the West). These missiles threatened Western European security gravely. In response, West Germany, Belgium, the Netherlands, and Luxembourg actively pushed Washington to deploy on their territories the new generation of short-range and very accurate Pershing II missiles, as well as the low-flying and difficult-to-detect cruise missiles. These deployments in 1983 marked the last serious confrontation between NATO and the Soviet Union (Gaddis 2006).

The rapid disintegration of the Soviet Union in 1991 left NATO without its original purpose. There was no longer a Soviet bloc or Soviet power to contain. Many experts believed that NATO had no future. However, realists argue, there were other reasons for this organization to survive.

The first was regional security. Small European states now feared the power of a unified Germany. Further, the political vacuum left by the Soviet disintegration triggered a civil war in Yugoslavia (1991–95). To maintain stability, Europe needed a strong security alliance. Thus in 1996–98, with energetic U.S. support, Poland, the Czech Republic, and Hungary became NATO members. In 2004, Estonia, Latvia, Lithuania, Slovenia, Slovakia, Bulgaria, and Romania acquired full membership, too. For them, NATO membership was "a return to Europe" and a security guarantee against Russia. To strengthen its international ties, NATO established an official partnership network with more than twenty countries, including Ukraine, Georgia, Moldova, and Montenegro. In 2009, Croatia and Albania joined in. (See Map 2-3.)

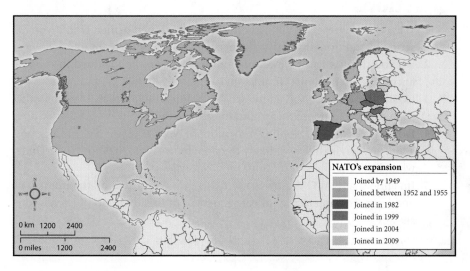

NATO's expansion

- Joined by 1949
- Joined between 1952 and 1955
- Joined in 1982
- Joined in 1999
- Joined in 2004
- Joined in 2009

0 km   1200   2400
0 miles   1200   2400

MAP 2-3 Belgium, the Netherlands, Luxemburg, France, the United States, the United Kingdom, Canada, Portugal, Italy, Norway, Denmark, and Iceland formed NATO in 1949. By 2009, NATO was an alliance made up of twenty-eight member countries.

The second reason was the perceived threats outside Europe, such as Iran's nuclear ambitions and instability in North Africa and the Middle East. This led to the movement to "globalize" NATO. Some European capitals and Washington hoped to use the economic, financial, and military power of the alliance to resolve international conflicts around the world. More than a dozen NATO states sent troops to fight in Afghanistan and helped the United States during its occupation of Iraq. In 2011, NATO launched a military campaign in Libya.

NATO's expansion and attempts to design new roles for the alliance also led to serious debates between defensive and offensive realists (Sloan 2010). The former argue that the expansion of the North Atlantic alliance was not necessary, because NATO did not face any realistic threat. The new NATO members, they suggest, deliberately exaggerated external threats, particularly from Russia. The momentum for NATO expansion was created by domestic political groups who pursued their interests and used the bogus justification of foreign threat (Goldgeier 1999). The advocates of defensive realism also point out that NATO's eastward enlargement triggered an anxious reaction in Russia, including the recent crisis in Ukraine. Followers of offensive realism disagree. They maintain that NATO has to be expanded and that Russia under the leadership of Vladimir Putin would have attempted to increase its power anyway.

Meanwhile, U.S. plans to use NATO as an instrument for unipolar international order ran into serious problems. The war in Iraq produced a serious split in NATO in 2003, forcing the Bush administration to rely on the United Kingdom and on new members from Central Europe and the Baltic States. With Russia invading Georgia in 2008 and taking over the Crimea Peninsula in 2014, any plans to enlarge NATO have been postponed. The alliance, some realists argue, has outreached its boundaries and revealed its limitations. The discussion continues.

Questions

1. What other threats, in addition to those mentioned earlier, would you describe to additionally justify, the necessity to strengthen NATO?
2. Do you think a Latin American country needs to be included in the alliance? If yes, which one? If not, why?
3. Could these threats be addressed by political or economic means other than strengthening the North Atlantic alliance?
4. Do you see Russia becoming a member of NATO? If you see this as a possibility, when is this most likely to happen: in 2020, 2025, or 2030? Under what domestic and international conditions?
5. Imagine that NATO dissolves itself this year. What will be the immediate and long-term international consequences of this dissolution (if you foresee any)?

CONCLUSION

For decades the realist view was predominant in discussions of international relations. Power and the reactions of states to international anarchy were seen as vital to explaining world security or insecurity. Ruling elites, watching the changing balance of power, saw realism as the only way to keep international order intact. The lessons of World War II backed realist arguments. If great powers had acted earlier to stop Nazism and fascism, the argument goes, seventy million people would not have perished.

Yet even while the Cold War lasted, realism began to change. In a way, the neorealist theory was a victim of its own success. It could almost ignore the debates that had given birth to realism in the first place—the great questions concerning human nature and values, morality and power, prudence and vision. The collapse of the Soviet Union left realists with a complex and often puzzling world. The United States was now the only great power, yet it failed to create a stable international order. It remains unclear whether the United States can remain the world's leader for long. What kind of realist policies will the future see? For this, we need to study emerging international realities and problems more closely. The debates will become more intriguing.

KEY TERMS

anarchy 41
bipolar order 49
Cold War (1946–89) 45
gross domestic product
    (GDP) 43

hegemony 43
international system 41
multipolar order 49
neorealism (structural
    realism) 47

power 41
predator state 60
realism 41
realpolitik 42
unipolar order 49

IDEAS

CHARACTERISTICS OF REALISM

- States are the main actors in international relations
- States focus on power, security, and national interests
- States try to avoid anarchy
- Neorealism emphasizes power structure and order

DEVELOPMENT OF REALISM

- States historically applied realist principles to balance out one another
- Realism explains the rise, fall, and evolution of great powers
- Realism explains the Cold War as a bipolar international order

ARGUMENTS

LESSONS OF REALPOLITIK

- States need a strong economy and military, efficient diplomacy, and few international commitments
- Predator states disregard international rules and must be dealt with
- Rapid power shifts threaten stability

LESSONS FROM MILITARY AND NONMILITARY RESPONSES

- Wars are likely yet avoidable
- States benefit from an international order that prevents large-scale wars
- States may act preventively to preserve an international order
- Diplomacy may prevent war

CONTEXTS AND APPLICATIONS

THE INDIVIDUAL DECISIONS CONTEXT

- Individual factors may play a role in power politics, but realists tend to overlook them

THE STATE POLICIES CONTEXT

- States' foreign policies are formed on two levels: the domestic and the international
- Domestic forces affect foreign policies of democratic and non-democratic states

THE GLOBAL CONTEXT

- Realists argue in favor of a consolidating force to keep global developments in check

Critical Thinking

❶ Explain the principles of realism in thirty seconds, and give at least one example of realpolitik.

❷ Apply principles of realpolitik to the United States' foreign policy toward any contemporary international conflict.

❸ What are the similarities and differences between realism and neorealism?

❹ Do you see the United States as a hegemonic power today? Why or why not?

❺ Why do realists associate bipolarity with international stability?

❻ How does realism explain individual foreign policy decisions? Give examples.

The Liberal Perspective 3

> *No state shall by force interfere with the constitution or government of another state.*

—IMMANUEL KANT

I N THE FALL OF 1987, MIKHAIL GORBACHEV RELEASED *PERESTROIKA: NEW THINKING FOR OUR COUNTRY AND THE WORLD.* MOST PRESIDENTS AND PRIME MINISTERS PUBLISH their memoirs *after* they leave office. But the Soviet leader's book was not a memoir. It was a call for a new world based on new principles of international relations. Gorbachev argued that to achieve global stability and peace, world leaders should change their thinking. First, they must reject the use of force in foreign policy. Second, they must put aside ideological differences in the name of nonviolence and cooperation. And third, they must build a new international community. As he said a year later from the podium at the General Assembly of the United Nations, states must "search for a consensus of all mankind."

Skeptics dismissed Gorbachev's rhetoric as an empty promise. How could one trust the top official of the Communist Party? They were wrong. In the next months, Poland and Hungary dismantled Communist regimes that the Soviet Union had protected for almost forty years. The Berlin Wall fell in November 1989, and a year later East Germany and West Germany declared re-unification. Throughout these momentous changes in Eastern Europe, Gorbachev refrained from using force or threats of force.

Western security experts feared that Soviet generals would try to stop changes initiated by Gorbachev. Instead, in December 1991 the Soviet Union peacefully dissolved into the Russian

Previous page: The Berlin Wall, built in 1961 by East Germany with Soviet assistance, became a dramatic symbol of Communism. The Wall fell in 1989, a ripple effect of Mikhail Gorbachev's "new thinking." This spectacular event demonstrates the importance of ideas of cooperation and common security in changing international relations. Which ideas today have the biggest impact on world politics?

Federation and fourteen other independent states. The stunning changes posed a serious challenge to realism. If power politics alone represent the essence of international relations, how was Gorbachev able to reject power politics and embrace a new norm?

Years have passed since the end of the Cold War. But have world leaders embraced universal principles of cooperation? The answer is inconclusive. Most countries today live in peace. However, military threats continue to affect international relations. Scores of unresolved conflicts could easily explode in open violence. In 2009, it was the U.S. president's turn to call for "a new era of engagement based on mutual interest and mutual respect." But did this call lead to a stable and peaceful world? If such a world is our common goal, why can't governments achieve it?

This chapter will examine an old alternative to the realist approach to international relations, *liberalism*, and its modern incarnation—*neoliberalism*. This view accepts the reality of anarchy and power politics but maintains that this reality can be transformed by spreading democratic norms, establishing the rule of law, and promoting economic and political cooperation. The ultimate goal is to establish common norms and institutions of international behavior. Liberalism also points to international and nonstate organizations as key players, along with states. This chapter will describe the origins, main modern strands, and principal applications of the liberal approach and its impact today.

▶ Describe the key features of liberalism and neoliberalism.
▶ Explain why and how liberalism seeks to overcome anarchy and power politics.
▶ Distinguish different approaches within neoliberalism.
▶ Apply neoliberal approaches to individual decisions, to specific policies of states and other actors, and to global developments.

Learning Objectives

Ideas

For centuries, power politics dominated international relations. Generations of political leaders, diplomats, military officers, and experts learned through trial and error the principles of power balance, spheres of interests, and military domination. Despite continuing conflicts, the ideals of religious tolerance, reason, and enlightenment spread across Europe and America. These led many politicians in the eighteenth and nineteenth centuries to believe that human beings and states alike are capable of reason and self-restraint—the foundations of stability. State leaders increasingly raised doubts about the capacity of realpolitik to provide long-lasting peace. With the spread of democratic governance in the twentieth century, more political leaders questioned the secrecy and lack of accountability in traditional diplomacy and foreign policy institutions. Not only state officials, but also citizens and their associations should be the actors of foreign policy, and the rule of law and the benefits of cooperation should override a permanent power struggle between state interests.

liberalism A school of thought based on the idea that international organizations, international economic cooperation, interdependence, and democracy allow states to avoid power politics and establish a lasting peace.

International liberalism, or simply **liberalism**, is an approach to international relations based on several fundamental and interconnected principles:

1. It does not believe that power politics is the inevitable source and outcome of international relations. One country's gain does not necessarily mean another country's loss.
2. It emphasizes international economic cooperation and interdependence.
3. It sees international organizations and nonstate actors as influences shaping state preferences and policy choices.
4. It believes that the spread of international law and democracy helps to secure lasting peace.

The Development of Liberalism

Will people ever live in a peaceful, prosperous world without fear and intimidation? How would *you* achieve these goals in practice? In the history of international relations, the stubborn reality of power politics and wars has constantly challenged supporters of liberalism.

INTELLECTUAL ROOTS

Liberal ideas are rooted in the rich philosophical and cultural traditions cultivated in Europe. First, liberalism emerged as a set of ideas of *enlightenment* and *humanism*. Enlightenment thinkers like John Locke (1632–1704) and David Hume (1711–1776) in England, Voltaire (1694–1778) and Montesquieu (1689–1755) in France, and scores of others argued that free individuals pursuing their interests could transform the nature of politics. To put it simply, a monarch would always fight other monarchs. Free and enlightened individuals, however, would have no reason to clash. The liberated individuals of free states, pursuing and prospering from mutually beneficial trade policies, were thus likely to pursue policies of mutual respect for the sake of shared benefits.

In *Perpetual Peace: A Philosophical Sketch* (1795), the German philosopher Immanuel Kant (1724–1804), whose words open this chapter, brought these ideas together. The essay imagines a federation of independent republics that would share mutual responsibilities, respect for the rule of law, and joint economic interests. Without the constraints of the law, the essay argues, states would behave like "savage people" in the wilderness. But the road to civilization demands a contract among states, which Kant called *a league of peace*. Like the police in a community, this league should be governed by law to secure freedom and peace.

His ideas provided key concepts for contemporary liberal perspectives of international relations. Modern liberals often summarize the ideas of Kant as the *Kantian Triangle*. It consists of a *republican constitution* (today we call it democracy), a *commercial spirit* of trade (economic interdependence), and *international law* (including the activities of international institutions that promote it) (Russett and Oneal, 2001). This triangle describes the three major brands of liberalism: legal, economic, and institutional.

Rapid industrialization in Europe and North America and the growth of global trade in the late nineteenth century provided support for the liberal view. Historians sometimes call this period *the first globalization*: An international economic alliance appeared as an alternative to destructive warfare. Liberal thinkers did not believe that war was a natural outcome of the struggle for power and territories. Rather, they thought war was unnatural and preventable.

The nineteenth and early twentieth century produced classic international liberal thought, such as the works of John Stuart Mill (1806–1873) and Giuseppe Mazzini (1805–1872). Liberal scholar and politician Norman Angell, in *The Great Illusion* (1910), denied that states prosper largely through power games and territorial expansion. Wars, he wrote, disrupt economic order. The territorial gains achieved by war cannot compensate for much greater losses in business and international trade. States would eventually learn this lesson. Cooperation would gradually lead to prosperity for an ever-growing number of countries and peoples.

Nevertheless, war would remain common so long as old political elites pursued power politics. Joseph Schumpeter, an economist from Austria-Hungary, wrote in *The Sociology of Imperialism* (1919) that the ever-greater prominence of the *bourgeoisie* (entrepreneurs and the middle class) would lead to the decline of military aristocracies and with it the disappearance of territorial expansionism and international violence. An educated and secure people would devote their energy to the production and satisfaction of rational needs. Confrontation, therefore, would become obsolete.

The ideas of Kant, Angell, and Schumpeter remained popular among liberal internationalists. In an open, democratic system, state leaders respond to peaceful, law-abiding citizens who are involved in economic exchanges (Doyle 1986). Thus, a democratic system of government was itself crucial to preventing international violence. Would this assumption prove correct?

In his 1795 essay *Perpetual Peace*, Immanuel Kant argued that the road to a stable international system demands a contract among states, which he called *a league of peace*. His ideas provided key concepts for contemporary liberal perspectives on international relations. Do they remain relevant today?

 Perpetual Peace has become a source of new ideas for many generations of scholars and politicians. Read it on the companion website.

On the companion website: "Kant, Immanuel," in *The Routledge Encyclopedia of Philosophy*. Arthur Schlesinger Jr., "Forgetting Reinhold Niebuhr."

CASE IN POINT > *Are Humans Inherently Selfish and Violent?*

Not all European intellectuals were captivated by ideas of liberalism and beliefs in an individual's propensity for peace and reason. Warfare was often associated with manhood as a component of a noble character. Immanuel Kant, for instance, who defended liberal principles, also wrote that "a prolonged peace favors the predominance of a mere commercial spirit, and with it a debasing self-interest, cowardice, and effeminacy, and tends to degrade the character of the nation." In the nineteenth and early twentieth centuries, people were intrigued by the ideas of influential philosophers such as Friedrich Nietzsche (1844–1900) and psychoanalyst Sigmund Freud (1856–1939). Nietzsche believed that only the strong and the power-driven rule the world. Freud argued that irrational forces dominate human behavior and, after the devastation of World War I, grew extremely skeptical about the ability of humans to preserve peace. Aggression, he believed, is embedded in the human *psyche*, and social institutions are often incapable of stopping hostility and violence.

CRITICAL THINKING

This is a centuries-old debate about human nature: If left to their own devices, are humans likely to choose peace and cooperation over egotism and rivalry, or will violence prevail? Let's look at this discussion from a different angle. Discuss conditions, both domestic and international, under which you think people are likely to choose cooperation over rivalry. Also discuss conditions that in your view are likely cause violence. To support your arguments, pick an ongoing international conflict to see if the conditions you have suggested are present there.

EARLY ATTEMPTS TO IMPLEMENT LIBERAL PRINCIPLES

Already in the nineteenth century, statesmen and scholars began to call for international organizations that could practice diplomacy based on mutual compromises. Public figures and influential liberal thinkers pressed governments to build a system of collective security and **global disarmament**, or states' elimination of their weapons. After all, if no state possessed weapons, none could start a war. Although the idea of total disarmament appeared impractical, many state leaders embraced the thought of serious limits on weaponry and war.

global disarmament
The universal and voluntary elimination by states of their offensive weapons.

As the first steps, an increasing number of government officials and international humanitarian organizations hoped to impose "civilized" constraints on warfare. In 1899 the first international disarmament conference was convened in the Netherlands at Russia's initiative, to negotiate limits on state possession of weapons. In 1899 and again in 1907, at the second disarmament conference, many European states signed the Hague Convention, which banned some lethal technologies in warfare and regulated the treatment of prisoners and civilians during wartime. For the first time, the principles of liberalism challenged realism in practice.

THE LESSONS OF WORLD WAR I

Agreements to limit warfare, not to mention disarmament agreements, suddenly seemed utopian when Austria-Hungary declared war on Serbia in July 1914.

Instead of mediation, the whole of Europe, and then the rest of the world, plunged into war. Millions of people waved national flags and volunteered to fight and die. World War I (1914–18) took the lives of more than sixteen million people, providing a frightening lesson to supporters of liberal ideas. During the war, most countries' leaders acted like predators and wanted nothing less than a military victory. Scores of European intellectuals who had previously denounced violence now rode the wave of nationalism and supported their war-hungry governments.

Their support did not last long. The war in fact prompted calls for liberalism. As a result of the conflict's devastating toll on societies across Europe, urgent calls for international cooperation were heard all over the world. U.S. president Woodrow Wilson, a former president of Princeton University, actively promoted cooperation among countries with the notions of free trade and equal respect. In 1917, with the United States entering the war, he began to tout a League of Nations, an international organization that would protect smaller countries from aggression and steer the world toward cooperation and peace. (MacMillan 2003). Wilson hoped that the spread of liberal principles of free trade could provide international stability, resolve conflicts, and reduce the likelihood of war. (Remember the ideas of Angell and Schumpeter.) Wilson also hoped that one day European great powers would free their colonies.

THE LEAGUE OF NATIONS

The League of Nations was formally established in 1919 at a peace conference in Paris. The League was the first global organization aimed at prevention,

Woodrow Wilson became the first American leader to promote the global ideology of liberal internationalism. He succeeded in creating the League of Nations but failed to win support for it in the United States. This photo shows Wilson on a speaking tour in St. Louis, Missouri, to promote the League, in September 1919.

mediation, and peaceful resolution of interstate conflicts, support of basic human rights, disarmament, and economic cooperation. Although the U.S. Senate, dominated by the "isolationists," refused to support Wilson's internationalist policies and the United States never joined the League, several nongovernmental associations, the religious society of the Quakers, business leaders, and politicians supported the League's global mission. Liberal internationalists in the U.S.—supporters of Wilsonian principles—proposed the Dawes Plan in 1924 and the Young Plan of 1929. These programs of financial assistance to the economically ailing Germany, the U.S.'s former foe, aimed to provide stability for Europe. American secretary of state Frank Kellogg received the Nobel Peace Prize for his efforts to negotiate an international pact banning war as an "instrument of national policy." The United States also took part in the World Disarmament Conference in Geneva from 1932 to 1934.

Britain and France, however, ignored Wilson's liberal principles. The Versailles Treaty of 1919 imposed on Germany the burden of paying punitive reparations to the victors, which constrained German, and consequently European, economic development. Europe became divided not only by war, but also by new border laws. When the former Austria-Hungary and Ottoman Empire were broken into many independent states, this partition exacerbated ethnic tensions and territorial claims. Under the pressure of economic crises and nationalism, political liberalism quickly failed in many European countries, giving way to authoritarian, militant regimes (Shirer 1990; Mazower 2000).

The League of Nations fell victim to discord among the great powers. It could not prevent several aggressions, including Japan's invasion of Manchuria and Italy's occupation of Ethiopia. Hitler's Germany, Mussolini's fascist Italy, and Stalin's Soviet Union brazenly defied the League. In September of 1939 Hitler and Stalin attacked Poland and divided its territory between themselves. France and Britain declared war on Germany, the Second World War started, and the League became a political corpse. Many critics of the League, among them the British journalist and historian E. H. Carr (1939), rejected the principles of liberalism. They claimed that the future belongs to powerful states. Those who still believed in international cooperation watched in despair.

1945: A NEW BEGINNING FOR LIBERAL PRINCIPLES

As often happens, tragic events became valuable lessons. They grew into beliefs that history should not repeat itself. Many liberal ideas formed the backbone of U.S. foreign policy during and immediately after World War II. In the 1940 election, Democratic president Franklin D. Roosevelt and his Republican rival Wendell Willkie agreed that the world needed a new beginning, one based on cooperation and restraint. In 1941, Roosevelt convinced British prime minister Winston Churchill to sign the Atlantic Charter, an agreement renouncing future territorial conquests and promising to restore sovereignty to all states. The charter revived Wilsonian principles: free trade, cooperation, and equality among nations. Roosevelt also entertained the idea that the

MAP 3-1 Europe pre- and post-WWI. Borders redrawn by the Versailles Treaty.

United States, the United Kingdom, the Soviet Union, and China could play the role of international police as part of a new international organization, the United Nations. A council of the great powers would have special responsibilities to preserve peace. Roosevelt's successor as president, Harry S. Truman, was an ardent supporter of liberalism, and carried in his pocket the poem "Locksley Hall" by Alfred Tennyson (1809–1892), describing a vision in which

> the war-drum throbb'd no longer, and the battle-flags were furl'd in the Parliament of men, the Federation of the World.

Roosevelt's advocacy allowed institutional liberalism to become reality. The United Nations (UN), a global international institution, was founded in San Francisco in April 1945, shortly after Roosevelt's death (see Chapter 6). Permanent members of the UN Security Council included the United States, the United Kingdom, the Soviet Union, France, and China. The preamble of the UN Charter reads:

> We, the peoples of the United Nations [are determined] to save succeeding generations from the scourge of war, . . . reaffirm faith in fundamental human rights, . . . promote social progress and better standards of life in larger freedom, . . . practice tolerance, and live together in peace with one another as good neighbours.

The economic strand of liberalism also flourished after World War II. The United States and Great Britain, learning from the mistakes of the Versailles Treaty, were against punishing Germany with heavy reparations. Instead, there were ideas to make Germany an engine of a pan-European economic revival. In 1945 U.S. and British politicians and economists launched the World Bank and International Monetary Fund (IMF). Their purpose was to lay the foundations of a lasting global financial system. Attempts to create an international trade organization to promote free trade were not at first successful, as we will see in Chapter 7. The later General Agreement on Tariffs and Trade (GATT) aimed to reduce or eliminate barriers to international trade.

Advocates of economic cooperation won another victory when the U.S. Congress approved the European Recovery Program, commonly known as the Marshall Plan (1947–51). Thanks to the efforts of Secretary of State George Marshall and policy planner George Kennan, among others, this program offered unprecedented financial help to a Europe devastated by war, revived European capitalism, and reactivated trade between Europe and the United States. From the 1950s through the 1980s, the World Bank, IMF, and GATT remained pillars of international capitalism. Even in a world divided by the Cold War, they put trade wars out of existence. With substantial U.S. assistance, Western European nations, including Germany, created institutions of cooperation that gradually evolved into the European Community and, in the 1990s, into the European Union.

Although the arms race dominated the foreign policy agenda during the Cold War, views of institutional and economic liberalism remained attractive to state leaders and nongovernmental organizations. It was becoming clear that foreign policy driven by mutual interests and promoted by international

Communist-led demonstrators in Germany carry posters saying "Against the Marshall Plan that brings unemployment and misery." The USSR and Communists in Europe fiercely opposed the Marshall Plan, depicting it as a tool for U.S. domination.

institutions could bring substantial benefits. In the 1950s and 1960s, free-market democracies enjoyed tremendous economic growth. The new realities of international organizations and European economic integration began to influence and even challenge the old realist agenda of power balance, deterrence, and containment.

 Read more about the Marshall Plan on the companion website.

✳ Neoliberalism

After the 1960s, the agenda of liberalism expanded and diversified. IR began to study the ability of international institutions to promote cooperation among countries. Some neoliberals began to regard multinational corporations, wrongly as it turned out, as players that might soon substitute for sovereign states (Haas 1964; Kindleberger 1970; Vernon 1971). Some insisted that even bitter opponents like the United States and the Soviet Union could cooperate. The two powers, they argued, shared a common interest in stability and the prevention of nuclear war. In *The Anarchical Society*, Australian scholar Hedley Bull argued that sovereign states always tend to develop a "civilized" international society with shared rules and norms. Bull showed that countries, despite a lack of trust, strive to develop and observe common regulations and institutions (Bull 1977; 1988).

The *Kantian Triangle*, as we discussed earlier, produced three influential strands of liberal theorizing: institutional, economic, and legal. The institutional strand became especially influential as a root of **neoliberalism**, also called **neoliberal institutionalism**. It challenged the ideas of neorealism by Kenneth Waltz and other realists. Neoliberals used complex arguments to

neoliberalism (neoliberal institutionalism) An approach that postulates that states prefer to seek security not through power politics but in the context of a complex interdependence among states.

support their idea that sovereign states prefer cooperation to power politics and do not seek short-term advantages if international institutions promise them a better outcome: lasting security. Neoliberals also postulate that states remain a main subject of analysis in international relations. However, states realize their interests in the new context of complex interdependence among states. This context, as supporters of this view argued, can become a model that would "provide a better portrayal of reality" compared to realism and neo-realism (Keohane and Nye 1989, p. 20). Complex interdependence has three main features. First, states interact through multiple channels including informal ties and economic, financial, and cultural contacts. Second, security is not always the primary agenda of state-to-state interactions. Different issues become important at different times, such as trade and currency regulations, human rights concerns, and the economic assistance of wealthy countries to poor ones. And third, military force is typically not used by countries against other countries.

The end of the Cold War brought new converts and arguments for neoliberal concepts. As you may remember from the introduction to this chapter, Soviet leader Gorbachev called for the rapid reduction of tensions between the United States and the Soviet Union. Scores of experts, from journalists to state officials, discussed possibilities for a world order based on freedom of choice. Some liberal critics even declared that the principles of neorealism could not be applied to developed democracies. According to these critics, states are not just billiard balls on a table, but rather are complex units consisting of individuals and voluntary groups. In a democratic country, individual citizens and groups elect their governments. In their foreign policy, these governments reflect the interests and preferences of many domestic actors. This strand of liberalism views states as institutions that are serving the needs and choices of individuals and groups. Therefore, states, like people, are capable of goodwill, self-restraint, and cooperation (Moravcsik 1993).

CHECK YOUR KNOWLEDGE

▶ Describe the three strands of modern liberalism.
▶ What are the main differences between the League of Nations and the United Nations?
▶ Why should states, according to neoliberalism, prefer cooperation to power politics?
▶ What are the features of complex interdependence?

Stop here!!!← **Arguments**

We turn now to a critical evaluation of modern liberalism. How does it compare with realism, and what are liberalism's strengths and weaknesses?

Comparing Liberalism and Realism

Liberalism is much more conceptually diverse than realism. Further, liberalism is not only *descriptive* when it criticizes realism as a framework for

TABLE 3-1 Liberal and Realist Views of International Relations

	The Liberal Tradition	The Realist Tradition
Actors	States are important but are not the only actors in international affairs. International institutions and nonstate actors are also important.	Sovereign states are the principal actors in international relations.
Achievement of Order and Stability	Order and stability are achieved through interdependence and by goodwill, mutual trust, and compromise.	Order and stability are achieved by power balancing among states and mutual fear of a major war.
Means	Military force is used to restrain the aggressor and only after international diplomacy fails.	Military force or threats to use force are the most efficient means of power balancing.

analyzing international relations. It is also *prescriptive*: It suggests how the world can and should function (Betts 2004, 119). How far does liberalism go in challenging realpolitik? Table 3-1 compares the liberal and realist traditions in international relations.

LIBERALISM AND WARS

One of the most compelling arguments of the liberal approach to international relations is that war is no longer the primary threat to the international order. Not only can anarchy diminish, but human beings can learn from their experience. American political scientist John Mueller wrote in *Retreat from Doomsday: The Obsolescence of Major War* (1989) that Europe had learned from its experience of two world wars, overcome national rivalries, and constructed a peaceful community. Europeans, he argued, had outlived a centuries-old principle that military confrontation is the most appropriate way to solve international disputes. Warfare had become as outmoded as duels and slavery (Mueller 1989).

At the same time, it would be wrong to argue that liberals completely exclude the use of military force as a feature of international relations. Most liberals today do not share the ideals of complete disarmament. It is instructive to look at the arguments and logic used by recent U.S. administrations when they engaged in war. In 1991 President George H. W. Bush started a military campaign against Iraq using a realist argument for the importance of restoring the balance of power in the Persian Gulf. President Clinton supported air strikes against Yugoslavia in 1999 using a liberal argument about the importance of stopping violence in that region. In 2003, the administration of George W. Bush, invaded Iraq using realist arguments: Iraq, they claimed, had acquired weapons of mass destruction. Then came a liberal argument: spread democracy in Iraq and through the Middle East. President Obama and his advisers supported a military campaign against Libya in 2011 and were close to starting a military campaign against Syria in 2013, claiming that the dictators in

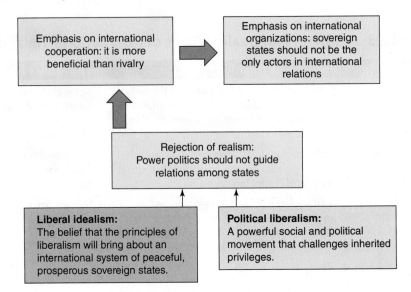

FIGURE 3-1 The logic
of liberalism.

those countries violated international norms and human rights. It may look
as if the United States used liberal arguments to advocate the use of military
force abroad—even when that force violated other countries' sovereignty
(Doyle 1986). (See Figure 3-1.)

LESSONS OF DIPLOMACY

diplomacy
The management of
international relations
through negotiations.

Diplomacy, which we began to discuss in Chapter 1, is the management of
international relations through negotiations. Sovereign states establish embassies in other states and keep channels of communication open to them.
Although these channels can be used for espionage, misinformation, and
intimidation, diplomacy helps to promote trust, avoid violent confrontations, prevent the use of force, and reduce the potential loss of property and
human lives. Liberalism argues that diplomacy can be effective in these ways
so long as state leaders act honestly, express goodwill, and aim for nonviolent
solutions.

Harold Nicolson, a British historian and diplomat, published *The Evolution of Diplomatic Method* in 1954. Diplomatic rules, procedures, and tech-
niques of negotiations changed over time, he wrote. And they continue
changing. Conducted in secrecy for centuries, diplomacy has become more
accessible to scrutiny. Once almost exclusively bilateral and regional, diplomacy has also become increasingly multinational and even global. During
the Cold War, the United States and the Soviet Union agreed that diplomatic
talks were preferable to accusations and standoffs. Historically, diplomacy
has played an increasingly important role in maintaining peace and stability
(Jonsson and Langhorn 2004).

DEBATE > WHEN SHOULD LIBERALS GO TO WAR?

Liberalism should not be understood as an outright rejection of realism. All versions of liberalism and neoliberalism accept some assumptions of realpolitik, including the importance of state sovereignty, the desire of states to avoid anarchy, and the power of professional diplomacy (Sharp 2009). Moreover, liberal concepts do not ignore the reality of war. The disagreement between realists and liberal internationalists is about when and how to use force in international relations. New generations of diplomats, politicians, and scholars change the tone and scope of this debate. What would be your position if you were president of the United States?

WHAT'S YOUR VIEW?

Discuss the following statements, and pick the one you think best reflects the way the liberal view should develop today.

❶ War must be avoided, so the United States should not use military force unless it is directly attacked.

❷ War should be avoided, but force can be used to stop significant loss of human life in other countries.

❸ War ought to be avoided, yet force should be used to protect human rights and promote democracy.

Libyans celebrate news of the death of longtime leader Muammar Qaddafi in October 2011, the result of a U.S.-supported campaign. Many cheered for the NATO support of the anti-Qaddafi forces in Libya, an example of liberal interventionism protecting human lives. Critics argued that NATO exceeded its international mandate, interfered in a civil war, and reduced Libya to anarchy, inviting violence and terrorism.

CASE IN POINT > *Diplomatic Efforts in an India-Pakistan Conflict*

In December 2001, in the wake of a terrorist attack on India's parliament for which India blamed a Pakistan-based Islamic terrorist group, India and Pakistan amassed over a million troops on the Indo-Pakistani border. These countries had gone to war several times before, most recently in 1971. Now they threatened each other with nuclear missiles. The entire international community joined urgent efforts to avoid imminent violence. After weeks of relentless diplomatic talks, the standoff eased and reciprocal concessions began. Pakistan's leaders promised to stop cross-border infiltrations of civilian combatants into India-controlled Kashmir. India, in exchange, withdrew its navy from the North Arabian Sea and lifted the fly-over ban imposed on Pakistani commercial jets. India also agreed to upgrade diplomatic ties with Islamabad. Indo-Pakistani relations remain tense and difficult, but international diplomacy proved its efficacy in easing military threats.

CRITICAL THINKING

❶ Why did diplomacy work in this particular conflict but fail in others, such as during the conflict between the United States and Iraq in 2003? Compare these two conflicts by paying attention to (a) the willingness of the involved governments to communicate with each other and (b) the ability of the international community to influence the conflicting sides. ❷ Can you think of other, more contemporary conflicts in which diplomatic efforts led to a peaceful resolution? Which international and domestic conditions contributed to this diplomatic success?

Indian and Pakistani foreign ministers meet in Islamabad, Pakistan, in 2015. These nuclear powers have fought several wars since gaining independence from Britain in 1947. Since then, they continue to have territorial disputes. Do you think that a third power should mediate these countries' negotiations?

Realists view diplomacy as an instrument of adaptation to the changing distribution of power in the international order. Liberals have a more proactive agenda for diplomacy: They view it as a tool for entities cooperating as complexly interdependent states, and maintaining international norms.

The liberal view of diplomacy includes more international actors than realpolitik. Not only great powers, but smaller states, the United Nations, and other international organizations and NGOs become important diplomatic actors. Liberals point out that small European countries, such as the Netherlands, played a crucial role in making human rights a basic concern for European diplomacy in the 1970s—while the United States and the Soviet Union still played realpolitik games. In 1975, the Conference on Security and Cooperation in Europe signed the Helsinki Final Act. This document bound the twenty-five states that signed it, including the United States and the Soviet Union, to respect and protect humanitarian concerns and human rights, such as the right to receive information, exchange ideas, or unify families across the state borders. It was a triumph of liberal internationalism (Thomas 2001). Liberals also view diplomacy not only as negotiations among states but as a type of "people's diplomacy," in which individuals and groups participate for the sake of international cooperation.

DEMOCRATIC PEACE

IR scholars have elaborated on Immanuel Kant's thesis on "perpetual peace." Professors of political science and IR, Michael Doyle (b.1948), Bruce Russett (b.1935), and James Lee Ray (b.1944) propose what is known as **democratic peace theory**. It suggests that although democratic states can go to war against non-democratic ones, democracies do not fight one another. Most twentieth-century wars took place between non-democratic countries or between democracies and authoritarian regimes. There is hardly a single case in which democratic countries governed by stable political institutions went to war against each other. Why? Democratic peace theory gives three reasons:

democratic peace theory The theory that democracies are not likely to fight one another.

- **First, the institutions of representative democracy discourage going to war against other democracies.** These institutions include parliaments, a free press, pluralist public organizations, and public opinion. Because of these factors, leaders are discouraged from plotting aggressive strategies, especially against other democratic countries (Owen 2005).
- **Second, because of shared values and shared norms of behavior, democratic states regard each other as partners rather than enemies.** Democratic states, unlike autocracies, develop a culture of compromise and negotiation. Consensus building at home translates into tolerance abroad. Mutual concessions help democracies address disagreements between themselves and resolve conflicts peacefully. In addition, because democracies are more open, they feel less threatened by one another (Maoz and Russet 1993).
- **Third, economic interdependence makes war unacceptable for economic reasons.** (As we saw earlier in this chapter, Norman Angell made the same point in 1910.) Many theorists and practitioners agree that peace and the prosperity of democratic states depend on free markets and international trade. Therefore, state leaders and business groups regard military conflicts as ruinous, because they damage a complex economic infrastructure (Oneal and Russet 1997; Gartzke 2007).

Democratic peace theory had an extraordinary impact on international relations during the last two decades. Many embraced it and recommended using it guide foreign policy. Critics, however, argued that this theory was incomplete and if used in practice could lead to dangerous consequences. We will return to this controversy later in this chapter.

SOFT POWER

In the 1980s, political scientist, diplomat, and intelligence analyst Joseph S. Nye (b.1937) argued that, besides the desires for power and security, states are also influenced by the examples set by other states, their governments and their people (Nye 1990). He called this influence "**soft power,**" in contrast to the economic and military power of a state, known as "hard power." Examples of economic and social success can include ideas, values, and, more broadly, a way of life. Soft power does not rely on intimidation; it wins hearts and minds without winning wars. It produces voluntary followers, not reluctant satellites (Nye 2004).

soft power   A state's ability to influence other state by example, through economic and social success.

It is not correct to attribute soft power only to democracy. During the early phases of the Cold War, for example, the Soviet Union had soft power as well. Communist models were popular in Asia, Africa, and Latin America, especially in countries struggling for independence from European colonial rule. India, Indonesia, Afghanistan, Burma, Algeria, Egypt, Angola, and many other countries turned to the Soviet model of state-driven industrialization and social egalitarianism (Westad 2007). Many political leaders and ordinary

---

CASE IN POINT > *Can "Democratic Peace Theory" Be Challenged?*

Imagine you are a researcher checking the hypothesis "Democracies are more peaceful to each other than non-democracies." Examine the list of military conflicts between 1945 and 2007 posted on the "Correlates of War" website. Make your own assessment of each country's involvement in warfare. Then try to divide the countries into democracies and non-democracies. You will immediately notice that it is not an easy task. Some states, like Iran or China, use democratic electoral procedures but their political systems are authoritarian. There are young and unstable democracies,

like in Bosnia or Georgia. There are states with democratic institutions but authoritarian policies, like Russia. The arguments of democratic peace theory become more complex if we try to assess the degree or scope of democratic development in the study's countries. To complicate your task even further, consider the following questions.

CRITICAL THINKING

❶ Overall, how many wars have been waged between democracies, according to this list? ❷ How many democracies were U.S. allies during the Cold War and opposed to the

Soviet Union? Have they had military conflicts among themselves during those years? If the Soviet threat was what united them, then the democratic peace theory is in doubt. ❸ Or is it? Prepare a list of interstate military conflicts over the past five to seven years. How many countries run by democratic governments have fought each other? How stable or advanced have those democratic governments been?

 Go to the companion website to view the dataset for "Extra-state War."

people in these countries saw the Soviet model as just, anticolonial, and as promising immediate results.

Soft power is volatile and fluid; it depends on changing circumstances. State actions or policies can erase or reshape the achievements of decades (Gause 2005; Mitzen 2005). The U.S.'s soft power experienced surfs of increasing strength and ebbs of decline. The Vietnam War in the 1960–70s, the occupation of Iraq in 2003, and the crisis of the global financial system in 2008–2011 were all serious blows. Still, in comparison to other countries, the U.S.'s still predominates soft power.

Soft power, unlike hard power, is difficult to calculate. It operates largely through *perceptions*. It is, however, generally observed that when one country emulates another country, both are unlikely to engage in mutual hostilities (See Figure 3-2.)

Soft power applies not only to states; IGOs and NGOs can serve as models, too. They demonstrate, as supporters of liberal internationalism hope, the advantages of liberal ideas over power politics. At the same time, it is incorrect to consider concepts of soft power tools of liberalism, and hard power the only instrument of realism. Supporters of realpolitik and liberals may use both of these powers in combination (Nye 2004).

After World War II, the United States replaced the United Kingdom as a financial, economic, and military leader, and gained soft power as well.

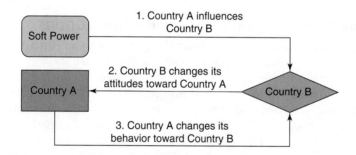

FIGURE 3-2 The effects of soft power. Sources: Nye, 2002, 2004.

DEBATE > WHICH COUNTRY HAS THE MOST SOFT POWER?

Some countries may gain soft power and squander it later. Some countries have been very successful at developing technologies, education, science, or trade. Others have provided excellent social conditions for their citizens. Still others are known for order, efficiency, and low crime rates.

WHAT'S YOUR VIEW?

❶ Which countries today, in your view, have effective soft power and why?

❷ Will the United States be able to keep and enhance its soft power or not? Defend your opinion.

❸ Does China today possesses significant or rather insignificant soft power and why?

❹ Which country's soft power would you like to significantly increase during the next five or ten years?

An IKEA store in Shanghai, China. Soft power has many facets and often appears in the form of successful economic models. IKEA is a Swedish company known for its efficiency and affordable prices. What other forms of soft power come from Scandinavia?

A devastated Europe, including Germany, in the late 1940s viewed the U.S. as a magnanimous and open-hearted nation. With the Marshall Plan, as we saw earlier in this chapter, the U.S. put the values of international peace and prosperity above narrow interests (Gaddis 2006). A democratic, non-hierarchical society like the U.S. promises opportunities for all (all people "are created equal"). The "American dream" had reached its apogee, and many Europeans yearned to see its ideals applied in their war-ravaged societies. Hollywood movies, the U.S.'s popular music, Coca-Cola, cars, and fashion all won millions of hearts worldwide. Even in the Communist Soviet Union in the 1960s, many young men and women sought to emulate the U.S.'s fashion, choice of music, and lifestyle.

The anti-Communist hysteria (McCarthyism) in the 1940s and 1950s, segregation policies, the Vietnam War in the 1960s and 1970s, the occupation of Iraq in 2003, and the crisis of the global financial system beginning in 2008 were all serious blows to the U.S.'s prestige.

International and Nongovernmental Institutions

Chapter 1 already defined international organizations as functional associations of several states or nongovernmental organizations joining together for the purpose of international cooperation. Neoliberal **institutionalism** argues that international order cannot be achieved without such international institutions, because they create mutual obligations, provide equal access to information, and reduce the uncertainty that countries face evaluating each other's policies (Keohane and Nye 1989; Keohane and Martin 1995). A common type is the **international governmental organization** or **intergovernmental organization** (IGO), which is typically composed of several sovereign member states. Several types of them exist. There are global international organizations open to any country, like the United Nations. There are regional organizations, like NATO, that include countries from a certain geographical area. In terms of their goals, IGOs can be security-related, economic, financial, cultural, educational, and so on. As an illustration, the Organization of the Petroleum Exporting Countries (OPEC) includes countries pursuing maximization of their profits through common production and pricing policies. We will examine the structure and functioning of several IGOs in the following chapters.

International security also benefits from **transnational cooperation**, or collaboration between nonstate agencies and groups of private citizens forming networks. These networks range from business and religious groups to athletes,

intergovernmental organization (IGO)
Association of several nation-states or nongovernmental organizations for the purpose of international cooperation.

transnational cooperation
The interaction of nonstate agencies, networks of states, and groups of citizens.

teachers, scientists, and artists. They are inherently interested in international exchange, open borders, and cooperation. By their activities, they strengthen the premises of liberalism and increase mutual understanding. These networks of people represent the liberal idea of people's diplomacy (see Table 3-2; Kavaloski 1990).

CROSS-NATIONAL NETWORKS

After World War II, Jean Monnet (1888–1979), a French political economist, businessman, and diplomat who never held a prominent government office, worked with influential international friends, including U.S., French, and German politicians and entrepreneurs, to promote French-German reconciliation. The first product of their collaboration, the European Coal and Steel Community (1951), united France, West Germany, Italy, Belgium, the Netherlands, and Luxembourg (Duchene 1994). It began the European integration that resulted in the European Union today.

Another example of a cross-national network was the Bilderberg group, created in the early 1950s by the Polish expatriate Józef Retinger (1888–1960) and the Dutch prince Bernhard zur Lippe-Biesterfeld (1911–2004). This group of influential people from different countries promoted "Atlantic identity" and cooperation among Western democracies. In the 1970s, the Trilateral Commission played a similar role. (Its best-known member, Polish-American

TABLE 3-2 Types of People's Diplomacy

Type of People's Diplomacy	Main Activities
Citizen delegations and socially responsible tourism	Cultivating ongoing contacts and understanding among individuals and social groups across borders
Sister cities projects	Organized interactions between residents of two cities from different countries
Cooperative peace projects	Grassroots initiatives to provide aid to people enduring war or to start transnational peace movements
Video-conferences and blogs	Communication projects allowing personal contacts between people of different countries via satellite or the Internet
Cultural, sport, and scientific exchange and cooperation	Sponsored tours, sport competitions with the aim of breaking the ice between states; joint research or cultural projects
Homestay organizations	A form of international tourism inviting foreign guests to lodge at families' homes
International youth camps and work brigades	Restoration, construction, or environmental protection in one country by youth from several countries
International humanitarian organizations	Education and training for international voluntary service

Source: Kavaloski 1990.

A member of the German Parliament (Bundestag) takes part in a protest rally in front of the embassy of Saudi Arabia in Berlin, 2015. The protest was organized by the NGO Amnesty International against the corporal punishment of Saudi blogger Raif Badawi. Should government officials take part in NGO activities? Why or why not?

political scientist and politician Zbigniew Brzezinski (1977–1981), later served as national security advisor in the Carter administration (1977–1981).) The commission brought together politicians, pundits, and corporate leaders from the United States, Western Europe, and Japan.

Other transnational networks transcended the divisions of the Cold War. For instance, periodic meetings of Soviet and Western physicists and other scientists, concerned with the nuclear arms race, influenced Gorbachev's decision to move toward nuclear disarmament and demilitarization of the Soviet Union (Evangelista 1999).

NONGOVERNMENTAL ORGANIZATIONS

Another major assertion of liberalism is that, in today's world, the power to make decisions in the international arena should shift toward nongovernmental organizations (NGOs). Their presence in international relations became particularly noticeable at the end of the last century (Keck and Sikkink 1998; Iriye 2002). Jessica Mathews (b.1946), former president of the Carnegie Endowment for International Peace, a foreign-policy think tank founded in 1910, argued that the power of contemporary states would further decline because of the growth of NGOs. Because of the Internet and other technological advances, governments would no longer have a monopoly on information or exercise control over as many spheres of human life (Matthews 1997). The spectacular proliferation of internationally operating NGOs over the past ten years has led many to envision them as a new force behind liberalism.

@ Freedom House in Washington, D.C., publishes annual reports on the degree of democratic freedoms in most countries. You will find links on the companion website.

As mentioned in Chapter 1, for example, Freedom House in Washington, D.C., is an internationally recognized nongovernmental organization. Based on experts' evaluations, its Freedom in the World survey provides an annual rating of a country's treatment of its citizens' most basic liberties. These ratings determine whether a country is labeled free, partly free, or not free. NGOs and governments frequently use such ratings to assess democratic developments in foreign states. Critics often point out that Freedom House's activities go beyond information gathering and resemble liberal interventionism. Critics also maintain that this NGO is biased against countries such as Iran, Russia, and China.

There are three major interconnected fields of international activity for NGOs today (Figure 3-3):

- **The first is information gathering and analysis.** In many cases, governments are incapable or unwilling to collect information about their own environmental problems, human rights violations, and other dangerous developments. NGOs then become valuable sources.

FIGURE 3-3 Three key fields of NGO activity.

- **The second field is advocacy and education.** Not only do many organizations collect information; they also appeal to public opinion, media, and governments to address international problems.
- **Third, NGOs organize and deliver humanitarian aid and support for environmental protection** (see Chapters 9 and 10). Of course, the activities of different NGOs can overlap.

▶ Democratic peace theory gives three reasons why democratic countries governed by stable political institutions do not fight one another. Name these reasons.

▶ What is soft power? Give an example.

▶ What is people's diplomacy? Provide at least two examples.

▶ Identify types of NGO activities, some controversial, others not.

CHECK YOUR KNOWLEDGE

Contexts and Applications

How well have liberal ideas stood the test of reality? We will examine liberal assertions in light of decisions by individual leaders, state policies, and the global context.

The Individual Decisions Context

In an attention-grabbing piece published in *Foreign Affairs*, professor of biology, neuroscience, and neurosurgery at Stanford University Robert Sapolsky (b.1957) argued using biological and anthropological evidence that humans are not naturally aggressive. People are not destined to fight in endless violent conflicts. Human choices are the product of rational calculation and social context. Rational choices by state leaders should therefore help avoid violence (Sapolsky 2006).

If people are by their nature inclined to peace, why do countries so often engage in devastating wars? One answer is that countries' leaders have a profound impact on international relations. The global and political context, the

CASE IN POINT > *To What Degree Does Partisanship Affect U.S. Foreign Policy?*

The U.S. president is expected to act as a national leader and as the commander-in-chief, regardless of partisanship. Quite often, especially during the Cold War, the U.S. president has claimed his foreign policy transcends differences between Republicans and Democrats. Yet bipartisan foreign policy often exists more in words than in deeds. Some presidents have chosen unilateral interventionism, others have chosen multilateralism. It is important to realize that the choice of foreign policy is not based exclusively on party affiliation. Foreign policy-making is a multistep process involving institutions, legal rules, and personal preferences. Specific events in other parts of the world affect policies, too. Both the Republican and Democratic Parties consist of diverse people with diverse views about diplomacy, agreements, and war. Still, we know these parties differ on the role the United States should play in the world and the methods to maintain its position in the world.

CRITICAL THINKING

❶ Can we make an educated judgment about whether and how these presidents' party affiliation affected their choices on war, peace, and international agreements? ❷ Were Democratic presidents more "peace committed" than Republicans? ❸ Give some recent examples of how politics affects foreign policy.

 Visit the companion website for relevant links.

life experience of decision makers, and their ability to withstand pressure from advisers, lobbies, and interest groups—all these affect individual choices and international politics. We will see that implementing the basic principles of liberalism requires political courage.

President Woodrow Wilson, who served as president from 1913 to 1921, faced serious opposition at home when he pushed for U.S. participation in the League of Nations. He did not succeed. Other presidents were more successful and skillful. Franklin Roosevelt who served as president from 1933 to 1945, was instrumental in establishing the United Nations. Dwight Eisenhower, who served from 1953 until 1961, and John Kennedy, who served as president from 1961 to 1963, knew in the late 1950s and the early 1960s that the United States had achieved economic and military superiority over the Soviet Union. Both presidents were under tremendous pressure to use this superior power for a pre-emptive nuclear strike. Yet they also knew from personal experience how devastating a war can be and acted prudently.

In West Germany in the 1970s (when Germany was divided into West and East), Chancellor Willy Brandt (1913–1992) pushed for engagement and collaboration with European Communist states. Brandt believed that "peaceful coexistence" would bring more positive results than war. He faced tremendous opposition from powerful political forces. The peaceful end of the Cold War vindicated those statesmen who advocated alternatives to a violent resolution.

More recently, in 2014 German chancellor Angela Merkel (b.1954) chose a liberal line to set Western policies toward Russian leader Vladimir Putin (b.1952) during the crisis in Ukraine. She surprised some realists who believed that Germany would not put aside its interests on behalf of liberal internationalism. Merkel speaks Russian and Putin speaks German, and both countries had productive economic relations, with the volume of trade exceeding $100 billion in 2012. Still, when the Obama administration proposed sanctions against the Russian economy and its leadership, Merkel supported the sanctions even though they were going against Germany's economic interests. Some argued that Merkel chose a tough line against Putin for personal reasons: she did not like Putin's "bullying" behavior. It is obvious, however, that the German leader chose to support trans-Atlantic solidarity and European cooperation. The Kremlin's attempts to deal separately with Germany to ease the sanctions—in the style of realpolitik—failed.

The future of the world may depend on the choices of political leaders, and they may or may not choose peace. Supporters of liberalism believe that it takes courage and wisdom to make rational decisions in the spirit of cooperation and engagement. Attractive principles remain only wishes unless they pass the test of domestic politics.

The State Policies Context

As we have just seen, domestic politics strongly influence international relations. As Princeton professor of politics Andrew Moravcsik (b.1957) wrote in "Taking preferences seriously: a liberal theory of international politics" (published in *International Organization* 51, Autumn 1997, pp. 513–53): "societal ideas, interests, and institutions influence state behavior by shaping state preferences." Liberal preferences helped Western European states integrate into the European Community and in 1991 into the European Union (Moravcsik 1997, p. 513).

German Chancellor Willy Brandt kneels before the monument to the Jews killed by the Nazis during the uprising in the Warsaw Ghetto in Poland. Brandt fought against the Nazis during World War II. Democratic, liberal Germany spent considerable resources to atone for the war crimes of the Third Reich and to build better relations with its eastern neighbors.

But does democracy always brings peace, stability, and interdependence? Consider democratic peace theory, introduced earlier in this chapter. It assumes that democratic states are unlikely to engage in war against one another (Christison 2002; Jervis 2002). However, Jack Snyder, professor of International Relations in the Department of Political Science and the Saltzman Institute of War and Peace Studies at Columbia, and Edward Mansfield, professor of Political Science and Director of the Christopher H. Browne Center for International Politics at the University of Pennsylvania, looked at countries that are not fully democratic but only *in transition* to democracy. These countries might actually be *more* prone to war compared to stable but authoritarian regimes. Why? We should look at domestic political factors. Democracy allows political groups to compete openly. If democratic institutions are immature and unstable, some of these groups may use nationalist, populist, and demagogic slogans and agendas to devastating effect (Mansfield and Snyder 1995; Snyder 2000). This happened in Germany in the 1920s, when Hitler was rising to power. This happened recently in Russia where democratic chaos in the 1990s produced the autocratic presidency of Vladimir Putin. In the Middle East, in Afghanistan, Iraq, Libya, or

Egypt, efforts to overthrow autocracies and replace them with democratic institutions brought instability and war (Gause 2005; Mearsheimer 2014).

Democratic peace theory has other limitations. Its supporters draw examples largely from Western Europe and North America and from just four decades after 1945 (Gowa 2000). War often finds support from public opinion in democratic countries (Chan 1997). Perhaps democracies in the recent past have had other reasons for not going to war against each other (Layne 1994). For instance, the Soviet Union provided a common enemy, the United States was the overwhelmingly strongest democratic state (discouraging others to challenge it), and devastating world wars had weakened two traditionally expansionist democracies, the United Kingdom and France. Instead of the expected confrontation over colonies and spheres of influence around the world, the Western powers formed the U.S.-led military and political bloc against the Soviet Union. This allowed them to resolve their differences peacefully.

PUBLIC SUPPORT FOR FOREIGN POLICY

Realists generally focus on the results of foreign policy and consider legitimacy just another factor associated with power (Morgenthau 1978). Realpolitik is not supposed to be bound by public opinion. However, most democratically elected leaders do feel the pressures of domestic and international opinion. To succeed, foreign policy may depend on public support (Kagan 2004).

Studies of the past two decades show that liberalism is likely to be implemented if it finds strong support in the public and the media. If a government decides to start a war without convincing moral or ideological justification, public opinion is likely to oppose it (Nacos et al. 2000). Since the war in Vietnam, the White House has hesitated to engage in protracted conflict with potentially high casualties. For example, the Clinton administration quickly withdrew soldiers from Somalia in October 1993 after guerrillas downed two Black Hawk helicopters and images of a dead U.S. soldier appeared in the media. Clinton was also reluctant at first to send American troops to Bosnia. Expensive and prolonged military action could have easily cost him reelection in 1996 (Sobel 2001).

When leaders lack public support, they may change policy—or seek to swing public opinion. In 2001, the Japanese government sent three military vessels to the Indian Ocean to help Western allies in the Afghan conflict. The government hoped that a more active role in world affairs would win the approval of the Japanese people. Yet only 8 percent of the Japanese people were in support of the move (Maddox 2001). The relationship between public opinion and foreign policy also depends on the structure of the parliamentary system, the views of elected officials, presidential leadership, and the elite's perception of public opinion (Shiraev and Sobel 2006). In summary, although public opinion does not necessarily direct foreign policy, it can constrain it. (See Table 3-3.)

policy climate
The prevailing sentiment among policy makers and other influential individuals.

POLICY CLIMATE

If individuals are capable of making rational decisions and avoiding war, then their collective opinion should matter too. The **policy climate** is the prevailing sentiment among policy makers and other influential individuals. It includes beliefs about what the government, international organizations, and

TABLE 3-3 The Impact of Public Opinion on Foreign Policy

The impact of public opinion on foreign policy is likely to increase if:	
(1)	A national election is scheduled in the near future and opposition is strong: Incumbent officials need public support for re-election.
(2)	Support or opposition to a certain foreign policy–related issue is overwhelming and consistent: Officials may argue that they have a "mandate."
(3)	Majority opinion agrees with decision makers: Officials are likely to use polls as justification for their action or inaction.
The impact of public opinion on foreign policy is likely to weaken if:	
(1)	No national election is scheduled in the near future and the political opposition is relatively weak.
(2)	Support or opposition is weak or inconsistent: Officials may argue that the public is uncertain or divided.
(3)	Majority opinion disagrees with decision makers: Officials are likely to ignore or downplay the polls.

Sources: Rosenau 1961; Holsti 1992; Sobel and Shiraev 2004; Yankelovich 2005

CASE IN POINT > *U.S. Public Opinion and the Use of Force Abroad*

Despite substantial reservations in principle to the use of force abroad, most Americans support short-term military action with limited casualties. From the 1990s to 2003, engagements in Kuwait, Kosovo, Afghanistan, and Iraq all had substantial public support—at least at the beginning. Conversely, with declining public support, military interventions have been scaled back in Korea, Vietnam, and more recently Iraq. No open military interventions have begun when public support was weak, as in Angola and Ethiopia. During the crisis in Darfur, despite most Americans' support for some military engagement, there was no direct U.S. military action in that region.

CRITICAL THINKING

❶ According to a 2007 poll by CNN/ORC, most Americans supported their country's military involvement to stop the massive loss of life in the Darfur conflict. Yet the Bush administration ruled out military action there. If you were president then, what reasons would you give for your noninvolvement? Consider other conflicts the United States was involved in at that time, the schedule of presidential elections in the United States, and the nature of the conflict in Darfur. What is the situation in Darfur today? ❷ According to a 2013 Gallup poll, most Americans (51 percent) did not support the United States taking military action against the Syrian government; only 36 percent supported this action. President Obama did not authorize the use of force against Syria. Again, if you were president then, what reasons would you give for your noninvolvement? Consider the situation in and around Syria as well as Obama's personal views and his other foreign-policy decisions.

nongovernmental groups should do on the international level—particularly faced with international conflict or security threats. Opinion leaders air their views in public debates, speeches, policy statements, televised interviews, printed publications, and the Internet. The principles of liberal internationalism may prevail within a favorable policy climate.

The policy climate can shape a country's foreign policy and international role. Consider two examples. Historically, the policy climate in Norway is sharply opposed to racial discrimination, ethnic violence, and religious intolerance. This has made Norway a leader in international human rights campaigns and peaceful conflict resolution. In Canada, from the beginning of the Bosnian conflict in 1991, the policy climate favored humanitarian intervention. As a result, the Canadian government took the lead in asking the United Nations to intervene and promised to contribute personnel and equipment (Carrière et al. 2003).

In summary, liberal internationalism is not exclusively the choice of individual politicians. It also depends on democratic principles of government, public opinion, and the policy climate.

The Global Context

globalization
The growing interdependence of countries and their economies, the growing importance of international exchanges of goods and ideas, and increased openness to innovation.

Globalization, or the growing interdependence of countries and their economies, not only brings opportunities, but also poses new challenges for the liberal approach to international relations. Economic liberalism must find better answers to how to face the growing threat of instability in global financial markets. For instance, a global financial panic may lead to a flight of capital from certain markets, resulting in diminishing investments, halted building projects, and massive unemployment. Only big states and states with great financial resources can resist the volatility of today's financial markets. These few include the United States, the members of the European Union, China, India, and several others.

China's state-owned Bright Food Group calls for international investments to help it bring in Western food and promote Chinese products abroad. Do you think food corporations will soon put small grocery stores out of business worldwide?

Institutional liberals supported NATO and the EU enlargement in the 1990s. They continued their support when both institutions experienced difficulties in the past several years. Still, they have to prove that these institutions would work in case of diminishing U.S. support. After all, the European Union and NATO could not stop Russia's takeover of Crimea in 2014 and the violation of Ukraine's sovereignty, international treaties, and legal norms. Will NATO be able to protect its smaller members—such as the Baltic states—if Russia threatens them?

Optimists in the liberal camp remain undaunted. From their point of view, the world's interdependence diminishes the ability of powerful states to act unilaterally, which reduces the chance of military conflict. Liberal institutionalists staunchly supported economic sanctions imposed on Russia in 2014 in retaliation for the Kremlin's actions against Ukraine. Although, as noted earlier, economic interdependence between Russia and the EU suffered due to these sanctions, policy makers, including German chancellor Angela Merkel and French president François Hollande, asserted that their goal was to continue the strategy of integrating Russia into the European economy and its institutions—provided Russia stopped acting as a predator state in Ukraine.

Globalization entails interconnectedness and, therefore, multiple interests. The complexity of and urgency of global problems may also support liberal ideas. International projects in the twenty-first century increasingly require the shared economic and financial resources of many states. Even the United States, the biggest economic and military power today, cannot police the world. The role of international and nongovernment organizations will increase simply because there are no alternatives.

As we have seen, democratic peace theory still has to be tested on a global scale. In today's world, states that try to borrow from Western democracy often fail in the face of corrupt bureaucracies, inertia, fierce opposition, and political, ethnic, and religious violence. Ukraine, Georgia, Colombia, Pakistan, Iraq, and Afghanistan have all had difficulty building democratic institutions. Does this mean that illiberal regimes, such as in Singapore and China, are better choices for poor and developing countries than French, British, and U.S.-style democracies?

The next decades may provide some answers. Robert Keohane at Princeton University believes that important remedies to domestic conflicts and violence are land reform, environmental cleanup, better education, and health care. These policies can best promote stability and prosperity. The military will still have a role to play, however, international organizations, economic support, and international cooperation can strengthen civilian public sectors and address ethnic and social problems (Keohane 2005). Although few would argue against better education and health care, a key challenge is to find sufficient resources to accomplish these projects.

Some ideas of liberal internationalism may sound quite revolutionary. Gidon Gottlieb (1932-2015), director of a pre-diplomatic Middle East Peace Project at the Hoover Institution of Stanford University, in 1994 offered an idea of "states plus nations": Ethnic groups should receive special legal status and the political status of a nation. A world of traditional states, in his view, would evolve into a system of many nations, not necessarily with physical borders. Citizenship in a nation could be granted to people living in separate states, such as people of Chinese descent in Europe, Asia, and the U.S. They would still pay taxes and serve in the military where they live, however, nationality would be a matter of cultural heritage, not of "motherland," and territorial conflicts would decrease. Massive migrations in the twenty-first century should put Gottlieb's proposal to the test.

@ Look up these abbreviations: G-3, G-5, G-7, G-8, G-10, G-20, and G-77. What do they represent, and what functions do they serve? How many still exist today? Are there any new groups with similar aims?

> ▶ Leaders applying principles of liberalism in foreign policy face domestic opposition. Why?
> ▶ How do public opinion and the policy climate affect foreign policy?

CHECK YOUR KNOWLEDGE

One project has already been tested by history—the European Community. Although the testing period has been relatively short so far, as we see next, many of its lessons have been compelling.

THE USES OF HISTORY: The European Community

Background

For three hundred years, prominent thinkers looked forward to European integration based on principles of humanism and peace. The first practical steps toward European integration according to the principles of liberalism were not taken until after the Second World War. In Western Europe, Cold War divisions led to strong leadership and a policy climate favoring international cooperation. In 1949, NATO forged a lasting defense alliance between Western Europe and the United States to contain the Soviet threat. With NATO in place, Western Europeans could focus more on economic cooperation and integration.

Of crucial significance was a new understanding, a *rapprochement*, between France and West Germany. In 1951, the European Coal and Steel Community (ECSC) (discussed on page 97 as an example of a cross-national organization) placed the power to make decisions about the coal and steel industries in the hands of an independent body.

President Truman, who served as president from April 1945 until 1953, and Eisenhower, who served from 1953 to 1961, as well as a majority in Congress, adhered to **Atlanticism**, the position that the United States–Western Europe relationship is a focus of national interest. Grants, loans, machinery, and equipment provided by the Marshall Plan helped the Western and Mediterranean parts of Europe recover after the war. The plan also envisaged a united European economic and trade market.

Atlanticism
The belief that the relationship between the United States and Europe is a focus of national interest.

With the United States' support, Jean Monnet, Robert Schuman, Ludwig Erhard, and others built on Western Europe's successful economic recovery and cooperation. In 1957, European leaders signed the Treaty of Rome, creating the European Atomic Energy Community (Euratom) and the European Economic Community (EEC). Member states removed trade barriers between one another, forming a free-trade zone informally called the *Common Market* (Haas 1958). Within the next decade Western European states abolished trade tariffs, partnered in the development of peaceful atomic energy, and created educational and academic exchanges. In 1967, the European Parliament was established. Originally, the members of the European Parliament came from state parliaments, but in 1979 the first direct elections took place, allowing the citizens of member states to vote for European representatives. Since then, there have been direct elections every five years. Common economic policies were followed by common financial policies. When the United States devalued the dollar in the early 1970s (making U.S. exports more competitive but imports sold at home more expensive), Western European states linked the value of their national currencies (the European "currency snake") to the dollar in a coordinated fashion.

In 1973 Denmark, Ireland, and the United Kingdom joined the EEC; Greece, Portugal, and Spain followed during the 1980s. Despite these advances (or maybe because of them), European integration ran into many difficulties. The United Kingdom revoked its plans to join the union. British officials feared losing economic and, possibly, political independence. This view found substantial public support at home. France's expensive domestic agricultural subsidies also created tensions: While supporting its farmers financially, the French government would make French agricultural products less expensive and thus more competitive in other countries. The sharp rise of oil prices in 1974 slowed economic growth and caused further political tension in the EEC (Hitchcock 2008). Economically successful members, like West Germany, believed that they contributed too much in relation to the less successful members, like Portugal and Greece. The latter, in turn, felt they received too little help.

After a difficult decade, European integration received a powerful boost at the end of the Cold War. Many factors contributed, including the end of economic stagnation, a reduction in oil prices, the successful internationalization of many European businesses, and the collapse of Communist regimes in Eastern Europe and the Soviet Union. Whatever its troubles, the European Community now looked like a shining success by comparison. High economic productivity, a common market, division of labor, and efficient technology sharing—all these had failed to occur under Communist regimes. After 1989, Eastern European countries, free from the Soviet bloc, rushed to participate in European integration. East Germany became integrated into West Germany.

European governments, especially France, to their credit, used this new political momentum. Any remaining fears of a united Germany spurred action toward a larger integrated Europe (Bozo et al. 2012). At the end of 1989 German chancellor Helmut Kohl (b. 1930) agreed to support the Economic and Monetary Union (EMU), which envisaged a common European currency and deeper economic interdependence. In 1992, just months after the Soviet Union's collapse and the reunification of Germany, European leaders signed the Treaty of Maastricht (named after the city in the Netherlands where it was signed) to put political, financial, economic, and even military integration on a fast track. It transformed the European Community into the European Union (EU) and entailed the implementation of the euro. All EU members now enjoy common European citizenship and the freedom to conduct business activities in any country of the union. The EU also acquired full-scale executive, legislative, and judicial institutions based in Brussels, Belgium, called the Council of the European Union, the

EU and local interests may clash. In front of the European Parliament in Brussels, Belgium, protestors speak out against the statutory German minimum wage act in 2015.

European Commission, and the European Court of Justice. Strasbourg, France is the official seat of the European Parliament. Luxembourg hosts the Secretariat of the European Parliament, although many sessions and committee meetings are held in Brussels.

The new "superstate" has a common currency (the euro, after January 1, 1999), flag, anthem, central bank, supreme court, parliament, president of the European Commission, developing armed forces, sizeable bureaucracy, and budget. By 2004, Austria, Finland, Sweden, Poland, the Czech and Slovak Republics, Hungary, the Baltic states (Estonia, Latvia and Lithuania), Slovenia, Cyprus, and Malta had joined the Union. Bulgaria and Romania became new members in 2007. With the Treaty of Lisbon that year, the EU attempted to set up a coordinated security and foreign policy. Still, the main decision-making bodies of the EU are legislative ones (Parliament and Council). There is no strong pan-European executive.

Analysis

While Europe is still far from acting with unanimity and resolve, the EU represents the greatest triumph of the liberal tradition. But is that triumph premature? Opponents of liberal internationalism tend to see it as a big bureaucracy and big ambitions. Compare the arguments of both.

State Sovereignty or "Central" Power in Brussels?

Supporters of the liberal view emphasize that the power of individual states has been gradually diminishing for fifty years. A deep interdependence among European national economies disincentivizes military confrontations among members of the EU. A new European identity is emerging (Moravcsik 1998).

Opponents of the liberal view believe that further erosion of state sovereignty is harmful. It transfers sovereignty to bureaucrats in Brussels and even further away from voters. Local authorities and communities can no longer decide what is right for *them*. Greater competition for jobs creates local resentment toward new immigration from Eastern Europe, the Middle East, and Africa. Opponents predict that future battles in Europe will be over nationalistic ideas and national identity. Political parties advocating nationalism have grown stronger in Europe since 2010.

The European financial crisis that began in 2009—and particularly the acute financial problems in Greece, Italy, Ireland, and Portugal—sharpens discussions of the future of the European Union. Some argue that a single European currency has made responding to the recession harder. Advocates of the EU's political integration argue that the euro should require a powerful central political authority to regulate it, preventing financial abuses by some member states of the EU. The experts in Germany, the largest donor into the EU common budget, argue that countries, particularly should be expelled from the Eurozone until their governments balance their budgets and stop taking loans they cannot repay. The future of the European Union depends on collective action to resolve these financial and economic problems. In 2010, member states created the European Financial Stability Facility to preserve financial stability of the union. In 2011 European leaders agreed on serious financial measures to avoid a deep crisis and obliged the governments of several countries to take serious austerity measures to reduce their national debt. (We will return to international political economy in Chapter 7.)

Free Trade or Economic Protectionism?

The European Union was created to defend four economic freedoms: the free flow of capital, labor, products, and services. Supporters of early unification argued that the integration of one functional area would almost necessarily lead to the integration of others (Haas 1958). Significant progress has been achieved. The European "superstate" invests heavily in education, health care, employment, and the environment.

Yet Europe's sluggish economy revealed problems with this liberal project. The austerity imposed by Brussels (and promoted by Germany), for the purpose of balancing the budgets of heavily indebted EU members, created oppressive unemployment among young people, especially in Italy, Spain, and Greece. In these countries, governments slashed down social and educational programs and raised taxes in order to accumulate state revenue. This helped political parties sharply critical of the EU policies. Many People in those countries began to view Germany as an economic "dictator." Political pressure in Italy and Spain grew to resist Germany-sponsored austerity policies.

Observers warned that populistic, nationalistic regimes would take over in much of Europe and weaken democracy (Art 2011). They may also weaken the transnational sense of belonging to Europe, rather than to specific territories and countries. A common European identity is widely shared by young and successful professional classes, and it is crucial for the future of the European project.

National Politicians or Euro-Technocrats?

A united Europe only partially substitutes for local and state institutions. The Union, supporters suggest, should work on just a few issues, such as criminal law, taxation, and standards in social policy— including unemployment benefits, pension plans, and funding for education. The Union should also have a central office in charge of EU foreign affairs and a small but viable military force.

Critics disagree. To them, the "red tape" of a sprawling Euro-bureaucracy is already a problem. There are too many offices, institutions, rules, and regulations in Brussels. Conservative nationalists believe that the more power is given to central institutions, the less efficient they become. Supporters of economic liberalism are particularly against increasing taxes and regulations. Socialist parties believe that a stronger central bureaucracy will help old political elites and international corporations gain even more power at the expense of factory workers and farmers. Still other critics think that new institutions are actually useless, because they cannot substitute for sovereign states.

The arguments on both sides, for and against further European unification, appear correct if you apply them selectively enough. Supporters look for facts proving their position, while opponents dismiss these facts and give attention to others. People's political affiliations and economic interests affect their opinions as well. *Eurobarometer*, a regular series of surveys in EU countries, shows overall a relatively stable level of support for membership, especially in economically successful states. Support diminishes, however, in countries going through economic difficulties. Global polls by the Pew Research Center reveal diminishing support for institutions and organizations when people feel that they are not well protected in the socioeconomic area.

Democratic Peace or Conflict with Neighbors?

Liberal thinkers have assumed that the EU does not need a coordinated foreign policy. They have argued that the main objective of Brussels is the promotion of liberal policies: complex economic interdependence, the rule of law, and democratization. In 2008, after the Russian-Georgian war, it became clear that Russia would resist further spread of NATO eastward to include Georgia and Ukraine. The EU Council then started promoting the idea of an Eastern Neighborhood. According to their liberal logic association with an Eastern Neighborhood would promote European values without antagonizing Russia.

The government of Vladimir Putin in the Kremlin, however, interpreted the Eastern Neighborhood as a security threat. In 2011, Russia created a rival project, the Eurasian Union, to integrate the countries in the EU Eastern Partnership, especially Ukraine. Putin regarded the EU's promotion of liberal principles as a tool for democratizing and absorbing countries once parts of the Soviet Union into Western sphere of influence. Brussels though did not anticipate a confrontation with Russia.

Yet in late 2013 through early 2014 this is what happened. Ukrainian President Viktor Yanukovich, when forced to choose between the Eastern Neighborhood and the Eurasian Union, opted for the latter. This resulted in a mass protest that swept Yanukovich from power. Putin reacted with violent and coercive policies aimed at destabilizing Ukraine. After a forced referendum, Russia annexed Crimea from Ukraine. Since the summer of 2014 Russia backed separatists in Ukrainian regions bordering Russia. Thousands were killed, and approximately a million people were displaced as refugees.

On the companion website, you will find links to more information about the European Union, opinion polls of EU countries, and Pew Global Surveys.

Questions

1. Discuss the view that Russia presented a great threat to European liberal values and norms by acting as a predator state.
2. Do you agree that the EU's only effective choice was economic sanctions on Russia? Which liberal policies may have been more effective?
3. Does a liberal "super-state" like the European Union require a coordinated foreign and military policy? Explain your view.
4. Do you think that the European Union will become stronger economically and politically by 2020, or do you think it will significantly decline? How will it evolve?

CONCLUSION

In the liberal tradition, state preferences, not state power, should define international relations. Countries, like humans, are capable of self-restraint and cooperation. Long-term moral purposes and values are more important in international relations than power-driven calculations. War and conflicts can be contained through diplomacy, economic interdependence, cultural exchanges, and transnational institutions. Contrary to realpolitik, supporters of the liberal tradition emphasize the growing importance of nongovernmental organizations in forming foreign policy. One of the reasons to be optimistic about the liberal approach is that in democratic countries, politicians usually pay serious attention to public opinion.

KEY TERMS

Atlanticism 106
democratic peace theory 93
diplomacy 90
global disarmament 82
globalization 104

intergovernmental
    organization (IGO) 96
liberalism 80
neoliberalism (neoliberal
    institutionalism) 87

policy climate 102
soft power 94
transnational cooperation 97

IDEAS

CHARACTERISTICS OF LIBERALISM

- Rejection of zero-sum power politics
- Emphasis on international cooperation
- Emphasis on international organizations and nonstate actors

DEVELOPMENT OF LIBERALISM

- 18th c.: political liberalism challenged nobility (Locke, Voltaire, Kant)
- 19th c.: rapid industrialization, growth of global trade
- 20th c.: Angell, Schumpeter

ATTEMPTS TO IMPLEMENT LIBERAL PRINCIPLES

- Disarmament conferences
- League of Nations
- Atlantic Charter
- World Bank, IMF, GATT
- United Nations
- Marshall Plan

FACETS OF LIBERALISM

- Neoliberalism: state interests are realized in the context of interdependence
- "End of History": no viable alternatives to liberal capitalism and global modernization

ARGUMENTS

PREMISES OF LIBERALISM

- Obsolescence of war
- Power of diplomacy
- Democratic peace theory
- Soft power

LIBERAL INSTITUTIONALISM

International order cannot be achieved without international institutions:

- IGOs (e.g., UN, NATO, OPEC)
- Cross-national networks
- NGOs

CONTEXTS AND APPLICATIONS

INDIVIDUAL DECISIONS CONTEXT

- The choices of political leaders affect outcomes of war and peace

STATE POLICIES CONTEXT

- Ideas, interests, and institutions influence states' foreign policies

GLOBAL CONTEXT

- Domestic and international opinion shape foreign policy

Critical Thinking

❶ Explain the principles of liberalism in thirty seconds, and give at least one example of liberal principles applied to foreign policy.

❷ Compare and contrast liberalism and realism. Which arguments does liberalism use to dismiss the principles of power politics?

❸ What are the differences among the various approaches and traditions within liberalism? Give examples.

❹ Apply principles of liberalism to the United States' foreign policy toward any contemporary international conflict.

❺ How does liberalism explain individual foreign policy decisions? Give examples.

Alternative Views 4

We are the 99%.
> —OCCUPY WALL STREET SLOGAN

AFTER SEPTEMBER 11, 2001, THE TALIBAN—AN ISLAMIC MOVEMENT THEN IN POWER IN AFGHANISTAN—REFUSED TO GIVE AWAY OSAMA BIN LADEN, THE MASTERMIND of that day's devastating attacks. In response, the United States and its allies threatened war. Had the Taliban leaders used strategic calculations and acted as realists, they would have realized that they could not possibly withstand the U.S. military. The balance of power was simply not on their side. Yet the Taliban rulers chose neither course. Rather, against enormous odds, they chose resistance and foreign occupation of their country.

About ten years later, a movement called the Islamic State of Iraq and Syria (ISIS) emerged in Iraq and Syria. In 2013, ISIS rapidly expanded control over a significant territory. Declared a terrorist group by the UN, ISIS conducted mass executions of Syrian and Jordanian soldiers and officers, civilians, and Western journalists. The movement proclaimed the Worldwide Caliphate—a global Islamic state. By its brutal actions, ISIS united against itself both Western and Arab states. In 2014, an international coalition was formed to conduct military operations against ISIS to prevent its continued expansion.

As you can see, the Taliban and ISIS leaders rejected any cooperation with the international community and did not practice realpolitik to bargain for their own survival. What motivated their seemingly self-destructive decisions? Why did they choose confrontation? Neither realism nor liberalism can competently answer this question. This chapter will explore alternative approaches that go beyond realism and liberalism in explaining international politics. We will

Previous page: Two children of Iraqi Christian refugees expelled from Mosul, Iraq, in 2014 by ISIS, which has systematically forced out the city's Christian population.

explore how identities, perceptions, social norms, conflicting economic interests, gender, race, and psychological factors shape the behavior of leaders and states.

▶ Describe the shortcomings of realism and liberalism and the necessity of other interpretations of world politics.
▶ Explain alternative views of international relations, including constructivism, conflict theories, feminism, identity formation, and political psychology.
▶ Give examples of how perceptions, conflicts, inequality, social norms, gender, race, political culture, nationalism, and psychological factors shape international relations.
▶ Apply alternative approaches to interpreting the behavior of leaders, states, and international organizations.

Learning Objectives

Ideas

Both realists and liberals explain international relations as the sophisticated and rational actions of states and organizations. But in actuality, how rational are the choices of international actors? Ideology, greed, honor, deep-seated beliefs, and misperceptions are the driving forces behind many decisions. This chapter presents approaches to international relations that go beyond realism and liberalism to explore causes and patterns of international relations:

- *Constructivism* argues that states develop their interests and notions of security according to diverse social norms and historical experiences. It posits that power, anarchy, and security have different meanings for different countries. One country, such as Israel, may see a certain development (like Iran's nuclear program) as a serious threat, while others (like Russia) see it as an acceptable reality. Like individuals, states can exaggerate external threats, underestimate dangers, or even completely overlook them. During the past twenty years, constructivism became a third major theoretical approach to international relations, and even became a serious rival to both realism and liberalism.

[handwritten margin note:] ex: China views vs U.S. views

- Other alternative theories focus on *conflict and inequality* as defining factors in international relations. For example, the world may be driven by the capitalist search for profit, as Marxist theories explore, or it may be defined by race and gender inequality, the focus of postcolonial and feminist theories. These approaches call for serious changes in the current international system; they are critical toward Western models of development and modernization.

- Another approach, close to constructivism, focuses on *identities*, or the ways people and institutions perceive themselves and others. Religious values, ethnic pride, nationalism, democratic norms of behavior—all can shape countries' diplomatic priorities. These factors sometimes affect political will to use force.
- Finally, *political psychology* focuses on decision makers—both individuals and groups—and how they react to international change, opportunities, and crises. This field explores the complex mechanisms of political behavior—including political leaders' individual life experiences, emotions, biases, misperceptions, rationality, and irrationality.

Arguments

If you saw two people fighting in the street, what would you do? You may choose not to get involved, of course, assuming that breaking up a fight is not your business. You may call for help. Or you may get involved directly. If you did, whose side would you take? Neither? Your decision, obviously, depends on many circumstances and factors, such as concern for your personal safety, whether other people are present, and who is fighting. For example, you probably would help a defenseless person rather than a bully, or a small child resisting a bigger one.

In the same way, actions of states and international organizations depend on circumstances. Canada and Cuba are neighbors of the United States. Yet one is an American partner and friend, and another was for many years an adversary. Obviously, the Cuban and the United States governments viewed the entire international order differently (Reus-Smit 2009).

The Constructivist View

constructivist view (or constructivism)
An approach to international relations that assumes that state actions and policies are based on how leaders, bureaucracies, and societies interpret, or *construct*, information.

Advocates of the **constructivist view** (or **constructivism**) argue that states' actions and policies are based on how leaders, bureaucracies, and societies interpret or *construct* the information available to them. Constructivism posits that *power, anarchy,* and *security* are not unchanging categories. Rather, they have different meanings for different states and organizations (Wendt 1992). A serious threat for one state may not be an issue for another: India and Pakistan are concerned about each other's nuclear weapons, but they express little concern about Russia's nuclear missiles. Like individuals, governments and societies can exaggerate external threats or overlook them (Buzan and Hansen 2009). As when you step in to break up a fight, countries act based on their ideas of what is fair or safe in international relations. If two countries agree on what is fair and secure, they are more disposed to cooperate.

States, of course, pursue their vital interests. Realists, as you will remember, assume that these interests always push states to react to anarchy by building up their power. Liberals insist, on the contrary, that interests in peaceful trade push states to cooperate. Constructivists raise a critical question: *Where do state interests come from?* Who defines which interests are to be respected as vital, legitimate, and essential—and which can be disregarded? To answer,

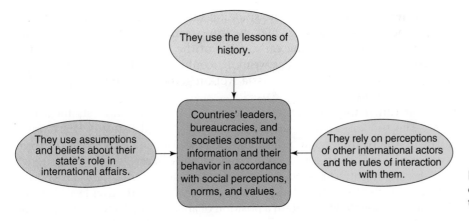

FIGURE 4-1 The constructivist approach to international relations.

constructivists emphasize the importance of social norms, perceptions, and rules in defining state interests (Wendt 1999; Checkel 1998). (See Figure 4-1.)

Leaders make foreign policy decisions based on at least three main factors (Hudson 1999; Hemmer 1999). First are assumptions and beliefs about their country's role in international affairs. Second are perceptions of other key actors in international relations and the rules of interaction with them. And finally come the lessons of history in past errors and accomplishments.

Constructivism does not contend, however, that beliefs, perceptions, and lessons just spring from the imagination. Rather, these are *collective* principles, developed and shared by powerful societal groups. A good example is a question constantly discussed in the United States: "What is our country's mission?"

▶ Describe the three main factors in foreign policy decision-making.
▶ What, in your view, is the role of the United States in international affairs today?
▶ Suggest the most powerful actors in international relations today. Are they friends or foes of the United States? What are their roles in global affairs?
▶ Name at least two significant accomplishments of U.S. foreign policy in the past ten years. Name at least two major errors. What lessons should Washington learn from these experiences?

CHECK YOUR KNOWLEDGE

SOCIALLY CONSTRUCTED MEANINGS

Socially constructed meanings have governed political decisions from ancient times. In the fifth century BC, Thucydides described how fear and honor, in addition to self-interest, provoked Greek cities to go to war. Constructivists would agree with much of what Thucydides wrote. Fear, of course, is a major factor in realism as well, for instance, fear of international anarchy. Yet the realist approach does not explain why a country's military power evokes intense fear of neighbors in one situation but not in another. For instance, Russia today has a much greater nuclear arsenal than the Soviet Union's during the 1950s. Yet in the early stages of the Cold War, Washington and Moscow assumed that nuclear weapons could be used against each other. Today, the United States and Russia work together on the assumption that nuclear weapons must never be used.

Pearl Harbor syndrome Individual attitudes and state policies focused on avoiding sudden and devastating attacks.

Fear can shape international interactions and state interests for a long time. The sudden Japanese attack against the United States in 1941 transformed American foreign policy for decades. To this day, **Pearl Harbor syndrome**—individual attitudes and state policies focused on avoiding sudden and devastating attacks—serves as a justification for American military power, which is greater than that of all other countries combined. After Pearl Harbor, Washington sought to maintain a position of absolute military superiority and often acted preemptively if it perceived a security threat from abroad. The September 11, 2001, attacks seemed to validate old fears of foreign attacks on American soil. Fear also adds an element of irrationality to human decisions. Did Washington overreact as a result?

From the viewpoint of constructivism, Thucydides' "honor" is also a social category that shapes international behavior. It is a state's search for respect, international credibility, prestige, and reputation. "Honor" can also take a warped expression. Saddam Hussein in 2003 refused to cooperate with the United Nations and the United States because he was afraid that

Pearl Harbor under attack, December 7, 1941. This event shaped American perceptions of national security for decades after. What milestone events have shaped your perception of international security and international politics?

concessions would reveal his weakness to his foes such as Iran and to his Arab allies (Woods et al. 2011). Hussein also wanted to maintain his image in the Arab world as an uncompromising fighter against Western powers (Primakov 2009). As Thucydides might have argued in ancient Greece, Hussein's defiance in the face of American power was a matter of fear and a warped sense of honor.

THREE TYPES OF INTERNATIONAL ENVIRONMENTS

Perceptions of how states should act—if these perceptions are shared by other states—translate into actions and shape a particular international environment:

- States may consider, for example, the international environment as a gigantic battlefield. Here individual states compete as enemies for power and resources, using all means necessary to win (Wendt 1992). This view of competing states recalls the violent and anarchic society described by English philosopher Thomas Hobbes (1588–1679) and is called the *Hobbesian model*.
- Other states may perceive their environment differently. To them, states are not necessarily enemies. Instead, they interact as reasonable opponents: They observe the rules of the game and try to compromise with one another to balance their interests. This view is the *Lockean model* and has its roots in the philosophy of English Enlightenment thinker John Locke (1632–1704).
- Finally, some states may see the world as driven by fundamental norms of ethics, based on recognition of the rights of others and a genuine desire to preserve international peace. This is the *Kantian model*, named after German philosopher Immanuel Kant (1724–1804). (See Table 4-1.)

At pivotal moments in history, especially at the end of major wars, dominant states and their leaders have to decide on the principles of a new postwar international environment. For instance, U.S., British, and Soviet leaders met in Yalta in 1945, a few months before the end of World War II. British prime minister Churchill clearly preferred the Lockean model. He wanted to maintain a strong British Empire and was prepared to divide a postwar world into separate spheres of influence. In his view, power balancing would contain any rivalry.

President Roosevelt gravitated instead toward a Kantian world view, with lasting institutional foundations for postwar peace and partnership. He hoped that a new global intergovernmental organization, supported by American wealth and goodwill, would consolidate the world. Soviet leader Stalin, however, tended to see a Hobbesian environment. He never believed in a lasting cooperation between the Communist Soviet Union and the capitalist powers; he wanted to expand Soviet territory and to build a security "buffer zone" between his country and the West. The three leaders could not agree on a common vision for the postwar world. As a result, fears grew, and the global confrontation known as the Cold War began (Plokhy 2010). (See Figure 4-2.)

TABLE 4-1 Key Assumptions by Type of International Environment

Type of Environment	Key Assumptions
Hobbesian (after Thomas Hobbes)	• States are enemies and rivals • They are engaged in power politics • Political conflicts have zero-sum outcomes • Self-interest and security are states' primary interests
Lockean (after John Locke)	• States are competitors that can be reasoned with • Force and compromise are used in combination • Mutual restraint is a norm of behavior • International treaties build security
Kantian (after Immanuel Kant)	• States are partners • Cooperation is the main mechanism of international relations • Nonviolence is a norm of behavior • Collective security is the ultimate goal of all states

Sources: Wendt 1992; 1999.

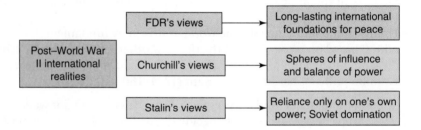

FIGURE 4-2 Three leaders, three worldviews: A post-Yalta world from the constructivist perspective.

HISTORICAL LESSONS

States draw different lessons from international relations and may have very different understandings of what constitutes a fair game. Why did Canada and Cuba choose and sustain different policies toward the United States, for example? Canada, a former British colony, was for a long time in confrontation with the United States yet achieved an equal relationship with Washington on the basis of common values and mutual trade. Cuba, a former Spanish colony, fell under the United States' economic domination and was run by U.S.-backed dictators until 1959. Fidel Castro and a group of young revolutionaries, when they came to power, rejected Washington's domination and allied with the distant Soviet Union. They adopted the Communist ideology and were eager to provide bases for Soviet nuclear missiles that targeted the United States (see "The Uses of History" at the end of this chapter).

For constructivists, history shapes the international environment. If diplomacy does not bring justice to the suffering, or if the world leaves an aggressor unpunished, then a Hobbesian environment is likely to take shape. In contrast, if states interact efficiently for a long time, support international institutions such as the United Nations, and make room for nongovernmental organizations, then a status quo can emerge based on trust, bringing humanity closer to the Lockean or Kantian ideal (Wendt 1992). Similar logic guided the United States and the European Union's member states in 2014 and later in their responses to Russia's violation of Ukraine's territorial integrity. They imposed economic sanctions on Russia, but not necessarily with the goal to contain and weaken the country. Rather, their goal was to maintain Kantian values in Europe and prevent Europe's eastern parts from descending into the Hobbesian environment due to Russia's actions. President Putin was offered the choice to build relations according to the principles of the Lockean environment: mutual restraint, respect for international treaties, and self-interested cooperation without integration (Blinken 2015).

CHECK YOUR KNOWLEDGE

▶ In which ways can fear affect the behavior of states? Suggest examples when countries underestimate and overestimate threats against them.

▶ Describe three environments in international relations. Discuss the environments established today in these regions: Western Europe, Central Asia, Southeast Asia, North Africa, and Central America.

▶ Explain key differences between the historical experiences of Canada and Cuba. Pick another country and discuss how its experiences have affected its foreign policy today. Suggested cases: Germany, Japan, and Russia.

Marxism and Conflict Theories

Some theories emphasize economic, social, and political inequality as primary sources of conflict and international tension. These theories highlight the roles of social classes, ruling elites, males, and other dominant groups in shaping foreign policy and global affairs. Dominant groups or states impose their will on less powerful groups or states, create an unequal order to serve their interests, and so generate conflicts, violence, and wars. Only liberation from this order and the end of inequality can reduce tensions both domestically and internationally.

MARXISM (AND LENINISM)

Marxism has been one of the most influential schools of political and economic thought during the twentieth century. Karl Marx (1818–1883) regarded human history as driven by the struggle between social classes—the *haves* and the *have-nots*. Marxism views a state as an instrument of the dominant classes or groups, such as aristocracy or capitalists, to oppress and exploit other classes, such as peasants or workers. The state conducts its foreign policy according to the interests of the ruling classes, which are to maximize their power and wealth at the expense of other social classes and of other states. Marxists see

Marxism A social, political, and economic theory that interprets international relations as a struggle between states representing ruling elites interested in control over territories, people, and resources.

international relations as a struggle between states' ruling elites over territories, people, and resources. Only a revolution of industrial workers, the *proletariat*, can save humanity from the eternal cycle of oppression and injustice, by establishing **Communism**—a classless political and social order of equals free from oppressive governments (Marx and Engels, [1848] 2011).

Vladimir Lenin (1870–1924) adapted Marxism to explain developments in the early twentieth century. According to Lenin, capitalism concentrates wealth in the hands of a few banks and industrial corporations. This, in turn, produces unbridled **imperialism**, a global aspiration and fight for territories and resources. According to Lenin, sovereign states participating in this struggle are just obedient "executive committees" of powerful corporations and banks expressing the interests of super-wealthy elites. In search of new markets and resources, Lenin argued, just a handful of capitalist countries of Europe and North America colonized Africa and Asia in the nineteenth century and kept Latin America in a state of dependency. Lenin called for a world revolution as the only way to save humanity from imperialism and war (Lenin, [1916] 1996).

Throughout the twentieth century, Communist revolutionaries justified violence as long as it was aimed against capitalism or the revolutionaries' opponents. Communist states included the Soviet Union, the People's Republic of China, parts of Eastern and Central Europe, Vietnam, Cuba, and North Korea. Marxism-Leninism promotes *distributive justice*, according to which the contemporary world's distribution of resources and power is fundamentally unfair and therefore should be changed. Marxism-Leninism rejects liberal values, political democracy, pluralism, and individualism in the same way it rejects the free-market economy. Capitalism here is viewed as a source of exploitation and inequality. Political democracy is ridiculed as a façade to deceive the oppressed and the poor, to divide them, and to rule over them (Ziegler 1981). (See Figure 4-3.)

After World War II many Communist parties in Western Europe distanced themselves from Leninist views. They turned instead to social-democratic models in which all social classes can share wealth and power. Lenin's theory of imperialism, however, remained particularly popular among the champions of anti-elitism, decolonization, and national liberation.

Communism
A classless political and social order free from oppressive government.

imperialism (Lenin's theory of) A global struggle among international corporations and banks for territories and resources.

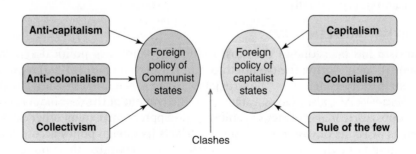

FIGURE 4-3 Marxist view of Communist and capitalist countries' foreign policy.

FROM DEPENDENCY THEORY TO OCCUPY WALL STREET

In the 1960s and 1970s, some Western thinkers turned to **neo-Marxism** to argue that world capitalism should not be destroyed but rather reformed through science and smart policies. In Asia, Africa, and Latin America neo-Marxists reacted against *liberal modernization*, which advised states to follow the American market-based model of economic and social development. Argentinean scholar Raúl Prebisch (1901–1986) argued that the structures of international relations—and trade in particular—make it impossible for countries to grow out of poverty. The free market keeps poor states dependent on rich states while supplying the latter with cheap labor and raw materials. Only by building its

An Indian folk singer performs at a Communist Party of India–Marxist rally on the eve of the party's West Bengal state convention in Kolkata, India, in 2015.

own industries and "substituting" for foreign goods by producing its own can a state emerge from dependency. These views became the foundation of **dependency theory**.

American sociologist Immanuel Wallerstein (b. 1930) formulated a related view known as *world-systems theory*. He used a Marxist concept, *hegemony*, which claims that a few industrial countries have an advantage in world affairs, whereas other states are kept behind (Wallerstein 1979). World-systems theory divides the world into a **core**, consisting of the developed states that exercise their hegemonic power, and the **periphery**, including former colonies and underdeveloped and chronically poor states. The core states, located mainly in North America and Western Europe, impose free-market rules on the poor states to keep the periphery in permanent poverty and dependence (Gereffi and Korzeniewicz 1993).

The interests of the core and the periphery are in conflict. The core states share an interest in maintaining the established economic order while eliminating challenges from the periphery. The Soviet Union and China in the twentieth century challenged the capitalist core. Yet the Soviets and Chinese could not reshape the global economic, financial, and trade systems. In the end, China and the Soviet Union (shortly before its collapse) decided to become part of a world system dominated by the United States, Western Europe, and Japan (Goldfrank 2000).

The financial global crisis that started in 2008 brought fresh attention to the issue of economic inequality. Radicals from the *antiglobalist movement* claimed that globalization, praised by liberal theoreticians during the 1990s, in reality benefitted only wealthy countries (sarcastically called "the golden billion"). A new round of development studies included discussions of how the global North can assist the global South (Wallerstein 2004; Arrighi 1994;

dependency theory The view that the world economic order is based on the flow of resources from a "periphery" of poor states to a "core" of wealthy states.

core In dependency theory, economically developed states that exercise their hegemonic power.

periphery In dependency theory, former colonies, and underdeveloped, chronically poor states.

Arrighi and Lu Zhang 2011). Rapidly increasing income disparity in the United States triggered the emergence in 2011 of *Occupy Wall Street*—a vast movement that united many people under the slogan "We are the 99%." The movement's activists asserted that most Americans, instead of benefitting from their country's position at the helm of globalization, were in fact losing out. At the same time, a tiny fraction of Americans—the "1 percent"—possessed most of the nation's wealth. The movement became international. Although the movement's long-term impact on **conflict theories** remains unclear, it gave these theories a fresh relevance. If social and economic inequality continues to grow, some new derivative of Marxism may come back and win the allegiance of millions around the world. We will return to these discussions in Chapter 7.

conflict theories Approaches that emphasize economic, social, and political inequality as a source of contradictions and tensions among social groups. Conflict theories highlight the role of social classes, ruling elites, and other dominant groups in shaping global affairs.

postcolonial studies The critique of Western domination in postcolonial Africa, Asia, and Latin America.

POSTCOLONIAL STUDIES

Using the assumptions of Marxism-Leninism, **postcolonial studies** critique Western domination in postcolonial Africa, Asia, and Latin America (the global South). Proponents cite the policies of the global North as the main source of global problems. According to this approach, European imperialism and racism have shaped the very language of international relations, which divides the world into "us" against "them" (Said 1994; Spivak 1999). Advocates of postcolonial studies argue that the West retains its dominance over the rest of the world through cultural and informational means and that state military agendas and international corporations perpetuate colonialist policies (Gregory 2004). Western thinkers and journalists define the West as a norm and depict attempts to overthrow Western domination as counterproductive and irrational (Said 1979; Fanon 2005). Further, this approach contends that the Cold War was mainly waged in Africa, Latin America, and Asia, preventing the development of these regions and causing the suffering of non-Western peoples (Chakrabarty 2007; Westad 2007).

CHECK YOUR KNOWLEDGE

▶ What are the key points of Lenin's theory of imperialism? Discuss whether these points are applicable today.
▶ Why did neo-Marxist scholars react against *liberal modernization*?
▶ Explain the core and the periphery in Wallerstein's arguments.
▶ Why are postcolonial studies discussed as a conflict approach?

GENDER AND INTERNATIONAL RELATIONS

Other conflict approaches focus not on social classes and wealth, but on social divisions such as gender and race. Again, social and political injustice are seen as a source of conflict in international relations.

feminism Critical approach arguing that men's political domination and their oppression of women shape international relations.

Feminism is the view that women do not have equal rights and opportunities to those of men, and that global changes are needed to achieve social justice. Feminist scholars have produced a wealth of work linking gender inequality to international relations. They argue that existing approaches reflect the gender bias of our male-dominated world (Hirschman 2010).

First, feminists say, men created legal and cultural rules, government institutions, and policies that systematically discriminate against women and satisfy men's needs. Global studies show that women not long ago filled fewer than 20 percent of parliamentary seats worldwide—and fewer than 15 percent of ministerial-level positions (Hunt 2007). Outside Western countries, women seldom play a significant role in policy-making in defense, security, or diplomacy. The task is therefore to give women institutional support to represent their interests in the policy-making process globally (Waylen 2010). (See Tables 4-2 and 4-3.)

Second, feminists say, defense and security policies reflect a masculine culture that accepts war and violence rather than consensus and peace (Cohn 1987). For centuries women's views of politics and conflict as well as their preferences for non-violent conflict resolution were not taken into consideration. And in fact studies show that women as a group tend to differ from men in their leadership style and understanding of security (Ayman and Korabik 2010). If women occupied more positions of power and if feminine qualities and attitudes rather than masculine ones were more valued, many feminists conclude, we all would live in a much more peaceful world (Hunt 2007).

Third, there is a strong correlation between violence against women and violence in foreign policy. Countries that tolerate aggression against women are more prone to use force abroad as well (Patterson 2006). Domestic gender inequality influences a state's choices between violence and cooperation, peace and war, even in democracies (Caprioli and Boyer 2001). In sum, feminist scholars argue, women should have the freedom and opportunities to make their own choices in everyday life and politics alike (Snyder-Hall 2010).

TABLE 4-2 Women in single and lower houses of parliament, percentage of total. Selected countries.

Rwanda	Bolivia	S. Africa	China	United Kingdom	United States	Russia	Brazil	Iran	Kuwait
64	53	42	23	23	19	14	9	3	1

Source: Inter-Parliamentary Union 2015

TABLE 4-3 Women on corporate boards, percentage of total. Selected countries.

Norway	Finland	France	United Kingdom	Denmark	United States	Spain	India	Japan
36	30	29	23	22	19	18	10	3

Source: CNN 2015

Researchers and advocates of feminism have directed attention to serious international issues—including modern sex slavery, the trafficking of women and children across borders, rape and other forms of sexual violence, the lack of protection for women and children in war zones, and AIDS (Buzan and Hansen 2009, 212).

Political Culture

culture A set of values, behaviors, and symbols shared by a group of people and communicated from one generation to the next.

political culture A set of values and norms essential to the functioning of international and national political institutions, including the attitudes of states toward each other and individual citizens.

Culture is a set of values and symbols shared by a large group of people, expressed in behavior and communicated from one generation to the next (Shiraev and Levy 2013). **Political culture** is the attitude of a community or country toward political authority and politics in general. This attitude is commonly embedded in behavior. Political culture is not a consensus or uniformity on political issues; people still tend to disagree on almost everything. Rather, it is a dominant perception concerning the rights and obligations of citizens—and the rules and practices of political participation. Applied to international relations, studies of political culture suggest at least two main points, one domestic and the other international. First, a country's foreign policy is rooted in its political culture. Second, different countries' political cultures affect the relationships between them and their abilities to influence each other.

We can identify at least three types of political culture (Almond and Verba 1963). In traditional or *parochial* political culture, citizens are only remotely aware of the presence of central government. Most of them make local decisions regardless of state policies. In *authoritarian* political culture, people obey the government in most areas of their life. They have little opportunity for feedback, dissent, or voluntary participation in politics. In *participatory* or democratic culture, the government may remain powerful, but citizens have the right to influence politics, elect their leaders, organize associations, and express their opposition. Also, mixed types of political cultures exist, especially when countries undergo political transition (Levitsky and Way 2010). (See Table 4-4.)

In the United States and France, the elements of participatory democracy are strong, whereas the elements of parochial or authoritarian culture are insignificant. In contrast, in Afghanistan and Iraq, parochial culture has dominated

TABLE 4-4 Types of Political Culture

Parochial	People are only remotely aware of the government; they do not form a political community
Authoritarian	People obey the government, act like subjects, and have little impact on its policies
Participatory or Democratic	People act like citizens, have the right to influence politics, elect their leaders, organize associations, and express their opposition
Mixed or Hybrid	Elements of two or three types of political cultures coexist

for centuries, and participatory culture had little opportunity to develop. This is one of the reasons why Washington's attempts to impose political reforms in these countries were not successful. Differences in political cultures are not of course the only factors affecting bilateral relations. Countries like Russia and Saudi Arabia show elements of all three political cultures, but authoritarian culture prevails. And yet Saudi Arabia and the United States remain strategic partners. Relations with Russia, meanwhile, have worsened.

In democratic countries, participatory political culture is part of people's everyday life. The governments of these countries base their policies toward one another on shared principles and avoid confrontation and war with each other (see arguments about democratic peace in Chapter 3).

Authoritarian states control the means of education and *communication* to spread information that may be politically useful; they use censorship to limit access to information that they think can hurt them. Authoritarian states can mobilize masses against other states, to distract them from domestic problems, using the slogans of violence and hatred (Fukuyama 2011).

With a monopoly on information, authoritarian governments could control the process of political mobilization. In the twenty-first century, the Internet, cellular phones, Facebook, and Twitter have eroded technological barriers and geographic distance. The popular revolts in Tunisia and Egypt in 2011 and in Ukraine in 2014 are examples of how modern means of communication can destabilize authoritarian states. These realities have caused authorities in China and elsewhere to censor their communication networks and limit the free flow of information.

▶ How does masculine culture relate to international relations? Suggest an example of a policy or decision rooted in a masculine culture.

▶ Explain *parochial*, *authoritarian*, and *participatory* political cultures. Why is a country's political culture relevant to international relations?

CHECK YOUR KNOWLEDGE

Identity Factors

Fire power and the size of economic investments can make a difference in global affairs. A country's military and economic power, however, is often not enough to affect values, beliefs, and affiliations. People tend to resist foreign influences simply because they are foreign and tend to defend their way of life and their identity. **Identity** refers to how people see themselves as members of national, ethnic, religious, gender, or political groups. Common identity comes from shared history, culture, and language—and can generate passions in state-to-state relations that economic self-interest cannot. Nationalist and religious passions can be particularly destabilizing and even dangerous. During the war in Vietnam, American leaders spoke of winning "hearts and minds"—and this is often more difficult than winning a military conflict. Successful foreign policy is impossible without attractive cultural symbols— the "soft power" we discussed in Chapter 3.

identity The characteristics by which a person is recognizable as a member of a cultural group, such as a nation, an ethnic group, or a religion.

A boy holds his stepsister in Nyamata, Rwanda, in 2004, ten years after the civil war that left him orphaned. The world's most powerful countries were late to respond to the extreme ethnic violence that took the lives of hundreds of thousands of Rwandan people. The consequences of that war are still felt today.

IDENTITIES AND CIVILIZATIONS

Identities are certainly broader than political cultures. Let's turn to the familiar example of Canada and Cuba. Can identity factors help us to understand the difference between their relations with the United States? Canada and the United States share common identity roots in the British Empire and in Anglo-Saxon traditions. Cuba has roots in the Spanish Empire, Catholicism, and the Caribbean culture. Do you think these factors played a role when the Castro government launched its anti-American policies and convinced its people of the threat of imperialism coming from the North?

Political scientist Samuel Huntington (1993) argued that cultural factors and identities became more important than political, military, and economic interests in international affairs. He believed that several countries could share common identities and form a "civilization" rooted in centuries of collective experiences and practices. Liberal-democratic political culture, Huntington argued, is a product of the Western civilization based on the classical legacy of Greece and Rome, Catholicism and Protestantism, European languages, the separation between religion and state, the rule of law, social pluralism, civil society, traditions of representative rule, and individualism. Other civilizations are based on values and experiences associated with Islam, Buddhism, Hinduism, Eastern Orthodox, and other religions. Whereas in Western

Christian countries politics became separated from religion, in Islamic countries a unity of religion and politics is often emphasized. Huntington believed that non-Western civilizations would resist the expansion of democracy and Western political culture. Like tectonic plates in geology, civilizations will have friction along their fault lines.

Huntington and other scholars argue that the major conflicts in world politics are not between states but rather between "civilizations" unified by cultural values. Iran and Saudi Arabia are rivals, in this view, not only because of their competition for leadership in the region but rather because of a deep-seated animosity between Persian and Arab civilizations. Similarly, Western Europe has treated Russia with great suspicion, not just because of its policies but because Europe views it as an alien, unpredictable, and dangerous civilization (Huntington 1993; Neumann 1996).

▶ How does identity (ethnic, religious, political, etc.) affect people's views and actions related to foreign policy and international relations? Give examples.

▶ According to Huntington, what are the roots of the liberal-democratic political culture?

CHECK YOUR KNOWLEDGE

RACE AND ETHNIC CONFLICT

Theories of **racial and ethnic prejudice** maintain that world politics remains rooted in the superiority of some racial, national, cultural, or ethnic groups over others. Racial and ethnic prejudices affect international relations in at least two general ways. First, political leaders interpret the world in racial or cultural terms; and second, dominant states primarily pursue the interests of white majorities.

We have already mentioned that postcolonial studies focus on how racism shapes international relations. Indeed, during the nineteenth and most of the twentieth century, theories of racial superiority, such as social Darwinism, justified European domination, slavery, and colonialism. Later anthropological and cultural studies rejected these ideas, emphasizing multiculturalism and equality.

Postcolonial studies, too, may point to sources of racial and ethnic conflict. In this view, Western powers have long represented a white culture of colonialism and racism. This leads to a double standard in their foreign policy. For example, the major powers took almost no action to stop the conflicts involving black Africans in Biafra in the 1960s and in Rwanda in 1994. Western powers may continue to doubt African countries' capabilities of self-governance, which results in the West's lack of commitment to Africa (Gates 1998).

NATIONALISM AND OTHER POLITICAL ATTITUDES

Identity-related attitudes affect politics especially when people express solidarity with social groups to which they belong in opposition to "others."

There are at least four kinds of such attitudes—nationalism, tribalism, xenophobia, and fundamentalism. They have a direct impact on diplomacy and global affairs.

nationalism
Individual and collective identification with a country or a nation. Nationalism also can become the belief in a nation's special role. Often, it is the belief that an ethnic group has the right to form an independent state.

Nationalism has many definitions, but generally it is an individual and collective form of identity with a country or a nation. Members of an ethnic group may never see one another yet view themselves as a unified group, particularly when threatened (Anderson 2005). Nationalism is often the belief that an ethnic group has the right to form an independent state. Nationalism can serve simultaneously as a consolidating and a dividing force (Muller 2008). Before 1948, Jews and Arabs in Palestine lived together under the British administration. When the British withdrew, the Jews in Palestine formed an independent state of Israel supported by the Soviet Union, the United States, and several Western countries. The neighboring Arab leaders went to war against Israel and lost. This led to the flight of the Palestinian Arabs from their lands and the formation of two sharply distinct national groups, Israeli Jews and Palestinian Arabs, which have remained in conflict for years (Fromkin 2009). In the 1990s, the collapse of Yugoslavia led to the spark of nationalism and the emergence of several new independent countries in Europe.

tribalism A way of thinking and a movement identifying itself not with nation-states, but rather with a religious or ethnic group.

National identity can coexist peacefully alongside other beliefs and patriotisms. Forms of nationalism, however, can become divisive and violent (Theiss-Morse 2009). One such form of nationalist hatred is *chauvinism*, an exaggerated belief in national superiority. Even more radical is neo-Nazism, a dangerous combination of anti-Semitism, militarism, and racism. National identity is a very powerful factor in political mobilization during conflicts and wars. People will put aside their political differences to stand shoulder-to-shoulder as citizens against another state. Political parties mend their differences to defend their country against a foreign threat. In its virulent, active form nationalism can be an effective substitute for a participatory political culture, especially in non-democratic states. During World War II many Germans followed Hitler to the end, for example. Despite their serious disapproval of the authoritarian leader Slobodan Milošević, the Serbian political opposition moved to his side during NATO's bombing campaign against Serbia in 1999.

xenophobia Fear and contempt of foreign countries and foreigners, helping politicians and regimes to mobilize public opinion, defeat political opposition, win elections, neutralize critics, or justify war.

English Defence League demonstration in Dudley, England, in 2015 against the building of a new mosque in the town. EDL insists it is a peaceful organization opposing Islamic extremism, but its past actions have often resulted in violence. Where else in Europe have nationalist parties and movements gained strength recently?

Both nationalism and **tribalism** may be associated with **xenophobia**, which is a deep-seated fear and hatred of foreign countries and foreigners. In Afghanistan, for example, resentment of any foreign military presence has a long history (Hopkirk 2004). Xenophobia exists in democracies as well. One example is a fear of immigrants. A 2011 study found that in the European Union,

DEBATE > WHO ARE PATRIOTS AND NATIONALISTS?

The labels "nationalist" and "patriot" are often confusing. Moreover, the terms *nationalist*, *patriot*, *patriotic*, or *unpatriotic* are often deliberately misused to boost one's popularity and scorn political opponents. Just what does it mean to be a Korean, Mexican, or American patriot? In public discourse, as research shows, being a "patriot" has always been more suitable than being a "nationalist" (Kosterman and Feshbach 1989). Some, however, consider "nationalism" and "patriotism" dangerous elements associated with people's obedience to authority.

WHAT'S YOUR VIEW?

Imagine that the president of the United States together with Congress have made a decision to send a significant number of military personnel to fight in an overseas conflict. Opinion polls show that the majority of Americans are in favor of this military action. Which of the following opinions would you consider most *patriotic*, and why?

❶ I support this decision because I love my country and believe we must support our president and our Congress in times of crisis regardless of what the public opinion reveals. ❷ I support this decision because I love my country and because the majority of Americans are in favor it. ❸ I oppose this decision because I love my country and do not want it to fight a foreign war.

almost fifty percent believed that immigrants "are taking employment opportunities from the local population" (Eurobarometer 2011).

Fundamentalism is a form of identity rooted in religious beliefs. Fundamentalists advocate a return to the past—often an imagined past, before modern influences came to undermine traditional values. To them, openness, globalization, and democracy threaten local cultures and their status. *Private* fundamentalism can be found among devout believers of Islam, Christianity, Judaism, and other religions. It has little impact on international politics. *Political* fundamentalism, in contrast, advocates its vision of how its government should function and the foreign policy it should conduct (Husain 2005). ISIS is an example of Islamic fundamentalism that has profoundly changed international relations. We will further examine fundamentalist beliefs and their impact on international relations in Chapter 8.

fundamentalism
A point of view or social movement distinguished by rigid adherence to principles rooted in tradition (typically religious tradition) and often by intolerance of individual rights and secularism.

▶ How does nationalism influence international relations? Give examples of positive and negative influences.
▶ Define xenophobia. Suggest the ways in which xenophobia can affect a country's foreign policy.
▶ Explain political fundamentalism.

CHECK YOUR KNOWLEDGE

Political Psychology

Every time the United States elects a new president, political strategists around the world start guessing. What are the views of the new president? Will there be a new foreign policy direction in Washington? After all, human beings make decisions and conduct policies on behalf of countries and international organizations. And these individuals may be proactive or passive, vindictive or forgiving, rely on ideology or on intuition, and turn to advisers or act alone. **Political psychology** studies the interactions between political and psychological factors in individual and group behavior.

Political psychologists use the behavioral and cognitive sciences to gather information about world leaders and analyze their policies (Houghton 2008). Some of their data comes from experimental studies. Most, however, comes from politicians themselves—their statements, interviews, press conferences, speeches, memoirs, and policy-making.

political psychology
The study of the interactions between political and psychological factors in individual and group behavior.

RATIONAL DECISION-MAKING

rational model
In political psychology, the view that politicians act, for the most part, logically, to maximize positive outcomes and to minimize negative outcomes.

According to the **rational model**, political leaders try to maximize the positive outcomes and minimize the negative consequences of their decisions. In other words, they tend to act, for the most part, rationally. If they act rationally, then mutual trust based on interpersonal contact becomes crucial, so that state leaders will act openly and sincerely (Cholett and Goldgeier 2002), try to narrow their differences, and arrive at a mutually acceptable solution. This process involves concessions, goodwill gestures, proposals, retractions, and compromises (Barner-Barry and Rosenwein 1985). In the difficult 1990 negotiations over the reunification of Germany, for example, decision makers were able to find reasonable compromises. The Soviet leader Mikhail Gorbachev agreed to withdraw troops from East Germany in exchange for West German financial assistance to the Soviet Union and pledges not to expand NATO eastward beyond Germany (Sarotte 2009). Some leaders prefer to take quick actions without reflection, whereas others prefer to be more careful. U.S. president Barack Obama, as some observers noted, generally erred on the side of caution, recognizing the high costs of quick and reckless decisions in foreign policy (Osnos 2014).

Approaches based on rational models also maintain that if we, as observers, had full access to information, we could explain international relations as a bargaining process. We could take stock of the participating sides' potential gains and losses. The problem, however, is that political leaders are guided not only by pragmatic calculations. They may have personal attitudes, aspirations, and ambitions that affect their policies as well.

BIASED DECISION-MAKING

prospect theory
Theory stating that people consistently miscalculate their chances of success and failure.

Decisions in international relations are too ambiguous and complex to explain by rational models alone (Hart 1991). Human thinking is not completely rational, even when people believe they act logically (Steinbruner 1974; Cutler 1981). **Prospect theory** (for which one of its developers, Daniel Kahneman, won the Nobel Prize in 2002) states that people, even when acting in a seemingly rational way, consistently miscalculate their chances of success and failure (Kahneman and Tversky 1979). Emotions and misperceptions affect how politicians evaluate the international situation (Larson 1985; 1997).

consistency bias   In cognitive theories, the rule that the human mind operates so as to keep beliefs, opinions, and ideas consistent.

What kind of biases occur and why? In **consistency bias**, new information is more likely to be accepted if it accords with an individual's prevailing opinions. Similarly, in **resistance bias**, people tend to stick to their decisions even when new evidence challenges their assumptions (Levy 2009; Heider 1959). Finally, **accessibility bias** occurs when people pick not the best option but one that is easily available and easily understood.

What do these biases mean for international relations? Biases tend to steer politicians to hawkish, violent choices more often than to nonviolent, reconciliatory strategies (Kahneman and Renshon 2007). They often exaggerate the evil intentions of their adversaries and underestimate peaceful initiatives. Leaders also tend to be uncritical of their own actions and reluctant to compromise. Former president George W. Bush might have displayed consistency and resistance bias when the United States started two wars, in Afghanistan in 2001 and Iraq in 2003. Bush's initial self-confidence led him to reject views critical of his foreign policy (Woodward 2007; Renshon 2009).

Another source of bias in foreign-policy decisions is **group pressure**: The presence of other people, such as cabinet members, alters individual decisions, *group inhibition*. Conversely, other people can encourage decision makers to act carelessly and recklessly, an example of *group facilitation*. People frequently care about competition with other group members, not necessarily about confronting the problems at hand (Deutsch and Krauss 1962).

Finally, biased decisions could be caused by a leader's own psychological problems as a result of significant stress, strong emotional commitment to an issue, or psychological illness.

German chancellor Angela Merkel (left), Ukrainian president Petro Poroshenko (center), and French president François Hollande shake hands during their meeting in Kiev, Ukraine, in 2015.

Russian president Vladimir Putin meets with U.S. president Barack Obama in 2012. Body language reveals how well these leaders get along.

POLITICAL SOCIALIZATION

Can we understand foreign-policy decisions better by studying how decision-making develops? **Political socialization** examines how individuals acquire and change their political knowledge and beliefs during their lifespan (Sears et al. 2003). Two types of studies of political socialization can be useful for international relations as a discipline. One is the study of generational changes in people's political beliefs, including views on foreign policy. For example, before the Vietnam War, U.S. citizens gave U.S. foreign policy had bipartisan support (Hilsman 1959). Since the late 1960s, however, U.S. citizens have tended to

resistance bias In cognitive theories, the rule that leaders resist changing their ideas about international relations.

accessibility bias In cognitive theories, the rule that a leader tends to pick the option that is most easily available.

group pressure In political psychology, the ability of other people to alter individual decisions.

political socialization The study of how individuals acquire their political knowledge and beliefs.

disagree on foreign-policy actions. Many factors affect people's views of international events. Why is it important to know about public opinion in the study of foreign policy? In democracies, leaders are aware of and try to influence public opinion. As we learned in Chapter 3, when leaders lack public support, they may change policy.

The second type of study in political socialization examines how leaders develop their views of politics and the world (Murray 1943; Erikson 1969).

Contemporary studies conclude that political leaders tend to form many of their beliefs early in life (Jost and Sidanius 2004). Some biographical evidence suggests that entire careers are shaped by the desire for recognition, achievement motivation, search for power, and redemption (Volkan and Itzkowitz 1984; Renshon 2011). Of course, this intriguing suggestion requires future critical discussion. (See Table 4-5.)

TABLE 4-5 Political Psychology: U.S. Presidents and Their Formative Years

President	Politics as a Way to Address Personal Issues
Richard Nixon	Lonely and anxious as a child, Nixon shunned people and used politics to compensate for personal insecurities. As president, he avoided the media and preferred closed-door deals, which led to success in some of his realpolitik designs but also to the Watergate scandal.
Jimmy Carter	From his youth, Carter was committed to doing "right" and to avoiding violence. These attitudes motivated him to put human rights at the center of his foreign policy. His idealism led to successes but also serious mistakes in foreign policy.
Ronald Reagan	Raised in a lower-class family, Reagan made his way up using his persistence, hard work, and excellent communication skills. He acquired strong conservative beliefs later in life.
Bill Clinton	Growing up as an orphan, the future president developed a profound ambition to distinguish himself. He was often brilliant in domestic politics and cautious in foreign policy, but reckless in his personal life.
George W. Bush	Raised in a secure upper-class environment, in a powerful family, Bush grew up with severe personal problems. He overcame alcoholism by turning to religion and work. He developed a sense of self-righteousness, which led him to seek limited feedback from others. As president, he saw the War on Terror as a global struggle between good and evil.
Barack Obama	As a biracial child growing up in such distinct social environments as Hawaii and Indonesia, he developed a respect for the world's diversity. His mother's death from cancer made him determined to reform healthcare. Obama became an overachiever and learned to navigate the American political system, often preferring compromise to confrontation in foreign policy.

Sources: Reeves (2001); Post (2005b); Glad (2009); Renshon (2004; 2011); Takiff (2010).

As you can see, there are parallels between political psychology and constructivism, in that both describe how political leaders construct and interpret information. Political psychologists, however, attempt to look inside the human mind through empirical research and experiments.

▶ Why don't rational models fully explain international political behavior?
▶ What are consistency, resistance, and accessibility biases in decision-making? Suggest examples.
▶ What do political socialization studies add to our understanding of foreign policy?

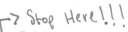

Contexts and Applications

How well do constructivist, conflict, feminist, and political psychology approaches hold up in practice? To judge, we have to apply them critically to actual cases and contexts in international relations.

The Individual Decisions Context

Constructivist views, with their emphasis on social meanings, and political psychology share a similar concern for how countries' leaders make decisions. Rich empirical data show the importance of individuals' character in shaping political choices (Sears et al. 2003). What do these studies reveal?

VISIONARIES, FANATICS, AND PRAGMATICS

Mikhail Gorbachev, the last leader of the Soviet Union, fundamentally changed international relations in 1988 with the idea that the United States, Canada, other NATO countries, and a reformed Soviet Union share similar values, including worldwide peace. Gorbachev called for nuclear disarmament and the renunciation of the use of force in international relations (Rey 2004). At the time, many realists dismissed Gorbachev's vision as unworkable, but his ideas were a catalyst for the peaceful overthrow of Communism in Eastern and Central Europe.

Gorbachev's visionary ideas were rooted in his individual character. First, he became convinced that the West was no longer an enemy. Second, Gorbachev turned to the West not only because of growing Soviet economic difficulties but also because he believed in Western economic and social models. Culturally, Gorbachev was a *Westernizer*, in sharp contrast with previous and contemporary leaders in Moscow (Rey 2004; Zubok 2007). A shift in values and perceptions, as constructivists would argue, changed Soviet foreign policy.

Adolf Hitler was a fanatic who challenged the entire international system. His beliefs and values in the 1930s and 1940s were xenophobic, anti-Semitic, and anti-elitist. He envisioned Germany's global domination and was obsessed with "racial purity" and the elimination of Jews. He hoped to restore an Aryan culture based on its mythic roots. Many Germans, disillusioned with liberal democracy and hoping that a strong state would solve their problems, followed him (Kershaw 2000). Whereas Gorbachev was a visionary of a transnational community based on Western values, Hitler was a fanatic of a dangerous myth promoting war, racism, and anti-Semitism. Both cases suggest that, at certain points in history, a single person's cultural values and identity can change the course of history.

In reality, visionaries and fanatics are few and far between. Most political leaders remain pragmatic, because they are dealing with domestic and international events based on practical calculations rather than value considerations. To most of them, avoiding crises and winning the next election are more important goals than adhering to a set of ideological beliefs.

THE ANATOMY OF DECISIONS

Political psychologists often assume that leaders make biased decisions caused by emotions, misperceptions, and the pressure of deadlines. Leaders may not always search for the best decision. Settle on the first acceptable or convenient alternative. Others may be stubborn—afraid of appearing weak or unwilling to lose credibility. As professor Jerrold Post, a former CIA analyst, wrote in a memorandum to Congress in 1990 describing Saddam Hussein of Iraq, "Saddam's worldview is narrow and distorted, and he has scant experience out of the Arab world" (Post 1990). Saddam presented himself as the only Arab leader to champion the Palestinian cause and was not afraid of the United States. He saw himself as engaged in a struggle that every great leader should endure. If need be, he was prepared to go down heroically. Neither negotiation nor surrender fit his image of the actions of a great revolutionary leader.

analogy The comparison of a new situation to a familiar one. Analogies may provide quick answers in place of a more lengthy discussion.

Decisions can also be biased by a reliance on **analogy**. Comparing new situations to familiar ones can provide quick answers. As we have seen, analogies in policy-making may reflect both rationality and bias (Jervis 1976; Cholett and Goldgeier 2008). After World War I, most European statesmen feared that any international crisis would lead to war. Constrained by this frightening analogy, British and French leaders signed a deal with Hitler in Munich in 1938, allowing him to dismember Czechoslovakia. In time their action became the basis of an analogy, too. President Lyndon Johnson and his advisers evoked the "Munich analogy" in sending U.S. troops to defend South Vietnam. The argument was that anything less would be appeasing Ho Chi Minh just as Britain and France had appeased Hitler. (Khong 1992). The Munich analogy was used again in 1991, when Iraq occupied Kuwait. President George H. W. Bush compared Saddam to Hitler to justify a U.S. invasion. Negotiations with the Iraqi dictatorship, he believed, would endanger regional and world peace. Yet again, critics used this analogy to point out the lack of action from the West to stop Russia's active engagement in the conflict in Ukraine in 2014–15.

Some leaders are driven by irrational motives. Illness can diminish an individual's ability to reason. So can extreme circumstances. Alexander George pioneered the study of leadership under stress or crisis. He found that a leader's psychological problems can fatally disrupt strategic decision-making (George 1969). Soviet leader Leonid Brezhnev's addiction to medication, for example, may have contributed to the fateful decision to send Soviet troops to Afghanistan in December 1979 (Zubok 2007).

Many countries lack legal mechanisms for replacing a sick or unstable leader. Authoritarian regimes have concealed the sickness of leaders out of fear of domestic instability. Cuban authorities did not reveal Fidel Castro's declining health until he passed authority to his brother Raúl in 2007. North Korea similarly refused to discuss the health of its leader, Kim Jong-il, in 2011. Even in a more transparent democratic society, a leader's personal problems may affect foreign policy, although there is less risk of national disorder.

The rise of terrorism also points to the importance of discussing irrationality in decision-making. We return to this discussion in Chapter 8.

LIFE EXPERIENCES

The evidence regarding the impact of early experiences on political leaders' decisions remains inconclusive. Did Castro's early beliefs about Cuba–U.S. relations shape his revolutionary policy for thirty years? Did Gorbachev's early experience of war make him averse to the use of violence when he became the Soviet leader? How did Obama's childhood affect his leadership during his presidency? Although early life events surely affect decisions, we have little reliable and verifiable evidence connecting a leader's formative experiences with specific actions (Post 2008; Kowert 1996). The political preferences of Castro, Gorbachev, and Obama may be better explained by many other factors that shaped their identities later in their lives. Biographical and psychological studies of political leaders, military commanders, and diplomats can be incomplete, selective, and sometimes misleading. Nevertheless they frequently provide important information.

ALTERNATIVE THEORIES TESTED

Marxists argued for a long time that once oppressive social classes are defeated, equality and justice can win. Yet in Cuba, the Castro revolutionary regime after 1959 became even more oppressive, relying on the arrest and execution of opponents. Iran after 1979 demonstrates that one-man dictatorship was replaced by dictatorship of a group of Ayatollahs and religious authorities, even more repressive and corrupt. If Marxists paid more attention to individual factors, they would have admitted that their Marxist social utopia was always brushed aside by people competing for power and money.

North Korean soldiers bow in front of bronze statues of late leaders Kim Il-sung (left) and Kim Jong-il in Pyongyang, North Korea, in 2015. In authoritarian countries, leaders' personal lives remain a state secret even after they die. Why do authorities maintain such secrecy?

What about the feminist idea that women would do better than men if they occupied positions of power? Women in power have not always engaged in peaceful policies. They often cannot eradicate corruption either. U.S. secretaries of state Madeleine Albright in the 1990s and Condoleezza Rice and Hillary Clinton in 2001 to 2013 did not steer foreign policy decisively on the path of peace. Albright and Rice had to justify military campaigns in Kosovo, Afghanistan, and Iraq. Clinton did not challenge Barack Obama's military actions in Libya and constant use of unmanned planes to kill militants in Pakistan and Afghanistan. Feminist scholars argue back when they discuss these examples: To succeed, a woman must adapt to a political and cultural environment created by men. Women, they argue, compared to male leaders, are likely to possess a more conciliatory approach to foreign policy (Schein 2002). Yet they may not have the immediate economic and political resources to reduce corruption and violence. They also have to work in a predominantly male atmosphere. Could you suggest other reasons as to why women often could not bring peace and address injustice even they occupied the most powerful political positions in their countries? (See Table 4-6.)

CHECK YOUR KNOWLEDGE

▶ Who are visionaries and fanatics in international relations? What are the differences between them, from your point of view?

▶ Explain the Munich analogy. Offer two contemporary examples to illustrate.

▶ Describe how socialization studies explain decision-making in international relations.

▶ Why is it important to monitor the psychological health of leaders?

TABLE 4-6 Critical Evaluation of Prominent Women in Power

Name, Country	Position and Years in Power	Examples of Corruption or Forceful Responses
Golda Meir, Israel	Prime Minister: 1969–74	Led Israel in the 1973 war against Arab states (the Yom Kippur War).
Indira Gandhi, India	Prime Minister: 1966–77; 1980–84	Led India in the 1971 war against Pakistan. Frequently used tough measures to deal with domestic and international issues.
Isabel Peron, Argentina	President: 1974–76	Accused of corruption and the disappearances and assassinations of opposition leaders.
Margaret Thatcher, United Kingdom	Prime Minister: 1979–90	In 1982, initiated a tough military response to Argentina's military presence in the Falkland Islands. Believed nuclear weapons help to keep peace.
Benazir Bhutto, Pakistan	Prime Minister: 1988–90; 1993–96	Charged with corruption while in office and was a key figure in Pakistan's nuclear program.
Yulia Tymoshenko, Ukraine	Prime Minister 2007–2010	Accused of corruption; sentenced to a prison term and released in 2014.

The State Policies Context

Alternative views can enrich our understanding of how state politics and institutions affect a country's international behavior. Most national leaders face a host of institutional and political forces that constrain their freedom of action and influence foreign policy.

BUREAUCRACY AND COGNITIVE MAPS

In most countries, decision-making is a result of **bureaucratic bargaining**. Political groups and institutions fight for their interests and make compromises. We looked at "log rolling" from the realist perspective in Chapter 2. The constructivist approach suggests many more ways through which bureaucracy can bias foreign policy. During the Cold War, for example, the *domino theory* became common wisdom in the United States: The loss of a single country to Communism in Asia or Latin America would trigger a chain reaction, and soon all neighboring countries would fall into Communist hands. After the end of the Cold War, democratic peace theory (Chapter 3) became nearly as influential in Washington.

Constructivism also helps in understanding how cognitive factors shape international behavior in authoritarian states. In the 1950s, U.S. analysts hoped to predict how the political beliefs of members of the Soviet Politburo would translate into foreign policy. **Cognitive maps**, or diagrams of information processing and decision-making, were used (often unsuccessfully) to predict Soviet decisions. We can use a cognitive map to explain a choice made by the Taliban in Afghanistan, a political movement based on revolutionary Islamist ideology (Husain 2005). The core of the Taliban's cognitive map is spiritual solidarity with Muslims fighting for a caliphate, a regional religious commonwealth. It was therefore inconceivable for the Taliban leadership to cede to U.S. pressure to hand over another Muslim, Osama bin Laden, after the attacks of September 11, 2001. In those circumstances, the Taliban leaders chose war. (See Figure 4-4.)

bureaucratic bargaining   The process by which political groups and institutions express their interests and make trade-offs and compromises.

cognitive map   Model of information-processing and decision-making.

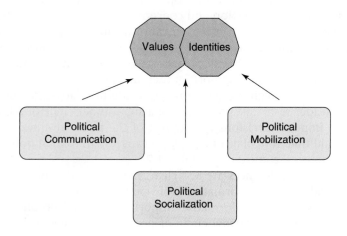

FIGURE 4-4 How values and identities related to politics are formed.

ACCESS TO INFORMATION AND STATESMANSHIP

State leaders have an important edge over rank-and-file officials, citizens, and the media—exclusive access to intelligence. This advantage does not, however, guarantee the most effective foreign policy. In many countries, intelligence experts avoid making policy suggestions because they are not supposed to influence decision-making. But political leaders often put pressure on intelligence efforts. Sometimes experts fail to contradict the erroneous perceptions of policy makers, who may have already decided on a course of action. Joseph Stalin and Saddam Hussein forced their advisers to tell them what they wanted to hear. The Bush administration, critics say, pressed the CIA to report that Iraq was on the verge of producing nuclear arms (Goodman 2008). The Obama administration officials in 2012, according to critics, were reluctant to call the assassination of the U.S. ambassador in Libya a terrorist act to avoid possible political fallout at home. Yet sometimes the realities on the ground change a country's foreign policy. France invaded Mali in 2013 despite French president Hollande's earlier objections to intervention. This policy change was caused by a rapidly deteriorating situation in this African country where Islamic fundamentalist fighters were about to take power by force.

Did the U.S. President's Daily Brief trigger war in Iraq? Visit the companion website for links.

The fast-growing volume and complexity of information is a serious challenge to any decision maker. Too much information can be a barrier to clear and accurate decision-making—just as too little information can be (Nye 2002). How can a leader take in an overwhelming amount of information before making policy decisions? The U.S. president begins the workday by reading a document called the President's Daily Brief (PDB), a procedure created during the Cold War. Reducing complex and voluminous evaluations to a short PDB provides much-needed simplicity. However, it also risks the loss of regional and local contexts or of crucial details.

THE DEMOCRATIC-AUTHORITARIAN CONTINUUM

In democracies, the decision-making process is relatively open to inquiry, scrutiny, criticism, and free discussion. Parliamentary factions, the media, nongovernmental groups, and public opinion play a role in the decision-making process. Political opposition and concerned groups can draw attention to foreign-policy issues and can serve as a restraining force on governmental decisions, especially those related to foreign aid or the use of military force abroad (Sobel 2001; Nacos et al. 2000). Leaders of democratic states should therefore tend to seek broad political support for their decisions.

In authoritarian regimes, decisions are made in relative secrecy. The authoritarian leader secures support among a small inner circle of reliable supporters and imposes decisions on the rest of the political elites. Individual leaders should therefore play a more significant role in foreign policy than in democratic political contexts. (See Table 4-7.)

In reality, the differences are less clear. Officials in democratic countries too may shield valuable information from public scrutiny (Goodman 2008). Since the 1940s, sensitive information important to U.S. decision-making has been disseminated to a narrow circle of people on a "need-to-know" basis.

CASE IN POINT > *Two-Level Games*

Political scientist Robert Putnam (1988) offers an aid to testing constructivist assumptions. His *two-level game* model suggests that leaders make foreign policy with one eye on international factors (the first level) and the other eye on domestic developments (the second level). State leaders operate on both levels. Domestic forces affecting policy decisions include legislative institutions, lobbying groups, political opposition, media, and often the military. The impact of these institutions depends on the country's constitution and democratic traditions. Democratic leaders have to think about reelection even in the midst of an international crisis. Most famously,

Winston Churchill and George H. W. Bush led their countries in military victories in Germany and Iraq, but lost elections, in 1945 and 1992, respectively.

The conflict between Israel and the Arab states provides an incredibly complex example of a two-level game. Israel cannot make too many concessions to the Palestinians without antagonizing a big part of the electorate. Among the Palestinians, the groups and leaders that support negotiations with Israel often face domestic backlash as well. At the same time, supporters of a tough approach on both sides risk losing broad popular support (Mahler 2004).

CRITICAL THINKING

❶ Domestic politics can affect foreign policy either positively or negatively. Can you illustrate some positive impacts of two-level games?
❷ According to the Treaty Clause of the United States Constitution, international agreements signed by presidents must be confirmed by a "super majority" (two-thirds) of the Senate. Would you argue for or against an amendment to change the required supermajority to a simple majority? If adopted, would this amendment, in your view, reduce or increase the impact of domestic politics on foreign policy?

TABLE 4-7 Decision-Making in Authoritarian and Democratic Contexts

	Authoritarian Context	Democratic Context
Political Environment	Decisions are made in political isolation and are not seriously scrutinized or influenced by other political forces.	Group decision-making is scrutinized and critically appraised by the media, political opposition, and public opinion.
Type of Political Support	The authoritarian leader secures support from a small inner circle of reliable supporters, secret police, and the military. The leader imposes decisions on the rest of the political elites.	Democratic leaders tend to seek broad political support for their decisions from government, the media, political parties, and public opinion.
Situational Factors	An individual leader's choices play a crucial role in decision-making.	Policy mistakes by an individual leader are likely to be prevented or corrected by other political actors, including individuals and institutions.

Strategic plans remain classified for decades and foreign-policy errors are rarely subject to independent investigation. The United States used secret diplomacy and covert operations against the Communist powers for years. Similar strategies are pursued today against international terrorist organizations.

two-level game
A model in which states react to both domestic and international politics.

A burqa-clad Indian woman checks her phone in Hyderabad, India, in 2015. India's top court affirmed people's right to online free speech by striking down a provision that had called for imprisoning people who send "offensive" messages. How could collective experiences of democratic freedoms affect international relations?

COLLECTIVE EXPERIENCES

Collective experiences may either help in democratic transitions—as we saw in the examples of Germany and Japan after World War II—or become obstacles to national reintegration. Although Germany has been a single state since 1990, citizens from former Communist East Germany continued for some years to harbor resentment toward fellow citizens and politicians from western parts. People in North and South Korea are still sharply divided by ideology and politics. Residents of Taiwan, although they may share a similar language with their counterparts in China, have vastly different collective experiences and attitudes than those who live in the People's Republic of China.

Collective experiences of the very same events naturally differ from country to country. Europe in the twentieth century lost tens of millions of lives in wars and suffered massive devastation. For the United States, despite heavy casualties, these conflicts were for the most part foreign wars, and the country emerged in 1945 as the strongest and wealthiest in the world. As a result, many Europeans take a much more cautious attitude toward the use of military force than Americans do (Costigliola 2000). This could have contributed to divisions within NATO after the United States invaded Iraq. (See Table 4-8.)

In time, collective experiences change. Germany occupied Ukraine and Russian lands twice in the twentieth century, causing large-scale destruction

TABLE 4-8 Collective Experiences and Foreign Policy: Comparative Cases

Country	Example
United States	The Great Depression shaped the identity of millions and helped the U.S. government abandon isolationism during and after World War II.
Soviet Union	Memories of the 1941 Nazi invasion in 1941 and the Great Patriotic War against Germany provided widespread popular support for the Soviet regime. Soviet leaders and the majority of citizens believed that they had the right to occupy Eastern Europe after World War II and to defend themselves against Western imperialism.
Cuba	U.S. attempts to overthrow Castro's government in the early 1960s rallied millions of Cubans to its support. Their collective memories were shaped by images of heroic struggle against the United States.
North Vietnam	First China, then France, and then Japan colonized Vietnam. Communists exploited this experience to win power in the 1950s and later to direct anticolonial sentiment against the United States.

and the deaths of millions of people. Yet, in 2011, 84 percent of Russians had a positive view of Germany. More than 70 percent of Russians believe the United States is their country's main enemy (Levada Center 2015). Most Vietnamese these days do not consider the United States an enemy. Direct U.S. investment in Vietnam has reached $16 billion and is increasing, and more than 13,000 Vietnamese exchange students attend U.S. colleges (Gang 2011). Conversely, after the American occupation of Iraq and Afghanistan, more people in Muslim countries began to view the United States as hostile (Pew 2015).

▶ What is bureaucratic bargaining in foreign policy? Suggest an example.

▶ What are cognitive maps? How do they help analyze a country's policies?

▶ What are the two levels in Robert Putnam's theory? Can foreign policy affect domestic policy?

▶ Read about the history of Iran, Argentina, or India and discuss how its citizens' collective experiences affect its foreign policy today.

CHECK YOUR KNOWLEDGE

The Global Context

GENDER AND CLASS PERSPECTIVES

Are feminist ideas being implemented globally? More countries now promote women to positions of power. France, for example, requires large companies to raise the proportion of female directors to 40 percent by 2020. In Spain, public and large private companies were required by law to reach that same goal in 2015. Norway introduced a similar requirement more than a decade ago (Beck 2011). Although few women are yet heads of state, more and more women, particularly young professionals from Western societies, are involved in nongovernmental organizations. Political psychologists say that women on average adapt better to intercultural communication, display greater tolerance, and work better in groups than men. Increasingly, educated and well-trained women successfully manage grassroots networking, humanitarian aid, and fundraising. This influx of women in NGOs may, in turn, signal monumental changes to come in the whole of international relations (Hunt 2007).

The financial crises in the first decades of the twenty-first century renewed world-systems arguments that the capitalist "core" serves the interests of just a few wealthy states. Since 2009 the United States has allocated hundreds of billions of dollars to support delinquent banks and insurance companies. At the same time, the old core, dominated by Washington, may be giving way to a new core in Asia. In China, the state has retained a firm grip on finances, accumulated multibillion-dollar reserves of Western currency, begun new economic transformations, and achieved impressive growth (Arrighi 2010). The new rich have appeared, but global poverty persists. We will return to this paradox in Chapter 7.

GLOBAL INTERESTS?

Earlier we saw that domestic social attitudes and political processes shape countries' interests and foreign policy. So do international structures, laws, norms of behavior, organizations, and institutions (Finnemore 1996). For example, in the past, states were concerned with accumulating wealth, viewing it as a "zero-sum game"—a game with clear winners and losers. However, by the end of the twentieth century, poverty was recognized as bad for global stability and for the well-being of wealthy states as well as poor ones. Global poverty became a global challenge.

In addition to changing structures, shifting global values may encourage states to see their interests differently. After the end of the Cold War in the early 1990s, the United States seemed the only superpower left, with military capabilities superior to all other states combined. The post–Cold War world devalued the use of military power, however, and valued humanitarian agendas, such as policies to relieve poverty, protect the environment, and fight infectious diseases. The United Nations received from an increasing number of states more authority to make global decisions. At the same time, Washington in more recent years began to turn to the United Nations and other international and transnational organizations to regain international legitimacy and leadership (Cholett and Goldgeier 2008).

In front of the U.S. Embassy in Moscow in 2015, a young couple protests U.S. support for human rights activists in Russia. Anti-Americanism became a means for the Kremlin to rally the Russian people and shut down NGOs that had Western funding.

REGIONAL RESPONSES

Globalization causes social, cultural, and ideological changes as well as political and economic ones. In response, some political elites have turned to *hybrid* political cultures, based on elements of authoritarian and traditional culture, and many authoritarian states practice some form of democracy (Krauthammer 2008). Some leaders prefer emphasizing local and regional values and contrast them with the liberal values of the West. In the 1990s, Singapore's leader, Lee Kuan Yew, spoke eloquently about Asian values. By advocating a form of capitalism based on Confucian values and strong authoritarian power, he sought to compete more effectively with the West (Mahbubani 2002). Russian leaders proposed what they called *sovereign democracy* to defend authoritarian forms of governance combined with some democratic principles (Shiraev 2013). After the Cold War, authoritarian countries switched to **competitive authoritarianism**— a strategy for preserving legitimacy and power (Levitsky and Way 2010). Under competitive authoritarianism, elections are regularly held, but a single leader or party dominates. The government uses police, courts, and tax agencies to harass the opposition, control the media, abuse state resources, and manipulate electoral results.

Economic liberalization does not necessarily cause democratization. Germany, Japan, and South Korea did abandon authoritarianism and turn to democracy in the twentieth century, but the lessons of these success stories may not apply universally. Today Venezuela, Kenya, China, and Russia all combine free-market economies with authoritarian policies. Many countries in fact use nationalism to argue against democracy on Western terms.

"Export" of democracy to other countries usually fails when there are no local conditions or actors to support it (McFaul 2009). Still, supporters of democracy should not become discouraged. Democracy has many faces and can adapt to many local conditions. And the outcome may not resemble the American, Canadian, or French models.

ON CLASHES BETWEEN CIVILIZATIONS

Samuel Huntington believed that "civilizations" based on different religious, cultural, and political foundations are unlikely to cooperate. He warned, as you remember, that future conflicts would happen, not between nation-states divided by interests, but between civilizations divided by values (Huntington 1993). The developments of the twenty-first century have neither confirmed nor contradicted this prediction so far.

On the one hand, critics find the idea of the "clash" a bit exaggerated. China ("Confucian civilization" in Huntington's typology) does not want to clash with anyone; its leadership speaks instead of peace and economic cooperation. Most Asian and Latin American leaders discuss global cooperation instead of competition with the West.

On the other hand, pessimists point to the strength of Islamist parties in Egypt; the rise of violent, religion-inspired fundamentalism; and the continuing clashes in Syria, Iraq, Yemen, Somalia, Nigeria, and Sudan. They predict that Islamic fundamentalism, despite its several setbacks, and anti-Western attitudes will flourish. We will return to this subject in later chapters.

competitive authoritarianism
A hybrid political culture with a competitive electoral system in which a single leader or party dominates. The government uses state power to defeat opposition and mobilize public opinion.

THE USES OF HISTORY: The Cuban Missile Crisis

Background

The Cuban Missile Crisis was one of the most dramatic events of the twentieth century. It also could have been one of the most tragic, because the world came very close to a nuclear war. Which lessons from the Cuban Missile Crisis could we apply today?

In 1962 the Soviet leadership decided to place a number of nuclear missiles in Cuban territory. The missiles, if launched, could have reached most major cities in the U.S. (See Map 4-1.) The Soviets moved the missiles surreptitiously and lied to the world community about their actions. President John F.

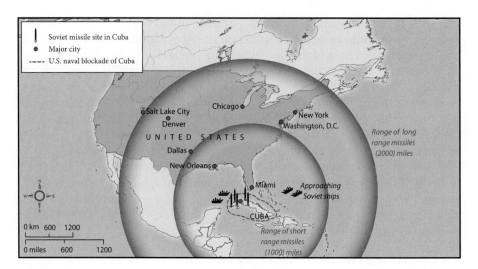

MAP 4-1 Range of missiles' penetration in the Cuban Missile Crisis

Kennedy issued an ultimatum to the Soviet premier Nikita Khrushchev, demanding a stop to the missiles' deployment. Kennedy ordered a naval blockade of Cuba to prevent the Soviet vessels carrying the missiles from entering the area. Khrushchev promised retaliation. The world was on the brink of a major confrontation between Moscow and Washington: a nuclear war seemed inevitable. Fortunately, both leaders found a way to resolve the conflict. How did they do this? What led to the conflict?

In *Essence of Decision* (1971), Graham Allison argues that bureaucratic politics provides the best explanation of the decision-making process during the Cuban Missile Crisis. For years, Allison's book remained a standard text for applying rational models of decision-making to crisis management in international relations. In the 1999 edition, based on new access to Soviet, Cuban, and American archives, the authors argued that both leaders acted rationally to pursue pragmatic goals: Khrushchev sought to improve Russia's position within the balance of power, and Kennedy sought to restore the international status quo without provoking a war (Allison and Zelikow 1999). (See Figure 4-5.)

Analysis

CONSTRUCTIVIST VIEW

What if we step aside from the traditional rational model and look at the Cuban Missile Crisis through a constructivist lens? If seen from this angle, Khrushchev's main motivation changed: It was first to shift the balance of power in Soviet favor, but later to defend Cuba from an American invasion. In 1961, the United States had trained Cuban nationals to invade Cuba, and the CIA had made plans to assassinate Castro. U.S. policy makers failed to understand that their provocative actions might have triggered Khrushchev's fears of a possible full-scale U.S. invasion of the island. For the Soviet leader, who boasted of the

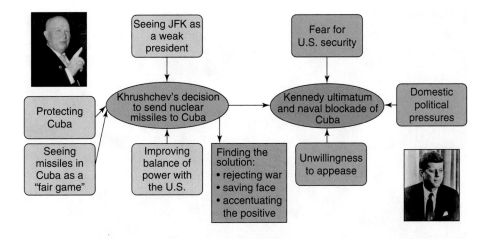

FIGURE 4-5
Perceptions and motivations of Khrushchev and Kennedy in the Cuban Missile Crisis.

inevitability of a global Communist victory, a successful U.S. invasion of Cuba and the defeat of Castro would have been an unacceptable blow to his prestige and to the position of the Soviet Union in the world. Policy makers in Washington could not imagine that the Soviet Union would care so much about Cuba and would dare send missiles and troops across the Atlantic. In accordance with consistency and resistance bias, the American analysts believed that the Soviets would not set up a military base within such close range of the United States.

FEMINIST AND MARXIST PERSPECTIVES

To a conflict theorist, both Kennedy's and Khrushchev's decisions were essentially human—and, as feminists would add, also male. The leaders stepped back from the abyss but only after they had brought the world to the brink of a war. And what if Castro, instead of Khrushchev, had been the main decision maker on the Communist side? What if he had control over nuclear weapons? Castro was a recent convert to Marxism-Leninism, but he was arguably more revolutionary minded than Khrushchev—he was prepared to sacrifice Cuba on the altar of the world revolution. Postcolonial studies might describe him as reacting to the white male Western world. Fortunately, Khrushchev in this case proved more realist than revolutionary.

POLITICAL PSYCHOLOGY PERSPECTIVE

The rational model assumes that Khrushchev, like Kennedy, would have acted logically in weighing cost-benefit options. The Soviet leader might have wanted, for example, to improve the strategic position of the Soviet Union with respect to the United States. Yet this interpretation is incomplete. It fails to reflect Khrushchev's personal insecurities caused by his policy failures. He was unable to force Western powers out of West Berlin from 1958 to 1961. Chinese Communists criticized him for ideological mistakes, and his reform of the Soviet economy failed to produce the expected results. Khrushchev was

On October 16, 1962, President John F. Kennedy announced that the United States had established a "quarantine" of Cuba, after discovering Soviet missiles there. The president promised that his country would deliver "a full retaliatory response upon the Soviet Union" if the Soviets attacked the United States.

therefore desperate to gamble for success in Cuba. He considered himself a clever decision maker, and his prestige depended on the outcome of this missile venture (Blight et al. 1993; Taubman 2004).

New evidence from archives also reveals that Khrushchev relied on erroneous assumptions about the United States' decision-making. He evaluated Kennedy in a biased way, viewing the president from the vantage point of his own life, shaped in the trenches of World War II. For Khrushchev, Kennedy was a spoiled "rich kid" from New England, a toy in the hands of hard-liners, and a pushover when it came to international affairs.

Kennedy and his advisers likewise knew very little about the top leadership and decision-making in the Soviet Union. Washington received contradictory messages from Khrushchev: some of them quite belligerent and cocky, some more conciliatory. Kennedy was lucky to have an adviser, Llewellyn (Tommy) Thompson, who had just served as the U.S. ambassador in Moscow. Thompson met Khrushchev many times and interpreted his decisions not just in accord with the rational model but with knowledge of Khrushchev as a person. In the end, Thompson was convinced that Khrushchev was bluffing and recommended that Kennedy suggest a way for Khrushchev to save face—the secret trade of Soviet missiles in Cuba for U.S. missiles in Turkey. Thompson was right. As it turned out, Khrushchev never contemplated using the nuclear weapons and tried to reduce the chances of accidental miscalculation. He even ordered his commanders to keep the nuclear warheads in storage facilities.

POLITICAL SOCIALIZATION PERSPECTIVE

As veterans of World War II, Kennedy and Khrushchev shared a crucial formative experience. For all their differences as individuals, in the domestic pressures they faced, and in their ideologies and biases, the U.S. and Soviet leaders shared a common fear—the fear of unleashing a world war with nuclear weapons. This fear dominated the influence of analogies. Kennedy rejected the Munich analogy which would have suggested he appease the Soviets. The last thing Khrushchev wanted was to provoke the United States, as the Japanese did at Pearl Harbor in 1941, into a full-scale war. For Khrushchev, nuclear weapons in Cuba were just a means of deterring U.S. aggression against Cuba.

We cannot guarantee that a dangerous crisis of similar proportions will never occur again. Yet we can reduce the potentially deadly consequences of any international crisis if we learn lessons from history. The main lesson of the Cuban Missile Crisis is that rational decision-making is very difficult under extreme stress, with a fluid situation and time constraints. In such conditions, politicians may turn to their emotions and biases. Another lesson is the need to avoid a dangerous chain reaction of decisions that could drive opponents to make dangerous decisions.

Questions

Consider one of the following scenarios. If you were president, how would you deescalate and resolve the crisis?

1. China attempts to take Taiwan militarily.
2. Iran directly threatens Israel.
3. India and Pakistan, both nuclear powers, plunge into war over Kashmir.
4. Russia makes the decision to build a big military base in Central America.

Remember, in your decisions you should take into consideration the impact of misperceptions, brush off the arguments of your most hawkish advisers, and add your knowledge of history—all to find a solution short of war.

CONCLUSION

International relations are influenced by a great number of factors, and theories going beyond realism and liberalism can help explain them. Constructivism does not necessarily challenge mainstream theories of international relations. Rather, it provides valuable information about how and why states develop policies and interests. Conflict theories claim that state interests are defined by ruling elites trying to secure power. Identities, formed by history, religion, and culture, can affect the foreign policy of states in many ways. And political psychology provides important information about how personal experiences, group influence, and other individual factors affect global affairs.

Some formative factors, group interests, identities, and perceptions in international relations are more important than others, and some circumstances are simply insignificant: but which ones? Only the careful study of international relations can provide answers.

KEY TERMS

accessibility bias 133
analogy 136
bureaucratic bargaining 139
cognitive map 139
Communism 122
competitive
   authoritarianism 145
conflict theories   124
consistency bias 132
constructivist view
   (constructivism) 116
core 123

culture 126
dependency theory 123
feminism 124
fundamentalism 131
group pressure 133
identity 127
imperialism (Lenin's
   theory of) 122
Marxism 121
nationalism 130
Pearl Harbor syndrome 118
periphery 123

political culture 126
political psychology 132
political socialization 133
postcolonial studies 124
prospect theory 132
rational model 132
resistance bias 133
tribalism   130
two-level game   141
xenophobia 130

Visual Review ALTERNATIVE THEORIES

IDEAS

SHORTCOMINGS OF LIBERALISM AND REALISM
- How do international actors define their interests?
- Why do they choose one policy over another?

CHOOSING ALTERNATIVE VIEWS
- Constructivism emphasizes social norms and historic experiences of states
- Conflict theories pay attention to different forms of inequality and discrimination
- Identity theories turn to values and perceptions
- Political psychology focuses on inner mechanisms of political behavior

ARGUMENTS

SOCIAL CONSTRUCTION
- State interests are constructed through interpretation of facts
- States create their international environment
- Countries draw different lessons from history

INEQUALITY
- Marxism
- Dependency and world-systems theories
- Feminism
- Theories of prejudice

IDENTITY FACTORS
- Political culture and identity are shaped by collective experience, religion, ethnicity, and other group and individual experiences
- Nationalism, tribalism, xenophobia, and fundamentalism complicate global affairs

POLITICAL PSYCHOLOGY
- Policy decisions are not necessarily rational
- Individual and group actors affect foreign policy

CONTEXTS AND APPLICATIONS

THE INDIVIDUAL DECISIONS CONTEXT
- Leaders' choices can be rational or biased, affected by both immediate and life experiences

THE STATE POLICIES CONTEXT
- Domestic bureaucracy, political competition, democratic contexts, and access to information affect foreign-policy decisions

THE GLOBAL CONTEXT
- Global developments affect state interests and policies, which in turn affect the world

Critical Thinking

1. What are the key shortcomings of realism and liberalism in understanding international relations?
2. Using the ideas of constructivism and political psychology, identify at least three of the most dangerous political leaders in today's world.
3. Why are the lessons of history important for constructivists? Why do decision makers often overlook these lessons?
4. Why have dependency and Marxist theories regained popularity in recent years?
5. Discuss in class: Imagine that in three months, all governments in all countries will be headed by female leaders: presidents, prime ministers, and queens. How much would world politics change, and in what ways? Explain your argument.

5 International Security

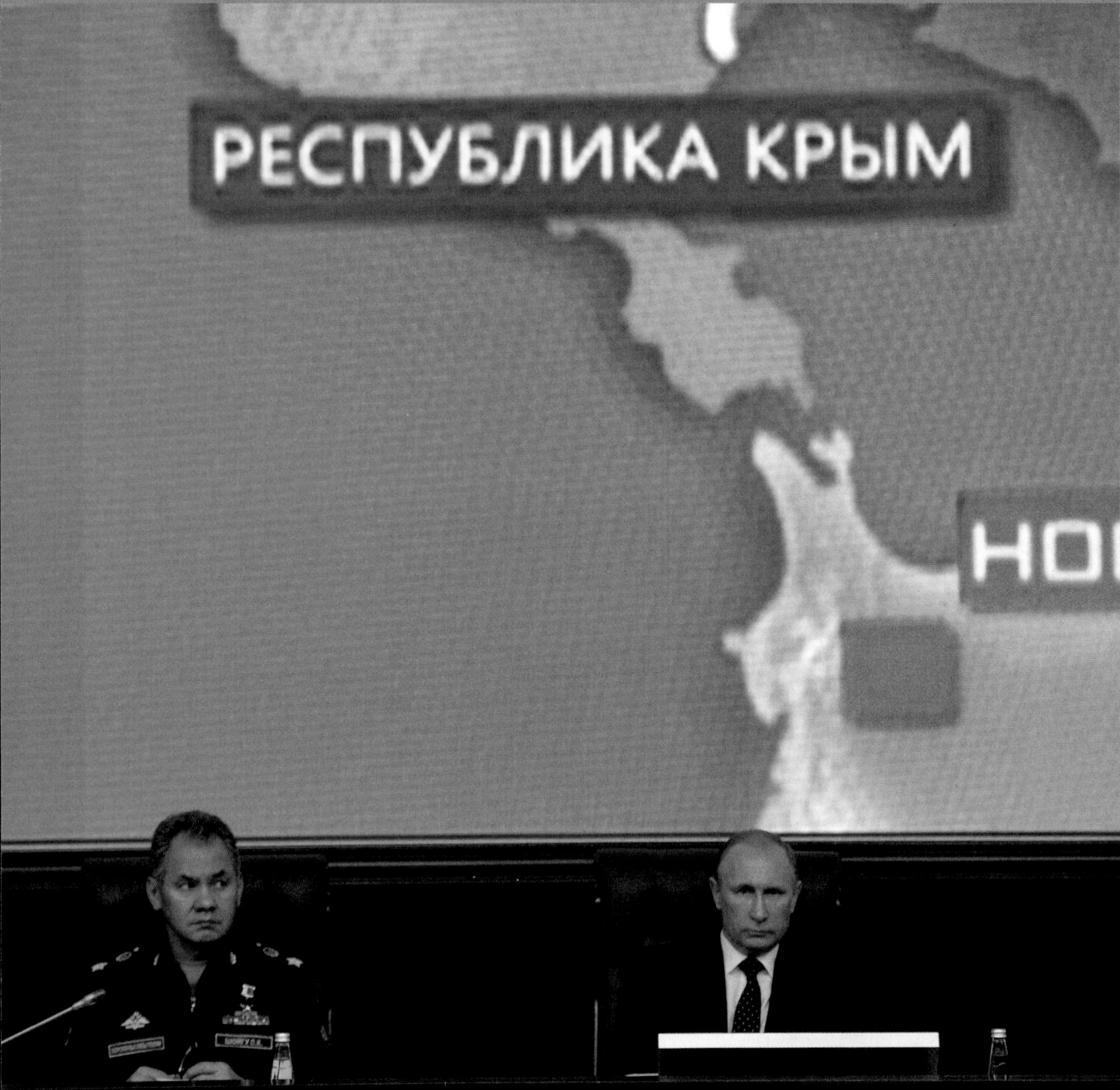

Eternal vigilance is the price of liberty.
—DEMOSTHENES (384–322 BC)

I N MARCH 2014, RUSSIAN PRESIDENT VLADIMIR PUTIN SIGNED A DECREE "TO ADMIT THE REPUBLIC OF CRIMEA" AND THE CITY OF SEVASTOPOL INTO THE RUSSIAN Federation. After the collapse of the Soviet Union in 1991, Crimea was part of Ukraine, a sovereign state. Putin argued that he acted in response to the will of people of Crimea, after they voted in a referendum. Putin also claimed that Russia protected the Russian-speaking population of Crimea against the Ukrainian nationalists who took power in Kiev following a violent coup.

Ukraine's political elites regarded this takeover as a blatant act of aggression and a violation of Ukraine's sovereignty. The United States, all members of the European Union, and the majority of UN members considered Russia's move an annexation and a gross violation of international norms. Danger of large-scale war in Eastern Europe became real. The Kremlin inspired and backed armed separatists in Donbass, an industrial region in southeast Ukraine with a mixed Russian-Ukrainian population. The Ukrainian government launched an "anti-terrorist operation" against the separatists. In response, the Russian military (without declaring war) engaged the Ukrainian forces in Donbass. The Ukrainian government asked Western countries to provide lethal weapons to stop Russian aggression.

This conflict created a profound sense of insecurity in Eastern Europe. NATO returned to action. The United States and

Left: Russian Defense Minister Sergei Shoigu (left) and President Vladimir Putin lead a meeting with top military brass in Moscow in 2014, with a map in the background showing Crimea. The United States, the European Union, and many other countries condemned Russia's takeover of Crimea, an event marking the end of a time of peace and stability in Europe.

the United Kingdom sent military equipment and troops to the Baltic countries and Poland to reassure them. In addition, the U.S. and the EU imposed economic and financial sanctions on Russia in an attempt to deter further aggression. Putin, however, viewed the conflict in Ukraine as a civil war, denied Russia's involvement in it, and promised a retaliatory response to the sanctions.

Did this conflict mark a new period of increased insecurity not only in Europe, but also globally? Liberals argue that Russia challenged the global order. What if other states begin annexing territories and supporting separatists overseas, claiming ethnic and religious "solidarity"? Realists suggest that Russia acted from a position of weakness and used force to reestablish its security interests in Eurasia. Most experts agree that 2014 marked the end of the post-Cold War period in Europe, when peace and stability were taken for granted. Journalists coined the phrase "a new Cold War."

It is clear that war and related fears of insecurity remain the foremost issues in international relations today. How do countries define and build their security strategies? Why do these strategies often lead to new threats and even wars? Is global security achievable, and by what means? In this chapter we will examine security challenges and policies in today's world.

Learning Objectives	▶ Describe the scope of national and international security.
	▶ Discuss security from realist, liberal, constructivist, and alternative perspectives.
	▶ Explain variation in security policies.
	▶ Apply major views of security to realities of international relations at each level of analysis.
	▶ Evaluate the effectiveness of particular security policies.

Ideas

Sovereign states act to protect their own sovereignty and territorial integrity from domestic and foreign threats. Some act alone, relying on their economic might and armed forces. But most seek help from foreign states and international organizations and prefer negotiations and compromise to avoid military conflict. Security policies of the twenty-first century are supported by gigantic bureaucratic and military machines, influenced by political parties and lobbying groups. To better understand the complexity of national and international security, we begin, as usual, by defining key terms.

Security

National security has traditionally been understood as the protection of sovereignty, territorial integrity, and interests. National security used to be treated as distinct from domestic security, which is commonly associated with fighting criminal activities and is handled by the police. Maintaining the state's armed forces, obtaining and modernizing weapons, keeping aircraft and battleships, training specialists, and developing mass-mobilization plans are essential for national security (Sarkesian et al. 2007). All of these aspects of security require a vast government infrastructure. Some countries also use their military to address domestic security concerns. In Turkey, for example, the army is frequently used to combat guerrillas fighting to create an independent Kurdistan. Russia used its military and massive internal security forces to defeat domestic separatist insurgencies in its southern provinces Chechnya and Ingushetia. These days, security increasingly involves the use of information in cyberspace. In response to WikiLeaks scandal, the United States' government created several centers to deal with cyber-intelligence and counterintelligence.

national security A state's need to protect its sovereignty, territorial integrity, and vital interests.

International security refers to mutual security issues involving more than one state. Security is *bilateral* when it involves two states and *multilateral* when it involves more than two states. NATO is the best known multilateral security organization, formed more than half a century ago. In Shanghai, China, in 1996, Kazakhstan, China, Kyrgyzstan, Russia, and Tajikistan signed the Treaty on Deepening Military Trust in Border Regions and later agreed to reduce their military forces in those areas. This security organization came to be called the Shanghai Cooperation Organization or *Shanghai Six* after Uzbekistan joined the treaty. Internationalization of security is natural in the era of globalization. Table 5-1 provides a sample of international security pacts.

international security Mutual security issues involving two or more states.

Threats to international security come from many directions and sources. Historically, they have primarily taken the form of direct intimidations and hostile actions of countries, leading to wars. Such wars still happen, even in Europe, as the Ukrainian-Russian conflict has demonstrated. Other threats to international security come from failing states and nonstate actors, such as the Taliban and ISIS which we discussed in the previous chapter. Failing states (often called fragile states) are those in which governments are incapable of exercising their major functions. Syria, Libya, Somalia, Chad, Sudan, Central African Republic, and several other countries may be considered failing. A **failing state** is marked by the inability to control territory and impose law and order. As a result, violence and lawlessness spread, terrorist groups operate freely, civil wars flare up, and the population suffers massively.

failing state A state in which the government is incapable of exercising its major functions, defending borders, or making key decisions.

TABLE 5-1 Examples of International Security Pacts

International Security Pact	Description and Major Goals
The Treaty of Friendship, Cooperation and Mutual Assistance (Warsaw Pact). Created in 1955.	Organized by the Soviet Union, this pact involved Communist states in Eastern Europe. Major goal: to keep Soviet military presence in Central Europe against NATO.
OAS: The Organization of American States. Formally created in the late 1940s.	Initiated by the United States, it includes the countries of North, Central, and South America. Major goals: security of the American continents, common action on the part of those states in the event of aggression.
ASEAN: The Association of Southeast Asian Nations. Created in 1967.	Includes countries located in Southeast Asia: Indonesia, Malaysia, the Philippines, Singapore, Thailand, Brunei, Myanmar, Cambodia, Laos, and Vietnam. Major goals: to contain Communism and have mutual protection.
CENTO: Central Treaty Organization. Created in 1955. Dissolved in 1979.	Included Iran, Iraq, Pakistan, Turkey, and the United Kingdom. Major goal: containment of the Soviet Union.
The Shanghai Cooperation Organization. Created in 1996.	Includes Kazakhstan, China, Kyrgyzstan, Russia, Tajikistan, and Uzbekistan. Major goals: keeping separatism in check, confronting terrorism, and balancing U.S. power in the region.

CHECK YOUR KNOWLEDGE

▶ The Fund for Peace regularly posts the Fragile State Index at www .fundforpeace.org/global. Which countries are in the "Very High Alert" category today? Ask your professor to discuss the situation in one of these countries in class. Also find on this site the countries that are "most improved."

▶ Explain bilateral and multilateral security.

Conflict and War

conflict An actual or perceived antagonism between states and international or nongovernment organizations.

Studying conflict is also essential for our understanding of national and international security. A **conflict** is any antagonism between states, IGOs, or NGOs over territory and resources, or because of differences in values and perceptions of security. Conflict typically reflects the inability of a state or an international organization to achieve its goals because of the resistance or unwillingness of other actors. Conflicts remain nonviolent if conflicting sides use no force to resolve them.

war An organized violent confrontation between states or other social and political entities, such as ethnic or religious groups.

Violent conflicts involve the use of force. Their ultimate form is **war**, an organized violent confrontation between states or other social and political entities, such as ethnic or religious groups. Victory in war is achieved by superior force and not by diplomatic negotiations or legal rulings. Only after hostilities end in an armistice do negotiations resume. If war ends in surrender, one side is forced to accept conditions imposed by the victors.

At the same time, wars do not exclude political bargaining. Prominent Prussian military thinker Karl von Clausewitz (1780–1831) wrote about war as "a continuation of policy by other means." He meant that states use wars as instruments in achieving their policy goals: to protect their strategic interests, and to reduce or eliminate domestic and international threats. During the Cold War and especially recently we have seen that the divide between war and nonviolent conflict became less evident: International actors began to practice new, hybrid forms of hostilities, often on a limited scale, to achieve their political goals.

A U.S. Marine (left) talks with South Korean Marines during U.S.–South Korea joint-landing military exercises, south of Seoul, South Korea, in 2015. South Korea historically relies on multilateral security and receives assistance from NATO and the United States. Which other countries in East Asia rely on Washington for security?

War, in other words, is a most extreme strategy in security policies. These security policies affect a broad range of international issues and, ultimately, the behavior of other states and international organizations. Security policies are born out of continuous debates among political elites, security officials, military experts, and the media. We shall start with the typology of wars as expressions of security policies.

Types of War

On September 1, 1939, German troops crossed the Polish border and advanced into the territory of a sovereign state. This is an example of an *offensive* war. For Poland, though, it was a *defensive* war. Labeling a war defensive or offensive is important for several reasons. One is international legitimacy, which affects other states' official reaction to the war. Defensive wars also evoke sympathy and support, whereas offensive actions typically lead to criticism, condemnation, or forceful resistance. It is common for countries to camouflage their offensive actions as defensive (Levy 1984). You can search for examples using the chapters you have read so far.

The intentions and policies leading to wars are complicated. Some states start **preventive wars** to protect themselves if they believe that other states might threaten them in the future. In 1914 Germany's elites acted on this logic to declare a war on Russia and France: They felt threatened by the Russian-French alliance and believed it was necessary to "knock out" Russia before it became stronger. There are also **preemptive wars**, which are launched to destroy the potential threat of an enemy when an attack by the adversary is believed to be imminent (Beres 2008). In 1967, Israel launched a surprise air attack against Egypt, Syria, and Jordan. The Israeli government was convinced that these Arab states were mobilizing to attack Israel. In 1999, NATO considered the bombing of Serbia preemptive operation to stop an imminent attack of the Serbian army against ethnic Albanians living in K-osovo. Some countries disagreed with Israel and NATO motives and explanations, and considered

preventive war
A war launched by a state to protect itself when it believes that other states might threaten it in the future.

preemptive war
A war launched to destroy the potential threat of an enemy when an attack by the adversary is believed to be imminent.

CASE IN POINT > *War in Angola*

An international conflict in Angola in 1975 started as a prolonged civil war among three rival political factions. Rapidly, the conflict began to attract the attention of other states out of concern for their security interests. The neighboring Zaire provided support for the FNLA (National Front for the Liberation of Angola), one of the feuding factions in Angola. Cuba supported the MPLA (Peoples' Movement for the Liberation of Angola), a left-wing group, with weapons, military advisers, and troops. South African troops entered Angola to fight against the Cubans and the MPLA from the south on behalf of the third faction, UNITA (National Union for the Total Independence of Angola). The Soviet Union began to provide financial and military support for Cuba's military actions. The United States also supported the FNLA, and then UNITA and South Africa. Thus, a conflict grew into a regional war.

It was also a **proxy war**, or armed conflict orchestrated by other, more distant countries using substitute forces to avoid a direct confrontation with each other. The Soviet Union and the United States were not directly involved in the hostilities in Angola, but they claimed that the war was important to their strategic security interests. For almost thirty years after foreign troops left Angola, other countries continued to fuel the civil war with illegal arms sales to the feuding sides. More than 500,000 people died in this conflict.

CRITICAL THINKING

❶ The war in Angola and other proxy wars are criticized for moral reasons. These criticisms are warranted. Discuss whether a proxy war may also be justified by a country's security interests. For many years the United States used the Colombian military to fight against the powerful local forces involved in drug trafficking. ❷ If you were president of the United States, under what specific circumstances would you approve a proxy war? ❸ Consider a case of a regional conflict (ask your professor to help choose) in which thousands of people are systematically slaughtered and the regional security is threatened. Would you approve of a proxy war to stop the unfolding war? Explain your reasoning.

those wars as acts of aggression. The subject of preventive and preemptive wars remains highly controversial, a subject to which we will return later.

In terms of their scope and consequences, wars can be *local*, *regional*, and *global*. Local wars typically involve two states, but a massive armed conflict within a country, such as a civil war, need not engage other neighboring states. Local conflicts, especially in today's world, are likely to draw in other countries in close geographic proximity. Take, for example, a conflict in Syria that began several years ago. Clear distinctions between a local and regional war would be difficult to draw.

Some local or regional conflicts grow into global wars, or *world wars*, with global consequences. World War I was triggered by the declaration of war on Serbia by the Empire of Austria-Hungary in 1914; in response, Russia declared mobilization, and Germany declared war on Russia and France. Germany's attack on Poland in 1939 made Britain and France—allied with Poland—to declare war against Germany. This launched the Second World War.

Wars, conflicts, and security threats in general, can be *symmetrical* or *asymmetrical*. A classic example of a symmetrical security conflict was the United States' long confrontation with the Soviet Union. In a symmetrical conflict, an attack by one state is likely to cause a comparable response from the other. During the last two centuries states prepared their armed forces to fight in symmetrical conflicts. An asymmetrical conflict does not involve regular armies but rather involves small groups of combatants who try to avoid open fighting (Fearon and Laitin 2003). **Guerrilla warfare** (often called irregular, unconventional warfare) uses irregular combat units who typically hide in difficult terrain (forest, mountains) and are usually not distinct from the civilian population (Boot 2009). Guerilla wars create significant security problems for states because they require special military strategies. The United States failed to win a guerilla war in Vietnam (1964–75), and the Soviet military had to withdraw from Afghanistan after a long war with local guerrillas (1979–88).

guerrilla warfare
Political violence by identifiable, irregular combat units, usually to seize state power, win autonomy, or found new states.

The Cold War can also be seen as a transition period from frequent and open hostilities to more complex, hybrid forms of war. In these newer forms, both sides cannot destroy each other but instead maintain mutual rivalry while engaging in diplomatic bargaining. The United States and the Soviet Union never broke diplomatic relations, signed many treaties, and even developed trade and economic relations with each other. At the same time, they were waging proxy wars against each other: in Korea, Vietnam, Ethiopia, Angola (see "Case in Point: War in Angola"), and other places.

After the Cold War ended, conflicts often included international terrorism. The impact of terrorism on international security and on international relations will be considered at length in Chapter 8.

 Learn more about Operation Desert Storm in video from the companion website. See how the world responded to a predatory war waged by the Iraqi government in 1990.

In the past, states commonly pursued territorial conquests and engaged in *predatory wars* for treasures, raw materials, trade routes, territories, and human beings as a workforce. Colonial expansion in the nineteenth and twentieth centuries—conducted by European powers such as France, Great Britain, Belgium, Italy, and Russia in Africa and Eurasia—is an example. Iraq occupied Kuwait in 1990 to gain possession of its vast oil resources and infrastructure. Other wars, called *retaliatory wars*, are waged by a state to weaken or punish another. China attacked Vietnam in 1979 to punish Hanoi for the occupation of Cambodia and removal of the Communist regime there. There are also *ethnic* and *religious wars* caused by conflicts between various groups struggling for their beliefs, rights, territories, and independence (Soeters 2005).

Our brief classification of wars need not be complete. Many types overlap, and you can add your own. For example, a war can be offensive, local, and preventive at the same time. Why are these definitions of war and conflict important? We will see in this and other chapters (in Chapter 6 in particular) that countries initiate their policies and wage war based on how they see and

The difference between offensive and retaliatory, preventive and preemptive wars is often unclear. Members of a U.S. Air Force munitions team assemble guided bombs in 2015 to support air war against the ISIS guerrillas who have taken over nearly a third of Iraq and Syria. The United States and eleven other nations formed a coalition carrying out bombing raids.

interpret international conflicts. These definitions allow governments to justify their actions.

Under most circumstances, states try to avoid war. Wars are risky and deadly, and they can lead to significant losses, defeat, and even destruction of a state. With this in mind, states usually design security policies that can help them achieve their goals short of war. We look next at these types of policies.

Security Policies

In Europe in the nineteenth and early twentieth centuries, many international actors tried to combine rationality and morality to develop an international system of rules and regulations for warfare and to ban the use of certain arms (we will turn to the concept of "just war" in Chapter 6). During World War I (1914–18) and World War II (1939–1945), however, states turned to the "total war" strategy to achieve unconditional defeat of the enemy. The concept of "total war" is generally rejected today. Moreover, states, IGOs, and NGOs develop policies to limit weapons of mass destruction (WMD)—nuclear, chemical, and biological. In 1968 the leading nuclear powers signed the Non-Proliferation Treaty (NPT) with the goal to stop the dissemination of nuclear weapons. In 1975, the Biological Weapons Convention banned development and possession of these weapons of mass destruction. A similar convention for chemical weapons entered in force in 1997. During the last decades, however, *conventional weapons* and computer technologies have been drastically upgraded so that they, too, can bring destruction on a large scale.

Countries' failure to choose the right strategy may have serious consequences. The United States during the Cold War often responded asymmetrically to the Soviet security threat; that is, it tried to achieve the position of absolute superiority using its wealth and economic growth. The Soviet Union, although its economy was much smaller, attempted to respond symmetrically, to achieve power parity with Washington in terms of the number of nuclear weapons (Gaddis 2006; Zubok 2007). This strategy weakened and undermined the Soviet economy. The variety of state responses to foreign threats only begins with symmetry–asymmetry. (See Table 5-2.)

Security policies can also be based on unilateralism and multilateralism. In **unilateral** policy, a state relies primarily on its own resources (Kane 2006).

unilateralism
Reliance on a state's own resources rather than support from others; acting alone in foreign policy.

TABLE 5-2 Types of War and Strategies

Intentions and Policies	Offensive, Defensive, Preventive, Preemptive, Symmetrical, Asymmetrical, Mixed
Purposes	Predatory, Retaliatory, Political, Mixed
Strategies	Conventional, Nonconventional, with Weapons of Mass Destruction; Symmetrical and Asymmetrical; Mixed
Scope and Consequences	Local, Regional, Global, Mixed

In contrast, states adopting a **multilateral** policy coordinate their efforts with other states or international organizations. Sometimes security policy can be a combination of both: In 2003 the United States unilaterally decided to start a war against Iraq and acted against the resolution of the United Nations. However, American diplomacy hastened to create "the coalition of the willing," involving several states who backed American actions and even sent their troops to Iraq.

Isolationism is a policy of noninvolvement in international alliances. It does not mean that an isolationist country always stays away from international conflicts; rather, it means that this country chooses to act as it wishes. Isolationism largely governed U.S. policy until World War I and remains a strong current in public opinion today: More than 50 percent of Americans say that their country should "mind its own business" internationally (Pew 2014a). Similarly, some states choose nonalliance with any military bloc or coalition. (See Figure 5-1.)

Interventionism is a policy of interference in other states' affairs and conflicts without regard for their consent. During the eighteenth and nineteenth centuries, European great powers including Britain, France, Russia, and then Germany intervened around the world, expanding their colonial empires. From 1898 until 1917, the United States, although "isolationist" toward Europe, intervened unilaterally in Central America (O'Brien and Clesse 2002). After 1895, Japan became the first modern Asian power to act in the same interventionist way in China and the Pacific. Japan's interventionism was a cause of its war with the United States.

Other states prefer a consistent policy of **cooperation** (Newman et al. 2006). In the 1950s the small democratic state of Finland chose to cooperate with its neighbor the Soviet Union. From Finland's viewpoint, it was a reasonable bargain, while the Soviet Union saw it as a way to declare its peaceful intentions toward other European states.

Most security policies involve a complex combination of foreign, defense, and domestic policies. In most countries, the head of state (president or prime minister) directs security policies with the help of a complex bureaucracy.

multilateralism
Coordination of foreign policy with allies; participation in international coalitions, blocs, and international organizations.

isolationism
A policy of non-involvement in international conflicts.

interventionism
A policy of interference in other states' affairs or international conflicts without regard for their consent.

cooperation
A foreign policy that addresses other states' concerns for their security.

 On the companion website, learn more about the types of security clearance and who can apply for it in the United States.

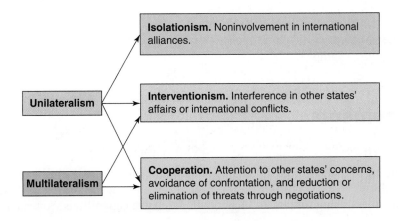

FIGURE 5-1 Basic security policies. *Sources: Wittkopf 1990; Sobel 2001; Hinckley 1992.*

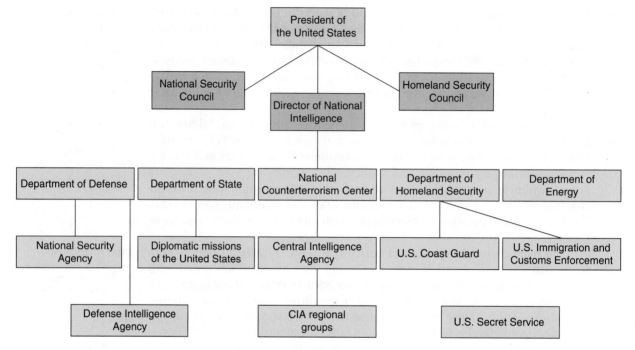

FIGURE 5-2 Major U.S. actors and agencies involved in national security.

In Washington, the National Security Council (NSC) is part of the Executive Office of the President of the United States. The presidents also directs the activities of other government departments, organizations, and agencies dealing with national security. (See Figure 5-2.)

CHECK YOUR KNOWLEDGE

▶ Explain the differences and similarities between predatory and retaliatory wars.
▶ Explain proxy war. Give an example.
▶ Can a country's isolationist policy be interventionist at the same time? Suggest examples.

Arguments

Realism

According to realism, security is the main and exclusive responsibility of states. They always try to maximize their power and tend to act according to their interests in assessing threats and their own defensive capabilities. States tend to observe international treaties only as long as these treaties do not conflict with state security and interests. When the international situation changes, states may abrogate their international commitments in the name of security. The core element of every state's security, according to realism, is power and the ability to use it.

REALIST PRINCIPLES OF SECURITY

Geography is frequently the subject of security concerns and policies. Oceans, rivers, and mountains can act as natural security barriers. For many years Japan, the United Kingdom, and the United States thought of the seas as protection from foreign intrusions, whereas Belgium, Poland, China, and Russia were more vulnerable. States are frequently involved in conflicts over international trade routes—such as the Strait of Gibraltar between Europe and Africa, the Suez Canal in Egypt between Africa and Asia, and the Dardanelles in Turkey between Europe and Asia.

Security, according to realism, also depends on the quantity and quality of the armed forces and their mobility. The centerpiece of British security policy from the seventeenth through the twentieth century was the Royal Navy. The acquisition of nuclear weapons in 1945 gave the United States absolute military superiority—until the Soviet Union tested its atomic weapon in 1949. Countries that pursue nuclear weapons today, including North Korea and Iran, think of them as a security guarantee. The concept of *revolution in military affairs* became a prevalent outlook on the future of war. It is based on debates about the vital necessity of using modern technology in warfare and security (Adamsky 2010; Table 5-3).

Smaller states have less room for diplomacy acting alone when they lack economic and military clout (Waltz 2001). They often try to receive security guarantees from more powerful states and organizations. Poland, Hungary, and the Czech Republic joined NATO in 1999 for a host of reasons—but above

TABLE 5-3 Examples of Realist Arguments Related to Security

Elements of Power	Example
Quantity of weaponry and military forces: numbers matter	The central goal of British security policy from the seventeenth through the twentieth century was ensuring that the Royal Navy was larger and more advanced than the largest navies of the other great powers.
Quality of weaponry: ability to destroy matters	Development of fast-moving motorized military units and new military tactics helped Nazi Germany achieve quick victories the first three years of World War II. Computer and other technologies give superiority to the United States today compared to other countries.
Presence of armed forces abroad	During the Cold War the Soviet Union and the United States kept their armies in Central Europe. The United States continues to keep its armed forces in military bases around the world.

all fear of Russia (Goldgeier 1999). In the twenty-first century, Vietnam and the Philippines rely increasingly on the United States to secure their interests in the South China Sea. The United States and its European allies consider Saudi Arabia a stabilizing factor in an extremely unstable region and assist it militarily (Friedrich 2011).

International security is a dynamic process. When individual states use force or act against existing treaties and international organizations, this affects the stability of the entire international system. The war in Iraq and the use of force in Libya destabilized the Middle East and North Africa. If North Korea and Iran develop nuclear weapons, this will destabilize regional balance of power. What about Russia's actions in Crimea in 2014? Political scientist John Mearsheimer argued that Russia's takeover of Crimea was not necessarily an act of aggression. Rather, it was a reaction to NATO's attempts at expansion to the East and to remove Ukraine from Russia's influence. Russia, he argued, was forced to build up its own security (Mearsheimer 2014). Critics argue that Russia's actions in Crimea and the resulting war in Donbass added to regional destabilization and insecurity, where both Ukraine and Russia would lose more than they gained.

THE SECURITY DILEMMA

security dilemma
A situation in which one state's efforts to improve its security cause insecurity in others.

The situation in which one country's efforts to improve its security causes insecurity in others is known as the **security dilemma**. One state, for example, may decide to improve its security by strengthening its defensive capabilities. But this makes a neighboring state see its security as diminished, and it may retaliate in kind.

The security dilemma helps in understanding why a disruption of the power balance or a change in the structure of the international system increases international tensions (Booth and Wheeler 2007). During the Cold War, for example, the United States built up its naval and air bases nearest the Soviet Union to contain the spread of Communism to Europe and Asia. The Soviet Union maintained a huge army in Central Europe ready to invade Western Europe in the event of an attack. Western countries, scared by the Soviet buildup, asked the United States to deploy nuclear missiles on their territory. The international system was bipolar at that time, which made this arms race very difficult to stop.

nuclear deterrence
Maintaining nuclear weapons with the intention not to use them but to deter others from nuclear attack.

NUCLEAR DETERRENCE

The security dilemma helps explain the policy of **nuclear deterrence**— maintaining nuclear weapons with the intention not to use them but to deter others from nuclear attack. In the 1960s, top politicians in the United States began to realize that attempts to achieve superiority in nuclear weapons did not guarantee security and could cause a global calamity. The United States therefore adopted a security strategy of **mutual assured destruction (MAD)**: If both countries had enough nuclear weapons to destroy the other even *after* a surprise nuclear attack, this would serve as deterrence. Some critics of this approach urged instead an unlimited arms race, including the construction of an antimissile defense. Other critics believed that nuclear weapons should be abolished altogether.

mutual assured destruction
(MAD) The U.S. doctrine that if two nuclear states have the capacity to destroy each other, they will not use nuclear weapons.

Robert McNamara remained defense secretary during the Kennedy and Johnson administrations and masterminded American military escalation in Vietnam. He believed that a "loss" of South Vietnam to the Communists would cripple American credibility and security globally.

MAD could not stop the arms race, and so Washington and Moscow began to negotiate rules for arms control. New nuclear weaponry and the bipolar structure of international relations quickly revived the security dilemma until 1987, when Mikhail Gorbachev and Ronald Reagan put a halt to the vicious circle (Leffler 2007).

@ Learn more about MAD (mutual assured destruction) on the companion website.

THE DOMINO THEORY

One practical application of realist principles to security was the **domino theory**. In this theory, the international system resembles a row of dominos standing on end. If a single domino falls, so will the rest. In the 1950s, President Dwight Eisenhower argued that Communist takeover in even a small country could initiate the "domino effect" and would be a major threat to international security (Boot 2007).

One of the most compelling reasons for U.S. involvement in the Vietnam War in the 1960s was fear of a domino-like fall of anti-Communist governments throughout Southeast Asia and beyond if the United States kept out of Vietnam (McNamara 1996). These fears were reasonable yet exaggerated: The domino effect did not correctly predict a massive Communist takeover in Asian countries.

domino theory
An American view during the Cold War that a seizure of power by Communists in one country will produce a chain reaction of Communist takeovers in other countries allied with the West.

SECURITY REGIMES

One way to avoid the domino effect is through multilateralism. In a **security regime**, powerful countries provide protection to other states in exchange for their cooperation (Jervis 1982). NATO emerged in 1949 as a security regime in

security regime
A region in which a powerful country provides protection to other states in exchange for their cooperation.

which the United States provided a nuclear "umbrella" protecting Western Europe from the Soviet Union. Less formally, the United States in the past decades became the security regime guarantor for Saudi Arabia, Kuwait, and the United Arab Emirates (the wealthiest Arab states), against Iraq, and later against Iran (Fouskas 2003) and the threats from the insurgents of the Islamic State (ISIS).

CHECK YOUR KNOWLEDGE

▶ Explain the security dilemma. Give an example.
▶ Apply the domino theory to explain each of the following:
    (a) the U.S. intervention in Iraq in 2003
    (b) the U.S. and its allies' military actions in Syria in 2014–15
    (c) Western sanctions against Russia for its actions in Ukraine in 2014–15

Liberalism

Supporters of international liberalism recognize the primary role of states in security policies but also point to the increasing role of international organizations and nonstate actors. They believe that the power of states and security regimes is no longer the only key to peace in today's world.

LIBERAL PRINCIPLES OF SECURITY

In the liberal view, neither economic nor military power alone can bring lasting security, and military threats are seldom the best choice of action. Instead, the necessity and the desire for mutually acceptable outcomes and the complexity of international problems give countries the incentive to cooperate (Bull 1977; 1988; Ikenberry 2011a).

Realists, as you should recall, assume that states have few choices; they either increase their power or align with some states against the others (Herrmann and Lebow 2004). Supporters of the liberal view maintain that states have other options, such as negotiated settlements to avoid war and the creation of new institutions and norms of international cooperation. When war happens, liberals argue, it is because the sides in the bargaining process face too much uncertainty, cannot avoid a temptation to use force against each other, and cannot agree on how to divide the contested resources (Fearon 1995).

According to the liberal view, security policies in democratic societies should be part of the democratic process: They should be transparent and accountable whenever possible. The decision-making process should be more open to discussion. Not only a small group of security professionals, but also representative institutions, the media, and nongovernment organizations should influence strategic security decisions affecting the lives of millions (Stoddard 2006).

liberal interventionism
An approach to international relations that accepts violence only if all diplomatic and nonviolent means are exhausted.

Liberals are not totally rejecting war. They tend to approve of use of force for liberal goals. **Liberal interventionism** means that a coalition of states and IGOs can act preventively against a predator state when international security is at stake. In principle, liberals believe that military force should be used only when diplomatic and nonviolent means are exhausted. But liberals do not always limit themselves by this belief. In recent years a new doctrine is gaining strength based on the "responsibility to protect" principle, which means that states should bear responsibility to intervene into affairs of sovereign states if their governments cause mass suffering of people. We will return to liberal interventionism and "responsibility to protect" in Chapter 10.

IGOs AND THE SECURITY COMMUNITY

The interdependence of economic, political, and environmental issues today, as liberals argue, makes a traditional balance of power, maintained by sovereign states, obsolete or out of fashion. In 1918 and 1919, U.S. president Woodrow Wilson's Fourteen Points already called for **collective security**, an arrangement in which security of one country becomes the concern of all who provide a collective response to threats. Collective security was supposed to replace a shaky balance of power in Europe (Adler and Barnett 1998). But how to make this collective security work? Historic record is mixed at best.

collective security
An arrangement in which the security of one country becomes the concern of others as well.

International organizations, such as the United Nations or international communities such as European Union are not designed to develop detailed security policies. And they are poorly designed to prevent military conflicts. The United Nations consists of 193 member states and all of them join, on a rotating principle, the UN Security Council. In reality, the five permanent members of the Security Council have the power to support or block any policy initiated by other UN members. The UN Secretary General is only a mediator among member-states: His authority and resources come from the most powerful members such as the United States. The European Union, a seemingly powerful IGO, has a vast bureaucratic structure with a substantial budget, but it does not have authority to develop a joint collective security and military policies including collective diplomacy. Perhaps the E.U. failed to think strategically about its relationship with Ukraine and Russia, and inadvertently made the Ukrainians choose between Europe and Russia—the choice that provoked the disastrous confrontation with Russia in 2014. Liberal scholars admit these limitations of IGOs and international community yet they insist that benefits overshadow the difficulties. The United Nations and the European Union generate greater legitimacy for their decisions because they are collective (Tavares 2009). We will return to this topic in Chapter 6.

An alternative to the security regime, endorsed by realists, is the **security community**—based not on force, fear, and secret agreements, but on mutual interests, voluntary cooperation, and open discussion. The idea of a security community rests in part on the sharing of rational and moral anticipations and dispositions of self-restraint in using force (Adler 2008; Deutsch et al. 1957). Security communities emerged relatively recently as governments, political leaders, and other influential groups agreed on joint action and nonviolent conduct to maintain security and avoid war. Western Europe is good example of a security community, as are the United States, Canada, and Mexico.

security community
A group of countries united by mutual security interests, arrangements, and common liberal values.

Constructivism

In the constructivist view, as you should remember, countries act according to historical experience, identities, perceptions, and social norms. Canada, for example, has no concerns about U.S. military superiority because the two countries remain at peace and have not intervened into each other's affairs for at least a century. In contrast, countries such as Latvia, Estonia, and Lithuania harbor security fears toward Russia because the Soviet Union annexed and incorporated them by force from 1940 until 1991.

PERCEPTIONS, IDENTITIES, AND BELIEFS

security policy
Principles of international behavior to advance a state's fundamental interests and ensure national security.

A **security policy** is inseparable from perceptions (or misperceptions) of other states, such as their *propensity to use force*. Countries may see each other as a friend, a distant partner, an isolationist, an outcast, or an enemy. For example, North Korea's development of nuclear weapons alarms South Korea and Japan because it has acted belligerently in the past.

An even more important factor in security policies is a state's international *identity*—the perceived role it plays in a regional or global community. The Soviet Union's identity was linked to international Communism and the defeat of capitalism, and for this reason Soviet security strategies remained unilateralist and interventionist on the global scale. The United States views itself as a beacon of freedom and democracy: This caused it sometimes to intervene unilaterally, but more fundamentally to build cooperation with other democratic states and allies. Security identities can be shaped by painful memories: Afghanistan's identity is linked to the constant attempts of foreign powers to control its territory. Yet security identities change; Japan changed its identity after 1945 from imperialist and aggressive to peacefully democratic and cooperative.

If countries learn to overcome the record of mutual resentment, they eliminate a source of the security dilemma. After World War II, France and Germany, two countries with a long history of mutual violence and mistrust, began to

Iranian students climb over the wall of the U.S. embassy in Tehran during the Iranian Revolution, November 4, 1979. The students went on to hold fifty-two of the embassy staff as hostages for 444 days. The U.S.–Iranian conflict affected American security policies in the Middle East and Central Asia for many years.

engage in economic and political integration that led to a united European market (see Chapter 3). Neither country now regards the other as a threat. Different developments occurred between India and Pakistan after their creation in 1947. For decades, each country saw the other as hostile, and their security policies reflected these attitudes. Most recently, Russia has developed a deep mistrust toward not only the United States, but also the European Union. As a result, in 2014 and later, the Russian elites and the majority of Russians viewed Western support of Ukraine as a hostile policy aimed against Russia's security interests (Mearsheimer 2014; Levada 2015).

A crucial feature of a country's security policies is its definition of security. Some countries may define their security only in military terms, while others include economic and environmental security as well (Buzan and Hansen 2009). We will discuss environmental security in Chapter 9.

MILITARISM AND PACIFISM

Militarism is an attitude of international security that glorifies war, conquest, domination, and weapons—puts a premium on the use of military force in response to most foreign threats. **Pacifism**, in contrast, is a principled opposition to war and the belief that international disputes should be settled by nonviolent means. This social attitude glorifies restraint, mutual concessions, respect, and peace (Zinn 2002). Militarism and pacifism reflect the never-ending argument between *hawks*, who support tough measures, and *doves*, who reject violence in foreign policy.

militarism
A tendency to rely on military force in response to foreign threats.

pacifism A principled opposition to war, and the belief that international disputes should be settled by arbitration and other nonviolent means.

Public attitudes shift constantly between militarism and pacifism. International events contribute to such shifts (Hanson 2001). As the result of the heavy U.S. casualties during the war in Vietnam, domestic political dissent and protests grew in the United States in the late 1960s and early 1970s. The term **Vietnam syndrome** stands for general unwillingness to engage in foreign conflicts because of the perceived negative impact of the previous war. This syndrome influenced the dovish attitudes of many decision makers for years. Today, the elites of most democratic countries include both hawks and doves. For example, in Israel the generally hawkish politicians of the Likud party must contend with the more dovish Labor party leaders. These attitudes evolve and may change with new threats on the horizon.

Conflict Theories

States maintain international security to protect key interests of the dominant social groups. Marxism, feminism, and other conflict theories have long criticized international security policies, claiming that they are state-centric, dominated by special interests, and gender-biased.

MARXISM

In the Marxist view, security policies reflect the interests of the ruling economic and political elites. To protect their wealth and power, these elites wage war, create international organizations, sign international treaties, and pursue their own interventionist or isolationist strategies. Marxists compare international security to an old colonial system of domination.

In the Soviet Union, Marxist-Leninist ideology reinforced Soviet imperialist policies (Shlapentokh et al. 2008). Soviet ruling groups felt insecure as long as the country was surrounded by non-Communist states. After winning World War II, the Soviet Union expanded its ideological vision of security by creating a security belt of Communist regimes; and after the 1950s, it began to help radical anti-Western regimes around the world (Zubok 2007). It also imposed tight security controls within its borders: The Soviet population was not supposed to know that living standards in Western countries were much higher.

Contemporary Marxist views on security go beyond the security policies of Communist states of yesterday and today. Today's Marxists claim that international politics reflects above all the interests of wealthy, well-organized groups. These interests are supported by the corporate media and global financial institutions; they are embedded in countries' educational systems.

Marxists often avoid the state-centered analysis of security and shift the discussion toward global aspects of security. Marxists challenge neoliberalism and the entire capitalist world order for generating an increasing economic disparity and insecurity of the vast majority of people. Unemployment, consistent financial troubles, and the erosion of the middle class are viewed as the most significant security problems of today (Davis 2011).

FEMINISM

Traditionally, feminism argued that in negotiation, diplomacy, or decision-making, women could add an important element of trust in international relations, something that men failed to achieve. The key problem was that few women were allowed to help shape military and security policy (True 2009). The past two decades have brought significant changes in the way some countries expanded the role of women in national security areas. At the same time, feminist views of security cannot be reduced to the issue of how many women serve in government offices. Rather, many feminists also seek to reframe the way we all understand security, not unlike Marxism.

Feminist challenges to traditional views, norms, and values of security emerged in the 1960s on the campuses of North American and West European universities. For more than half a century already, feminists criti-

German Defense Minister Ursula von der Leyen greets German helicopter pilots in Mazar-i-Sharif, Afghanistan, in 2014. Historically, very few women have served as defense ministers, even in advanced democracies.

cize the government monopoly on security issues. They were particularly wary of realism because it defined national and international security in terms of state sovereignty and domination—two key values associated with masculinity. During the 1980s and later, feminists argued that the male-dominated narrative of force and war should be replaced with other narratives including individual safety, interdependence, agreement, and shared power (Reardon 1985; Enloe 2000 and 2007; Wibben 2011). Feminists call to reconsider and reject the whole concept of war as a "natural" way by which sovereign states protect themselves from threats. Security specialists must consider the value of the Golden Rule: Do to others what you would have them do to you. Security policies also need to be "gender mainstreamed": More women must be involved in institutional policies, and masculine views of conflict and war must be questioned and rejected (Stiehm 2009).

When the Cold War ended, feminists shifted the discussion from *national* security to *global* security, focusing on the problems of violence, gender and racial discrimination, and environmental degradation. Feminists also argued that the understanding of security as the absence of war is incomplete. There should be *positive peace*—with guarantees of basic social and economic rights to all (Hirschman 2010; Tickner 1992).

No discussion of security today can be complete without "gendering," or analyzing from the feminist perspective, every major element of traditional approaches and issues (Sjoberg 2009).

▶ Describe the differences between security regimes and security communities. Provide an example.
▶ Explain liberal interventionism.
▶ Explain "Vietnam Syndrome." Does something opposite to this syndrome exist in politics?
▶ What is the propensity to use force?

CHECK YOUR KNOWLEDGE

Contexts and Applications

The U.S. Constitution gives the president authority in the areas of national security and international relations. Yet evaluating security risks and seeking adequate responses must take place at several levels, only beginning with individual leaders. These different contexts help in understanding the complexity of defining and building international security.

The Individual Decisions Context

During the Cold War, the U.S. president accumulated extraordinary power to decide on the issues of national security. The U.S. Congress even granted the White House discretion to start wars, for instance in Vietnam, without congressional authorization. As a result, almost every U.S. president since 1945 has significantly altered national security strategy (Gaddis 1982). The trend continued after the end of the Cold War, when President Clinton conducted a major reevaluation of global threats. Whereas President George W. Bush brought his own vision of security threats, focusing on international terrorism and the rogue regimes of Iraq and Afghanistan, President Barack Obama moved to more traditional realist strategies. In other countries with strong executive power, such as France and Russia, new leaders introduce new security agendas. In Russia, for instance, former president Boris Yeltsin (1991–1999) pursued a strategy of security cooperation with the United States and NATO. After the enlargement of NATO in the 1990s and later, and after the events in Ukraine, president Putin began to view policies of Washington and NATO as a security threat.

LEADERS AND ADVISERS

Waging a war is often the individual choice of a political leader and close associates, but only within limits. In democracies, there are constitutional limits on power. Political opposition, public opinion, and the media limit the choices too. In non-democracies, leaders' choices to wage war seem unrestrained. Yet their lives and safety are often under threat if they leave office (Goemans et al. 2009). They may therefore choose war simply to secure political power. Statistical analysis suggests that non-democratic leaders indeed have a higher propensity to wage war because of political insecurity (Debs and Goemans 2010). (See Table 5-4.)

Moreover, decision makers seldom act alone on security issues. They depend on analysts and advisers who may have their own theories about how the country should evaluate and respond to security threats. The policy of containment, formulated by George Kennan in 1946–47 (see Chapter 2), was especially influential. Kennan, a State Department official, believed that Communism would eventually collapse under the weight of its contradictions. In contrast, Paul Nitze, another U.S. security official, believed that the United States needed significant peacetime rearmament to fight the Soviet threat (Thompson 2009). The competition between these two views lasted for many years.

TABLE 5-4 Views of National Security: Selected U.S. Presidents and Soviet/Russian Leaders, 1945–2016

U.S. President	Views of National Security	Soviet/Russian Leader	Views of National Security
Harry Truman 1945–53	Containment of Communism requires economic and military aid to governments that can be victims of Soviet expansion	Josef Stalin 1945–53	Soviet security dictates creation of a "security belt" consisting of the countries where Communist regimes are imposed
Richard Nixon 1969–74	Complex agreements with the Soviet Union and China, delegation of responsibilities to regional allies	Leonid Brezhnev 1964–82	Military build-up, accompanied by arms control agreements and the creation of the European security system, combining NATO and the Soviet Union
Ronald Reagan 1981–89	Military build-up to apply pressure on the Soviet Union; support of anti-Communist forces in the Third World; pursuit of nuclear disarmament	Mikhail Gorbachev 1985–91	Rejection of Stalin's and Brezhnev's policies, adoption of a defensive military doctrine; the Soviet Union should join the "common European home" of economic and political cooperation; pursuit of nuclear disarmament
Bill Clinton 1993–2001	Enlargement of NATO; peace-keeping missions abroad, but without casualties	Boris Yeltsin 1991–99	Alliance with Western democracies, integration of Russia into the international system as a great power
George W. Bush 2001–09	Unilateralist preemptive wars against "global terror"; further enlargement of NATO and promotion of democratic transitions	Vladimir Putin 2000–08	Defense of territorial integrity; main security threat is the expansion of NATO and domestic terrorism
Barack Obama 2009–17	The United States must act in accordance with international law and in close cooperation with other states	Dmitry Medvedev 2008–12; Vladimir Putin 2012–	Protecting authoritarian rule at home and around the world. Confronting the West in a wide range of international issues.

PEACE PSYCHOLOGY

To some political psychologists international security is achievable primarily through education and good will. They develop **peace psychology**, which tries to understand the ideological and psychological causes of war and find practical applications of their findings (MacNair 2003). Their goal is to

peace psychology
The study of the ideological and psychological causes of war, in order to develop educational programs to reduce the threat.

CASE IN POINT > *Are Veterans More Likely Than Non-Veterans to Support the Use of Force?*

A detailed study of the U.S. foreign policy elite in the nineteenth and twentieth centuries found that politicians with a military background were less likely to support the use of force than non-veteran leaders (Gelpi and Feaver 2002). In fact, the more military experience policy makers possessed, and the greater the percentage of veterans serving in government, the less likely a military response. Once a military response was underway, however, veterans were more supportive of greater use of force for a longer period. In contrast, non-veterans tended to become less supportive of the use of force as a conflict continued.

CRITICAL THINKING

Why do you think veterans are less inclined toward the use of force? And why do you think veterans are more supportive of wars once a military response is under way? Ask those who have served in the military (and especially those who served in Iraq or Afghanistan) to share their views.

Sources: Dubnik 2010; Gelpi et al. 2002.

Paper lanterns float along the Motoyasu River in front of the Atomic Bomb Dome in Hiroshima, Japan, in 2014.

develop educational programs to reduce the threat of violence. Certainly, more often than not, political leaders read intelligence reports through the prism of preconceived beliefs. Yet leaders and ordinary people, they believe, can look beyond old images of "the enemy" and find possibilities for dialogue. Peace psychology made important contributions to U.S.–Soviet relations during the Cold War and the relaxation of international tensions in the 1980s (Greening 1986). They organized face-to-face meetings between officials, students, teachers, and other professionals in the United States and the Soviet Union to promote trust. At the end of this chapter, we will see how both institutional and psychological factors brought about the end of the Cold War.

Should women in high offices be psychologically prone to peaceful conflict resolution? As we noted in Chapter 4, with so few women in charge of foreign policy, it is difficult to know how much women in high offices would make a difference. But in the past Golda Meir in Israel, Indira Gandhi in India, and Margaret Thatcher in the UK were more prone to use force than some of the male politicians that surrounded them. In the United States, Madeleine Albright, Condoleezza Rice, and Hillary Clinton acted very tough as secretary of states.

CHECK YOUR KNOWLEDGE

▶ What does peace psychology study?
▶ Explain graduated reciprocation in tension-reduction.

DEBATE > GRIT AND THE SPIRAL OF INSECURITY

During the Cold War, advocates of nuclear disarmament argued for an exit from the cycle of mutual insecurity. Frustrated by the superpowers' inability to guarantee international security, they believed that real policy change could begin with small, incremental steps. Such goodwill gestures would include student exchanges, trade deals, and joint projects and interviews. An American psychologist, Charles Osgood, developed the **graduated reciprocation in tension-reduction** (GRIT) model in the 1960s, and Soviet leader Mikhail Gorbachev relied on it during 1987 to 1989 when he transformed the security doctrine of the Soviet Union. The result was the end of the Cold War.

WHAT'S YOUR VIEW?

❶ If GRIT was so successful in some cases, why don't political leaders use it to settle today's international conflicts? ❷ Which of the following points of view would you defend, and why?

a. This strategy should and eventually will work. International tensions cannot be resolved by force or domination. GRIT also requires political leaders who are visionaries.

b. This strategy does not work. Peace should be imposed: International tensions must be reduced first by military or political means. Only after that can symbolic acts and goodwill gestures be utilized.

The State Policies Context

As realists insist, a country with massive military power has more security options than a weaker state. However, military strength alone is not a guarantor of security. A country also needs trustworthy allies, domestic political stability, and national unity. During the American Revolution, the Americans' alliance with France compensated in part for their military weaknesses. French political disunity in the late 1930s allowed Hitler to crush France and its allies quickly in 1940. These examples show the importance of domestic factors in foreign and security policy (Walt 1991).

graduated reciprocation in tension reduction (GRIT) Small goodwill steps by one or two sides in an international conflict that help to build trust and reduce international tensions.

PUBLIC OPINION

In democratic countries, national security is the subject of public debate, and political pressures exert considerable influence (Nacos et al. 2000). Yet during the time of international tensions or when a war appears imminent, public tends to "rally around the flag." Experts call it *rage militaire*—euphoric expectations of a confrontation and a quick victory. Knowing that effect, some political leaders may engage in a *diversionary war*, to distract domestic public opinion from pressuring problems at home. Ideally, this war should distract from a domestic problem and strengthen the government's position in power (Sobek 2008). Yet usually the military fervor does not last long. After the Vietnam War the public in the United States no longer supported long war and military commitments overseas, and developed very low tolerance for casualties (Shiraev and Sobel 2006). (See Table 5-5)

There are cycles in public opinion, which are related to generational experience. Before World War II, Americans were largely isolationists. Most

TABLE 5-5 Confrontations, Hostilities, and Public Support

Country, Period	Descriptions of Public Reaction
Britain, mid-1850s	Fear of Russia was rampant among decision makers and the educated public, who viewed Russia as a danger to British colonies. The two countries fought between 1853 and 1856.
China, 1965–69	The Chinese Communist Party launched a massive propaganda campaign, blaming the Soviet Union for selling out Socialist values. The campaign fueled a wave of anti-Soviet sentiment in China and led to bloody skirmishes on the Sino-Soviet border in 1969.
Iran, 1979–	Western pressure and economic sanctions against Iran have fueled and maintained an anti-Western sentiment among a significant portion of the population.
Russia, 1999–	NATO military strikes against Serbia, condemnation of Russian actions in Georgia, and economic sanctions against Russia for its actions in Ukraine led to anti-American outbursts and the Russian government's abandonment of its pro-Western course in foreign policy. After 1999, Russia began to regard NATO as an adversary.

believed that their country's security did not depend on the situation in Europe or elsewhere. After World War II, American public opinion tended to be more interventionist. Consensus in support of interventionist policies lasted until the middle of Vietnam War, roughly 1968, when Americans became divided.

IDEOLOGY

In today's democratic societies, according to opinion polls and electoral results, people on the left are more likely to oppose military confrontations, in accord with liberal views of international relations. Those on the right are more likely to be nationalistic and pro-military, in accord with the realist perspective. These views are reflected in popular perceptions of the major political parties. In the United States, Democrats are often seen as "soft" and Republicans as "hawkish." Studies show that conservative presidents' foreign policy tends to be hawkish (Dueck 2010). In Germany, Christian Democrats (a conservative party) are frequently viewed by opponents as too tough in dealing with international threats and Social Democrats (a liberal party) as too weak (Shiraev and Sobel 2006).

These perceptions are not always accurate. Conservative governments, which are generally reluctant to raise taxes to subsidize the military, frequently choose diplomacy, coalition building, and bargaining with adversarial states (Narizny 2003). Liberals recently became more supportive of the use of military force against governments perceived to be capable of atrocities against their own people. The constructivist perspective offers another explanation for why liberals do not necessarily express soft attitudes and conservatives hawkish ones. People tend to respond to national security threats according to their *self-perceptions*. Conservatives may feel more comfortable in the foreign-policy arena because they already support a forceful defense and therefore do not need to use force all the time (Reeves 2001). Liberals, who may feel less secure about their ability to mount a military response, may overreact.

LOBBYING AND SECURITY BUREAUCRACY

Lobbying is activity by individuals, groups, and corporations to influence public officials in support of legislation or policies. Its methods include mail campaigns, mobilizing voters, funding political campaigns, and op-ed pieces in the media. Advocates of conflict theories argue that lobbying helps the ruling classes determine foreign and security policy. During the twentieth century, however, lobbies represented different approaches toward securities. Some business groups pushed for American economic and military expansion. During the Cold War, Quakers and other groups promoted negotiations with Soviet leaders to prevent nuclear war, while ethnic Americans from Eastern Europe and Catholic organizations were anti-Soviet and supported federal spending to maintain U.S. military superiority. A powerful pro-Israeli lobby emerged between 1967 and 1973 and used strategic security goals to justify U.S. support for Israel (Mearsheimer and Walt 2007).

lobbying Activities with the goal of influencing public officials in support of legislation or policies.

During the Cold War, government security bureaucracy and industrial corporations shared their common interest in the perpetuation of the arms race and confrontation with the Soviet Union. In 1960, President Dwight Eisenhower spoke of the "military-industrial complex" that had come to dominate his country's security policies (Eisenhower 1960). After the terrorist attacks of 2001, a new powerful bureaucracy emerged. Homeland security as a policy now combines domestic and national security tasks. The long-term impact of homeland security bureaucracy on foreign policy decision-making is yet to be seen, but it clearly represents a powerful new factor in security policies.

The Global Context

With the increasing interconnectedness of economies and policies, more and more events and factors have implications for national and international security. The essence of international relations becomes not just about state and regional politics, but about energy resources as well.

GEOPOLITICS

For centuries, sovereign states struggled for territorial and geographic advantage. Many of them used **geopolitics**—the theory and practice of using geography and territorial gains to achieve political power or seek

Rep. Elise Stefanik, R-N.Y., participates in the House Armed Services Committee hearing on the United States' Defense budget. The committee votes for the allocation of billions of dollars every year for security-related contracts. Some large contracts create tens of thousands of jobs in the United States.

geopolitics The theory and practice of using geography to achieve political power or seek security.

security. Geographical position gave some countries clear advantages in security matters, while others remained vulnerable. New research in history suggests that geopolitics played a crucial role in the rise and fall of the great world powers (Morris 2010). In Afghanistan, the country's vast and rough terrain and underdeveloped infrastructure pose significant challenges for military operations to achieve stability in this country. At the same time, an unstable Afghanistan is a source of regional and global insecurity.

A significant change took place after the end of the Cold War. Irregular wars (conflicts involving guerillas, instead of regular military) proliferated in the second half of the twentieth century. In the 1990s, wars had shifted away from Asia and Latin America and toward Eurasia, the Middle East, and sub-Saharan Africa. This shift was caused, in addition to some domestic political and economic factors, by a massive dissolution of political regimes in these regions following the end of the Cold War (Kalyvas and Balcellis 2010, 423).

International terrorism altered the face of irregular warfare. It does not respect geographical boundaries. (We will discuss terrorism in Chapter 8.) Small nuclear weapons can now be delivered to cities in a suitcase, and nuclear proliferation is now an acute security issue. Because a *dirty bomb* (one that combines radioactive material with conventional explosives) does not need sophisticated means of delivery, the spread of nuclear materials could have global consequences. Countries have few options other than cooperation on security and law enforcement. The gathering and sharing of intelligence has become crucial. Over the last decade international organizations over the last decade have played a greater role in global security.

REGIONAL SECURITY

Territorial integrity and sovereignty remain important issues affecting global security. A country's breakup or the interference of neighboring countries can create regional instability—especially in multiethnic zones with weak governments. As we saw in the introductory example to this chapter, India, for example, supported the partition of neighboring Pakistan and the creation of the independent country of Bangladesh in 1971; Pakistan quickly retaliated and war broke out. These days, ethnic and religious violence in West Africa and the Middle East may become the most significant threats to global security for years.

Some multilateral steps toward regional security have already been taken, such as the Central America Regional Security Initiative (CARSI 2015). This collective effort of governments, law-enforcement agencies, and NGOs aims to prevent the spread of illicit drugs, the violence associated with them, and transnational threats. The initiative attempts to reduce the flow of narcotics, arms, weapons, and bulk cash generated by drug sales and to confront gangs and criminal organizations. If efforts like this succeed, they will demonstrate the importance of international organizations and coordinated policies.

@ Learn more about the Central America Regional Security Initiative from the companion website. What is the U.S. role in this program? If you were president, what would you change in this program to make it more efficient?

ENERGY, RESOURCES, AND SECURITY

In the twentieth century, the struggle for access to oil contributed to international conflicts. During periods of robust economic growth, when the demand for fuel is high, any disruption in the production of oil has serious consequences. The Arab oil embargo against the West in the 1970s contributed to a serious, widespread recession (Bryce 2009). For the United States, dependence on foreign oil has been a security challenge. Energy self-sufficiency is likely to be a major strategic goal of future administrations. In terms of new strategic relations in the twenty-first century, new political alliances are likely to emerge. Former ideological and political allies may turn away from their former partners and gravitate toward energy-rich nations, thus weakening strategic security regimes. New emerging energy alliances could easily be perceived as threats to other states' security (Guérot 2010).

About 35 percent of the world's seaborne oil shipments go through the Strait of Hormuz, between the Gulf of Oman and the Persian Gulf. This image from Iranian state TV shows damage to a mock U.S. aircraft carrier during military drills by Iran's Revolutionary Guard in 2015. The U.S. Navy downplayed this episode, but protecting energy supply lines will likely remain a serious international security issue.

Energy independence does not guarantee security for the United States, however. The twenty-first century has marked the rapid economic growth of China, India, and Brazil—so-called emerging economies. They too need an uninterrupted supply of oil and natural gas, at the lowest possible price, and they are likely to make substantial investments in their militaries to protect it. China's economic growth could contribute to global tension in other ways as well: Its massive exports could undermine other countries' economies and key manufacturing industries, weakening their job markets (Peerenboom 2008). The competing principles of realpolitik and cooperation will be tested once again.

> ▶ What are the relative roles of public opinion and lobbies in security policies?
> ▶ Explain GRIT.
> ▶ What is the "military-industrial complex"?
> ▶ What is the Central America Regional Security Initiative?
> ▶ Why has oil become a global security issue?

CHECK YOUR KNOWLEDGE

THE USES OF HISTORY: Ending the Cold War

Background

Why did the Cold War, a global conflict that had lasted for decades, end so suddenly and without significant violence? In the early 1980s, the future of global security appeared bleak. The most common assumption among professional analysts and politicians was that the next decade would be the most dangerous period since World War II. This expectation was driven in part by the logic of the security dilemma: The U.S. military buildup under President Ronald Reagan was believed to lead to a Soviet buildup, and more tension (Gray 1982). Yet in 1987 and 1988 the fear and insecurity faded away. President Ronald Reagan and the new Soviet leader Mikhail Gorbachev established mutual trust. In the Intermediate Range Nuclear Forces (INF) treaty of 1987, they agreed to destroy missiles of intermediate and shorter range (from 500 to 5,000 kilometers). And in 1989–90, Soviet troops began to pull out of Eastern Europe. Early in 1990 Gorbachev agreed that Germany should be peacefully reunited; a few months later the Soviet leader consented to Washington's position that a unified Germany should remain inside NATO.

The peaceful transformation of the security landscape and the entire international system in 1988–91 took most experts by surprise. *Triumphalists*, mostly conservatives in the United States, were quick to claim a U.S. victory, an expected result of the military buildup and constant pressure against the Soviet Union. By creating a military deadlock for the USSR in Afghanistan, supporting Solidarity (an anti-Communist, anti-Soviet movement) in Poland, building advanced military systems, encouraging Saudi Arabia to reduce oil prices (the main source of Soviet finances), and taking a belligerent stand in the war of ideas, the United States undercut the Soviet Union's power bases, undermined its self-confidence, and forced it to surrender in the Cold War.

U.S. President Ronald Reagan and Soviet General Secretary Mikhail Gorbachev meet in 1986.

Analysis

Declassified documents and interviews made clear that the triumphalist thesis is simplistic. Soviet archives reveal that the key to a security transformation was Gorbachev's desire for domestic reforms and his refusal to see the world through the prism of the security dilemma. The Soviet leader acted from the position of growing weakness: Soviet economy and finances were in disarray. But he also wanted to build an international community in Europe and Asia that would include NATO countries. The Soviet leader spearheaded a new image of a just, secure world and a path to achieve it—what he called the "new thinking." Liberals in the West proclaimed Gorbachev their champion. They acknowledged that he shared many ideas with the neoliberal domestic and transnational intellectual communities (English 2000; Evangelista 1999). Among them was Charles Osgood's GRIT model. By applying these ideas to international relations, Gorbachev succeeded in breaking the deadlock of the security dilemma. Many all over Europe and the world applauded the Soviet leader when he declared at the United Nations in 1988 that international security is "one and indivisible" and rejected the use of force in international relations.

One can even reassess the role of U.S. president Ronald Reagan in the light of liberal theories. Although the Reagan administration initially did not trust Gorbachev's intentions, Reagan recognized that the Soviet threat was disappearing and seized the opportunity to build a new framework of agreements and cooperation with the Soviet Union. The emerging mutual trust between Reagan and Gorbachev helped to break the cycle of insecurity. They proceeded despite the resistance of powerful national forces, including the most belligerent members of the military on both sides and government officials with hostile attitudes about the other country. (Chernyaev 2000; Leffler 2007).

Realists and neorealists too began to search for more sophisticated explanations of the end of the Cold War. They argued that the Soviet Union's uncertain role in the new structures of international relations and its weakening stand in the global balance of power affected the behavior of the Soviet leaders. A younger generation of Soviet leaders, including Gorbachev and foreign minister Eduard Shevardnadze, realized that the Soviet Union had to avoid a new round of arms race that it could not win. Because the USSR could not prevail over the West, it decided to join the West (Wohlforth 2003). Gorbachev's new perception of common security emerged as an alternative to confrontational policies seen as dangerous, expensive, and counterproductive (Herrmann and Lebow 2004).

Constructivist assessments help explain the evolving ideas on security by the Soviet and U.S. political leadership. Gorbachev, unlike the older generation of Soviet leaders, no longer identified himself with a Soviet military superpower. In contrast, he viewed nuclear weapons as ensuring Soviet security against foreign threats. Nor was he obsessed with memories of World War II that had left Soviet elites deeply insecure when it came to the West. Gorbachev's personal aversion to the use of force and his preference for nonmilitary means to respond to security challenges were almost pacifist. In the end, Gorbachev not only accepted that a unified Germany would become an anchor of peace and prosperity in Europe, but also based his strategy on integrating the reformed Soviet Union into a "common European home"—the term used to describe a new structure for security and economic integration that included North America. (Rey 2008; Zubok 2014).

Liberals, neorealists, and constructivists agree that a peaceful resolution like this one does not come about exclusively from military pressure. It takes rethinking national security after traditional approaches end in crisis or deadlock. The colossal military power of the Soviet Union was undermined by a corrosion of ideology and political will (Lévesque 1997, 252). Influential Soviet elites became convinced that Western models based on political freedoms, private entrepreneurship, and consumerism had more to offer. Had the Soviets and Americans had different political leaders, most probably the Cold War would have continued. Yet not just the Kremlin, but ordinary people had begun to think differently. They were no longer prepared to shed blood for a cause they did not believe in and an empire they did not benefit from. In the end, ideas and values transformed international security.

Advocates of alternative approaches to international relations draw different lessons from the peaceful end of the Cold War. Marxists argue that the Soviet Union was never a truly Socialist country (Shlapentokh et al. 2008). Gorbachev and Soviet elites simply shifted from one mode of domination and insecurity to another neoliberal model based on global capitalist exploitation, inequality, and again, insecurity. Feminist critics argue that the narrative of the end of the Cold War should not revolve around the actions and thoughts of just a few male leaders, such as Gorbachev, Reagan, and Bush. Moreover, the global outcomes of 1989 were not nearly as revolutionary: Instead of building peace and cooperation, Western statesmen preserved and expanded NATO, perpetuating the same old security agenda (Sarotte 2009).

Drawing lessons from the end of the Cold War is not easy. It stands as a unique case—the meltdown of a major power. Yet it has generated rich and valuable discussions that reopen and reassess the tenets of national and international security today.

Questions

1. The relations between Russia and the West have recently deteriorated. Which side would you hold most responsible for the tensions, and why: the West, Russia, or both?
2. Which domestic factors in Russia could have contributed to international tensions?
3. Which domestic factors in the United States and the West in general could have contributed to tensions with Russia?
4. Do you predict that the new Cold War will be over soon? Why or why not? Which individual, political, and global conditions from the end of the Cold War exist today, and which do not?

CONCLUSION

For centuries, states' security policies were secret. Monarchs and prime ministers defined national interest as political sovereignty and territorial integrity. As soon as national interest was protected, the state could pursue other interests through foreign policy. This view of security is generally supported by realists, who identify the goal of security policies as a favorable international balance of power.

Supporters of international liberalism believe that realist considerations lead to actions that undermine national and international security. Rather than relying on force, they seek a greater role for international and nongovernment organizations. Public opinion is important, too, but only if it can be expressed freely. Western Europe has shown the world that democratic states can build a stable peace based on security communities.

Why do some state leaders choose military actions while others seek peaceful solutions? In part, these attitudes are socially constructed. Values, fears, and misconceptions guide policy makers through the maze of international and domestic politics and a constantly changing world.

International security may seem like a gigantic chess game. It takes knowledge, skill, and intelligence to understand all the moves. It takes a heart, however, to recognize that behind all these pieces are human beings.

KEY TERMS

collective security 167
conflict 156
cooperation 161
domino theory 165
failing state 155
geopolitics 178
graduated reciprocation
   in tension reduction
   (GRIT) 175
guerrilla warfare 159
international security 155

interventionism 161
liberal interventionism 166
isolationism 161
lobbying 177
militarism 169
multilateralism 160
mutual assured destruction
   (MAD) 164
national security 155
nuclear deterrence 164
pacifism 169

peace psychology 173
preemptive war 157
preventive war   157
security community 167
security dilemma 164
security policy   168
security regime 165
unilateralism 160
war 156

IDEAS

KEY CONCEPTS
- **National security:** protection of a state's sovereignty, territorial integrity, and interests
- **International security:** bilateral or multilateral
- **Conflict:** antagonism between states or international organizations
- **War:** organized violent confrontation

TYPES OF WAR
- **Intentions and policies:** offensive, defensive, preemptive, preventive
- **Scope and consequences:** local, regional, global
- **Strategies:** conventional, nonconventional, weapon types
- **Purposes:** predatory, retaliatory, political, ethnic, religious

SECURITY POLICIES
How many states are involved in the policy?
- unilateral
- multilateral

How do states address foreign threats?
- isolationism
- interventionism
- cooperation

ARGUMENTS

REALISM
- Security depends on the quantity and quality of armed forces and their mobility
- States try to maximize their power
- Security dilemma: A state's attempt to improve its security creates insecurity in other states

LIBERALISM
- Neither economic nor military power alone can bring lasting security
- States almost always have options for negotiation
- Collective security: The security of one state is the concern of all

CONSTRUCTIVISM
- States act according to experience, ideologies, perceptions, and social norms
- Militarism: glorifies war, conquest, domination
- Pacifism: principled opposition to war; disputes should be settled nonviolently

ALTERNATIVE AND CONFLICT THEORIES
- Security policies reflect and protect the key interests of the dominant social groups
- Marxism: critical of political and economic elitism
- Feminism: critical of exclusion of women from policy-making

CONTEXTS AND APPLICATIONS

INDIVIDUAL DECISIONS CONTEXT
- Leaders and advisers
- Peace psychology and goodwill

STATE POLICIES CONTEXT
- Public opinion
- Ideology
- Lobbying

GLOBAL CONTEXT
- Geopolitics
- Regional security
- Global energy and resources

Critical Thinking

❶ In one sentence each, describe the realist, liberal, constructivist, and other perspectives on security.

❷ Explain two applications of security policies in the context of individual decisions.

❸ Give an example of a country's security policy you consider effective and one you consider ineffective. Explain your choices.

❹ Would a total ban on nuclear weapons increase or decrease international security? Why?

International Law

Insofar as international law is observed, it provides us with stability and order and with a means of predicting the behavior of those with whom we have reciprocal legal obligations.

—J. WILLIAM FULBRIGHT (1905–1995)

I N JULY 2001, THE GOVERNMENT OF ISRAEL BEGAN TO BUILD A SECURITY BARRIER SEPARATING ISRAEL FROM THE PALESTINIAN TERRITORIES. THE WALL, WHICH IS about 450 miles (720 km) long, is in fact a 160- to 330-feet-wide (50–100 m) engineering project. It consists of a fence with electronic sensors, a ditch up to 13 feet (4 m) deep, a two-lane asphalt patrol road (the "trace strip") built parallel to the fence with sand smoothed to detect footprints, and barbed wire. No longer could people cross the fenced area through a checkpoint without a permit issued by Israeli authorities.

The Palestinian government has long considered this construction project illegal and repeatedly asked the Israeli government to stop it. The General Assembly of the United Nations decided to investigate in 2003, and the UN International Court of Justice decided by a majority vote that the wall was "contrary to international law." The court obliged Israel to cease construction without delay and to repeal all laws associated with it. Israel was also under an obligation to make reparation for all damage caused by construction. Other countries were advised not to give assistance to Israel in advancing the project, and the UN Security Council was asked to consider further action.

What happened next? Israel did not halt construction of the fence, but instead completed most of it. The government submitted a written statement justifying the fence as a security measure against terrorist attacks. Legal scholars in Israel wrote

Previous page: Runners taking part in the Palestine Marathon pass by the Israeli separation barrier in the West Bank city of Bethlehem in 2015.

that a sovereign state might construct a temporary security barrier in an occupied territory. The Israeli Supreme Court ruled that the fence was legal. Still, it ordered some changes in the barrier route to accommodate Palestinians. A new route would return some 140 acres (approx. 0.5 square km) to the Palestinians.

Which side's legal arguments appear stronger in your view? Should the governments of sovereign states obey the decisions of international organizations, including courts? Under what circumstances do countries have the right to disagree? How do you coordinate international law with the interests of independent states? These questions have critical significance in today's global world. This chapter deals with the principles and consequences of international law and its role in international relations (ICJ 2004. Israel High Court Ruling 2005).

> ▶ Explain the principles, sources, and evolution of international law.
> ▶ Describe the opportunities as well as the limitations of international law.
> ▶ Outline the principal differences among various views and approaches to international law.
> ▶ Apply key principles of international law to individual decisions, state policies, and global developments.

Learning Objectives

Ideas

In general terms, a *law* is a rule either prescribed or recognized as binding. **International law** is a set of principles, rules, and agreements that regulate the behavior of states and other international actors. In theory, states and international organizations should agree on a set of general rules and then enforce them properly. In reality, it is a daunting mission.

international law
Principles, rules, and regulations concerning the interactions between countries and other institutions and organizations in international relations.

Law, the Role of IGOs, and International Relations

There is no formal document or code to set forth worldwide legal principles. Nor is there a global constitution, global supreme court, or worldwide law-enforcement agency. International legal regulations are effective only as long as key international actors recognize and follow them rather than ignore or reject them. As we have seen already, Israel rejected international law when it refused to halt construction of a security barrier. Is it really necessary, then, or even practical, to have international law? The answer is *yes*, absolutely. At least three reasons explain why.

A need for a secure international environment. Sovereign states, organizations, businesses, and ordinary people need a secure environment rather than lawlessness (Bull 1977). States and international organizations set rules and establish sanctions against violations of such rules. Take piracy, for example. It disrupts maritime communication, inhibits trade, and endangers lives. The United States has appealed to international legal norms to fight piracy since the end of the eighteenth century. A significant increase of piracy near Somalia and the Horn of Africa about a decade ago created a collective international response to uphold and enforce international anti-piracy laws (Boot 2009).

A need for conflict resolution. Although international actors constantly engage in disputes, they realize that force alone is not the most efficient way to resolve them. Wars are destructive and lead to further conflicts. International law can also serve as an instrument of new states' creation. Internationally observed rules help countries to resolve border issues and property rights so that agreements are kept without violence (Linklater 2009). In the 1990s, Yemen and Eritrea disputed over control of the Hanish Islands in the Red Sea. Violence was about to erupt. In 1998, the Permanent Court of Arbitration, one of the oldest institutions for dispute resolution, determined that the archipelago belonged to Yemen. Eritrea accepted this legal decision, and violence was avoided. (See Map 6-1.)

@ On the companion website, you can examine several cases showing the interaction between countries' legal systems.

A need to coordinate domestic laws in a global world. States have different constitutional, administrative, criminal, contract, family, and property laws. Numerous disagreements naturally emerge, especially in an era of global trade and travel (Keohane 2005). Think of divorce and custody disputes, trademark

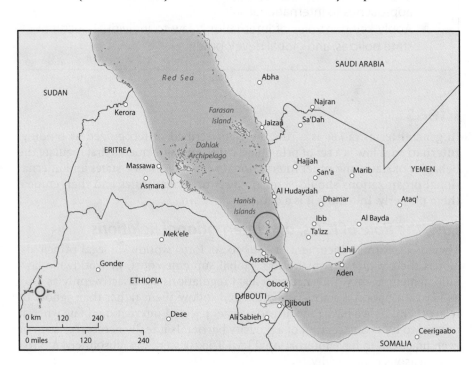

MAP 6-1 Previously disputed Hanish Islands belong to Yemen now, thanks to international arbitration.

violations, contract violations, financial obligations, and compensations for faulty products or services. International law should also be applied to fight transnational organized crime including extortion, drug and human trafficking, kidnapping, and money laundering. Because countries have different constitutional, administrative, criminal, contract, family, and property laws, numerous practical problems and disagreements naturally emerge, especially in an era of global trade and travel. International law is therefore essential in regulating the relationships (a) among private citizens living in different countries, (b) between private citizens and foreign governments or organizations, and (c) among international organizations.

A Japanese Maritime Self-Defense Forces pilot patrols the Gulf of Aden off Somalia in 2014. Japan began such missions as anti-piracy measures in 2009.

Principles and Sources of International Law

International law establishes legal principles—or general rules of law application—for two, several, or even all countries (Kahler and Lake 2003). For example, international law applies only within its **jurisdiction**, which defines how far it can reach. Anti-piracy laws have universal jurisdiction because they apply everywhere. Other laws are more specific. The European Union, for example, restricts certain food products imported to its countries (Rankin 2010). Switzerland, a non-member, is free to use its own food regulations.

To become subject to international law, a state must be *sovereign*, which means that its government should be lawful and exercise supreme authority within its territory (see Chapter 1). International organizations are subject to international law too. They, as well as sovereign states, are engaged in *diplomacy*—the managing of international relations by means of negotiations. Rules of *diplomatic protocol* are based on centuries of tradition and prescribe how these activities between states and organizations should be performed.

Where do the legal principles and rules regulating international relations come from? As we see next, the **sources of international law** include treaties, customs, general principles, and the actions of courts and other international organizations. (See Table 6-1.)

International treaties (also called *agreements, charters, pacts, covenants,* and *conventions*) are formal, written commitments between international actors, and they often suggest sanctions if those commitments are violated or ignored. A state or organization usually can cancel, or *abrogate*, a treaty—especially if the treaty has term limits. In 2002, soon after the terrorist acts of September 11, 2001, the United States abrogated the Anti-Ballistic Missile Treaty, concluded with the Soviet Union in 1972, so that Washington could build an antimissile defense. Generally, however, countries do not walk out of treaties.

jurisdiction The right and authority to make decisions and apply justice.

@ When is a foreign diplomat subject to arrest for breaking U.S. law? Must a diplomat pay taxes? Can countries declare a diplomat unacceptable or unwelcome? Visit the companion website to learn about *diplomatic immunity* and *persona non grata.*

sources of international law Treaties, customs, general principles, the actions of international courts and other organizations, and other processes that regulate international relations.

TABLE 6-1 Sources of International Law

International Treaties	Formal, written commitments between international actors. Example: The New Strategic Arms Reduction Treaty, signed by Russia and the United States in 2010, limits the nuclear arsenal capabilities of both countries.
International Customary Law	Derives from the past practices of sovereign states. Example: Diplomatic representatives and members of their families are free from criminal persecution and civil liability in countries where they work and live unless their governments revoke such "immunity."
General Principles of Law	Widely accepted principles of morality and common sense. Examples: An international agreement is supposed to be honored; a sovereign state has the right to control the use of resources within its territory; a sovereign state has the right either to recognize or not to recognize another country.
Resolutions of International Organizations or Judgments by International Courts	Examples: Resolutions of the United Nations, the International Court of Justice, NATO, or the European Union.

international treaties Written agreements between nations (also called agreements, charters, pacts, covenants, and conventions).

customary law Law derived from the past practices of sovereign states in the absence of repeated objections from other states.

general principles of law Cross-cultural principles of morality and common sense.

By their lasting nature, these documents help protect the international community from sudden changes.

International **customary law** derives from the past practices of sovereign states. International actors simply come to see these "customary actions" as normal and expected under particular circumstances. For example, every sovereign state with access to the sea is expected to claim jurisdiction over its territorial waters, which extend 12 nautical miles or 22 kilometers—originally, they extended the distance of a cannon shot fired from the shore. States are expected not to deploy weapons in earth orbit (Gangale 2009).

A third source is **general principles of law**, which are common, cross-cultural principles of morality and common sense. Legal decisions, for instance, should be passed based on *equity*—the need to be balanced and impartial. States have the right of self-defense, but their actions should be proportional to the aggression. If states, organizations, and businesses damage the environment of other states, they should compensate. In 2010, oil company British Petroleum immediately offered compensation to people and organizations for the damages caused by a massive oil leak in the Gulf of Mexico that lasted more than one hundred days. Overall the company paid more than $40 billion in legal fines and cleanup costs (BBC 2014).

The judgments of international organizations along with works by legal scholars and political analysts are another source of international law. In 1980, following Israel's decision to make Jerusalem its capital, the UN Security Council issued Resolution 478, declaring the Israeli law a violation of international law. In part because of this resolution, almost all foreign embassies in Israel remain in Tel Aviv.

Most contemporary international agreements, treaties, and rules derive from a rich legal history. We turn to that history now.

▶ Explain three arguments in support of international law. Come up with your own example to justify the importance of international law.
▶ Explain the jurisdiction principle. Give two examples related to yourself and to your own country.
▶ Name four sources of international law. Would you consider the "eye for an eye" principle (the custom of retaliation) as part of customary law?

Development of International Law

The Treaty of Westphalia established an early foundation of international law in 1648, as you will remember from Chapter 1. The acquisition of new lands also required justification. During the period of colonial expansion, European rulers often used the legal term *terra nullius*, or land belonging to no one, to claim lands such as Australia as their lawful possessions (Lindkvist 2007). Much later, this term was applied to Antarctica, the moon, outer planets, and the deep seabed—but now to prevent claims of sovereignty by other countries.

LAWS OF THE SEA

The Laws of the Sea are among the oldest in international law. States involved in overseas commerce had to deal with competition, the safety of shipments, and financial disputes. They needed the freedom to travel by sea and to trade with other countries, and rules became a necessity, to minimize preventable losses. These laws are based on agreements, practical needs, and legal scholarship. Hugo Grotius (1583–1645), a Dutch diplomat and thinker, in *Mare Liberum* (1609) formulated one central principle, **freedom of the seas**: A state's sovereignty ends at the edge of its territorial waters and the high seas are open to all countries. Although not every state accepted these principles at first, they eventually did, and these rules survived for centuries. Today, outside of territorial waters of other states, countries and individuals have the right to navigate, conduct scientific research, use aircraft, and even lay cable or pipelines. In the second half of the twentieth century, many new agreements were reached to regulate international navigation and sea borders. New agreements also regulate exploration of the ocean surface, its seabed, and protect its flora and fauna. After the 1970s countries began to claim and enforce legal rights over the exploration and use of marine resources within their *exclusive economic zone* (EEZ), which stretches to 200 nautical miles (370 km) from the country's coast.

freedom of the seas
The principle that countries have the right to travel by sea to, and trade with, other countries; each state's sovereignty ends with its territorial waters.

@ On the companion website, you can read classic laws of the sea and learn what they mean. Notice how detailed and specific some of those rules are. Most of these rules continue to regulate the international behavior of states and organizations.

LAWS OF WAR

In the eighteenth and nineteenth centuries, a consensus emerged among ruling elites on the need to regulate war and to minimize its increasingly deadly consequences. Influenced by the philosophy of "just war," in 1899 Czar Nicholas II of Russia and Queen Wilhelmina of the Netherlands assembled an

Frenchmen meet Australian Aboriginals in this drawing, done between 1818 and 1820. European great powers often used the legal term *terra nullius*, or land belonging to no one, to colonize new territories.

unprecedented international conference in The Hague (in the Netherlands). The First Hague Conference involved representatives from twenty-six states, including high-level delegations from the United States and Japan. The Second Hague Conference was called in 1907 with forty-four states present.

The participating countries agreed that war must be the last resort in settling international disputes, and the right to declare it should be limited. Limits must also be put on the use of violence during war. Poisoned gases, for example, were banned because they caused great suffering to soldiers and civilians. The documents also recognized the rights of prisoners of war and outlawed using the enemy's flag and military uniform for deception. Pillaging, bombarding towns not defended by the military, punishing civilians, and refusing to care for wounded enemy soldiers were all deemed illegal. (See Figure 6-1.)

laws of war
Common principles that states should follow in case of an armed conflict.

The Hague Conference outlined the **laws of war**—common principles that states should follow in case of an armed conflict. For example, a state should declare whether it initiates hostilities against another state with a *declaration of war*. A state at war has *belligerent rights*, such as the right to visit and search merchant ships, seize cargo of the enemy, or attack and destroy military forces and equipment of the enemy. States at war also expect to have their soldiers and officers treated in accordance with the decisions of the Hague Conference, regardless of who started the conflict or who has moral right to use violence. A suspension of hostilities was called **armistice**. A country's formal surrender should stop all military actions, but the victors could impose the conditions of peace, as happened later with the end of World War I in 1918 and World War II in 1945.

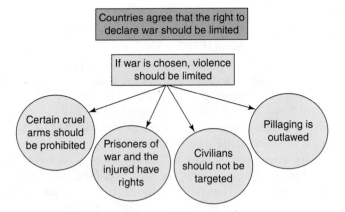

FIGURE 6-1 Major decisions of the Second Hague Conference (1907).

It was acknowledged that a state could choose **neutrality** by rejecting any formal military or political alliance. Several states today have proclaimed neutrality, including Costa Rica, Finland, Sweden, and Switzerland. They are obliged to use all means to ensure that their territory is not used by other countries to stage aggression or to engage in hostile actions, such as spying.

The Hague Conferences seemed to signal a new era in international relations. Yet for all their declarations, the conferences brought only few practical results. For one thing, talks reached an impasse over the issue of appointment of international judges. Every delegation wanted to see a representative of its state appointed, and bigger states wanted a bigger share of votes. Worse, many legislatures back home, mostly for domestic political reasons, failed to ratify the Hague resolutions or attached serious amendments, making the resolutions ineffective.

neutrality Rejection of any formal military or political alliance (see isolationism).

HUMANITARIAN ISSUES

Declaring limits on the use of war was nevertheless an important step in the development of international law. The concerns grew about the fate of ordinary people in wars—both combatants and civilians (Abrams 1957). Who can protect them from excessive violence and harm? There was a growing agreement that all human beings, regardless of their nationality or creed, have basic rights that international law must protect.

In 1863, Swiss citizen Jean Henri Dunant (1828–1910) founded the International Committee of the Red Cross (ICRC) to help all wounded soldiers on the battlefield. The Red Cross was instrumental in the first Geneva Convention for the Amelioration of the Condition of the Wounded in Armed Forces in the Field, signed in August 1864 by fourteen states, on the humane treatment of captured and wounded soldiers. Dunant became the first winner of the Nobel Peace Prize. The International Federation of the Red Cross and Red Crescent Societies was formed in 1919, and the 1864 Geneva Convention was the precursor of three more agreements signed in Geneva in 1906, 1929, and 1949. Together, the Geneva Conventions legalized the rights of the captured and wounded, as well as civilians and other noncombatants (Borch and Solis 2010).

On the companion website, you can find the Geneva Convention for the Amelioration of the Condition of the Wounded in Armies in the Field and other international treaties on the fate of combatants and civilians. What did these agreements suggest about their enforcement?

HUMAN RIGHTS

human rights
Fundamental rights with which all people are endowed regardless of their race, nationality, sex, ethnicity, religion, or social status.

In the twentieth century, a powerful argument about **human rights** gained strength. These are fundamental rights with which all people are endowed regardless of their race, nationality, sex, ethnicity, religion, or social status. The United Nations became a major vehicle for producing and promoting international legal norms on human rights. In 1948, the UN General Assembly adopted the Universal Declaration of Human Rights. The Covenant on Civil and Political Rights and the Covenant on Economic, Social, and Cultural Rights, adopted in 1966, came into force in 1976. A year earlier, the Conference on Security and Cooperation in Europe, which included the United States and the Soviet Union, signed the Helsinki Final Act. This document bound the twenty-five states that signed it to respect and protect humanitarian and human rights, such as the right to receive information, exchange ideas, or unify families across the state borders. It was a triumph of liberal internationalism (Thomas 2001).

The concept of human rights tied international law to natural law: All humans, by their nature, are entitled to some basic rights. Why, then, can't states create a system to encourage the observance of human rights globally? The Carter administration (1977–81), supported by nongovernment groups and legal scholars, made human rights a key goal of its foreign policy. International law, it argued, should allow interference with the affairs of states found responsible for massive and systematic human-rights violations.

The evolution of attitudes toward human rights is a remarkable success of international law. The fourth Geneva Convention of 1949 and the Genocide Convention of 1948 have become widely recognized treaties. The 1948 Convention defined **genocide** as the deliberate extermination or prosecution of national, racial, ethnic, and religious groups, whether in war or in peacetime. The term "genocide" was coined in 1944 by a Polish lawyer of Jewish descent, Raphael Lemkin. These and other humanitarian agreements aim at limiting suffering and death during military conflicts. They protect prisoners of war and civilian noncombatants against indiscriminate violence against them. These laws also assume that states, even non-democratic ones, must respond today to the international community if authorities engage in arbitrary arrests for political reasons, systematic torture, rape, or the deliberate killing or injury of civilians. These deliberate offenses became known as *crimes against humanity*.

genocide The deliberate extermination or prosecution of racial, ethnic, religious, or social groups, whether in war or in peacetime.

EARLY LEGAL INTERNATIONAL INSTITUTIONS

The Hague conferences established the Permanent Court of Arbitration (known as the Hague Tribunal) to make binding decisions on disputes between cooperating states, IGOs, and private parties. The idea of international arbitration was very popular in the United States as well in the early twentieth century, and President Theodore Roosevelt asked the Court to settle a dispute with Mexico. The Permanent Court of Arbitration remains the oldest legal institution for international dispute resolution. Although most of the cases adjudicated in this court involve boundaries between countries, some of the decisions involve international business disputes. In 2014, for example, the court awarded $50 billion to shareholders of Russian oil company Yukos, which had been seized by the Russian government.

In the nineteenth and the early twentieth century, other international organizations were established to promote cooperation in technology, communication, and law enforcement. Among them were the International Telegraph Union (founded in 1865), the International Telecommunication Union, and the Universal Postal Union (formed in 1874). The countries joining the Universal Postal Union pledged to cooperate in setting prices and standards for delivering mail, both domestic and international. The International Criminal Police Commission, founded in 1923 in Austria following consultations with law enforcement professionals from several countries, was not a global

A Scottish policeman addresses the media during a news conference in 2014 at the police headquarters near Manila, Philippines. Philippine police, backed by Interpol, have arrested dozens of suspected members of an online extortion syndicate.

police force. Nonetheless, *Interpol* (as the organization is called today) has eased cross-border police cooperation to prevent and combat international crime. Both the Universal Postal Union and the International Telecommunication Union are today UN agencies, and Interpol has become one of the largest international organizations.

@ Online, look up the most recent activities of the Universal Postal Union, the International Telecommunication Union, and Interpol. Are they useful and practical? Do countries need these organizations, or can they coordinate their legal efforts independently?

FROM THE LEAGUE OF NATIONS TO THE UNITED NATIONS

The League of Nations officially came into existence in January 1920. This was the first global organization, as you will remember from Chapter 3, born out of practical calculations and idealist thinking. The League's structure included the Council (its top executive body, with both permanent and nonpermanent members), the Assembly (which included all representatives), and the Secretariat (playing supporting and administrative functions). Autonomous but closely connected to the League were the Permanent Court of International Justice and the International Labour Organization. The League also operated several committees and commissions on health, refugees, slavery, and other issues (Henig 2010). It had some success in taking care of refugees fleeing wars and revolutions, settling some international disputes, and fighting slavery. Unfortunately, the League's inability to stop several wars in Africa, Europe, and the Pacific undermined its authority; and during World War II the League of Nations was replaced by the United Nations.

The term *United Nations* was coined by U.S. president Franklin D. Roosevelt. On January 1, 1942, representatives of twenty-six states signed the Declaration of the United Nations and pledged to continue fighting together against Nazi Germany, fascist Italy, and imperial Japan (Schlesinger 2003). In 1945, representatives of fifty countries met in San Francisco to draw up the UN Charter, signed on June 26, and the United Nations officially came into existence on October 24. Membership was open to all states that accepted the charter. The first session of the General Assembly of the United Nations convened in March

On the companion website, read more about the ICJ, composed of fifteen judges elected to nine-year terms by the United Nations General Assembly and the Security Council.

1946 in London, with representatives of fifty-one states. In 1952 the UN moved to its new headquarters in New York City.

From the start, the UN Charter and decisions of the United Nations, its agencies, and affiliated international organizations became an important source of international law. The United Nations does not have legislative power to enact binding rules of international law. It cannot force countries to change their domestic laws. However, its recommendations have been crucial to the development of international principles of human rights and their defense. The United Nations created the International Court of Justice (ICJ), located in The Hague, to resolve legal disagreements submitted by states. Its role is "to settle legal disputes submitted to it by States and to give advisory opinions on legal questions deferred to it by authorized United Nations organs and specialized agencies."

CHECK YOUR KNOWLEDGE

▶ Explain the *freedom of the seas* principle of international relations.
▶ What are crimes against humanity?
▶ Why did the League of Nations fail?
▶ What is the International Court of Justice?

Arguments

The Realist View of International Law

The realist approach to international law makes several interconnected assumptions. First, sovereign states by definition have no higher authority over them—not even international law. Second, international law can regulate relations among states, but it should not undermine a sovereign country's core interests, including security. Finally, without proper enforcement, international law is simply ineffective (Morgenthau 2006). Because the task of enforcement cannot be granted to a global organization (as you should remember, realists believe that sovereign states have no authority above them), individual countries and their coalitions should remain the guarantors of global security. (See Figure 6-2.)

FIGURE 6-2 The realist view of international law.

The realist approach does not advocate lawlessness. The anarchical nature of today's global international system, realists argue, makes international law important, but also difficult to implement. To be effective, realists argue, international law should be considered in each of the contexts we have mentioned: state sovereignty, state interest, and means of enforcement.

SOVEREIGNTY

Imagine for a moment that the United Nations passes a resolution outlawing the death penalty in all countries, once and for all. Does this mean that sovereign states recognizing capital punishment must now follow this new international law? Realists dismiss this possibility, because the UN has neither jurisdiction nor power to enforce such a resolution. Each state is bound only by those rules of international law to which it has consented (Vattel 2001). Thus Israel could accept or reject the ICJ's decision about its security barrier, discussed at the start of this chapter, because it is a sovereign country. Moral objections to Israel's policies are a separate issue.

In cases of aggression, realists continue, the victim state does not have an obligation to consult with international law about how to respond. It has the right to defend itself and to seek help from others. Nor does a state have an obligation to defend other states in the absence of a defense agreement. The United States must defend Japan against aggression because of agreements signed between these two countries. But no international law can compel, for instance, Poland or Ukraine to send their armed forces to defend one another.

STATE INTEREST

The goal of the 1997 Kyoto climate change conference was to commit governments to reduce greenhouse gas emissions. Although the United States signed this agreement, it has not been submitted to the Senate for *ratification*, or approval, because of strong domestic political opposition.

Governments typically reject any international law that may undermine their interests or impose undesirable legal, financial, or other obligations. Realists believe that states have the right to choose their own policies toward international organizations, including the United Nations. The main provisions of certain international laws are ambiguous exactly because they leave room for states to interpret them in the way they want, to avoid conflict with opposition at home or from other states (Morgenthau 1978). Governments, as a rule, condemn violations of international law highly selectively. When such violations do not affect a country's national interest, these breaches are routinely ignored. After the attacks of 9/11, the United States removed sanctions on Pakistan and India that had been imposed earlier against their developing nuclear weapons. Washington needed help from Pakistan, but the sanctions were removed from both countries to avoid objections from India (Sathasivam 2005).

LAW ENFORCEMENT

International law can be enforced under certain conditions. For instance, decisions of international organizations could be enforced by **international mandate**, or legal permission to administer a territory or enforce international law.

international mandate Legal permission to administer a territory or enforce international law.

CASE IN POINT > *The International Criminal Court*

The International Criminal Court (ICC) is the first permanent international world court. It was established less than two decades ago to try individuals accused of war crimes, crimes against humanity, genocide, and aggression. However, the 2002 *American Service Members' Protection Act* (ASPA) limits U.S. government support and assistance to the ICC because the court does not sufficiently protect constitutional rights of U.S. citizens working and serving abroad (Elsea 2006). This U.S. policy has enthusiastic supporters and avid critics. Supporters argue that this court's jurisdiction could indeed violate constitutional rights of Americans, including protection from double jeopardy, trial by a jury of one's peers, and the right to confront one's accuser. Critics maintain that the United States upholds double standards on international behavior: It advocates international criminal justice for others, but refuses to subject its own officials and citizens to the same rules. Although the United States participates in the Court's activities and ongoing prosecutions, Washington has no intention to join the ICC (Simons 2013).

CRITICAL THINKING

❶ In your view, should there be a uniform, global standard of justice that every country must follow? If no, why? ❷ If yes, how would you as president reconcile the Court's jurisdiction (the applicability of it decisions in other countries) with the Constitution of the United States? ❸ Is a compromise between the U.S. Constitution and the ICC possible, and if so, what would it look like?

In the 1920s, France and Great Britain, the two most powerful members of the League of Nations at that time, established such mandates to rule on a vast area of the former Ottoman Empire. The territories where now you find Iraq, Palestine, Israel, and Jordan were entrusted to Great Britain. France took control of Lebanon and Syria. Under the assumption that the people of those territories were not ready to govern themselves, the French and British governments declared the legal right to "administrative advice and assistance." This system of mandates survived World War II, but by now almost all mandated territories have become sovereign states. These days, the United Nations issues international mandates for its peacekeeping missions.

The Liberal View of International Law

The liberal tradition challenges realpolitik and pays more attention to the advantages and opportunities provided by international law. It makes three main arguments, and we'll look at each in turn. First, states, like individuals, are capable of managing their relations based on shared principles. Second, international institutions can play a bigger legal role in international affairs by applying the principles of extraterritoriality and supranationalism. Last but not least, a state's claims of a legal right to wage war should be limited, as well as a state's sovereignty to commit atrocities against its people. (See Figure 6-3.)

REASON AND SHARED PRINCIPLES

International law, liberalism argues, is not an artificial creation of lawyers and politicians. It addresses our common and compatible needs that cement the fabric of international relations.

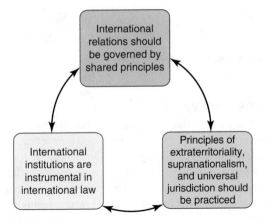

FIGURE 6-3 The liberal view of international law.

Interdependence, mutual consent, and legal obligations are the products of common reason backed by common law (Gruber 2000). For instance, the laws that regulate our lives do not rely on coercion alone. Most people observe domestic criminal laws not only because they are afraid of jails or expect retribution from their neighbors. They accept the law mostly out of a sense of social duty, shared rules, and moral principles. True, some citizens commit illegal acts and, if caught and convicted, pay penalties. Yet in general even laws that carry little threat of sanction for their violation are observed.

States and international organizations, for similar reasons, tend to observe international law. Like domestic common law, international customary law is supported by daily, habitual, and voluntary transactions. International finance, trade, and commerce all work because they are based on international rules without which the global economy could not function—especially given the growing complexity of global interdependence. International law thus becomes an increasingly practical alternative to local laws, which are enforceable only within a limited territory.

EXTRATERRITORIALITY AND SUPRANATIONALISM

If sovereign states exercise supreme authority within their territories, what legal argument can be made in support of international law? The liberal view invokes the principle of **extraterritoriality**, or exemption from the jurisdiction of local law. In the past, some foreign residents living in certain areas were free from the jurisdiction of local courts. Merchants from Genoa and Venice who traveled to Istanbul, for example, were exempted by the Ottoman rulers from following the Sharia, or Islamic law. Similarly, many Americans lived in China under a combination of U.S., European, and local ordinances (Scully 2001). Today, extraterritoriality applies to heads of states, diplomatic missions, and foreign military bases.

extraterritoriality
Exemption from the jurisdiction of local law.

Supporters of the liberal view further argue that, with the advancement of international organizations, ever-increasing travel, international commerce, and electronic communications, territoriality becomes increasingly difficult to enforce. The sheer necessities of our daily interactions will encourage states and businesses to turn to extraterritoriality.

DEBATE > WHY CAN'T WE OUTLAW WAR?

Could the United Nations pass an international law to ban wars altogether? Realists use history to argue that such a law would be ineffective unless it is enforced. A 1928 international agreement known as the Pact of Paris (or Kellogg-Briand Pact) was signed by fifteen nations, including Canada, France, Germany, Great Britain, India, Japan, South Africa, and the United States. The agreement stated that war should be abolished forever as a means of resolving international conflicts. Yet it remained empty without proper enforcement.

Right after the Pact of Paris was signed, the U.S. Senate ratified the treaty. However, the lawmakers made it clear that the United States would not be compelled to use force against countries that violate the treaty. In other words, Washington promised not to punish future aggressors, and so aggressive wars could continue. And they did. In the 1930s, the world community did not stop aggression by Japan against China, Italy against Ethiopia, or the Soviet Union against Finland (Oppenheim 2008). The League of Nations could not stop hostilities between Paraguay and Bolivia. International law enforcement became, under the critical eye of

realists, a serious problem of international law.

WHAT'S YOUR VIEW?

Let's assume that next year most countries of the United Nations, including the United States, agree to legally ban wars between states altogether. Based on what you have read, argue in favor of one of these positions:

Ⓐ The global legal ban on war not only is possible, it will be successfully implemented. Suggest several conditions under which this law would be effective. For example, which country or organization could be capable of enforcing this law and how? Ⓑ The global legal ban on war is absolutely unrealistic. Explain why is this law impossible and impractical.

Important: In the course of discussion, try not to defeat the opposing point of view; instead, try to reconcile arguments A and B, finding a reasonable compromise.

@ The Office of the Historian of the U.S. Department of State provides information about earlier legal attempts to outlaw war.

The signing of the Kellogg-Briand Pact in 1928, which renounced aggressive war and prohibited the use of war as an instrument of national policy except in matters of self-defense. Despite their support of the pact, German, Italian, and Soviet leaders started aggressive wars in the next decade.

Liberal theorists understand that lack of enforcement is a major weakness of international law. Therefore, liberalism turns to **supranationalism**—the delegation of authority from sovereign states to international institutions or organizations. Supranationalism does not mean that states give up their sovereignty once and for all. They merely delegate some of their sovereignty to an international institution that assumes the role of a supranational power (Close 2000). Such an institution can regulate international relations based on shared principles, which can be expanded or amended as needed. The European Union, for example, has a long history of such gradual changes and legal adjustments (Mak 2008).

supranationalism
International treaties, international customary law, and general principles of law recognized by civilized nations.

UNIVERSAL JURISDICTION

The arguments about human rights discussed earlier advanced the idea about international law allowing interference with the affairs of states engaged in massive and systematic human-rights violations. Liberalism advanced the concept of **universal jurisdiction**: Government officials and political leaders— even individuals with diplomatic immunity—who are perpetrators of heinous crimes against their own people should not escape justice when they leave their countries. Universal jurisdiction justifies their arrest and extradition. Although a country's government is typically not liable for crimes committed in its name, individuals such as politicians or military commanders who commit certain acts can be held personally liable. In the past, a similar concept, *hostes humani generis* ("enemies of the human race"), was applied to pirates, hijackers, or hostage takers operating outside any state's jurisdiction. In recent times, former Chilean dictator Augusto Pinochet, former head of Yugoslavia Slobodan Milošević, and the president of Sudan Omar al-Bashir have been legally charged for human rights violations they committed in their countries. We look in depth at their cases and others at the end of this chapter, and we return more broadly to humanitarian issues in Chapter 10.

Sudanese President Omar al-Bashir addresses Parliament in Khartoum in 2013. Al-Bashir has been legally charged for human rights violations committed in his country.

THE LEGALITY OF WAR

Liberalism refers to the principles of "just war" as a means to limit violence in international affairs. What are these principles? First, only sovereign states may pursue their strategic goals by the means of war. Second, war is justified only when it is based on the principle of proportionality in the use of force. Third, even if two states are at war, they should respect humanitarian concerns for honesty and mercy (Lauterpacht [1933] 2011). Liberalism also argues that wars can be significantly limited if sovereign states turned to the principles of international law to justify war. Countries may start wars in self-defense, but they may not use aggression, to which international law gives special attention.

universal jurisdiction   The principle that the perpetrators of certain crimes cannot escape justice by moving to another country and invoking its sovereign immunity.

Aggression is an attack by a state aiming at retribution, territorial expansion, or conquest. In 1974 a UN special committee named seven offenses falling in this category. (See Figure 6-4.) However, if these actions are sanctioned by the United Nations, they are not considered aggression.

aggression   An attack by a state aiming at retribution, expansion, or conquest.

Supporters of the liberal tradition do not rule out war. States may use violence as their last resort or if they are under attack. Any use of force, in their

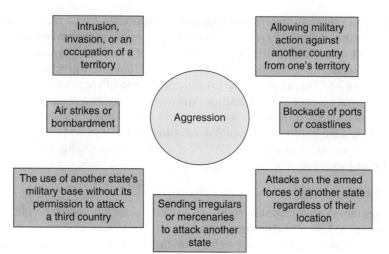

FIGURE 6-4
Aggression as defined by the United Nations.

opinion, is justified to restrain an aggressor or to stop systematic and deliberate violence, especially against ethnic or religious groups. Compelling legal arguments, however, are needed to sanction military intervention. The Charter of the United Nations (Chapter VII) suggests three conditions necessary for the use of military force: threats to peace, breaches of the peace, or acts of aggression.

CHECK YOUR KNOWLEDGE

▶ How can the principle of universal jurisdiction be applied to you personally? Under what conditions?
▶ Why has the United States never joined the International Criminal Court?
▶ Have there been any legal attempts to ban war globally? If so, name one.
▶ Explain universal jurisdiction. Give one example.

Constructivism and Other Views of International Law

Supporters of other approaches share some assumptions with the realist and liberal traditions. However, they pay most attention to specific factors and contexts to explain international law.

CONSTRUCTIVISM'S VIEW OF IDEOLOGY AND LAW

States have their own expectations and create their own norms when it comes to international law. Revolutionary governments or radical movements usually reject the existing norms; their key goal is to change the system, not to uphold it. The leaders of the French Revolution in the late eighteenth century denounced the Westphalian *balance of power* system and sought to liberate Europe from royal tyranny in the name of universal rights. After the Russian revolution in 1917, the Bolshevik government canceled unilaterally all international treaties that the Russian Empire had previously signed.

Ideology and values are another important factor; driven by them, states can reject or embrace international agreements and organizations. For example, NATO, as a defense organization, rested on more than a shared perception of the Soviet threat. Gradually, NATO members, different as they were, developed a common understanding of international law, based on respect for national sovereignty and respect for plurality of opinions. This ideology cemented the alliance for many years (Schmidt 2001). Advocates of NATO insist that today it has a greater goal than common defense: It supports a community of legal norms, based on common values.

Constructivists also argue that the common values of social improvement and the desire to eliminate hunger and diseases, and to stop genocide, could serve as a foundation for an efficient international legal system. The challenge is to agree on such goals and their implementation.

PERCEPTIONS OF INTERNATIONAL LAW

A key argument of constructivism is that international law is based on shared values and perceptions. Here constructivists turn to political psychology to interpret those factors (Reus-Smit 2009). For example, the United Nations gives a general definition of aggression, but leaders may interpret aggression according to their own interests. They often claim to initiate hostile actions as an act of self-defense; in this way, they hope to avoid sanctions against them.

NATO's 1999 war in Kosovo illustrates the importance of perceptions in international law. Here a group of countries challenged the right of Serbia to retain the territories of the former Yugoslavia. In the eyes of Serbia, however, NATO countries were attacking its sovereignty within its legitimate borders. The Serbian military sought to restore control over the province of Kosovo and to defeat the Kosovo Liberation Army, which was composed of Albanian fighters who often acted violently against the Serbian population. The Clinton administration and the governments of other NATO countries rejected Serbia's explanations. They accused Serbia of aggression against the Albanians, who were the ethnic majority in Kosovo, and demanded that the Serbian army stay out of this region. When the UN Security Council couldn't pass a resolution to approve international sanctions or military action because of opposition from Russia and China, NATO bombed Serbia. To justify war, Washington claimed that Serbian officials had initiated a terror campaign against ethnic Albanians, and air strikes were the only option to stop genocide (Ramet 2005). Serbia, Russia, and China sharply disagreed. They claimed that accusations of human-rights violations should not allow international law to trample laws of sovereign states. In fact, the number of refugees and casualties among Albanians and Serbs substantially increased as a result of NATO bombing campaign. In Russia's opinion, NATO created a precedent: Any states or groups of states now could justify their aggression by humanitarian reasons. To Serbia, human-rights violations in Kosovo took place precisely as a result of the NATO's strikes.

What was the most important outcome of this conflict? An independent state in Kosovo was created in 2008, protected by NATO troops. Thousands of ethnic Serbians were forced out of Kosovo by the Albanian forces. More than one hundred and ten countries including the United States and Canada had recognized Kosovo by 2015. The 1999 events in the former Yugoslavia are just one dramatic example of different interpretations of and disputes over international law and universal jurisdiction. (Compare again the views of NATO, Russia, and Serbia.)

Russian authorities explicitly used the Kosovo case as a legal precedent to justify war against neighboring Georgia in 1988; they claimed that they were protecting an endangered ethnic region of South Ossetia from Georgia's armed forces. Russian authorities later recognized South Ossetia and Abkhazia, another ethnic enclave of Georgia, as two sovereign territories. Again, Moscow was citing Kosovo's independence as a legal precedent to justify Russia's actions. The United States and other NATO countries denounced this behavior as a violation of Georgia's sovereignty and claimed that the two cases were different. The vast majority of countries did not recognize South Ossetia and Abkhazia as sovereign states.

 An article in *The Economist* presents the opinions from both sides but argues that the cases of Kosovo and Ossetia are dissimilar: "South Ossetia is not Kosovo," August 28, 2008. See the companion website.

CONFLICT THEORIES

Conflict theories maintain that international law is, for the most part, a convenient instrument to serve the interests of powerful social groups. For Marxists, governments, corporations, banks, and even big international organizations create legal rules that benefit mostly the rich (Miéville 2006). The entire international legal system is designed to maintain the economic and political superiority of a few West European and North American states at the expense of the rest of the world. For example, with the exception of China, all permanent members of the UN Security Council are nuclear states of Europe and America.

South Ossetian separatist fighters rest during the Russian-Georgian war of 2008. Russia supported ethnic separatists and defeated Georgia, which wanted to rout them. This war raised serious tensions in the relations between Russia and NATO.

Although international humanitarian law made significant progress, powerful states and groups pay only selective attention to violations.

Theories of racial and ethnic prejudice make similar points but from a different perspective. Instead of pointing to class interests, they insist that, deliberately or not, international law is consistently used to promote the interests of the privileged countries of Europe, North America, and Japan. The big powers support international law so long as it does not threaten the status quo—and their superiority (Blanchard 1996). These powers generally reject any attempt to give more power to countries in South and Southeast Asia, Africa, and Latin America. They are unwilling, for example, to reform the United Nations and other international organizations, and they often abuse the principle of universal jurisdiction to justify acts against less powerful states. As an illustration, in 1984 the International Court of Justice held the United States responsible for violating international law by an armed rebellion against the Nicaraguan government and by mining the country's harbors. Washington blocked the

---

DEBATE > FROM KOSOVO TO THE RUSSIAN-UKRAINIAN CONFLICT

On February 21, 2014, Ukrainian president Viktor Yanukovych fled the capital city, Kiev, in the aftermath of violent unrest. Suddenly, the opposition was in power in Ukraine. A few days later, Russian armed units—they were without insignias, yet it was a generally accepted view that they were Russian troops—swiftly occupied strategic locations across Ukraine's Crimean Peninsula (Crimea), including airports, television stations, and the parliament buildings. A referendum on whether to join Russia was quickly held on March 16, and the voting results supported seceding. Two days later, Russian president Vladimir Putin signed a law making Crimea and the city of Sevastopol, a naval base located on the peninsula, part of the Russian Federation. The West denounced this move as an annexation of the territory of a sovereign country. To the West, this was a fundamental violation of

international law, of treaties that Russia had signed with Ukraine, and of the Budapest memorandum of 1994, in which the United States, the United Kingdom, France and Russia pledged to respect Ukraine's territorial integrity.

WHAT'S YOUR VIEW?

Russia insists that the unification of Crimea with Russia was perfectly legal and should not be called "annexation," which is the forcible takeover of another country's territory. Russia also insists that it was the will of the people that provided the legal foundation for the unification. Moreover, Russians compared the case of Crimea with the case of Kosovo, in which the people voted to secede from Yugoslavia. The West had supported this decision. Moscow also argued that after Yanukovych's flight from Kiev, there was not a legitimate government in Ukraine, so Russia was protecting

the Russian-speaking minorities in Crimea against possible violence.

Most Western leaders, IGOs, NGOs, and independent observers disagreed. They declared the referendum invalid because of Russia's military pressure and because the referendum violated the Ukraine's constitution. A wide range of international sanctions against Russia followed.

❶ As a lawyer, argue the case on behalf of Russia and on behalf of the United States, which opposes Moscow's position. ❷ As an independent legal observer, which position do you think appears stronger from the perspective of international law? Why? ❸ Which arguments not mentioned here could both sides use to strengthen their arguments? ❹ Could you suggest a legal compromise? Discuss its applicability today.

enforcement of this decision using its veto power in the UN Security Council (Schulte 2005).

From the feminist perspective, gender relations are an integral part of international politics and international law (True 2009). Historically, international law was based on an exclusively masculine perspective focusing on power, the use of force, and ultimately war. Women's expectations and values were commonly excluded, or their importance was diminished, in early legal agreements among states. Significant progress was made in the past century to promote legal foundations for gender equality, civil rights, and humanitarian issues. The law specifically protects women as victims of violence during ethnic and social conflicts. However, international law does not go far enough in protecting the rights of women globally. Segregation, sex exploitation, slavery, and systematic abuse continue. In many countries, women are routinely denied the same legal protection that men receive. Often these violations are explained by local authorities as cultural traditions, and the extraterritoriality principle of international law is ignored (Chappel 2008). Feminist scholars underline the importance of extraterritoriality in support of *care ethics* in international relations, which focuses on the responsibility for all for the suffering of human beings and, to a lesser degree, for all issues related to state sovereignty and power.

CHECK YOUR KNOWLEDGE

▶ Why are perceptions of international law important in international relations?

▶ What were the most significant outcomes of the Kosovo conflict in relation to international law?

▶ What is care ethics in international relations?

Contexts and Applications

The Individual Decisions Context

It takes individual leaders to initiate, interpret, and enforce international law. They may see direct personal benefits from the application of international law to their countries' foreign policy. In the past, neither realism nor liberalism paid enough attention to the role of individuals. Constructivism provides important insights here.

POLITICAL AUTHORITY

autocratic rulers
Leaders who use unlimited power and who follow international and domestic law only if it suits them.

The political authority exercised by leaders at home often shapes their attitudes about international law, treaties, and bilateral agreements. **Autocratic rulers**, who claim unlimited power, typically follow international and domestic law only when it suits them. They often refer to a sense of mission, religion, or ideology to justify their actions. Mobutu Sese Seko, the ruler of Zaire (today part of the Congo) from 1965 to 1997, declared that "democracy is not for Africa." He also rejected democratic principles of government at home, allowed his associates to violate business agreements with foreign companies, illegally redistributed the resources of foreign companies, and imprisoned opponents without a trial (Wrong 2002).

An extreme form of autocratic ruler is a **tyrant**—another word for a dictator. Like Hitler and Stalin, tyrants are not constrained by laws, not even those they themselves impose. They use unlimited power to oppress the people of their own country or its foreign possessions (Wallechinsky 2006). Saddam Hussein of Iraq and Kim Jong-il of North Korea can be also regarded as dictators for their brutal and illegal policies. These examples may suggest a major weakness of international law: Many autocratic rulers in the past simply ignored international agreements and global conventions, especially when it comes to human rights (Burt 2010).

Democratic leaders, by contrast, tend to pursue their policies within the framework of domestic and international law. Their behavior thus provides support for democratic peace theory and the liberal approach to international relations. However, contemporary developments in many countries present a significant challenge to this view. Some authoritarian leaders, as we saw in Chapter 3, run for elections and allow limited civic freedoms in their countries. Other leaders make a travesty of elections and democratic procedures at home, creating a "hybrid" regime that combines democratic legitimacy with authoritarian practices. In their foreign policy, they are likely to take a cynical view of international norms and treat international law arbitrarily, according to little more than immediate interests (Singh 2010). Yet other leaders may use authoritarian means domestically but respect international law, as happened in Egypt in 2013 when the military dismissed the country's elected president.

Go online to find the current Democracy Index compiled by *The Economist*, listing the world's most authoritarian countries. Try to establish which countries on this list have friendly relations with the United States. Does Washington support most of them or only a few of them?

tyrant A ruler who uses unlimited power to oppress the people of the ruler's country or its foreign possessions.

democratic leaders Leaders who treat the letter and spirit of the law as the core of their domestic policy and, in most circumstances, foreign policy.

Dictator of Zaire Mobutu Sese Seko (1930–1997) routinely ignored international agreements on human rights. Dictators pose significant challenges to international law because frequently, they simply disregard it.

The State Policies Context

Realists argue, most often correctly, that states treat international law in the context of domestic politics, policy, and security strategies. For example, South Africa, Israel, India, and Pakistan refused to sign a nonproliferation treaty and North Korea withdrew from it mostly because the treaty would have placed legal restrictions on their development of nuclear weapons. In another case, take Article 2(4) of the UN Charter, which tells all states to refrain from the use of force that violates the territorial integrity or political independence of another country. Two exceptions exist: the UN Security Council's authorization or self-defense. However, the last sixty years show that democratic governments do not necessarily follow Article 2, which prohibits violence, but turn instead to Article 1 of the UN Charter, which allows the prevention and removal of threats to the peace (Loyola 2010). In other words, countries often choose legal uncertainties and contradictions to justify their policies including war.

INTERNATIONAL LAW AND THE UNITED STATES

The U.S. president or secretary of state may not enter into obligations to other nations that are binding on Congress. The constitutional powers of the legislature cannot be given away to other branches of the government, and Congress may or may not ratify a treaty. Ever since the Jay Treaty (named after Chief Justice John Jay) in 1795, a treaty requires a two-thirds vote in the U.S. Senate. The rules are a bit easier for trade deals; for them, *executive agreements* need only a majority vote in both houses of Congress. Sometimes, when opposition in the legislature is strong, as it was in 2015 against a massive trade pact with Pacific nations known as the Trans-Pacific Partnership, the executive branch may not want to engage in a political battle. The Clinton administration, for instance, did not push for ratification of the 1997 Kyoto Protocol to fight global gas emissions. But even after Congress ratifies a treaty, the legislature can render it ineffective by not allocating funds—or by attaching restrictions on how funds are to be used (Grimmett 1999).

Presidents may also reconsider their position on international law under pressure from Congress or constituencies. In 1993, President Clinton pledged to link trade to China's policies toward human rights, in compliance with the U.S. Trade Act. However, Clinton turned away from his pledge as opposition grew, thanks to growing profits from trade and investments, as well as increasing consumer reliance on inexpensive goods manufactured in China.

Conflicts can also arise between U.S. and international law. We have already reviewed Washington's reluctance to fully participate in the International Criminal Court. Some U.S. federal laws may be inconsistent with international laws. For example, section 201 of the 1974 Trade Act states that the president may impose temporary trade barriers if an increase in imports would hurt domestic industry. Such actions may violate the rules of the World Trade Organization prohibiting trade barriers. However, because of powerful lobbies and the need to get the votes of people with manufacturing jobs, presidents from time to time impose trade barriers to help certain domestic industries including steel and tire manufacturing. International law is pushed aside to pursue domestic goals.

At other times, conflict with U.S. law may mean that a treaty's ratification is postponed indefinitely (Moravcsik 2001). Congress did not ratify the American Convention on Human Rights, signed by President Carter, because it challenged federal and state laws by placing serious restrictions on abortion rights and implementation of the death penalty. Even existing agreements may be reconsidered. For example, the Optional Protocol to the Vienna Convention on Consular Relations lets the International Court of Justice make the final decision when citizens have been illegally detained abroad. The United States initially backed the measure as a means to protect its own citizens overseas. It successfully sued Iran for taking fifty-two hostages from the embassy in Tehran in 1979. But the United States withdrew from the accord in 2005 after some countries that had abolished capital punishment successfully complained before the ICJ that their citizens were sentenced to death in the United States. The U.S. State Department argued that international law might interfere with domestic criminal law (Jordan 2005).

Finally, some agreements are signed but later rejected for apparent irrelevance or ambiguity. The Convention on the Elimination of All Forms of Discrimination Against Women disallows all forms of exploitation of women and girls; it also guarantees equal access to education, employment, and health care. The Senate has held hearings on this agreement several times since 1980 but failed each time to bring the treaty to a vote (Baldez 2013). Why didn't the United States ratify this treaty? Both Republican and Democratic administrations argued that U.S. law already protects against discrimination, whereas women in other countries have little or no legal protection. Declarations without proper global enforcement, they declared, are useless and often counterproductive (Kirkpatrick 2002). Signing the treaty has not prevented many countries from violating most basic of women's rights. (See Figure 6-5.)

 On the companion website, learn more about international treaties signed by the United States but later delayed or not ratified by Congress. See how domestic politics and law affect international agreements.

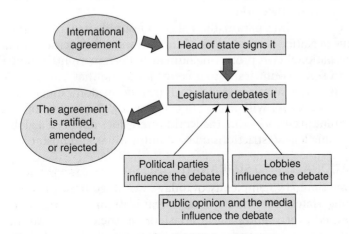

FIGURE 6-5 Domestic factors and international treaties. In most democratic countries, international agreements signed by executive leaders must be approved (ratified) by the legislation. Influenced by political, economic, and other interests, legislators may approve, amend, or reject treaties.

The Global Context

For centuries, international law was instrumental in economic exchanges between states, organizations, and individuals. (We return to economic issues in the next chapter.) International agreements have settled many territorial disputes and probably prevented many wars. The laws of war—especially those dealing with the humane treatment of civilians, captured or wounded soldiers, and nonmilitary personnel—have saved millions of lives. International agreements today protect travel, property, family rights, due process, and the well-being of many around the world. Studies show that under the right conditions, international law becomes a more powerful force than military action in bringing stability, order, and peaceful change (Huth et al. 2011).

What are other signs of the global impact of international law? International law concerning genocide and war crimes continues to attract attention. The creation of the International Criminal Tribunal for the former Yugoslavia (ICTY) in 1993 in The Hague was a remarkable event. The idea came from German foreign minister Klaus Kinkel, and Resolution 827 of the UN Security Council created the institution. The court has jurisdiction over certain crimes committed on the territory of Croatia, Bosnia, and Herzegovina, which were parts of the disintegrated Yugoslav state after 1991. The court hired its staff from many countries.

The ICTY served a model for the second similar tribunal—the International Criminal Tribunal for Rwanda (ICTR). It was created in 1994 by the UN Security Council (Resolution 955) to prosecute those responsible for the mass killings and violence in Rwanda during a civil war there. Because the continuing tensions in Rwanda make fair decisions based on domestic law almost impossible, it was imperative to apply international law under the watch of the ICTR.

Although critics rightly complain about the high cost and bureaucratic inefficiency of international courts, these institutions were generally successful. They gave many victims an opportunity to seek justice. Most governments and millions of people around the world support the courts' work and consider them legitimate. Carla del Ponte, a former Swiss attorney general who served as prosecutor for ICTY and ICTR, became one of the most recognized and respected lawyers in the world.

On the companion website, read more about Carla del Ponte and her work.

The success of international law should not hide its failures and excesses. The League of Nations ended up as a failure. Wars and atrocities still take place. Many international laws protecting human rights remain little more than declarations in some countries. Other countries argue that human rights violations just give the West an excuse to intervene in domestic affairs of other sovereign states (as we will discuss in Chapter 10). Opponents of "big government" at home argue, too, that the world surely does not need a global government imposing legal restrictions on communications and business.

FROM NATIONALISM TO SUPRANATIONALISM

At the same time, the complexity of today's world requires a greater coordination among states and international organizations. Urgent environmental issues, global poverty, and natural disasters—as the events of the past twenty years have shown—demand responses from across the global community.

In The Hague in 1998, Bosnian Serbs accused of serious crimes sit behind their defense lawyers prior to a session at the International Criminal Tribunal for the former Yugoslavia. The court has jurisdiction over certain crimes committed on the territories of Croatia and Bosnia—parts of the pre-1991 Yugoslavia. Since 1994, the Court indicted more than 160 and sentenced more than 65 persons.

So does worldwide financial instability, as demonstrated by the global financial crisis of 2008–2011. It should be imperative to hold global financial actors accountable to certain international rules that should be designed. State bureaucracies remain corrupt and inefficient. These and other trends will almost certainly require strengthening and expanding international law, which also highlights the importance of NGOs and international organizations in a growing number of global issues.

Supporters of supranationalism point to the success of the European Union and the **East African Community** (EAC). In 2000, Tanzania, Uganda, Burundi, Kenya, and Rwanda formed this economic and political union, with the goal of a common market for goods, labor, and capital, a single currency, and one unified federation by 2023 or even earlier. Although a similar plan collapsed back in the 1970s, steps thus far suggest that these countries are on the path to achieve their goal. Most important, the EAC example, if it is a success, should show that the participating countries accept binding legal rules, put aside religious, tribal, and political differences, and move toward a common strategic goal.

East African Community (EAC)
An economic and political union between five countries (Tanzania, Uganda, Burundi, Kenya, and Rwanda).

UNRESOLVED OBSTACLES

The concepts of supranationalism and universal jurisdiction find significant support. They also have been under criticism for some time. Who should implement international law? Critics have complained for some time that too many NGOs and IGOs, staffed by unelected officials, remain slow, expensive, and inefficient (Queenan 2013; Kissinger 2001). Moreover, supporters of conflict theory, including feminist scholars, mention that many NGOs promote an agenda set mostly by the educated upper class from Western countries. Lack of accountability of unelected professionals is yet another problem, even if they act with the best of intentions (Wapner 2002).

Universal jurisdiction, as you remember, assumes that individuals are legally responsible for certain illegal actions regardless of where they live. Critics of universal jurisdiction are skeptical that judicial procedures alone without proper debate will be effective in international politics. Of course, acts of genocide or other blatant human rights violations should not be left unpunished, but only when they are proven and carefully investigated. Otherwise, legal decisions may be motivated by politics or ideology. In other cases, some individuals and organizations may simply misinterpret international law because they are acting out of their own interests (Agier 2010). Moreover, some legal decisions or initiatives can be simply impractical.

Realism provides a strong argument against supranationalism: To be effective, a law must always be enforced. Unfortunately, in many cases, IGOs and NGOs rely instead on goodwill and the expectation that legal norms will be followed. Take global nuclear policies. The Nonproliferation Treaty has slowed the spread of nuclear weapons, but the United Nations has not stopped North Korean and Iranian nuclear programs (Pelligrini 2010).

Another argument against the expansion of international law comes from critics of globalization. They contend that any global law would primarily benefit wealthy countries and big international corporations. Predictions emphasized that the global gap between the rich and the poor would increase. Liberal

CASE IN POINT > *Rwanda and Belgium Law*

A 1993 Belgian war crimes law was aimed at protecting civilians in time of war by relying on the principle of universal jurisdiction. Neither the accused nor the accuser needed to be Belgian citizens for a case to go forward. In addition, anyone could bring a criminal complaint, which a local magistrate was required to investigate to determine whether further action was warranted.

The law was first put to use after mass slaughter in Rwanda, a former Belgian colony. Eric Gillet, a prominent human rights lawyer, filed suit, accusing several Rwandans living in Belgium of horrible war crimes. Soon cases were filed against former Israeli prime minister Ariel

Sharon, then-Iraqi president Saddam Hussein, the late Congolese ruler Laurent Kabila and his foreign minister, Rwandan president Paul Kagame, former Iranian president Ali Akbar Hashemi Rafsanjani, and several generals from Guatemala. Suits were also filed against international oil companies accused of connections with the military rulers of Burma, the Palestinian leader Yasser Arafat, Cuba's president Fidel Castro, and former U.S. president George H. W. Bush. Altogether, according to the Belgian justice ministry, more than thirty complaints were on file.

Things rapidly took an absurd turn. One British citizen arrived at

the Belgian embassy claiming that the BBC, the British Broadcasting Corporation, was seeking to assassinate him. In an attempt to avoid a serious diplomatic crisis and stop frivolous suits, the Belgian government dismissed the law.

CRITICAL THINKING

Can you suggest a few political and legal measures to prevent similar misuses of international legal rulings? Considering this case, would you have imposed high application fees for the plaintiffs to eliminate many frivolous lawsuits? For the same purpose, would you narrow down the definition of a war crime? Discuss these and other possibilities.

democracy of the Western type would be frequently forced on other countries, often against their will and often with counterproductive results. Also, some claim that human rights violations can be used as an excuse to wage aggressive wars (Bricmont 2006).

THE USES OF HISTORY: War Crimes, Genocide, and the Legacy of Nuremberg

Background

Attempts to use international law to stop genocide and limit the deadly effects of war began more than one hundred years ago. These early efforts were ineffective and frustrating from the start. The most significant change took place at the end of World War II.

During World War II, Germany, Japan, and the Soviet Union imposed violence against civilians on a scale unprecedented in modern times. *The Holocaust* (in Hebrew, *Shoah*), which was the deliberate extermination of the Jews by the Nazi government, is one of the most profound cases of genocide in history. At the same time, the Japanese government massacred tens of thousands of civilians in China and was responsible for widespread rape and torture in Nanking in 1937. Soviet authorities deported millions from the annexed territories in the Baltic region and Poland in 1939; they also deported large ethnic groups living in the Crimea and Caucasus in 1944. The German invasion of the Soviet Union that began in June 1941 quickly turned into a genocidal war, in which hundreds of thousands of people of various ethnic groups were massacred. Small states in wartime Yugoslavia also practiced genocide against civilians. British and American carpet bombing of German and Japanese cities and the nuclear attacks on Hiroshima and Nagasaki in 1945 were clear violations of the Hague Conventions as well. The British-American massive bombing campaign aimed at causing unacceptable damage to Germany and Japan, to force unconditional surrender (Hitchcock 2008).

After several meetings, the leaders of the United States, the USSR, and the United Kingdom agreed to hold the political and military leaders of Nazi Germany and imperial Japan responsible for crimes against humanity. But how could the government of a sovereign state be put on trial? The London Charter, announced by the Big Three on August 8, 1945, provided the legal arguments. It stated that the German government had lost its political authority, and the Allied states had the right to establish a special court to apply the laws of war against Germany. The court would have jurisdiction only over crimes that took place after the start of the war in 1939. Legally, the Charter followed up on the decisions of the 1907 Hague Conference. It became the grounds for the Nuremberg trials against Nazi criminals in 1946, with German political leaders charged on four counts:

- *Conspiracy to wage aggressive war*—a premeditated plan to commit war crimes.
- *Crimes against peace*—wars of aggression in violation of international law.
- *War crimes*—profound violations of the laws of war, including mistreatment of prisoners of war and slave labor.
- *Crimes against humanity*—actions in concentration camps and on occupied territories in Europe.

Judges were appointed, defense lawyers hired, and witnesses called. After testimonies and deliberations, the court handed death sentences to eleven top German officials. Two others were acquitted. The rest received long prison sentences.

Analysis

The Nuremberg tribunals had a profound and lasting influence on international law. Similar trials were held in Japan, China, Australia, the Philippines, and other countries. For example, the 1946 International Military Tribunal for the Far East (also known as the Tokyo Trials) sentenced to death seven former top Japanese officials responsible for genocide and seventeen more to lengthy prison terms. In China thirteen separate trials were held. Over five hundred defendants were convicted and 149 executed. Gradually, expanded definitions of war crimes were accepted and agreements to implement them were signed. The United Nations adopted the Convention on the Prevention and Punishment of the Crime of Genocide (General Assembly Resolution 260) in 1948. Based on these international precedents and documents, the term *genocide* entered international law to mean the deliberate extermination or prosecution by any government of national, racial, ethnic, and religious groups—whether in war or in peacetime.

Nuremberg had a lasting impact on international law. The trials initiated a series of developments to establish a permanent international criminal court. (It took almost half a century, though, before its statute was adopted.) The trials also served as a precedent for UN guidelines for determining war crimes. For example, if a country's laws do not impose a penalty for a war crime, this country's officials and even its head of state—if accused of committing war crimes—can be prosecuted under international law. So can ordinary citizens.

Advocates of liberalism and many influential nongovernment organizations have long demanded greater enforcement of international law, including the arrest and prosecution of state leaders who commit war crimes or similar acts. These demands gained momentum in the early 1990s, with support from many states and international organizations including the United Nations, and practical steps followed. The International Criminal Tribunal for the former

Nazi leaders on trial in Nuremberg, Germany, in 1945. The Nuremberg Trials (1945–46) had a profound and lasting influence on international law.

Yugoslavia (ICTY), created under the auspices of the United Nations, during almost a decade of work indicted 161 individuals and sentenced sixty-four. (Three died while serving their sentences.) In 1999, Slobodan Milošević, the former leader of Yugoslavia, was put on trial in The Hague by ICTY. Milošević was charged on sixty-six counts of genocide, crimes against humanity, and war crimes in Croatia, Bosnia and Herzegovina, and Kosovo between 1991 and 1999. The trial lasted four years, and Milošević died in jail in 2006.

The court also focused on atrocities committed by leaders of the paramilitary Bosnian Serbs in Bosnia—including those accused of killings, torture, and running concentration camps. After many years in hiding, the Bosnian Serb commanders Radovan Karadžić, Ratko Mladić, and Goran Hadžić were brought before the court. Their case may be investigated for years before judgment is passed. At the same time, the Tribunal on Rwanda (ICTR), now located in Arusha, Tanzania, finished fifty trials and convicted twenty-nine persons accused of war crimes and crimes against humanity. More trials are in progress.

In 1998, 120 countries adopted the Rome Statute, the legal basis for establishing the International Criminal Court, a permanent institution that "shall have the power to exercise its jurisdiction over persons for the most serious crimes of international concern." The ICC is located in The Hague in the Netherlands and is not part of the United Nations. The Rome Statute went into force in 2002, and the ICC opened investigations in several countries. In 2009

Go online to find current cases at the International Criminal Court.

the ICC brought charges against the president of Sudan, Omar al-Bashir, for crimes against humanity, war crimes, and genocide. Whenever al-Bashir visited another country, he could be arrested and brought to The Hague for justice. In 2011 the Court brought charges against six officials from Kenya over their alleged involvement in the 2007–2008 electoral violence in that country. Some charges were later dropped, but others were sustained.

Realists, of course, have been skeptical about the effectiveness of international law. Yet they supported the Nuremberg trials, because these were initiated and enforced by powerful states—the United States, the USSR, and the UK. Realists note, too, that it took NATO's massive military campaign against Yugoslavia, including the bombing of cities, to put former president Milošević on trial. And al-Bashir, even under formal indictment from the ICC, remained in his country.

During the Nuremberg trials, the Soviet Union used falsified documents to accuse the Nazis of massacring twenty thousand Polish officers in the Katyn Forest in Russia. This crime, as the Russian government acknowledged a few years ago, was in fact committed on Stalin's order by the Soviet secret police (Sanford 2009). The Soviets' own acts of genocide and mass deportations were not so much as mentioned during the Nuremberg trials. Moscow literally got away with murder because it was powerful and victorious.

For all its flaws and inconsistencies, however, the Nuremberg trials have played an important role in the development of international law. They have led to more than sixty years of international agreements. They serve as a model for future international trials as well, based on the principles of extraterritoriality and universal justice. The trials created a *legal precedent*—a ruling that international courts may develop in future prosecutions. Last but not least, Nuremberg gave hope that fundamental rights will be protected and justice will, eventually, be served. (See Figure 6-6.)

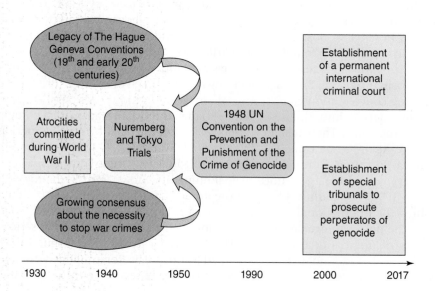

FIGURE 6-6
International law and the legacy of the Nuremberg Trials: A chronological snapshot.

Questions

1. What would you do—as president—to make sure that international tribunals maintain the democratic standard of protection for the individual? In democratic societies, for example, an accused murderer or rapist is only a *suspect*, not a criminal, before conviction in a court of law.

2. Are international tribunals truly impartial? International courts, critics fear, can easily become a stage for *victors' justice*—in which a victorious country applies one set of rules to judge its own actions and applies different rules to judge the defeated enemy. (You have read about the Soviet Union's actions before the Nuremberg trials.) How can the international community make sure that the tribunals are not used to settle political scores with the accused under pressure of influential governments?

3. Would it be beneficial, in your view, to discuss, design, and enforce a new international code of laws, instead of relying on legal precedents from the past? Explain.

CONCLUSION

There is neither a universal world constitution nor written principles suggesting how states should act. No single judge or court is empowered to decide when a state violates international law. As we saw at the start of this chapter, Israel refused to accept the decision of an international court. Still, in many other cases states adhere to legal principles and to agreements with other states or international organizations. Everywhere, treaties are signed, trade agreements are made, and disputes are settled by legal means. Critics of international law stress its vagueness, inconsistency, and biases, along with the frequent objections of individual states. However, the rule of law has made substantial progress during the last century and a half. History shows that law prevails through agreement, and not solely through coercion, because it provides most citizens with a sense of security, brings them hope and stability, and makes the world a more open, free, and comfortable place to live. The world faces an even bigger challenge now: to make these rules work.

KEY TERMS

aggression 201
autocratic rulers 206
customary law 190
democratic leaders 207
East African Community
   (EAC) 211
extraterritoriality 199
freedom of the seas 191

general principles of law 190
genocide 194
human rights 194
international law 187
international mandate 197
international treaties 189
jurisdiction 189

laws of war 192
neutrality 193
sources of international
   law 189
supranationalism 201
tyrant 207
universal jurisdiction 201

Visual Review INTERNATIONAL LAW

IDEAS

KEY CONCEPTS, PRINCIPLES, AND SOURCES OF INTERNATIONAL LAW

- International law refers to principles, rules, and agreements that regulate the behavior of states and other international actors
- Territoriality and jurisdiction principles define how far laws can reach
- Sources of international law: treaties, customary law, general principles of law, and rulings by international organizations and courts

THE DEVELOPMENT OF INTERNATIONAL LAW

- The Treaty of Westphalia established an early foundation of international law in 1648
- The Laws of the Sea dealt with competition, the safety of shipments, and financial disputes
- The Laws of War dealt with common principles that states should follow in case of an armed conflict
- Early international legal institutions and organizations dealt with humanitarian issues and disputes among states

ARGUMENTS

REALISM

- International law should not undermine a sovereign state's key interests
- Without proper enforcement, international law is ineffective

LIBERALISM

- Interdependence, mutual consent, and legal obligations are necessary
- Evolving principles: supranationalism, universal jurisdiction, and extraterritoriality

CONSTRUCTIVISM

- Historical and socioeconomic conditions, values, and identities determine perceptions of international law

OTHER THEORIES

- In conflict theory, international law serves the interests of a few at the expense of others
- In self-organization theory, justice administration and law enforcement require a "world state"

CONTEXTS AND APPLICATIONS

THE INDIVIDUAL DECISIONS CONTEXT

- Leaders' choices strengthen or weaken international law

THE STATE POLICIES CONTEXT

- States treat international law in the context of domestic politics, policy, and security strategies

THE GLOBAL CONTEXT

- Most states have a strong interest in developing and maintaining international legal norms

Critical Thinking

❶ What are the main limitations of international law?
❷ Compare and contrast the realist and liberal views of international law.
❸ Why did Nazi Germany and Imperial Japan withdraw from the League of Nations? Thought experiment: Discuss the consequences of the U.S.'s withdrawal (hypothetical) from the United Nations today.
❹ Give arguments for and against universal jurisdiction.
❺ Suggest examples of extraterritoriality that you find useful and acceptable.

International Political Economy 7

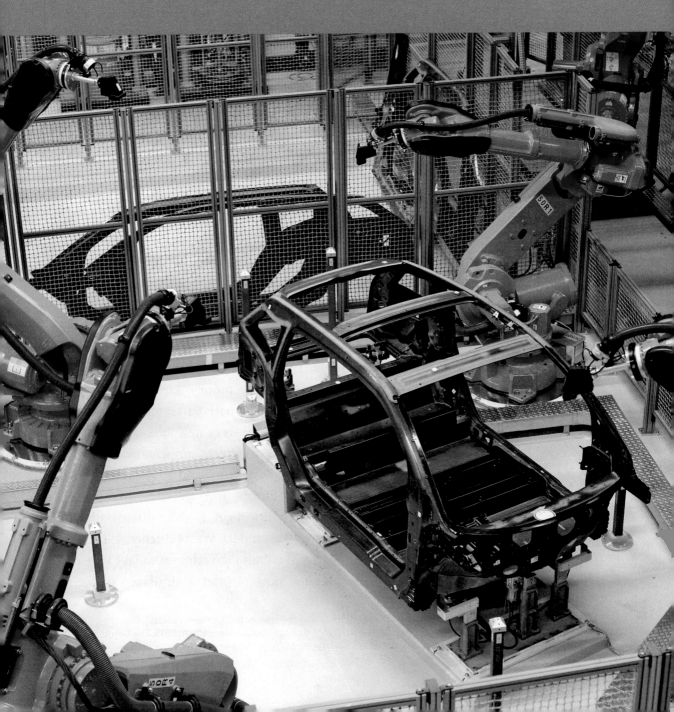

Practical men, who believe themselves to be quite exempt from any intellectual influence, are usually the slaves of some defunct economist.

—JOHN MAYNARD KEYNES

IN 1947, MANY EUROPEAN CITIES LAY IN RUINS AFTER WORLD WAR II. ECONOMIES BEGAN TO REVIVE BUT STILL STRUGGLED. UNEMPLOYMENT WAS RAMPANT. LACK OF FUEL, FOOD, AND clothing was endemic. In France and Italy, the threat of Communist coups grew. Chaos and insecurity reigned from Poland to Greece.

In June of that year, the U.S. secretary of state, George Marshall, announced an assistance program to Europe that became known as the Marshall Plan. In 1948, Congress approved the first $5 billion in aid. By 1952 the United States had spent $13.5 billion in sixteen countries, an equivalent of about $120 billion today. It was a massive "stimulus" to stabilize finances and sustain economic growth, which increased by 35 percent.

Why did Washington provide this help? The ultimate goal of the Marshall Plan was to prevent Communism from spreading over Western Europe. The Marshall Plan was also good for the U.S. economy: Using American money, Europeans began to purchase American equipment, spare parts, technologies, and know-how. Hundreds of thousands of new jobs were created in America. The Plan helped to resurrect European liberal democracy, threatened by hunger, instability, and political radicalism. The plan pulled Western Europe into the U.S. financial and trade orbit, but also the political orbit, and initiated a host of institutions that shaped the modern West (Hitchcock 2008).

Are the lessons of the Marshall Plan relevant today? Why can't today's wealthy economic powers offer a similar plan for the

Previous page: An electric BMW i3 during the start of production in Leipzig, Germany. The i3 was the first electric car put into high-volume production by BMW in 2013. The German automobile industry benefited from the liberal system of trade after World War II.

countries that desperately need investments? Back in the 1940s, European countries receiving American funding mostly decided for themselves how to spend it. They had to comply with only one condition: keep Communists away from power. Now, assistance from the International Monetary Fund (IMF) comes with many strings attached. Should countries themselves, rather than international organizations, decide how to spend such funds? Should they follow the example of the United States and other liberal democracies? China never complied with the IMF regulations yet successfully combined private entrepreneurship with state controls, with remarkable results. (See "The Uses of History" on p. xx.) Can other countries emulate China's success story, or is it unique?

In this chapter, we discuss the economic and financial aspects of international relations. We consider the influence of economic interests on foreign policy agendas; the impact of states and their policies on international economy, finances, and trade; the opportunities and challenges of global economic interdependence; and the problem of wealth and poverty from a global perspective.

Learning Objectives

▶ Explain the major factors of international political economy.
▶ Explain the principles of mercantilism, economic liberalism, constructivism, and conflict theories in the context of international economic policies.
▶ Evaluate the impact of states on the international economy, finances, and trade, as well as the challenges of global economic interdependence.
▶ Apply major economic views to realities of international relations within three contexts of analysis.

Ideas

International political economy (IPE) is the study of how politics and economics interact in an international context. For decades, IPE was considered a less essential field of international relations, less important than security studies or diplomacy. From the end of the Cold War, however, this field rapidly advanced. Successful economic and financial policies—as many realized—are likely to guarantee material security of a country and contribute to international stability

international political economy (IPE) The ways in which politics and economics interact in an international context.

and peace. The failure of such policies could lead to a political and social crisis. Today, with the world so interdependent or "globalized," the financial or economic failure of just one state can have profound international consequences. The crises in the United States in 2008–2011 and the prolonged economic slowdown in the European Union in the second decade of the century created uncertainty and tension in the entire international system.

How do state economic policies affect international relations? Which economic models are most successful in today's global economy and why? To answer these and other questions, political economists analyze such activities as production, consumption, finances, and trade.

The Major Factors of IPE

PRODUCTION AND CONSUMPTION

production The process of creating goods and services with market value.

Economic **production** is the creation of goods and services with market value. For centuries, states accumulated resources and territories to enhance their power. States also controlled, funded, or regulated their productive capacities— from gold mines and oil wells to factories and trade companies. In the modern world, the power of states is measured in the size and growth of their **gross domestic product** (GDP), which is the monetary value of the goods and services produced at a given time. To compare, the GDP of the United States is close to $17 trillion, China's is about $9 trillion, and South Korea's and Mexico's are around $1.3 trillion (World Bank 2015).

gross domestic product (GDP) The total market value of all the goods and services produced within the borders of a nation during a specified period.

In the twenty-first century more production is shifting from older economic powers—the United States, Japan, and Western Europe—toward emerging markets, or countries in the process of rapid economic growth, such as China, India, and Brazil. For the past couple of decades, mainly because of their lower wage costs, these and other countries, such as Malaysia and Chile, have substantially increased their share of global manufacturing, reaching more than half the world's exports. Emerging markets have recently accounted for nearly half of global retail sales, and their share is growing (Woodall 2011).

consumption The selection, adoption, use, disposal, and recycling of goods and services.

A country's power is also inseparable from its scale of **consumption**, which is the selection, adoption, use, disposal, and recycling of goods and services. A country's consumption patterns affect its *imports*, or the products and services it purchases abroad. For example, the United States is the third largest crude oil producer in the world. However, through most of the 2000s, about 50 percent of its consumed oil (the United States is the biggest oil consumer in the world) comes from other countries, which creates dependency. This dependency on foreign oil is in sharp decline now, thanks to the innovative oil explorations on U.S. territory. In recent years, more attention has been paid to the byproducts of consumption—*waste* and *pollution*, which have become global problems. China still lags behind major developed countries in consumption, but its industries became major polluters (Economy and Levi 2014; Economy 2010b).

FINANCES

Historically a state's financial resources, or *finances*, consisted of gold reserves, stored in well-protected places (e.g., Fort Knox in the United States). The more gold a country had, the more power it was thought to possess. These days, finances most often mean the value of stocks and bonds traded on markets, and financial wealth is measured in paper notes or more complex indicators, tracked electronically and up to the minute.

For centuries, states sought to control and augment their finances. Financially wealthy states could pay for a large military force and lend money to other states in exchange for political favors and loyalty. Great Britain dominated the world financial system in the nineteenth and first half of the twentieth century, but it lost much of its wealth during World War II and dismantled its vast empire shortly after. The United States assumed the dominant financial role in the 1940s. Today it is still the wealthiest nation in the world by many standards, but over the last decade its expenses have surpassed revenues, and the U.S. dollar now depends on the financial

Anti-austerity protest in Rennes, France, in 2015. Approximately 2,500 protesters were on the streets. The EU financial crisis put governments of individual member-countries between angry citizens and strict demands from Germany and the EU bureaucracy in Brussels.

backing of China. China, in turn, needs a stronger U.S. economy capable of paying the debt back to China. World finances are now so complicated that no state can manage and regulate them alone.

National **currencies**—dollars, euros, yuan, pesos, and rubles—can be converted into other currencies at what is called an *exchange rate*. From 1945 until 1971 the value of the U.S. dollar was fixed to the price of gold (the so-called gold standard). Now, the dollar and other national currencies fluctuate vis-à-vis each other and gold; their exchange rate depends on many factors, including GDP growth, exports and imports, and political as well as economic events. The consequences of volatility of currency exchange rates may have significant impact on international trade and seriously affect all businesses and ordinary citizens. (See Table 7-1.)

currency The physical component of a country's money supply, comprising coins, paper notes, and government bonds.

TABLE 7-1 Consequences of Shifting U.S. Currency Exchange Rates

International Security Pact	Consequences
More Expensive Than Previously	Good news for people who travel abroad because they can get more for their dollars. However, U.S. products will cost more abroad, and fewer products will be exported. This could easily cause a decrease in production and a loss of jobs in the United States. That's bad news for domestic manufacturers.
Less Expensive Than Previously	Bad news for tourists traveling abroad: They get less for their money. A weaker currency, however, means that U.S. exports can increase as they become less expensive and thus more competitive on the global market. That's good news for domestic manufacturers.

FINANCIAL GLOBALIZATION

The globalization of finances is a developing trend. Countries' economies are becoming more interconnected and the movement of capital across borders is increasing. The effects of financial globalization are yet to be certain. Despite the seeming openness of the financial markets that embrace millions of traders daily, only a few financial centers continue their domination including London, New York, and Hong Kong. Most of us feel the effects of financial globalization when we use our credit cards overseas. Entrepreneurs, too, use electronic international transfers to other banks. On the other hand, the possibilities for fraud and tax evasion have skyrocketed. Also, international terrorist organizations use modern financial transaction methods to finance their activities. To combat tax fraud and other illegal activities, countries introduce tough new regulations thus slowing down the momentum for financial globalization.

Countries have to constantly adapt to the realities of financial globalization. Some governments have powerful financial tools, including interest rates, which banks use to lend money to private citizens and corporations. In 1978, Washington hiked up interest rests to reduce high inflation at home. As a result, other countries and financial organizations, in anticipation of high returns, began to send their money to U.S. banks. Most countries try to adjust to currency exchange rates, which may weaken or strengthen their economies. Some countries used fixed exchange rates to prevent their national currency from fluctuating against other currencies. The goal of this practice is partly to protect the price of the country's products from declining in foreign markets (see the concluding section on China).

TRADE

International trade is another volatile factor in international relations. Under most circumstances, states try to stimulate and expand their exports—goods and services that the country sells officially on the international market. And most states depend on their imports—goods and services that the country has to bring in from outside. The difference between the value of exports and imports is the **balance of trade.** It is positive when exports surpass imports and negative if a country buys more than it sells. Before the 1970s the United States had a positive balance of trade, but it has slipped into an ever-growing trade deficit, largely a result of goods imported from China and the import of oil from the Persian Gulf.

balance of trade
The difference between the size of exports and imports of a country.

Why are trade deficits so important in international relations? For decades, trade imbalances created inequality in the distribution of wealth between wealthy and poor countries. African and most South American countries exported agricultural products and raw materials to developed countries at low prices, whereas the latter exported sophisticated products and services at high prices. As a result, poorer states owed substantial amounts of money to wealthy ones. Economic and political dependency became intertwined. In the past twenty years, the rapid growth of manufacturing in China, India, Brazil, and elsewhere has altered the global trade balance. Now consumers in Western countries owe money to China, where

DEBATE > GLOBAL INTERDEPENDENCE AND LOCAL PRICES

Currency exchange affects almost all of us, immediately and directly. When we buy inexpensive goods with the label "made in China," we often save money—or so it seems. In reality, we pay another, hidden price—American jobs. Chinese goods are inexpensive because the cost of labor in China is cheap and because the Chinese state deliberately maintains a low exchange rate between its national currency, the yuan, and two major currencies—the dollar and the euro. As a result, factories in China manufacture goods that cost significantly less than if they were produced in, say, Boston or Paris (Meyerson 2010).

And Western firms move their production to China or other countries because it is cheaper to manufacture there. As a result, in the twenty-first century, the Western world is no longer the leading manufacturer. Millions of industrial jobs have been lost over the past twenty years.

WHAT'S YOUR VIEW?

What are the consequences for the United States? What would you do about manufacturing jobs? What would you decide if you were president? Consider the possibilities. ❶ Would you initiate policies to stop the continuing loss of manufacturing jobs to foreign countries, even if the result was a 10 percent increase in the cost of most products? ❷ Or, would you allow a significant number of manufacturing jobs to disappear in order to ensure that the average consumer does not pay more? ❸ Could there be a third way? Suggest a "hybrid" strategy that would combine these two policy options.

 Visit the companion website for a list of products made in the United States.

goods are manufactured. The ability of states to control the movements of goods and capital has declined sharply, especially in the era of the Internet. Many corporations move their production to China, Vietnam, or Malaysia, which offer a large pool of cheap, educated, and disciplined labor. This shift affects manufacturing jobs in wealthy countries, though economists disagree on how. Some argue that losing manufacturing jobs to foreign countries should encourage people to pursue occupational training in search better jobs and opportunities at home (Cowen 2014).

MAIN ACTORS

The world's economy and finances stem from the dynamics and trends of the global market economy and from the purposeful policies and strategies of the most powerful actors. The main actors of IPE are states and intergovernmental organizations. There are also multinational corporations, the organizations that own or control productions of goods or services in several countries. Among the biggest are Google, Apple, Toyota, Microsoft, Walmart, and British Petroleum. States' governments use their economic and financial power to influence other countries and their economic and financial policies. We already described how the United States used its exceptional economic power to introduce the Marshall Plan and aid to West European countries. This policy certainly aided American economic and political interests. Intergovernmental organizations such as the World Trade Organization, North American Free Trade Agreement (NAFTA), and the Transatlantic Economic Council create international structures and facilitate policies of global significance. The most spectacular example so far, as you should remember, has been a set of intergovernmental agreements that created the European Union (Moravcsik 1997).

Main actors' policies, of course, are dependent on market trends. Yet they are also shaped by domestic politics, countries' security interests, individual choices, and various short-term factors. Last but not least, these policies are defined by economic theories and models. University-trained economists and financial experts play a prominent role in countries' actions related to production, finances, and trade. To understand contemporary IPE we have to comprehend how these ideas and models occurred, how they developed, and how they are applied.

<table>
<tr><td>

CHECK YOUR KNOWLEDGE

</td><td>

▶ What is GDP? Why do countries have different GDPs?
▶ Explain the positive and negative balance of trade. How does the negative balance of trade affect you personally?
▶ Who are the major actors in international political economy? What factors shape their interactions?

</td></tr>
</table>

Arguments

We can take several different types of arguments and approaches to studying international political economy. Here, we will look at mercantilism (often linked with realism), economic liberalism, constructivism, and conflict theories. (See Figure 7-1.)

Mercantilism: A Prequel to IPE

mercantilism The economic view that emphasizes the accumulation of resources and capital by states, as well as state regulation of trade.

Mercantilism as one of the oldest economic approaches calls for the accumulation and protection of available resources under full control of a sovereign country. This economic theory was widely accepted several centuries ago, when

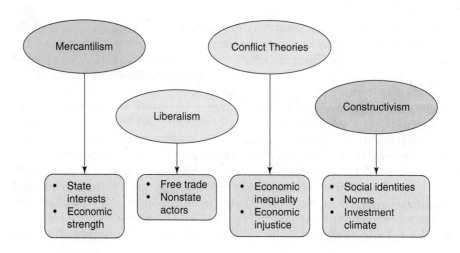

FIGURE 7-1 Major approaches of international political economy.

absolute monarchies such as France, followed mercantilist recipes to aggrandize power at the expense of their neighbors. At the heart of mercantilism is the view that maximizing net exports is the best route to national prosperity. Many countries, including the United States, later used mercantilism along with nationalist rhetoric (O'Brien and Clesse 2002), and mercantilist arguments are making a comeback today.

PRINCIPLES OF MERCANTILISM

Mercantilists assume that, globally, wealth is limited and does not grow or shrink fast. To succeed, states should compete for territories, resources, and colonies. Their economic policies should therefore aim at accumulating natural resources and gold reserves, territorial expansion, establishing exclusive trade with colonies, and payments from defeated enemies.

Mercantilist principles can be applied to the production, distribution, and consumption of resources and products (Ekelund and Hébert 2007). First, states must make sure that most of the products and services they need are produced domestically and that natural resources—such as coal, gas, and oil—are primarily for domestic consumption. This encourages employment and limits other countries' opportunities to sell their products there. States should accumulate precious metals and stimulate overseas trade to ensure the flow of gold and silver into the state's treasury. These metals are important to stabilize finances, maintain armed forces, and fight wars.

Mercantilism says that imports of foreign goods should be limited, but in reality this principle is difficult to achieve. States should therefore maintain a positive balance of trade: They must sell more than they buy from foreign countries. Governments should also discourage foreign traders by establishing tariffs on imported goods, thus making them overly expensive. A foreign debt is a state's serious vulnerability.

Finally, it is necessary to support domestic manufacturers and merchants. Today, when international competition cannot be ignored, governments increase their subsidies for domestic producers. They keep the value of their currencies artificially low to make manufactured products cheaper and thus more competitive on international markets. (See Figure 7-2.)

PRACTICES OF MERCANTILISM

Mercantilism used to be linked with realism, just as a country's economic strengths were commonly associated with its military capabilities (Thurow 1992; Gilboy 2004). Like realists in the past, mercantilists argued that economic rivalry among states is only natural. In fact, it is a **zero-sum game**: Mutual benefits are seldom achievable, giving states two options—either win or lose (Harrison and Prestowitz 1990). For example, many European states long considered the struggle for colonies as vital to their economies and national security. Later, the control of oil and gas resources and pipelines came to be as seen as a serious security issue.

The trade balance, too, can be seen in this way. China, for example, makes its trade surplus a top strategic priority. To limit foreign competition, China's government gave local company UnionPay a near monopoly over the handling

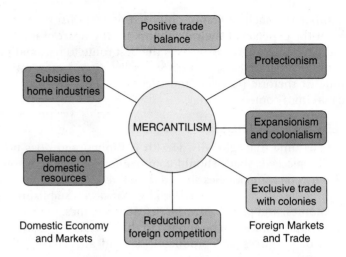

FIGURE 7-2 Mercantilism: A snapshot.

of payments between individual merchants and banks. (We look more at China's economic success story at the end of this chapter.) India for many years banned foreign supermarkets on its territory that sell products more cheaply than their Indian competitors. Mercantilism may appear as an outdated theory and most university-trained economists discard it. Yet, politicians, especially populists, continue to use mercantilist arguments to defend domestic consumers and homegrown businesses.

Mercantilism supports **protectionism**—the policy of restricting or discouraging imports and encouraging domestic production. One way to do it is through **tariffs**—fees on imported goods, to make them more expensive. This gives domestic producers a chance to sell their goods, protects domestic workforce, and may reduce the negative trade balance. The United States practiced protectionism for most of its history and most harshly during the Great Depression of the 1930s. Another form of protectionism is direct subsidies to domestic industries, to keep jobs and make products more competitive abroad (Zahariadis 2008). States also protect their industries by legislating import quotas or negotiating with other countries to voluntary limit their exports. The United States pursued both these policies to limit Japan's car exports in the 1970s and Japanese Datsuns and Toyotas were better designed and more fuel-efficient, which threatened American automobile corporations. Protectionist policies also stem from mercantilist logic and are supported by strong domestic lobbies, such as wine producers in France, rice growers in Japan, and steel workers and fishermen in the United States (Haas 2012; Anderson 2005).

Countries may also use **economic sanctions** against other states—that is the deliberate withdrawal, or threat of withdrawal, of customary trade and financial relations, to put pressure on a government to change its policies. The ultimate form of economic sanctions is an *embargo*, or the prohibition of trade. Usually these policies do not last, but the United States imposed an embargo on Cuba from 1960 until 2014 and on Iran beginning in 1979. In the past,

protectionism
Economic restrictions by the state to discourage imports and encourage domestic production including "import substitution."

tariff   Tax or financial charge imposed on imported goods.

economic sanctions
The deliberate, government-driven withdrawal, or threat of withdrawal, of customary trade and financial relations in an effort to change another country's policies.

economic sanctions often preceded or followed a war. In the twentieth century, however, they began to play a role as an alternative to violence. They may be used in an attempt to restrain a belligerent government, punish aggression, contain a civil war, influence policies, or simply make a political statement.

American legislation, for example, allows economic and trade sanctions against countries that expropriate U.S. property, organize coups against elected governments, and support terrorism. Countries that violate human rights, harbor international war criminals, engage in nuclear proliferation, or fail to cooperate sufficiently with U.S. antinarcotics efforts may also become targets of economic sanctions. The Office of Foreign Assets Control of the U.S. Department of the Treasury administers and enforces economic and trade sanctions. Many of them are based on UN and other international mandates. (Malloy 2015; Hufbauer and Oegg 2003).

THE KEYNESIAN APPROACH

A serious attempt to advance and adapt mercantilist logic to the modern world was made by John M. Keynes (1883–1946), a British economist. Keynes was a founder of **macroeconomics,** which looks at the structure and performance of the entire economy. In *The General Theory of Employment, Interest and Money* ([1936] 1965), he argued that, contrary to the assumption of the efficiency of free markets, governments should regulate business and especially finances. According to **Keynesian economics,** national governments can ease the undesirable effects of economic recessions by spending more money than their revenues allow. By putting money into the economy, government can fuel business transactions and purchases, stimulate production and consumption, lower unemployment, and create a prosperous middle class. Keynes' principles played a key role in the understanding of the structure and performance of economics for half of the twentieth century. Today some economists argue in favor of returning to Keynesian economic policies, in view of unstable international markets and because of the decline of middle classes in some developed countries under the pressure of globalization.

Following Keynes' ideas, states abandoned the gold standard and started to manipulate the supply of money through banking interest rates—a process known as **monetary policy.** For instance, the Federal Reserve, the central banking system in the United States, is responsible for maintaining the stability of the financial system. The Federal Reserve can determine the rise or fall of interest rates, thus making credit either more expensive or less, and so opening or closing the flow of capital into the economy. The government can also use government spending or taxes to influence the economy—an approach called **fiscal policy.** States can raise taxes and use this money to create jobs while at the same time fighting *inflation*, a rise in the prices. In the 1970s and 1980s, Keynesian principles came under heavy criticism from the advocates of liberal economic theories. But after the global financial and economic crisis that started in 2008, the discussion began about whether the Keynesian policies should be revived gain.

macroeconomics The study of the structure and performance of the entire economy, including the interrelationship among diverse sectors.

Keynesian economics The principle that national governments should conduct expansionary fiscal and monetary policies whenever necessary to ease the undesirable effects of economic recessions.

fiscal policy The use of government spending or revenue collection to influence the economy, jump-start it out of recession, or create jobs.

Economic Liberalism and the Formation of IPE

economic liberalism
The belief and theory that only free market, free trade, and economic cooperation can lead to a peaceful and prosperous world.

International political economy today is largely shaped by **economic liberalism**—the belief that international economic connections, globalization of finances, production, and labor are not only the main source of economic development, but also a vital source of international cooperation, stability, and peace. Liberal economists maintain that the dynamics and structures of international trade, and globalizing markets of finances and labor, would remain the key realities that would shape economic developments and the distribution of power in the international system.

THE ROOTS AND PRINCIPLES OF ECONOMIC LIBERALISM

Scottish economist and philosopher Adam Smith (1723–1790) was one of the founders of economic liberalism. In *An Inquiry into the Nature and Causes of the Wealth of Nations* (1977), published in 1776, he opposed restrictions on international trade, arguing that commerce brings prosperity and peace among nations. A noted follower, David Ricardo (1772–1823), believed that free trade is the best regulator of labor and natural resources. Another economic liberal, Friedrich List (1789–1846), suggested that commercial unions among states make trade flourish and enrich all participants (List, [1841] 2006).

Economic liberalism gradually replaced mercantilism as a dominant trend in economic policies in the second half of the nineteenth century. However, liberal economic ideas came under serious attack during the Great Depression and the rise of Communism, fascism, and social democracy from the 1920s through the 1950s. This was the time when the Keynesian approach became dominant in the United States as the main economic rationale for the New Deal—a series of domestic programs to deal with the devastating impact of a severe economic crisis. Yet economic liberals challenged Keynes' ideas as a potentially dangerous aberration. In *The Road to Serfdom* ([1944] 2007), the Austrian economist Friedrich von Hayek (1899–1992) sharply criticized the idea of state regulations of markets. Hayek influenced American economist Milton Friedman (1912–2006), who in his *Capitalism and Freedom* (1962) renounced Keynesianism as an outdated theory that did not reflect international economic dynamics. Friedman, who taught at the University of Chicago, argued that the state should abandon

A pedestrian walks past an advertisement for Apple's iPhone 6 and 6 Plus smartphones in Yichang City, central China, in 2014. Chinese state officials may no longer use the world's leading technology brands. The Chinese government says it is protecting against Western cybersurveillance and shielding Chinese home phone brands against foreign competition.

protectionist policies and make sure that the amount of money in circulation would gradually grow—an idea called *monetarism*.

Economic liberalism influenced politics. British prime minister Margaret Thatcher, who pushed for fundamental economic reforms in the United Kingdom after 1979, and President Reagan in the United States were followers of economic liberalism. The deregulation of economic activities in the United Kingdom and the United States in the 1980s, combined with government control over the flow

Jubilant crowds offer a cluster of hands for Britain's reelected prime minister, Margaret Thatcher, in 1983. Thatcher pushed for economic deregulation. Her policies drew both fierce resistance and enthusiastic support in the United Kingdom.

of money through changing interest rates, remained the dominant policy of many countries.

Free trade through international cooperation is the key goal of liberalism. An early argument in its defense comes from the principle (often called the law) of **comparative advantage**. It explains why it is beneficial for two countries to specialize in production of only certain goods and then buy other goods on international markets rather than produce everything at home. This principle is attributed to Robert Torrens (1815), but David Ricardo made it famous two years later. Imagine England and Argentina making textiles and corn. In England, production of both takes less time than in Argentina, so it has an economic advantage over Argentina. Mercantilists would ask why, in this case, England needs to import anything from Argentina. The principle of comparative advantage seems to go against common sense.

Actually, the law suggests that both countries would benefit from mutual trade: If Britain would import corn from Argentina, it would save more labor time and resources to focus on textiles and improving their quality. In the same way, Argentina would gain from focusing on the production of corn while importing British textiles. In both countries, consumers would be better off because prices of both products would be lower and their quality higher.

In the same spirit, economic liberals argue that the benefits obtained from protecting domestic producers against foreign competitors are insignificant compared to the damage to the domestic economy as a whole: People have to pay much higher prices for domestic goods, plus protected businesses have less incentive to develop, modernize, and be competitive internationally. Economic liberals also argue that economic cooperation reduces the chance of war: Businesses are likely to lobby for cooperation and international law (Oneal and Russett 1997; Rogowski 1990). This will induce states to choose cooperation. (See Figure 7-3.)

INTERNATIONAL ORGANIZATIONS

Economic liberalism, with Keynesian modifications, inspired the creation of international institutions to facilitate trade and provide financial stability worldwide. More efficient institutions, their supporters believed, would lead to a more prosperous and peaceful world (Ikenberry and Grieco 2002; Keohane 2005).

comparative advantage   A theory that explains why it is beneficial for two countries to trade with each other instead of relying on their own domestic production.

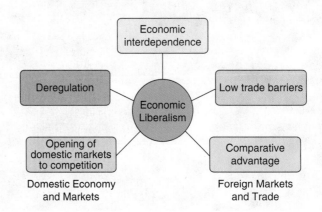

FIGURE 7-3 Economic liberalism: A snapshot.

The Great Depression of the 1930s, a period characterized by high protective tariffs and the breakdown of global markets, offered strong reasons to build international economic and financial institutions. Many believed that protectionism had slowed economic recovery and provoked extreme nationalism, led to a struggle for territory and resources, and ultimately contributed to World War II. In 1944, representatives of the United States, the United Kingdom, the Soviet Union, France, and China met in Bretton Woods, New Hampshire, leading to the creation of the International Monetary Fund (IMF) and the International Bank of Reconstruction and Development (IBRD) (Peet 2009). After the Soviet Union backed out of the Bretton Woods agreements in 1946, both institutions became the pillars of Western capitalism. Participating states agreed to contribute parts of their gold reserves to a global "pool" to maintain the balance of payments in international trade. The United States, the wealthiest contributor, played the leading role in the functioning of these institutions.

The IMF has grown more than four times from forty-five members in 1945. Its goals are to maintain stable exchanges between national currencies and to provide financial help to countries in trouble. The IBRD (commonly called the World Bank) involves almost all states (except for Cuba, North Korea, and a few others) and makes loans to developing countries for long-term projects. In both institutions the wealthiest donors have more authority. The IMF and World Bank provide financial help conditionally: Usually, the recipient of assistance must reform its finances according to these institutions' prescriptions. These prescriptions, which commonly involve privatization and deregulation—often draw criticism. For example, it is argued that the key lending institutions do not pay enough attention to the local conditions of recipient countries (Strand 2013). The prescriptions may also stimulate the growth of certain industries yet cause the decline of others, thus sparking unemployment and economic disparities.

Other liberal international institutions created after the Bretton Woods agreements were the *General Agreement on Tariffs and Trade (GATT)*, signed in 1947 in Geneva, and the *International Trade Organization (ITO)*, created the next year in Havana. The members of GATT held periodic trade negotiations, gradually leading to reductions of tariffs. The ITO failed, however, because the U.S. Senate rejected its charter: Many American politicians feared that it would become a kind of global government. However, GATT became successful during the 1960s and in 1995 was renamed the World Trade Organization (WTO), which is today a global organization with membership exceeding one hundred and sixty countries.

The WTO is the main international organization today designed to promote economic development and growth through the removal of tariffs and the opening of national markets to international trade. It also helps enforce their agreements and resolve trade disputes (World Trade Organization 2015). It does not act as a global government and does not negotiate on behalf of states but rather provides a framework for negotiations. The WTO insists that countries should adhere to the principles of nondiscrimination, reciprocity, and transparency in their trade policies (Hoekman and Kostecki

2010). This means that countries should have equal access to foreign markets, imported products should be treated no less favorably than domestically produced goods, and no secret deals or domestic regulations should restrict free trade.

Supporters of the WTO hope that free trade will reduce poverty, improve standards of living, create employment, and provide new economic opportunities for billions (Narlikar 2005). Critics offer at least three main arguments. First, they believe that free trade benefits mostly rich countries of the global North while leaving underdeveloped countries of the South to produce raw materials and supply cheap labor (see more about it later in this chapter). Second, small countries can exercise less influence in the "rounds" of talks that produce new WTO rules. Finally, these rules harm small business: In free trade, critics maintain, only big multinational corporations can thrive. Critics also stress that the organization offered no new solutions to the global financial crisis that started in 2008 (Cottier and Elsig 2011).

 Visit the companion website to learn more about the World Trade Organization and the World Bank.

REGIONAL TRADE AGREEMENTS

regional trade agreements Mutual commitments that bind several neighboring countries to pursue common economic and financial policies.

Regional trade agreements are rules and mutual commitments based on international treaties that bind countries to pursue common economic and financial policies. They usually deal with tariffs and their reduction and elimination. They also deal with transportation, communications, intellectual property, environmental standards, investments, and trade policies. In 2015, there were more than six hundred regional trade arrangements and their number is likely to grow (WTO 2015). One is the NAFTA, which went into effect in 1994. In it, the United States, Mexico, and Canada agreed to gradually eliminate most trade and investment barriers in dealing with one another. In 2014, twelve countries (the United States, Australia, Canada, Japan, Mexico, Brunei, Chile, Malaysia, New Zealand, Peru, Singapore, and Vietnam) expressed interest in and negotiated forming the Trans-Pacific Partnership. Potentially, its possible members could together produce more than 40 percent of the world's GDP.

Why do countries need such agreements? They gain from lower prices. States also seek to secure access to each other's markets and products. Many less developed countries need economic security and pursue trade agreements with developed states. Wealthy countries seek cheaper products and services and expect new consumers' markets to grow (Whalley 1997). The profiles of several of the most important regional organizations based on free trade are displayed in Table 7-2.

CHECK YOUR KNOWLEDGE

▶ Explain the comparative advantage principle.
▶ What is the main idea of economic liberalism?
▶ What is the main goal of key international trade organizations?
▶ Explain the three main arguments of WTO critics.

TABLE 7-2 Examples of Regional Trade Agreements

Regional Agreement	Main Features
European Union (EU)	The EU is the most ambitious project in economic and political integration, with a population of 500 million and a GDP of $17 trillion. It has a common currency and central banking system (the euro and the European Central Bank), and it has taken steps to develop a common foreign and security policy. (We examined the European Union in Chapter 3.)
Southern Common Market (MERCOSUR)	Comprising Argentina, Paraguay, Uruguay, Brazil, and Venezuela (since 2006), the Southern Common Market represents a total population of 190 million people—all living in an area larger than the European continent. The organization promotes the movement of goods, people, and currency among these countries.
Asia-Pacific Economic Cooperation (APEC)	This group of twenty-one Pacific Rim countries, including the United States, meets regularly to improve economic and political ties among member states. The group has working committees on a wide range of issues, from communications to fisheries.

Constructivism and IPE

Material resources and economic policies, constructivism argues, are often seen through the prism of collective values and socially constructed priorities (Reus-Smit 2009). The goals and structure of economic policies change from country to country depending on social, political, and cultural conditions in these countries (Evans 1998). Ideologies and customs also influence economic policies. For instance, free trade may be viewed as a positive or negative development, depending on a country's role in the world market (Copeland 1996).

Using constructivist ideas, one can see the Marshall Plan as not only an economic policy but also a way to promote beliefs in free markets and free trade—as opposed to mercantilism, not to mention Communism. The Marshall Plan fostered cooperation, mutual acceptance, and the willingness of European states to become what we commonly call "the West." Economic interests and policies are socially constructed by governments, influential elites, lobbies, and societies at large. This may explain in part why some countries practice protectionism more often than others, or why some states use fixed exchange rate in their international trade, and other states prefer flexibility.

NATIONALISM AND ECONOMIC POLITICS

Governments and business elites cannot ignore domestic and international politics. Decision makers have to justify their economic and financial policies from the viewpoint of a **national purpose**—a major economic goal that political and business elites want to achieve for their country. A vision of the country's future

national purpose
In the constructivist view, a major economic goal that political and business elites want to achieve for their country.

A man kicks an effigy of Guatemalan vice president Roxana Baldetti during a protest sparked by a recent corruption scandal in Guatemala City in 2015. Authoritarianism, corruption, and criminalization of economic life create a bad climate for international investments.

may affect people's common identity, which becomes a powerful guide of policies. This guide can be stronger than the logic of rational economic benefits (Abdelal 2001). When the Soviet Union imploded in 1991, some new post-Soviet countries—such as Estonia, Latvia, and Lithuania—turned rapidly away from Russia, despite their historic economic interdependence. Belarus and Kazakhstan, both former Soviet republics, preferred cooperation: For decision-making elites there, it did not conflict with how they saw the national purpose of their own countries.

Countries constantly redefine their national purpose and economic interests. India, for example, beginning with its increasing economic rivalry with China in the 1990s, sought a stronger role in world affairs. It turned from longstanding protectionist policies to international cooperation and interdependence, allowed foreign investments, and promoted economic openness (Alamgir 2008). According to constructivism, India's massive economic reforms were strongly influenced by its policy makers' perception of what India should be, especially in comparison with China (Smith 2013).

ECONOMIC CLIMATE

economic climate
A set of values and practices, such as the level of trust, transparency, or corruption that encourages or discourages economic investments.

States, regions, and the global community develop an **economic climate**, or set of values and practices that may or may not support official economic policies and visions of national purpose. According to economic liberalism, manufacturers, sellers, and consumers act in accord with the rules of supply and demand. In reality, constructivists say, scores of other factors affect their behavior.

Laws that protect the ownership of private property lead to a functioning free market unless a majority of the population follows them. An unfriendly business climate lacks a legal foundation, custom, and trust. The lack of tradition in legal protection of private property severely limits the functioning of a country's market economy, which affects the country's participation in international economic activities. Authoritarianism, corruption, and criminalization of economic life create a bad climate for international investments. In the most extreme cases, producers stop trading openly, and prefer transactions in cash only. Conversely, in the established democracies with market economies, backed by strong legal system, foreign investments increase, and producers supply goods based on trust, without advance payments.

A favorable economic climate means lower cost to business. International investors are likely to bring their money to a country in which they feel protected. In contrast, insecurity and corruption drive international investors away. Places perceived as corrupt, as a rule, lose international investors. Therefore, a country's foreign economic policies become inseparable from its domestic social policy and how it is perceived by others.

@ Go online to find out more about Transparency International and its annual surveys of the world's corruption.

Marxism and Conflict Theories: Radical Criticisms of IPE

Conflict theories, as you know from Chapter 4 maintain that the world's economic structure unfairly benefits dominant social classes and groups, such as the wealthy, males, and whites. Such economic order, according to conflict theories, should be replaced by a new and fairer one through revolution or reforms.

MARXISM

Supporters of Marxism argue that despite a wide range of democratic changes in the past century, the gap between a few rich countries and the rest of the world, between the global North and South, remains profound. Today, international corporations and banks, not the governments of sovereign states, are the true holders of global power because of their financial resources. States serve the interests of the ruling class of billionaires using diplomacy, international agreements, and international law to manage international relations, which in effect should lead to higher profits. Free-trade agreements are designed to enrich the international ruling class and give nothing to the middle class, workers, and peasants. But what do Marxists suggest? Their old recipes, urging violent revolutions and nationalizations of large banks and big corporations, lost their credibility after many attempts and failures in the past. The failure of the economies of the Soviet Union, Cuba, North Korea, and other Communist countries disenchanted many Marxist sympathizers. Today, Marxists cannot offer a viable alternative to global capitalism. They do, however, support the antiglobalist movement that demands high taxes on the rich and rigorous social control over banks and corporations, as discussed in Chapter 4.

ECONOMIC DEPENDENCY

Dependency theory has its roots in the research of an Argentine economist, Raúl Prebisch (1901–1986), and a German economist, Hans Singer (1910–2006). In their view, technology-driven developed nations, called the *core*, have been receiving more benefits from international trade than technology-deprived developing countries, called the *periphery*. Singer and Prebisch showed that core nations, but not periphery, benefit significantly from improvements in technology. Moreover, periphery countries cannot catch up with core nations under the conditions of free trade (Prebisch 1989; Singer 1999). The wealth of core countries is almost constantly increasing, whereas the wealth of the periphery is flat or decreasing.

Supporters of these views maintain that the discriminatory structure of the world's economy and trade is the main cause of global inequality and chronic poverty. According to these views, elites from the periphery reap the benefits, and the rest remain in abject poverty while working for transnational corporations. Dependency theorists began to use terms such as "global North and South" and "North–South divide" to direct attention to the failures of economic realism and liberalism. The poor, agricultural nations of the **South** (so-called although not all are in the Southern hemisphere) are totally dependent on the developed industrial **North**, both economically and politically. The latter is the core of the capitalist system, and the former remains on the

dependency theory
The belief that the world economic order is based on the flow of resources from a "periphery" of poor states to a "core" of wealthy states.

South (global)
Predominantly agricultural countries that are dependent on the rich and technology-driven (global) North.

North (global) In dependency theory, predominantly rich and technology-driven countries that benefit from the raw materials and cheap labor of the (global) South.

periphery. These, as you will remember from Chapter 4, were main the points of world-systems theory (Wallerstein 1979).

In the 1960s and 70s, many economists in the Third World became influenced by dependency theory, and some of their recommendations produced visible results. The rise of Brazil's economic power in the twenty-first century can be credited to some of their prescriptions (Sweig 2010). Supporters of dependency theory accept private property and acknowledge the importance of some elements of a free-market economy. Nevertheless, they believe that the rules governing markets should change and the world's economic order should be restructured (Scott 2001).

CHECK YOUR KNOWLEDGE

▶ What is the main idea of the Marxist view on IPE ?
▶ Explain the *core* and the *periphery*.
▶ What is economic climate? How does it affect investments?

CASE IN POINT > *Fair Trade*

Fair trade (known also as *trade justice*) initiatives suggest that developed countries should agree that developing nations can sell their products, primarily agricultural goods and resources, at assured prices. Manufacturers and distributors must not use child labor, slavery, an unsafe workplace, or other forms of abuse and discrimination. *TransFair USA*, a nonprofit organization, certifies and labels products manufactured under fair trade principles. Thanks to fair trade, certified coffee, tea, cocoa, fresh fruit, rice, and sugar are all available at tens of thousands of retail locations. Fair trade standards are set by a Germany-based umbrella group, *Fairtrade Labelling Organizations International* (FLO).

CRITICAL THINKING

❶ Would you support the mandatory application of fair trade principles to all food imports to the United States? Critics argue that you must then pay a higher price for food. Proponents of fair trade reply that in Norway and Germany, for example, higher food prices do not seem to devastate family budgets. ❷ Assignment: For a week, write down the price and country of origin of every food product you consume. If a product is foreign, add 10 percent to its price. (For example, if you buy a cup of Columbian coffee for $2.00, add $0.20.) Tally the total at the end of the week: this is how much you would pay for participating in *fair trade*. Would a 10 percent price increase be acceptable, given *your* financial situation? How have these calculations affected your views of trade justice?

Yukiko Doi, head of the Fair Trade Nagoya Network, Japan, campaigns to have Nagoya win the status of a "Fair Trade Town," helping manufacturers in developing countries achieve better terms of trade.

 Read more about fair trade on the companion website.

Contexts and Applications

Few economists predicted the massive financial and economic crisis that peaked in 2008. As banks collapsed and property values plummeted, stock markets fell, and unemployment soared. Even fewer economists predicted how long the crisis would last. Signs of recovery appeared in 2010, when the economies of China, India, and Brazil showed some encouraging annual growth numbers, up to 10 percent. Brazil's economy slowed down five years later, but the United States picked up and became a major growing economy again.

What are the international lessons of the crisis? Some were quick to blame the free market and unregulated capitalism. They urged a return to tight state regulations or even mercantilism, to stop states from running negative trade balance and deficits. Liberal economists fought back, defending free trade, but not its excesses. Politicians in many developing countries looked instead to dependency theory. They faced a difficult dilemma: Which economic path of development should they accept—one with more state regulations or less control? Should it be the free market so eagerly promoted by the West? Or should it be a Chinese model rooted in heavy state regulations but seemingly secured economic growth?

No single economic crisis, even the deep one that the world has witnessed, can prove success or failure for certain economic policies. Still, it is important to find out why states choose particular policies rather than others—and when these policies become effective. We must look at the individual, state, and global contexts and circumstances in which these policies developed.

The Individual Decisions Context

Many theories of international business and trade are tested on the level of **microeconomics**—the field of economics that considers the behavior of consumers, companies, and industries. Here individual decisions play a big role. Similarly, a choice of international economic policies may be rooted in the decisions of individual state leaders and the leaders of major international financial institutions. But how? Among the factors affecting decisions are leadership, ideology, and the economic climate.

microeconomics
The field of economics that considers the behavior of individual consumers, companies, and industries.

POLITICAL LEADERSHIP

If policies were based only on ideology, a country's decisions would be predictable. A Communist leader promoting an isolationist foreign policy is likely to reject economic cooperation or trade with capitalist countries. And in fact Albania from the 1950s through the 1980s insisted on complete economic self-reliance; so has North Korea for more than sixty years. Their leaders assumed that a true Communist country is capable of building a prosperous economy alone. This policy, called **autarky**, has failed miserably: These states could barely provide the minimum resources for their populations.

Political leaders decide on economic policies based on a variety of ideas. (See Table 7-3.) They cannot afford isolation, but they still have to choose between multilateralism and unilateralism, cooperation and noncooperation with the international system. With the increasing price of oil and oil products in the mid-2000s, some oil-producing states began to act as unilateralists. After

autarky   A long-term policy of national self-sufficiency and rejection of imports, economic aid, and cooperation.

TABLE 7-3 National Leaders and Economic Policies

Name	Country	Years in Office	Economic Decisions
Kim Il-sung (1912–1994)	North Korea	1948–94	An authoritarian, Communist leader, he hoped to build a prosperous, independent state based on the ideology of *Juche* (spirit of self-reliance)—a blend of autarky, extreme centralization, and nationalism. Private property was prohibited and foreign trade was limited.
Fidel Castro (b. 1926)	Cuba	1959–2011	In his long tenure in government, Castro's economic policies were based on his belief in state planning and an inevitable confrontation with capitalism. Cuba, however, had to be subsidized heavily by the Soviet Union, and after the Soviet collapse, by Venezuela.
Mohammad Reza Pahlavi (1919–1980)	Iran	1941–79	Pahlavi remained a reliable supporter of the United States, the free-market economy, and international trade. His reforms spawned massive corruption. He was expelled during the Islamic revolution.
Deng Xiaoping (1904–1997)	People's Republic of China	Approximately 1981–92	After the economic and social disaster of the Cultural Revolution, Deng concluded that the Chinese economy could be restored only by a combination of state planning and market initiative. Deng's reforms set the foundations for the "economic miracle." With significant foreign investments, China became a leading economic power. It preserves, with few modifications, the old political system.
Margaret Thatcher (1925–2013)	United Kingdom	1979–90	Thatcher began to dismantle state regulation of the economy and weakened trade unions. She also resisted the UK's integration into the European Community, fearing that its regulations would reverse her reforms.
Lech Wałęsa (b. 1943)	Poland	1990–95	Wałęsa opposed Communist rule and led the independent trade union "Solidarity" against it. As president, he promoted free-market principles but hoped to avoid its excesses. He lost power in the midst of a Polish economic recession.
Robert Mugabe (b. 1924)	Zimbabwe	Since 1980	An authoritarian ruler, Mugabe advocated a blend of anticolonialism and nationalism. His economic policies were erratic and mostly mercantilist. Under his leadership, Zimbabwe remained one of the poorest countries in Africa.

TABLE 7-3 (Continued)

Hugo Chávez (1954–2013)	Venezuela	1999–2013	An exemplary Latin American populist, Chavez built his economic policies on a blend of Socialist ideas, anticolonial and anti-imperialist messages, and Bolivarianism (the unification of Latin America). A believer in dependence theory, he repeatedly tried to use his country's oil profits to finance anti-American policies.
Muammar Qaddafi (1942–2011)	Libya	1969–2011	Qaddafi's economic policy of "Islamic Socialism" established government controls of large industries but permitted small business. In practice, most national wealth, especially the oil revenues, went to him and his supporters. During his last years in power, Qaddafi improved relations with Western countries, hoping to benefit even more from high oil prices. He was overthrown by a popular insurrection supported by the West.

2006, Iran openly pushed the development of its nuclear program. Iranian leaders stated that Western countries would not dare to impose sanctions on their country because the West needed Iranian oil. Yet they miscalculated, even as they understood that unilateralism could be risky.

MICROECONOMICS

Microeconomics can show how the behavior of individual consumers affects international markets and overall international stability. After the terrorist attacks of September 11, 2001, the world's stock markets fell drastically. Scores of investors decided to sell their stocks and put their money in what they perceived as a more secure investment, such as cash or gold. It was an instant emotional reaction to the crisis. Most people were not under direct threat but still felt insecure; acting on their instincts and impulses, they created a global financial disruption that lasted for months. The same cycle repeated in the fall of 2008, when the stock market plummeted. In 2010 and 2011, rumors that Greece, a member of the European Union, might default on its national debt, thus threatening the euro, created fears pushing people to buy state bonds and U.S. dollars. Usually, such "stampedes" are short-lived and help speculators to gamble on the fluctuations in value between currencies. The currency speculation, however, can destabilize the international financial system in the long run. Some European governments began to lobby for a tax on any exchange of foreign currency, to discourage currency speculation.

Even without speculators, financial markets can become volatile. News headlines, elections results, and statements made by leaders affect decisions by both individuals and companies. Millions of individual decisions, affected by mass reactions, produce greater financial volatility. Government officials generally comment as little as possible about economic problems, to avoid investors' panic.

CASE IN POINT > *Discoveries and Innovation*

Not only financial speculators and mass reactions affect international political economy; scientists and engineers do so as well. Discoveries, innovations, and other accomplishments may dramatically affect travel, trade, and the ways products and services are exchanged (Yergin and Stanislaw 1998). The steam engine made possible rail and ship transportation—moving people and goods safer and faster across countries, continents, and oceans. In 1819, the American steamship *Savannah* crossed the Atlantic. It was the beginning of a new era of trade between the continents. It influenced global migration as well. In 1832, American inventor Samuel Morse developed a single-wire telegraph system; and after 1865,

telegraph cables were laid across the floor of the Atlantic between the continents. The spread of these technologies powered a dramatic expansion of world trade.

CRITICAL THINKING

❶ Not including the obvious example of the Internet, what are some other prominent innovations and discoveries of the past twenty years that, in your view, have had the most significant impact on international trade and commerce? ❷ Which of today's innovations do you think would revolutionize international markets in 2025 and why? How could Facebook or Twitter play a bigger role in world politics? ❸ How would upcoming innovations affect international

relations in 2025? Offer your creative assessment.

Diptanshu Malaviya, 15, demonstrates a machine that picks up garbage during an innovation exhibition in New Delhi, India, in 2015. Diptanshu made this with help from his brother Mukul Malaviya. How realistic is the expectation that the center of technological innovation moves from Western countries to new economies?

The State Policies Context

State leaders are commonly seen as people who make reasonable decisions. However, most leaders represent business and financial interests, and they make their economic decisions based on political obligations. In a democratic society, politics is often about promoting economic interests (Olson 1971).

THE BUSINESS CYCLE AND COUNTRIES' ECONOMIC POLICIES

From the nineteenth century on, market economies developed in cycles. The growth of investments, employment, and economic capacities is called *expansion*, and the absence of growth is commonly called *recession*. Keynesian economics became the first economic model that provided countries with policies to try to end recessions and stimulate expansion. The policies of the New Deal in the United States were partially inspired by these ideas. After the end of World War II, many countries held modified Keynesian ideas about increased budgetary expenses and budget deficits. Advocates of Keynesian ideas—such as the Truman, Kennedy, and Johnson administrations in the United States—argued that these policies helped reduce the negative impacts of the business cycle. Some even claimed that the era of business cycles was over.

But the world recession of the 1970s disproved those optimistic claims. Later, the longest period of expansion lasted from the early 1990s until 2008.

The following recession was the longest since the Great Depression of the 1930s. However, after 2013, the American economy began to expand again. This time, advocates of liberal monetarism argued that consistently increasing the amount of money in circulation helped overcome the recession. Critics of liberal monetarism, however, argue that what really helped was heavy state spending on social programs. Others pay attention to America's technological innovations and new oil and gas extracting technologies (such as "fracking") that have freed the United States from dependence on foreign oil (Cowen 2014). Today, countries' economic policies have become extremely complex and increasingly dependent on international developments.

DOMESTIC POLITICS

Scores of domestic political factors affect a state's economic and financial policies, its international trade, and the country's overall international situation. In turn, economic factors influence politics. In the West today, some political groupings are likely to reject government economic regulations and to support market-oriented policies. Their political opponents are more likely to support state regulations and policies to protect the domestic labor force and various social groups against the perceived harms of the market.

It is difficult to promote deregulation and free-market policies in countries and regions devastated by poverty, violence, social neglect, and rampant corruption. These policies can produce more negative immediate effects than positive ones. It takes time to develop infrastructure, to find investors, to create jobs, and to develop a favorable business climate. Most governments do not have the luxury of time to experiment with free-market reforms. They need to show immediate and positive results. Therefore, many choose regulation.

In the United States, where labor costs are high, many manufacturing workers oppose open global competition. For two decades the U.S. economy has been steadily losing high-paid industrial jobs, as companies move their production facilities to countries where there are fewer regulations and labor is cheap—a practice called **outsourcing** (Bergsten 2005). In response to complaints from labor and struggling middle class families, Presidents George Bush and Barack Obama issued temporary protectionist measures to help the steel, tire, and automotive industries.

outsourcing The practice of moving business and jobs to other countries and regions where labor costs are lower.

SURPLUS OR MANAGEABLE DEFICIT?

Domestic political and social factors affect the attitudes about *surplus-oriented* and *trade deficit-tolerant* economic policies. Surplus, as you will remember, was a core objective of traditional mercantilism. A trade deficit is generally acceptable in free-market economies. Consider several examples of how states deal with their deficit or surplus.

The role of state planning and surplus was crucial to the *Asian development model*, which originated in the 1950s out of cooperation between Japan's government and private businesses. Japan's Ministry of International Trade and Industry (MITI) identified potential overseas markets and then worked with private industries to assist them with their exports. The state also helped with market information, access to foreign technology, licensing, loans and subsidies, and, when necessary, state tariffs. This relationship between government and business helped Japan, after the economic devastation of World War II, turn into the economic powerhouse of Asia. During the 1960s, this model was adopted in Singapore, Hong Kong, Taiwan, and later Malaysia and South Korea, with remarkable results.

For years, East Asian economies were driven by policies to ensure a massive trade surplus. Political parties in these countries, despite a host of differences in their domestic platforms, maintained similar views about exports (which had to be stimulated) and imports (which had to be regulated). Yet the negative consequences of such policies eventually appeared—just as they did for the eighteenth-century's French mercantilism. The trade surplus pushed up labor wages and costs for services. As a result, Japan's exports became more expensive compared to exports from China and other countries. This contributed to Japan's recession in the 1990s and more than a decade of slow economic growth. The entire effectiveness of the Asian developmental model was in question.

In the twenty-first century, manufacturing boomed in countries with cheaper labor, and their share in world imports dramatically increased. This pushed trade deficits to a new high in many developed countries, especially the United States.

What about models that allow trade deficits? American and Western European economies tend to tolerate deficits, after several decades of economic growth, mutually beneficial trade, and Keynesian regulatory policies. For many economists and investors, however, the U.S. negative trade balance is a dangerous development: It means that foreign countries have accumulated U.S. dollars. What if foreign holders no longer want to keep them? Will it be a serious problem? At least three possibilities have been proposed (DiMicco 2015; Levey and Brown 2005).

A pessimistic forecast suggests that at some point the dollar will drop sharply in value against other currencies. A global panic will cause the dollar to tank further and interest rates to skyrocket. The global economy will be dragged into a deeper crisis.

A less dramatic forecast predicts only a slow, moderate rise and decline in the dollar. A short-term recession, combined with the cheaper dollar, will eventually reverse the negative trade balance: Americans will buy fewer expensive foreign products. Yet American products—including cars, software, and computers—will become more affordable in other countries. When dollar rises, American products should become more expensive and thus less competitive globally.

In a more optimistic view, America will return to manufacturing. Emerging economies will need to import advanced technologies, software, and equipment from the United States and other developed countries to build new manufacturing facilities and to improve their living standards. International investors and consumers will continue to invest, convinced that future technological innovations and successful business methods will help the United States to remain an economic leader.

Which view appears more realistic to you? We return to the debate over the role of trade at the end of this chapter.

The Global Context

Economic policies succeed or fail depending on global business cycles, conflicts, and individual decision of political leaders. International conflicts affect business activities around the world. The terrorist attacks on September 11, 2001, shut down not only the Wall Street but also business and financial activities globally. Fears of an escalating military conflict in the Middle East may drive oil prices up in a matter of hours. Optimistic reports about the United States' employment immediately attract global investments into the U.S. economy. The world markets are increasingly interconnected.

WHICH ECONOMIC POLICY?

Aside from conflicts, terrorist attacks, and promising employment numbers, many important decisions affecting the global economy come from the centers of economic and financial power in the wealthiest countries of the word. The battles over the direction and scope of economic policies in the era of globalization are continuous and passionate. Advances in high frequency trading and new technological advances suggest the early signs of another industrial revolution (Marsh 2012). Yet will it provide stable economic growth for all countries?

In times of peace and prosperity, the principles of economic liberalism gain strength. People begin to believe that "a rising tide lifts all boats"—an aphorism attributed to President Kennedy. The classic liberal approach often falls out of favor, however, during tough economic times. Reacting to the Great Depression and the ideological challenge from Communism, the Roosevelt, Truman, and Eisenhower administrations accepted Keynesian policies. This was a setback for free-market principles, but for some time it guaranteed capitalism's stability. Nevertheless, at least two problems were on the horizon.

Keynesian economics assumed that a well-educated elite could decide what is best for national and international economies. Yet the state often takes on an obligation to carry too many increasingly expensive welfare programs including pensions and unemployment benefits. (See Figure 7-4.) The second and larger problem was inflation and a decline in growth, as Keynesian support for full employment required state investments and higher taxes. The combination of high inflation and no growth in the late 1970s, called *stagflation*, led the Federal Reserve (the central banking system of the United States) to sharply raise the interest rate to 11 and then even 20 percent (check today's rates to compare). President Ronald Reagan combined some elements of Keynesianism with deregulation of many industries, weakening of labor unions, and lowering taxes. These measures brought an unprecedented amount of foreign capital to the United States, curbed inflation, and boosted the economy for some time.

In the early 1990s economic liberalism reigned practically unopposed. Its principles have also been boosted by "democratic peace theory" (see Chapter 3): Economic liberals began to claim that the spread of free-market practices contributes to the spread of democracy—and ultimately lessens the probability of war among states (Gartzke 2007). The IMF and World Bank began to stipulate

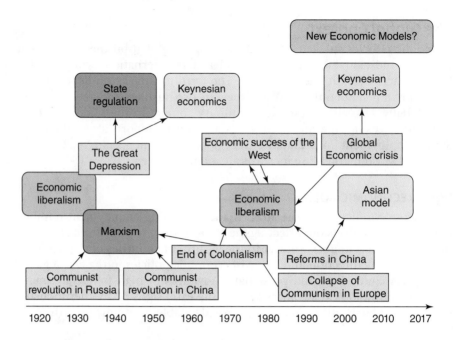

FIGURE 7-4 Economic theories and policies: A snapshot.

that developing countries receiving their loans must implement such neoliberal economic policies as liberalization of trade, direct foreign investments, privatization of state enterprises, and deregulation of business.

A serious discussion continues about the direction of economic politics and the revision of the economic and political guidelines offered to developing countries in the past (Birdsall and Fukuyama 2011). One such approach has been the maximum deregulation of production and finances to jumpstart stagnant and inefficient economies of a wide range of countries. This approach has been called the *Washington Consensus* (because the International Monetary Fund and other financial institution that advocated this "consensus" are located in Washington, D.C.). How successful were such policies? Although liberal economists continue emphasizing the benefits of the "free market," many criticisms of the Washington Consensus deserve attention and careful analysis. Critics, for example, argue that the rigid application of the Washington Consensus may unintentionally destroy the middle class, bring instability, jeopardize democracy, and give excessive power to transnational corporations and export-oriented lobbies. In the end, a few enrich themselves at the expense of many others. Economic inequality between countries and regions has always been an important topic of discussion in international relations.

In the early 1990s, the failure of state-planned Communist economies provided fresh arguments for supporters of government deregulation. Russia and other former Communist countries were adopting capitalism. China allowed elements of a free-market economy in a Communist society in which private property was prohibited for decades. Indian economic elites (which at times had looked with sympathy at the Soviet model of industrialization) also moved away from state economic planning and control. Indian economists concluded that even the most brilliant government bureaucrat could not consistently make great economic and business decisions (Bhagwati 2004).

NORTH–SOUTH DIVIDE AND DEVELOPMENT

Dependency theory, as you remember, predicted that market capitalism and free trade would not reduce the gap between the South and North. Indeed, most countries of Africa and Latin America remained suppliers of cheap resources and services to the North. The *brain drain*, or the exodus of the most educated and skilled individuals from poor countries to developed countries, continued. Some critics of liberalism claimed that deregulation of capital accounts in the 1980s–90s destabilized the global South even more: More individuals tended to keep their money in the banks of the North, and this created the "flight" of capital from the poorer countries. Also, global financial speculators ruined the currencies of Thailand and Argentina in 1998 (Stiglitz 2002).

At the same time, developments of the last twenty to thirty years complicated North–South arguments. In Asia, Hong Kong, Singapore, Taiwan, and then China broke out of poverty and joined the countries of the North in wealth and development. By the 1990s, leaders of most developing countries gained greater access to global finance, markets, trade, and industrial production. Some states of the South, such as Brazil and India, began to integrate their economies into regional and global networks. This complicated the argument about North–South divide and the strategies of economic development.

More than one billion people today in the global South still live on less than a dollar per day. Should the elimination or substantial reduction of poverty become a global policy? If yes, how it should be managed? There are at least three points of view regarding the fight against global poverty. Jeffrey Sachs (2005; 2015), an adviser to the UN from Columbia University, maintains that the solution lies in large direct and sustainable investments to eliminate a global political-economic injustice. Poor countries cannot escape the "poverty trap" without substantial help from the North. In *The End of Poverty*, Sachs argues that poverty would be completely eliminated if the rich countries would pay around $200 billion for twenty years.

William Easterly (2001; 2006) of New York University and economist Dambisa Moyo (2010) represent another view. They believe that foreign direct help may destroy initiative, contribute to corruption, and create a culture of dependency instead of private entrepreneurship. The poverty trap, Easterly and Moyo maintain, is avoidable only if the poor are given freedom and the right incentives.

Pakistani children play in a stream polluted by sewage from nearby localities, in a suburb of Islamabad in 2015. The UN estimates that more than one in six people worldwide do not have access to 20–50 liters (5–13 gallons) of safe, fresh water a day to ensure their basic needs for drinking, cooking, and cleaning. Some economists suggest that reducing global poverty requires better understanding and addressing of people's needs on the grassroots level.

Finally, economists Abhijit Banerjee and Esther Duflo (2011) turn to micro-economics. They maintain that both economic aid and private entrepreneurship may work only if we better understand how the poor make financial and economic decisions. Help should be delivered, but the donors should know when and how it should be distributed and cases in which local initiatives and choices should be supported. An important key to success here is education and access to information. We will return to this subject again in the concluding chapter.

GLOBAL INTERDEPENDENCE

Developments after the Cold War—and especially the growth of international cooperation and financial transactions—have led to a new economic and political interdependence (Doremus et al. 1998). Decisions on the national level can have a profound impact on others as well. A mortgage crisis in the United States in 2008 and a financial crisis in the European Union in 2010 and 2011 threatened the financial and economic stability of much of the world economy. Public debt, or the debt of a country's central government, surpassed many countries' GDPs. (See Table 7-4.) These countries often need substantial international help to avoid a financial disaster. In the case of large economies like Italy or Japan, international institutions like the IMF are helpless. This chain of problems could easily result in disastrous financial and economic instability. A rising tide may lift all boats, but in stormy waters it is dangerous to be tied to the ship.

On paper, the path to global economic prosperity may look easy. The United States should have an export-led expansion, and it should reduce import-based consumption. Europeans and Asians should slow their exports and buy more from the United States. The U.S. government should decrease its spending and increase interest rates. These steps will reduce consumer spending

TABLE 7-4 Public debt as percent of GDP, selected countries.

Country	Estimates, 2012–2015
Japan	212%
Zimbabwe	209%
Greece	167%
Iceland	133%
Lebanon	129%
Italy	126%
Canada	84%
United States	72%
China	31%
Russia	15%

Sources: Woodall 2011, 107; CIA World Factbook 2015.

and encourage savings. However, instead of decreasing, U.S. government spending increased dramatically from 2001 to 2015. In the long run, this situation is likely to threaten the position of the dollar as the world's reserve currency and further destabilize world finances. Meanwhile, the Chinese government is reluctant to permit their currency to rise against the dollar. These measures would make China's exports to the United States more expensive, and U.S. products would cost less in China. However, such policies are difficult to implement because of China's surplus-oriented and job-generating strategies. Instead, unlike the euro, the yuan is still pegged to the dollar.

Finally, Europe could reduce interest rates and regulations to promote investments. It could also trim social programs that weigh heavily on state budgets. However, lower interest rates would reduce the money supply to European banks. And cuts in social programs would require serious political sacrifices, which almost no political parties are willing to accept.

MULTINATIONAL CORPORATIONS

In the 1970s, the growing interdependence among economies of the most developed countries created possibilities for large companies to invest internationally, transfer their production and research facilities abroad in search of cheaper labor, and create joint enterprises outside their homeland. Royal Dutch Shell, British Petroleum, and Exxon, among others, became what we call today *multinational corporations*. Japanese companies Toyota and Honda opened their American and European branches to sell cars while avoiding protectionist barriers. Soon South Korean giants Hyundai and Daewoo followed the pattern. In the sphere of global consumption, McDonalds, Walmart, and Starbucks became the largest multinational corporations. What role do these and other multinational corporations play in the global economy?

On the one hand, as some scholars argue, multinational corporations have become new powerful and stateless actors affecting state and IGO policies. Unlike most public officials in democratic countries, who are elected by popular vote, powerful CEOs of international corporations are not. Yet their decisions affect billions of people. Corporations may negatively affect small businesses and may overlook violations of human rights in poor countries (Ruggie 2013). On the other hand, multinational corporations create new jobs and invest in local infrastructure. Despite their wealth and power, they are subject to national and international regulations. Multinational corporations must also maintain their public image and conduct policies that are in line with public opinion.

INTERNATIONAL INSTITUTIONS AND THE GLOBAL ECONOMY

Whereas many countries are unwilling to implement tough economic measures to combat global poverty, every economy is becoming increasingly interdependent. Does the world therefore need new institutions to take charge of the global economy and trade? Some suggest that we already have such a system, but an imperfect one.

Although the IMF, the World Bank, and the WTO are backed by the governments of the economically strongest states, they and other international institutions face strong criticism for the way they operate (Peet 2009; Blustein 2009).

Critics point to corporate bureaucracy and a lack of transparency. Some argue that these organizations act largely on behalf of a few wealthy state members (Stiglitz 2002) and neglect the increasing importance in international trade of countries in Asia, Latin America, and Africa. Countries vote in global organizations based on their position in the world economy, an arrangement that evokes increasing criticism (Hoekman and Kostecki 2010; Rapkin and Strand 2006).

Loans are another focus of debates. Supporters of the IMF believe that loans help states of the South create independent economic and banking systems, develop efficient government institutions, build social infrastructure, and more. Critics argue, however, that the IMF dictates to sovereign states how they should run their banking systems and economies (Woods 2007).

The classic assumptions of economic theories may need a fresh look today. Global trade means the erosion of state power and the increasing influence of nonstate institutions and even individuals, such as financial speculator George Soros, a famous philanthropist and sponsor of nongovernment organizations. Studies show that global corporations can make a profit and contribute to social policies at the same time (Hartman and Werhane 2009). Yet governments may no longer protect their citizens economically, and corporations may choose to benefit their shareholders first before making responsible economic decisions (Madeley 2009).

 Go online to read about George Soros's Open Society Foundations.

ECONOMIC GLOBALIZATION AND CONFLICT

How does economic and financial globalization affect international conflicts? In the first decade of the 1900s, European economies were growing; countries placed fewer limits on imports, exports, immigration, and the exchange of products (Yergin and Stanislaw 1998). Yet a global war broke out in 1914. Does this example mean that globalization cannot prevent another global conflict?

Concerns continue about the possibility of new international conflicts caused by economic fears. In the United States, some people wonder if China's growing economic power will lead to a conflict. Such fears are fed by historical analogies, but also by the logic of mercantilism. Yet, contrary to some predictions, the early twenty-first century shows that mutual trade creates interdependence and increases the chances for cooperation. And, as we have learned, mercantilism is often flawed. For instance, according to its logic, future wars are likely between countries that have vast oil and gas resources (such as Russia, Saudi Arabia, and the United States) and countries that consume these products but don't have them (such as Japan, China, or India). In this reasoning, oil and gas are strategic products that directly affect a nation's security. However, nothing says that such a scenario lies ahead these days.

CHECK YOUR KNOWLEDGE

▶ What is outsourcing?
▶ Explain the *Asian developmental model*. Why can't the United States apply this model domestically?
▶ What is the main argument of the book *The End of Poverty*?
▶ What are the differences between macroeconomics and microeconomics?

THE USES OF HISTORY: China as a Free Rider of Liberal Globalization

Background

China's transformation from a country ravaged by Communist experiments into an economic and financial giant is a most dramatic story of recent times. During the century's first decade, China's economy grew by up to 9 percent each year, and its exports increased even faster. China is now the second-largest exporting country in the world, after quickly surpassing the United Kingdom and Germany. In 2010, it became the second largest economy in the world, outpacing Japan. China's contribution to global economic growth grew from 2.6 percent in 1981 to 9.7 percent in 2001 and should reach 28 percent in 2016. Even the global crisis that started in 2008 did not significantly affect Chinese ascendancy, contrary to pessimistic expectations of many economists. If it continues this way, some economists argue, China in twenty years may replace the United States as the vehicle of international economic development.

For students of international political economy, China's rise poses important questions. What were the domestic and international wellsprings of this success? Which economic theories and policies "worked" for China? What impact will China's rise have on international relations?

Socialism w/ chinese aspects

China's "economic miracle" is rooted in the 1978 reforms of the Communist leader Deng Xiaoping (1904–1997). He broke with Communist dogma by allowing small private property, retail trade, and profit-making. More surprisingly, Deng's reforms showed that the Communist regime could shift from a state-directed economy that barred private property to a state-directed economy with private property—all without significant social disturbances. Chinese politicians and economies learned from the mistakes that contributed to the collapse of the Soviet Union. Unlike Mikhail Gorbachev, Deng did not combine economic liberalization with a shift from one-party rule to democracy. The Chinese leaders, like Gorbachev, wasted billions of dollars to keep afloat existing state-run industries. But in contrast to the Soviet leader, they shepherded the emergence of a new economy, privately owned and run on market principles.

Analysis

What were the key elements of China's economy and international trade policies? This economy from the start was focused on producing consumer goods for export. At first, China produced cheap, poor-quality clothing, toys, and other goods. During the 1990s, however, Chinese export became technologically advanced, using Japanese, German, and American know-how, for instance, to produce electronic goods and household durables. As a result of thirty years of uninterrupted economic growth, from three to four hundred million people, many of them peasants, have risen from poverty to the middle class.

Soviet leader Mikhail Gorbachev (L) shakes hands with Chinese senior leader Deng Xiaoping 16 May 1989 in Beijing. Both leaders inspired and managed dramatic economic reforms in their countries with dramatically different results.

China became the first big country in the global South to move rapidly to the position of an economic superpower, avoiding many of the social and economic problems that plague other developing economies on the way up. China has not faced mass unemployment. It has not become dependent on foreign imports and loans. Instead, China has made the leading developed states, including the United States, dependent on *its* exports. Chinese leaders chose the export-oriented model of East Asian "tigers"—Taiwan, Singapore, and Hong Kong—combining the advantages of cheap educated labor with foreign investments and technologies.

Domestic Factors

There were several domestic factors behind China's success. First, China had a strong authoritarian government, ruled by the Communist party. It could conduct long-term policies practically unchallenged domestically. The Communist leadership continued its economic reforms without democratization. Second, China had an almost unlimited supply of hard-working labor, mostly peasants. Moreover, unlike in most other poor countries, they were educated, thanks to a compulsory educational system modeled after the Soviet Union's in the 1950s. China today also has one of the largest pools of skilled professionals. Many of them receive college degrees abroad and come back. Third, this workforce and their incomes remain under tight control of the party leadership, which maintains the *household registration system* in which people must obtain a government permit to establish residence. All employees in the city have to belong to *danwei* (the work unit) and receive their wages and benefits from it, including housing and medical coverage. Party leadership established a monopoly on large capital investments through a system of state-licensed banks—above all, the Bank of China. All peasants and city dwellers must deposit their wages into these banks.

Such arrangements would upset the vast majority in the United States, where they would quickly be branded as state Socialism. In fact, the Chinese leadership calls its policies "Socialism with Chinese characteristics." The government keeps financial, economic, and labor policies under its tight control. For many years, the Communist Party suppressed destructive social conflicts and prevented workers from demanding more rights and higher wages (Gong 2009).

China's policies resemble mercantilism, yet the strategies aim at capitalizing on the liberal economic policies in economy and finances. In a word, China's version of mercantilism worked well only because Beijing acts as a free rider of a Western-built liberal international economic system. If other countries had

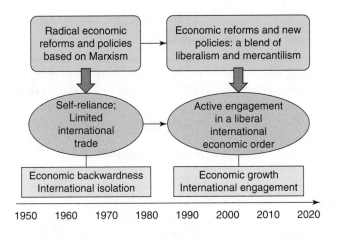

FIGURE 7-5 China's economic policies and international trade: A chronological snapshot.

used the same policies as China has done, or if countries used tariffs and other trade restrictions, Chinese export-oriented growth would have been impossible. (See Figure 7-5.)

International Factors

Several international factors helped China. First, the United States after 1971 stopped treating China as a Communist enemy. In fact, after 1979 it began to treat China as a strategic partner in the Cold War against the Soviet Union. As a result of its improved relations with the West, China successfully negotiated the return of Hong Kong, a prosperous British colony, to Chinese jurisdiction in 1997.

Second, China's alliance with the United States allowed ethnic Chinese from Taiwan, Hong Kong, and Singapore to invest in the Chinese economy. This policy brought massive foreign investments to China's export-driven economy—not only from other states, but from individuals and companies as well.

Third, the United States opened American markets to Chinese goods, and in 1994 President Clinton abolished all restrictions on Chinese exports. The United States made no systematic attempt to prevent outsourcing of American high-tech industries to China. Other Western states practiced outsourcing as well, in competition with the United States.

What, then, can be the impact of China's growth on international relations? As a popular German journal stated, "China is seeking to engage with the West, but on its own terms" (*Der Spiegel* 2010). It looks like the Chinese leadership would try to pursue a "free-rider" policy as long as it could afford. During the last decade Beijing sought to turn China into the largest manufacturing center in the world—becoming essentially what the United States was in the 1920s through 1950s. In addition to importing Apple iPods, Ford trucks, and Heineken, it also seeks to create competitive Chinese models (Aaronson 2010). This policy, economists argue, helps China steal millions of jobs from countries with high-paid labor (Krugman 2009).

Forecasts

From a realist perspective, China may also challenge Western security. Due to Washington's financial obligations, the financial health of the United States is dependent, at least in theory, on decisions made by the party leadership in Peking. Chinese military expenditures rose to $130 billion in 2014, and they continue to grow. It has the second largest military budget in the world. Of course, the U.S. military budget is about eight times bigger, but China has the resources to increase its spending even more. Security experts point to China's ambitions to control the seas around it. What would Washington do if China decides one day to take Taiwan by force?

Liberal economists dismiss these arguments. Chinese economic progress, liberals argue, has brought hundreds of millions in China out of poverty. Hundreds of millions of consumers all over the world benefit from the low price of Chinese goods. During the 2000s China became the engine of economic growth elsewhere as well, as China invested in Africa, America, and Southern Asia (Zoellick 2012). By this logic, Chinese society will gradually evolve as a large middle class pushes for political reform. If China practices neo-mercantilism, that is no more than necessary at this stage to provide stability (McKinnon 2010).

China increasingly complies with international organizations and international norms of behavior. After all, it does not want to contest the basic rules of the liberal international order (Ikenberry 2011a; 2011b). China wants to be not only an important international player. It wants to be a good player with a sound global strategy (Economy 2010a). Fears of China's financial takeover may be mistaken. After all, China provides American consumers with affordable goods in exchange for "pieces of paper." The dollar reserves accumulated by the Bank of China are the savings of Chinese people—the fruits of their hard work. No Chinese leadership would risk ruining the U.S. Treasury by "failing" the dollar. Liberals write about the United States and China as mutually dependent—although some of them admit that China benefitted from this dependency much more than its trade partner (Ferguson 2010).

From the constructivist view, too, China is unlikely to become a global adversary. China has never pushed for world domination. After decades of poverty and suffering, China developed a very different national purpose—achievement and excellence—as an economic, not political superpower. This may explain China's extraordinary efforts to modernize everything from airports and superhighways to high-speed trains. The Chinese government turned the 2008 Summer Olympics in Beijing into a demonstration of national pride but also modernity. The legitimacy of the party rests ultimately not on ideology or political promises but rather on economic improvements and growing consumption. Per capita income in China is barely one-tenth of America's (which is close to $50,000). But consumption and living standards grow every year. In 2009, China became the world's largest market for automobiles.

World systems theorists, as you should remember, believe that China is bent on replacing the United States in a few decades as the core of the global capitalist system. These assumptions echo postcolonial studies, which would expect former colonies to demand an end to Western global domination (Arrighi and Li Zhang 2011). The global financial crisis gave more credibility to such views. The crisis hit the West; China's GDP in 2009 grew by 8.7 percent, largely because the Bank of China provided a $587 billion stimulus package to the domestic economy. Domestic consumption and construction soared. This was a fine example of Keynesian economic policies comparable to the Marshall Plan.

Liberal economists argue back that China's state-run capitalism still has to demonstrate its lasting ability to generate innovation. If the West declines, they argue, then China's export would either decline or turn to domestic consumption. Chinese salaries would grow—meaning that China would become more "Americanized." Chinese Communist authorities may yet run up against the global trend toward openness and individualism. Already, China is trying to reduce its brain drain by offering incentives to its citizens who return to China after studying in the West. Moreover, top Chinese leaders are reportedly in training to learn more about world economic trends (Pin-Lin 2010, 10).

In the absence of political opposition, and with a monopoly on power, party leaders can make decisions with relative ease. Their real challenge is to keep economic growth going. And, as history teaches, no success lasts forever.

Zhou Qunfei, Chairwoman of Lens Technology, is one of the richest women in China. Her personal wealth exceeded $10 billion in 2015. Will China's economic growth continue to reduce poverty, or will it increase social polarization between rich and poor?

Questions

1. How successful, in your opinion, will the Chinese economic model be? How many countries will follow China's example? What specific features do some other countries lack that China has?

2. Does China have enough "soft power" to peacefully conquer people's hearts and minds globally? How can China increase its soft power and promote its economic policies?

3. Individual freedoms and economic security are not mutually exclusive. Yet as we could see throughout this chapter, specific countries' policies may emphasize one at the expense of the other. If you had to choose, what is more important to you: to have fewer individual freedoms but be economically secure, or to have only some economic security but be able to exercise all individual freedoms?

4. A thought experiment: Which particular individual liberty (e.g., freedom of speech, freedom to form a party, freedom to travel) could you sacrifice for one particular economic guarantee (such as a full-time job, paid tuition, a pension)?

CONCLUSION

Economic theories rise and fall with the tides of history. Global interdependence challenges past theories, formed when a few wealthy states could define economic and financial policies for others as well. For decades, free-market principles worked well in Western Europe, Japan, and North America. In the twenty-first century, many Asian countries have adopted free-market policies too. However, "one size fits all" free-market policies can often damage rather than help countries with their unique financial, governmental, and social institutions. For example, Singapore and China did not simply turn to liberal democracy, and Russia's attempts to shift rapidly to both a free-market economy and liberal democracy cost it dearly; its productive capacities declined dramatically and the population suffered. Today's experience suggests that sound economic policies require knowledge of each country's political, social, and cultural conditions.

KEY TERMS

autarky 239
balance of trade 224
comparative advantage 232
consumption 222
currency 223
dependency theory 237
economic climate 236
economic liberalism 230
economic sanctions 228

fair trade 238
fiscal policy 229
gross domestic product (GDP) 222
international political economy (IPE) 221
Keynesian economics 229
macroeconomics 229
mercantilism 226

microeconomics 239
national purpose 235
North (global) 237
outsourcing 243
production 222
protectionism 228
regional trade agreements 234
South (global) 237
tariff 228

Visual Review INTERNATIONAL POLITICAL ECONOMY

IDEAS

INTERNATIONAL POLITICAL ECONOMY
- Interaction of politics and economics in an international context

DEVELOPMENT OF LIBERALISM
- States' production, consumption, finances, and trade

ARGUMENTS

MERCANTILISM
- Accumulating resources
- Protecting domestic markets

ECONOMIC LIBERALISM
- Classical: Free production, trade, and consumption
- Keynesian: Governments should play an active role
- Reliance on international economic and financial institutions, as well as trade agreements

CONSTRUCTIVISM
- Economic policies depend on the social, political, and cultural conditions in which these policies are implemented

OTHER THEORIES
- Marxism: The world is dominated by a ruling class, which owns the major means of production
- Dependency: Technology-driven developed nations have been receiving more benefits from international trade

CONTEXTS AND APPLICATIONS

THE INDIVIDUAL DECISIONS CONTEXT
- Political leadership affects economic choices
- Microeconomics: Behavior of individual consumers influences international markets

THE STATE POLICIES CONTEXT
- Domestic factors affect *surplus-oriented* and *trade deficit-tolerant* economic policies

THE GLOBAL CONTEXT
- Global economic and financial cooperation has led to both greater economic and political interdependence and new tensions and conflicts

Critical Thinking

❶ Compare and contrast mercantilism and economic liberalism.
❷ Would economic liberals support international trade sanctions, and if so, under what circumstances? Use one contemporary example.
❸ Why are tariffs harmful for international trade? Can tariffs be helpful, and who would benefit from them?
❹ Why are the International Monetary Fund and the World Bank often considered tools of the global North to dominate the global South?
❺ If the United States and European Union imposed 100 percent tariffs on all Chinese goods, how would it affect China and the West? How would it affect you personally?

8 International Terrorism

We learned about an enemy who is sophisticated, patient, disciplined, and lethal.

—FINAL REPORT OF THE NATIONAL COMMISSION ON TERRORIST ATTACKS UPON THE UNITED STATES, 2004.

O N SEPTEMBER 11, 2001, A RADICAL GROUP CALLED *AL-QAEDA* CARRIED OUT TERRORIST STRIKES AGAINST THE UNITED STATES. THE GROUP DESTROYED THE World Trade Center in New York and a portion of the Pentagon near Washington, D.C. The terrorists hijacked four civilian airplanes and flew them into their targets, dying along with their victims. One plane crashed in Pennsylvania. Fifteen of the hijackers were from Saudi Arabia, and four came from other Arab countries of the Middle East. The attackers were trained in al-Qaeda camps in Pakistan, Sudan, and Afghanistan. The Bush administration issued an ultimatum to the Taliban government, the religious group that controlled Afghanistan at that time and that gave refuge to al-Qaeda. The ultimatum called for immediate delivery of Osama bin Laden and his associates to an American court. The Taliban offered to try bin Laden in Afghanistan in an Islamic court instead. The White House rejected the offer, and U.S. and British troops launched a war in Afghanistan.

The allied troops quickly established control over the country yet failed to capture bin Laden and destroy the Taliban and al-Qaeda completely. In 2003 the United States sent troops to Iraq. It took ten years to hunt down and kill bin Laden in his hideout in Pakistan. Al-Qaeda, however, was not destroyed; it maintained its lethal potential. And new violent groups, including the Islamic State, al-Shabaab, and others, appeared and strengthened their positions in the Middle East, as well as in several countries in Asia and Africa.

Left: Light beams in place of New York City's World Trade Center, which was destroyed in the terrorist attacks of September 11, 2001.

The military operations and political decisions triggered by 9/11 had a profound and lasting impact on international relations. The United States and other countries committed enormous resources to these efforts. Some analysts believe that these types of decisions and policies, to be effective, should be significantly improved, and that the United States should show its global strength and leadership. Others emphasize the necessity for the United States and its allies to scale back, end the "War on Terror," let other countries solve their own political problems, and focus on more pressing problems of the economy. Yet others argue that although the struggle against terrorism should continue, it should increasingly move to the nonmilitary phase, when law enforcement, IGOs, and NGOs turn to legal, economic, and social issues that spawn terrorism.

Which argument is stronger? How dangerous is international terrorism, and how does it affect the world? Let's take a close look at the theories explaining international terrorism and explore how states, international organizations, and the entire global system deal with the challenge.

Learning Objectives	▶ Define terrorism, explaining its logic, strategies, and methods.
	▶ Explain how states, international organizations, and the entire global system deal with the challenge of terrorism.
	▶ Distinguish among different views of terrorism and counterterrorist policies.
	▶ Apply your knowledge about terrorism and counterterrorism in three contexts of analysis.

Ideas

Leaders of most countries agree that the problem of international terrorism needs immediate attention. They disagree, however, as to how terrorism can be defeated. Journalists and security experts debate definitions and policies to deal with terrorism. Governments and international organizations have committed huge resources to study, understand, and combat it. Thousands of people have died. Many areas of our lives, including public safety procedures and international travel, have been altered. In this chapter we will define terrorism, examine its historical roots, discuss counterterrorism, and critically examine various views of terrorism and counterterrorism.

Terrorism and Counterterrorism

Terrorism is violence by nonstate actors, such as individuals or groups, to achieve radical political goals. Terrorism is thus a form of *political radicalism*—ideas and methods to produce rapid, dramatic change in the social or political order. Terrorism can be state sponsored, in that a foreign government can provide financial, military, or logistical support to terrorists to further its policy goals. Yet in essence it remains a nonstate phenomenon.

As a means to achieve political goals, terrorism can be viewed as domestic or international. **Domestic terrorism** pursues domestic political goals such as the dismantling of a government or a change in state policies. This does not necessarily present a direct danger to other states or international organizations. **International terrorism**, which is the main focus of this chapter, challenges international stability by threatening one country or a region. It rejects international law and defies international organizations. The distinctions between domestic and international forms are imprecise, however; some apparently domestic acts of terrorism have regional or even global consequences.

International terrorism differs from guerrilla warfare, gangsterism, or piracy. **Guerrilla warfare** is political violence by identifiable, irregular combat units, usually to seize state power, win autonomy, or found new states (see Chapter 5). *Gangsters* and *pirates* may practice random killing, extortions, and kidnappings, but their goal is not political: It is profit (Boot 2009). International terrorism usually sets no limits on violence and targets civilians in the name of extreme political goals.

States and international organizations develop measures, called **counterterrorism**, to prevent and combat international and domestic terrorism. This is a government's policy, with a budget, conducted according to legal rulings, and exercised by a special agency in coordination with other offices, international organizations and alliances, NGOs, or independent contractors. In the United States many federal institutions are involved in counterterrorism, above all the Department of Homeland Security, the CIA, and the NSA (see Chapter 5). They gather information, pursue and eliminate terrorist groups, and disrupt their activities including their financial operations (Priest and Arkin 2010a). The price tag of their operations is measured in hundreds of billions of dollars.

Why Definitions Are Important

There are serious consequences to the use of the labels *terrorism* or *terrorist*. The policy choices of states and international organizations often depend on how terrorism is defined. Also, violent individuals, groups, and governments typically avoid being associated with terrorism and often contest its definitions (Hoffman 1998; Sloan 2006).

LEGITIMIZATION OF MILITARY ACTIONS

Because terrorism is considered an illegal form of violence, countries may choose extreme measures to deal with it. By labeling a group an international terrorist organization or a violent act as an act of international *terror*, a government can establish a justification for violent countermeasures, just as in times

---

terrorism Random violence conducted by non-state actors, such as individuals or groups, against governments or their citizens to achieve political goals.

domestic terrorism Terrorism to achieve domestic political goals, such as dismantling a government or a change in policies.

international terrorism Terrorism that involves international groups, interaction between countries, or international organizations, often with regional or global consequences.

guerrilla warfare Political violence by identifiable, irregular combat units, usually to seize state power, win autonomy, or found new states.

counterterrorism Long-term policies and specific short-term measures to prevent and combat international and domestic terrorism.

Members of the Jordanian women's police special operations team wait to compete against elite anti-terrorism squads from eighteen countries during the 2015 Annual International Warrior Competition. Will the coalition of Arab states be able to stabilize the Middle East by themselves, without the military assistance of Western countries?

On the companion website, you will find links to terrorist designation lists, the National Consortium for the Study of Terrorism and Responses to Terrorism, and the RAND database of worldwide terrorist incidents.

of war. Even an invasion of foreign territory can be labeled self-defense if it targets terrorists. In the wake of September 11, 2001, there was evidence that the Afghani government provided asylum and created conditions beneficial to the al-Qaeda terrorists. This gave the United States a justification to send troops to Afghanistan, with support of the international community. Note that the decision to label an act as *terrorism* or an organization as *terrorist* remains a prerogative of governments. The U.S. Department of State maintains an official list of foreign terrorist organizations, which is regularly updated.

MOBILIZATION OF INTERNATIONAL LAW

International law generally favors cooperation against terrorist groups or states accused of sponsoring terrorism. In 1988, a terrorist act against civilian Pan Am Flight 103 over Lockerbie, Scotland, killed 270 people. When it was established that a Libyan official had been involved, Western countries imposed sanctions on Libya. Its leader, Muammar Qaddafi, was kept away from international meetings, including UN sessions. Only after Libya formally apologized and offered compensation to the victims' families were sanctions lifted (Bergman 2008).

Also according to international law, individuals suspected of terrorist acts are subject to *extradition*, or removal from one country to another (where they committed their violent acts) to face charges. Many states cooperate with one another and extradite suspects. For example, in 2015, a British suspect was extradited to the United States to face trial there for running a training camp when he had lived in the United States. Turkey apprehended and returned to the UK three British schoolgirls who had run away to join ISIS. Governments revoke the travel passports of individuals accused of terrorist activities

(Abelson 2015; Wright 2006). Saudi Arabia chose to detain terrorism suspects in specially organized rehabilitation camps (Stern 2010).

Overall, the need to combat international terrorism has created an unprecedented network of new bilateral and international military, economic, and intelligence sharing and financial agreements. In a word, the threat of terrorism is changing international relations.

JUSTIFICATION OF OTHER POLICIES

Some states may use swift counterterrorist measures questionable from the viewpoint of international law. For example, after the assassination of Israeli athletes during the 1972 Olympic Games in Munich by Palestinian militants, the Israeli government set up a special squad to scout and kill the perpetrators. The squad frequently acted illegally, using almost the same violent means as the hunted terrorists. (It was the subject of the controversial film *Munich*, directed by Stephen Spielberg.) Countries may also unilaterally toughen domestic security laws including street surveillance, passenger screening at airports, and travel restrictions for foreigners. Some view most forms of counterterrorism as justifiable because terrorists are "outside the law" (Klein 2005). Others disagree on legal grounds. After 9/11 many criticized the U.S. government for suspending normal juridical norms for suspects in terrorism, keeping them in special prisons, such as at the U.S. base at Guantanamo in Cuba, and even using torture to obtain information. Critics also claimed that the "Patriot Act," a set of domestic counterterrorist policies signed by President George W. Bush in October 2001, limited civic freedoms at home. In 2011, President Barack Obama signed a four-year extension of three key provisions in the act. In 2015 some parts of the law were renewed through 2019.

The graves of five murdered Israeli athletes in Tel Aviv. Palestinian terrorists kidnapped and killed eleven Israeli athletes at the Munich Olympics in 1972 in a crime that shocked the world. Israel launched covert operations to retaliate for the murder.

CASE IN POINT > *The Terrorism Label Can Be Misused*

Because policies are frequently based on how terrorism is defined, the term is subject to misuse. First, some governments use the label to combat domestic opposition. The Chinese government used this tactic in Tibet to crush public protests against oppressive Communist rule.

Second, governments may argue that international law does not apply when terrorism is at stake. For example, after 2001, U.S. authorities identified many suspected terrorists as "illegal combatants" and disregarded the Geneva protocols, which prohibit indefinite detention of prisoners of war. For years, prisoners were kept at a U.S. military base at Guantanamo. This precedent caused serious domestic and international criticism of both the George W. Bush and Obama administrations.

Third, governments could use the *terrorism* label to settle personal scores with political or business opponents. By accusing a group or individuals of terrorist activities, a government can delegitimize them in the eyes of the courts and public opinion.

CRITICAL THINKING

❶ Suggest examples of the potential misuse of the term *terrorism*.
❷ Search the Web for "We are not terrorists" (in quotation marks). You will find an amazing diversity of quotes, speeches, and statements. Select five cases representing different groups. What arguments do the authors of these statements use to separate themselves from terrorism? If they are not terrorists, what do they call themselves? Why do they need to defend their image, and to whom do they appeal?

CHECK YOUR KNOWLEDGE

▶ Define political radicalism. Can political radicalism be nonviolent?
▶ How does terrorism differ from gangsterism and guerrilla warfare?

How Terrorism Works

When we ask how terrorism works, we should look not only at methods, such as suicide bombing. We should also look at assumptions and supposed justifications.

ASSUMPTIONS AND METHODS

Terrorism by definition is rooted in an assumption that it is practically impossible to defeat states and international coalitions in an open military battle. Governments have support from businesses, intelligence, armed forces, and law-enforcement institutions. Therefore, terrorists rely on unconventional methods to cause fear among the population of a targeted country or a group of states (Chaliand and Blin 2007). They rely on secrecy and the ability to keep their cells invisible from the governments. The Internet often becomes an asset to terrorist groups because governments have little control over it (Kello 2013; Horgan 2009, 2).

Terrorist groups are often extremely difficult to infiltrate. Most are in reality *networks*, or loose collectives. Members of one group may not know members from others. Instead of building a formal hierarchical structure, they rely on loyalty and mutual surveillance. Their sense of collective involvement is reaffirmed by spiritual and material rewards for devotion—and merciless punishments for betrayal (Miller 2013; Gunaratna 2002).

Terrorist groups use violence or threats of violence to influence governments or key decision makers. Government officials are not always the direct targets. Terrorists often target civilians, including children, using random killings, bombings in public places, and attacks on shopping malls, television stations, or hotels (Nacos 2009). Everyone is potentially vulnerable. For example, Boko Haram, a violent Islamist movement based in northeast Nigeria, kidnapped over two hundred schoolgirls in 2014 from a secondary school. The girls were targeted because Islamists viewed all women educated in schools as violating the Sharia law. Many of the captured girls were later moved across international borders as slaves.

Future terrorist attacks may attempt to use weapons of mass destruction (WMD): nuclear, biological, or chemical weapons. A small suitcase nuclear device in the hands of a terrorist can destroy New York, Washington, Moscow, Tokyo, or London. Preventing nuclear proliferation and a leak of nuclear know-how to terrorist organizations, therefore, remains a priority for the international community (Howard and Forest 2008; Hoffman 2010). The Internet and other communication networks add the possibility of **cyberterrorism**—paralyzing attacks online on political, financial, and economic centers. Threats may range from significant theft of data and disruption of computer operations to more deadly attacks that destroy entire systems and physical equipment (Kello 2013; Gertz 2011). Cyberterrorism poses a significant threat to a country's military capabilities by threatening its logistics network, stealing its operational plans, or obstructing its ability to deliver weapons on target. Even when a cyberterrorist is identified, it is difficult to retaliate (Lynn 2010). We will address these threats later in the chapter. Table 8-1 summarizes the most common methods of terrorism.

cyberterrorism
Paralyzing online attacks on political, financial, and military centers.

The face of international terrorism changed irrevocably after September 2001. Before, terrorists usually relied on **coercion** and **extortion** to get what they wanted from governments—while promising not to use coercion in the future if their demands are satisfied. Negotiations between states and terrorists were possible (Bueno de Mesquita 2005). Bin Laden and his associates created a new brand of terrorism: They aimed to cause a moral and political defeat to the West, to create a new political order, and rejected negotiations.

coercion and extortion The use of force and threats of force to compel others to comply with demands.

Terrorists look for publicity, or *public exposure*. By committing an act of violence, a radical group is likely to attract the attention of millions. This is important for at least two reasons. First, the group may rapidly publicize its agenda to seek sympathy (Pape 2003; Pillar 2001). Second, public exposure often helps a terrorist group to recruit supporters, sponsors, and new members. Copycat terrorist acts may also follow (Coleman 2004). Figure 8-1 summarizes the methods of terrorism.

THE "LOGIC" AND STRATEGIES OF TERRORISM

Terrorism is a means to achieve a particular political goal. Most terrorist groups use relatively similar arguments to justify their violence. Terrorism is explained as a method of *last resort*. Terrorism is portrayed as a desperate response to an acute problem. Once the source of injustice is removed, then violence will end. The Mau Mau groups in Kenya in the 1950s used terrorism to fight British

TABLE 8-1 Methods of Contemporary Terrorism

Methods	Examples
Attacks against civilians in public places	In 2005, a series of coordinated suicide attacks in London took the lives of fifty-six people. Prerecorded statements from the perpetrators claimed that the attacks were in response to UK participation in the wars in Iraq and Afghanistan. In 2014, three Israeli teenagers were kidnapped at the Israeli settlement in the West Bank, as they were returning home. They have been killed.
Targeting journalists	In 2015 two gunmen—both radical Islamists—broke into the office of the satirical cartoon journal *Charlie Hebdo* in Paris and in cold blood killed twelve journalists and cartoonists. Around this time ISIS executioners in Syria staged executions of several Western journalists and posted the scenes of the killings on the Web.
Attacks against government offices	In 2011, terrorists attacked the American diplomatic compound in Benghazi, Libya, killing U.S. Ambassador J. Christopher Stevens and U.S. Foreign Service Officer Sean Smith.
Attacks against military targets	In October 2000, two suicide bombers killed seventeen U.S. sailors and damaged the Navy ship, USS *Cole*, in Aden Harbor in Yemen. The terrorist group al-Qaeda took responsibility for the attacks.
Hostage taking	On June 27, 1976, a plane on its way from Tel Aviv through Athens to Paris was hijacked and 248 passengers were taken hostage; the plane landed in Entebbe, Uganda. The terrorists demanded the release of their fellows—mostly Palestinians—from various prisons.
Cyberterrorism	In May 2007, Russian hackers became enraged by Estonia's decision to remove the monument to a Soviet soldier from World War II from a central square in Tallinn, the Estonian capital. A massive cyberattack paralyzed the Estonian government for days. In 2013, several cyber attacks that originated in North Korea hit South Korean financial institutions.

forces and local civilians collaborating with them. The terrorists promised to stop their attacks if the British left. Terrorists often argue for *collective responsibility*. If civilians die in a terrorist act, it is claimed, they paid the price for being on the side causing injustice. Osama bin Laden, in his *Letter to America* in 2002, claimed that those who died in terrorist attacks on September 11, 2001, including Muslims, were guilty because they supported U.S. policies as taxpayers and consumers.

Finally, terrorism is justified by those who use it as an act of *retaliation*. Terrorist groups often call their attacks a payback for grievances. The Marriott Hotel bombing in Pakistan in 2008 was an act of retaliation from local terrorist groups for Pakistan's cooperation with the United States. The two perpetrators of the 2013 terrorist act in Boston reportedly vented their grievances

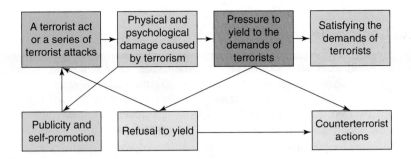

FIGURE 8-1 The process of terrorism.

against U.S. foreign policy. The 2015 brutal attack of the terrorist group al-Shabaab on a Kenyan college that took the lives of 147 people was an act of retaliation against the Kenyan government for its earlier crackdown against al-Shabaab.

Terrorist groups may pursue different goals, but most of their strategies remain consistent. There are at least five such strategies: (1) intimidation, (2) attrition, (3) provocation, (4) spoiling, and (5) outbidding (Kydd and Walter 2006). Using intimidation and attrition, terrorists show their strength and willingness to destroy. Using provocation, terrorists "invite" overreaction and violence to keep the situation unstable. Provocations often force governments, international organizations, and individuals to respond in ways that aid the terrorists' cause. When terrorists turn to spoiling, their aim is to expose their enemies' weaknesses and the inability to stop terrorism. The outbidding strategy helps terrorists demonstrate their willingness to persevere and appear undefeatable.

> ▶ Explain "collective responsibility."
> ▶ Name and explain the five key strategies of terrorism.

CHECK YOUR KNOWLEDGE

Terrorism: In the Name of What?

Before turning to terrorism, groups and individuals share certain goals. Such goals derive from *ideologies*, or comprehensive principles and beliefs. We briefly examine four major ideologies that inspired terrorists around the world: anarchism, radical socialism, extreme nationalism, and religious fundamentalism. (See Table 8-2.)

ANARCHISM

As a political philosophy and a global movement, **anarchism** seeks to create a borderless, peaceful society of free communes in which people generate and distribute wealth without government control. There are peaceful and violent types of anarchism. Among chief theorists of the latter was Mikhail Bakunin (1814–1876), who rejected any form of state, whether monarchy or liberal republic. Anarchists believe that government offices, banks, and capitalist enterprises must be destroyed and that sovereign states should be dissolved.

anarchism An ideology and movement that seeks to create a borderless, peaceful, self-governing society of free, local communes in which people generate and distribute wealth without government control.

TABLE 8-2 Tactics and Goals of Terrorism Driven by Ideology

Ideology	Tactics of Terrorism	Goals of Terrorism
Anarchism (mostly in the 19th and early 20th centuries)	Acts against government officials and civilians to create panic and paralyze government and society.	Destruction of all state institutions. Creation of a self-governing society of free communes.
Extreme Nationalism (mostly throughout the 20th century)	Acts against government officials and civilians of another nation to break their will. Acts against other ethnic groups.	Creation of a nation-state. The eviction of other ethnic groups.
Radical Socialism (mostly throughout the 20th century)	Acts against governments, to unleash a revolution of the masses.	A new society based on the abolition of private property and the destruction of privileged groups.
Religious Fundamentalism (throughout history)	Acts against those viewed as enemies of a religious order.	A religious revolution. A theocracy in one country or transnational religious order.

Anarchists have used political assassinations and other acts of terrorism as a means to reach political goals. Their belief was that such acts would inspire people to rise up against injustice and then turn to anarchism, but that conclusion has never come to pass. While anarchism was a source of violent radicalism for many years, it has always been fragmented and poorly organized. A less dangerous yet influential form of anarchism today is the radical anti-globalization movement.

EXTREME NATIONALISM

In the context of international relations, nationalism is an ideology aimed to create a nation-state. Nationalist militants have used terrorist methods for many years. In July 1914, in the Bosnian city of Sarajevo, Serbian nationalists assassinated Archduke Franz Ferdinand, heir to the Austro-Hungarian (Habsburg) throne, and his wife Sophia, thus triggering a harsh response from Austria. The failure of European governments to resolve this crisis resulted in World War I. Nationalism-motivated terrorism was predominant throughout the twentieth century. Nationalist-motivated terrorism has stirred dramatic events in Northern Ireland, Palestine, Korea, Vietnam, Kenya, Algeria, Kosovo, and elsewhere. In the twenty-first century, one of the most active radical groups remains the PKK (Kurdistan Workers' Party). It continues its violent struggle (using tactics including terrorism) against the Turkish government to create a sovereign Kurdistan.

RADICAL SOCIALISM

Radical socialism seeks to destroy capitalism and liberal democracy in the name of social and economic equality (see Chapters 4 and 7). During decolonization

in the 1950s and 1960s, many radical Socialist groups in Latin America and Africa used
terrorism and targeted authoritarian governments, which often relied on Western support. Ernesto Che Guevara (1928–1967), an
Argentinean doctor, believed that random
acts of deadly violence would spark revolutions across Latin America. Another Socialist, Abimael Guzmán, a former university
professor in Peru, formed a radical Maoist
group called Shining Path (*Sendero Luminoso*)
that began a bloody campaign of terror
against government institutions and officials (Burt 2009). Government forces in
Bolivia tracked down, captured, and killed
Guevara in 1967. Guzmán was captured and
imprisoned for life in Peru in 1992.

Kurdish supporters of the Kurdistan Workers' Party, known as
PKK, hold up portraits of the jailed Turkish Kurdish guerrilla
leader Abdullah Öcalan as they push their children in strollers
during a demonstration demanding his release, in Beirut,
Lebanon in 2015. For thirty years Turkey considered the Kurdish
guerillas to be terrorists. Will Turkey's attitude change?

In the 1970s the *Red Army Faction* (RAF)
in West Germany and the Red Brigades
(*Brigate Rosse*) in Italy targeted bankers and
government officials to create instability and chaos. In 1978, Italian terrorists
kidnapped and killed former prime minister Aldo Moro. Gradually, the wave
of terrorism abated. Some of its leaders, including RAF's founder Ulrike Mein-
hof, committed suicide. Others were killed or captured. Only a few Socialist
groups today use terrorism as a method of struggle against capitalism.

ISLAMIC FUNDAMENTALISM

Islamic fundamentalism is one of the main ideologies inspiring terrorist activities today. **Fundamentalism** is a set of beliefs and behaviors based on strict
adherence to religious principles. A number of Islamic groups have organized
terrorist acts to advance their political agenda—the creation of an Islamic state.
In recent years, Salafism, a radical version of Islam, has inspired anti-Russian
guerrillas in Northern Caucasus (Hahn 2012). *Al-Qaeda*, an international underground network, wants the establishment of a global Muslim state (called a
caliphate) governed by the Sharia law (Desai 2007). *ISIS* too claimed its intention to create a caliphate in Iraq, Syria, and other countries (Weiss and Hassan
2015). *Jemaah Islamiyah* is a Southeast Asian radical organization attempting to
establish an Islamic state to include Brunei, Malaysia, Singapore, Indonesia,
and the southern Philippines. The *Taliban* is a Sunni political movement operating primarily in Afghanistan and Pakistan and using both terrorism and insurgency to build an Islamic state in Afghanistan. *Hamas* is a political movement
in Palestine hoping to create an independent Islamic Palestine; it is still formally committed to destroying Israel as a state. This group, especially its military wing, has been engaged in violence and terrorism. *Hezbollah* is a Shiite
group operating from Lebanon and targeting Israel and its supporters. (Sunnis
and Shiites are different branches of Islam.) Radical groups inspired by
Buddhism appeared in Myanmar (Beech 2013).

**religious
fundamentalism**
A set of beliefs and
behaviors based on strict
adherence to religious
principles.

DEBATE > DO VIOLENT GROUPS CHANGE?

True or false? "Every fundamentalist or radical group supports terrorism." *False.* Many fundamentalist groups reject violence. Most nationalist or socialist groups also categorically reject terrorist methods.

True or false? "Radical groups disagree about the methods they use." *True.* It is important to distinguish moderate and nonviolent wings in any movement from more radical wings.

True or false? "Violent groups don't change." *False.* Some groups abandon terrorism for the sake of international legitimacy. Nationalists often shift from violence to negotiations if they see their ultimate goal, the creation of a nation-state, acknowledged by the international community.

WHAT'S YOUR VIEW?

Hezbollah, or the Party of God, and Hamas are groups operating in the Middle East; the first is in Lebanon, and the other is predominantly in the Gaza Strip. They are organizations of Islamists that pledge for many years the destruction of the state of Israel. On the other hand, these find significant support among local residents. As president of the United States would you rather:

❶ Pursue a strategy to change these groups' ideologies over time and open up every opportunity for negotiations with them; or ❷ Neutralize and defeat them because although some violent groups may change, it is too risky for the region and the world to rely on this expectation.

If you attempt both strategies, which one would you consider most important and why?

 On the companion website, learn more about Hezbollah and Hamas.

This brief classification does not exhaust the long list of beliefs that can motivate terrorists. Even a belief in the need to protect nature can move some individuals to violence, or "ecoterrorism" (as we will see in Chapter 9).

CHECK YOUR KNOWLEDGE

▶ Explain the strategic goals of anarchism, radical socialism, extreme nationalism, and religious fundamentalism, especially Islamist groups.
▶ Suggest the ways to achieve these goals by peaceful means.

Arguments

The Realist View of Terrorism

Understanding international terrorism has been a challenge to realists. First, the main focus of realism is on power relations among sovereign states and not on informal networks. Second, realism's models for decision-making tend not to take into account the ideological or religious motivations that drive terrorist networks. Still, realism's framework of *power balance* and *asymmetrical threats* is useful in explaining international terrorism. Also, realism justifies the preventive use of force to neutralize terrorist threats.

POWER BALANCE

Nonstate actors can disrupt the balance of power much like states. Inaction in response to terrorism, realists argue, may weaken a targeted state's power and encourage terrorist groups to strike again. Terrorism may thus be used as a powerful tool of international destabilization.

Let's return to the 1914 Sarajevo assassination. The Serbian nationalists who killed Archduke Ferdinand did not act officially on behalf of Serbia, and the Serbian government condemned the terrorist act. However, the Austrian government in Vienna decided to punish the Serbs because otherwise it would have encouraged Serbia, and its ally Russia, to reduce the influence of Austria-Hungary in Europe and in the Balkans. So Vienna made the fateful decision to declare war on Serbia. An unstable power balance in Europe, divided into two blocs, contributed to the decision of other countries—Russia, then Germany, and then France and the United Kingdom—to join the war. A nonstate group of nationalists had interfered in an international power balance and achieved an extraordinary result.

ASYMMETRICAL THREATS AND PREVENTIVE ACTIONS

Realism teaches that in a stable world, there is a *symmetry*, or balance of forces and threats: An attack by one state could cause a response from other states, and balance is restored. Terrorism, however, poses an **asymmetrical threat** to sovereign states (Reynolds 2012; Cordesman 2002). Terrorists cannot build expensive weapons, such as submarines, stealth fighters, or aircraft carriers to pose a significant threat. As in case of cyberterrorism, a few determined computer programmers can, if they find a vulnerability to exploit, threaten any country's financial resources and military capabilities (Lynn 2010). Because terrorists do not represent a state, countries may find it difficult to identify the perpetrators and retaliate effectively. Terrorist groups therefore try to provoke governments to overreact or launch futile responses. Some say that the U.S. reaction to the 9/11 attacks was also exaggerated and led to a costly "war on terror" without any definite outcome.

International terrorism may destabilize a balance of forces in unpredictable ways. As you can see, the Serbian terrorists provoked European states to go to war that destroyed the existing international order. Realism maintains that responses to a terrorist act can drag various forces into a wider conflict, as in Europe in 1914. (See Figure 8-2.) Terrorist acts in Sarajevo in 1914 and on September 11, 2001, in the United States are nearly a hundred years apart yet they seem to share some similarities because of their international dynamics. In both cases, nonstate groups committed acts of violence with extraordinary consequences. Both Austria-Hungary and the United States went to war against

asymmetrical threat The danger imposed by terrorism because a state cannot effectively retaliate and restore a balance of power.

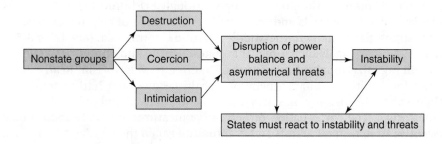

FIGURE 8-2 Terrorism from the realist perspective.

the countries (Serbia and Afghanistan, respectively) harboring terrorists. We can see why states use military power in response to terrorist acts but also why the result of their actions is often unpredictable.

In the context of asymmetrical threats, the key realist idea of international security based on deterrence (Chapter 5) becomes essentially ineffective. Because states cannot effectively retaliate against terrorism in "an eye for an eye" fashion, they should instead engage in preventive and punishing measures. States should use force preventively, whenever a verifiable evidence of an imminent terrorist threat emerges.

COUNTERTERRORISM

Realist strategies for counterterrorism include *monitoring* and *prevention*. Intelligence gathering ranges from electronic monitoring to infiltration into terrorist organizations. In the United States, more than eight hundred information technology companies were not long ago involved in counterterrorism intelligence (Priest and Arkin 2010b; 2011). These policies also include elaborate measures to prevent terrorist groups from acquiring sophisticated military technologies, including WMD. The United Nations' High-Level Panel on Threats, Challenges and Change also reported in 2004 that countries may conceivably justify the use of force, "not just reactively but preventively and before a latent threat becomes imminent" (United Nations 2004).

preemptive policies
Action against terrorists before they strike.

Other policies are *preemptive* and *punitive*. **Preemptive policies** take action against terrorists before they strike. These policies range from the physical elimination of groups to the disruption of their financial operations. Since 2001 scores of al-Qaeda militants have been detained or killed—mostly by unmanned aerial vehicles (UAV), commonly known as drones. From the realist viewpoint, such actions do not violate other countries' sovereignty for two reasons. First, governments often secretly grant permission for such actions. Second, some governments, such as in Pakistan, Sudan, or Afghanistan, do not exercise full control over their territory.

Another set of policies is called *homeland security*, after the American example. The September 11 attacks required a costly refurbishing and expansion of the U.S. government. New government structures were created to increase the control of borders and immigration, screen millions of visitors, monitor electronic communications, and investigate suspects. After 2001 and particularly after the 2004 bombing in Madrid and the 2005 bombing in London, most governments of the European Union implemented tougher immigration policies, stricter deportation procedures, and additional legal restrictions to monitor the flow of people through EU borders. These policies were aimed at individuals and organizations suspected of helping terrorist organizations, particularly in the Middle East and Central Asia. (See Table 8-3.)

In summary, realism assumes that states identify and eliminate the physical and organizational infrastructure of international terrorism. Realists also stand for punitive military operations against states that harbor terrorists. There should be pressure on states that provide financial and political support to terrorism. The combination of preventive measures and force should take incentive from terrorist hands and eventually weaken them.

TABLE 8-3 Counterterrorist Policies: Realist Targets and Methods

Targets	Methods: Monitoring, Preemption, and Homeland Security
Camps and other facilities used for training or to stage a terrorist attack	Political pressure on governments where such facilities exist; direct military strikes against camps or facilities
Financial assets of suspected terrorists	Confiscation, blocking, or control of assets used to support international terrorism
Terrorist networks and cells	Search and surveillance; operations against the existing networks; tougher immigration policies
Weapons of mass destruction and delivery systems	Safeguarding the sites where WMD are stored; protection of technologies to prevent their use by terrorists; ensuring nonproliferation of WMD beyond current nuclear states

A bus destroyed by the July 2005 terrorist attack in London. This attack along with others in the London Underground took the lives of more than fifty people. The British government soon tightened security and immigration procedures, most of which are still in place today.

How can we measure the effectiveness of realist policies? Most obviously, the absence of new terrorist attacks may indicate that these policies have worked. There are, however, both obvious and hidden side effects. These include the high financial costs of counterterrorism, its impact on the economy, loss of individual freedoms, and the impact on democratic governance itself. We will address these issues later in this chapter.

The Liberal View of Terrorism

To understand terrorism, liberalism argues, we have to examine the conditions that breed political radicalism. Terrorism cannot be defeated by military means alone. It takes understanding the causes of terrorism and using legal and economic means of international cooperation to defeat it. States combating terrorism are likely to succeed when they act together to create a better international environment and engage international institutions and nonstate actors.

UNDERSTANDING CAUSES OF TERRORISM

A key question is why terrorism takes place. Liberalism treats terrorism as a complex phenomenon exploiting acute social and political problems. This view finds support in a 1977 UN resolution stating that economic and social problems cause some people to turn to terrorism. This was not a justification of terrorism, but an attempt to explain and eventually defeat it.

The logic of liberalism is this: People turn to terrorism for a reason, even if it appears to be a distorted one. Foreign occupation, chronic unemployment, the injustices of daily lives, and profound inefficiency in addressing social problems all contribute to radicalism. From the liberal point of view, policies that address these causes can dry up the reservoir of violent radicalism and isolate terrorists from the rest of the population that may justify the terrorists' activities. It takes time and patience to implement such policies.

CRIMINALIZING TERRORISM

criminalization of terrorism
Considering terrorism a form of criminal behavior in the context of domestic and international law.

In a liberal point of view, in what is called the **criminalization of terrorism**, a democratic society should not apply one set of legal rules for its own citizens and another set for groups labeled terrorists. The main point is that illegal violent actions should not cause illegal counteractions. International law can be used in addition to domestic laws to qualify terrorist actions as crimes and deal with them using a broad domestic and international consensus (Schultz 2004). If legal rules are not in place, they have to be set. Inside their countries, governments should not limit the rights of law-abiding citizens and should draw a clear line between monitoring terrorist activities and the surveillance of people's daily activities. They should coordinate their policies and rely on international law against terrorist groups and their sponsors. The rule of law, in the end, is the best way to confront the lawlessness that is the breeding ground of radicalism and terrorism (Samuel 2013). Figure 8-3 shows the steps in analyzing terrorism from the liberal perspective and choosing the appropriate counterterrorism option.

LIBERALISM AND COUNTERTERRORISM

Supporters of the liberal view do not promise quick results of their policies. Rather, they emphasize gradual improvements because social changes take time to implement. Liberalism does not reject military actions against known terrorist groups and individuals. The difference between the liberal and realist approaches is in the priorities they assign to negotiations, consensus, legal means, and the use of force. (See Table 8-4.)

Any action against terrorist groups should be strictly legitimate. It must be conducted in accordance with international law and include, whenever possible, international cooperation. Counterterrorist measures should be a combination of negotiations, law-enforcement operations, and military actions

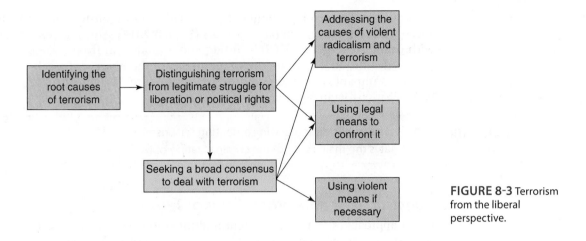

FIGURE 8-3 Terrorism from the liberal perspective.

TABLE 8-4 Fighting International Terrorism: The Liberal Perspective

Target	Method of Handling International Terrorism
Violent radical groups	Deterrence by propaganda and legal policies. Differentiation and marginalization of extremists. Attempts to negotiate with others.
Conditions and root causes of terrorism	The improvement of social and economic conditions of the population, reduction of potential social support for radical groups.
Terrorist propaganda, justified by nationalist and other legitimate goals	International condemnation of terrorism, outlawing groups that resort to terrorist methods. Support of national liberation and other legitimate causes through international organizations.
Anti-Western radicalism, especially Islamic fundamentalism	Educational campaigns. Cooperation with nonextremist Islamic and other religious organizations. Coordination of policies with local authorities.

(if necessary)—all under the guidance of local and international rules. Such policies should legitimize counterterrorism.

Counterterrorism should include strategic cooperation between states, international organizations, and NGOs (Cronin 2002). *Public diplomacy*, or the achievement of policy goals by engagement with the local communities and elements of civil society, should become an efficient form of counterterrorism. Public diplomacy seeks to separate terrorist and other radical organizations from their popular base (Simon and Martini 2004). Public diplomacy thus relies on soft power (see Chapter 3) to win the "hearts and minds" of ordinary people and leaders alike. However, without NGOs and local authorities, public diplomacy will be ineffective.

The liberal principles should not be applied without considering the actual social, cultural, and geographical factors (Kaplan 2012). American experience with counterinsurgency (COIN) in Iraq and Afghanistan from 2006 to 2015 provided additional facts and new arguments for the liberal approach. Abject poverty, rampant corruption, and infiltration of foreign fighters could play a very negative role in fighting terrorism.

CHECK YOUR KNOWLEDGE	▶ What is public diplomacy in combating terrorism? ▶ What is the main point of the criminalization of terrorism?

Constructivist and Other Views of Terrorism

Other approaches focus on different interpretations of terrorism's causes and suggest new approaches to counterterrorism. These include constructivism and conflict theories.

THREE PILLARS OF TERRORISM

States and organizations, supporters of constructivism claim, define terrorism and conduct antiterrorist policies based on their perceptions. As perceptions change, so do policies. Counterterrorism is a product of social construction: It is based on ideological beliefs, the quality of information available to the decision makers, and the way they interpret it. Above all, constructivism attempts to understand the motivations of terrorists, their identities, and their ideas.

Violent radical groups pursue many different political goals and hold diverse creeds. Yet the choice of terrorism has three basic motives. We can call them the *three pillars of terrorism*. (See Figure 8-4.)

1. *"We see a profound problem."* Terrorists generally believe that some profound injustice has occurred or is occurring now. It might be a foreign occupation, ethnic or religious oppression, social and economic exploitation, imprisonment of certain individuals, or a devastating military defeat of their country.

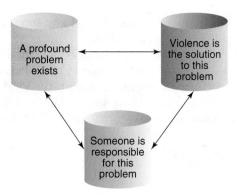

FIGURE 8-4 The constructivist view: The three pillars of terrorism.

CASE IN POINT > *Northern Ireland*

International attempts to deal with the sources of terrorism in Northern Ireland demonstrate a potential for the liberal approach, and limitations of it. Northern Ireland, a division of the United Kingdom, suffered for decades from a conflict between Roman Catholic and Protestant groups. The Irish Republican Army (IRA) and its successors sought to remove British influence from Northern Ireland and used terrorist acts to achieve this goal. Patient negotiations, mediation from other governments, the involvement of religious and secular groups, a referendum, legal reforms, and economic assistance seemed to bear fruit. In the 1990s, the British and Irish governments, with the help of Washington, reached a series of agreements that Ireland (the Republic of Ireland *and* Northern Ireland) could be unified only by peaceful means—and only if the majority of Northern Ireland voted for it. In 2005 the IRA promised to lay down its arms for good. Yet international agreements could not resolve the problem completely: Violent nationalist passions go beyond economic interests and legal reforms. They can flare up at any moment and require a very long time to pass away.

CRITICAL THINKING

❶ Discuss factors that contributed to policies to help control sectoral violence and terrorism in Northern Ireland. Consider geography, socioeconomic conditions, efforts of other countries, and the role of education. Suggest other factors as well. ❷ Discuss the possibilities of applying lessons from Northern Ireland in other places such as Afghanistan, Iraq, and Syria. What are the most significant obstacles to this application?

IRA terrorist volunteers at a camp near Dublin in 1966. After decades of violence, it appears that terrorism is finally eradicated in Northern Ireland. Can other countries learn from this case?

2. *"We know who is responsible."* Terrorists see their targets as solely responsible for this injustice. They may identify the source of the injustice as their own government, a foreign state, a political regime, or the international order in general. In an ethnic conflict, for example, they see one side as an innocent victim and the other as a villain. There are no gray areas.

3. *"Violence is the solution."* Terrorists believe that only violence can direct attention to the injustice or even put an end to it. In their eyes, violence should destroy the source of the injustice, force others to deal with it, and awaken public attention. Most radical groups pay less attention to what they are going to do politically after the violent act is "successful" and their goal of destruction is achieved.

The Basque conflict in Spain may be a fine illustration of constructivist arguments. In the 1930s, the fascist regime of Francisco Franco (1892–1975) eradicated Basque autonomy. Franco banned public display of the Basque flag, celebration of Basque holidays, speaking the Basque language in public places, and teaching it in schools. Even baptizing children with non-Spanish names became illegal. For the Basque people, these policies were seen as a profound injustice (pillar 1). The Franco regime in Madrid was seen as solely responsible for this injustice (pillar 2). Most people resisted these policies through nonviolent means. However, several groups saw no other means but violence (pillar 3). Terrorism caused more than eight hundred deaths in the struggle for an independent Basque state.

To fight the Franco regime with arms, several radical groups emerged, including the ETA (short for *Basque Homeland and Freedom*, as translated). In the 1960s, the ETA became a charismatic "spokesperson" for Basque nationalism (pillar 1). After a liberal republic replaced the Franco regime in 1975, the Spanish government applied liberal economic solutions to the problem of Basque separatism, including significant investments in the region and tax breaks. As a result, the Basque territories became among the most prosperous in Spain, and terrorist attacks abated. But terrorism did not end: A new violent faction later emerged, replacing the old ETA militants. The new terrorists no longer benefit from the grassroots support the ETA had, but they cling to their identity as uncompromising fighters (pillar 3).

In 2010, the group declared a new ceasefire but called on the Basque people to "continue in the struggle" on the path to freedom. In 2011, ETA declared that the ceasefire would be permanent and that international observers might monitor it. The group also declared that it would use democratic means to achieve its political goals. Yet the tensions may continue for some time. In 2015 Spain's Interior Ministry announced the arrest of sixteen individuals for alleged connections with ETA.

IDEOLOGY, IDENTITY, AND INTERNATIONAL CONTEXT

Constructivists argue that not every case of perceived injustice produces terrorism. Without a powerful ideology justifying random violence and individual sacrifice, terrorism cannot exist. The rise and fall of these ideologies should be

The 1972 attack on Israeli athletes and coaches during the Olympic Games was considered in the West a barbaric terrorist act. Heads of most countries condemned it. Yet others refused to do so. The bodies of the five Palestinians participating in the Munich massacre were flown to Libya, where they were buried with full military honors.

In 1994, Baruch Goldstein, an Israeli citizen, walked into a mosque in Hebron and killed twenty-nine Palestinian worshipers. Although the Israeli government condemned the massacre, Goldstein's tomb has become a place of worship for many Jews. The tombstone reads: *Here lies the saint, Dr. Baruch Kappel Goldstein; Blessed be the memory of the righteous and holy man; May the Lord avenge his blood, which devoted his soul to the Jews, Jewish religion, and Jewish land. His hands are innocent and his heart is pure. He was killed as a martyr of God.*

Have you heard the expression, "Your *terrorists* are our *freedom fighters*"? Do you completely agree with it? Do you accept an assumption that there is no distinction between moral or immoral acts because all our judgments are subjective? Or are there universal moral values applicable to all people regardless of their religion or nationality?

WHAT'S YOUR VIEW?

At least two options are possible.

1 Any violence is immoral, especially terrorism. Every terrorist act is unacceptable. "Freedom fighters" become terrorists when they use terrorist methods. It does not matter which side the fighters are on.

2 Not every act of violence is immoral. There are conditions under which some forms of violence are acceptable. In this case, one may justify specific violent acts but not others.

Which view would you likely support, and why?

@ On the companion website, read more about the events leading up to the 1983 attack in Lebanon: "Chapter 6: Lebanon: 1982–1984," by John H. Kelly, from *U.S. and Russian Policymaking with Respect to the Use of Force* (1996), edited by Jeremy Azrael and Emil A. Payin. Also read the *New York Times* article about the aftermath of the 1994 Hebron attack: "WEST BANK MASSACRE: The Overview; Rabin Urges the Palestinians to Put Aside Anger and Talk," by Clyde Haberman, March 1, 1994.

regarded in an international context. Consider Japan and Germany after their defeat in World War II. The United States and other powers occupied both countries for years, and the Japanese and German people never resorted to terrorism. Why not?

Above all, the war defeat and terrible destruction undermined any support in Germany and Japan for extreme nationalism. Also, from the viewpoint of international relations, both countries quickly became allies of the United States: Americans became their defenders against the Soviet Union and assisted their economic recovery. As a result, the identity of those countries rapidly changed: They were no longer defeated enemies but instead became part of "the free world" and the U.S. allies. Both military defeat and international realignment of these countries helped to marginalize violent nationalist identities.

In contrast, at the end of the twentieth century, the societies of the Middle East became a meeting point between ideological versions of Islam (and scores of Muslim scholars consider these versions non-Islamic) and the people who looked for violent identities. The radical versions of Islam, funded by Saudi Arabia—*Wahhabism* and *Salafism*—sought to shape the identity of people in

Afghanistan, Pakistan, and the Northern Caucasus from the 1980s through the 2000s. The al-Qaeda ideologues, including bin Laden, used the wars in Afghanistan and Iraq to promote an extremely violent type of Islamic identity. They argued that there was a centuries-long war between "Crusaders" from the West and the forces of Islam. They regarded the Soviets in Afghanistan in 1980 through 1988, and then the Americans in Saudi Arabia after 1991, as the "Crusaders" and were determined to defeat them at any cost.

MARXISM AND CONFLICT THEORIES

Conflict theories explain terrorism as a form of political struggle against oppressors. Classical Marxism generally supported terror against the class of capitalists, supporters of the capitalist system, and governments representing it. However, disagreements among Marxists persisted about specific policies. Lenin and the Bolsheviks (see Chapter 4) supported mass terror against "class enemies" in Russia and in other countries, but not individual acts of terror. Other disagreements existed between the Soviet Union and newly formed Socialist countries, such as Cuba in the 1960s and Kampuchea (Cambodia) or Ethiopia in the 1970s. The Soviets did not endorse random killings, kidnappings, and other terrorist acts committed by radical Communist groups. At the same time they did not condemn them publicly and supported some of the terrorist groups financially. Today's Marxists do not endorse terrorism by Islamic radical groups but do see it as a reaction to unjust policies. Modern conflict theorists, particularly those who regard international relations in terms of "North vs. South" may regard terrorism as an inevitable consequence of the structural inequality in the world. For them, only radical distribution of resources to the more poor regions can help to reduce terrorist activities.

CHECK YOUR KNOWLEDGE

▶ Name the three pillars of terrorism.
▶ Explain the Basque conflict from the position of the "three pillars."

Contexts and Applications

No approach fully explains terrorism. No single theory offers universally effective methods of counterterrorism. Realism emphasizes security and power politics but overlooks ideology, social causes, and individual motivations of terrorists. Liberalism pays attention to terrorism's causes but often overrates the chances for cooperation with radical groups. Constructivism helps to understand terrorists' motivations and identities, but often lacks practical solutions. The individual, state, and global contexts allow us to compare the applications of different theoretical approaches.

The Individual Decisions Context

How well do theories and hypotheses work to explain the behavior of individual terrorists and terrorists groups? Let's summarize the most significant findings. At the end of this chapter, we will return for a historical perspective to the case of al-Qaeda.

THE TERRORIST'S PROFILE

Do terrorists share common behavioral features? Law-enforcement professionals have long used behavioral profiling of criminal behavior. Can something similar be done with terrorism?

The answer is not encouraging. Attempts to create a single universal profile of the terrorist have so far been unsuccessful. Studying individuals accused of or convicted for terrorism is challenging for logistical and ethical reasons (Horgan 2011). Terrorists come from different backgrounds and are influenced by many special circumstances. What about the liberal assumption that poverty is the main source of terrorism? Actually, studies based on statistical analyses have found a complicated correlation between a country's economic conditions and individual motivations of terrorists (Krueger 2007; Abadie 2006). Most organizers and leaders of terrorist networks never lived in poverty and even came from well-to-do families (Bernstein 2009). At the same time, their "foot soldiers" are still likely to be poor (Pape 2003).

Studies also contest a popular assumption that most terrorists are deeply disturbed. Although extreme violence such as suicide attacks seems irrational, terrorists believe that they act with complete rationality (Crenshaw 2000; 2010). An individual's decision to commit a terrorist act appears rational within its social context: Injustice must be eliminated (Asal and Blum 2005). Terrorists tend to believe that their actions have a deeper personal and spiritual meaning. (See Table 8-5.)

Theories of group influence also find empirical support. Marc Sageman (2004) examined the biographies of members of radical violent organizations. They were strongly influenced by *group pressure* from peers. Other studies show that individuals join extremist groups for the same reasons that people join gangs—to gain a sense of belonging. Only later do they acquire extremist views (Horgan 2009). Refugee camps around Israel and in other parts of the world are a recruiting ground for terrorism because young people there develop an overwhelming sense of unity and a desire to fight together for a common goal. Casualties among members of these groups only contribute to greater solidarity (Post 2004).

The constructivist view's three pillars of terrorism seem to be valid. An individual is deeply convinced that violence should be committed to address a perceived injustice. A group or organization then provides the necessary tools and means to satisfy the craving for destruction and self-sacrifice. (See Figure 8-5.)

REHABILITATION AS COUNTERTERRORISM

The destruction of terrorists and their networks has been a major task of counterterrorism. But what do we know about **rehabilitation**, the process of assisting someone engaged in radical acts to return to the community? Is it possible to reeducate and change former radicals? Supporters of liberalism, in theory, believe in rehabilitation methods, but do they have facts to back their assumptions?

rehabilitation
Helping someone who has been involved in a radical or terrorist group return to the community.

TABLE 8-5 Is There a Terrorist Profile?

Factor	Findings
Age	Rank-and-file terrorists tend to be younger individuals. Globally, younger people commit the greatest number of violent crimes of any nature.
Gender	Terrorists are mostly males. Yet women join their ranks frequently and for a variety of reasons.
Occupation	There are no direct links between a person's occupation and terrorism. Unemployment, however, is a factor.
Poverty	There is no direct correlation between a country's economic conditions and terrorism. However, poor people in areas with high levels of unemployment are more vulnerable to recruitment by radical groups.
Mental illness	No evidence exists for elevated rates of mental illness among terrorists. Partial evidence exists for depression and stress-related problems that influence an individual's search for glory and martyrdom.
Psychological insecurity	Evidence exists for low-self-esteem, heightened insecurity, and elevated anger directed at other people.
Group pressure	Evidence exists that group pressure is a factor contributing to terrorism. However, some individuals disengage from such pressure.
Radical ideology	Most terrorists are radicalized in their choice of action. However, radicalization is often a result of group pressure, not the other way around.

Sources: Horgan 2014; 2009; Crenshaw 2010; Post 2004; 2008.

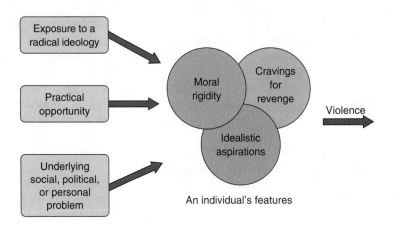

FIGURE 8-5 The inner world of a terrorist. As an individual becomes increasingly alienated from society, he or she may contemplate violent action to address the perceived injustice (Sageman, 2004).

Special "de-radicalization" government centers in Saudi Arabia and Iraq (run by American Task Force 134) bring cautious but optimistic results. Such centers base their work on the assumption that many individuals had been radicalized despite having little knowledge of Islam, politics, and history. With education and psychological counseling, these people can change their political views. Others simply need to find jobs (Stern 2010). How effective are such rehabilitation programs? Of 120 Saudi nationals who have been repatriated back to their country from the Guantanamo detention center, about 80 percent went back to normal life (Boucek 2009). Others, however, returned to terrorist activities in Afghanistan, Syria, and elsewhere. Of course, time and studies are needed to know more.

The State Policies Context

Terrorism is influenced by a variety of domestic factors. In turn, the threat of terrorism compels countries to amend their policies. We have already seen in earlier chapters how Presidents Bush and Obama were influenced by domestic politics. Let's see how the state context helps understand the complexity of counterterrorism as well as terrorists' motivations.

DOMESTIC COSTS OF COUNTERTERRORISM

After 2001, the United States committed considerable resources to enhance national security. The debates continue about how much the counterterrorism activities cost the American taxpayers. The Congressional Research Service estimated the cost of operations in Iraq, Afghanistan, and other places under the umbrella of the global "War on Terror" to be $1.7 trillion (deRugy 2015). Independent estimates including long-term medical and other costs pushed up the price from $3 trillion to $5 trillion (Stiglitz 2011). These calculations included

U.S. Presidents George W. Bush and Barack Obama on the day of Obama's first inauguration, January 20, 2009. Were there differences in their views on terrorism? How were these views shaped by their life experiences?

the cost of new government institutions and practices, such as the Department of Homeland Security and airport security checks, but also the cost of military and nonmilitary engagements in Iraq and Afghanistan—and even future medical and social welfare expenses of the veterans of these wars.

The debates about the cost of counterterrorism bring us back to the discussion of asymmetrical responses to terrorism. The main goal of international terrorism, as you remember, is to weaken the international order. Terrorists also hope to trigger excessive and costly reactions from the countries they attack. Critics of U.S. counterterrorist policies claim that international terrorism in the twenty-first century is succeeding because of the cost Americans pay to combat it. The attacks of September 11 and the anxiety they generated caused long-term damage not only to the American budget but to the economy as well. Excessive airport security and visa scrutiny also diminished tourism to the United States for several years after 2001. The aftermath of the attacks brought a fundamental change to national priorities and policies. Without this shift, American government would not have fought two costly wars and could have invested more into its own infrastructure, research, and education.

TERRORISM AS A MEANS TO GAIN STATE POWER

Both realist and liberal commentators rightly mention that not every radical or fundamentalist group becomes a threat to international security (Cooper 2004). Nationalist-driven terrorism tends to focus on domestic goals: gaining autonomy, independence, or establishing a new state. Once the goal is achieved, the reasons for further violence no longer exist. A study of four hundred terrorist groups in the twentieth century found that 124 of them eventually established ties to legitimate political parties (Weinberg and Pedahzur 2003). In the past thirty years, many formerly radical political groups in Latin America have renounced violence and turned to politics. In Jordan, the Muslim Brotherhood, which had renounced violence, gained about one-third of the seats in parliament. The moderate wing of the Muslim Brotherhood in Egypt also denounced the use of violence in 1971 (Herzog 2006). The Egyptian Brotherhood, after it was legalized in 2011, was victorious in parliamentary and presidential elections. (The group was outlawed again in 2013 in the aftermath of the military coup. Its leaders received harsh sentences.) However, nationalist movements could transform into terrorist groups pursuing fundamentalist agendas. In other cases, terrorist groups use instability to gain political power and form an independent state. The low-intensity conflicts fought since the 1990s in the North Caucasus transformed a secular struggle for independence from Russia into a holy war to establish an Islamist state (Saradzhyan 2010). A civil war in Syria created a power vacuum there and contributed to the rise of ISIS, which violently pursued its own independent state.

DEMOCRATIC GOVERNANCE AND TERRORISM

We already mentioned democratic peace theory and its possible implications for terrorism. Another issue for discussion is effectiveness of democracies in combatting terrorist threats. It may appear that authoritarian states can be more effective: They have fewer constraints than democracies in using harsh measures against terrorists. Yet history shows that authoritarian regimes cannot defeat terrorism: They just drive terrorists underground. Authoritarian states may also use the threat of terrorism as an excuse to attack the political opposition. Chinese antiterrorist laws, for example, could facilitate future human rights abuses committed in the name of counterterrorism (Human Rights Watch 2015). The Chinese government to this day cites the threat of global terrorism to justify its crackdown on separatist forces in Xinjiang, a predominantly Muslim region, and Tibet.

Liberal democracies appear more vulnerable to terrorism than authoritarian regimes because of their openness and decentralization. Democracies often lack a political consensus on how to fight terrorism. We already mentioned that after 9/11 critics of the Bush administration claimed that its policies expanded government prerogatives at the expense of civil liberties. The phones of terrorism suspects were tapped, their Internet correspondence was monitored, and habeas corpus (the constitutional right to be brought before a judge) was suspended (Ignatieff 2004). The challenge is to create effective counterterrorist policies without compromising democratic governance and freedoms.

Yet in the long run democracies tend to resist radical violence more successfully than nondemocratic regimes. Democratic means create legitimacy and help gain popular support for counterterrorism. The decline of the IRA in Northern Ireland and the defeat of the Red Brigades in Italy and the RAF in Germany in the 1970s showed that democratic states could overcome terrorism without compromising their democratic principles.

Emerging democracies may be most vulnerable to terrorism because they lack effective institutions and a functioning civil society. They also are likely to

Volunteers carry an injured child to safety after soldiers stormed a school seized by heavily armed terrorists near Chechnya in 2004. More than 300 hostages died, including 156 children, amid explosions and machine gun fire. What caused such a high number of casualties? We can blame the terrorists, but the counterterrorism operation by the Russian government was arguably inept.

suffer from corruption, nepotism, and tribalism. Some members of the police, the security services, and the public may actually sympathize with terrorist causes. For instance, in Pakistan both democratically elected leaders and the military dictators there had a poor record of dealing with terrorist groups. Officials from the Pakistani secret service (ISI) have long supported radical Islamists in Afghanistan and India. Pakistani domestic politics remain vulnerable to radical Islamism (Husain 2011; Rashid 2008).

CHECK YOUR KNOWLEDGE
- ▶ Which characteristics are commonly included in the "terrorist profile"?
- ▶ If the main goal of terrorist groups is political, why don't most of them switch to the legitimate political process?

The Global Context

Assessments of terrorism and counterterrorist policies must also take into account their global impact. That includes terrorist strategies and the effectiveness of global counterterrorism. At the same time the global context allows us to see how international terrorism challenges or promotes international interdependence—political and economic.

THREATS TO THE GLOBAL ORDER

Do terrorists achieve their goals? Is terrorism effective in disrupting the global order? The conclusions are mixed. Particularly when the demands of violent groups are specific and limited, governments tend to cooperate. Sometimes they even pay ransom money for hostages. Most of the time, however, states and international organizations refuse to negotiate with terrorist groups, which do not achieve their political goals. In fact, terrorism is likely to delay the solutions of international conflicts or social problems:

- The anarchist movement, even at the height of its activities in the nineteenth and early twentieth century, failed to destroy government institutions or establish direct democracy. To the contrary, after World War I, new and powerful authoritarian states arose.
- Socialist radicalism of the 1960s and 1970s attained only limited success. A global alternative to liberal capitalism never materialized, and "red terrorism" abated.
- Terrorism has also delayed the resolution of many legitimate claims for national sovereignty including statehood for Palestinians.

The effectiveness of international terrorism in the name of Islam deserves some discussion. As we already mentioned, the damage of the September 11 attacks was considerable and lasting. Terrorism and its threats affected the lives of hundreds of millions of people. At the same time, al-Qaeda and similar groups did not even come close to achieving their global goals. Polls show that religiously motivated terrorism, because of the destruction it caused for several decades, had alienated the majority of Muslims even in the areas where it had initially won many sympathizers (Horowitz 2009). According to a global survey of attitudes in Muslim countries, 67 percent of Muslims were concerned about Islamic extremism (Pew 2013a). Fundamentalist Islamic movements challenged but did not overthrow the authoritarian regimes in the Middle East targeted by al-Qaeda. Although the influence of al-Qaeda and similar radical groups has been in decline all around the Islamic parts of the world early this century (Husain 2005; Pew Research Center 2011), several new groups have emerged in the Middle East, North Africa, Nigeria, Somalia, and other countries.

Neorealists, liberals, and constructivists concur that terrorism will remain a difficult challenge. However, the international system today is generally more resilient than in the past, and terrorists cannot trigger a global calamitous war, like they had done in 1914. From neorealist perspective, there is a concert of great powers to act internationally against terrorist threats, even when some great powers may differ on specific details. Liberals correctly point to the role of the United Nations and its numerous institutions, as well as a host of nongovernment organizations: Terrorists may temporarily overwhelm weak or failing states, yet with the help of international cooperation—not excluding international intervention—these states no longer remain safe and lasting havens for terrorists. And some constructivists argue that with the exception of militant Islamic fundamentalism, there is a general decline of violent ideologies around the world. We can only hope that this trend continues.

GLOBAL WAVES

Are there distinct tides and ebbs of terrorism around the world? As we saw earlier, anarchism motivated a wave of terrorism in the late 1800s. A second wave, inspired by anticolonialism and nationalism, began in the 1920s and lasted for several decades. The late 1960s witnessed the birth of the terrorist attacks of radical Communist groups in Europe as well as Sri Lanka, Peru, and Colombia. This wave dissipated by the end of the last century, but a new wave, mainly religious terrorism, had already begun in the 1980s (Rapoport 2004; Post 2005a). It spreads beyond sovereign borders, and its motives are rooted in a cultural, anti-Western sentiment (Wieviorka 2007).

The differences among these waves of terrorism are not only ideological. International terrorism since the Cold War, sometimes called *new terrorism*, has several distinct features (Crenshaw 2000; Kaplan 2012). First, terrorists have increasingly resorted to attacks on civilian populations to achieve greater carnage and more headlines. There is an increased focus on destruction; the means of terrorism has become its goal (Brandt and Sandler 2010). Second, terrorism's operations have become increasingly global. Third, terrorists more often operate in small, loosely connected groups without a centralized command. These groups are difficult to penetrate and liquidation of one group does not bring down the whole terrorist network. Terrorist leaders urge their followers not to negotiate or accept bargains.

The willingness of some terrorist groups, particularly Islamists, to embrace religious martyrdom is a frightening development. In addition, terrorism has embraced new technologies, including the Internet. Instead of revolvers and dynamite, terrorists today use sophisticated explosives, civilian aircraft, ships, and high-speed trains to cause maximum damage to people and infrastructures.

In Buenos Aires, Argentina, demonstrators hold up a sign that reads in Spanish "No more terrorism, no more violence, no more kidnapping, no more FARC." FARC is a radical terrorist organization from Colombia.

A miniaturized nuclear device could have catastrophic consequences anywhere at any time. There are serious concerns that Iran, after it develops nuclear weapons, will pass them on to terrorist organizations. In addition, unstable states, such as Pakistan, may not be able to maintain effective controls over their nuclear facilities.

Will there be another wave of terrorism? Where will it come from? Should we prepare for a series of nuclear attacks or anticipate a cyber assault against financial institutions and communication networks? Preventive policies may include the use of force. Yet most important, they will need coordinated policies of all responsible states and international organizations.

CHECK YOUR KNOWLEDGE

▶ Has terrorism been an effective tactic of political change?
▶ Name and describe three waves of terrorism in history.
▶ Describe the characteristics of the most contemporary wave.

GLOBAL COUNTERTERRORISM

September 11, 2001, marked a turning point for global counterterrorism. At the same time, as a result of the wars in Iraq and Afghanistan, people in democratic countries may have become tired of precautions and fear of terrorists. The experience and wisdom, however, demands that the structures and institutions of global terrorism should be made more efficient, not dismantled.

Significant international efforts will be needed to strengthen central authority in some countries. Both realists and liberals accept the view that failing states provide a breeding ground for terrorism. Yemen and Afghanistan are two examples. Building a stronger state becomes a counterterrorism policy (Boucek 2010). Another important policy is pressure on political regimes, such as Iran, suspected of supporting international terrorism.

Part of the solution must come from within countries and regions that breed radicalism. For example, many Islamic scholars today denounce the ideology of violence, which, in their view, has nothing to do with Islam and its basic values. Killing terrorists, as liberals argue and as the U.S. government learned in Afghanistan and Iraq, will not end the problem of radical violence because it feeds on ideologies rooted in deep social and political problems. If these problems are addressed, the threat of terrorism diminishes.

Effective policies should combine several interconnected strategies. One is the reasonable and multilateral use of force to change the perceptions of the regional or global balance of power. Another is persistent attention to social and economic problems that provide mass backing for terrorist radicals. Serious work should be done to reappraise international law and law enforcement procedures to criminalize terrorism. There must be coordinated information policies to encourage others not to glorify violence. Some of these policies may be ineffective, and tactical corrections will be necessary (Post 2005b).

Another important issue in global antiterrorism policies is moral. Are deadly drone strikes against known terrorists acceptable if innocent people die as a "collateral damage"? The New America Foundation (NAF 2012) estimates that of all people killed by U.S. drones in Pakistan, 5 to 10 percent could be innocent bystanders, including children or hostages. This number was higher a few years earlier when the aerial attacks began. In April 2015 President Obama publicly apologized after a drone unintentionally killed Italian and American hostages in Pakistan, along with the targeted terrorists.

Most experts writing about terrorism underline the need to understand strategies that perpetrators of asymmetrical conflicts use. Guerrilla warfare, for example, is not a brand new form of military struggle. In twentieth century conflicts, quite a few political leaders gained power in their countries by launching protracted guerilla wars. History shows that most guerilla movements hoped push the superior, better organized and better equipped enemy close to physical and psychological attrition. New international context may favor insurgents and complicate the attempts of states to deal with guerillas. Because mass media in democratic countries report heavily on casualties and destruction caused by insurgency's actions, public opinion in such countries may fast develop a negative view of an ongoing conflict (Boot 2013). This may exhaust the will of democratic countries to engage in protracted counterinsurgencies, especially outside their own territory, and heighten the ability of insurgents to survive even after suffering grave military setbacks.

Effective counterterrorism depends on knowledge of its ultimate targets. Are we fighting against specific individuals or against the ideologies that inspire them? Will the physical elimination of a potent radical group solve the problem of terrorism? To approach these questions, we turn to the case of al-Qaeda. Understanding its motivations and actions in the past is crucial for building effective defense, security, and foreign policies of the future.

THE USES OF HISTORY: Al-Qaeda

Background

caliphate   A global Islamic state (one of the ultimate goals of al-Qaeda).

The name *al-Qaeda* ("the base") is forever linked to the terrorist attacks of 9/11. Al-Qaeda is an international terrorist network rooted in fundamentalist Islamic principles. It fights to create a global Islamic state, or **caliphate**. An effective way to understand al-Qaeda is to look at the careers and views of its founders—above all, at Osama bin Laden (1957–2011), who was born and grew up in Saudi Arabia. His father, born in Yemen, became a prominent real estate and commercial developer who made hundreds of millions of dollars on government construction projects in Saudi Arabia and elsewhere. This wealth and status helped bin Laden. However, instead of following in his father's footsteps, and despite opportunities resulting from his high social status, bin Laden grew increasingly frustrated with the Saudi society. From his late teens, the main point of his frustration was that the society was progressively distancing itself from the fundamentalist principles of Islam (Bodansky 2001). Contemporary music, dance, entertainment, mass media, ideas of democracy and equality between men and women—all bothered him immensely (Dennis 2002).

Among those who strongly influenced bin Laden and his future al-Qaeda associates was an Egyptian fundamentalist thinker Sayyid Qutb (1906–1966), a member of the Egyptian organization *Muslim Brotherhood*. Qutb traveled in the United States and returned home a virulent enemy of American society and Western cultural influences. He was especially disgusted by social equality between men and women (Qutb, [1964] 2007).

- A true and just social system can be created only on the basis of the Sharia, or Islamic law. Islam knows only two kinds of societies, Islamic and un-Islamic, or *Jahiliya*. This inferior society—which cares for neither Islamic beliefs, values, laws, morals, nor manners—is, according to Qutb, the contemporary world.
- A true Islamic society would have no rulers because Muslims need neither judges nor police to obey divine law. Any secular authority or legal system must be repulsive to Muslims. Any secular system—authoritarian or democratic, nationalist or Communist, the free market or a planned economy—is illegitimate unless it follows the Sharia.
- Muslims should use preaching and *Jihad*, the duty to wage a holy war, to overthrow secular governments—even if they are ruled by Muslims. As a result, people will be free from their servitude to other men and ready to serve God.
- The present Muslim generation had laid down its spiritual arms defeated by secularism.

From Qutb, the young bin Laden and other founders of al-Qaeda learned about offensive *jihad*, which is the right and duty to inflict violence to advance spiritual and political beliefs (Coll 2009).

Key Formative Events

The Soviet invasion of Afghanistan in 1979 gave a number of young educated and radical Saudis, including bin Laden, their first battlefield. They began to raise money and volunteer to fight against the Soviets. This new Jihad, against foreign invaders supporting the Communist Afghani regime, launched a "brotherhood" of militants. When the Soviet Union withdrew from Afghanistan in 1988, these militants considered it their historic victory over "the Satan." At this point bin Laden met with Ayman al-Zawahiri, an Egyptian doctor. Born in 1951 to a prominent family, he also was influenced by the ideas of Sayyid Qutb. Around 1988, al-Zawahiri and bin Laden formed a group, which a decade later became known as al-Qaeda. Al-Zawahiri provided ideas for its organizational structure and trained members; bin Laden supplied ideas and money. This group already aimed beyond the Soviet Union and against the "Great Satan"—the United States (Wright 2006).

Bin Laden and his associates interpreted the Gulf War of 1991, in which the international coalition led by the United States evicted Iraqi troops from Kuwait, as another "crusade" of the West against Islam. They vowed to expel American troops from the "sacred land" of Saudi Arabia. Bin Laden grew increasingly critical of the Saudi royal family and government, to the point of mutual hostility. He had to leave Saudi Arabia and founded a new training base for al-Qaeda militants in Sudan. After 1996, the Taliban movement seized power in Kabul, and bin Laden and al-Zawahiri moved their base to Afghanistan. From Afghanistan, they planned the attack on the United States.

Analysis

The National Commission on Terrorist Attacks upon the United States (known commonly was the 9/11 Commission) aptly summed up the essence of al-Qaeda's goals and methods: "The enemy rallies broad support in the Arab and Muslim world by demanding redress of political grievances, but its hostility toward us and our values is limitless. Its purpose is to rid the world of religious and political pluralism, the plebiscite, and equal rights for women. It makes no distinction between military and civilian targets. Collateral damage is not in its lexicon." (National Commission on Terrorist Acts, 2002).

The main goal of the founders of al-Qaeda is the creation of a global Islamic state. As you will remember, nationalist groups also pursue the creation of sovereign states. Yet their goals are quite different from al-Qaeda's. To achieve a global Islamic state, the entire global order must be destroyed. In their plan, nation-states will disappear, and a new stateless uniform Muslim society will emerge. (Compare this with anarchism's goals.) In the process, several regional caliphates will unify Muslims living in Europe, Africa, and Eurasia. In particular, caliphates could unify Arab states in the Middle East, North Africa, the Caucasus, Pakistan, Afghanistan, Indonesia, and Southeast Asia.

The most significant obstacle to these goals, al-Qaeda believes, is Western civilization, especially its individualism, materialism, secularism, and gender equality. Followers believe that Western societies are decadent and weak; they

Bin Laden is dead, yet the radical ideology he supported is not. In Istanbul, Turkey, in 2015, members of pro-Islamic groups hold a banner that reads, "If there is no limit to our freedom of expression, then prepare yourselves for our limitless freedom to act."

can therefore be terrorized, undermined, and eventually overwhelmed.

This second enemy is the Jews and the state of Israel. Al-Qaeda beliefs borrow heavily from the old conspiracy theories about the Jewish "world dominance," including their control of the world's economic and financial system. Key is the Palestinian problem, and to solve it the state of Israel must be eliminated; and Israel's main supporter, the United States, must be undermined. In speeches, bin Laden and his associates frequently referred to their enemies as "Jews and Crusaders."

The third obstacle is corrupt regimes in Muslim countries. Their grip on power must be weakened and their secular governments eventually abolished. Although it is a daunting task, enemies can be weakened and defeated with the right methods.

The United States, seen as the main source of Western decadence and a key sponsor of Israel, became the main target of al-Qaeda's wrath. Al-Qaeda leaders became convinced that, despite America's strength, the country was built on a weak secular foundation. Methods of terror could bring the entire Western civilization down. Terror attacks by suicide bombers (a terrorist tactic frequently attributed to al-Zawahiri) must strike the West and its allies repeatedly and in the most vulnerable places. "We will use your laws against you," bin Laden boasted. A weakened West would not be able to support Israel, and the global system would crumble.

Lessons

Based on what we know about al-Qaeda, what conclusions and recommendations can we form related to future counterterrorism?

Although some reports portrayed bin Laden as a typical political player who simply despised America's policies (Hamud 2005), most viewed him as uncompromising and obsessed. In the past, such individuals as Che Guevara or Guzmán (described earlier in this chapter) were rigid in their judgments and inflexible in their actions. They were ready to sacrifice their lives for the sake of an ideological agenda. As for bin Laden, Washington followed the realist logic. It concluded that talks were counterproductive, and President Obama ordered him killed on May 2, 2011, in a bold operation by U.S. Special Forces.

But the struggle against al-Qaeda-inspired terrorism continues. New leaders and organizations have emerged, including the Islamic State. Terrorism is too complex a social and political problem to simply go away. Much depends on the transformations in Muslim countries and on the future evolution of Islam. In some countries of the Middle East, North Africa, and elsewhere, conditions of extreme poverty and misery—alongside government corruption and injustice—have created a fertile ground for fundamentalism.

Questions

1. What potential developments in Muslim countries do you think would discourage the continuation and growth of radical movements and terrorist organizations?
2. What specific foreign policy changes should the United States and the West as a whole implement to discourage radical movements and terrorist organizations?
3. How strongly do you support the view that al-Qaeda, ISIS, and other groups are largely "products" of the "clash of civilizations" (Chapter 4) and therefore not susceptible to preventive policies?

CONCLUSION

The global struggle against terrorism cannot succeed if it is not supported by the international community, nongovernment organizations, and public opinion. In their counterterrorism policies, states should combine a variety of methods—including military action, surveillance, public diplomacy, economic sanctions, economic aid, law enforcement, education, training, and international law. It is also necessary to address the causes of terrorism, including unsettled territorial disputes, rampant poverty, injustice, and discrimination. This is a task not only for government but for all of us.

KEY TERMS

anarchism 267
asymmetrical threat 271
caliphate 290
coercion and extortion 265
counterterrorism 261

criminalization of
  terrorism 274
cyberterrorism 265
domestic terrorism 261
guerrilla warfare 261

international terrorism 261
preemptive policies 272
rehabilitation 281
religious fundamentalism 269
terrorism 261

IDEAS

KEY CONCEPTS
- Terrorism: A form of violent political radicalism by non-state actors
- Counterterrorism: Policies and measures to prevent and combat international and domestic terrorism

KEY STRATEGIES OF TERRORISM
- Intimidation
- Attrition
- Provocation
- Spoiling
- Outbidding

KEY IDEOLOGIES OF TERRORISM
- Anarchism
- Radical socialism
- Nationalism
- Religious fundamentalism

ARGUMENTS

REALISM
- Terrorism disrupts the power balance
- Asymmetrical threat
- Counterterrorism involves monitoring and prevention

LIBERALISM
- To fight terrorism one should better understand its causes
- Criminalization of terrorism
- Emphases on broad international cooperation and public diplomacy

CONSTRUCTIVISM AND OTHER APPROACHES
- Terrorism is based on beliefs, available information, and interpretations
- Motives: a problem, an assigned responsibility for the problem, and absence of nonviolent choices
- Conflict approaches explain terrorism as a form of political struggle against oppressors

CONTEXTS AND APPLICATIONS

THE INDIVIDUAL DECISIONS CONTEXT
- No universal profile of a terrorist, yet most crave revenge, display moral rigidity, and have idealistic aspirations
- Terrorists' motivations may change
- Political leaders differ in how they understand terrorism and counterterrorism

THE STATE POLICIES CONTEXT
- Terrorism is influenced by a variety of domestic factors, including its perceived cost
- Terrorism may be considered as a means to gain power
- Democracies and non-democracies are affected by and respond to terrorism differently

THE GLOBAL CONTEXT
- Terrorism as a method has a mixed record of accomplishing its goals
- There are several global "generations" of terrorism
- Global efforts should improve counterterrorism's effectiveness

Critical Thinking

1. Compare and contrast terrorism and guerrilla warfare. Give examples.
2. Explain why terrorism is an asymmetrical threat.
3. Provide examples of preemptive but not violent counterterrorist policies.
4. Suggest arguments for and against criminalization of terrorism.
5. How and why have the tactics of terrorism changed over time?
6. Is it possible to eradicate terrorism completely? Why or why not?

Environmental Problems and International Politics

Nature provides a free lunch, but only if we control our appetites.
—WILLIAM RUCKELSHAUS

D O YOUR HAIRSPRAY AND REFRIGERATOR HAVE ANY-THING TO DO WITH INTERNATIONAL POLITICS? BELIEVE IT OR NOT, THEY DO. SCIENTIFIC RESEARCH HAS SHOWN that certain chemicals in air conditioning and cooling units, known as aerosol spray propellants, dangerously affect the atmosphere. With improving living standards and increased consumption in the second half of the past century, hundreds of millions of people began to use cooling and heating devices and aerosol sprays. Slowly, the protective ozone layer of the atmosphere began to deplete, and the sun's radiation increased, thus causing skin cancer and many other dangerous consequences. In 1985, twenty leading industrial countries signed the Vienna Convention for the Protection of the Ozone Layer to regulate some dangerous chemical substances used in sprays and coolants. In 1987, forty-three countries signed the Montreal Protocol to stop production of specific chemicals or reduce them substantially by 1999. Industries received incentives to phase out old chemicals and develop new, cleaner products. After this agreement came into force, the concentrations of the chemicals contributing to the ozone depletion have gradually leveled off.

Today's world faces an overwhelming range of environmental challenges. They are acknowledged not only by scientists but also by the vast majority of governments around the world. The international community launched new environmental programs and initiatives. A whole new dimension of international relations

Previous page: Aerial view of a junkyard piled high with scrapped vehicles in Hangzhou City, China, in 2015. In an increasingly affluent society, more consumers are buying cars. The Chinese government has vowed to control air pollution, actively pushing for green upgrades to vehicles and setting ambitious carbon-cutting targets.

has emerged. The agreements on the ozone layer were successful because several powerful countries set aside their differences and agreed to act together. Agreements for today's environmental problems appear to be more difficult to reach. Many proposed actions are vigorously contested for a host of reasons. Finding and implementing global environmental policies may be one of the greatest challenges of our century.

In this chapter, we will discuss how environmental problems and the debates around them affect international relations and policies of countries, international organizations, and NGOs.

▶ Identify today's key environmental problems and major policies to address them.

▶ Explain how environmental problems and the debates surrounding them affect international relations.

▶ Describe similarities and differences among several approaches to environmental problems.

▶ Apply your knowledge to analyze individual decisions, state policies, and global developments on environmental problems.

Learning Objectives

Ideas

Environmental problems and policies are a relatively new subject in international relations. For many years, the consensus was that sovereign governments had full authority to deal with the land, water, air, and natural resources of their countries as they pleased. Countries reached agreements on the environment mostly to get more profits from the extraction and sale of mineral resources. Even today, states usually do not ask for permission from others to drill for oil or to burn forests. During the last few decades, however, the attitudes of international organizations and most countries toward environmental problems began to change fundamentally in part due to the realization that the world is not just a combination of countries but rather a complex **ecosystem**, which includes complex interactions between life and its surroundings. A *country's ecosystem*, like that of the United States or Mexico, is part of a *regional ecosystem*, such as North America. It is also part of the *global ecosystem*—and all three are interconnected. Large-scale natural disasters, such as volcanic eruptions or massive oil spills, affect the ecosystem instantly. Other changes take time to develop.

Environmental politics includes the activities of political leaders, parties, NGOs, scientific laboratories, and others to influence environmental policy.

environmental politics   The activities of political leaders, parties, NGOs, scientific laboratories, and others to influence environmental policy.

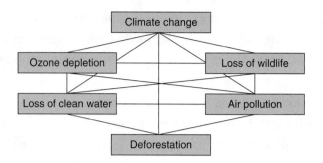

FIGURE 9-1 Main environmental problems.

contamination   The byproducts of human and nonhuman activities affecting air, water, and soil.

depletion   The serious reduction of essential elements of an ecosystem, such as loss of forests, fresh water, or entire species.

These policies address at least two types of problems: *contamination* and *depletion*. **Contamination** is any by-product of human and nonhuman activities affecting the air, water, and soil. **Depletion** is the serious reduction of essential elements of the environment, such as loss of fresh water, clean air, forests, or entire species. As we will see in this chapter, climate change is mainly caused by one form of contamination called greenhouse gases. At the same time, even ordinary garbage can be another source of contamination. Natural processes and natural disasters may cause contamination and depletion as well. (See Figure 9-1.)

Environmental Problems

AIR POLLUTION

Volcanic eruptions and forest fires have polluted the atmosphere for centuries. Industrialization and the growth of cities created new sources of pollution—including coal-burning factories, massive garbage dumps, animal wastes, and open sewer systems. Smog, an obvious form of air pollution, became unmistakable in Europe and the United States in the nineteenth century and later appeared in big cities all over the world. Not long ago, soot from burning was detected even in the ices of Greenland and high in the Himalayas ("Time to Call the Sweep?" 2010).

In the twenty-first century, the largest sources of air pollution are power plants using coal: They produce almost a quarter of the pollution worldwide. The second largest cause is deforestation, or loss of forests due mostly to human activities. Transportation (including planes, ships, and cars), a third source, produces about 14 percent of emissions. (See Figure 9-2.)

acid rain   The accumulation of acids in clouds, rain, snow, sleet, and, subsequently, lakes and rivers owing to sulfur dioxide, nitrogen oxides, and other pollutants in the atmosphere.

One of the serious consequences of air pollution is **acid rain**, which is caused by high concentrations of *sulfur dioxide, nitrogen oxides*, and other pollutants in the atmosphere. Acid rain pollutes lakes and rivers, killing many small life forms; it damages buildings and historic monuments, corroding metal constructions; and it affects crops: A higher content of oxides in food is dangerous to our health.

Early negotiations regarding acid rain began in the 1970s between the United States and Canada. These two countries signed a major treaty (often called the *Acid Rain Treaty*) in 1991 to limit cross-border air pollution. Other countries signed treaties leading to automobile and factory emission controls.

CASE IN POINT > *A Disappearing Sea*

In the 1960s, the Soviet Union began an ambitious construction project. To irrigate cotton plantations and other agricultural projects, the government partially diverted two rivers that bring fresh water into the Aral Sea, a body of water shared by Kazakhstan and Uzbekistan (two Soviet republics that later became independent nations). The result was depletion, as the water supply to the sea declined significantly, and shallow streams quickly evaporated. By the 1980s, the fishing industry in the Aral Sea was in serious decline; today it is almost destroyed, being only 10 percent of its original size. The vast area around the Aral Sea including

river deltas is covered with salt and toxic substances as the result of receding water and pesticide runoff. Thousands of square miles of dry land have appeared, contributing to dust storms and damaging the environment of the region even further. The people living in the area experience a shortage of fresh water and suffer from respiratory and other health ailments.

The territory of the Aral Sea is shared by Kazakhstan and Uzbekistan. Kazakhstan is attempting to save the northern part of the sea, already separated from the rest of the sea. Uzbekistan will not stop the irrigation of its cotton plantations and is more interested in

searching for oil and gas on the exposed seabed. The depletion of the sea continues.

CRITICAL THINKING

1 What lessons can we draw from this case? **2** Who should be responsible for saving the disappearing sea? Kazakhstan and Uzbekistan, another country, an NGO, or an IGO? **3** Suppose you served as chair of an international organization called Save the Sea, and you had significant resources at your disposal. What would you do with the sea? **4** Is this particular environmental battle worth fighting? Why or why not?

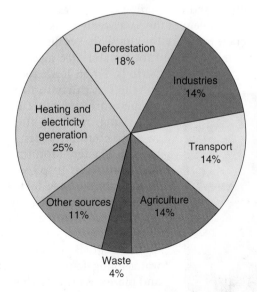

FIGURE 9-2 Sources of air pollution in the world.

Because of these efforts, the problem has somewhat diminished in urban areas but persists in many industrial regions.

Air pollution causes many respiratory problems and may also produce other serious long-term health consequences, especially in urban and industrial areas.

The poor, who typically lack access to health care, are the most vulnerable to the effects.

OZONE DEPLETION

ozone depletion
Steady decline in the amount of ozone in the stratosphere, allowing the sun's damaging ultraviolet radiation to reach the earth.

The ozone layer is a part of the atmosphere that protects humans and animals from the sun's deadly ultraviolet radiation. Scientists have registered a steady decline in the total amount of ozone in the earth's stratosphere—an estimated 3 percent per decade since the 1980s. This is called **ozone depletion**. Ozone "holes" have appeared over Antarctica and Australia. Research and coordinated international actions have significantly slowed the process by focusing on a major cause of ozone depletion, the chemicals that are produced naturally by marine organisms and are used in air conditioning and cooling units, as aerosol spray propellants, and for cleaning electronic equipment. No country can create a "shield" to guard its own atmosphere, which makes ozone depletion a global issue (Roan 1989). As you will remember from the introduction to this chapter, the Vienna Convention and the 1987 Montreal Protocol limited production of certain chemicals contributing to ozone depletion. Additional international agreements aim at phasing out and eliminating these chemicals entirely from industrial use.

CLIMATE CHANGE

climate change
A significant and lasting alteration of global weather patterns.

Climate change is a significant and lasting alteration of global weather patterns (Gerrard 2007). It most often means *global warming*, or rising temperatures, but also includes the increasingly frequent abnormalities in climate conditions, such as frequent storms and devastating heat waves. It has been the most debated environmental problem of the past twenty years.

The earth's average temperatures have always fluctuated to some degree. The earth's history has included four major "ice ages" as well as warmer periods, when flora and fauna flourished. For the last thirty to forty years, however, temperatures have been steadily and rapidly rising, reaching the warmest level in twelve thousand years. According to the World Glacier Monitoring Service (see them online at http://www.wgms.ch) glaciers globally have lost up to 10 percent of their mass over just the last decade, and ice that for centuries blocked northern seas is retreating. The retreat of glaciers in other areas affects the availability of water for agriculture as well as for animals and plants. As the earth warmed in the last half of the twentieth century, 1,700 plant, animal, and insect species moved closer to the poles, at about four miles per decade (Parmesan and Yohe 2003). The World

The People's Climate March in London in 2015 was one of 2,500 events in 166 countries calling for action on climate change. Do such symbolic actions make any difference?

Wide Fund for Nature publishes a list of animals threated by climate change (WWF 2015).

When did debate over global climate change begin? In 1896 a Swedish chemist and physicist, Svante Arrhenius, was one of the first to establish a connection between global temperatures and human activities. He calculated that air pollution from factories could double CO_2 levels in the atmosphere in three thousand years, warming the planet significantly. In 1938, Guy Callendar, a British engineer, also predicted a global rise in the world's temperature because of CO_2. Yet those projections were dismissed by the scientific community and essentially forgotten. Only with the start of the environmental movement in the early 1970s did attitudes begin to change. The first public hearings on global warming in the U.S. Congress took place in the mid-1970s. The policy makers, the scientific community, and ordinary citizens continue to debate climate change, its causes, and policies to address it.

What causes climate change? According to the widely accepted hypothesis, climate change is caused by a combination of factors including solar activity and variations in the Earth orbit. One of the most significant factors is the *greenhouse effect*, as the sun's radiation becomes trapped by the atmosphere, much as in a greenhouse. Instead of the glass ceiling of a greenhouse, however, this absorption results from pollutants in the atmosphere, including carbon dioxide (CO_2), methane (CH_4), and other so-called greenhouse gases. These gases affect an atmospheric layer that traps some of the sun's heat that warms the planet. Burning of fossil fuels caused the levels of CO_2 to increase by approximately 30 percent since the eighteenth century. At present, a few industrial countries emit more CO_2 than do all developing countries together. (See Figure 9-3.)

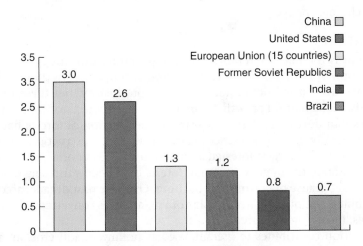

FIGURE 9-3 Assessment of gas emissions in 2025 (projected, if no major changes take place). Billions of tons.

Greenhouse emissions are the by-products of burning to produce energy, heat homes, cook food, and make machines work. In the 1850s, the burning of wood generated almost 90 percent of the world's energy. At the start of twentieth century, coal produced 70 percent of the world's energy; in the 1950s, oil and coal each had about a 40 percent share. In the twenty-first century, oil still generates 40 percent of greenhouse gas emissions, followed by natural gas (25 percent), coal (25 percent), and nuclear reactions (about 5 percent) (EIA 2015; World Resources Institute 2015).

Skeptics argue that global warming is caused by a combination of factors, including not just human activities but also natural processes taking place in space, on the sun, in the atmosphere, and in the oceans (Jacques 2009). Skeptics acknowledge the alarming signs of the major environmental changes but discount the scope and severity of the consequences. But even skeptics agree that even small changes in the ecosystem can have global effects. To illustrate, in the Little Ice Age of the fifteenth century, the earth's average temperature dropped by just 1°F (approximately 5°C). The Thames River in England froze, and Alpine glaciers touched villages as far south as modern Austria and Switzerland.

Although other factors may impact the temperature, the greenhouse hypothesis has received support from many authoritative scientists. What are the consequences of climate change? The most dramatic forecasts predict a 10°F (5.5°C) climb in global temperatures during this century and a 39-inch (1 m) rise in global ocean levels due to melting ice. Even more moderate forecasts project a rise of 3 inches (8 cm). Any scenario would have catastrophic consequences for low-level inhabited territories. New Orleans, London, Amsterdam, and many other cities would have to build storm-surge defenses to avoid flooding. Experts also project more frequent climatic abnormalities including heat waves, hurricanes and typhoons, as well as severe winters in some typically warm areas. Prominent politicians supported scientists' call for the urgency of addressing climate change.

DEFORESTATION

deforestation
The massive removal or disappearance of forests, owing to the thinning, changing, and elimination of trees, bushes, and other vegetation.

Deforestation is the massive removal or disappearance, thinning, changing, and elimination of trees, bushes, and other vegetation (Williams 2006). Fires and flooding have caused deforestation throughout history, but these losses were replenished by natural growth. Humans too contributed to deforestation for centuries, but during the last fifty years the destruction of forests has increased significantly, as a consequence of agriculture and construction, including some of the earth's largest forested areas—in Brazil, Equatorial Africa, and Indonesia. In Brazil, the huge Amazonian forests have been shrinking rapidly since the 1950s because of cutting and burning. Over the past decade, according to the United Nations, an area the size of England was converted each year to other uses, mostly agriculture.

desertification
The expansion of deserts into places previously available for agriculture.

Deforestation contributes to greenhouse gas pollution, soil erosion, and **desertification**—the expansion of deserts into places previously available for agriculture. Desert expansion contributes to illness, hunger, and poverty (Johnson et al. 2006; Rechkemmer 2004).

LOSS OF WILDLIFE

Deforestation, urban development, tourism, mining, and commercial hunting and fishing threaten animal life. Hunters illegally kill rare species of monkeys, tigers, turtles, and rhinoceros for pleasure, profit, or souvenirs. Climate change also affects animals globally, and many of them cannot adapt to the changing natural conditions (Schellnhuber et al. 2006). In the last decade, more than 16,000 species were threatened with extinction. According to the Living Planet Index (http://www.livingplanetindex.org), populations of vertebrate species have halved in the past forty years. If current trends continue, between 15 percent and 37 percent of species will disappear by 2050 (Thomas et al. 2004). Perhaps the largest threat is the growing indifference of the public to wildlife, conservation and environmental issues in general. Environmental protection still draws support among Americans, for example, yet more people are concerned about potential costs (Pew 2015).

LOSS OF CLEAN WATER

Chronic droughts, industrial and agricultural activity, waste, and overpopulation can all lead to water contamination and shortages. Today approximately one billion people have no access to clean running water. Hundreds of millions drink unclean water directly from nearby rivers. The most troubling problems persist in India, China, and Mexico. Worldwide, agriculture is the main consumer of water, and the world's population is growing. By 2050, if trends continue, the demand for water for agriculture will double relative to 2000. Another problem comes from climate change. If the warming trend remains, more ice will melt. The disappearance of glaciers in the Tibet-Himalaya area may lead to substantial losses of river water for all neighboring countries. Because of changes in weather patterns, the Mediterranean region can expect a drop in precipitation of 25 to 30 percent by the middle of the century (Stern 2007).

Water pollution is another major by-product of human activity, including sewage from towns and farms, discharges from power stations, and industrial silt. Rivers, lakes, and even seas are threatened by chemical waste. Especially dangerous are toxic heavy metals (such as mercury, lead, and cadmium) and oil spills. Unclean water contributes to serious illnesses in humans and kills living organisms in rivers, lakes, and oceans (Black 2011; Pearce 2007). China's rapid industrial development has dumped significant waste into major rivers, thus creating significant health hazards (Moore 2014; Economy 2010b).

Disasters and Accidents

Natural disasters, such as earthquakes or erupting volcanoes, can have devastating impacts. Yet man-made accidents, too, can have catastrophic environmental consequences. Natural disasters cannot be prevented, but their damaging consequences can be diminished through effective preparations, international assistance, and cooperation. For instance, the 2004 tsunami caused a significant loss of human life in many Asian countries because the affected countries had almost no early warning systems and lacked many adequate preparations. The governments could not rescue many victims. Medical help

water pollution
The byproducts of human activities that are harmful to rivers, lakes, seas, and underground water.

natural disaster
A natural hazard such as an earthquake or a volcano eruption with devastating impact on the ecosystem.

 The International Program on the State of the Ocean (IPSO) is a consortium of scientists and other experts to identify problems and develop workable solutions to alter the degradation trajectory of the world's oceans. Find out more on the companion website.

was often limited. Fresh water was absent, because salt water and sewage infiltrated many water reservoirs (Helm 2005). Although international forces (including the United States Navy) provided prompt and effective relief efforts, the local governments were often inefficient.

Human-created disasters include chemical leaks, radioactive leaks, and oil spills. In December 1983 in the Indian city of Bhopal, almost fifteen thousand people died and tens of thousands were injured by toxic gas leakage from a chemical refinery owned by a U.S. company, Union Carbide. At least one million people suffered serious health consequences. Union Carbide, which settled the case with the Indian government, continues to insist that the disaster was not an accident but a deliberate act of sabotage (D'Silva 2006).

The most devastating leak of radioactive materials took place at the Chernobyl nuclear plant in the former Soviet Union in 1986. The largest series of oil spills in history took place during the Iraq's takeover of Kuwait in August 1990 and the Persian Gulf War in January 1991 between the United States and Iraq. Retreating Iraqi troops destroyed Kuwait's oil rigs, setting fires and creating giant oil lakes. Between six and eight million barrels of oil spilled into the Persian Gulf. The biggest marine oil spill in history took place in the Gulf of Mexico in 2010, when an explosion in an oil platform operated by British Petroleum took the lives of eleven workers. From three to five million barrels of oil went into the water, causing serious damage to wildlife and contaminating the U.S. coastline. The economic impact was estimated at between $3 billion and $12 billion. Studies suggest that this was not just one accident associated

@ The Historical Incidents database project funded by the National Oceanic and Atmospheric Administration's Environmental Services Data and Information Management Office includes the most significant oil-spill disasters since 1978. Find the link on the companion website.

Reporters wearing protective suits and masks visit the troubled Fukushima No. 1 nuclear power plant of the Tokyo Electric Power Co. in Okuma, Fukushima Prefecture, in 2012. Even wealthy Japan needed international help to deal with the consequences of the tsunami.

with one oil company. Although these accidents are preventable, they may happen again and with even more devastating environmental consequences (Juhasz 2011).

CHECK YOUR KNOWLEDGE

▶ What lesson did the 1985 Vienna Convention and the 1987 Montreal Protocol provide for today's governments and international organizations?
▶ Which environmental problem does the Aral Sea case illustrate?
▶ When and where did the largest series of oil spills in history take place?

Environmental Policies Today

Efforts to protect the environment include regulations and restrictions, green investment, and more comprehensive policies. Financial regulations, taxation, economic incentives, and legal directives all play a role.

RESTRICTION AND REGULATION

In 1900 the Lacey Act banned trade in wildlife, fish, and plants that have been illegally obtained, transported, or sold. This act is effective to this day, and the last amendment to it in 2008 expanded its protection to additional plants and plant products and also prohibited import of illegal timber to the United States. In 1986 the International Whaling Commission banned commercial whaling. Other policies in many countries regulate legal business activities that may be environmentally harmful. To reduce deforestation, for example, nearly 40 percent of the Amazon River basin is legally protected, including approximately 25 percent in private hands. Owners must keep 80 percent of their land forested. These are examples of **conservation**—regulatory policies to protect and preserve natural resources, plant and animal species, and their habitat. Conservation is not necessarily a combination of bans and restrictions imposed by governments. Conservation is also a form of social ethics supporting recycling, care, restoration, and preservation of nature (Hambler and Canney 2013).

conservation
A policy of protecting and preserve natural resources, including plant and animal species and their habitats.

Taxation and other financial incentives for environmental protection have gained recognition as well (Nordhaus 2008). An example is *emissions trading* to limit pollution. Here companies and countries receive "credits," giving them the right to emit a pollutant, but only up to a limit. Those who cannot cut pollution that far are required to buy additional credits from others that pollute less (Fusaro and James 2006). (See Figure 9-4.)

The United Nations took up a major initiative to globalize policies on climate change. In June 1992 the international meeting in Rio de Janeiro, commonly known as the Earth Summit, produced the UN Framework Convention on Climate Change (UNFCCC). The goal of this treaty was to stabilize greenhouse gas concentrations in the atmosphere. Since then, UN conferences on climate change have met periodically. A milestone was the conference in Kyoto, Japan, in 1997, when the participants signed the **Kyoto Protocol** to the UNFCCC. Most industrial countries agreed to reduce greenhouse gas emissions

Kyoto Protocol
A 1997 international agreement to limit air pollution and reduce global warming.

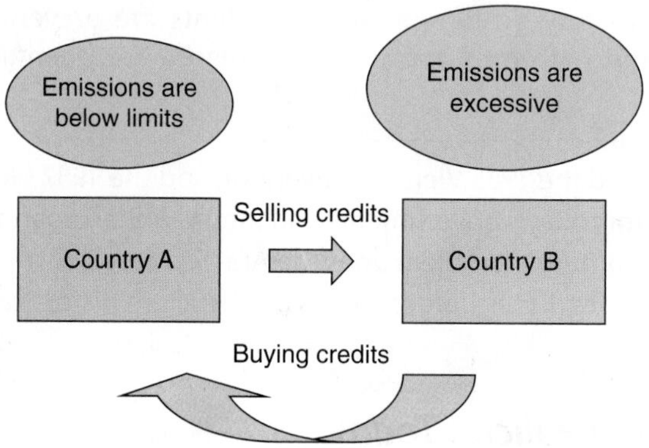

FIGURE 9-4 Emissions trading. Countries that limit their emissions can receive financial rewards. Countries that fall short of cutting their emissions pay a penalty.

by an average of 6 to 8 percent below 1990 levels by 2012. Later governments agreed in Doha, Qatar, to extend the Protocol to 2020.

Some countries, small and big, do not participate in the Kyoto Protocol. Some are ready to cut their emissions but would not participate in emission trading. Canadian officials argued it was too expensive for Canada to contribute $7 billion per year—the price of carbon credits for this country—at a time of economic recession (van Loon 2011). The U.S. Congress during the Clinton, Bush, and Obama administrations did not ratify the Kyoto Protocol. China and India, as well as dozens of developing countries, are exempted from the treaty. A major objection was that the required emission cuts would hurt these countries' economic situation. Without the participation of the world's biggest polluters, the UN effort was incomplete.

GREEN INVESTMENTS

Green investments are business ventures in which companies are involved in activities reducing contamination and depletion and introduce environmentally friendly practices. Typically but not always, green investments require governmental policies to stimulate private business. In most cases, these are investments in environmentally friendly technologies, business methods, and agricultural practices. Green investments go beyond simple restrictions. Many countries, for example, invest in reforestation to make up for lost trees and other vegetation. In China and Costa Rica, policies are being set for agriculture: The fewer trees farmers cut, the more trees farmers plant, the more money they get in form of subsidies. In the same way, **geo-engineering** aims at technological solutions of environmental problems (Victor et al. 2009; Victor 2006). One strategy for reducing the existing accumulation of greenhouse gases involves releasing particles into the air to reflect more sunlight back into space. Another strategy includes collection and storage of carbon gases from coal plants. Germany, for example, draws new carbon capture and storage laws (CCS) to allow companies to store CO_2 indefinitely in underground storage facilities. Regions that host such facilities would receive financial compensation (German Energy Blog 2015).

Wind-powered electricity generators have become common in many countries. In Denmark, 26 percent of the electricity comes from wind-powered generators. In Germany, the figure is nine percent. In the United States, according to the Department of Energy, it is only three percent. Why does the United States lag behind?

Unlike coal or oil, **renewable energy** is replaced naturally as fast as it is consumed (Kemp 2006). It draws on such alternative sources as wind, the sun, tides, and geothermal power—the natural heat within the earth. Wind-powered electricity generators, solar thermal plants, and photovoltaic power stations are examples of new technologies producing renewable energy. Between 2005 and 2015, British Petroleum pledged to invest up to $8 billion in "renewables." General Electric's growth strategy, called *ecomagination*, commits the company to using wind power, diesel-electric hybrid locomotives, new efficient aircraft engines and appliances, and advanced water-treatment systems. Another area of investment is *biofuels*, made from plants, vegetables, or celluloid (Brown and Brown 2012; Soetaert and Vandamme 2009). Brazil has reduced its dependence on oil and gas by producing biofuels from sugar cane. The Chinese government makes significant investments in wind technologies, electric cars, and electric vehicle charging stations (Shahan 2014). India has recently created National Solar Mission and is working to increase dramatically the use of the sun's energy. The government is providing up to 90 percent support for setting up solar power plants. One of the specific goals is to install twenty million solar lights around the country.

India has its own Ministry of New and Renewable Energy. Find the link on the companion website. Read about and discuss the ministry's main accomplishments.

The costs associated with this "green revolution" are still considered to be prohibitively high for many countries, especially poor ones. The International Energy Agency estimated that to reduce global oil consumption by a quarter and cut global greenhouse gas emissions in half by 2050, the world would need to invest $50 billion to $100 billion each year in clean-energy technologies, compared to about $10 billion a year spent recently (Levi et al. 2010).

Even within the European community only the most prosperous countries, such as Germany and the Netherlands, can afford to spend significant funds on renewables. Newer members of the community—Bulgaria, Romania, Poland, Latvia, Estonia, and Lithuania—have asked for assistance.

Global Environment Facility (GEF) An independent financial organization established in 1991 that provides grants to developing countries for projects that benefit the global environment and promote sustainable development.

Usually the poorer the country is, the less inclined it is to invest in geo-engineering and renewables. That places increasing pressure on wealthy countries to provide financial support through loans or grants (Shah 2014; Esty and Winston 2006). The **Global Environment Facility (GEF)**, created in 1991, provides funds for projects in six areas: climate change, biodiversity, pollution in international waters, land degradation, ozone depletion, and persistent *organic pollution*—such natural contaminants as fish and animal waste (French 1994). From the start, the GEF has supported almost two thousand environmental initiatives in countries that otherwise would not have had the financial resources. About 20 percent of the funding is distributed through nongovernmental organizations.

Without coordinated international efforts, the green revolution would be ineffective. Yet China, Japan, and the United States for many years refused the leadership role in environmental policies, citing the threat of economic slowdown. The European Union remains the most active actor in international environmental politics (see next section).

COMPREHENSIVE POLICIES

sustainable development A comprehensive policy that meets the needs of the present without sacrificing the ability of future generations to meet their own needs. This policy is about stimulating economic growth while protecting the environment and natural resources.

A more comprehensive policy is **sustainable development** that meets the needs of the present without sacrificing the ability of future generations to meet their needs. This policy is about stimulating economic growth while at the same time protecting the environment and natural resources (Blewitt 2014; Rogers et al. 2007). The idea of sustainable development emerged partly in response to a 1987 report, *Our Common Future*. Prepared by the UN-sponsored World Commission on Environment and Development, it argued that helping local economies, protecting natural resources, and ensuring social justice for all people are not contradictory but rather complementary goals. (See Figure 9-5.)

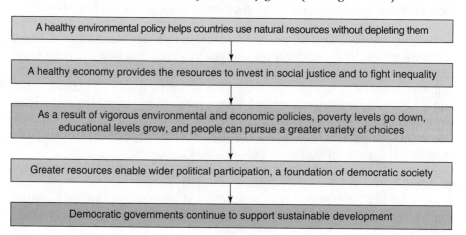

FIGURE 9-5 Main conclusions of the *Our Common Future* report.

A healthy environmental policy helps countries use natural resources without depleting them

A healthy economy provides the resources to invest in social justice and to fight inequality

As a result of vigorous environmental and economic policies, poverty levels go down, educational levels grow, and people can pursue a greater variety of choices

Greater resources enable wider political participation, a foundation of democratic society

Democratic governments continue to support sustainable development

The European Union is the world's leader in designing and implementing comprehensive environmental policies. Starting in the 1970s, many environmentalist groups began to have a significant impact on Europe's political life. From the 1990s, practically all discussions of the EU's economic development focused on the environment and sustainable development.

In 2007 through 2009, the EU Climate Change program established the 20-20-20 targets (often called the *2020 Climate and Energy Package*): 20 percent of the energy consumed in Europe must come from renewable sources, and countries must reduce gas emissions by up to 20 percent by 2020. To accomplish these ambitious goals, the EU will have to impose tougher pollution restrictions, encourage low-emission vehicles, expand emissions trading, and invest in public transportation and low-energy construction. The main problem is a lack of resources to meet these targets, especially after the financial crisis and economic slowdown of the past several years. Although the supporters of the *2020 Climate and Energy Package* believe this should be a model for other countries to follow (Wurzel and Connelly 2012), skeptics also argue that, even if the 20-20-20 targets are met, their impact on climate change will be insignificant.

Many unresolved issues remain. It is unclear how key developing countries—Brazil, India, and China—will cooperate with UNFCCC initiatives. It is also unclear how to combine comprehensive, global environmental policies with many countries' desire for financial security, economic growth, and guaranteed employment.

POLICY IMPLEMENTATION

Environmental policies often run up against the realities of everyday life. The United States depends heavily on coal and oil; a switch to renewables is impossible without a long transitional period and huge investments. Federal and trade deficits make it extremely difficult to pay for more costly alternatives to coal and oil. Sweden, despite more than a three-decade-long ban on new nuclear plants and the decision to close all nuclear plants by 2010, cannot close its nuclear facilities because there are no realistic and environmentally friendly replacements. A growing demand for energy forces the country to continue using nuclear reactors and replacing the existing ones with new reactors. Environmental policies require imagination and innovation, but there are limits. People continue to buy cars that run on gasoline—and they are becoming more efficient and less polluting, and, compared to hybrid and electric cars, still less expensive.

▶ Define renewable energy. If the benefits of renewable sources of energy are obvious, why haven't all countries switched to renewables?

▶ What is sustainable development? Why did the 20-20-20 EU targets appear as an example of sustainable development?

CHECK YOUR KNOWLEDGE

Arguments

Realism

States traditionally struggled for natural resources and considered nature as an asset to conquer and exploit. Experts and politicians trained in realpolitik acknowledged the environmental issues but still treated them as marginal. In their view, states maintain **environmental sovereignty**—the right to use and protect their environment and natural resources. At the core of environmental sovereignty is a country's pursuit of its interests, in light of domestic politics. After the 1970s, however, many realists began to connect the problems of depletion and contamination to national interests and security threats. It became clear that uncontrolled use of national resources and inattention to environmental problems could undermine international stability.

environmental sovereignty
The right of states to use and protect their environment and natural resources.

ACCIDENTS, DISASTERS, AND SECURITY

Natural and human-created disasters are serious events affecting security and military policies, especially if they cause massive casualties and significant environmental damage. In turn, governments now accept a greater responsibility than ever for dealing with the consequences. After the 2004 tsunami in Asia and the earthquake in Haiti in January 2010, several countries committed their military forces to the rescue operations, and U.S. naval vessels delivered humanitarian assistance. However, any deployment of foreign troops in another country, regardless of their mission, can become a source of security concerns, and international tensions can easily arise. Natural disasters can trigger significant security concerns and changes in environmental policies. After the Fukushima nuclear power plant was damaged by the 2011 tsunami, the coalition government in Germany—influenced in part by the events in Japan—decided to close all nuclear plants in Germany by 2022.

Environmental disasters may quickly worsen existing social problems, especially in poor countries like Haiti, triggering political violence and instability. (We discuss similar cases in the next chapter). Conversely, wars and political turmoil may have catastrophic consequences for the environment. Terrorist groups seeking to cause significant damage may focus on nuclear reactors, chemical plants, hydroelectric stations, or dams (Levi 2009). These facilities' protection thus becomes part of a government's environmental security policies.

Depletion of natural resources is a potential cause of conflict. Realists argue that the constantly increasing demands for natural resources, clean water, and agricultural lands could become a major source of local

This oil rig in the North Sea is one of many new ones in the Arctic region. There may be a scramble for control of this region among several countries. Will it become a major source of regional conflict?

and regional conflicts. Scarcity of natural resources is often a security issue (Le Billon 2006). Israel, for example, controls most freshwater reservoirs, including underground aquifers, in the Gaza and the West Bank. While Palestinians demand full access, Israel considers water a strategic asset and uses it to put pressure on the other side. In the 1980s, Turkey began to construct hydroelectric dams using water from the Euphrates River to rotate turbines to produce electricity. These dams reduced the water flow in Syria, Iran, and Iraq, which was protested (Homer-Dixon 1991). China's similar projects in Tibet caused serious concerns in India and other neighboring countries (Economy 2010b).

GLOBAL COMMONS

The **global commons** includes areas not under any one country's sovereign control, such as the open ocean, the seabed, the atmosphere, the outer space, and Antarctica. The idea of the global commons has found significant international support. However, commons have also emerged as potential sites of conflict around the world (Nonini 2007). Without international regulations, private companies or predator states could endanger the environment in the global commons and deplete its resources. And without international agreements, disputes over environmental and other policies in the global commons are likely (Grover 2006). One such area of concern is the Arctic: The polar seas began to thaw, thus allowing countries to navigate in the area during summer and explore natural resources there (Zellen 2009; Borgerson 2008). International agreements have long protected the global commons from hostile takeovers and depletion. This policy has become a strategic priority for the United States and other developed democratic states.

global commons
Geographical areas not under any nation's sovereign control.

The 1959 Antarctic Treaty prohibits any economic exploration and military operations, including nuclear tests, on the sixth continent. No country may claim a territory in Antarctica. Additional agreements regulate research, economic, and military activities on the continent. For example, the 1991 Madrid accord bans coal mining and oil exploration in Antarctica for fifty years. Some business activities such as tourism are allowed, so long as they are regulated and the profits are shared. In the realist view, denying privileged access to Antarctica benefits international security because it maintains the existing balance of power.

▶ What is environmental sovereignty? Give an example.
▶ What are global commons? Give examples.

CHECK YOUR KNOWLEDGE

In sum, supporters of realism acknowledge the importance of environmental policies and international environmental cooperation. At the same time, realism continues to view environmental issues in the context of security interests and the balance of power.

Liberalism

Liberal models treat environmental issues as requiring a sustained and coordinated international effort. Unlike realism, liberal internationalism treats environmental policies as a central feature of modern-day international relations. As you will remember from earlier chapters, many liberals claim that the destructive nature of contemporary wars should make them obsolete as a policy option. Similarly, the depth and scope of today's environmental problems should change the traditional, power-driven approach to international politics. Liberals strongly believe in environmental agreements, institutions, and the involvement of nongovernment organizations (Harris 2004).

INTERNATIONAL TREATIES AND ORGANIZATIONS

An early wave of environmental treaties came in the 1970s. They were mostly regional, signed by countries with shared concerns about contamination, conservation, and the protection of endangered species. The Amazon Cooperation Treaty of 1978 provided guidelines to eight Latin American countries for water use, transportation, environmental research, tourism, and commercial developments in the Amazon region. In Western Europe, with the help of newly formed green parties, Environmental Action Programs (EAP) were launched. Governments allocated funds for massive cleaning efforts in rivers and lakes. In one successful international action, countries banned chlorofluorocarbons (CFCs) in aerosol spray cans and refrigerators in response to ozone depletion.

From the very start, the most ambitious goal of environmental advocates was to develop a global policy framework under the UN umbrella. In 1973, the United Nations Environment Programme (UNEP) was founded, with its headquarters in Nairobi, Kenya. Its activities covered protection of the atmosphere and global ecosystems, the promotion of environmental science and education, and an early warning and emergency response system in cases of environmental disasters. UNEP has developed guidelines and treaties on international trade in harmful chemicals, cross-border air pollution, and contamination of international waterways (UNEP 2010). In 1988, the United Nations funded the Intergovernmental Panel on Climate Change (IPCC) to evaluate the most recent science and human activities related to climate change. During the 1990s, the agenda of international environmental politics broadened. Now it included global environmental agreements. We have already discussed the 1992 UN Conference that created the UNFCCC. For the first time, a true global environmental institution was formed, with 172 countries participating. Ten years later, the Earth Summit of 2002—the World Summit on Sustainable Development—took place in South Africa.

The signing of the Kyoto Protocol in 1997 was a shining moment for global environmental politics (McGovern 2006). More than 190 countries later ratified this agreement and pledged to reduce their emissions of carbon dioxide and five other greenhouse gases. Many countries considered emissions trading. The next decade, however, was largely disappointing for environmentalists and their supporters. Powerful forces in the United States, China, Canada, and other countries began to view emerging environmental policies as a threat to their countries' economic interests. Skeptics attacked the environmental movement, warning that climate control would end in a global bureaucratic regime and huge expenditures without effect (Lomborg 2010).

Despite the global financial crisis and recession of the past decade, global environmental politics has not waned—just the contrary. In April 2009 the leaders of the United States, China, the European Union, India, Russia, and twelve other major economic powers, as well as the United Nations and Denmark, created the Major Economies Forum on Energy and Climate (MEF). The group made a strong effort to boost the UNFCCC negotiations, culminating in a December 2009 conference in Copenhagen. The Copenhagen Accord set several important goals. First, the countries pledged to keep global temperatures from increasing to more than 2°C (3.6°F) above preindustrial levels. Next, they promised to allocate up to $100 billion a year by 2020 to help developing countries deal with climate change. They also promised *transparency*: assured methods so that others could verify whether they are cutting emissions. Finally, the accord required that all but the poorest countries produce specific plans for curbing emissions (Levi 2010a).

The 2010 Cancun Agreement by 193 countries confirmed the key goals established by the Copenhagen Accord. To achieve those goals, industrialized countries would have to cut their emissions between 25 and 40 percent compared with 1990 levels by 2020. These cuts would be voluntary and subject to international inspection. A new Green Climate Fund under UN auspices was established, to manage billions of dollars in support of climate action (Levi 2010b). In 2012, countries reached a global agreement to extend the provisions of the Kyoto Protocol until 2020. Further, a new agreement should be negotiated and reached to replace the Kyoto Protocol. The major problem remains: Facing financial and economic difficulties of the past several years, witnessing the oil prices raise and fall, countries remained reluctant or unable to cut their emissions when significantly faced with domestic political and economic pressures (Levi 2014).

On the companion website, you can read descriptions of the Kyoto Protocol and the Copenhagen, Cancun, and other Agreements, along with assessments of their impact on policies and the environment.

NONGOVERNMENT ORGANIZATIONS

Environmental NGOs first emerged to advocate environmental policies in areas neglected by the public or the government. Some, like Greenpeace, choose provocative and attention-grabbing strategies (see Uses of History: A Greenpeace Story in the end of this chapter). Others, like the Sierra Club and the National Audubon Society, focus mainly on education. The Centre for Science and Environment (CSE) is named after a successful media campaign against air pollution in large Indian cities. Partly because of this group's pressure, the government decided to use compressed natural gas as the main fuel in the capital city's buses and taxis. Still other NGOs focus on funding. The GEF, for one, provides grants to developing countries for projects that benefit the global environment and promote sustainable developments in local communities. The GEF helps countries address such problems as biodiversity, greenhouse gas emissions, pollution in international waters, land degradation, the ozone layer, and persistent organic pollutants.

Visit the companion website to learn more about nongovernment environmental organizations that have appeared during the last decade.

NGOs, according to liberal theories, advance democratic governance and represent a wide range of interests and opinions not represented in large bureaucratic structures. They also monitor environmental policies and reveal problems that governments often overlook or ignore. NGOs educate and influence the public, launch direct actions, and enhance awareness of environmental problems.

PUBLIC AWARENESS

In a democratic society, public opinion should affect policy-making, and education can shape public opinion (Hobley 2012). The more people know and care about the environment, the more supportive they are of environmental policies. The liberal view thus favors sustained educational efforts and public discussions about the environment.

Global public opinion, despite fluctuations, is generally warming up to environmental issues. Global climate change was the top-rated concern in a thirty-nine-nation Pew Research Center survey in 2013: 54 percent across these surveyed countries said global climate change was a *major* threat to their country. A slightly fewer number of people mentioned international financial instability as their top concern (Pew 2013). In 2015, 64 percent Americans said that they favored stricter limits on emissions to address climate change (Pew 2015). Specific economic circumstances, however, affect public opinion. During an economic slowdown, most Americans prioritized economic growth (54 percent) over environmental protection (36 percent; Jones 2011). The same 2015 Pew survey also revealed that Americans increasingly worry about the costs to protect the environment.

"ENVIRONMENTAL OFFENDERS"

The World Wildlife Fund (WWF) assesses consumption habits in different countries and publishes a list of "environmental offenders." The residents of

The mall of the Emirates in Dubai, UAE includes an artificial mini-ski resort and is a shopping and recreational paradise. Critics admit that this mall consumes too much energy to entertain just a few consumers. How should governments of countries labeled "environmental offenders" address the criticism?

the United Arab Emirates (UAE) top the list. Each person in the UAE needs 12 hectares (30 acres) of biologically productive land and sea to sustain life— area needed for the production of vegetables, fish, fruit, or rice and to absorb waste. The United States was the second-worst "offender," with a requirement of 9.6 hectares. The average global requirement, according to the WWF, is 2.2 hectares per person, but the available supply is only 1.8 hectares.

What is the main point of such a list, and how effective is the publication of the list? Could you reduce your personal consumption habits, at least for a short period? How? In your view, will doing so affect the environment in any measurable way?

CHECK YOUR
KNOWLEDGE

▶ What are the key differences between realist and liberal views of environmental policies?
▶ What is the Kyoto Protocol?
▶ For how long was the Kyoto Protocol extended?
▶ How could public awareness affect the environmental policies of governments?
▶ Who are "environmental offenders" according to the WWF, and what are their offenses?

Constructivism

Why did international environmental politics emerge only in the last decades of the twentieth century and not earlier? Policies stem from social and political debates and reflect people's changing values and identities and new awareness of the environment.

Mastery values encourage individuals to exercise control over nature and exploit its resources. **Harmony values** encourage a different attitude—one of preservation and care (Smith and Schwartz 1997). In the constructivist view, both harmony and mastery values affect the environmental policies of different countries and in different periods.

For centuries, mastery values dominated politics. They were behind policies of rapid industrialization and the extraction of natural resources in the twentieth century. Market competition and mass consumption reinforced mastery values in democratic societies, but these values influenced Communist countries as well. Harmony values, in contrast, encourage conservation and environmental protection. They are attached to concerns for the common good inherent in liberal democracy.

International environmental policies are most effective when they adjust to local political, social, and cultural contexts and address local concerns. Environmentalism is strong in the Canadian province of Quebec, which generates eco-friendly hydroelectricity that it sells it to other provinces and the United States. Elsewhere, environmental policies often run into local resistance. In Indonesia, many African countries, and Brazil, peasants oppose attempts to ban *slash-and-burn* farming—a method of farming that contributes to

mastery values
The view that individuals may exercise control over and exploit natural resources.

harmony values
The view that the environment should be preserved and cherished rather than exploited.

 Visit the companion website to learn more about intellectual movements in philosophy, art, sociology, and science that reflect harmony and mastery values: utilitarianism, progressivism, romanticism, and others.

deforestation and air pollution—because they desperately need new farmlands (Waters 2006). To stop slashing and burning, the structure of the local economies must change. New jobs for local farmers are needed, which requires significant investment. Other countries can help if they face no serious economic problems themselves. But during a recession, investments decrease.

Strong resistance to environmental policies in the United States is a more complicated case, but it too points to the connections among politics, values, and economic interests. Power companies and carmakers are not thrilled about policies limiting gas emissions because they may limit profits. The Bush and the Obama administrations allowed the use of new technologies like hydraulic fracturing. "Fracking," as it is commonly known, mainly because of the unknown environmental consequences of this method, sparked protests by environmental organizations and some communities, but it has also made the United States self-sufficient in terms of oil and gas (Levi 2013). Environmental policies are even more difficult to implement in countries exporting oil, gas, and coal. Saudi Arabia, Russia, and other oil and gas producers are genuinely interested in having other states dependent on these energy sources. A reduction in oil consumption due to environmental policies will mean a loss of profit.

Constructivism argues that changing the structure of economic incentives should go hand in hand with enhancing environmental education and awareness. However, changing values could be a more complicated task than introducing new taxes or bringing new managers.

Alternative and Critical Views

environmental discrimination
Actions and policies of the global North that sustain the contamination and depletion of the environment in the global South.

For conflict theories, economic discrimination is embedded in today's international environmental politics. **Environmental discrimination** refers to actions and policies of the global North that sustain the contamination and depletion in the environment in the global South. Facing tough environmental policies at home, corporations continuously moved their industrial facilities to less-developed countries and shipped toxic waste there for inexpensive recycling (Grossman 2007). Most climate control efforts contribute to global inequality. Rich countries can afford to slow production, cut emissions, and adopt tough conservation measures. However, poor countries would suffer from tough new regulations, which would depress their economies. These countries were not given a chance to develop in the past because of colonialism. Environmental policies imposed by the North would have a similar effect.

Critics of imperialism and colonialism argue that, for centuries, powerful Western nations ignored environmental policies while depleting the natural resources of the rest of the world. Today, the disparity in consumption of energy between the rich North and the poor South is staggering. The United States has less that 5 percent of the global population, but it consumes almost 25 percent of the world's energy. On average, U.S. residents consume six to ten times as much energy as do people in rapidly developing countries like India and China—and twenty times as much as people in poor states like Bangladesh.

What would be a solution? There should be global *environmental justice* based on the equal protection from environmental problems and a fair distribution of environmental benefits (Walker 2009). The main investment in global environmental policies should come from the North (Roberts and Parks 2006). Because wealthy countries remain the main consumers of energy and the chief global polluters, they should cut their emissions first. This should allow less-developed states to increase energy consumption and develop their economies. Some scholars argue that such policies will be impossible to implement unless major structural changes take place across countries. Today's environmental problems, they maintain, have their roots in the inability of the capitalist system, with its emphasis on consumption, to address the accelerating threat to life on the planet (Magdoff and Foster 2011).

CHECK YOUR KNOWLEDGE

▶ Compare mastery and harmony values. Can there be a compromise between these two sets of values?

▶ What is slash-and-burn farming? Could you suggest an alternative to it?

▶ Explain environmental discrimination.

Contexts and Applications

The Individual Decisions Context

In the United States, former senator and vice president Albert Gore received the Nobel Peace Prize for his global environmental advocacy. Yet former president of the Czech Republic, Vaclav Klaus, openly criticized "global warming hysteria." What makes political leaders strong defenders or entrenched skeptics of environmental policies?

ENVIRONMENTALISM AND SKEPTICISM

Views of the environment can be understood as a continuum. (See Figure 9-6.) On the one side of this continuum is **environmentalism**, the belief in the necessity of urgent and comprehensive actions to protect the environment. Environmentalists support conservation of natural resources, push for measures

environmentalism
Belief in the necessity of urgent and comprehensive policies to protect the environment.

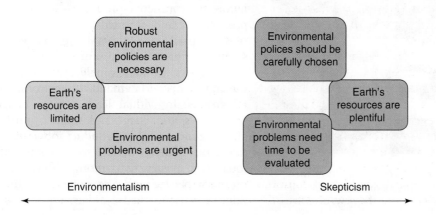

FIGURE 9-6 The spectrum of attitudes: Environmentalism and environmental skepticism.

against contamination, and endorse sustainable development. They believe that many environmental problems are urgent, and the earth's natural resources are limited (Cullen 2010). Commercial activities harmful to the environment should be regulated or banned. Environmentalism is associated with harmony values and a belief in growth through preservation. Environmentalism finds support among many scientists with international standing and is also rooted in *progressivism*, or the belief in deliberate social action for the sake of the common good. This social action must be ecologically sound. Environmentalists also insist that the world's environmental problems are extremely serious and that countries should do significantly more to protect the environment (Davis 2007).

environmental skepticism
A questioning of environmentalism from the point of view of science or practicality.

At the other end of the continuum is **environmental skepticism.** Skeptics can be conservatives as well as liberal individualists who are likely to adopt mastery values and to believe that current environmental policies are too costly to be feasible and effective (Lomborg 2007; 2010a). They support conservation on a smaller scale and believe in the priority of business and market forces over government regulations (Walley and Whitehead 1994). Skeptics maintain that protecting the environment is important, other serious problems including terrorism, diseases, and hunger should receive more urgent care.

Political leaders' education, family experiences, and other circumstances contribute to their choices. Al Gore's concern for nature was enhanced by his experience as a student, when one of his professors made him aware of rising global temperatures, and as a father, when his son was hit by a car and recovered only after a coma. Environmentalism often finds reinforcement in religious values. *Evangelical environmentalism* treats environmental problems and climate change in particular as a serious moral issue. Many members of all religions believe people have a spiritual duty to protect the environment (Jenkins 2008).

Scientists and politicians often disagree about the gravity of environmental problems. They also argue about which policies should be launched to deal with these problems. However, it is incorrect to portray environmental debates as a battle between government bureaucrats—old, conservative, and uneducated "dinosaurs" eager to ignore environmental problems—and young, progressive, and talented activists. In fact, over the past twenty years, there has been a significant change in environmental attitudes: State leaders are increasingly susceptible to the arguments and demands of environmental groups. Individual leaders may change their views, too. Large and small countries alike are more likely to conduct robust environmental policies because of a major shift today from mastery to harmony values among ordinary people and the governing elites. Education has sparked awareness and brought

A photograph of Rachel Carson hangs from supports on the bridge now bearing her name in Pittsburgh, Pennsylvania. Her environmental book *Silent Spring* affected the views of millions.

DEBATE > ALARMING AND SKEPTICAL VOICES

Contemporary environmental discussions resemble the longtime debate between *cornucopians* (a reference to the "cornucopia," or horn of plenty), who believed that natural resources are practically limitless, and neo-Malthusians, the followers of the nineteenth-century British scholar Thomas Robert Malthus (1766–1834), who predicted that the inevitable depletion of natural resources would generate conflicts (Homer-Dixon 1991).

James Lovelock, a British environmental scientist, drew wide attention for his *Gaia hypothesis*, named after a Greek goddess. Every grain of sand, drop of water, or breath of air is a particle in this immense, interdependent structure—a structure whose disturbance could lead to disaster. In fact, Lovelock believes that if nothing is done during the next fifty years, global warming will make most of the planet uninhabitable, and civilization will perish. Lovelock proposes, among other things, urgently switching to nuclear energy and building giant pipes to transfer carbon dioxide from the atmosphere to the ocean (Lovelock 2015).

Bjørn Lomborg, a Danish political scientist, calls himself a "skeptical environmentalist." In *Cool It* (2007), he admits that the environment is under serious stress, but more research and thinking are needed before launching multi-billion-dollar projects. If the European Union adopts all the policies it wants to control noxious emissions, he says, it would cost taxpayers $250 billion, but the results would be negligible (Lomborg 2010). His organization, the Copenhagen Consensus Center, supports the idea of cost-efficient environmental policies.

WHAT'S YOUR VIEW?
This debate, like the debate between the neo-Malthusians and the cornucopians, appeals to both emotions and common sense, but it is not always based on solid research. Academics and mainstream environment experts often hesitate to support Lovelock's doomsday scenarios, and they question Lomborg's expertise. Still, the publications of both authors continue to attract great public attention.
❶ What are the weakest and strongest arguments of the neo-Malthusians and the cornucopians?
❷ Suggest several arguments that both the neo-Malthusians and the cornucopians would agree on.
❸ Propose a policy (such as an investment or conservation strategy) that could address the concerns of both the neo-Malthusians and the cornucopians.

changes in the ways both regular people and politicians see the environment. The political climate is warming toward environmental issues even faster than the global temperature is rising.

A SENSE OF MISSION AND LEADERSHIP

The success of international environmentalism testifies to the role of individual scientists, activists, and political leaders. In 2015, former Chinese state television reporter Chai Jing produced a documentary where she expressed her concern about significant pollution in China's cities. Within a few weeks about 100 million people, mostly in China, watched this video online, which sparked new debates about the insufficient environmental policies of the Chinese government (Tran 2015). The impact of this documentary was compared with the historic impact of *Silent Spring*. When Rachel Carson published *Silent Spring* in 1962, warning about the use of pesticides in agriculture, the book became an immediate sensation, affecting the views of millions in the United States and globally. Individuals embrace environmentalism for various reasons. Some see the problems that other people do not or don't want to see. Some, like the

Canadian ecologist Bill Darnell, came to environmentalism because of their opposition to nuclear war and nuclear testing. Darnell came up with a powerful combination of words, *green* and *peace*, and cofounded one of the most famous environmental organizations, Greenpeace.

Many student radicals of the 1960s saw environmental protection as society's next frontier, and many of them later became prominent politicians. Brice Lalonde, leader of the French National Union of Students and a former minister, established Friends of the Earth. Daniel Cohn-Bendit and Joschka Fischer, prominent European politicians and legislators, helped in 1981 to write the political agenda for the Green Party in Germany. In the United States, President Jimmy Carter became a convinced environmentalist because of his experience as an engineer on a nuclear submarine and as a farmer in Georgia. In May 1977, he proposed a host of environment policies, ranging from conservation to new energy research. To set an example, Carter installed solar panels on the roof of the White House to heat some of its water boilers. At the dedication ceremony in 1979, he predicted that these panels would supply "cheap, efficient energy" twenty years later (Biello 2010).

In Europe, environmental policies have had support from conservative and liberal political leaders; in the United States, personal differences have mattered more. When Ronald Reagan came to power, many of Carter's environmental programs were discontinued. The solar panels on the White House were dismantled in 1986 and sold at auction. After Al Gore became vice president in the Clinton administration in the 1990s, he did much to revive a federal environmental agenda. When George W. Bush was in the office, he was unenthusiastic about the Kyoto Protocol and treated the UNFCCC with strong reservations. President Obama attempted to return to a more active environmental agenda after 2009 but later redirected his priorities due to the country's many other economic problems (Tumulty 2011).

The State Policies Context

Why do political leaders in Germany and Sweden enact proactive environmental policies, regardless of the political party in office? Why do China and the United States frequently appear not to do enough? Domestic politics, in addition to individual values, plays a strong role, including the impact of political institutions and political affiliations (Economy 2010b; Kamieniecki and Kraft 2007).

NATIONAL PURPOSE AND PARTISAN POLITICS

Sometimes countries reduce their sovereignty in exchange for financial benefits. They agree, for example, on **debt-for-nature swaps**. These are international deals allowing a financially struggling state to designate an area for environmental conservation in exchange for, say, a reduction in its foreign debt. The World Wide Fund for Nature pioneered the idea of building national parks in exchange for financial incentives. In Guatemala, the $24-million debt-for-nature swap should finance conservation policies through 2021 and thus protect the tropical forest for many years. Guatemala's debt to the United States was invested in conservation efforts (Grandia 2012; ENS 2006).

debt-for-nature swaps Agreements to designate an area for environmental conservation in exchange for a reduction in the country's foreign debt.

The environment's place in a country's priorities depends on how that country sees its *national purpose*. For three decades, starting in the late 1940s, China defined its national purpose in terms of industrial development and rapid economic growth. Chinese Communists believed the environment must be put into the service of the revolution. Forests had to be felled, mountains leveled, and rivers reversed in their courses (Shapiro 2001). As a result, the Chinese government did not consider depletion or air and water pollution to be urgent problems. More recently, the Chinese Communist Party changed its environmental strategies to address many rapidly emerging problems (Dutta 2005). To date, the results of this policy are inconclusive.

The United States has gone through policy cycles, depending on national purpose and priorities. This "seesaw" environmental history can be explained not only by individual presidents but also by the ideological polarization between the two major political parties—especially after the 1980s. The Republicans have defined national purpose primarily in terms of economic liberalism and rejected most federal intervention. They argue that strict environmental regulations could weaken American businesses and make the United States less competitive with other countries (McGovern 2006). In contrast, the Democrats see national purpose in terms of economic regulation and robust environmental policies. They argue that green policies will create jobs and help to avoid serious future problems. There is no robust bipartisan strategy on environmental policies in Washington, and none is likely to emerge any time soon. At the same time, as we have mentioned, both the Bush and Obama administrations agreed to support new methods of drilling for oil and gas. Such methods in combination with several other factors will provide for the United States' energy self-sufficiency. This also means that fossil fuels continue to be the major source of energy globally.

Partisan divides on environmental issues are associated with ideology and politics. In democratic societies, parties associated with social-democratic programs tend to support environmentalism to a greater extent than conservative groups. In many European countries, Green Parties have gained strength and won seats in legislatures. Meanwhile parties supporting industrial interests are usually skeptical about environmentalism. Agricultural parties maintain a mixed position: They support environmental protection but oppose costly regulations. The balance in partisan politics can shift considerably, depending on a country's economic situation: With high unemployment and a stagnant economy, as opinion polls show, environmental concerns are often put aside. Economic prosperity allows more people to support dynamic environmental policies.

Environmental advocates, including the Philippine Coast Guard and a group of Miss Earth Philippines beauty candidates, conduct coastal cleanup along the shores of Freedom Island to mark World Earth Day, 2015. Can collective actions make people more environmentally responsible?

THE DEMOCRATIC CONTEXT

Democratic context can be favorable or unfavorable to environmental policies. Already in the 1970s, when the international environmental movement emerged, its opponents called it "elitist." The majority of voters may not understand adequately the scientific arguments behind environmental policies, but immediately see that they are expensive. In times of economic and financial recession, the general public tend to vote for their pockets more and listen less to the warnings of environmental scientists.

In democracies, policies that require state appropriations also require support from voters. A major problem is a gap between the knowledge gathered by environmental scientists on the one hand and general public on the other (McCarthy 2011). And there are too many interest groups that doubt environmental studies and criticize their conclusions as either unreliable or exaggerated (Murray 2008). Also the high cost of the proposed international environmental actions alienates many voters who fear losing their jobs or do not want to pay for these policies from their own pocket.

In non-democracies, environmental activism faces significant problems including censorship and suppression. In 1995, the Nigerian military government executed "Ken" Beeson Saro-Wiwa, a prominent activist who exposed environmental abuse committed in his country by oil companies. This reminds us that environmental activities, protected and even encouraged in democratic countries, may be dangerous in authoritarian and corrupt states. In democracies, where the media and public opinion carry more weight, environmental policies are debated more openly than in countries run by authoritarian regimes. Highly publicized public protests and petition campaigns halted the construction of nuclear power plants in many European countries. In the 1980s, media-driven public pressure against the use of CFCs in refrigerators and aerosol sprays influenced governmental regulations and international agreements and forced companies to look for more environmentally friendly technologies. (See Figure 9-7.)

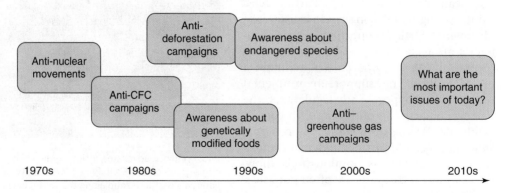

FIGURE 9-7 Environmental activism: A few examples.

The Global Context

Environmental policies face at least three challenges at the global level. The first is the need to balance environmental policies and economic development. The second is the necessity for sustained global effort by governments and NGOs. The third is the need for new effective strategies to deal with the consequences of climate change if current policies fail.

THE ENVIRONMENT AND BUSINESS

Supporters of environmentalism generally argue they are not against honest business practices but only against greed and ignorance that the free market cannot control. Supporters of businesses say that they want to protect the earth but oppose harsh regulations that halt economic growth (Pielke 2010). Can environmentalism and economic interests be reconciled?

Realists point out that, as long as oil and coal remain the least expensive sources of energy, countries will continue to use them. Renewables are simply too expensive. According to the International Energy Agency, in the United States, electricity from new nuclear power plants is 15 to 30 percent more expensive than electricity from new plants using coal. Wind power is more than twice as expensive as coal, whereas solar power costs about five times as much. In other countries, like China, renewables may cost even more (Levi et al. 2010). And global demands for energy are rising. In response, supporters of realism and liberalism may agree: Governments and the private sector must invest more in cleaner energy sources.

One way to reconcile business and environmental interests is **socially responsible investing** (SRI), a business strategy combining the pursuit of the social good, environmental protection, and profits—all at the same time. Today, many businesses support SRI as part of their marketing strategies. In many countries, national parks are an example of SRI. They tend to spark tourism, stimulate environmental research, and create jobs (Gaston and Spicer 2004).

socially responsible investing (SRI)
A business strategy combining the pursuit of the social good, environmental protection, and profits.

green certification
The grant of certificates to companies that pursue responsible environmental policies, in order to make their products more competitive in the market.

Green certification is another way to merge business and environmental interests. Companies that pursue responsible environmental policies receive a certificate that is supposed to make their products more attractive to consumers and thus more competitive. Logging companies, for example, are invited to apply for green certificates if they promise sustainable development. The Forest Stewardship Council, an NGO based in Germany, has drawn up rules for sustainable forestry.

THE NEED FOR GLOBAL EFFORTS

How will all these programs be financed, and how will they fit into strategies for global development? Massive environmental

Solar panels are set on the rooftop of the green mosque opened in Dubai, United Arab Emirates, in 2014. The UAE's first eco-friendly mosque has integrated various methods to combat its energy consumption.

investment in the least prosperous countries must play a major part in any international effort. The 2009 UN climate conference in Copenhagen pledged to set aside $30 billion a year to help the world's poorest countries deal with climate change. Rich countries also agreed, as we have seen, to allocate $100 billion per year and to direct funds from the global North to the global South to pay for emissions reduction (Levi 2010a; Levi 2010b). Many projects remain ambitious and expensive but also necessary. Desertec, an initiative backed by German firms, plans to build by 2050 one hundred solar power plants and scores of wind farms in northern Africa. The project that started in 2009 will sell, if everything goes well, much of the electricity generated to Europe. In the end, consumers will pay for clean energy, and African countries will benefit economically (Desertec 2015).

Support for new environment-friendly technologies can also take place on a global scale, and research and implementation will both benefit from multilateral efforts. Renewables, for example, supplied around 15 percent of world energy in the first decade of the 2000s, and this share is going up. Wind power is booming in Europe and the United States thanks to private investment and government subsidies.

Enforcement of environmental policies, too, shows the need for global efforts. As realists argue, international agreements remain useless unless they are enforced. For example, the 1976 Convention on International Trade in Endangered Species (CITES) prohibited trading in rhino horn. More than 170 countries joined the treaty, including the countries most involved in horn importing—China, Japan, Vietnam, and Yemen. Unfortunately, trade simply moved onto the black market, and hunters continue to kill these rare animals.

Last, global solutions may help where government bureaucracies are slow to respond (Ebrahim 2006). After the 2004 tsunami in the Indian Ocean killed so many, UNESCO took leadership, and in 2005 an international agreement with twenty countries was reached to create the Indian Ocean Tsunami Warning System, emulating the U.S. system in the Pacific. It is hoped that such a system would be able to prevent many negative consequences of natural disasters in the future.

New environmentally friendly technologies and other innovations have difficulty moving from the research laboratory to the market. Multibillion-dollar funding itself often creates problems. Instead of pursuing long-term environmental policies, countries frequently create their own arbitrary "wish lists" of projects to be funded by international organizations (Spector 2005). The main goal is to control the money. Take, for example, water policies. The Consultative Group on International Agricultural Research showed that small, direct investments in projects designed to help regions lacking water are very effective. However, many governments insist on large investments under *their* control. This strengthens liberal claims for the importance of NGOs and independent activism in keeping pressure on decision makers.

GLOBAL POLICIES

Global cooperation is needed to address climate change and other environmental challenges. A single, even economically advanced, country cannot

What if the world is slow to turn to renewables and fails to address climate change? What if its consequences become inevitable? Let's draft a list of the most significant environmental consequences in the near future. For example:

- Heat waves will become more frequent and harsh.
- Desertification will affect already dry places.
- Rains will fall harder in other places, thus increasing flooding.
- Many more species will be endangered. More ice will melt and sea levels will keep rising.

WHAT'S YOUR VIEW?

❶ What does the world have to do to adjust to these and other severely worsening conditions? What strategies should be implemented? Discuss three policies related to safe infrastructure, food security, and population policies. Feel free to either support or criticize them. Explain your reasons. ❷ Countries will have to take responsibility for creating a safe infrastructure, including dams, housing insulated against heat and cold, and reliable communications. Every wealthy country will be responsible for its own environmental security, but poorer countries should be helped. Do you agree or not that the funding priority related to the environment should be increasingly given to protection instead of prevention? ❸ Food security—the guaranteed availability of food—will be another challenge in poor agricultural regions. The right to sufficient, healthy, and nutritious food must be satisfied regardless of environmental and social constraints (McDonald 2011). Yet food security is difficult to achieve without genetically modified food: plants and grains that can sustain harsher climatic conditions. Would you support investments in these products? Why or why not? ❹ Some parts of the planet will face significant depopulation, while others will become overcrowded. To avoid massive social problems, coordinated immigration and population policies may be needed, challenging traditional conceptions of state sovereignty. Would you agree to divert some environmental funds to resettle affected populations in safer geographical areas? ❺ Which other global policies would you suggest as replacements or additions to this list?

produce the clean-energy innovation for the world. Countries must cooperate to sustain policies that are environmentally just and do not benefit the wealthiest countries only (Walker 2012). Different countries' efforts can build on one another. The United States can learn from China and Germany about clean-coal technologies. U.S. labs can help India with its massive solar energy projects. Brazil will need the research of European chemical labs to increase its production of biofuels from sugar cane (Levi et al. 2010).

The responsibility of major industrial powers for greenhouse emissions is obvious. However, cutting emissions in the North and allowing them to climb in the South is probably not a good idea. The world should turn more to cleaner technologies, renewable energy sources, and policies of sustainable development.

Keep in mind that the world also needs coordination between global environmental and energy policies (Levi 2013). But the most far-reaching global environmental policy will also sustain economic growth, provide opportunities, and improve social conditions around the world.

CHECK YOUR
KNOWLEDGE

▶ Explain environmentalism and skepticism. Can these points of view be reconciled?

▶ What is a country's national purpose referring to the environment? Give examples.

▶ Explain green certification.

THE USES OF HISTORY: A Greenpeace Story

Over the past forty years, Greenpeace has drawn significant support from all over the world and inspired enthusiastic critics. Many admire its dramatic style of environmental activism. Others see it as dubious and self-promoting. To achieve its goals, Greenpeace often chooses confrontational and controversial methods. What, then, is the real Greenpeace?

Background

Greenpeace traces its roots to 1971, when several young people grew increasingly frustrated over nuclear testing. Early "green peaceniks" sailed on an old fishing boat from Vancouver, Canada, to Amchitka, a small island near Alaska's west coast, with the hope of disrupting underground nuclear testing. The protesters were intercepted and the nuclear testing went on. However, many copycat groups have emerged.

In the 1970s, such groups launched a worldwide campaign against commercial whaling and seal hunting, sparking public condemnation and political pressure against the whaling industries. In 1986 the International Whaling Commission banned commercial whaling. Meanwhile other activists were turning against toxic waste and pollution.

In the late 1970s regional groups formed Greenpeace International to oversee the goals and operations of regional organizations. Other groups chose to remain independent but to tackle similar environmental problems. Greenpeace today is a global NGO, with its headquarters in the Netherlands and offices in more than forty countries. The organization receives hundreds of millions of dollars in donations from almost three million individual supporters and grants.

Greenpeace activists use nonviolent protest to raise the level and quality of public debate about the environment. The group promotes harmony values (Greenpeace 2015). Two of its key and interconnected methods are direct action and public education.

Activists disrupt business activities by picketing, blocking roads, jamming communications, or staging sit-ins. They also aim to raise awareness of environmental issues by sponsoring lectures, research, and educational programs. Greenpeace uses litigation and scientific research to back up its claims.

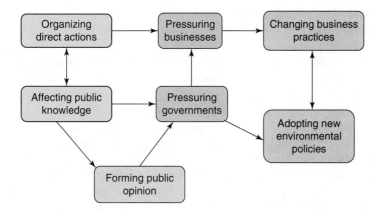

FIGURE 9-8 Methods of Greenpeace.

In the 1980s, it pushed for a global moratorium on radioactive waste dumping at sea. In 2003, intense lobbying efforts by Greenpeace resulted in the UN sanctions on Liberia for illegal logging. In 2005, Sony Ericsson under pressure from Greenpeace and other groups began to phase toxic chemicals out of its products. In 2010, after years of lobbying by Greenpeace, food giant Nestlé agreed to stop purchasing palm oil, the production of which destroys Indonesian rainforests. Greenpeace's *Go Beyond Oil* campaign aims at significant reducing, and eventually ending, the world's consumption and production of oil. Greenpeace sponsors research in the area of renewable energy. It also develops its own technologies, such as Greenfreeze—a refrigerator free of chemicals that contribute to ozone depletion and global warming. Greenpeace currently sponsors a global campaign to stop deliberate deforestation by 2020. Rainbow Warrior II is the organization's motor-assisted yacht is used for protest actions as well as research and awareness campaigns. (See Figure 9-8.)

Governments show different attitudes toward Greenpeace activities. Russia, for example, reacted harshly in 2013 to Greenpeace disruption of the work of an oil rig in the Russian part of the Arctic. A Russian law enforcement unit seized the Greenpeace ship *The Arctic Sunrise*, towed it to the Russian port Murmansk, and detained twenty-eight activists and two journalists on charges of "piracy" and "hooliganism." They were all released after being detained for three months.

Greenpeace activists unfold a banner reading: "Do not burn, should be recycled" in St. Petersburg, Russia, 2015. Greenpeace activists were protesting against the construction of four waste incineration plants on the outskirts of the city. Can environmentalism flourish in non-democratic conditions?

Analysis

Critics acknowledge Greenpeace's role in environmental activism but question the significance of its efforts. Realists argue that governments are unlikely to support environmental policies that threaten their core interests. Greenpeace almost certainly exaggerated the success of its anti-nuclear campaign. The United States, the Soviet Union, and France stopped nuclear testing in the atmosphere and underground, but not necessarily because of pressure from environmentalists; these countries had changed their long-term strategic nuclear plans for other reasons. U.S. nuclear policies, for example, were influenced mainly by negotiations with the Soviet Union. Greenpeace also claims that its relentless efforts to oppose nuclear waste shipments from France to Russia ended in victory, but Russia has said Greenpeace had little to do with its decision. Nestlé agreed not to buy palm oil from questionable sources, but these deals already accounted for less than 1 percent of the global trade of palm oil. Finally, is passing an environmental law enough? Monitoring this law's implementation is a difficult and tedious task that many environmental groups didn't focus on much in the past.

Greenpeace sometimes chooses form over substance, flashy labels over serious efforts to educate. Its promotional materials speak of "dirty energy," "deadly fuels," the "oil fuels war," "climate-destroying oil and coal companies," and "genetic pollution" (Greenpeace 2015). Greenpeace sometimes, as critics say, chooses the wrong battles. Some activists claim that the real source of environmental problems is capitalism itself with its pursuit of profit. Yet the arguments that Greenpeace uses are protected by law. In market societies, political groups can express their opinions freely and influence politics by a wide range of lawful means. In authoritarian countries, where governments regulate and control business, environmental groups are ignored, their actions suppressed, and their activists jailed. This does not mean that capitalism eagerly embraces environmental values simply because this is the right thing to do. Not many people thirty years ago understood Greenpeace, its ideology, or its methods. It took a generation to attract supporters globally. Environmental policies are the product of long and difficult battles for hearts, minds, and pockets.

From the first, Greenpeace embraced the tactics of the peace campaign and civil rights movement of the 1960s, including individual acts of disobedience and appeal to moral foundations. Yet it has also evolved. Today Greenpeace relies on help from lawyers and scientists to function effectively within democracy. Online fund-raising is a key to its success as well.

Greenpeace's evolution reflects broader political and cultural changes as well. It began its journey by fighting for causes that many people then opposed or misunderstood—from radioactive waste dumping at sea to illegal logging, genetically modified foods, and sustainable agriculture. All these causes are increasingly acceptable. Greenpeace's tactics in the past probably alienated many more people than they attracted. But where Greenpeace once had just a few members, it can now draw on the energy of tens of thousands of volunteers, researchers, and lawyers and a multimillion-dollar budget. Greenpeace and other groups have changed many of their tactics and targets, but they remain loyal to the goal of environmental protection.

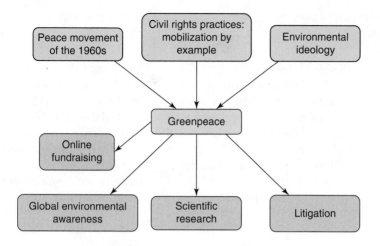

FIGURE 9-9
Greenpeace: Sources and actions.

Questions

1. Visit Greenpeace International's main website and scroll down to "Get involved" (www.greenpeace.org). Examine the list of activities and projects. Which of these do you consider the most important today, and why? Which would you support the least, and why?

2. What problem that is not addressed in this list would you want Greenpeace to focus on next? Discuss. Could you submit your ideas to Greenpeace now?

3. For many decades Greenpeace has campaigned against certain polices and decisions of big corporations. However, in the twenty-first century, Greenpeace has become a very large international corporation with an annual revenue of more than $400 million. Do you support or oppose the idea of creating an independent international NGO to monitor the activities of big nongovernment organizations? The goal of this group will be monitoring the transparency and accountability of NGOs. Do we need such a group, or should global NGOs monitor themselves? (See Figure 9-9.)

CONCLUSION

In "The Tragedy of the Commons," published in *Science* in 1968, the prominent ecologist Garrett Hardin argued that even the most rational individuals acting independently from one another will eventually deplete a limited resource they share together. Our global environment is truly a limited resource, and to secure our future countries must act together. The opening of this chapter illustrated how a collective effort and mutual compromises solved one serious environmental problem twenty-five years ago. But are countries today ready to cooperate and sacrifice even more? The debates about global environment and environmental policies will continue to reflect who we are and what we stand for socially and politically. Action must follow, but it is up to you what kind of action that will be.

KEY TERMS

acid rain 298
climate change 300
conservation 305
contamination 298
debt-for-nature swaps 320
deforestation 302
depletion 298
desertification 302
environmentalism 317

environmental
  discrimination 316
environmental politics 297
environmental skepticism 318
environmental sovereignty 310
global commons 311
Global Environment Facility
  (GEF) 308
green certification 323

harmony values 315
Kyoto Protocol 305
mastery values 315
natural disaster 303
ozone depletion 300
socially responsible investing
  (SRI) 323
sustainable development 308
water pollution 303

IDEAS

ENVIRONMENTAL POLICIES

- Interconnected threats to ecosystems, including climate change, deforestation, loss of wildlife, and loss of clean air and water

DISASTERS

- Natural calamities and man-made accidents that may have catastrophic environmental consequences

ENVIRONMENTAL POLICIES

- Two major categories of problems: contamination and depletion
- Regulations and restrictions, green investment, and more comprehensive policies

ARGUMENTS

REALISM

- Environmental policies should not undermine state sovereignty
- Some environmental problems can become security threats
- Countries should cooperate regarding global commons

LIBERALISM

- Environmental policies are a central feature of IR
- International organizations and treaties play a key role in policies
- Nongovernment organizations' role should increase
- Public awareness brings change

CONSTRUCTIVISM

- Environmental policies are socially constructed and reflect values as well as interests

OTHER THEORIES

- Conflict and dependency theories: Rich countries must accept a greater responsibility for the environmental problems they have created

CONTEXTS AND APPLICATIONS

THE INDIVIDUAL DECISIONS CONTEXT

- Individual values, education, and leadership affect leaders' choices in their environmental policies

THE STATE POLICIES CONTEXT

- Political institutions and partisanship
- In democracies, environmental policies are debated openly
- Authoritarian governments tend to regulate environmental debates or ban them altogether

THE GLOBAL CONTEXT

- Countries try to balance environmental policies and economic development
- They continue sustained global efforts and seek new strategies

Critical Thinking

1. Using an empirical case of your choice, analyze a depletion problem that has led or might lead to an international conflict.
2. Realists argue that governments are unlikely to support environmental policies that threaten their core interests. Discuss this argument from a constructivist view, focusing on countries' "core interests."
3. How important are renewable energy strategies? Should governments have a separate ministry in charge of these issues, such as in India?
4. Should developing countries have the right to pollute for some time to end poverty and catch up with the industrialization process? Discuss.

The decision to intervene in any country or crisis [must be] based solely on an independent assessment of people's needs—not on political, economic, or religious interests.

  —DOCTORS WITHOUT BORDERS

I N MAY 1967, SECESSIONISTS IN THE SOUTHEASTERN PROVINCES IN NIGERIA DECLARED INDEPENDENCE AND THE CREATION OF A NEW COUNTRY CALLED BIAFRA. IN RESPONSE, the central government blockaded Biafra to defeat the secessionists. As food supplies failed to reach the region, famine and violence spread. Two to three million people died over three years, yet the rest of the world simply stood by. There was no international intervention to stop the atrocities. The news about Biafra soon disappeared from the front pages of major newspapers.

About twenty-five years later, a violent conflict broke out in Bosnia, a territory of former Yugoslavia that had disintegrated in 1991. Militants representing three local ethnic groups first targeted each other, and then the violence spiraled. More than one hundred thousand people died on all sides as a result of massive atrocities against civilians. Violence of this scope had not been seen in Europe since World War II. In response, NATO and the UN launched significant military initiatives, including airstrikes. A peace agreement was reached in 1995, and an 80,000 multinational military contingent occupied Bosnia.

Why did NATO and the UN respond with force in Bosnia but not in Biafra? These two cases highlight a few core questions of international relations. How does a country's location affect the way such crises are perceived? When one country faces a

Left: Syrian refugee Amani Abdul-Qadir, 27, is seen through a broken window as she sits inside her former classroom at the Al-Rama Public School in the Lebanese-Syrian border village of Al-Rama. More than eleven million Syrians were driven away from their country or internally displaced by the atrocities of the civil war.

tragic loss of life, do other states have an obligation to intervene? Should other countries and the UN be allowed to use force in a country without the express permission of its government?

A consensus has grown among Western powers that in such crises, the use of force is necessary to save civilian lives. As U.S. President Obama said in 2011, "Some nations may be able to turn a blind eye to atrocities in other countries. The United States of America is different. And as president, I refused to wait for the images of slaughter and mass graves before taking action." These words explain the 2011 military action in Libya, when the United States joined forces with NATO and other states in support of rebels. Yet other states, including Russia and China, were quick to criticize, claiming that such responses violate sovereignty and cause instability. Indeed, it often takes long years for a country to return to order after military interventions. The challenge is to make sure that the pursuit of immediate goals does not cause long-term negative consequences.

This chapter covers international efforts to prevent and stop massive human suffering. These efforts pose new questions and spark new discussions.

Learning Objectives	▶ Explain major humanitarian challenges and their causes. ▶ Discuss humanitarian policies to address these challenges. ▶ Outline similarities and differences among key approaches to humanitarian challenges. ▶ Explain leaders' choices, countries' political conditions, and global contexts affecting humanitarian challenges and policies.

Ideas

humanitarian crisis
Incident or problem that threatens the health, safety, security, and well-being of many people, usually in a single geographic area.

Suffering is inseparable from human existence. However, many forms of suffering caused by identifiable sources are preventable and can be alleviated. At this very moment, millions of people suffer from political and ethnic violence, natural disasters, persistent food shortages, acute infectious diseases, and forceful migration. These are **humanitarian crises**—incidents or continuing problems threatening the health, safety, security, and well-being of many, usually in a distinct geographic area. A conflict causing massive civilian deaths, like the ones in Biafra and Bosnia, are a humanitarian crisis. Rapidly spreading

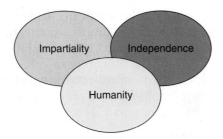

FIGURE 10-1 Three principles of humanitarian policies. Alleviate suffering first (humanity), play no favoritism (impartiality), and do not allow self-interested agendas (independence).

infectious diseases, acute water shortages caused by a drought, or massive hunger as a result of a flood or earthquake are other examples.

Countries, as well as international and nongovernment organizations, plan, develop, and conduct policies to deal with these crises. Humanitarian policies are based on three fundamental principles: humanity, impartiality, and independence. *Humanity* means that policies first of all must save lives and alleviate suffering. *Impartiality* means no preferences for any political leader, country, or group. *Independence* means that humanitarian policies are not guided by open or veiled political, economic, or military objectives of participating states (United Nations 2006; Young 2010). (See Figure 10-1.)

Humanitarian interventions are the actions of foreign powers in a humanitarian crisis with or without the approval of a legal authority controlling the area (Roberts 2000). Besides bringing relief, humanitarian interventions also attempt to eliminate the sources of the crisis, especially human causes. Some interventions involve armed forces. In cases of natural catastrophes, governments usually welcome foreign aid and rescue groups. However, when political disputes or ethnic-religious strife is involved, states are much more reluctant to invite foreign countries to intervene. Countries also choose to participate or not get involved in international humanitarian actions.

By international law, all countries have **humanitarian sovereignty**—the right to accept or reject humanitarian interventions on their territories. The UN Charter of 1945 states in article 2(7) that "nothing . . . shall authorize the United Nations to intervene in matters which are essentially within the domestic jurisdiction of any state. . . ." Humanitarian sovereignty (which is a facet of state sovereignty) is an essential principle of international relations restricting interventions. However, as we shall see, this principle faces practical as well as moral and political limitations (Weiss 2012).

Types of Humanitarian Challenges

Many humanitarian crises affect large groups of people and spread across borders. They quickly become regional and even global problems.

PANDEMICS AND INFECTIOUS DISEASES

Infectious diseases are maladies caused by biological agents such as viruses, bacteria, or parasites. Outbreaks of infectious diseases in a large population are called **epidemics**. An epidemic spreading over a continent or globally is a **pandemic**.

humanitarian intervention Assistance with or without the use of military force to reduce the disastrous consequences of a humanitarian crisis.

humanitarian sovereignty A country's responsibility for its own humanitarian policies and the right to accept or reject humanitarian interventions.

infectious diseases Serious maladies caused by a biological agent such as a virus, bacterium, or parasite.

epidemic An outbreak of infectious disease in a large population.

pandemic An international epidemic that spreads across national borders.

For centuries, our ancestors were practically defenseless against pandemics. In the 1300s the Black Death killed almost a quarter of Europe. Around the same time, a pandemic killed millions in China, Central Asia, and India. Infectious diseases brought to America by European colonizers also caused the deaths of Native Americans five hundred years ago. Between 1918 and 1920, the Spanish flu killed from 50 million to 100 million people, including 500,000 in the United States, 400,000 in Japan, 200,000 in Great Britain, and over 17 million in India.

The Ebola virus outbreak in Africa in the 1970s and again in 2014, the cholera epidemic in Latin America, and the plague in India in the 1990s are just a few recent examples of pandemics. The World Health Organization recognizes today more than 1,400 infectious diseases. Among the deadliest are lower respiratory infections, HIV/AIDS, and infections causing diarrhea, tuberculosis, malaria, and measles. These illnesses cause the death of some ten to twelve million people each year. Malaria alone kills an estimated one million people a year, mostly African children. When deadly forms of influenza rapidly appeared, such as SARS in 2002 and H5N1 (Avian flu) in 2009, states took costly measures out of fear that the illness would spread (Karesh and Cook 2005).

Epidemics and pandemics are undoubtedly international problems. First, they cause significant loss of life and trigger global disruptions. They can directly affect the functioning of governments and the preparedness of armed forces, firefighters, paramedics, and the police (Lakoff 2010; Stewart 2006). Second, without international cooperation, governments may overreact to a rapidly developing pandemic. As a disease spreads, death tolls rise, and medication runs low, and governments could close international borders and stall trade. Finally, many governments lack the resources or proper management to protect their populations from preventable diseases. International involvement could save millions of lives (Wolfe 2011).

Indian counselors from an AIDS Healthcare Foundation examine the blood of a person for HIV during an awareness program on International Condom Day in New Delhi, India, in 2015. How can national customs and cultural habits help or thwart the effectiveness of such campaigns? In which ways?

AIDS

AIDS is a disease of the immune system characterized by increased vulnerability to infections. The *human immunodeficiency virus* (HIV) is its cause. Although AIDS develops much more slowly than influenza, it is a pandemic. According to UNAIDS and the World Health Organization, the total number of people infected by HIV in the second decade of the century could be between 35 million and 48 million. Nearly 25 million people have died from AIDS. Around 400,000 children are infected with HIV each year, most of them in Africa. Sub-Saharan Africa is the region with the highest prevalence of HIV: Almost two-thirds of all individuals with HIV live there (UNAIDS 2015). Every day, approximately 8,000 people

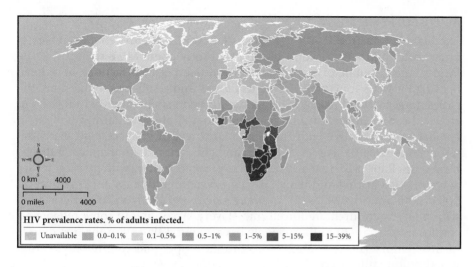

MAP 10-1 Worldwide HIV prevalence rates. *Source: The United Nations*

die of AIDS-related illnesses, mostly in underdeveloped countries, and more than 1,400 of them are children, according to Doctors Without Borders. HIV infection rates have reached 25 percent in some areas of southern and eastern Africa. In some countries, the rate is declining; yet in central Asia and Eastern Europe, the rate is growing. (See Map 10-1.)

AIDS is a serious global problem, but it is generally preventable and treatable with international cooperation. Wealthy countries have been able to stop the rapid spread of the HIV infection and provide medication for the infected. Globally, deaths due to AIDS have declined since 2007. Approximately $16 billion is spent on AIDS prevention and treatment every year in low-income countries; half the money is foreign aid. Yet people in countries without efficient health systems continue to suffer ("A Strategic Revolution in HIV," 2011). Poor hygiene and unsafe sex practices contribute to the problem.

CHRONIC STARVATION AND MALNUTRITION

Malnutrition is a severe medical condition resulting from constant food shortages. Chronic malnutrition leads to hunger and *starvation*. The last devastating **famine**—severe food scarcity—in Western Europe, in the 1840s, caused mass deaths and a wave of immigration to the United States, particularly from Ireland and Scotland. In the twentieth century, famine continued to break out in less-developed countries: in India, Russia, and China in the first half of the century; in some African countries (such as Nigeria, Ethiopia, and Angola) in the second half. According to the UN **Food and Agriculture Organization** (FAO), from 700 million to one billion people suffer from malnutrition at this very moment. According to the UN World Food Programme (WFP 2015), about 800 million people in the world do not have enough food to maintain a healthy lifestyle. In sub-Saharan Africa, at least one person in four suffers from malnutrition. The problem of malnutrition relates not only to the availability but also to the quality of food. The balanced diet largely available in industrially developed nations is out of reach for at least three billion people, who do not receive proper protein, vitamins, and minerals.

malnutrition
A medical condition resulting from famine or chronic food shortages.

famine Severe food scarcity causing malnutrition, starvation, disease, and increasing mortality.

Food and Agriculture Organization (FAO) A UN agency that coordinates international efforts to overcome hunger.

ACUTE SUFFERING

The Biafran catastrophe of the 1960s is just one of the extreme examples of acute suffering that the world has allowed to happen. More recently, in the Democratic Republic of Congo, where multiple political factions have been fighting for years for control of the territories and resources, civilians are the easiest targets. Those fleeing violence are forced to spend months and years in crowded camps under constant fear of death and physical harm. Civilians in combat zones also live with the persistent threat of violence, and many develop stress-related disorders. Women and children remain the most vulnerable groups. Rape is particularly devastating, because along with physical injury it brings long-lasting and demoralizing psychological trauma (Ritchie et al. 2005; Roth and Rittner 2012). In many places, especially in countries ridden with poverty, children are forced into slavery. According to some reliable accounts, more than 20 million people have endured slavery in the first decade of this century (Bales et al. 2009). Without proper and continuous international action, millions could suffer for years.

CASE IN POINT > *A Massacre As the World Watched*

In April 1994, an explosion of mass violence shook the republic of Rwanda, a small African country of 11 million people. Germany and then Belgium had ruled this country as colonial powers for decades, but in 1962 it became an independent state. Unfortunately, political and ethnic tensions brewing for many years grew into a civil war in 1990. Rwanda comprised three ethnic groups—the Twa, the Hutu, the Tutsi—of which the Hutu are in the distinct majority. After Rwanda gained independence from Belgium, a conflict between the Hutus and the Tutsis began. Dormant for decades, it degenerated into genocidal killings. Most victims were Tutsi men, women, and children pursued by Hutu militia and violent mobs. Some terrified Tutsis fled to the marshlands, where their rivals found them and killed them with machete knives. In a matter of weeks, an estimated 800,000 Tutsi were brutally killed. The surviving women were raped. Four million civilians fled to refugee camps in neighboring Burundi, Tanzania, Uganda, and Zaire. There were French paratroopers in Rwanda on a peacekeeping mandate, but they did not have power to prevent the carnage.

Meanwhile, the countries that could quickly intervene—in Europe or North America—watched from a distance. Only the appeals of the neighboring African states flooded by refugees—mostly the Hutus who feared revenge—triggered a delayed action from the international community. Big powers, including France, the United Kingdom, and the United States, failed to act.

CRITICAL THINKING

We often hear calls to "do something" so that the tragedy of Biafra or Rwanda does not repeat itself over and over in different parts of the world. However, many political leaders judge that such tragedies are not their concern.

❶ Do you think the world needs a unified international policy to immediately stop mass violence when it suddenly erupts? If yes, what would this policy be? If not, why? ❷ Consider the idea of a small and well-trained international military unit (let's call it the IMU), the only function of which is to stop violent conflicts that cause acute suffering in large groups of people. How large would the IMU have to be? Which countries would you suggest as contributors to it? ❸ Which country or organization should manage the IMU? Suggest legal rights and responsibilities that the IMU should have.

 Learn more about humanitarian crises on the companion website.

Causes of Humanitarian Crises

"When it rains, it pours." Humanitarian crises often have multiple causes, and one serious problem can lead to another. The earthquake in Japan in March 2011, the worst in a century, produced a disastrous tsunami that destroyed entire towns and killed thousands of people. A quarter of a million people lost homes. The tsunami also damaged the Fukushima nuclear plant, causing a significant radioactive threat. Although Japan is a wealthy country with an efficient government, the disaster was devastating. In less-developed countries and regions, natural disasters can lead to infectious diseases, hunger, and other forms of acute suffering, like what happened in Haiti in January 2010 after an earthquake that took the lives of more than 100,000 people, or in Nepal in 2015, also after an earthquake. Mismanagement, a lack of resources, rampant corruption, and political violence worsen humanitarian problems and delay their solution (Farmer 2012).

NATURAL DISASTERS

In the twentieth century alone, an estimated 70 million people died from natural disasters, including droughts, floods, and earthquakes. Today, economic development and technology help in dealing with severe droughts. However, earthquakes, tsunamis, hurricanes, and floods continue to pose grave danger, especially in less-developed countries. In 2004 the Indian Ocean tsunami killed over 230,000 people because regional early warning systems failed or were absent. During the 2010 Haitian earthquake in January 2010, the death toll was about 150,000 people and 250,000 houses and commercial buildings have been destroyed—many of which were constructed in violation of antiseismic standards. By contrast, in the Japanese earthquake of 2011, most dwellings remained intact and only the tsunami caused significant casualties.

In the immediate aftermath of a natural disaster, most social services are absent or in short supply. Natural health hazards continue to bring devastation to millions of people, especially in remote or overpopulated regions. Some countries provide effective care, whereas others do not; and so international assistance plays an crucial role (Woods and Woods 2007).

MISMANAGEMENT

In today's world, a drought should not cause mass suffering: A state can always purchase food from abroad or ask for assistance. Indian economist Amartya Sen, winner of the 1998 Nobel Prize in economics, showed that the main cause of famine in today's world is inefficient bureaucracy. In 1942, for example, a cyclone hit a vast area of Bengal and Orissa (now territories of Bangladesh and India) and destroyed virtually all rice harvests. Although food supplies remained significant, the incompetence and inaction of corrupt authorities took almost three million lives (Sen 1981).

Weak and collapsing state structures can be a serious cause of mismanagement. When its central state collapsed in the 1990s, Somalia fell into the hands of warlords. A fragile order was preserved by brutal force or by tribal loyalties (Mohamoud 2006), but major elements of the social infrastructure disintegrated, including health care services. Multiple international sources estimate that Somalia has one of the lowest average life expectancies in the world—under fifty years old.

Corruption and fraud also contribute to humanitarian problems. Emergency food supplies often end up in the hands of criminals, and money meant for medication is often used to buy weapons. Although effective anti-malarial drugs are available on the market, many Africans have very limited access due to mismanagement and fraud (Webb 2014; Singer et al. 2005).

Mismanagement in failing states, just like mass killings, sooner or later becomes an issue on the agenda of governments, IGOs, and NGOs.

POLITICS

Political leaders may deliberately cause acute suffering in their country's population for their own purposes. In the twentieth century, the Soviet Union and China caused the largest human-made famines in modern history. During the Soviet campaign of collectivizing the peasantry from 1929 through 1932, authorities seized land and property, including horses and cattle, and forced peasants to join *collective farms*. When the farms failed to meet unrealistically high quotas for delivery of agricultural products to the state, the government seized all food. Troops blockaded many agricultural areas, particularly in the Ukraine, preventing starving peasants from fleeing to cities where food could still be found. The resulting famine killed from five to seven million in the Ukraine, southern Russia, Kazakhstan, and other parts of the former Soviet Union (Martin 2001; Khlevniuk 2008). Another human-made famine arose in Communist China from 1960 to 1962 when the authorities forced peasants into agricultural labor communes and seized their crops. About 30 million people, mostly in the countryside, died from harvest failures and starvation (Becker 1998).

An aid worker shouts out names as he distributes aid packets to families in the destroyed village of Pokharidanda, near the epicenter of the massive Nepal earthquake in 2015. Practically no country can cope with large-scale natural disasters without international assistance.

MASS VIOLENCE

War or an ongoing political conflict can also lead to a humanitarian crisis. Civilians caught up in the conflict zone are typically deprived of medical care or humanitarian aid. When Sri Lanka launched an all-out military assault on Tamil Tiger rebels in 2009, the fighting caused massive civilian casualties. Civilians from two of India's northeastern states, Assam and Manipur, suffered from recurring ethnic and religious violence for years. Tens of thousands fled to crowded refugee camps, where malaria, measles, and other infectious diseases became widespread. As you will remember, international law allows humanitarian interventions to stop genocidal violence and to take legal action against the perpetrators.

In Syria, after the 2011 unrest against the President Bashar al-Assad's government, the authorities launched a lethal campaign against the rebels. They were deliberately targeting the civilian population of the rebellions regions, destroyed homes and schools, and killed tens of thousands civilians in the process. A bit later, the radical ISIS movement, that emerged in the midst of the Syrian civil war, started its own campaign of brutal violence against civilians in Syria, including Kurdish Muslims and Christians. Struggling for power in the region, the Syrian government and the extremist groups provoked a massive humanitarian crisis (Stern and Berger 2015). More than 11 million Syrians have been displaced, which was nearly half of Syria's entire population (Peçanha and Wallace 2015).

EXTREME POVERTY

About one billion people live today in **extreme poverty**, defined by the World Bank as $1.25 per person per day. One and a half billion live on no more than $2 per day. This numerical criterion is certainly vague so that many organizations recently started including malnutrition, lack of access to a basic education, and other criteria as important features of extreme poverty (Payne 2013). For most of the twentieth century, the world was divided into the richer North and the poorer, underdeveloped South. Although extreme poverty is now rare in Europe, the United States, Canada, and Japan, where taxpayers support generous welfare systems, almost 40 percent of sub-Saharan Africa is extremely poor. The rise of China improved the situation with poverty in the global South dramatically. Still, one-fourth of the world's poor live in India, the most populous democratic country.

As a group, the extremely poor are also the most defenseless against disease, starvation, and physical and psychological abuse. Of all economic groups they face the highest risk of injury or death. Poverty is a social trap, and the extremely poor are the most likely victims of a humanitarian crisis (Myers-Lipton 2015; Sachs 2005). (See Map 10-2.)

extreme poverty
A profound lack of resources and the inability to gain access to them.

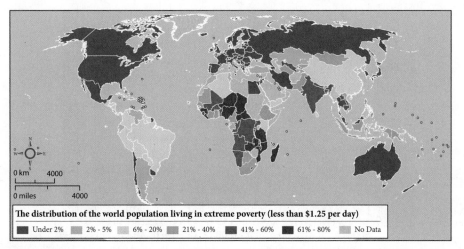

The distribution of the world population living in extreme poverty (less than $1.25 per day)

| Under 2% | 2% - 5% | 6% - 20% | 21% - 40% | 41% - 60% | 61% - 80% | No Data |

MAP 10-2 The distribution of the world population living in extreme poverty (less than $1.25 per day). *Source: The United Nations.*

OVERPOPULATION

overpopulation
A high concentration of people within a region, threatening its subsistence, or the minimum conditions to sustain a reasonable quality of life. It can cause serious environmental and social problems.

Overpopulation is a high concentration of people within a region threatening its *subsistence,* or the minimum conditions to sustain a reasonable quality of life. Around 1800, the world population was close to 1 billion. It grew to 1.6 billion in 1900 and to 3 billion by 1960 (United Nations Population Division 2004). It is about 7 billion now and projected to grow to 8 billion by 2025. (See Figure 10-2.)

Overpopulation can lead to serious health, environmental, and social problems, as in the city of Lagos in Nigeria. The population of this industrial and commercial center has reached 20 million, and thousands of new job seekers arrive each month. Lagos became a giant agglomeration of many communities—with a prosperous middle and upper class—surrounded by sprawling of slums lacking parks, recreational areas, plumbing, and modern health facilities. Although the vast majority has access to electricity, running water is limited and its quality is very poor. Human waste is commonly disposed of by the drainage of rainwater into open ditches. Many overpopulated areas are also prone to social instability, violence, and environmental problems (Angus and Butler 2011).

A rapid concentration of people does not automatically lead to overpopulation, especially in economically advanced countries. New York City, London, Sydney, Tokyo, Shanghai, Hong Kong, and Moscow are densely populated cities and may have their share of problems but they do not fail because of the lack of resources. On the contrary, they attract greater resources and attain greater economic success (Cohen 2005). However, where high density and poverty coexist, problems occur, as the example of Lagos suggests.

Does a high concentration of people mean poverty? Not necessarily. Monaco, a small country in Europe, has the highest population density in the world (23,000 people per square kilometer), and yet its citizens are among the

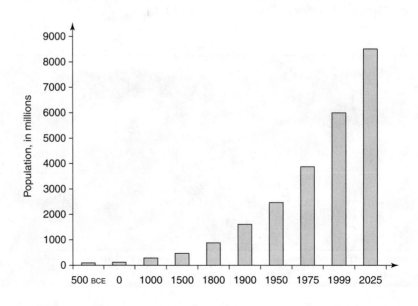

FIGURE 10-2 Global population growth.

wealthiest. At the same time, scarcely populated areas can be very poor. Cambodia, according to the World Bank, has only seventy-eight people per square kilometer but an average per capita GDP of just $2,600—about thirty times less than Monaco's.

INVOLUNTARY MIGRATION

Violence, hardship, or the threat of it can also displace people within or across state borders in search of *asylum*, or a place of safety. This forced relocation is **involuntary migration**, and when it comes to ethnic groups, authorities may make it a political goal. *Ethnic cleansing* is the forced removal or outright extermination of groups based on their origin and identity. Migrants fleeing from one country to another become **refugees**. They are typically willing to return to their home country, but only as soon as the threats there diminish. International help in these cases is essential. Turkey, Pakistan, Somalia, and Lebanon combined had around 5 million refugees in 2015. . Nearly 60 million people were displaced around the world in 2015 because of military conflict and threats to their lives, possibly the largest number ever recorded since 1945 (Peçanha and Wallace 2015).

Internally displaced persons (IDP) are involuntary migrants who do not cross international borders. They unwillingly leave their homes or region under threats of death, starvation, or imprisonment (Phuong 2010). In the past ten years there were over 20 million IDPs, most of them in Columbia, Sudan, Democratic Republic of the Congo, Iraq, Syria, and Azerbaijan. (See Table 10-1.)

Human trafficking is the illegal international trade in human beings for the purposes of exploitation. The U.S. Department of State (2014) estimated that that as many as 27 million men, women, and children are trafficking victims at any given time. Half are minors, and more than 80 percent are girls and women. People are trafficked for sexual purposes, arranged marriages, and labor exploitation. Some are ordered to beg on the streets or steal for money. Others, especially children, become soldiers. Yet others are sacrificed for their organs. The vast majority of victims are poor and uneducated. They have no means to resist injustice and cruelty. Human trafficking is one of the fastest growing global crimes. The international criminal groups use fraud, extortion, and bribery of officials to move people across the borders (Shelley 2010).

INTERCONNECTED PROBLEMS

One humanitarian challenge almost inevitably leads to another. More than one billion people today, according to the United Nations, lack access to running water. For another billion, 75 percent of the water comes from nearby rivers without proper filtering. Unclean water contributes to epidemics, and hunger worsens their deadly impact. Unhealthy populations living in poverty are especially vulnerable. Violent conflicts in a natural disaster area add to food shortages and massive starvation. Chronic suffering also contributes to disabilities.

Take AIDS, for example. A middle-class individual in a developed country today may live with AIDS for thirty to forty years or more, thanks to early

involuntary migration Relocation within or across state borders due to violence, hardship, severe suffering, or a significant threat of these.

refugees Involuntary migrants under threats of political or religious persecution or ethnic and religious violence.

internally displaced persons Those who involuntarily leave their home and region under threats of death, starvation, or imprisonment.

human trafficking The illegal trade in human beings for purposes of exploitation.

TABLE 10-1 Genocide and Forced Migration

Time, Place	Events and Consequences
1915 The Ottoman Empire	The Ottoman government, abetted by extreme nationalists, began to resettle 1.5 million Armenians from Anatolia to Palestine. Many of them died on the way from starvation and brutality. Many consider these actions an act of genocide.
1922 Turkey-Greece	Millions of Greeks and Turks from the former Ottoman Empire were forced to relocate from the places where they lived for centuries.
1939–49 The Soviet Union	Soviet dictator Joseph Stalin forcibly relocated about 3 million people from the Baltic states, Western Ukraine and Belarus, the Crimea and Southern Caucasus into Siberia and Kazakhstan. Many perished in the process.
1941–45 Germany and Territories Under Its Occupation	Nazi Germany killed 12 million civilians (among them 6 million Jews) and sent 6 million people from various parts of Europe, mostly Eastern Europe, to Germany to work as slaves. When Germany lost the war, almost 13 million Germans were forcibly relocated; many of them died along the way.
1975–79 Cambodia	The regime of Pol Pot and his associates killed about 1.5 million Cambodians as part of a political campaign.
1980–89 Afghanistan	Two million Afghan refugees established temporarily settlements in Pakistan and Iran during the Soviet occupation in the 1980s.
1995 Rwanda	1.7 million ethnic Hutus, fearing reprisals from the ethnic Tutsis, fled from Rwanda into Zaire and Tanzania.
1999 Serbia	About 700,000 Kosovo Albanians fearing the Serbian military crossed the Yugoslav border into Albania and Italy.
2006 Central African Republic	As a result of an ongoing political conflict, approximately 150,000 Central Africans remained internally displaced, and more than 70,000 have fled into neighboring Chad and Cameroon.
2003–16 Iraq	Over two million Iraqis have left their country since Operation Iraqi Freedom began in 2003. Millions more have been internally displaced due to ethnic cleansing by ISIS.
2011–16 Syria	About three million people fled Syria to the neighboring Turkey, Lebanon, Iraq, Jordan, and other countries as a direct result of violence.
2014–16 Ukraine	Over one million people fled from the conflict-ridden southeastern regions of Ukraine after Ukrainian forces clashed with local separatists backed by the Russian military.

Sources: Naimark 2002; Ramet 2005; Benvenisti et al. 2007; Hitchcock 2008; Muller 2008; Guterres 2015

diagnosis and treatment. Poverty and corruption shorten the lives of AIDS patients in other countries. In Africa, half of poor infants diagnosed with HIV die before the age of two. In the sixty-eight poor countries with the most AIDS-related childhood deaths, only 22 percent of mothers had access to treatment that prevents mother-to-child transmission of the virus ("A Strategic

Environmental pollution and trash scattered in the crowded Makoko neighborhood of Lagos, Nigeria. Although megalopolises grow rapidly, in the countries where governments are inefficient and economic infrastructure is poor, acute environmental problems are inevitable.

Revolution," 2011). Malnutrition often makes effective AIDS treatment nearly impossible because medications do not work properly in a body weakened by hunger.

The complexity of humanitarian problems not only makes international assistance imperative, but also raises questions. What kind of assistance can be most effective—and who should be responsible, individual states or international organizations? How far can international actors go, and should they always have consent from the states affected by the problems?

▶ Define a humanitarian intervention.
▶ What is a pandemic?
▶ Who are the *internally displaced*?
▶ What is human trafficking?

CHECK YOUR
KNOWLEDGE

Humanitarian Policies

There are three types of humanitarian policies. First, international interventions may remove the immediate cause of suffering or a potential threat. Second, relief efforts can help victims of a humanitarian disaster. Third, preventive measures may avert future crises. These policies, of course, frequently overlap. They can be unilateral or multilateral, depending on the involvement of states, NGOs, and intergovernmental organizations. They can also be nonmilitary or armed.

HUMANITARIAN INTERVENTION

peacekeeping
Military or nonmilitary intervention to stop violence (peacemaking) and to create the conditions for lasting peace (peace building).

 You can find out more about UN-sponsored peace-keeping operations on the companion website.

Humanitarian intervention, as we discussed earlier in the chapter, is the most controversial of these policies. In **peacekeeping**, the armed forces of one or several countries cross state borders in response to genocidal violence. This intervention has two goals: to stop violence (peacemaking) and to create the conditions for lasting peace (peace building) (Bellamy and Williams 2010). The UN Security Council can authorize peacekeeping operations if all five permanent members agree. UN peacekeeping is guided by three basic principles: consent of the involved governments and groups, impartiality, and the use of force only in self-defense. In 2015, there were sixteen peacekeeping missions worldwide including Haiti, Kosovo, Afghanistan, Timor, Mali, Liberia, South Sudan, Democratic Republic of the Congo, and one in Jammu and Kashmir observing the ceasefire between India and Pakistan.

After the failure to act in Rwanda, American and European politicians began to argue that countries might act preemptively to prevent genocide by using military force and even in violation of state sovereignty. On the basis of this argument, in Yugoslavia in 1999 and Libya in 2011, NATO forces acted against the Serbian leader Slobodan Milošević and the Libyan leader Muammar Qaddafi. Russia and China, both permanent members of the UN Security Council, objected. Critics claim that NATO humanitarian interventions are based on biased or incomplete information and tend to target some countries but not others.

How does humanitarian intervention and peacekeeping warfare differ from aggressive warfare? First, the states involved do not plan to occupy permanently or annex another state's territory. Neither do they pursue, in most cases, regime change in another country or act solely on behalf of their own strategic interests. Second, humanitarian interventions aim at political forces that use deadly violence against a population or pose an immediate threat of violence. And finally, such interventions require legitimacy, in the form of an international mandate—such as a UN Security Council resolution (Welsh 2004). In a civil war, UN resolutions do not authorize directly targeting any of the feuding factions and do not sanction the removal of political authorities. The UN admits that success in peacekeeping is difficult to guarantee because peace-keeping missions go to the most difficult social and political environments.

How can we balance respect for a country's sovereignty with the urgent need to stop a humanitarian disaster? The question remains much debated in the theory and practice of humanitarian interventions and peacekeeping missions.

RELIEF EFFORTS

Relief efforts provide immediate and direct aid to a country without violating its sovereignty and usually with its cooperation. After the 2004 tsunami destroyed coastal communities in Sri Lanka, Indonesia, and elsewhere, U.S. military personnel delivered 2.2 million pounds of emergency supplies. Twenty-five ships and ninety-four aircraft participated in the effort. After a 2005 earthquake, hundreds of relief workers arrived in Pakistan (Kashmir) bringing food, medical supplies, tents, and blankets. Governments welcomed the assistance and helped to distribute the supplies.

NGOs, private companies, and influential individuals contribute to international humanitarian relief efforts too. The American Relief Administration (ARA), led by Herbert Hoover, gave help to European countries, including Russia, early in the twentieth century, after the devastation of World War I. The ARA shipped more than four million tons of relief supplies, saving millions of lives. In the 1960s, a group of young French physicians, dismayed by the world's inaction in Biafra, started Doctors Without Borders. Since 1971, this organization has delivered aid in more than seventy countries affected by armed conflict, epidemics, and disasters (Bortolotti 2006). It sent more than two hundred medical volunteers after the 2004 tsunami disaster alone. In the United States, private companies and individuals also gave over $500 million in humanitarian assistance to the victims of the tsunami. Immediately after the 2011 tsunami in Japan, more than 130 countries contributed money and sent teams of search and rescue specialists, emergency medical personnel, and engineers to devastated regions. In 2015, after the tropical cyclone Pam devastated Vanuatu in the South Pacific, scores of NGOs sent supplies and medications to the island. The American Red Cross immediately set up a page for monetary donations, which showed their amounts as well as the people and organizations that donated.

CRISIS PREVENTION

Most infectious diseases can be controlled. Well-off countries have practically eradicated malaria, for example, by eliminating large bodies of standing water—the most common breeding grounds for the single-celled parasites that cause the illness. In countries with well-organized and well-funded medicine, medication to treat malaria is easily available as well. But less economically advanced countries need significant help—and a coordinated global effort.

The **World Health Organization** (WHO) finances the development and distribution of preventive vaccines, along with educational materials. For more than sixty years WHO has monitored influenza worldwide (Garrett 2005). Because many infectious diseases are easily spread from animals to humans, the WHO collaborates with the UN Food and Agriculture Organization (FAO), as well as the World Organisation for Animal Health (WOAH), to track disease outbreaks in animals. These organizations advise governments on animal commerce, quarantines, and vaccination.

Individual countries—often acting in accord—also contribute to disease prevention. Consider international initiatives in the fight against AIDS. In 2006, leaders of the most economically developed nations (the G-8) announced that, by the end of the first decade of the twenty-first century, AIDS medication should be available to all who need it. The UN has also set an ambitious target—to halve the number of cases of sexual transmission of HIV by 2015 (see if this goal has been achieved), to ensure that no child will be born with HIV, and to get fifteen million more people onto treatment ("A Strategic Revolution," 2011). And the Global Fund to Fight AIDS, Tuberculosis, and

Malaria (GFATM) has committed over $22 billion in 150 countries to fight these three diseases.

NGOs play an increasing role in disease prevention. The Bill & Melinda Gates Foundation, founded in 2000, is the largest charitable organization in the world today, attracting and distributing tens of billions of dollars in donations. The foundation conducts HIV and agricultural research, conducts sanitation programs, and coordinates testing of new vaccines (Peters et al. 2010).

POPULATION AND MIGRATION POLICIES

Several policies deal with devastating consequences of overpopulation (Brown 2006). Some aim at improving living conditions—constructing new homes, providing access to running water, building sanitation systems, and offering health care. Others focus on education, to help men and women plan their families. These policies help people learn about the physiology of pregnancy, childbirth, and contraceptives. They educate and empower women to play a greater role in family planning, and they teach families about their rights and responsibilities. The logic of family planning is straightforward: As the United Nations Population Fund insists, families with few children are better off economically than families with many. The Fund also works to prevent sexually transmitted diseases, to eliminate the educational gap between men and women, and to reduce maternal and infant mortality.

Some countries, such as China, use state-mandated policies of birth control. In 1980, China, facing poverty and overpopulation, launched the **one-child policy**. Each family was permitted to have no more than one child; couples with more must pay substantial fees. Exceptions do exist. Parents in

Go online to read about the Bill & Melinda Gates Foundation. How effective are the foundation's initiatives? Also read about the WHO and GFATM. Where have AIDS prevention policies succeeded? What are the remaining difficulties?

one-child policy
China's policy initiated in 1979 limiting the number of children that a family can have.

The skyline of Shanghai, China, population 23 million (and growing) as of the 2011 census. The Chinese government sees overpopulation as a serious problem and uses legal means to limit births.

rural areas and several big cities, including Beijing, may have two children. Some ethnic minorities and couples with advanced college degrees are also exempt—but even they are allowed no more than two children (Fong 2006).

In 2013, when the economic situation in many regions of China vastly improved, the government relaxed some rules. Now couples may have two children if one parent was an only child. These measures (along with other factors, of course) have slowed population growth in China, which now has approximately three to four hundred million fewer people than it could have had otherwise (China's population was 1.4 billion in 2015). There are many drawbacks to such measures, however. As a result of the one-child policy, fewer people have entered the labor force. Many Chinese families preferring boys over girls have turned to selective abortion of female fetuses. Western critics also point at the gender bias of these policies: Families are also allowed to have two children if the first child is a girl. Feminist experts view the one-child policy as a form of state violence against women's rights (Pohlman 2013). This policy was sustained, even though it targeted seemingly the most deep-seated values and cultural practices, because the Communist Party for years tightly controlled the school system, the media, and local governments. Opposing views were not allowed and were effectively suppressed.

DEBATE > REGULATING MIGRATION

Consider these three points:

❶ Governments can sometimes restrict migration within their countries. These days China enforces *hukou*, a system of household registration regulating migration within the country, especially from rural to urban areas. ❷ Sometimes, governments can limit their citizen's travel abroad. During the Cold War, most Communist countries did not allow their citizens to emigrate permanently and restricted even short-term travel abroad. The governments of Cuba and North Korea maintained such rules for more than fifty years (Munz 2003). ❸ Even more commonly, almost universally, governments regulate and restrict immigration, which is the movement of people into a non-native country in order to settle there. Politics and economic necessities affect immigration policies (Art 2011).

WHAT'S YOUR VIEW?

States have to regulate migration policies. They have to balance between pursing humanitarian goals and avoiding overpopulation, between offering new opportunities and reducing human trafficking. There is a growing opinion that in a world with increasingly porous borders, governments must prepare a new, globally coordinated migration policy. As you know, governments work together to address environmental problems, so why don't they cooperate on migration policy? Defend one of the following options, or suggest your own.

Option 1. A global migration policy shall set mandatory quotas for governments of wealthy countries to accept a certain number of migrants each year. Every state will also be mandated to regulate migration within their borders to avoid overpopulation crises. Poor states will receive subsidies from a specially set global fund.

Option 2. Only sovereign countries establish their migration policies and have full rights to restrict immigration and extradite illegal immigrants. Countries should coordinate such policies and make compromises from time to time, but only voluntarily. Besides, a global migration policy is likely to fail because of corruption, red tape, and local politics.

ANTIPOVERTY POLICIES

Experts turn to science and continue to discuss the causes of poverty and the most effective policies to reduce it (Banerjee and Duflo 2011). Disagreements remain. Some advocate international trade and development strategies; they hope that cheap labor in poor regions will attract private investments from wealthy countries. Others ask for greater investment in poor regions. Still others suggest a global redistribution of wealth from the rich countries to the poor ones. Jeffrey Sachs (2005; 2015), professor and an adviser to the UN from Columbia University, maintains that the solution to global poverty is in direct and large investments into poor countries, which are locked in a "poverty trap." They cannot escape from this trap without receiving substantial help from wealthy countries. In *The End of Poverty* and other publications he argues that poverty would be completely eliminated if the rich countries would invest around $200 billion to poor countries each year for twenty years. So, direct economic assistance remains the most common policy. The United States, the UK, Germany, and France all provide direct help to dozens of countries. The UN FAO funds assistance projects, conducts negotiations to stimulate trade, and distributes funds to help developing countries modernize agriculture and fishing.

Meanwhile, as many argue, direct assistance is a short-term remedy, it makes people dependent on outside help and does not attack the roots of poverty. Since the start of the twenty-first century, global poverty rates are in steady decline. Yet hundreds of millions in China, India, Brazil, and Turkey have risen above the poverty level not because of Western help, but because of the success of their economies. Still, market reforms alone can deepen inequality without eradicating poverty. A combination of economic aid, long-term investments, and economic reforms is probably the best way to approach the issue of global poverty.

Read more about Grameen Bank and Foundation on the companion website. Did you notice that the vast majority of the bank's clients are women? Why does the bank maintain this policy?

The Grameen Bank, founded in Bangladesh, is an innovative approach to help the chronically poor. This bank makes small loans to the needy. Called *microcredit*, such loans are given without requiring *collateral*—property or valuable items that traditional banks take over if a loan is not repaid (and that most loan applicants in Bangladesh don't have). But money is not given away either. Each loan must be paid back with interest. How does the bank operate without "solid" financial guarantees? It turns to communities. Every borrower must belong to a local group, which provides support and helps its members pay back their loans. Most of the bank's loans go to women—who still, compared to men, have fewer opportunities to generate an income or to obtain a commercial bank loan. In 2006, the founder of the bank, Muhammad Yunus, and his organization, received the Nobel Peace Prize.

REFUGEE POLICIES

States, IGOs, and NGOs provide temporary sanctuaries for refugees until they can safely return back to their homes (Agier 2010, 36). Some sanctuaries are temporary, such as shelters for flood victims. Others exist for decades, under protection from governments or international organizations. Some refugee camps even become integrated into their communities.

The UN High Commissioner for Refugees, established in 1950, coordinates international policies to protect refugees. The agency has helped tens of millions to find temporary asylum or resettle. It also has a mandate to help refugees without citizenship (UN High Commissioner for Refugees 2012).

Every country has its own refugee policies. In the United States and most European nations, asylum was long granted to people who are already in the country and unable or unwilling to return home because of a well-founded fear of persecution. Several years ago, however, some European states began to introduce admission tests, quota systems, and other legal barriers to asylum (Hainmueller and Hiscox 2007).

A recent crisis with refugees in the Mediterranean Sea demonstrates the complexity of the choice between action and inaction. Libya that plunged into a civil war after the fall of Muammar Qaddafi in 2011, became a haven for human-smuggling criminal rings. These groups profit from unsafely transporting tens of thousands of refugees from Syria, Libya, Iraq, and other countries of the Middle East and Africa to E.U. countries. Most of these refugees reach Italy and Malta and then go to Germany, where they hope to be granted political asylum or work as illegal immigrants. Thousands die in the process. The worst incident to date was in April 2015, when a ship carrying migrants capsized and nine hundred people died. Italy and Malta urged E.U. members to start a "nonmilitary intervention" against Libya's traffickers. The United Nations has called the Mediterranean crisis "a tragedy of epic proportions." Expectedly, Germany and other European countries faced record numbers of political refugees and asylum seekers, putting pressure on national budgets (Almukhtar et al. 2015). Does the European Union have to develop a coordinated and balanced response to this crisis? What should it be in your view?

> ▶ How does peacekeeping differ from aggressive warfare?
> ▶ Explain the differences between peacemaking and peacekeeping
> ▶ What are the goals and consequences of China's one-child policy?
> ▶ How does the Grameen Bank operate? Which approach did the Grameen Bank introduce related to loans?

CHECK YOUR KNOWLEDGE

Arguments

Realism

In the realist view, states have primary responsibility for resolving humanitarian crises within their territory. Realists do not reject humanitarian intervention as a policy option. They recognize the need for international relief efforts and preventive measures. However, they argue that states should always put their national interests first. (See Figure 10-3.)

Realists see humanitarian interventions as warranted in two cases. First, a country may intervene if a foreign humanitarian crisis directly affects its sovereignty or security (Holzgrefe and Keohane 2003). In 1971, India sent its

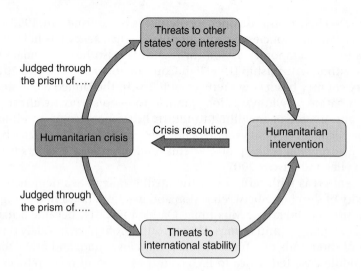

FIGURE 10-3 The realist view of humanitarian interventions. A country, realists argue, may intervene in a foreign humanitarian crisis if it directly affects the country's sovereignty or security. States may intervene in other countries' humanitarian crises if they cause significant regional destabilization.

military to East Pakistan, struck by a natural disaster, after about ten million refugees moved from there to India. Second, states may intervene in humanitarian crises if they cause regional destabilization. During the crisis around Biafra in the 1970s, the United Kingdom helped the central government in Nigeria to deal with the separatists. London wanted to prevent a chain of tribal secessions in Africa.

Realists warn that humanitarian interventions may create security dilemmas (see Chapter 5) and even contribute to instability and new wars. India's humanitarian intervention (such as a significant influx of refugees to India) in East Pakistan led to a war between India and Pakistan, producing an international crisis that drew attention from the United States, China, and the Soviet Union. The balance of power in the region changed in India's favor, when India won the war and helped set up the new state of Bangladesh in place of East Pakistan. In 1979, the Vietnamese invasion of Cambodia removed from power the genocidal government of Pol Pot responsible for the deaths of hundreds of thousands of Cambodians. Yet it also provoked China to attack Vietnam in retribution. The tension in Southeast Asia lasted a decade, until Vietnam agreed to pull out its troops.

Other actions, too, have drawn criticism from realists. In barely a decade, these included the military operations of NATO in Yugoslavia on the side of the Kosovo Albanians in 1999, the U.S. intervention in Iraq in 2003, and the NATO actions in Libya in 2011. Realists argued that those operations hurt international stability and increased insecurity of some countries. Humanitarian reasons alone could not justify the use of military force. In Yugoslavia, they feared, an independent Kosovo could destabilize the entire Balkans and produce new humanitarian problems. In Iraq, realists point out, the fall of Saddam shifted the balance of power in the Persian Gulf in favor of Iran, which was not in the interests of the West. Worst-case scenarios for Kosovo did not happen, but violence and terrorist activities continued in Iraq and Libya.

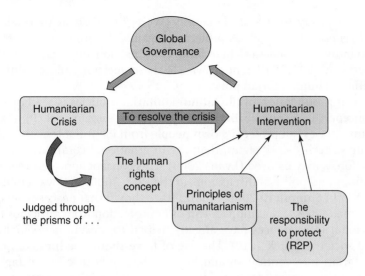

FIGURE 10-4 The liberal view of humanitarian interventions. The principles of humanitarianism, human rights, and the responsibility to protect justify humanitarian interventions.

Liberalism

Liberalism emphasizes not just dangers but opportunities in humanitarian interventions. Liberals believe that preventing genocides and curbing genocidal autocrats must be a priority. This policy should strengthen an international community based on law, interdependence, and peaceful cooperation. Even state sovereignty can be put aside for the sake of humanitarian principles. (See Figure 10-4.)

THEORETICAL PRINCIPLES

The liberal approach draws on a rich intellectual and legal tradition. The **humanitarian tradition**, or *humanitarianism*, states that human beings, regardless of their origin and social status, are morally responsible to help those who suffer (Festa 2010). Applied to international relations, this means that states have the responsibility to protect their citizens from the consequences of natural disasters, mass violence, starvation, or infectious diseases. Humanitarianism also claims that countries have the moral right to intervene for humanitarian reasons and not just out of strategic or security considerations (Power 2002). Liberals criticize policy that puts state interests above morality (Buchanan 2003; 2010).

Human rights (discussed in Chapter 6) provide a second intellectual and legal foundation for the liberal view. The 1948 UN Universal Declaration of Human Rights stated these rights broadly, and disagreements exist about specific rights. There are narrow and broad interpretations of these rights. Are human rights limited

Rescued Indian child laborers stand in a queue to board a train to be reunited with their parents in Bihar, one of India's poorest states, at a railway station in Hyderabad, India, 2015. Police have rescued hundreds of children working in hazardous industries in southern Indian cities despite laws that ban child labor.

to individual safety and physical integrity (Weiss 2012)? Or are there additional *civil and political rights*, such as protection against discrimination and repression? Do individuals have a right to food, clothing, housing, health, and education (Madigan 2007)? Different answers to these questions allow politicians to draw different humanitarian policies.

responsibility to protect (R2P)   The principle that if a sovereign country does not protect its own people from identifiable causes of death and acute suffering, then other countries and the international community must take action.

The third foundation of liberal humanitarian policies is a relatively new legal concept, the **responsibility to protect** (often known as **R2P**). If a sovereign country does not protect its own people from identifiable causes of death and acute suffering, R2P states, then the international community must act. Military forces may be used (Evans 2009). This concept appeared in scholarly publications and political discussions in the early 2000s and was embraced at the UN World Summit in 2005. Studies have shown that peacekeepers, when properly mandated and equipped, can offer protection from atrocious crimes. International interferences have already helped to prevent genocidal acts in troubled societies (Luck 2010). The use of force should be limited, however. Humanitarian intervention should be launched only in cases of large-scale loss of life or a manifest danger of it. The countries involved in humanitarian actions should use force only as a last resort and only if they have reasonable prospects of succeeding (Weiss 2004; 2012). These actions also should receive support from the United Nations.

The responsibility to protect is an evolving concept. It is based on politics, values, identity, current contexts, and other factors. Values often shape diplomatic priorities, and sometimes affect the political will to use force. In 2014, Russia claimed that the Ukrainian government's actions against separatists in Eastern Ukraine caused a humanitarian crisis requiring Russia's humanitarian intervention. Western courtiers sharply disagreed, accused Russia of destabilizing the region, and punished Russia by economic sanctions.

GLOBAL GOVERNANCE

global governance   The global cooperation of international actors with little or no power of enforcing compliance. This approach is based on the mutual interdependence of nations, the idea that global issues should be addressed by a collective effort, and the assumption that there is no single formula for solving all humanitarian problems.

Another relatively new concept may provide still more room for effective humanitarian policies (Rosenau et al. 2005; Hulme 2015). **Global governance** is global cooperation with little or no power to enforce compliance. This means that humanitarian issues should be addressed voluntarily and collectively, through a sustained international effort (Forsythe et al. 2004; Keck and Sikkink 1998).

Global governance is not a kind of world government that would substitute for individual countries and dictate policies on poverty, infectious diseases, or human trafficking. Global governance does not create a system of mandatory policies and practices. It uses existing structures, such as the United Nations or other international organizations (Rosenau 1999). Participating states have equal status when it comes to decision-making, but NGOs are particularly important. According to the UN Development Program (UNDP), the number of humanitarian NGOs reached 37,000 (Polman 2010, 10). The more power international law gives them, liberals argue, the more effective they become. *Universal jurisdiction* and *extraterritoriality* (discussed in Chapter 6) are thus essential.

No single formula or ideology, liberals insist, can solve all humanitarian problems. Each country has a unique history and politics. Free markets and strict government regulations each have their place. (See Tables 10-2 and 10-3.)

Constructivism

Humanitarian policies, constructivists argue, depend on perceptions. Humanitarian policies played an increasing role in international relations during the last century as many societies became more open, democratic, and interconnected. A country's interests are more often shaped not only by fear or aspirations for

TABLE 10-2 Some Features of Global Governance

Mutual Interdependence	Humanitarian issues should be addressed collectively.
Universal Jurisdiction	Global humanitarian aid, when necessary, is justified by the legal principles of extraterritoriality.
Equality Among States	Equality and fairness apply, with no single international authority such as a state or a small group of states.
An Increasing Role for Nongovernmental Organizations	NGOs can address some local humanitarian problems more efficiently than states.
Pragmatism and Flexibility in Finding Solutions	No single formula or ideology can solve all humanitarian problems. Local conditions must be considered.

TABLE 10-3 Global Compact as an Element of Global Governance

Global Concerns	Governance Principles
Human Rights	Principle 1. Businesses should respect human rights. Principle 2. They must not be complicit in human rights abuses.
Labor Standards	Principle 3. Businesses should respect freedom of association and the right to collective bargaining. Principle 4. Compulsory labor must be eliminated. Principle 5. Child labor should be abolished. Principle 6. Discrimination in employment and occupation must end.
Environment	Principle 7. Businesses should support a precautionary approach to environmental challenges. Principle 8. They should promote greater environmental responsibility. Principle 9. They should encourage green technologies.
Anticorruption	Principle 10. Businesses should work against all forms of corruption, including extortion and bribery.

Source: United Nations Global Compact: www.unglobalcompact.org

CASE IN POINT > *Global Compact*

United Nations Global Compact is an initiative that urges companies together with UN agencies and nongovernmental organizations to address humanitarian and social challenges. (See Table 10-3.) Participation is voluntary. Business leaders join Global Compact because they believe that traditional solutions to humanitarian problems may not work. Corruption, abuse, and neglect linger. Global Compact supports new labor, environmental, and anticorruption standards.

CRITICAL THINKING

What is your view of a joint effort by corporations and NGOs? Can it make a significant impact on the international system? Many believe that in the era of growing transparency corporations do not have an alternative but to care more about their public image. The competition is unfolding among businesses not only for the markets and shares but also for the ability to help and impact human lives in a positive way. Many disagree. In their view,

corporations ultimately are about profit, and not about humanitarian actions. It would be naive to expect them adopt the features of global governance without being pressured to do that (Table 10-2).
❶ Do you support the policy encouraging or mandating corporations increasingly contribute to humanitarian policies, or ❷ would you rather leave humanitarian policies exclusively for governments and IGOs?

power, as realists often argue, but by concern for humanity as a whole. Relatively small countries, such as Norway and Canada, are commonly the most active in humanitarian policies. In public opinion polls, Canadians tended to see themselves as more caring, less individualistic, and less selfish than their neighbors in the United States (Carrière et al. 2003). Russia and China are more cautious when it comes to foreign humanitarian initiatives. This reflects their security interests and concern about sovereignty, and their mistrust of the West.

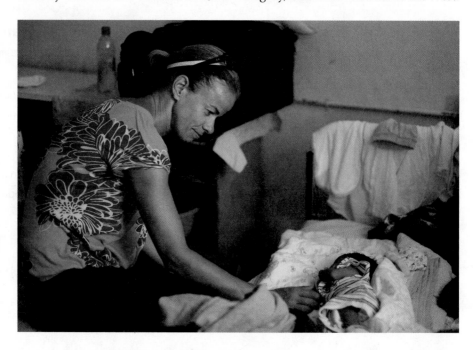

A Canadian aid worker checks on a baby she helped deliver at a hospital in Haiti in 2011. Historically, Canada has actively participated in humanitarian actions overseas. Some countries are very active in humanitarian missions, while others are not. Why?

Perceptions, in turn, are inseparable from the international context. During the Cold War, humanitarian actions were largely subordinate to geopolitical interests—above all the strategic interests of the United States and the Soviet Union (Weiss 2007, 31). The superpowers—the United States and the Soviet Union—also provided humanitarian assistance to build positive images of their countries (Westad 2007).

A country's elites tend to react to international events selectively, constructivism contends, in line with their identity, their interests, and their emotions. Political leaders and elites consider the plight of people of their own race, ethnicity, or religion as more compelling and important than the suffering of others (Finnemore 2004). During the war in Bosnia in the early 1990s, the Arab media focused on atrocities committed against Bosnian Muslims, whereas the Russian media emphasized atrocities against the Christian Serbs (Sobel and Shiraev 2003).

The evolution of societal norms helps governments and international organizations mobilize public support for humanitarian missions. So does, hopefully, the diminishing power of racism and xenophobia. Still, it is often difficult for political leaders to argue for massive humanitarian assistance to countries that do not evoke public sympathy.

Conflict Theories

Conflict theories maintain that inequality is the most important cause of humanitarian problems. "Inequality" means the lingering gaps between social groups, rich and poor, or wealthy countries and the rest of the world. Rescue operations and emergency aid are necessary, but no short-term act can address the structural issues.

Conflict theories also prescribe policies to rectify structural problems. In *The Wretched of the Earth* (2005), Frantz Fanon rejected European humanism as a model for the Third World. The victims of suffering in poor countries, Fanon wrote, must rise up and fight for their own security and prosperity. Others insist that the world needs global affirmative action. Wealthy nations must restructure their relations with the rest of the world. These prescriptions, you should remember, represent the *dependency theory* of international relations (Chapter 6). Take hunger, for example. Most countries could feed their own people, but international trade and finance compel them to export food instead. Paradoxically, food-exporting poor states depend on the financial assistance of food-importing rich powers (Lappe et al. 1998). To change this unfair order, the world's richest states must allow all countries to exercise sovereignty.

Some theorists believe that Western states use humanitarian intervention not just to address suffering, but rather to advance their strategic interests. Capitalist countries are commonly accused of wrapping expansionist designs in humanitarian rhetoric (Weiss 2007; Bass 2009). The global governance proposed by liberals is criticized as a way for powerful institutions and countries to impose their rules and interests on the rest of the world.

Feminism notes that humanitarian problems disproportionally affect women, and yet they do not receive due attention from the international community. Women over the past several years were also the most common victims of the HIV pandemic. Women and girls are targets of mass atrocities, human trafficking, and sexual assault. Rape is a form of intimidation and humiliation during violent conflict. This can also be a type of genocide when it is deliberately and systematically used against a particular ethnic or religious group. Sexual violence against women has long been widespread and underreported. It was widespread during the Armenian massacre in 1915, the partition of India in the 1940s, in armed conflicts in Latin America in the 1970s, and in African conflicts in Angola, Liberia, Sierra Leone, Rwanda, Somalia, and Sudan. Wars in East Timor, Sri Lanka, Myanmar, and Syria involved mass rape of civilians. Rape was also rampant during the war in Bosnia, a European country, in the 1990s (Leatherman 2011). Feminism encourages scholars and politicians to expand their traditional state-centered view of international security (see Chapter 5) and focus more on the security concerns and protection of the individual, including women (Kuehnast et al. 2011).

CHECK YOUR KNOWLEDGE

▶ Explain global governance.
▶ What is Global Compact?
▶ What does R2P mean?

Contexts and Applications

We can apply theories of international relations to humanitarian problems only if we take into account the complexity of world politics. Which theories provide a road map to more efficient policies? What are the proper roles of institutions, structures, and culture in all this?

The Individual Decisions Context

Humanitarian policies and their acceptance are often based on the choices of individuals. Political leaders may act out of conviction, ideology, or personal interest.

LEADERS' CHOICES

Some leaders are actively involved in humanitarian issues because of their deep-seated convictions. Kofi Annan from Ghana was devastated by the UN failure to stop genocide in Rwanda in 1994. Later, as UN secretary general from 1997 to 2006, he became an advocate of the responsibility to protect (R2P). Moral intentions and political calculations are often interconnected. Former British prime minister Tony Blair supported the U.S. invasion of Iraq in 2003 arguing for humanitarian reasons. At the same time, he believed that this support would also consolidate the alliance between the United States and the United Kingdom (Blair 2010).

Historically, stronger powers tend to underline their right to interfere in humanitarian issues, whereas officials from less powerful countries tend to choose caution (Bass 2009). Ultimately, however, specific circumstances shape a leader's choice. The record of the United States' policies demonstrates this. President Clinton failed to stop the genocide in Rwanda but used force to stop the ethnic cleansing in Kosovo several years later. President Bush rejected a humanitarian intervention in Darfur because he didn't want to overcommit the United States, which was already involved in wars in Iraq and Afghanistan. President Obama used the R2P doctrine in 2011 to justify the use of force to overthrow the government in Libya. On the other hand, he backed

United Nations Secretary-General Kofi Annan in 1997. After the UN failed to stop the genocide in Rwanda in 1994, Annan became an advocate of the responsibility to protect (R2P).

off in the similar situation in Syria two years later. These choices are based on many interconnected factors.

DENYING OR HIDING PROBLEMS

Leaders of the Soviet Union and other Socialist states were concerned for building a positive image of Communism. They were thus reluctant to admit to devastating problems in their own countries. They censored reports of natural disasters, epidemics, and human rights violations. During the 1930s and 1940s, Stalin effectively covered up massive hunger in the Soviet Union and rejected international assistance. Many years later, in the twenty-first century, Communist governments in Cuba and North Korea blocked information about serious humanitarian problems in their countries.

Authoritarian leaders facing little opposition at home tend to underemphasize the severity of crises in their countries. In the mid-1990s a prolonged famine devastated North Korea causing hundreds of thousands of deaths. North Korean leaders, however, were frequently blocking desperately needed international humanitarian relief (Haggard and Noland 2009). President Robert Mugabe of Zimbabwe often criticized international humanitarian efforts to help his country as imperialist ploys. Ideology or preoccupation with their country's prestige caused several African leaders to interfere with attempts to fight the AIDS epidemics there. These leaders also accused the international community of using the AIDS crisis as a pretense to expand Western domination.

The State Policies Context

Humanitarian policies are often inseparable from a country's domestic politics, including ideological beliefs, competition among political parties, media coverage, and lobbying efforts.

THE POLITICAL CLIMATE

When the substantial majority of the public in a democratic country is not interested in a crisis overseas, then the government is under less pressure to intervene. Politicians may in fact use public opinion to justify inaction. During the genocidal violence in Bosnia in the 1990s, as it was discussed in the opening case, European leaders at first refrained from intervention. In the United States, the Bush and then Clinton administrations also used negative public opinion as one of the reasons not to intervene (Sobel 2001).

At the same time, political elites can change the policy climate. From 1995 to 1999 the Clinton administration helped convince Americans that the United States should intervene in former Yugoslavia, where violence had already cost 100,000 lives. Politicians in France, Germany, the Netherlands, and the UK also grew frustrated over the inaction of their governments. NGOs and the media argued for a moral duty to launch a humanitarian military action. Finally, in 1995, a military coalition intervened.

The refugee policies of Europe's political parties reflect humanitarian principles but also electoral concerns. Parties of the left traditionally support generous immigration policies, particularly for the victims of repression (Sniderman et al. 2004). The left also recruits heavily from immigrant communities. Moderate social democratic parties, with their reliance on middle and lower middle class members, tend to support refugees so long as they do not threaten jobs. Parties of the political center support immigration by those with job skills, especially in the professions, but not the open-door immigration policies of the European Union. Parties on the right try to limit immigration for ideological reasons. They also point to the tight job and housing markets and the need to preserve a distinct European or national identity (Mral, et al. 2013). Libertarians generally believe in a universal right to travel and settle in the country of one's choice so long as one accepts that nation's rules and customs.

FAVORABLE CONDITIONS

Why are some humanitarian missions more effective than others? Effective humanitarian assistance requires favorable social and economic conditions, the absence of violence, local customs, and low levels of corruption and fraud. Securing these, however, is difficult. In countries such as North Korea, Syria, Afghanistan, and Somalia, humanitarian missions are much more difficult. Armed forces may stop violence, but they often contribute to protracted local conflicts and may even bring new violence (Young 2010).

Much of sub-Saharan Africa has long lacked the conditions for successful humanitarian missions. Weak and corrupt institutions as well as some political leaders in these countries usually support traditional customs and biases, not seek to change them. When it comes to AIDS, for example, most women have little control over their sex lives and many suffer from domestic abuse. Married women who are faithful to their husbands are at risk of contracting HIV, too, because men often have multiple sex partners. Local leaders tend to resist attempts to promote contraceptives, insisting that abstinence is the only proper preventive behavior. As a result, not long ago women were close to

60 percent of adults living with HIV. People with HIV are commonly stigmatized, which limits their access to health care: They choose to keep their symptoms secret or refuse testing and treatment (Trinitapoli and Weinreb 2012; Patterson 2006).

The Global Context

A more global world is likely to face a range of old and new humanitarian problems. Will future problems affect more people than ever? What are the main lessons of past policies, and how can the future be better?

NEW AND EVOLVING CONCERNS

Globalization brings new opportunities. However, globalization may also create new problems or deepen existing ones. Consider just a few developments—travel, migration, and climate change. Feel free to add your own ideas.

Global travel creates new health risks. Take infectious diseases as an example. With international travel expanding, people can carry a dangerous infectious disease to the far side of the world before the first symptoms appear. Insects and small animals can spread disease as well. Trade in animals and animal products includes hundreds of species of wildlife (Wolfe 2011; Karesh and Cook 2005).

Global migration also brings new problems and deepens old ones. Whereas wealthier families tend to move to comfortable and less-crowded places, new megacities in the developing world, like Lagos in Nigeria, attract millions of migrants from poorer areas. Natural disasters and epidemics find most of their victims in such crowded places. The epidemics may spread rapidly. Globally, the poor remain the most vulnerable to threats to their health and safety.

Global climate change (see Chapter 9) may lead to more frequent floods and droughts. Wealthy countries and regions may adjust to these changes, but others—and there will be hundreds of millions of them—will suffer unless certain preventive polices are set.

Most people in developed countries are accustomed to a stable income, a good education, medical care, and generous social benefits. Their comfortable lives may leave them more open to considering the suffering of others. The recent global recession and the following economic slowdown in most countries, however, may have changed that. To many people, a country torn apart by tribal violence may appear more distant and their problems less significant. Others may lose their faith in the possibility of solving global problems— including humanitarian problems. The temptation to turn away is not new. Nevertheless, calls for humanitarian action continue despite some people's indifference. And that indifference may well increase if humanitarian polices do not produce significant results.

POLICY ARGUMENTS

Recall from the start of this chapter the principles behind humanitarian intervention—humanity, impartiality, and independence. Although these principles have international recognition, debates continue about how to apply them. Many question the legitimacy of intervention for humanitarian reasons without another country's consent (Chandler 2006; Rieff 2006). Realists and liberals may agree on the need to enforce the rule of law and to save lives. But, they insist, sovereignty can be suspended only temporarily and only as part of a sustained international effort (Keohane 2003). Because the United Nations tends to apply R2P to humanitarian crises, there is a growing need for international enforcement. But because the United Nations has no armed forces, countries with strong militaries are likely to remain the global "enforcers." Other countries commonly reject these developments.

Another challenge to R2P is the blurring boundary between humanitarian assistance and military intervention to achieve political goals (Orbinski 2009). Some critics insist that R2P is just a clever cover for Western interference (Weiss 2004). The debates flared up again in the spring of 2011, when France and Britain, supported by the Obama administration, led the attacks against the dictatorial regime in Libya. They acted to protect Libya's population from slaughter and had UN Security Council authorization. Yet critics, including Russia and China, argued that the military strikes violated a UN mandate prescribing neutrality in a civil war. Humanitarian interventions continue to split the international community.

EFFICIENCY OF AID

The level of international humanitarian response rose to the record $22 billion in 2013 after falling in previous years due to, among other factors, a global economic slowdown (GHA 2014). Government donors contributed three quarters of the funding, and the private donors donated the rest. Is humanitarian aid effective, and how can we measure its effectiveness? With all the praise heaped on NGOs, criticism has become increasingly audible.

One issue is global coordination. A dozen large NGOs control the majority of nongovernmental humanitarian funding (Agier 2010, 35). Unfortunately, their efforts may duplicate one another. They also do not coordinate their programs effectively with the Red Cross, Red Crescent, and other UN-funded organizations.

Another problem is accountability. American and European NGOs have spent hundreds of millions of dollars on humanitarian assistance in Iraq and Afghanistan—but how effective was it? How much of each dollar and euro is spent on humanitarian aid, and how much is wasted, owing to corruption and fraud? This is not easy to judge. NGOs are usually audited in their countries of origins, but aid recipients are often not audited at all. Fighting factions often use

Easton Fowler, age 3, looks at his father, Capt. Scott Fowler, as they become reacquainted. Fowler returned with fifty-four other soldiers from West Africa in 2015, where they were helping to deal with the consequences of the deadly Ebola epidemic. They rejoined their families after a twenty-one-day period of controlled monitoring.

financial aid to continue the violence. The BBC found that Ethiopian warlords used millions of dollars in Western aid meant for victims of the famine of 1984 and 1985 to buy weapons. The rebels posed as merchants and met with charity workers to obtain relief money (BBC 2010). Some warlords also manipulate donors for personal enrichment (Polman 2010). Transparent bookkeeping does not always solve the problems of corruption.

SUSTAINABILITY OF SUCCESS

Short-term interventions alone cannot solve today's humanitarian problems. Rather, successful term policies must be *sustainable*. What, then, are the ingredients for long-term success in a global world?

One feature of successful policies is a *participatory approach*. NGOs, for example, can act as effective lobbyists for humanitarian actions. Ordinary people, too, can contribute money and become volunteers. The Web and social media have become effective mobilization tools as well.

Transparency and accountability are another feature. Without addressing corruption, humanitarian aid programs are ineffective. Again NGOs and other independent participants are important.

Wealth creation is another feature of successful humanitarian policies. For example, the creation of a stable market economy can help combat poverty. The recent experiences of Chile, Botswana, India, and South Korea show that private enterprise can deliver essential goods, food, and services. As poverty rates go down, the middle class grows, and the quality of social services improves. The decline in fertility rates in the world's poorest regions since the 1960s is probably contributing to improving living standards.

New international policies will probably emerge. Disease prevention is also a security issue, but *global health security* requires a serious global effort. Some countries have already begun to care for the health of other nations ("International Health Regulations," 2007). For example, countries have started sharing information about new viruses and infectious diseases. *Humanitarian medicine* is a new field concerned with diseases that affect primarily the poorest countries, where the public health infrastructure is in dire condition or nonexistent. It brings today's diagnostic and pharmaceutical tools to people who otherwise wouldn't get treatment (Lakoff 2010, 60).

Effective humanitarian policies are also linked to the development of international law (Buchanan 2010), to legitimize efforts to fight pandemics, hunger, or the consequences of civil wars. Once again, the role of NGOs and international organizations can only increase (Ayittey 2005).

▶ Explain the debates around R2P policy: How do supporters and opponents perceive R2P? How do they assess the consequences of humanitarian interventions?

▶ What is humanitarian medicine?

▶ What is the participatory approach to humanitarian policies?

CHECK YOUR KNOWLEDGE

THE USES OF HISTORY: Celebrities in Action

Background

Fridtjof Nansen (1861–1930), a Norwegian scientist and bold Arctic explorer, made headlines more than a century ago, but many still discuss his voyages. Fewer recall that he later received the Nobel Prize for his humanitarian efforts. In 1921 the League of Nations appointed Nansen as high commissioner for refugees. He helped millions of victims of World War I, the Russian Civil War, and other conflicts. He proposed a temporary certificate to allow residence in countries where refugees were not citizens. These "Nansen passports," recognized by over fivfty countries, helped millions to find new homes and survive mass violence. Nansen led the life of a celebrity while directing the world's attention to the fate of prisoners of war, refugees, and famine victims. He became one of the first humanitarian activists. His decisions had a global significance.

Celebrity activism is the involvement of famous individuals—primarily from the arts, science, sports, or entertainment—in humanitarian action. In the past, celebrities came from privileged groups including royalty. In the nineteenth and the early twentieth centuries, they raised money and organized hospitals during wartime to aid soldiers of their own countries. Today's celebrities deal with similar and different problems, including poverty, human trafficking, land mines, AIDS, hunger, and human rights. They are also not from the aristocracy but rather "media darlings" who can attract global attention almost instantly—far more quickly, in fact, than most politicians. When actress Angelina Jolie traveled to Cambodia, she reminded the world of the plight of refugees and the victims of land mines—legacies of the lethal Pol Pot regime. When she co-sponsored the Preventing Sexual Violence Initiative, it attracted a wave of sponsors and volunteers. When Bono, the singer from U2, met with top British and U.S. officials to discuss Africa, the events made headlines. When singer Katy Perry visited Madagascar in 2013 to assist children there with education and nutrition, scores of reporters followed to make sure that millions would be aware of the children's problems.

Thanks to Twitter, Facebook, and hundreds of blogs, celebrity activism is always "breaking news." But does it make a difference?

Actress Angelina Jolie Pitt, UN High Commissioner for Refugees special envoy and co-founder of the Preventing Sexual Violence Initiative, walks with her son as they visit a refugee camp in Myanmar in 2015. How effective can high-profile individuals be in helping to solve humanitarian issues?

Analysis

Celebrities routinely give away tens of thousands of dollars to schools, hospitals, refugee camps, and rehabilitation centers all over the world. Joey Cheek, the Olympic speed skater, donated $40,000 of his prize money to refugees in Darfur. A fashion show generated $170,000 for the Rainforest Foundation, founded by the British singer Sting. Angelina Jolie gave $500,000 to the National Center for Refugee and Immigrant Children foundation, to pay for legal care of orphaned asylum-seekers. Together with Brad Pitt, she gave $1 million to relief efforts in Haiti after the deadly earthquake there. Actor Nicolas Cage pledged $2 million to help former child soldiers and exploited kids. Bob Geldof, an Irish singer and songwriter, organized six free concerts in Europe and in North America involving Elton John, Madonna, Faith Hill, Stevie Wonder, Paul McCartney, Coldplay, U2, and Bon Jovi to raise money for Africa. Bono had a role in powerful nations' joint decision to write off $40 billion of debt owed by eighteen countries, mostly in sub-Saharan Africa.

Often celebrities are excellent fundraisers. Many of the wealthy (and not so wealthy) commonly reach for their wallets. Some are moved by the eloquent appeals of singers and actresses, and sponsor international projects. Others donate for the privilege of meeting them or simply joining them in a common cause.

Celebrity activism is not only about money. Celebrities also raise public awareness by helping to educate and mobilize public opinion. Years ago, actress Audrey Hepburn began her engagement with the United Nations International Children's Emergency Fund (UNICEF). At that time, not many people knew about the fund or her involvement in it. Today's celebrity appearances can draw the instant attention of hundreds of millions of viewers. Celebrities themselves blog or go on Twitter to organize grassroots campaigns. A global campaign cofounded by Bono calls on "citizens, voters, and taxpayers" to tell their governments to help Africa defeat poverty, malaria, and AIDS and to restructure its debts. One of its goals is to make sure that no child in Africa is born with AIDS.

 You can learn about the One campaign on the companion website.

More celebrities see their role as promoting awareness for specific causes. The Creative Coalition even offers training to prepare the rich and famous for public roles as social advocates. Supermodel Heather Mills and the late Princess Diana were engaged in the campaign against land mines. George Clooney and Ashley Judd work for AIDS education; Woody Harrelson and Josh Lucas chose environmental issues. Leonardo DiCaprio turned to global clean water problems. Because of Angelina Jolie, many people learned about refugee camps around the globe.

Celebrities make humanitarian organizations and their efforts more recognizable and, probably, more effective. P. Diddy (Sean Combs) contributed to the World Wildlife Fund. Ben Affleck calls for global attention to the violation of human rights in the Democratic Republic of Congo. Many small humanitarian groups need more international attention, which famous individuals could provide instantaneously. Many celebrities have relatively easy access to national political leaders and top government offices.

Critics, however, are harsh. At least two points are made. First, critics maintain that celebrity activism, despite its success, is not necessarily and always what it appears to be. Most of celebrity activists have tens or hundreds of millions of dollars in assets. A team of "advisers" and lawyers monitors a star's every financial move. They often recommend charitable donations that make sense financially. Tax incentives, especially in the United States, encourage celebrities to contribute to humanitarian causes. Celebrities also use their humanitarian activities and the media attention they generate to promote their products. A foreign trip can help advertise a forthcoming album or film. In other words, critics maintain that celebrities have plenty of ulterior motives to do humanitarian work.

Second, even if celebrities are true altruists, and profits or lower taxes are not their top priority, their efforts are superficial. They often want to show the world the immediate effects of their work, but humanitarian problems require a sustained effort. It takes years to achieve real, not superficial, change in the struggle against poverty and disease. Celebrities also lack sufficient expertise. They may believe that their opinions on social and political issues are valuable simply because *they* express them. And what if they display "celebrity activism complex"—a desire to do something important simply because it feels good? Sure, celebrities make people listen to what they sing and say. But their actions could be misguided. For example, in the past, substantial sums of money generated by rock concerts went to organizations under the control of corrupt governments.

People who live in the spotlight are easy to admire or to criticize. Liberals may criticize celebrity activism for its flashy style and inattention to the deeper social causes of humanitarian problems. Others may disapprove of celebrities for advocating controversial ideas. Yet celebrity activism indeed may bring public attention to serious problems faster and more efficiently than governments do. Humanitarian aid provided by famous people makes a difference. Food for the starving, shelters for the refugees, medications for children—they all matter. In the end, why celebrities donate their money and time is less significant than the results.

Questions

1. What are the potential benefits of reintroducing the policy of "Nansen Passports"—issuing documents for individuals suffering form humanitarian disasters? These documents should help thousands survive mass violence and find new homes. What if, to start, the UN issued 300,000 of such passports annually to help the most desperate and abused? To which countries would you send these individuals, and on what legal grounds?

2. What are the drawbacks of such an initiative?

3. Actor Matt Damon made headlines by staging a mock press conference for World Toilet Day (November 19). To draw attention to the global sanitation and clean water problem, he pledged (jokingly) not to use the bathroom for the day. Although many viewed Damon's action as a prank, some suggested that it should have made a difference. How might it have? Suggest several ways that this and similar flamboyant instances of celebrity "activism" can be useful locally and globally.

CONCLUSION

Overall, global awareness of real and potential humanitarian problems has advanced, although the focus of this heightened awareness is still very selective. The necessity of protecting human rights in foreign policy and international law are increasingly accepted, but not always implemented. The prevailing view is that more consistent humanitarian policies are necessary to allow people to develop their full potential and lead dynamic and peaceful lives in accord with their needs, cultural demands, and communities. A strong moral case remains for forceful humanitarian intervention in desperate cases. Yet the critical arguments related to R2P reveal that it is not enough to prevent or stop a humanitarian catastrophe; the international community has to do significantly more to address the sources of such disasters.

We began the chapter with questions. When one country faces a tragic loss of life, do other states have the obligation to intervene? When hunger strikes, is there a right or responsibility to help? When people face the overwhelming and destructive forces of nature, they must do everything they can to help. But who should protect people from the mismanagement, neglect, and abuses of their fellow human beings—and how? And what should be done to diminish global poverty? The global jury is still out.

KEY TERMS

epidemic 335
extreme poverty 341
famine 337
Food and Agriculture
   Organization (FAO) 337
global governance 354
human trafficking 343
humanitarian crisis 334

humanitarian intervention 335
humanitarian sovereignty 335
infectious diseases 335
internally displaced persons
   (IDP) 343
involuntary migration 343
malnutrition 337
one-child policy 348

overpopulation 342
pandemic 335
peacekeeping 346
refugees 343
responsibility to
   protect (R2P) 354

IDEAS

KEY ISSUES

- Incidents or continuing problems threatening the health, safety, security, and well-being of many
- Pandemics, chronic starvation and malnutrition, other forms of acute suffering

HUMANITARIAN PROBLEMS

- Environmental disasters and accidents
- Politics, mismanagement, neglect, and mass violence
- Extreme poverty, overpopulation, and involuntary migration
- Mostly interconnected

HUMANITARIAN POLICIES

- Intervention: the actions of foreign powers in a humanitarian crisis with or without the approval of a legal authority controlling the area
- Relief efforts: aid to a country without violating its sovereignty
- Prevention

ARGUMENTS

REALISM

- A country may intervene if a foreign humanitarian crisis directly affects its sovereignty or security
- States may intervene in humanitarian crises if they cause regional destabilization

LIBERALISM

- Policies rooted in three principles: humanitarianism, responsibility to protect, and human rights
- Emphasis on international cooperation and global governance

CONSTRUCTIVISM

- Countries build their humanitarian policies on their evolving values and perceptions, and their concern for humanity as a whole

OTHER THEORIES

- Conflict theories: economic and political inequality is the key cause of humanitarian problems
- Feminism: humanitarian problems disproportionally affect women, yet women do not receive due attention

CONTEXTS AND APPLICATIONS

THE INDIVIDUAL DECISIONS CONTEXT

- Leaders' choices are rooted in values or affected by individual circumstances that affect humanitarian policies

THE STATE POLICIES CONTEXT

- Humanitarian policies are connected to a country's domestic politics, including competition among political parties, media coverage, and lobbying efforts

THE GLOBAL CONTEXT

- Global challenges such as migration, travel, and climate change affect humanitarian problems and policies to alleviate them
- Efficiency and sustainability of global humanitarian efforts remain key challenges

Critical Thinking

❶ Discuss the benefits and drawbacks of humanitarian interventions. If you were president and had to choose three humanitarian interventions to support, which would you choose, if any, and why?

❷ What social and political conditions, in your view, are necessary for global governance to succeed?

❸ Should authoritarian, nondemocratic methods be used to address the most acute humanitarian problems? Under what circumstances?

❹ Does celebrity activism make a difference in the global efforts to fight illness, poverty, violence, or injustice? If so, in what way? If not, why not?

Conclusion: Forecasting the World of 2030

T HE SCIENCE OF INTERNATIONAL RELATIONS IS LIMITED IN ITS PREDICTIVE POWER. BECAUSE SO MANY FACTORS (BOTH KNOWN AND HIDDEN) INFLUENCE WORLD POLITICS, it is very difficult to make accurate forecasts. For example, few experts anticipated the implosion of Communism in 1989. Very few predicted the global financial meltdown that began in 2008 in the United States and the Eurozone crisis of 2011 and 2012. Not many could foresee the revolutionary turmoil in the Arab world that started in 2011. Even fewer anticipated a violent confrontation in Ukraine in 2014, involving Russia. The list goes on.

Why are there so few accurate forecasts in international relations? We can point to two main reasons. The first lies in what we call *intellectual conformism*: The majority of experts tend not to dissent from the majority opinion, even when facts and indicators urge them to. To battle intellectual conformism, it is always important to compare different, even sharply diverging views on the future of international relations.

Second, forecasts cannot be too specific, because they suggest only probabilities of events. These probabilities are based on scientific methods examining many variables and factors—economic, political, cultural, psychological, and so on. The complexity of such variables means there can be no absolutely "correct" or "incorrect" prognostic theories. These theories simply address the future with varying degrees of relevance. Mistakes in predictions are plentiful, but we can try to learn something from them about the workings of the international system.

And although it is easy to miss emerging trends, we shouldn't be discouraged. There are ways of making reasonably reliable forecasts in international relations. Every event has specific causes, and every development is set in a context. Wars, revolutions, international treaties, economic miracles, and great alliances—they all have precedents. Their lessons can be thoroughly studied and applied. The keys to success are your knowledge and a measure of imagination.

It is time for a final exercise. Using this book as a guide, try to make a few predictions. Your task is to discern certain patterns in international relations and creatively extrapolate them into the future. Use the key concepts and theories from Chapters 1 through 4, and then look to other chapters as relevant for your forecasts.

1. Will sovereign states survive as main actors or agents of international relations by 2030? While protecting stability, how will the strong states treat the weak states?

Globalization increasingly challenges states' sovereign power, and international laws advocated by IGOs and NGOs eat away at state sovereignty. The European Union's institutions are incapable of replacing the individual countries when it comes to taxation, law enforcement, education, welfare policies, and the inability to pay debts. But expectations of states' inevitable demise are premature. By all indications, states will continue to be major actors in the international system. Most countries will continue to retain their sovereignty without delegating it to the United Nations or to any other supranational organization. Bureaucratic traditions, the interests of ruling elites, national and cultural identities, and other factors will continue to reinforce individual states and their role in international relations. Do you disagree?

States will differ in their ability to deliver essential functions—such as collecting taxes, enforcing the law, maintaining stability, and protecting the population—as measured by the *index of state capability*. By this measure, the United States or most countries of the European Union are fairly strong states. In contrast, in many areas of Africa and Central Asia, states are either weak or very weak. Some of them are failing. Unstable and filled with tensions, these states often need urgent international assistance simply to survive. Somalia and Afghanistan have long been regarded as failing states.

What will happen to the relationships between strong and weak states in the next ten years? After reading this book and learning many facts and theories, answer the following questions. To support your answers, refer to Chapters 2 and 6.

A Cuban woman holds up a handwritten sign against the U.S. embargo during a march in Revolution Square marking May Day, in Havana, 2015. This was the first major national event since the start of U.S.–Cuba diplomatic talks. Who could accurately predict the results of these negotiations back in 2015?

a) In your view, how likely or unlikely is the possibility of two global "worlds" in 2030: one composed of strong and stable countries, and the other representing weak and unstable ones?

b) Will strong states like the United States continue to maintain international stability? What will prevent them from simply taking over the weak and unstable states?

2. Will countries continue making territorial claims?

Most countries today have settled their borders, but others continue to make territorial claims. There are unresolved border disputes between Azerbaijan and Armenia, Israel and its neighbors, India and Pakistan, India and China, and Georgia and Abkhazia—to name just a few examples. Ukraine does not recognize the loss of Crimea to Russia in 2014. These disagreements are likely to continue as sources of international tensions. The quest for oil and other natural resources will remain another potential trigger of territorial disputes. In those parts of the world where oil or other minerals are an economy's only resources, conflict is almost assured. If the ice continues to melt over the Arctic, the competition among nearby countries such as Russia, Norway, Canada, and the United States will intensify. South Sudan may face a long-lasting conflict with Sudan over the more than six billion barrels of oil reserves discovered on the territory between these two newly separate countries.

Other tensions over territorial sovereignty may be driven by economic calculations and nationalism. One region to watch is Southeast Asia. China, Taiwan, Vietnam, Malaysia, Brunei, and the Philippines have territorial claims in the South China Sea. China has published maps marking many islands as its own and has sent a submarine to plant a Chinese flag two miles deep in the South China Sea.

a) Which countries do you predict may make new territorial claims, and where? Use evidence to support your prediction.

b) Do you think that the world needs a global agreement to settle borders once and for all? Will this agreement (let's plan it for 2020) help end and prevent conflicts? Explain your view.

3. Will a powerful coalition emerge to challenge the United States?

Some supporters of realism argue that the United States is unlikely to remain an unchallenged global power for a long time. A coalition of states is likely to emerge to test America's supremacy. Other realists disagree and contend that these threats are exaggerated because the United States' hegemony is "stable" (Chapter 2). They believe that we live in the world where the most powerful, democratic states such as United Kingdom, France, Germany, and Japan have no interest in challenging Washington's power and supremacy. Partly as a result of America's relatively good historical record, many countries are likely to prefer Washington's hegemony to that of their neighbors (Walt, 2005b). Other experts think states like Russia and China are simply incapable of throwing a serious challenge either now or in the near future.

Which one of these two arguments do you see as more plausible than the other? To answer, browse the pages from Chapters 2, 3, and 4 referring to state power, power balancing, multipolarity and unipolarity, identity, and security regimes.

Now consider three hypothetical scenarios. How probable are they to you?

a) To challenge the United States' domination, China, Russia, India, and Brazil form a Transcontinental Economic Alliance in 2020. Its members control prices for most manufactured goods, establish economic sanctions against the United States, and start a new global currency to compete against the dollar.

b) Iran, Kazakhstan, China, and Russia, accompanied by several Central Asian states, build a new political and military pact called the *Eurasian Alliance*. Its key goal is to resist the "export of democracy" from Washington to Eurasia. They also keep American companies in Eurasia under control, keep Western NGOs out, and act jointly in the United Nations to advance their global interests. The United States agrees in 2021, under political pressure from its allies, to coordinate all its Eurasian policies with the Eurasian Alliance.

c) Several oil-producing authoritarian countries such as Venezuela, Nigeria, and Iran form the *New Energy Alliance* and drastically reduce their oil shipments to the United States and Western Europe. Most oil tankers in 2019 are redirected to Asia and Africa instead. The alliance calls for a "fair" distribution of global energy resources and refuses the United States' and British oil companies to operate in its countries.

Which of these scenarios do you consider plausible, somewhat probable, or barely possible? Are there, in your opinion, other potential alliances that could emerge in several years, and will they be successful?

4. In which areas will NGOs replace governments?

Supporters of liberal internationalism (Chapter 3) argue that NGOs are becoming the most significant and capable actors in international relations. NGOs use vast networks of volunteers and highly skilled professionals, and are often more efficient than government agencies. NGOs are usually more transparent than the large bureaucratic institutions. They also work closely with local populations and often have firsthand knowledge about the countries and regions in which they operate. Acting as global "whistleblowers" and "watchdogs," they can more effectively discover problems and attract immediate international attention.

a) In your view, in which areas of international relations would NGOs have the most influence? Will it be in international security (Chapter 5), international trade (Chapter 7), environmental protection (Chapter 9), humanitarian aid (Chapter 10), or other areas? Support your answer with facts and examples.

b) In which areas do you think states and coalitions of states will retain their superior decision-making power?

5. How will social media change international relations?

Supporters of liberalism (see Chapter 3) also believe that today's innovations in electronic communications should help in weakening authoritarian governments globally. The more access people have to the information exposing corrupt and abusive governments, the less authority and legitimacy these governments have. In the course of the past ten years, people in the Philippines, Ukraine, Lebanon, Tunisia, and Egypt were using smartphones and the Internet to organize resistance and push their corrupt governments out of power. Authoritarian governments can certainly push back. And they do.

Supporters of constructivism (Chapter 4) think the actual results of the ongoing technological changes are not that clear. True, the global informational revolution changes international relations. Yet these changes are not necessarily advancing democracy. For instance, during the political turmoil in the Middle East and North Africa in recent years, the "Twitter revolution" benefited in the end political Islam and not necessarily liberal democracy. Authoritarian governments in Iran, Zimbabwe, and China seek to control Internet and Web-based social networks. Moreover, in China, the Web allows nationalists to express their anger against the West and Japan, as well as hostility toward Tibetans, Muslim Uighurs, and other ethnic minority groups. Violent separatist and terrorist groups use the Web and mobile devices to launch attacks and threaten international security (see Chapters 5 and 8).

a) Five years down the road, what will be several key political outcomes of the global "media revolution"? Focus on the effects in one country or region.

b) Do you expect that authoritarian governments will increasingly use new media to go on the offensive and to bring down attempts at democracy in their countries?

c) Do you believe that free information always leads to democratization? Should free information always mean more political transparency and more accountability of officials?

6. Who would benefit from the globalization of the economy? Will poverty end?

Supporters of world systems and dependency theories (Chapters 4 and 7) have long maintained that the North (particularly Western Europe and the United States) draws the most benefits from the emerging global economy, whereas the South gets only what is left. Most recently, certain theorists started to speak about the "Chinese miracle." In this view, China has learned to benefit from the international economic system, and the United States appears to be a loser. Supporters of economic liberalism (Chapter 7) disagree with these conclusions. Their argument is that in today's global economy both the United States and China, along with many other countries, should benefit from economic openness and trade. A new technological revolution may change a global economic forecast and thus affect international relations in general (Evans-Pritchard, 2011). Consider *3D printing*, a technology that "copies" three-dimensional objects from a digital file. In a few years, giant assembly lines and big factories may no longer be needed: Many goods will be produced on demand, locally. This means that 3D printing may undermine the manufacturing capacity of countries, such as China and India. They manufacture and sell cheap products relying mostly on low-wage labor. 3D printing should challenge the whole global economic situation by making many manufacturing jobs obsolete.

a) Which countries will benefit the most from 3D printing? Which will lose out? Could every country benefit, and if so, how?

b) Will the current North–South divisions persist in ten years, and if so, how deep will they remain?

c) In your view, which countries would benefit the most in an emerging international economic order? Why?

7. A democratic peace—will it actually be "peaceful"?

Liberalism embraces the idea that democracies do not fight one another (Chapter 3). More democracy means more peace and international security. We learned in Chapter 1 that Japan and Germany transformed into wealthy and peaceful democracies after they had been occupied by the United States. During the Cold War, NATO encouraged its members, including Greece and Turkey, to become more democratic to avoid war with each other.

However, democratization is a very complicated process. Realists and constructivists argue that far away from Washington or Paris, the political outcome of democratic transitions becomes even more complicated. The experiences of Iraq, Afghanistan, and some other countries show that democratization does not necessarily stop violence (Chapter 8). Democratic reforms do not rapidly end pervasive poverty (Chapter 7). A quick transition away from authoritarianism and, vice versa, reversal of democratic development often produces ethnic or religious clashes and constant violence. Free elections may bring to power religious fundamentalists or ultra-nationalists, sworn enemies of liberal democracy (Chapter 4). Moreover, some emerging democracies tend to be more war-prone than authoritarian states.

We also should not overlook the threat of international terrorism. If democratization continues to spread around the world, some groups may continue to use terrorism and other forms of violence to achieve their political goals. As we know the early attempts at building democracy in Iraq led to sectarian ethnic violence, which inspired terrorist groups including al-Qaeda. The removal of the authoritarian regime in Libya had several unintended consequences for Algeria and Mali, where violent groups unleashed terrorism against governments.

a) Will the world in ten years be more democratic or less democratic compared to 2016?

b) Will the world become more stable and have fewer military conflicts if most countries become democratic?

c) Do you anticipate that the West will support an authoritarian but stable Middle East and Africa, or will it instead support democratic yet unstable governments there? Explain your reasoning.

8. Will the global reversal of democratic development possible? What demographic, social, and economic changes can contribute to this?

Almost seven decades ago, the English writer George Orwell published *Nineteen Eighty-Four*. This widely acclaimed novel describes a vision of the world in which all power belongs to an "inner party," an authoritarian and well-organized clique. The masses are obedient, terrorized, and distracted by government propaganda and cheap entertainment. Experts from different fields have used *Nineteen Eighty-Four* as an allegory for pessimistic scenarios of international relations.

Today, however, deeply pessimistic forecasts alluding to a global revival of authoritarianism are rare. In fact, an opposite trend—many forecasts filled with optimism and confidence—has emerged in scholarly predictions. For example, one prediction is that the complexity of interconnected problems will lead to the gradual reduction of countries' sovereignty in favor of a global government. Yet this will not be an authoritarian system: This government will comprise global international institutions and be rooted in international law (Wendt, 2003).

Many others too see no viable alternative to a global democracy. They predict that even authoritarian countries have no choice but to play by the rules set by economic and political liberalism. For example, China, they argue, would not challenge the liberal order because the Chinese leaders want to benefit from its policies, practices, and institutions while being in the center of the global liberal system. More countries are acting as "stakeholders" in the international system of the twenty-first century: pursuing multilateral cooperation, assuming greater responsibilities, and exercising influence through peaceful means (Ikenberry, 2014).

a) Which scenario is more likely, in your view? The one proposed in *Nineteen Eighty-Four* and suggesting global authoritarianism, or other projects suggesting global democracy?

b) If democracy prevails, will it be, in your view, a global democratic state, or will there mostly be sovereign democratic countries?

Scenarios

What will the world be like in future decades? Let's look at some scenarios for 2030. Based on what you have learned in this course, how plausible does each of these seem to you? Which aspects of these fictional developments would you consider (a) really possible, (b) somewhat possible, or (c) unlikely?

Beijing, China. *A new chairperson of the Microsoft Corporation, Shen Yang, said during today's press conference that the company needed to restore the confidence of its customers. To stay on the path of innovative research and development, it needs new ideas. After a new generation of Chinese "wallpaper computers" that transform our entire surroundings reached the market, Microsoft nearly lost its global competitiveness.*

It has therefore agreed to transfer its headquarters from the United States to China. The company will close some factories in Asia and build new ones in the United States and Canada, where labor has become cheaper than in Asia.

New York. *The incoming UN Secretary General, Evo Morales, former president of Bolivia, said that his top priority would be expanding the permanent membership of the UN Security Council. A longtime advocate of the inclusion of a country from Central America, he favors the candidacy of Cuba, which had its first multiparty elections last year. Radical reform of the United Nations should continue, he added, with elimination of the veto power of Security Council members. The UN will have its armed forces permanently stationed in all continents. Following the example of Canada and Sweden, countries should amend their constitutions to comply with the decisions of the United Nations and other international organizations.*

Ankara. *Top government delegations from Turkey and Iran have signed a mutual protocol on nuclear energy, as well as on educational, scientific, and professional exchanges between the two countries. For the first time in history, female leaders represent the Turkish and Iranian governments. They both studied in the United States and received their advanced degrees in international affairs.*

Moscow. *Russian President Vladimir Putin, the longest-serving leader in Russian history, met with the leaders of the New Eurasian Alliance, a political-military security organization formed just last year and including three former republics of the Soviet Union: Russia, the Ukraine, and Belarus. Putin underscored that the alliance is not a threat to Europe and welcomed countries like Finland, Poland, and Romania to join after meeting common requirements. Public opinion in many European countries reveals significant concern after the withdrawal of the United States from NATO. Putin also promised that, with Chinese and Russian leadership, there would be success in the next round of multilateral negotiations to create a global cartel of oil-producing countries, including Saudi Arabia, Iran, Venezuela, the United States, and Russia.*

Pyongyang. *The new capital of the unified Korea is rapidly becoming a booming modern metropolis. Using electric cars and solar-driven public transportation, Pyongyang has managed to avoid the traffic and pollution problems that beset the old capital, Seoul, for decades. The Korean Green Party in Parliament, which includes a number of former Communist officials, is urging a comprehensive ban on the use of gasoline-driven vehicles in five years.*

What do you think about these fictional news stories? Make your own assessment of how probable these developments are: very probable, somewhat probable, or not probable at all. Glance back at this book's table of contents to identify the pages that would be most helpful in assessing each of these hypothetical events. Will the UN be seriously reformed in a decade, and if so, in what way? Will North and South Korea merge without a conflict? Will China emerge as the second superpower? Will the United States keep its global economic leadership, and will NATO and trans-Atlantic partnerships survive? Will Beijing or Moscow successfully challenge Washington's interests around the world? Could Iran radically reform its regime and open its doors to the West? None of us has a crystal ball, yet some developments are more likely than others. Which ones, and why?

Careers in International Relations

STUDYING INTERNATIONAL RELATIONS SHOULD BE INTELLEC-
TUALLY CHALLENGING AND EMOTIONALLY REWARDING. YOU
CAN EXPAND AND IMPROVE YOUR CAREER POSSIBILITIES
through a critical and comprehensive knowledge of international relations. In fact, you will find many benefits in understanding diverse
points of view about past and present events.

Careers in IR can take many paths, several of which we briefly explore
below. At minimum, a bachelor's degree is required for careers in diplomacy,
international business, international development, intelligence analysis, and
defense or foreign policy. A graduate degree or a professional degree (such as in
law or business) is strongly recommended and increasingly required; obtaining an advanced degree may help expand your employment opportunities.
Most importantly, your success will depend on your knowledge, individual
skills, integrity, volunteer and research experience, and ability to work with
others.

Diplomacy

Diplomatic work has traditionally been one of most attractive fields of employment in international relations. In this field, you might remain within your
own country in its foreign policy offices, or you could be sent overseas to work
on a diplomatic mission. Diplomatic work is highly competitive, and the selection process is rigorous. Although the rules may be changing, most people
applying for diplomatic work in the United States have to pass a special

comprehensive exam (the Foreign Service Officer Test or FSOT) and go through a rigorous interview process, which usually requires additional studying and training. Why don't you initiate a study group at your college or university to better prepare for the Foreign Service Officer Test?

NGOs, IGOs, and Think Tanks

Working for nongovernmental organizations (NGOs), international governmental organizations (IGOs), and think tanks is becoming increasingly important and popular. As in diplomatic fields, if you work for an NGO, you might remain in your home country or move abroad for some time. You could work on projects ranging from conducting research and teaching to delivering humanitarian aid, guiding negotiations, and settling ethnic or religious tensions in local communities. One of the best ways to learn more about NGOs and test your commitment and skills is to obtain an internship in one of those organizations. Check this book's Facebook page for regular updates about internships: https://www.facebook.com/InternationalRelationsTextbook

Defense and Security

Many people pursuing a military or national security career also need training in political science and international relations. Conducting humanitarian and peacekeeping operations, assessing foreign threats, gathering military intelligence, working with allies, or analyzing regional and local conflicts—all these and many other activities of today's military offices require advanced knowledge of IR theory and practice. There are also many jobs within the government and private organizations requiring analytical skills and knowledge of foreign policy, policies of foreign countries, international law, the nature of ethnic conflicts, and negotiation strategies.

Law

Working as an attorney, you may specialize in cases involving negotiations, agreements, extradition, international consulting or litigation, such as family affairs, business, commerce, property rights, or investments. You could also be an immigration lawyer. If you develop expertise in international law, you may work for government and international institutions. Many students who apply to law or business school should study international relations simply because of the nature of their future employment.

Teaching and Research

A Ph.D. is typically required for teaching international relations at colleges and universities in the United States and Canada. Recipients of this degree may also seek out research or consulting positions in government or nongovernmental organizations. Teaching at a university frequently becomes a springboard to various fields of policy-making. Many U.S. secretaries of state have taught political science or international relations at the college level, including Condoleezza Rice, Madeleine Albright, George Shultz, and Henry Kissinger.

Journalism

Working as a journalist also requires advanced knowledge of international issues and regional conflicts, a deep and critical understanding of very complex information, and the ability to explain it to thousands or even millions of viewers, readers, or listeners. Foreign correspondents and international reporters today have to be proficient in two or more languages. As a journalist, you should know the history and current status of diplomatic ties between countries, international conflicts, understand various IR theories, and be familiar with their contemporary applications.

Online Resources

Career opportunities and internships in IGOs:

The United Nations: https://careers.un.org
UNESCO: http://www.unesco.org/new/en/unesco/join-us/
UNICEF: http://www.unicef.org/about/employ
The World Bank: www.worldbank.org/jobs
The European Union: http://eu-un.europa.eu/articles/articleslist_s83_en.htm
NATO: http://www.nato.int/cps/en/natohq/recruitment.htm

Career opportunities and internships in NGOs and think tanks:

The Woodrow Wilson Center: http://www.wilsoncenter.org/opportunities
The Brookings Institution: http://www.brookings.edu/about/employment
The Chicago Council on Global Affairs: http://www.thechicagocouncil.org/about/browse-job-openings
The Washington Center for Internships and Academic Seminars: http://www.twc.edu/
Arms Control Association (Washington, D.C.): http://www.armscontrol.org/internships
ECPAT-USA: http://ecpatusa.org/opportunities
Greenpeace: http://www.greenpeace.org/usa/en/about/jobs/
The World Wildlife Fund—United States: http://worldwildlife.org/internships
Doctors Without Borders: http://www.doctorswithoutborders.org/work-with-us

U.S. government career opportunities and internships (general search):

USA JOBS: http://www.usajobs.gov

U.S. government career opportunities and internships (selected departments and agencies):

The U.S. Department of State: http://www.careers.state.gov/

The Central Intelligence Agency: https://www.cia.gov/careers/index.html

The U.S. Environmental Protection Agency: http://www.epa.gov/internships/

The U.S. Department of Homeland Security: http://www.dhs.gov/student
-opportunities

The U.S. Department of Defense: http://godefense.cpms.osd.mil/internships
.aspx

Glossary

accessibility bias In cognitive theories, the rule that a leader tends to pick the option that is most easily available.

acid rain The accumulation of acids in clouds, rain, snow, sleet, and, subsequently, lakes and rivers owing to sulfur dioxide, nitrogen oxides, and other pollutants in the atmosphere.

aggression An attack by a state aiming at retribution, expansion, or conquest.

analogy The comparison of a new situation to a familiar one. Analogies may provide quick answers in place of a more lengthy discussion.

analysis Breaking down a complex whole into smaller parts to understand its essential features and their relationships.

anarchism An ideology and movement that seeks to create a borderless, peaceful, self-governing society of free, local communes in which people generate and distribute wealth without government control.

anarchy From a realist perspective, a condition of international relations that requires states to rely only on their own power.

antiglobalization Resistance to globalization, or an active return to traditional communities, customs, and religion. (See also **globalization**.)

asymmetrical threat The danger imposed by terrorism because a state cannot effectively retaliate and restore a balance of power.

Atlanticism The belief that the relationship between the United States and Europe is a focus of national interest.

autarky A long-term policy of national self-sufficiency and rejection of imports, economic aid, and cooperation.

autocratic rulers Leaders who use unlimited power and who follow international and domestic law only if it suits them.

balance of trade The difference between the size of exports and imports of a country.

bipolar order A type of world organization based on two centers of power or influence.

bureaucratic bargaining The process by which political groups and institutions express their interests and make trade-offs and compromises.

caliphate A global Islamic state (one of the ultimate goals of al-Qaeda).

climate change A significant and lasting alteration of global weather. It most often means *global warming*, or the rising temperatures and increasing number of abnormal and unseasonable climatic phenomena such as devastating storms and heat-waves.

coercion and extortion The use of force and threats of force to compel others to comply with demands.

cognitive map Model of information-processing and decision-making.

Cold War (1946–89) The state of tensions and competition between the Soviet Union and its allies on one side, and on the other, the Western world, including the United States, Western Europe, and their allies.

collective security An arrangement in which the security of one country becomes the concern of others as well.

Communism A classless political and social order free from oppressive government.

comparative advantage A theory that explains why it is beneficial for two countries to trade with each other instead of relying on their own domestic production.

competitive authoritarianism A hybrid political culture with a competitive electoral system in which a single leader or party dominates. They use the state power to defeat opposition and mobilize public opinion.

conflict An actual or perceived antagonism between states and international or nongovernment organizations.

conflict theories Approaches that emphasize economic, social, and political inequality as a source of contradictions and tensions among social groups. Conflict theories highlight the role of social classes, ruling elites, and other dominant groups in shaping global affairs.

conservation A policy of protecting and preserve natural resources, including plant and animal species and their habitats.

consistency bias In cognitive theories, the rule that the human mind operates so as to keep beliefs, opinions, and ideas consistent.

constructivist view (or constructivism) An approach to international relations that assumes that state actions and policies are based on how leaders, bureaucracies, and societies interpret, or *construct*, information.

consumption The selection, adoption, use, disposal, and recycling of goods and services.

contamination The byproducts of human and nonhuman activities affecting air, water, and soil.

content analysis A research method that systematically organizes and summarizes both what was actually said or written and its hidden meanings (the manifest and latent content).

cooperation A foreign policy that addresses other states' concerns for their security.

core In dependency theory, economically developed states that exercise their hegemonic power.

counterterrorism Long-term policies and specific short-term measures to prevent and combat international and domestic terrorism.

criminalization of terrorism Considering terrorism a form of criminal behavior in the context of domestic and international law.

critical thinking A strategy for examining, evaluating, and understanding international relations on the basis of reasoning and valid evidence.

culture A set of values, behaviors, and symbols shared by a group of people and communicated from one generation to the next.

currency The physical component of a country's money supply, comprising coins, paper notes, and government bonds.

customary law Law derived from the past practices of sovereign states in the absence of repeated objections from other states.

cyberterrorism Paralyzing online attacks on political, financial, and military centers.

debt-for-nature swaps Agreements to designate an area for environmental conservation in exchange for a reduction in the country's foreign debt.

deforestation The massive removal or disappearance of forests, owing to the thinning, changing, and elimination of trees, bushes, and other vegetation.

democratic leaders Leaders who treat the letter and spirit of the law as the core of their domestic policy and, in most circumstances, foreign policy.

democratic peace theory The theory that democracies are not likely to fight one another.

dependency theory The view that the world economic order is based on the flow of resources from a "periphery" of poor states to a "core" of wealthy states.

depletion The serious reduction of essential elements of an ecosystem, such as loss of forests, fresh water, or entire species.

desertification The expansion of deserts into the places previously available for agriculture.

diplomacy The management of international relations through negotiations.

domestic terrorism Terrorism to achieve domestic political goals, such as dismantling a government or a change in policies.

domino theory An American view during the Cold War that a seizure of power by Communists in one country will produce a chain reaction of Communist takeovers in other countries allied with the West.

East African Community (EAC) An economic and political union between five countries (Tanzania, Uganda, Burundi, Kenya, and Rwanda).

economic climate A set of values and practices, such as the level of trust, transparency and corruption that encourages or discourages economic investments.

economic liberalism The belief and theory that only free market, free trade, and economic cooperation can lead to a peaceful and prosperous world.

economic sanctions The deliberate, government-driven withdrawal, or threat of withdrawal, of customary trade and financial relations in an effort to change another country's policies.

environmental discrimination Actions and policies of the global North that sustain the contamination and depletion of the environment in the global South.

environmental politics The activities of political leaders, parties, NGOs, scientific laboratories, and others to influence environmental policy.

environmental skepticism A questioning of environmentalism from the point of view of science or practicality.

environmental sovereignty The right of states to use and protect their environment and natural resources.

environmentalism Belief in the necessity of urgent and comprehensive policies to protect the environment.

epidemic An outbreak of infectious disease in a large population.

experiment A research method that puts participants in controlled testing conditions. By varying these conditions, researchers can examine the behavior or responses of participants.

extraterritoriality Exemption from the jurisdiction of local law.

extreme poverty A profound lack of resources and the inability to gain access to them.

eyewitness accounts Descriptions of events by individuals who observed them directly.

failing state A state in which the government is incapable of exercising its major functions, defending borders, or making key decisions.

fair trade (or trade justice) Initiatives arising from a belief that free trade alone cannot solve such lingering problems as chronic poverty, diseases, and environmental troubles.

famine Severe food scarcity causing malnutrition, starvation, disease, and increasing mortality.

feminism Critical approach arguing that men's political domination and their oppression of women shape international relations.

fiscal policy The use of government spending or revenue collection to influence the economy, jumpstart it out of recession, or create jobs.

focus group A survey method involving small discussion groups used intensively in foreign policy planning, conflict resolution analysis, and academic research.

Food and Agriculture Organization (FAO) A UN agency that coordinates international efforts to overcome hunger.

foreign policy A complex system of actions involving official decisions or communications related to other nation states, international institutions, or international developments in general.

freedom of the seas The principle that countries have the right to travel by sea to, and trade with, other countries; each state's sovereignty ends with its territorial waters.

fundamentalism A point of view or social movement distinguished by rigid adherence to principles rooted in tradition (typically religious tradition) and often by intolerance of individual rights and secularism.

general principles of law Cross-cultural principles of morality and common sense.

genocide The deliberate extermination or prosecution of racial, ethnic, religious, or social groups, whether in war or in peacetime.

geopolitics The theory and practice of using geography to achieve political power or seek security.

global commons Geographical areas not under any nation's sovereign control.

global disarmament The universal and voluntary elimination by states of their offensive weapons.

Global Environment Facility (GEF) An independent financial organization established in 1991 that provides grants to developing countries for projects that benefit the global environment and promote sustainable development.

global governance The global cooperation of international actors with little or no power of enforcing compliance. This approach is based on the mutual interdependence of nations, the idea that global issues should be addressed by a collective effort, and the assumption that there is no single formula for solving all humanitarian problems.

globalization The growing interdependence of countries and their economies, the growing importance of international exchanges of goods and ideas, and increased openness to innovation.

graduated reciprocation in tension reduction (GRIT) Small goodwill steps by one or two sides in an international conflict that help to build trust and reduce international tensions.

green certification The grant of certificates to companies that pursue responsible environmental policies, in order to make their products more competitive in the market.

gross domestic product (GDP) The total market value of all the goods and services produced within the borders of a nation during a specified period

group pressure In political psychology, the ability of other people to alter individual decisions.

guerrilla warfare Political violence by identifiable, irregular combat units, usually to seize state power, win autonomy, or found new states.

harmony values The view that the environment should be preserved and cherished rather than exploited.

hegemony One state's overwhelming power in relation to other states.

human rights Fundamental rights with which all people are endowed regardless of their race, nationality, sex, ethnicity, religion, or social status.

human trafficking The illegal trade in human beings for purposes of exploitation.

humanitarian crisis An incident or problem that threatens to the health, safety, security, and well-being of many people, usually in a single geographic area.

humanitarian intervention Assistance with or without the use of military force to reduce the disastrous consequences of a humanitarian crisis.

humanitarian sovereignty A country's responsibility for its own humanitarian policies and the right to accept or reject humanitarian interventions.

identity The characteristics by which a person is recognizable as a member of a cultural group, such as a nation, an ethnic group, or a religion.

imperialism (Lenin's theory of) A global struggle among international corporations and banks for territories and resources.

infectious diseases Serious maladies caused by a biological agent such as a virus, bacterium, or parasite.

intelligence Information about the interests, intentions, capabilities, and actions of foreign countries, including government officials, political parties, the functioning of their economies, the activities of nongovernmental organizations, and the behavior of private individuals.

intergovernmental organizations (IGO) Association of several nation-states or nongovernmental organizations for the purpose of international cooperation.

internal affairs Matters that individual states consider beyond the reach of international law or the influence of other states.

internally displaced persons Those who involuntarily leave their home and region under threats of death, starvation, or imprisonment.

international law Principles, rules, and regulations concerning the interactions between countries and other institutions and organizations in international relations.

international mandate Legal permission to administer a territory or enforce international law.

international political economy (IPE) The ways in which politics and economics interact in an international context.

international politics The political aspects of international relations. The emphasis on politics suggests the primary focus of these studies: power-related interests and policies.

international relations The study of interactions among states, as well as the international activities of nonstate organizations.

international security Mutual security issues involving two or more states.

international system Checks and balances among states as they exercise their power to promote their interests.

international terrorism Terrorism that involves international groups, interaction between countries, or international organizations, often with regional or global consequences.

international treaties Written agreements between nations (also called agreements, charters, pacts, covenants, and conventions).

interventionism A policy of interference in other states' affairs or international conflicts without regard for their consent.

involuntary migration Relocation within or across state borders due to violence, hardship, severe suffering, or a significant threat of these.

isolationism A policy of noninvolvement in international conflicts.

jurisdiction The right and authority to make decisions and apply justice.

Keynesian economics The principle that national governments should conduct expansionary fiscal and monetary policies whenever necessary to ease the undesirable effects of economic recessions.

Kyoto Protocol A 1997 international agreement to limit air pollution and reduce global warming.

laws of war Common principles that states should follow in case of an armed conflict.

liberal interventionism An approach to international relations that accepts violence only if all diplomatic and nonviolent means are exhausted.

liberalism A school of thought based on the idea that international organizations, international economic cooperation, interdependence, and democracy allow states to avoid power politics and establish a lasting peace.

lobbying Activities with the goal of influencing public officials in support of legislation or policies.

macroeconomics The field of economics that considers the behavior of individual consumers, companies, and industries.

malnutrition A medical condition resulting from famine or chronic food shortages.

Marxism A social, political, and economic theory that interprets international relations as a struggle between states representing ruling elites interested in control over territories, people, and resources.

mastery values The view that individuals may exercise control over and exploit natural resources.

mercantilism The economic view that emphasizes the accumulation of resources and capital by states, as well as state regulation of trade.

microeconomics The field of economics that considers the behavior of individual consumers, companies, and industries.

militarism A tendency to rely on military force in response to foreign threats.

multilateralism Coordination of foreign policy with allies; participation in international coalitions, blocs, and international organizations.

multipolar order A world with multiple centers of power or influence.

mutual assured destruction (MAD) The U.S. doctrine that if two nuclear states have the capacity to destroy each other, they will not use nuclear weapons.

nation A large group of people sharing common cultural, religious, and linguistic features and distinguishing themselves from other large social groups. A nation may also refer to people who have established sovereignty over a territory and set up international borders recognized by other states.

national purpose In the constructivist view, a major economic goal that political and business elites want to achieve for their country.

national security A state's need to protect its sovereignty, territorial integrity, and vital interests.

nationalism Individual and collective identification with a country or a nation. Nationalism also can become the belief in a nation's special role. Often, it is the belief that an ethnic group has the right to form an independent state.

natural disaster A natural hazard such as an earthquake or a volcano eruption with devastating impact on the ecosystem.

neoliberalism (neoliberal institutionalism) An approach that postulates that states prefer to seek security not through power politics but in the context of a complex interdependence among states.

neorealism (structural realism) The theory that each state seeks a secure place in the international system according to the distribution of power.

neutrality Rejection of any formal military or political alliance (see isolationism).

nongovernmental organization (NGO) Public or private group unaffiliated formally with a government and attempting to influence foreign policy, to raise international concerns about a domestic problem or domestic concerns about a global issue, and to offer solutions.

North (global) In dependency theory, predominantly rich and technology-driven countries that benefit from the raw materials and cheap labor of the (global) South.

nuclear deterrence Maintaining nuclear weapons with the intention not to use them but to deter others from nuclear attack.

nuclear proliferation The spread of nuclear weapons, material, information, and technologies to create nuclear weapons.

one-child policy China's policy initiated in 1979 limiting the number of children that a family can have.

outsourcing The practice of moving business and jobs to other countries and regions where labor costs are lower.

overpopulation A high concentration of people within a region, threatening its subsistence, or the minimum conditions to sustain a reasonable quality of life. It can cause serious environmental and social problems.

ozone depletion Steady decline in the amount of ozone in the stratosphere, allowing the sun's damaging ultraviolet radiation to reach the earth.

pacifism A principled opposition to war, and the belief that international disputes should be settled by arbitration and other nonviolent means.

pandemic An international epidemic that spreads across national borders.

parochialism A worldview limited to the small piece of land on which we live or to the narrow experience we have.

peace psychology The study of the ideological and psychological causes of war, in order to develop educational programs to reduce the threat.

peacekeeping Military or nonmilitary intervention to stop violence (peacemaking) and to create the conditions for lasting peace (peace building).

Pearl Harbor syndrome Individual attitudes and state policies focused on avoiding sudden and devastating attacks.

periphery In dependency theory, former colonies, and underdeveloped, chronically poor states.

policy climate The prevailing sentiment among policy makers and other influential individuals.

political culture A set of values and norms essential to the functioning of international and national political institutions, including the attitudes of states toward each other and individual citizens.

political psychology The study of the interactions between political and psychological factors in individual and group behavior.

political socialization The study of how individuals acquire their political knowledge and beliefs.

postcolonial studies The critique of Western domination in postcolonial Africa, Asia, and Latin America.

power A state's ability to protect its own security and impose its will on other states and actors.

predator state A state conducting policies of systematic disregard for international rules and turning to belligerent actions in the international arena.

preemptive policies Action against terrorists before they strike.

preemptive war Military action launched to destroy the potential threat of an enemy when an attack is believed to be imminent.

preventive war Military action states take to protect themselves if they believe that other states might threaten them in the future.

production The process of creating goods and services with market value.

prospect theory Theory stating that people consistently miscalculate their chances of success and failure.

protectionism Economic restrictions by the state to discourage imports and encourage domestic production including "import substitution."

rational model In political psychology, the view that politicians act, for the most part, logically, to maximize positive outcomes and to minimize negative outcomes.

realism An approach to international relations that focuses on states and their interests, balance of power, and the structure of international relations.

realpolitik Policy rooted in the belief that the foundation of a nation's security is power and the threat of its use.

refugees Involuntary migrants under threats of political or religious persecution or ethnic and religious violence.

regional trade agreements Mutual commitments that bind several neighboring countries to pursue common economic and financial policies.

rehabilitation Helping someone who has been involved in a radical or terrorist group return to the community.

religious fundamentalism A set of beliefs and behaviors based on strict adherence to religious principles.

resistance bias In cognitive theories, the rule that leaders resist changing their ideas about international relations.

responsibility to protect (R2P) The principle that if a sovereign country does not protect its own people from identifiable causes of death and acute suffering, then other countries and the international community must take action.

security community A group of countries united by mutual security interests, arrangements, and common liberal values.

security dilemma A situation in which one state's efforts to improve its security cause insecurity in others.

security policy Principles of international behavior to advance a state's fundamental interests and ensure national security.

security regime A region in which a powerful country provides protection to other states in exchange for their cooperation.

separatism The advocacy of or attempt to establish a separate nation within another sovereign state.

socially responsible investing (SRI) A business strategy combining the pursuit of the social good, environmental protection, and profits.

soft power A state's ability to influence other states by example, through economic and social success.

sources of international law Treaties, customs, general principles, the actions of international courts and other organizations, and other processes that regulate international relations.

South (global) Predominantly agricultural countries that are dependent on the rich and technology-driven (global) North.

sovereignty The supremacy of authority exercised by a state over its population and its territory.

state A governed entity with a settled population occupying a permanent area with recognized borders.

state government An institution with the authority to formulate and enforce its decisions within a country's borders.

supranationalism International treaties, international customary law, and general principles of law recognized by civilized nations.

survey The investigative method in which groups of people answer questions on a certain topic.

sustainable development A comprehensive policy that meets the needs of the present without sacrificing the ability of future generations to meet their own needs. This policy is about stimulating economic growth while protecting the environment and natural resources.

tariffs Taxes or financial charges imposed on imported goods.

terrorism Random violence conducted by non-state actors, such as individuals or groups, against governments or their citizens to achieve political goals.

theory A general concept or scheme that one applies to facts in order to analyze them.

transnational cooperation The interaction of nonstate agencies, networks of states, and groups of citizens.

tribalism A way of thinking and a movement identifying itself not with nation-states, but rather with a religious or ethnic group.

two-level game A model in which states react to both domestic and international politics.

tyrant A ruler who uses unlimited power to oppress the people of the ruler's country or its foreign possessions.

unilateralism Reliance on a state's own resources rather than support from others; acting alone in foreign policy.

unipolar order A world with only one center of power or influence.

universal jurisdiction The principle that the perpetrators of certain crimes cannot escape justice by moving to another country and invoking its sovereign immunity.

war An organized violent confrontation between states or other social and political entities, such as ethnic or religious groups.

water pollution The byproducts of human activities that are harmful to rivers, lakes, seas, and underground water.

weapons of mass destruction (WMD) Nuclear, chemical, and biological weapons that can quickly and indiscriminately kill tens of millions of people.

xenophobia Fear and contempt of foreign countries and foreigners, helping politicians and regimes to mobilize public opinion, defeat political opposition, win elections, neutralize critics, or justify war.

References

A Strategic Revolution in HIV and Global Health (Editorial). 2011. *The Lancet* 377 (9783) June 18: 2055.

Aaronson, Susan Ariel. 2010. Is China Killing the WTO? *International Economy*, Winter.

Abadie, Alberto. 2006. Poverty, Political Freedom, and the Roots of Terrorism. *American Economic Review* (Papers and Proceedings) 96 (2): 50–56.

Abdelal, Rawi. 2001. *National Purpose in the World Economy*. Ithaca, NY: Cornell University Press.

Abelson, Rashad. 2015. Locked Out: The (Un)Constitutionality of Revoking the Passports of Americans Fighting for ISIS. *National Security Law Brief.* January 27. Online at http://www.nationalsecu ritylawbrief.com/locked-out-the-unconstition ality-of-revoking-the-passports-of-americans -fighting-for-isis/ (accessed April 10, 2015).

Abrams, Irwin. 1957. The Emergence of the International Law Societies. *Review of Politics* 19 (3): 361–80.

Adamsky, Dima. 2010. *The Culture of Military Innovation: The Impact of Cultural Factors on the Revolution in Military Affairs in Russia, the US, and Israel*. Stanford, CA: Stanford University Press.

Adler, Emanuel and Michael Barnett, eds. 1998. *Security Communities*. Cambridge, UK: Cambridge University Press.

Adler, Emanuel. 2008. The Spread of Security Communities: Communities of Practice, Self-Restraint, and NATO's Post-Cold War Transformation. *European Journal of International Relations* 14 (2): 195–230.

Agier, Michel. 2010. Humanity as an Identity and Its Political Effects. *Humanity* 1 (1): 29–46.

Akçam, Taner. 2007. *A Shameful Act: The Armenian Genocide and the Question of Turkish Responsibility*. New York: Picador.

Alamgir, Jalal. 2008. *India's Open-Economy Policy: Globalism, Rivalry, Continuity*. London: Routledge.

Aldous, Richard. 2007. *The Lion and the Unicorn: Gladstone vs. Disraeli.* New York: W.W. Norton.

Allison, Graham and Philip Zelikow. 1999. *Essence of Decision: Explaining the Cuban Missile Crisis.* 2nd edition. New York: Longman.

Allison, Graham. 1971. *Essence of Decision: Explaining the Cuban Missile Crisis.* 1st edition. New York: Little, Brown, and Company.

Almond, Gabriel and Sidney Verba. 1963. *The Civic Culture.* Boston: Little, Brown and Company.

Almukhtar, Sarah, K.K. Rebecca Lai, Sergio Peçanha, Derek Watkins and Jeremy White. 2015. What's Behind the Surge in Refugees Crossing the Mediterranean Sea. *The New York Times.* May 5. Online at http://www.nytimes.com/interactive/2015/04/20/ world/europe/surge-in-refugees-crossing-the-medi terranean-sea-maps.html (accessed June 22, 2015).

Anderson, Kym, ed. 2005. *The World's Wine Markets: Globalization at Work.* London: Edward Elgar.

Angell, Norman. 1910. *The Great Illusion: A Study of the Relation of Military Power in Nations to Their Economic and Social Advantage.* London: Heinemann.

Angus, Ian and Simon Butler. 2011. *Too Many People?: Population, Immigration, and the Environmental Crisis.* Chicago: Haymarket Books.

Arrighi, Giovanni and Li Zhang. 2011. Beyond the Washington Consensus: A New Bandung? In *Globalization and Beyond: New Examinations of Global Power and Its Alternatives*, eds. Jon Shefner and Patricia Fernandez-Kelly. University Park: Pennsylvania State University Press, 25–57.

Arrighi, Giovanni. 1994. *The Long Twentieth Century: Money, Power, and the Origins of Our Times.* New York: Verso.

Arrighi, Giovanni. 2010. The World Economy and the Cold War, 1970–1990. In *The Cambridge History of the Cold War*, Vol. 3, ed. Melvyn P. Leffler and

Odd Arne Westad. New York: Cambridge University Press.

Art, David. 2011. *Inside the Radical Right: The Development of Anti-Immigrant Parties in Western Europe.* Cambridge, UK: Cambridge University Press.

Asal, Victor and Andrew Blum. 2005. Holy Terror and Mass Killings? Reexamining the Motivations and Methods of Mass Casualty Terrorists. *International Studies Review* 7 (1): 153–155.

Ayittey, George B. N. 2005. *Africa Unchained: The Blueprint for Africa's Future.* New York: Palgrave Macmillan.

Ayman, Roya and Karen Korabik. 2010. Why Gender and Culture Matter. *American Psychologist* 65 (3): 157–170.

Baldez, Lisa. 2013. U.S. drops the ball on women's rights. *CNN.* Online at http://www.cnn.com/2013/03/08/opinion/baldez-womens-equality-treaty/ acessed April 25, 2015.

Baldoni, John. 2004. *Great Motivation Secrets of Great Leaders.* New York: McGraw-Hill.

Bales, Kevin, Zoe Trodd, and Alex Williamson. 2009. *Modern Slavery: The Secret World of 27 Million People.* London: Oneworld.

Banerjee, Abhijit and Ester Duflo. 2011. *Poor Economics: A Radical Rethinking of the Way to Fight Global Poverty.* New York: Public Affairs.

Barner-Barry, Carol and Robert Rosenwein. 1985. *Psychological Perspectives on Politics.* Prospect Heights, IL: Waveland.

Bass, Gary. 2009. *Freedom's Battle: The Origins of Humanitarian Intervention.* New York: Vintage Books.

Beck, Barbara. 2011. All Aboard: Women Will Get a Lift to the Top. *The Economist.* November 17. Special edition: The World in 2012, 99.

Becker, Jasper. 1998. *Hungry Ghosts: Mao's Secret Famine.* New York: Owl Books.

Beech, Hannah. 2013. The Face of Buddhist Terror. *Time,* July 1. Online at http://ti.me/10zStLO (accessed July 17, 2013).

Bellamy, Alex and Paul Williams. 2010. *Understanding Peacekeeping.* Cambridge, UK: Polity.

Benvenisti, Eyal, Chaim Gans, and Sari Hanafi, eds. 2007. *Israel and the Palestinian Refugees.* Berlin: Springer.

Beres, Louis R. 2008. On Assassination, Preemption, and Counterterrorism: The View From International Law. *International Journal of Intelligence and CounterIntelligence* 21 (4): 694–725.

Bergman, Ronen. 2008. *The Secret War with Iran: The 30-Year Clandestine Struggle Against the World's Most Dangerous Terrorist Power.* New York: Free Press.

Bergsten, C. Fred. 2005. Rescuing the Doha Round. *Foreign Affairs* 84 (7). Special WTO edition. Online at https://www.foreignaffairs.com/issues/2005/84/7 (accessed August 1, 2015).

Bernstein, Richard. 2009. Upper Crust Is Often Drawn to Terrorism. *The New York Times.* December 30. Online at http://nyti.ms/6S5b73 (accessed June 25, 2013).

Beschloss, Michael. 2007. *Presidential Courage: Brave Leaders and How They Changed America, 1789–1989.* New York: Simon & Schuster.

Betts, Richard. 2004. *Conflict after the Cold War: Arguments on Causes of War and Peace.* 2nd edition. New York: Longman.

Betts, Richard. 2008. *Conflict after the Cold War: Arguments on Causes of War and Peace.* 3rd edition. New York: Longman.

Betts, Richard. 2011. Institutional Imperialism. *The National Interest.* May/June: 85–96.

Bhagwati, Jagdish. 2004. *In Defense of Globalization.* New York: Oxford University Press.

Biello, David. 2010. Where Did the Carter White House's Solar Panels Go? *Scientific American.* August 6. Online at http://www.scientific american.com/article.cfm?id=carter-white-house-solar-panel-array (accessed September 25, 2012).

Birdsall, Nancy and Francis Fukuyama. 2011. The Post-Washington Consensus: Development after the Crisis. *Foreign Affairs* 90 (2): 45–53.

Black, Richard. 2011. World's Oceans in "Shocking" Decline. *BBC News.* June 20. Online at http://www.bbc.co.uk/news/science-environment-13796479?print=true (accessed September 25, 2012).

Blair, Tony. 2010. *A Journey: My Political Life.* New York: Knopf.

Blanchard, William. 1996. *Neocolonialism American Style, 1960–2000.* New York: Praeger.

Blewitt, John, 2014. Understanding Sustainable Development

Blight J. G., B. J. Allyn, and D. A. Welch. 1993. *Cuba on the Brink: Castro, the Missile Crisis, and the Soviet Collapse.* New York: Pantheon Books.

Blinken, A. 2015. Transatlantic Cooperation and the Crisis in Ukraine: Keynote and Discussion with U.S. Deputy Secretary of State Antony J. Blinken. Hertie School Of Governance. Online at http://www.hertie-school.org/mediaandevents/events/events-pages/05032015-transatlantic-cooperation-and-the-crisis-in-ukraine/ (accessed April 2, 2015).

Blustein, Paul. 2009. *Misadventures of the Most Favored Nations: Clashing Egos, Inflated Ambitions, and the Great Shambles of the World Trade System.* New York: Public Affairs.

Bodansky, Yossef. 2001. *Bin Laden: The Man who Declared War on America.* Roseville, CA: Prima Lifestyles.

Boot, Max. 2007. Another Vietnam? *Wall Street Journal.* August 24. Online at http://www.cfr.org/publication/14083/another_vietnam.html (accessed July 18, 2013).

Boot, Max. 2009. Pirates, Then and Now: How Piracy Was Defeated in the Past and Can Be Again. *Foreign Affairs* 88 (4): 94–107.

Boot, Max. 2013. The Guerilla Myth: Unconventional Wars Are Our Most Pressing National Security Concern. *The Wall Street Journal.* January 18. Online at http://www.wsj.com/articles/SB10001424127887323596204578243702404190338. (accessed April 12, 2015).

Booth, Ken and Nicholas Wheeler. 2007. *The Security Dilemma: Fear, Cooperation and Trust in World Politics.* New York: Palgrave Macmillan.

Booth, Ken and Nicholas Wheeler. 2008. *The Security Dilemma: Fear, Cooperation and Trust in World Politics.* New York: Palgrave Macmillan.

Borah, Rupakjyoti. 2011. BRICS: The New Great Game. *ISN Insights.* June 23. Online at http://bit.ly/12QmLUU (accessed July 19, 2013).

Borch, Fred and Gary Solis. 2010. *Geneva Conventions.* New York: Kaplan Publishing.

Borgerson, Scott G. 2008. Arctic Meltdown: The Economic and Security Implications of Global Warming. *Foreign Affairs* 87 (2) March/April.

Bortolotti, Dan. 2006. *Hope in Hell: Inside the World of Doctors Without Borders.* Buffalo, NY: Firefly Books.

Boucek, Christopher. 2009. Saudi Detainee-Rehab Program Mostly Successful. NPR's *All Things Considered.* December 31. Online at http://bit.ly/12Hel2h (accessed June 30, 2013).

Boucek, Christopher. 2010. Al Qaeda in 2010. *The Diane Rehm Show.* January 5. Online at http://bit.ly/15QPRqj (accessed July 18, 2013).

Bozo, Frederic, Marie-pierre Rey, Berndt Rother, and Ludlow N. Piers, eds. 2012. *Visions of the End of the Cold War in Europe, 1945–1990.* New York: Berghahn Books.

BP Found "Grossly Negligent" in 2010 Gulf Oil Spill. 2014. *BBC News.* September 4. Online at http://www.bbc.com/news/business-29069184 (accessed March 7, 2015).

Brandt, Patrick and Todd Sandler. 2010. What Do Transnational Terrorists Target? Has It Changed? Are We Safer? *Journal of Conflict Resolution* 54 (2): 214–36.

Bricmont, Jean. 2006. *Humanitarian Imperialism: Using Rights to Sell War.* New York: Monthly Review Press.

Brown, Paul. 2006. *Notes from a Dying Planet, 2004–2006: One Scientist's Search for Solutions.* Lincoln, NE: iUniverse, Inc.

Brown, Robert and Tristan Brown. 2012. *Why are We Producing Biofuels?* Ames, IA: Brownia LLC.

Bryce, Robert. 2009. *Gusher of Lies: The Dangerous Delusions of "Energy Independence."* New York: PublicAffairs.

Buchanan, Allen. 2003. Reforming the International Law of Humanitarian Intervention. In *Humanitarian Intervention: Ethical, Legal, and Political Dilemmas,* eds. J. L. Holzgrefe and Robert Keohane. New York: Cambridge University Press, 130–74.

Buchanan, Allen. 2010. *Human Rights, Legitimacy, and the Use of Force.* New York: Oxford University Press.

Buchanan, Patrick. 2008. *Churchill, Hitler, and the Unnecessary War: How Britain Lost Its Empire and the West Lost the World.* New York: Crown Publishers.

Buchanan, Patrick. 2009. *Day of Reckoning: How Hubris, Ideology, and Greed Are Tearing America Apart.* New York: St. Martin's Griffin.

Bueno de Mesquita, Ethan. 2005. Conciliation, Counterterrorism, and Patterns of Terrorist Violence. *International Organization* 59 (1): 145–176.

Bull, Hedley, ed. 1988. *Intervention in World Politics.* New York: Oxford University Press.

Bull, Hedley. 1977. *The Anarchical Society: A Study of Order in World Politics.* New York: Columbia University Press.

Burt, Jo-Marie. 2009. Guilty as Charged: The Trial of Former Peruvian President Alberto Fujimori for Grave Violations of Human Rights. *International Journal of Transitional Justice* 3 (3): 384–405.

Burt, Jo-Marie. 2010. *Political Violence and the Authoritarian State in Peru: Silencing Civil Society.* New York: Palgrave Macmillan.

Buzan, Barry and Lene Hansen. 2009. *The Evolution of International Security Studies.* New York: Cambridge University Press.

Caprioli, Mary and Mark Boyer. 2001. Gender, Violence, and International Crisis. *Journal of Conflict Resolution* 45 (4): 503–518.

Carpenter, Ted. 2006. *America's Coming War with China: A Collision Course over Taiwan*. New York: Palgrave Macmillan.

Carr, Edward H. 1969. *Twenty Years' Crisis, 1919–1939: An Introduction to the Study of International Relations*. 2nd edition. New York: Palgrave Macmillan. Originally published in 1939.

Carrière, Erin, Marc O'Reilly, and Richard Vengroff. 2003. "In the Service of Peace": Reflexive Multilateralism and the Canadian Experience in Bosnia. In *International Public Opinion and the Bosnia Crisis*, eds. Richard Sobel and Eric Shiraev. Lanham, MD: Lexington Books, 1–32.

CARSI. 2015. The Central America Regional Security Initiative. U.S. Department of State. Bureau of Public Affairs. Online at http://www.state.gov/p/wha/rt/carsi/ (accessed February 25, 2015).

Carson, Rachel. 1962. *Silent Spring*. New York: Houghton Mifflin.

Chakrabarty, Dipesh. 2007. *Provincializing Europe: Postcolonial Thought and Historical Difference*. Princeton, NJ: Princeton University Press.

Chaliand, Gerard and Arnaud Blin. 2007. *The History of Terrorism: From Antiquity to Al Qaeda*. Berkeley: University of California Press.

Chan, Steve. 1997. In Search of Democratic Peace: Problems and Promise. *Mershon International Studies Review* 41 (1): 59–91.

Chandler, David. 2006. *From Kosovo to Kabul and Beyond: Human Rights and International Intervention*. Ann Arbor, MI: Pluto Press.

Chappel, Louise. 2008. The International Criminal Court: A New Arena for Transforming Justice. In *Global Governance: Feminist Perspectives*, eds. Shirin Rai and Georgina Waylen. New York: Palgrave Macmillan.

Checkel, Jeffrey. 1998. The Constructivist Turn in International Relations Theory. *World Politics* 50 (2): 324–348.

Chernyaev, Anatoly. 2000. *My Six Years with Gorbachev*. Translated and edited by Robert D. English and Elizabeth Tucker. University Park: Pennsylvania State University Press.

Cholett, Derek and James Goldgeier. 2002. The Scholarship of Decision-Making: Do We Know How We Decide? In *Foreign Policy Decision-Making*, eds. Richard Snyder, H. W. Bruck, and Burton Sapin. Originally published in 1962, "revisited" by eds. Valerie Hudson, Derek Cholett, and James Goldgeier in 2002. New York: Palgrave Macmillan.

Cholett, Derek and James Goldgeier. 2008. *America Between the Wars: From 11/9 to 9/11: The Misunderstood Years between the Fall of the Berlin Wall and the Start of the War on Terror*. New York: PublicAffairs.

Christison, Bill. 2002. Former CIA Officer Explains Why the War on Terror Won't Work. *CounterPunch* (an online magazine) March 45. Online at http://bit.ly/14bei54 (accessed July 14, 2013).

Christison, Bill. 2002. Former CIA Officer Explains Why the War on Terror Won't Work. *Counterpunch* (an online magazine) March 45. Online at http://www.counterpunch.org/2002/03/04/former-cia-officer-explains-why-the-war-on-terror-won-t-work/ (accessed June 11, 2015).

CIA The World Factbook. Online at: https://www.cia.gov/library/publications/the-world-factbook/ (accessed June 17, 2015).

Clarke, Peter. 2008. *The Last Thousand Days of the British Empire: Churchill, Roosevelt, and the Birth of the Pax Americana*. New York: Bloomsbury.

Close, Paul. 2000. *The Legacy of Supranationalism*. New York: Palgrave Macmillan.

Cobham, Alex. 2013. Corrupting Perceptions. Why Transparency International's flagship corruption index falls short. Foreign policy, July 22. Online at http://foreignpolicy.com/2013/07/22/corrupting-perceptions/ (accessed February 21, 2015).

Cohen, Joel E. 2005. Human Population Grows Up. *Scientific American* 293 (3): 48–55. Online at http://bit.ly/OUTbgQ (accessed July 15, 2013).

Cohn, Carol. 1987. Sex and Death in the Rational World of Defense Intellectuals. *Signs* 12 (4): 687–718.

Coleman, Loren. 2004. *The Copycat Effect: How the Media and Popular Culture Trigger the Mayhem in Tomorrow's Headlines*. New York: Pocket.

Coll, Steve. 2009. *The Bin Ladens: An Arabian Family in the American Century*. New York: Penguin Press.

Cooper, Barry. 2004. *New Political Religions, or An Analysis of Modern Terrorism*. Columbia: University of Missouri Press.

Copeland, Dale. 1996. Economic Interdependence and War. *International Security* 20 (4): 5–41.

Cordesman, Anthony. 2002. *Terrorism, Asymmetric Warfare, and Weapons of Mass Destruction: Defending the U.S. Homeland*. Westport, CT: Praeger.

Corruption Perception Index. 2015. Online at https://www.transparency.org/cpi2014/results (accessed June 15, 2015).

Costigliola, Frank. 2000. "I Had Come as a Friend": Emotion, Culture, and Ambiguity in the

Formation of the Cold War. *Cold War History* 1 (1) August: 103–128.

Cottier, Thomas and Manfred Elsig, eds. 2011. *Governing the World Trade Organization: Past, Present and Beyond Doha*. New York: Cambridge University Press.

Cowen, Tyler. 2014. *Average Is Over: Powering America Beyond the Age of the Great Stagnation*. New York: Plume.

Crane, George and Abla Amawi. 1997. *The Theoretical Evolution of International Political Economy: A Reader*. New York: Oxford University Press.

Crawford, Michael and Jami Miscik. 2010. The Rise of the Mezzanine Rulers: The New Frontier for International Law. *Foreign Affairs* 89 (6) November/December: 123–132.

Crenshaw, Martha. 2000. The Psychology of Terrorism: An Agenda for the 21st Century. *Journal of Political Psychology* 21 (2): 405–420.

Crenshaw, Martha. 2010. *Explaining Terrorism: Causes, Processes, and Consequences*. New York: Routledge.

Cronin, Audrey. 2002. Behind the Curve: Globalization and International Terrorism. *International Security* 27 (3) Winter: 30–58.

Cronin, Audrey. 2010. The Evolution of Counterterrorism: Will Tactics Trump Strategy? *International Affairs* 86 (4): 837–856.

Cronin, Bruce. 1999. *Community under Anarchy: Transitional Identity and the Evolution of Cooperation*. New York: Columbia University Press.

Cullen, Heidi. 2010. *The Weather of the Future: Heat Waves, Extreme Storms, and Other Scenes from a Climate-Changed Planet*. New York: Harper.

Cutler, Robert. 1981. Decision Making and International Relations: The Cybernetic Theory Reconsidered. *Michigan Journal of Political Science* 1 (2): 57–63. Online at http://bit.ly/1aqXjeY (accessed July 16, 2013).

D'Silva, Themistocles. 2006. *The Black Box of Bhopal: A Closer Look at the World's Deadliest Industrial Disaster*. Victoria, BC: Trafford Publishing.

D'Souza, Dinesh. 2010. *The Roots of Obama's Rage*. Washington, DC: Regnery Publishing.

Davis, David H. 2007. *Ignoring the Apocalypse: Why Planning to Prevent Environmental Catastrophe Goes Astray*. Westport, CT: Praeger.

Davis, Mike. 2011. Spring Confronts Winter. *New Left Review*. Online at http://newleftreview.org/II/72/mike-davis-spring-confronts-winter (accessed July 15, 2013).

de Rugy, Veronique. 2015. *Wars in the Middle East Have Cost Taxpayers Almost $1.7 Trillion*. Online at http://mercatus.org/publication/wars-middle-east-have-cost-taxpayers-almost-17-trillion (accessed April 11, 2015).

Debs, Alexandre and H. E. Goemans. 2010. Regime Type, the Fate of Leaders, and War. *American Political Science Review* 104 (3): 430–445.

Dempsey, Gary. 2002. Old Folly in a New Disguise: Nation Building to Combat Terrorism. Cato Institute. March 21. Online at http://www.cato.org/pub_display.php?pub_id=1288 (accessed September 25, 2012).

Dennis, Anthony. 2002. *Osama bin Laden: A Psychological and Political Portrait*. Lima, OH: Wyndham Hall.

Der Spiegel. 2010. Staff. Beijing's High-Tech Ambitions: The Dangers of Germany's Dependence on China. Online at http://bit.ly/12kRVsf (accessed July 16, 2013).

Desai, Meghnad. 2007. *Rethinking Islamism: The Ideology of the New Terror*. New York: Palgrave Macmillan.

Desertec. 2012. Online at http://www.desertec.org/ (accessed July 19, 2013).

Desertec. 2015. Online at http://www.desertec.org (accessed June 19, 2015).

Deutsch, Karl W., Sidney A. Burrell, and Robert A. Kann. 1957. *Political Community and the North Atlantic Area: International Organization in the Light of Historical Experience*. Princeton, NJ: Princeton University Press.

Deutsch, Morton and Robert Krauss. 1962. Studies of Interpersonal Bargaining. *Journal of Conflict Resolution* 6 (1): 52–76.

DiMicco, Dan. 2015. *American Made: Why Making Things Will Return Us to Greatness*. New York: Palgrave Macmillan.

Donnelly, Jack. 2009. Realism. In *Theories of International Relations*, ed. Scott Burchill, et al. New York: Palgrave Macmillan.

Doremus, Paul N., William W. Keller, Louis W. Pauley, and Simon Reich. 1998. *The Myth of the Global Corporation*. Princeton, NJ: Princeton University Press.

Dower, John. 2000. *Embracing Defeat: Japan in the Wake of World War II*. New York: Norton.

Doyle, Michael. 1986. Liberalism and World Politics. *American Political Science Review* 80 (4): 1151–1169.

Dubik, James. 2010. Prudence, War and Civil-Military Relations. *Army*, September. Online at http://bit.ly/1ChKNLL (accessed June 20, 2015).

Duchene, Francois. 1994. *Jean Monnet: The First States-man of Interdependence.* New York: W. W. Norton.

Dueck, Colin. 2010. *Hard Line: The Republican Party and U.S. Foreign Policy Since World War II.* Princeton, NJ: Princeton University Press.

Dutta, Manoranjan. 2005. *China's Industrial Revolution And Economic Presence.* Hackensack, NJ: World Scientific Publishing Company.

Easterly, William. 2001. *The Elusive Quest for Growth: Economists' Adventures and Misadventures in the Tropics.* Cambridge, MA: MIT Press.

Easterly, William. 2006. *The White Man's Burden: Why the West's Efforts to Aid the Rest Have Done So Much Ill and So Little Good.* New York: Penguin Press.

Ebrahim, Alnoor. 2006. *NGOs and Organizational Change.* Cambridge, UK: Cambridge University Press.

Economy, Elizabeth and Michael Levi. 2014. By All Means Necessary: How China's Resource Quest is Changing the World. New York: Oxford University Press.

Economy, Elizabeth. 2010a. The Game Changer: Coping with China's Foreign Policy Revolution. *Foreign Affairs* 89 (6) November/December: 142–152.

Economy, Elizabeth. 2010b. *The River Runs Black: The Environmental Challenge to China's Future.* Ithaca, NY: Cornell University Press.

EIA (U.S. Energy Information Administration). 2015. Online at http://www.eia.gov/

Eisenhower, Dwight. 1960. Public Papers of the Presidents, Dwight D. Eisenhower. 1035–1040. Online at http://www.h-net.org/~hst306/documents/indust.html (accessed August 1, 2015).

Ekelund, Robert B., Jr. and Robert F. Hébert. 2007. *A History of Economic Theory and Method.* Long Grove, IL: Waveland Press.

Elsea, Jennifer. 2006. U.S. Policy Regarding the International Criminal Court. CRS Reports for Congress. Online at http://fas.org/sgp/crs/misc/RL31495.pdf (accessed March 3, 2015).

English, Robert D. 2000. *Russia and the Idea of the West: Gorbachev, Intellectuals and the End of the Cold War.* New York: Columbia University Press.

Enloe, Cynthia. 2000. *Bananas, Beaches, and Bases. Making Feminist Sense of International Politics.* Berkeley: University of California Press.

Enloe, Cynthia. 2007. *Globalization and Militarism.* New York: Rowman & Littlefield.

ENS. 2006. U.S. Swaps Guatemalan Debt for Forest Conservation. *Environmental News Service.*

October 3. http://bit.ly/197W7PT (accessed July 19, 2013).

Erikson, Erik. 1969. *Gandhi's Truth: On the Origins of Militant Nonviolence.* New York: W.W. Norton.

Esty, Daniel and Andrew Winston. 2006. *Green to Gold: How Smart Companies Use Environmental Strategy to Innovate, Create Value, and Build Competitive Advantage.* New Haven, CT: Yale University Press.

Eurobarometer. 2011. *Migrant Integration: Aggregate Report.* Conducted by TNS Qual+ at the request of Directorate General Home Affairs. Online at http://bit.ly/noM7CG (accessed June 16, 2013).

Evangelista, Matthew. 1999. *Unarmed Forces: The Transnational Movement to End the Cold War.* Ithaca, NY: Cornell University Press.

Evans, Gareth. 2009. *The Responsibility to Protect: Ending Mass Atrocity Crimes Once and for All.* Washington, DC: Brookings Institution Press.

Evans, Peter. 1998. Transnational Corporations and Third World States: From the Old Internationalization to the New. In *Transnational Corporations and the Global Economy,* eds. Richard Kozul-Wright and Robert Rowthorn. New York: St. Martin's Press, 195–224.

Evans-Pritchard, Ambrose. 2011. World Power Swings Back to America. *Telegraph.* October 23. Online at http://bit.ly/ptenjk (accessed September 25, 2012).

Fanon, Frantz. 2005. *The Wretched of the Earth.* New York: Grove Press. Originally published in French in 1961.

Farmer, Paul. 2012. *Haiti After the Earthquake.* New York: PublicAffairs.

Fearon, James and David Laitin. 2003. Ethnicity, Insurgency, and Civil War. *American Political Science Review* 97 (1): 75–90.

Fearon, James. 1995. Rationalist Explanations for War. *International Organization* 49 (3): 379–414.

Fearon, James. 1998. Bargaining, Enforcement, and International Cooperation. *International Organization* 52 (2): 269–306.

Ferguson, Niall. 2004. *Empire: The Rise and Demise of the British World Order and the Lessons for Global Power.* New York: Basic Books.

Ferguson, Niall. 2010. The End of Chimerica: Amicable Divorce or Currency War? Testimony before the Committee on Ways and Means U.S. House of Representatives, March 24. Online at http://belfercenter.ksg.harvard.edu/publication/20029/end_of_chimerica.html (accessed September 22, 2012).

Festa, Lynn. 2010. Humanity without Feathers. *Humanity* 1 (1): 3–27.

Figes, Orlando. 2012. *The Crimean War: A History*. New York, NY: Picador.

Finnemore, Martha. 1996. *National Interests in International Society*. Ithaca, NY: Cornell University Press.

Finnemore, Martha. 2004. *The Purpose Of Intervention: Changing Beliefs About The Use Of Force* (Cornell Studies in Security Affairs). Ithaca, NY: Cornell University Press.

Fong, Vanessa L. 2006. *Only Hope: Coming of Age Under China's One-Child Policy*. Palo Alto, CA: Stanford University Press.

Forsythe, David, Roger Coate, and Thomas Weiss. 2004. *The United Nations and Changing World Politics*. Boulder, CO: Westview Press.

Fouskas, Vassilis. 2003. *Zones Of Conflict: U.S. Foreign Policy in the Balkans and the Greater Middle East*. Sterling, VA: Pluto Press.

Fredrik, Logevall and Andrew Preston, eds. 2008. *Nixon in the World: American Foreign Relations, 1969–1977*. New York: Oxford University Press.

French, Hilary. 1994. GEF replenishment. *World Watch* 7 (4): 7.

Friedrich, Hans-Peter. 2011. An Interview of German Interior Minister. *Der Spiegel*, August 9. Online at http://bit.ly/oz01L0 (accessed July 17, 2013).

Fromkin, David. 2009. *The Peace to End All Peace*. New York: Henry Holt.

Fukuyama, Francis. 1993. *The End of History and the Last Man*. New York: Penguin Books.

Fukuyama, Francis. 2011. *The Origins of Political Order: From Prehuman Times to the French Revolution*. New York: Farrar, Straus, and Giroux.

Fursenko, Aleksandr and Timothy Naftali. 1997. *"One Hell of a Gamble": Khrushchev, Castro, and Kennedy, 1958–1964*. New York: W. W. Norton.

Fusaro, Peter C. and Tom James. 2006. *Energy & Emissions Markets: Collision or Convergence*. Hoboken, NJ: Wiley.

Gaddis, John Lewis. 1982. *Strategies of Containment: A Critical Appraisal of Postwar American National Security Policy*. New York: Oxford University Press.

Gaddis, John Lewis. 2006. *The Cold War: A New History*. New York: Penguin Books.

Gang, Ding. 2011. War's Legacy Still Tints Vietnam's View of US. *Global Times*, July 6. Online at http://bit.ly/nH5USI (accessed July 15, 2013).

Gangale, Thomas. 2009. *The Development of Outer Space: Sovereignty and Property Rights in International Space Law*. Westport, CT: Praeger.

Garrett, Laurie. 2005. The Next Pandemic? *Foreign Affairs* 84 (4) July/August.

Gartzke, Erik. 2007. The Capitalist Peace. *American Journal of Political Science* 51 (1): 166–191.

Gaston, Kevin and John Spicer. 2004. *Biodiversity: An Introduction*. Malden, MA: Blackwell Publishing.

Gates, Nathaniel, ed. 1998. *Race and U.S. Foreign Policy During the Cold War*. New York: Routledge.

Gause, F. Gregory. 2005. Can Democracy Stop Terrorism? *Foreign Affairs* 84 (5): 62–76.

Gelpi, Christopher and Peter Feaver. 2002. Speak Softly and Carry a Big Stick? Veterans in the Political Elite and the American Use of Force. *American Political Science Review* 96 (4): 779–793.

George, Alexander. 1969. The "Operational Code": A Neglected Approach to the Study of Political Leaders and Decision-Making. *International Studies Quarterly* 13 (2): 190–222.

Gereffi, Gary and Korzeniewicz, Miguel, eds. 1993. *Commodity Chains and Global Capitalism*. New York: Praeger.

German Energy Blog. 2015. Online at http://www.germanenergyblog.de/?p=18231 (accessed March 23, 2015).

Gerrard, Michael, ed. 2007. *Global Climate Change and U.S. Law*. Chicago, IL: American Bar Association.

Gertz, Bill. 2011. Computer-Based Attacks Emerge as Threat of Future, General Says. *The Washington Times*, September 13. Online at http://bit.ly/mYp915 (accessed July 17, 2013).

GHA. 2014. Global Humanitarian Assistance. Annual Report. Online at http://www.globalhumanitarianassistance.org/report/gha-report-2014 (accessed April 3, 2015).

Gilboy, George. 2004. The Myth Behind China's Miracle. *Foreign Affairs* 83 (4) July/August: 33–48.

Gilpin, Robert. 1981. *War and Change in International Politics*. Cambridge: Cambridge

Glad, Betty. 2009. *An Outsider in the White House: Jimmy Carter, His Advisors, and the Making of American Foreign Policy*. Ithaca, NY: Cornell University Press.

Glaser, Charles 2013. How Oil Influences U.S. National Security. *International Security* 38 (2): 112–46.

Gleijeses, Piero. 2003. *Conflicting Missions: Havana, Washington, and Africa, 1959–1976*. Chapel Hill, NC: University of North Carolina Press.

Goemans, Henk E., Kristian Skrede Gleditsch, and Giacomo Chiozza. 2009. Introducing Archigos: A Data Set of Political Leaders, 1975–2003. *Journal of Peace Research* 46 (2): 269–83.

Goldfrank, Walter. 2000 Paradigm Regained? The Rules of Wallerstein's World-System Method. *Journal of World-Systems Research* 6 (2): 150–95.

Goldgeier, J. and P. Tetlock. 2001. Psychology and International Relations Theory. *Annual Review of Political Science* 4: 67–92.

Goldgeier, James. 1999. *Not Whether but When: The U.S. Decision to Enlarge NATO*. Washington, DC: Brookings.

Gong, Sasha. 2009. Those Uppity Peasant Workers: The End of the Era of Cheap Chinese Labor. *The International Economy* Winter: 10–11, 83.

Goodman, Mel. 2008. *Failure of Intelligence: The Decline and Fall of the CIA*. New York: Rowman & Littlefield.

Gottlieb, Gidon. 1994. Nations without States. *Foreign Affairs* 73 (3) May/June.

Gowa, Joanne. 2000. *Ballots and Bullets: The Elusive Democratic Peace*. Princeton, NJ: Princeton University Press.

Graber, Doris and Johanna Dunaway. 2014. *Mass Media and American Politics*. 9th edition. Washington, DC: CQ Press.

Graber, Doris. 2010. *Mass Media and American Politics*. 8th edition. Washington, DC: CQ Press.

Grandia, Lisa. 2012. Enclosed: Conservation, Cattle, and Commerce Among the Q'eqchi' Maya Lowlanders. Seattle, WA: University of Washington Press.

Gray, Colin. 1982. *Strategic Studies: A Critical Assessment*. Westport, CT: Greenwood Press.

Greening, Thomas. 1986. Passion Bearers and Peace Psychology. *Journal of Humanistic Psychology* 26 (4): 98–105.

Greenpeace International. 2015. About Greenpeace. Online at http://www.greenpeace.org/international/en/about/ (accessed March 17, 2015).

Greenpeace International. 2015. About Greenpeace. Online at http://www.greenpeace.org/international/en/about/ (accessed June 17, 2015).

Greer, John Michael. 2005. *How Civilizations Fall: A Theory of Catabolic Collapse*. Online at http://ecoshock.org/transcripts/greer_on_collapse.pdf (accessed June 16, 2015).

Gregory, Derek. 2004. *The Colonial Present: Afghanistan, Palestine*. Malden, MA: Blackwell.

Grimmett, Richard. 1999. Foreign Policy Roles of the President and Congress. U.S. Department of State. June 1. Online at http://fpc.state.gov/6172.htm (accessed September 25, 2012).

Grossman, Elizabeth. 2007. *High Tech Trash: Digital Devices, Hidden Toxics, and Human Health*. Washington, DC: Island Press.

Grotius, Hugo. 2005. *The Freedom of the Seas*. New York: Adamant Media Corporation.

Grover, Velma, ed. 2006. *Water: Global Common and Global Problems*. Enfield, NH: Science Publishers.

Gruber, Lloyd. 2000. *Ruling the World: Power Politics and the Rise of Supranational Institutions*. Princeton, NJ: Princeton University Press.

Guérot, Ulrike and Mark Leonard. 2011. The New German Question: How Europe Can Get the Germany It Needs. Online at http://www.ecfr.eu/page/-/ECFR30_GERMANY_AW.pdf (accessed August 1, 2015).

Gunaratna, Rohan. 2002. *Inside Al Qaeda: Global Network of Terror*. New York: Columbia University Press.

Guterres, Anthony. 2015. Written text of speech to the UN Security Council. United Nations High Commissioner for Refugees. 26 February. Online at http://www.unhcr.org/print/54ef66796.html (retrieved March 31, 2015).

Haaretz Service. 2010. Germany's Deutsche Bank Divests from Israel Firm Linked to West Bank Separation Fence. May 30. Online at http://bit.ly/ccUg5s (accessed July 17, 2013).

Haas, Dieter. 2012. *Agricultural Policies in the EU and US: A Comparison of Policy Objectives and their Realization*. Saarbrücken, Germany: AV Akademikerverlag.

Haas, Ernst B. 1958. *The Uniting of Europe: Political, Social, and Economic Forces, 1950–1957*. Stanford, CA: Stanford University Press.

Haas, Ernst B. 1964. *Beyond the Nation-State: Functionalism and International Organization*. Stanford, CA: Stanford University Press.

Haberman, Clyde. 1994. West Bank Massacre: The Overview; Rabin Urges the Palestinians to Put Aside Anger and Talk. *The New York Times*. March 1. Online at http://nyti.ms/15RT6Qw (accessed July 19, 2013).

Haggard, Stephan and Marcus Noland. 2009. *Famine in North Korea: Markets, Aid, and Reform*. New York: Columbia University Press.

Hahn, Gordon. 2012. Global Jihadism Comes to Russia's North Caucasus. *Fair Observer*, July 12. Online at http://bit.ly/1LWJwRs (accessed August 1, 2015).

Hainmueller, Jens and Michael Hiscox. 2007. Educated Preferences: Explaining Individual Attitudes Toward Immigration in Europe. *International Organization* 61 (2): 399–442.

Hambler, Clive and Susan Canney. 2013. *Conservation*. New York: Cambridge University Press.

Hamud, Randall, ed. 2005. *Osama Bin Laden: America's Enemy in His Own Words*. San Diego, CA: Nadeem Publishing.

Hanson, Victor. 2001. *Carnage and Culture: Landmark Battles in the Rise of Western Power*. New York: Doubleday.

Hardin, Garrett. 1968. The Tragedy of the Commons. *Science* 162 (3859): 1243–1248.

Harris, Frances. 2004. *Global Environmental Issues*. West Sussex, UK: Wiley.

Harrison, Selig and Clyde Prestowitz, Jr. 1990. Pacific Agenda: Defense or Economics? *Foreign Policy* 79 (Summer): 60.

Hart, Paul. 1991. Irving L. Janis' Victims of Groupthink: A Psychological Study of Foreign Policy Decisions and Fiascoes. *Political Psychology* 12 (2): 247–278.

Hartman, Laura and Patricia Werhane. 2009. *The Global Corporation: Sustainable, Effective and Ethical Practices, A Case Book*. New York: Routledge.

Hayek, Friedrich. 2007. *The Road to Serfdom*. Chicago: University of Chicago Press. Originally published in 1944.

Heider, Fritz. 1959. *The Psychology of Interpersonal Relations*. New York: Wiley.

Held, David. 2007. *Globalization/Anti-Globalization: Beyond the Great Divide*. Cambridge, UK: Polity.

Helm, Dieter, ed. 2005. *Climate Change Policy*. Oxford, UK: Oxford University Press.

Hemmer, Christopher. 1999. Historical Analogies and the Definition of Interests: The Iranian Hostage Crisis and Ronald Reagan's Policy toward the Hostages in Lebanon. *Political Psychology* 20 (2) June: 267–289.

Henig, Ruth. 2010. *The League of Nations: The Makers of the Modern World*. London: Haus Publishing.

Herrmann, Richard K. and Richard Ned Lebow, eds. 2004. *Ending the Cold War: Interpretations, Causation, and the Study of International Relations*. New York: Palgrave Macmillan.

Herzog, Michael. 2006. Can Hamas Be Tamed? *Foreign Affairs* 85 (2) March/April: 83–94.

Hilsman, Roger. 1959. The Foreign-Policy Consensus: An Interim Research Report. *Journal of Conflict Resolution* 3 (4): 361–82.

Hinckley, Ronald. 1992. *People, Polls, and Policymakers: American Public Opinion and National Security*. New York: Lexington Books.

Hindmoor, Andrew. 2006. *Rational Choice* (Political Analysis). New York: Palgrave Macmillan.

Hiro, Dilip. 2010. *After Empire: The Birth of a Multipolar World*. New York: Nation Books.

Hirschman, Nancy. 2010. Choosing Betrayal. *Perspectives on Politics* 8 (1) March: 271–78.

Hitchcock, William I. 2008. *The Bitter Road to Freedom. A New History of the Liberation of Europe*. New York: Free Press.

Hitchcock, William I. 2010. The Marshall Plan and the Creation of the West. In *The Cambridge History of the Cold War*, vol. 1, *Origins*. Melvyn P. Leffler and Odd Arne Westad, eds., London: Cambridge University Press, 154–174.

Hobley, Marcus. 2012. Public Opinion Can Play a Positive Role in Policy Making. *Guardian*, September 3. Online at: http://www.theguardian.com/public-leaders-network/2012/sep/03/public-opinion-influence-policy (accessed June 19, 2015).

Hoekman, Bernard and Michel Kostecki. 2010. *The Political Economy of the World Trading System*. New York: Oxford University Press.

Hoffman, Bruce. 1998. *Inside Terrorism*. New York: Columbia University Press.

Hoffman, David. 2010. *The Dead Hand: The Untold Story of the Cold War Arms Race and Its Dangerous Legacy*. New York: Anchor.

Holsti, Ole. 1992. Public Opinion and Foreign Policy: Challenges to the Almond-Lippmann Consensus. *International Studies Quarterly* 36 (4): 439–466.

Holsti, Ole. 2004. *Public Opinion and American Foreign Policy*. Revised edition. Ann Arbor: University of Michigan Press.

Holzgrefe, J. L. and Robert O. Keohane, eds. 2003. *Humanitarian Intervention: Ethical, Legal, and Political Dilemmas*. Cambridge, UK: Cambridge University Press.

Homer-Dixon, Thomas. 1991. On the Threshold: Environmental Changes As Causes of Acute Conflict. *International Security* 16 (2): 76–116.

Hopkirk, Peter. 1994. *The Great Game: The Struggle for Empire in Central Asia*. New York: Kodansha International.

Horgan, John. 2009. *Walking Away from Terrorism: Accounts of Disengagement from Radical and Extremist Movements*. New York: Routledge.

Horgan, John. 2011. Interviewing the Terrorists: Reflections on Fieldwork and Implications for Psychological Research. *Behavioral Science of Political Aggression and Terrorism* 4(3): 195–211.

Horgan, John. 2014. *The Psychology of Terrorism*. New York: Routledge.

Horowitz, Juliana. 2009. Declining Support for bin Laden and Suicide Bombing. Pew Global Attitudes Project, September 10. Online at http://www.pewglobal.org/2009/09/10/rejection-of-extremism/ (accessed June 11, 2015).

Houghton, David. 2008. *Political Psychology: Situations, Individuals, and Cases.* New York: Routledge.

Howard, Russell and James Forest, eds. 2008. *Weapons of Mass Destruction and Terrorism.* Dubuque, IA: McGraw-Hill.

Hudson, Valerie. 1999. Cultural Expectations of One's Own and Other Nations' Foreign Policy Templates. *Political Psychology* 20 (4): 767–801.

Hufbauer, Gary and Barbara Oegg. 2003. Beyond the Nation-State: Privatization of Economic Sanctions. *Middle East Policy* 10 (2): 126–34.

Hulme, David. 2015. *Global Poverty: Global Governance and Poor People in the Post-2015 Era.* New York: Routledge.

Human Rights Watch. 2015. Chiba: Draft Counterterrorism Law A Recipe For Abuses. Online at http://www.hrw.org/news/2015/01/20/china-draft-counterterrorism-law-recipe-abuses (accessed April 11, 2015).

Hunt, Swanee. 2007. Let Women Rule. *Foreign Affairs* 86 (3): 109–120.

Huntington, Samuel. 1993. The Clash of Civilizations. *Foreign Affairs* 72 (3): 22–28.

Husain, Irfan. 2011. *Fatal Faultlines: Pakistan, Islam and the West.* Rockville, Maryland: Arc Manor.

Husain, Mir Zohair. 2002. *Global Islamic Politics.* New York, NY: Longman.

Husain, Mir Zohair. 2005. *Global Islamic Politics.* New York: Longman.

Huth, Paul, Croco, Sarah, and Appel, Benjamin. 2011. Does International Law Promote the Peaceful Settlement of International Disputes? Evidence from the Study of Territorial Conflicts since 1945. *American Political Science Review* 105 (2): 415–436.

ICJ (International Court of Justice). 2004. Legal Consequences of the Construction of a Wall in the Occupied Palestinian Territory. General List No. 131. July 9.

Ignatieff, Michael. 2004. *The Lesser Evil: Political Ethics in an Age of Terrorism.* Princeton, NJ: Princeton University Press.

Ikenberry, G. John and Joseph M. Grieco. 2002. *State Power and World Markets: The International Political Economy.* New York: W. W. Norton & Co.

Ikenberry, G. John. 2011a. The Future of the Liberal World Order. *Foreign Affairs* 90 (3) May/June: 56–68.

Ikenberry, G. John. 2011b. *Liberal Leviathan: The Origins, Crisis, and Transformation of the American World Order.* Princeton, NJ: Princeton University Press.

Ikenberry, G. John. 2014. The Illusion of Geopolitics: The Enduring Power of the Liberal Order. *Foreign Affairs.* May/June, 93 (3): 80–90.

International Health Regulations: The Challenges Ahead (editorial). 2007. *The Lancet* 369 (9575) May 26: 1763.

Inter-Parliamentary Union. 2015. Online at http://www.ipu.org/wmn-e/classif.htm (accessed July 24, 2015).

Iriye, Akira. 2002. *Global Community: The Role of International Organizations in the Making of the Contemporary World.* Berkeley: University of California Press.

Ismay, Hastings Lionel. 1960. *The Memoirs of General Lord Ismay.* New York: Viking Adult.

Israel High Court Ruling. 2005. Docket H.C.J. 7957/04 International Legality of the Security Fence and Sections near Alfei Menashe. September 15, 2005. Online at http://www.zionism-israel.com/hdoc/High_Court_Fence.htm

Jackson, Robert. 2005. *Classical and Modern Thought on International Relations: From Anarchy to Cosmopolism* (Palgrave Macmillan History of International Thought). New York: Palgrave Macmillan.

Jacques, Peter. 2009. *Environmental Skepticism* (Global Environmental Governance). London: Ashgate.

Janis, Irving and L. Leon Mann. 1977. *Decision-Making: A Psychological Analysis of Conflict, Choice, and Commitment.* New York: Free Press.

Jarausch, Konrad. 2008. *After Hitler: Recivilizing Germans, 1945–1995.* New York: Oxford University Press.

Jenkins, Willis. 2008. *Ecologies of Grace: Environmental Ethics and Christian Theology.* New York: Oxford University Press.

Jervis, Robert. 1976. *Perceptions and Misperceptions in International Politics.* Princeton, NJ: Princeton University Press.

Jervis, Robert. 1982. Security Regimes. *International Organization* 36 (2): 357–78.

Jervis, Robert. 2002. Theories of War in an Era of Leading-Power Peace. *American Political Science Review* 96 (1): 1–14.

Jervis, Robert. 2003. The Compulsive Empire. *Foreign Policy,* August, 137: 82–87.

Joffe, Josef. 2009. The Default Power: The False Prophecy of America's Decline. *Foreign Affairs* 87 (5) September/October: 21–35.

Joffe, Josef. 2013. *The Myth of America's Decline: Politics, Economics, and a Half Century of False Prophecies.* New York, NY: Liveright.

Johnson, Pierre M., Karel Mayrand, and Marc Paquin, eds. 2006. *Governing Global Desertification: Linking*

Environmental Degradation, Poverty, and Participation. London: Ashgate.

Jones, Jeffrey. 2011. Americans Increasingly Prioritize Economy over Environment. March 171. Online at http://www.gallup.com/poll/146681/Americans-Increasingly-Prioritize-Economy-Environment.aspx (accessed June 16, 2015).

Jonsson, Christer and Richard Langhorne. 2004. *Diplomacy*. Thousand Oak, CA: Sage.

Jordan, Darla. 2005. Spokeswoman of the U.S. State Department. Comments on the U.S. Withdrawal from the International Court of Justice. March 10. AFP.

Jost, John and Jim Sidanius. 2004. *Political Psychology: Key Readings*. New York, NY: Psychology Press.

Juhasz, Antonina 2011. Black Tide: *The Devastating Impact of the Gulf Oil Spill*. New York: Wiley.

Kagan, Robert, 2003. *Of Paradise and Power: America and Europe in the New World Order*. New York, NY: Knopf.

Kagan, Robert. 2004a. America's Crisis of Legitimacy. *Foreign Affairs* 83 (2): 65–87.

Kagan, Robert. 2004b. *Of Paradise and Power: America and Europe in the New World Order*. New York: Vintage.

Kagan, Robert. 2012. *The World America Made*. New York, NY: Vintage.

Kagan, Robert. 2012. *The World America Made*. New York: Vintage.

Kahler, Miles and David Lake, eds. 2003. *Governance in a Global Economy: Political Authority in Transition*. Princeton, NJ: Princeton University Press.

Kahneman, Daniel and Amos Tversky. 1979. Prospect Theory: An Analysis of Decisions under Risk. *Econometrica* 47 (2): 263–292.

Kahneman, Daniel, and Amos Tversky. 1972. Subjective Probability: A Judgment of Representativeness. *Cognitive Psychology* 3: 430–454.

Kahnemen, Daniel and Jonathan Renshon. 2007. Why Hawks Win. *Foreign Policy* 158: 34–38.

Kalyvas, Stathis and Laia Balcellis. 2010. International System and Technologies of Rebellion: How the End of the Cold War Shaped Internal Conflict. *American Political Science Review* 104 (3): 415–429.

Kamieniecki, Sheldon and Michael Kraft, eds. 2007. *Business and Environmental Policy: Corporate Interests in the American Political System* (American and Comparative Environmental Policy). Cambridge, MA: MIT Press.

Kane, Thomas. 2006. *Theoretical Roots of U.S. Foreign Policy: Machiavelli and American Unilateralism*. New York: Routledge.

Kant, Immanuel. 2003. *To Perpetual Peace: A Philosophical Sketch*. Indianapolis, IN: Hackett Publishing. Originally published in 1795.

Kaplan, Jeffrey (2012). Terrorist Groups and the New Tribalism: Terrorism's Fifth Wave. New York: Routledge.

Kaplan, Robert. 2012. *The Revenge of Geography: What the Map Tells Us About Coming Conflicts and the Battle Against Fate*. New York: Random House.

Karesh, William and Robert Cook. 2005. The Human-Animal Link. *Foreign Affairs* 84 (4) July–August.

Kaufman, Stuart, Richard Little, and William Wohlforth, eds. 2007. *Balance of Power in World History*. New York: Palgrave Macmillan.

Kavaloski, Vincent C. 1990. Transnational Citizen Peacemaking as Nonviolent Action. *Peace and Change* 15 (2) April: 173–94.

Keck, Margaret and Kathryn Sikkink, eds. 1998. *Activists Beyond Borders: Advocacy Networks in International Politics*. Ithaca, NY: Cornell University Press.

Kello, Lucas. 2013. The Meaning of the Cyber Revolution. *International Security* 38 (2): 7–40.

Kelly, John. 1996. Chapter 6: Lebanon: 1982–1984. In *U.S. and Russian Policymaking with Respect to the Use of Force*, eds. Jeremy Azrael and Emil Payin. Conference Proceedings. Rand Corporation. Online at http://bit.ly/16P1Fc6 (accessed July 18, 2013).

Kemp, William. 2006. *The Renewable Energy Handbook: A Guide to Rural Energy Independence, Off-Grid and Sustainable Living*. Tamworth, Canada: Aztext Press.

Keohane, Robert and Joseph Nye. 1989. *Power and Interdependence*. 2nd edition. New York: Harper-Collins.

Keohane, Robert and Lisa Martin. 1995. The Promise of Institutionalist Theory. *International Security* 20 (1): 39–52.

Keohane, Robert. 1989. *International Institutions and State Power*. London: Westview Press, Inc.

Keohane, Robert. 2003. Political Authority after Intervention: Gradation in Sovereignty. In *Humanitarian Intervention: Ethical, Legal, and Political Dilemmas*, eds. J. L. Holzgrefe and Robert Keohane. New York: Cambridge University Press, 275–298.

Keohane, Robert. 2005. From International to World Politics. *Perspectives on Politics* 3 (2): 316–17.

Kershaw, Ian. 2000. *The Nazi Dictatorship: Problems and Perspectives of Interpretation*. New York: Bloomsbury.

Keynes, John M. 1965. *The General Theory of Employment, Interest and Money.* New York: Harcourt, Brace & World. Originally published in 1936.

Khlevniuk, Oleg. 2008. *Master of the House: Stalin and His Inner Circle.* New Haven, CT: Yale University Press.

Khong, Yuen Foong. 1992. *Analogies at War: Korea, Munich, Dien Bien Phu, and the Vietnam Decisions of 1965.* Princeton, NJ: Princeton University Press.

Kindleberger, Charles. 1973. *The World in Depression: 1929–1939.* Berkeley: University of California Press.

Kirkpatrick, Jeane. 2002. Convention on the Elimination of All Forms of Discrimination against Women. Testimony before the Senate Foreign Relations Committee, Washington, DC. June 13.

Kissinger, Henry. 2001. The Pitfalls of Global Jurisdiction. *Foreign Affairs* 80 (4) July/August: 86–96.

Klein, Aaron J. 2005. *Striking Back: The 1972 Munich Olympics Massacre and Israel's Deadly Response.* New York: Random House.

Koseki, Shoichi. 1998. *The Birth of Japan's Postwar Constitution.* Translated by Ray Moore. Boulder, CO: Westview Press.

Kosterman, Rick and Seymour Feshbach. 1989. Toward a Measure of Patriotic and Nationalistic Attitudes. *Political Psychology* 10 (2): 257–274.

Kowert, P. 1996. Where *Does* the Buck Stop?: Assessing the Impact of Presidential Personality. *Political Psychology* 17 (3): 421–452.

Krauthammer, Charles. 2008. Crooked Roads to Democracy. *The Washington Post.* January 4, A21.

Krueger, Alan. 2007. *What Makes a Terrorist: Economics and the Roots of Terrorism.* Princeton, NJ: Princeton University Press.

Krugman, Paul. 2009. Chinese New Year. *The New York Times,* December 31.

Kuehnast, Kathleen, Chantal de Jonge Oudraat, and Helga Hernes, eds. 2011. *Women and War: Power and Protection in the 21st Century.* Washington, DC: United States Institute of Peace Press.

Kydd, Andrew and Barbara Walter. 2006. The Strategies of Terrorism. *International Security,* 31 (1): 49–80.

Kydd, Andrew and Walter, Barbara. 2006. The Strategies of Terrorism. *International Security,* Vol. 31 (1): 49–80

Kydd, Andrew. 2005. *Trust and Mistrust in International Relations.* Princeton, NJ: Princeton University Press.

Lakoff, Andrew. 2010. Two Regimes of Global Health. *Humanity* 1 (1): 59–79.

Lappe, Frances M., Joseph Collins, and Peter Rosset. 1998. *World Hunger: Twelve Myths.* New York: Grove Press.

Larson, Deborah. 1985. *Origins of Containment.* Princeton, NJ: Princeton University Press.

Larson, Deborah. 1997. *Anatomy of Mistrust: U.S.-Soviet Relations During the Cold War.* Ithaca, NY: Cornell University Press.

Lauterpacht, Hersch. 2011. *The Function of Law in the International Community.* New York: Oxford University Press. Originally published in 1933.

Laver, Michael. 1979. *Playing Politics.* London: Penguin.

Laver, Michael. 1997. *Playing Politics: The Nightmare Continues.* New York: Oxford University Press.

Layne, Christopher. 1994. Kant or Cant: The Myth of the Democratic Peace. *International Security* 19 (2): 5–49.

Le Billon, Philippe. 2006. *Fuelling War: Natural Resources and Armed Conflicts.* New York: Routledge.

Leatherman, Janie. 2011. *Sexual Violence and Armed Conflict.* Cambridge, UK: Polity.

Leffler, Melvyn. 2007. *For the Soul of Mankind: The United States, the Soviet Union, and the Cold War.* New York: Farrar, Straus and Giroux.

Lenin, Vladimir. 1996. *Imperialism as the Highest Stage of Capitalism.* New York: Pluto Press. Originally published in 1916.

Levada Center. 2013. Online at http://bit.ly/19M6xlO (accessed August 1, 2015).

Levada Center. 2015. Various polls referring to the United States. http://www.levada.ru/

Lévesque, Jacques. 1997. *The Enigma of 1989: The USSR and the Liberation of Eastern Europe.* Berkeley: University of California Press.

Levey, David and Stuart Brown. 2005. The Overstretch Myth. *Foreign Affairs* 84 (2) March/April: 2–7.

Levi, Michael, Elizabeth Economy, Shannon O'Neil, and Adam Segal. 2010. Globalizing the Energy Revolution. *Foreign Affairs* 89 (6) November/December: 111–21.

Levi, Michael. 2009. *On Nuclear Terrorism.* Cambridge, MA: Harvard University Press.

Levi, Michael. 2010a. Beyond Copenhagen. *Foreign Affairs.* Postscript. February.

Levi, Michael. 2010b. Reinforcing Climate Promises in Cancun. An Interview. Council on Foreign Relations. November 24. Online at http://www.cfr.org/

publication/23453/reinforcing_climate_promises_in_cancun.html?cid=rss-analysis-briefbackgroundersexp-reinforcing_climate_promises_i-112410 (accessed September 25, 2012).

Levi, Michael. 2013. *The Power Surge: Energy, Opportunity, and the Battle for America's Future*. New York: Oxford University Press.

Levi, Michael. 2014. The Obama-China Climate Deal Can't Save the World. So What? *Council of Foreign Relations*, November 21. Online at: http://www.cfr.org/environmental-policy/obama-china-climate-deal-cant-save-world-so-/p33831 (accessed March 29, 2015).

Levitsky, Steven and Lucan Way. 2010. *Competitive Authoritarianism: Hybrid Regimes After the Cold War*. New York: Cambridge University Press.

Levy, David. 2009. *Tools of Critical Thinking: Meta-Thoughts for Psychology*. Long Grove, IL: Waveland Press.

Levy, Jack. 1984. The Offensive/Defensive Balance of Military Technology: A Theoretical and Historical Analysis. *International Studies Quarterly* 28 (2) June: 219–238.

Liberman, Peter. 2006. An Eye for an Eye: Public Support for War against Evildoers. *International Organization* 60 (3) July: 687–722.

Lieven, Anatol and John Hulsman. 2006. *Ethical Realism: A Vision for America's Role in the World*. New York: Pantheon.

Lindkvist, Sven. 2007. *Terra Nullius: A Journey Through No One's Land*. New York: New Press.

Linklater, Andrew. 2009. The English School. In *Theories of International Relations*, ed. Scott Burchill et al. New York: Palgrave Macmillan, 86–110.

List, Friedrich. 2006. *National System of Political Economy. Volume 1: The History*. New York: Cosimo Classics. Originally published in 1841.

Lomborg, Bjørn, ed. 2004. *Global Crises, Global Solutions*. Cambridge, UK: Cambridge University Press.

Lomborg, Bjørn. 2007. *Cool It: The Skeptical Environmentalist's Guide to Global Warming*. New York: Knopf.

Lomborg, Bjørn. 2010. An Interview. *Financial Times*, December 9. Online at http://www.lomborg.com/news/financial-times-europe-needs-real-vision-on-climate (accessed August 1, 2015).

Lomborg, Bjørn. 2010a. *Smart Solutions to Climate Change, Comparing Costs and Benefits*. New York, NY: Cambridge University Press.

Lovelock, James. 2015. *A Rough Ride to the Future*. New York, NY: Overlook Books.

Loyola, Mario. 2010. Legality over Legitimacy. *Foreign Affairs* 89 (4) July–August. Online at http://fam.ag/13TtFQO (accessed July 18, 2013).

Luck, Edward. 2010. The Responsibility to Protect: Growing Pains or Early Promise? *Ethics & International Affairs* 24 (4): 349–65.

Lundestad, Geir. 1986. Empire by Invitation? The United States and Western Europe, 1945–1952. *Journal of Peace Research* 23 (3) September: 263–277.

Lundestad, Geir. 2012. *The Rise and Decline of the American "Empire": Power and its Limits in Comparative Perspective*. New York: Oxford University Press.

Lynn, William J. 2010. Defending a New Domain. The Pentagon's Cyberstrategy. *Foreign Affairs* 89 (5) September/October: 97–108.

MacMillan, Margaret. 2003. *Paris 1919: Six Months That Changed the World*. New York: Random House.

MacNair, Rachel. 2003. *The Psychology of Peace: An Introduction*. Santa Barbara, CA: Praeger.

Maddox, Bronwen. 2001. Japan Dips Toe in Military Waters. *Times* (London), November 29: News 1.

Madeley, John. 2009. *Big Business, Poor Peoples: How Transnational Corporations Damage the Global Poor*. London: Zed Books.

Madigan, Janet. 2007. *Truth, Politics, and Universal Human Rights*. New York: Palgrave Macmillan.

Magdoff, Fred and John B. Foster. 2011. *What Every Environmentalist Needs to Know about Capitalism*. New York: Monthly Review Press.

Mahbubani, Kishore. 2002. *Can Asians Think? Understanding the Divide Between East and West*. South Royalton, VT: Steerforth.

Mahler, Gregory. 2004. *Politics and Government in Israel: The Maturation of a Modern State*. Lanham, MD: Rowman & Littlefield.

Mak, Geert. 2008. *In Europe: Travels Through the Twentieth Century*. New York: Vintage.

Malloy, Michael. 2015. ed. *Economic Sanctions*. Cheltenham, UK: Elgar Research Collection.

Mansfield, Edward D. and Jack Snyder. 2007. *Electing to Fight: Why Emerging Democracies Go to War*. Cambridge, MA: MIT Press.

Maoz, Zeev and Bruce Russett. 1993. Normative and Structural Causes of Democratic Peace, 1946–1986. *The American Political Science Review* 87 (3): 624–638.

Marrar, Khalil. 2008. *The Arab Lobby and U.S. Foreign Policy*. New York: Routledge.

Marsh, Peter. 2012. *The New Industrial Revolution: Consumers, Globalization, and the End of the Mass Production.* New Haven, CT: Yale University Press.

Martin, Terry. 2001. *The Affirmative Action Empire: Nations and Nationalism in the Soviet Union, 1923–1939.* Ithaca, NY: Cornell University Press.

Marx, Karl and Friedrich Engels. 2011. *The Communist Manifesto.* SoHo Books. Originally published in 1848.

Matthews, Jessica. 1997. Power Shift. *Foreign Affairs* 76 (1): 50–66.

Mazower, Mark. 2000. *Dark Continent: Europe's Twentieth Century.* New York: Vintage.

McCallum, M. L., and G. W. Bury. 2013. Google Search Patterns Suggest Declining Interest in the Environment. *Biodiversity and Conservation.* Published online March 30. Online at: http://link.springer.com/article/10.1007%2Fs10531-013-0476-6#page-1 (accessed March 30, 2015).

McCarthy, Michael. 2011. Global Warning: Climate Sceptics Are Winning the Battle. *The Independent*, October 11. Online at http://ind.pn/oakpOW (accessed July 18, 2013).

McDonald, Bryan. 2011. *Food Security.* Cambridge, UK: Polity.

McFarlane, Robert. 1998. An Interview. In *Cold War: The Complete Series. Episode: Star Wars. Warner Home Video*, 2012.

McFaul, Michael. 2009. *Advancing Democracy Abroad: Why We Should and How We Can.* New York: Rowman & Littlefield.

McGovern, Joe. 2006. *The Kyoto Protocol.* Pittsburgh, PA: Dorrance Publishing Co.

McKinnon, Ron. 2010. A Reply to Krugman. *International Economy*, Winter.

McNamara, Robert. 1996. *In Retrospect: The Tragedy and Lessons of Vietnam.* New York: Vintage.

Mearsheimer, John and Stephen Walt. 2007. *The Israel Lobby and U.S. Foreign Policy.* New York: Farrar, Straus and Giroux.

Mearsheimer, John J. 2014. Why the Ukraine Crisis is the West's Fault: The Liberal Delusions That Provoked Putin. *Foreign Affairs*, September/October, 93 (5), 77–89.

Mearsheimer, John. 1990. Why We Will Soon Miss the Cold War. *The Atlantic Monthly* 266 (2) August: 35–50.

Mearsheimer, John. 2003. *The Tragedy of Great Power Politics.* New York: W. W. Norton & Company.

Meyerson, Harold. 2010. Time to Stand Up to China on Trade. *The Washington Post*, September 15, 23.

Miéville, China. 2006. *Between Equal Rights: A Marxist Theory of International Law.* Chicago: Haymarket Books.

Milgram, Stanley. 1963. Behavioral Study of Obedience. *Journal of Abnormal and Social Psychology* 67 (4): 371–378.

Miller, Martin. 2013. *The Foundations of Modern Terrorism: State, Society and the Dynamics of Political Violence.* New York: Cambridge University Press.

Mitzen, Jennifer. 2005. Reading Habermas in Anarchy: Multilateral Diplomacy and Global Public Spheres. *American Political Science Review* 99 (3): 401–417.

Mohamoud, Abdullah. 2006. *State Collapse and Post-Conflict Development in Africa: The Case of Somalia 1960–2001.* West Lafayette, IN: Purdue University Press.

Monroe, James. 1823. Seventh Annual Message to Congress, December 2. Online at http://miller center.org/president/ speeches/detail/3604 (accessed June 15, 2015).

Moore, Scott. 2014. Pollution Without Revolution. *Foreign Affairs*. June 10. Online at: http://www.foreignaffairs.com/articles/141559/scott-m-moore/pollution-without-revolution (accessed March 29, 2015).

Moravcsik, Andrew. 1997. Taking Preferences Seriously: A Liberal Theory of International Relations. *International Organization* 51 (4): 513–53.

Moravcsik, Andrew. 2001. Why Is the U.S. Human Rights Policy So Unilateralist? In *Multilateralism and U.S. Foreign Policy*, eds. Stewart Patrick and Shepard Forman. Boulder, CO: Lynne Rienner.

Moravcsik, Andrew. 2001. Why Is the US Human Rights Policy So Unilateralist? In *Multilateralism and U.S. Foreign Policy*, ed. Stewart Patrick and Shepard Forman. Boulder, CO: Lynne Rienner Publishers.

Morgenthau, Hans J. 2006. *Politics among Nations: The Struggle for Power and Peace.* 7th edition, revised by Kenneth W. Thompson and W. David Clinton. New York: McGraw-Hill. Originally published 1948.

Morgenthau, Hans. 1978. *Politics Among Nations: The Struggle for Power and Peace*, 5th edition, Revised, New York: Alfred A. Knopf.

Morris, Ian. 2010. *Why the West Rules—For Now: The Patterns of History and What They Reveal about the Future.* New York: Farrar, Straus and Giroux.

Moyo, Dambisa. 2010. *Dead Aid: Why Aid is Not Working and How There Is a Better Way for Africa.* Vancouver, BC: Douglas & McIntyre Ltd.

Mral, Bridgitte, Majid Krosravnik,, and Ruth Wodak. Eds. 2013. *Right-Wing Populism in Europe: Politics and Discourse.* New York: Bloomsbury Academic.

Mueller, John. 1989. *Retreat from Doomsday: The Obsolescence of Major War.* New York: Basic Books.

Muller, Jerry. 2008. Us and Them: The Enduring Power of Ethnic Nationalism. *Foreign Affairs* 87 (22) March/April: 18–35.

Munz, Rainer. 2003. *Diasporas and Ethnic Migrants: Germany, Israel and Russia in Comparative Perspective.* London, UK: Routledge.

Murray, Henry. 1943. *Analysis of the Personality of Adolf Hitler: With Predictions of His Future Behavior and Suggestions for Dealing with Him Now and After Germany's Surrender.* October. Cornell University Law Library. Online at http://library2.lawschool .cornell.edu/donovan/pdf/Batch_15/Vol_XC.pdf (accessed August 1, 2015).

Murray, Iain. 2008. *The Really Inconvenient Truths: Seven Environmental Catastrophes Liberals Don't Want You to Know About—Because They Helped Cause Them.* Washington, DC: Regnery Publishing.

Myers-Lipton, Scott 2015. Ending Extreme Inequality: An Economic Bill of Rights to Eliminate Poverty. Boulder, CO: Paradigm Publishers.

Nacos, Brigitte, Robert Shapiro, and Pierangelo Isernia, eds. 2000. *Decision-Making in the Glass House.* Boulder, CO: Rowman & Littlefield.

Nacos, Brigitte. 2009. *Terrorism and Counterterrorism. Understanding Threats and Responses in the Post–9/11 World.* 3rd edition. New York: Longman.

NAF (New America Foundation). 2012. The Year of the Drone. An Analysis of U.S. Drone Strikes in Pakistan, 2004–2012. Online at http://counter-terrorism.newamerica.net/drones (accessed August 8, 2012).

Naimark, Norman. 2002. *Fires of Hatred: Ethnic Cleansing in Twentieth Century Europe.* Cambridge, MA: Harvard University Press.

Narizny, Kevin. 2003. Both Guns and Butter, or Neither: Class Interests in the Political Economy of Rearmament. *American Political Science Review* 97 (2): 203–220.

Narlikar, Amrita. 2005. *WTO: A Very Short Introduction.* New York: Oxford University Press.

National Commission on Terrorist Acts upon the United States. 9-11 Commission Report. November 27, 2002. Online at http://www.9-11commission .gov/report/index.htm (accessed September 25, 2012).

Nau, Henry. 2002. *At Home Abroad: Identity and Power in American Foreign Policy.* Ithaca, NY: Cornell University Press.

Nelson, Anna Kasten. 1992. Review of the American "Empire": And Other Studies of U.S. Foreign Policy in a Comparative Perspective by Geir Lundestad. *The American Historical Review* 97 (2): 641–642.

Neumann, Iver. 1996. *Russia and the Idea of Europe: A Study in Identity and International Relations.* London: Routledge.

Newman, Edward, Ramesh Thakur, and John Tirman. 2006. *Multilateralism Under Challenge?: Power, International Order, and Structural Change.* Tokyo: United Nations University Press.

Nonini, Donald, ed. 2007. *The Global Idea of "The Commons."* New York: Berghahn Books.

Nordhaus, Richard. 2008. *A Question of Balance: Weighing the Options on Global Warming Policies.* New Haven, CT: Yale University Press.

Nye, Joseph. 1990. *Bound to Lead: The Changing Nature of American Power.* New York: Basic Books.

Nye, Joseph. 2002. *The Paradox of American Power: Why the World's Only Superpower Can't Go It Alone.* Oxford, UK: Oxford University Press.

Nye, Joseph. 2004. *Soft Power: The Means to Success in World Politics.* New York: Public Affairs.

O'Brien, Patrick Karl and Armand Clesse, eds. 2002. *Two Hegemonies: Britain 1846–1914 and the United States 1941–2001.* Aldershot, UK: Ashgate.

Olson, Mancur. 1971. *The Logic of Collective Action: Public Goods and the Theory of Groups.* Cambridge, MA: Harvard University Press.

Oneal, John R. and Bruce M. Russett. 1997. Classical Liberals Were Right: Democracy, Interdependence, and Conflict, 1950–1985. *International Studies Quarterly* 42 (2) June: 264–294.

Oppenheim, Lassa. 2008. *Oppenheim's International Law.* 9th edition, eds. Robert Jennings and Arthur Watts. New York: Oxford University Press.

Orbinski, James. 2009. *An Imperfect Offering: Humanitarian Action for the Twenty-First Century.* New York: Walker & Company.

Organski, A. F. K. 1968. *World Politics.* New York: A. Knopf. Originally published 1958.

Osnos, Evan. 2014. The Biden Agenda. *The New Yorker*, July 28. Online at: http://www.newyorker.com/magazine/2014/07/28/biden-agenda (accessed August 1, 2015).

Owen, John M. 2005. Iraq and the Democratic Peace. *Foreign Affairs* 84 (6) November/December.

Page, Benjamin and Robert Shapiro. 1988. Foreign Policy and the Rational Public. *Journal of Conflict Resolution*. 32: 211–47.

Pant, Harsh. 2011. China and Pakistan: A New Balance of Power in South Asia. *ISN: International Relations and Security Network*. June 20. Online at http://bit.ly/1VTGzpE (accessed August 1, 2015).

Pape, Robert. 2003. The Strategic Logic of Suicide Terrorism. *American Political Science Review* 97 (3): 343–361.

Parker, Kathleen. 2010. Obama, Our First Female President. *The Washington Post*, June 30. Online at http://wapo.st/cHTwjC (accessed July 15, 2013).

Parmesan, Camille and Gary Yohe. 2003. A Globally Coherent Fingerprint of Climate Change Impacts across Natural Systems. *Nature* 421: 37–42.

Patterson, Amy. 2006. *The Politics of AIDS in Africa*. Boulder, CO: Lynne Rienner.

Payne, Ruby. 2013. A Framework for Understanding Poverty; A Cognitive Approach. Highlands, TX: aha! Process.

Pearce, Fred. 2007. *When the Rivers Run Dry: Water— The Defining Crisis of the Twenty-First Century*. Boston, MA: Beacon Press.

Peçanha, Sergio and Tim Wallace. 2015. The Flight of Refugees Around the Globe. *The New York Times*, June 20. Online at www.nytimes.com/interactive/2015/06/21/world/map-flow-desperate-migration-refugee-crisis.html (accessed June 22, 2015).

Peerenboom, Randall. 2008. *China Modernizes: Threat to the West or Model for the Rest?* Oxford, UK: Oxford University Press.

Peet, Richard. 2009. *Unholy Trinity: The IMF, World Bank and WTO*. 2nd edition. London: Zed Books.

Pelligrini, Dominick, ed. 2010. *Nuclear Weapons' Role in 21st Century U.S. Policy*. Hauppage, NY: Nova Science.

Peters, Anny, Maja Micevska-Scharf, Francien Van Driel, and Willy Jansen. 2010. Where Does Public Funding For HIV Prevention Go To? The Case of Condoms versus Microbicides and Vaccines. *Globalization and Health* 6 (1): 23. Online at http://www.globalizationandhealth.com/content/6/1/23 (accessed September 25, 2012).

Pew Research Center. 2009. U.S. Seen as Less Important, China as More Powerful. December 3. Online at http://bit.ly/10Op1jG (accessed July 19, 2013).

Pew Research Center. 2010. Americans Spending More Time Following the News: Ideological News Sources: Who Watches and Why. September 12. Online at http://bit.ly/rlXOQ8 (accessed July 19, 2013).

Pew Research Center. 2011. Confidence in Osama bin Laden. Online at http://www.pewglobal.org/2011/05/02/osama-bin-laden-largely-discredited-among-muslim-publics-in-recent-years/ (accessed August 1, 2015).

Pew Research Center. 2013. Climate Change and Financial Instability Seen as Top Global Threats. Online at: http://www.pewglobal.org/2013/06/24/climate-change-and-financial-instability-seen-as-top-global-threats/ (accessed March 30, 2015).

Pew Research Center. 2013a. *Muslim Publics Share Concerns about Extremist* Groups. Online at http://www.pewglobal.org/2013/09/10/muslim-publics-share-concerns-about-extremist-groups/ (accessed April 12, 2015).

Pew Research Center. 2014. How Social Media is Reshaping News. Online at http://www.pewresearch.org/fact-tank/2014/09/24/how-social-media-is-reshaping-news/ (accessed February 19, 2015).

Pew Research Center. 2014a. Americans: Disengaged, Feeling Less Respected, but Still See U.S. as World's Military Superpower. Online at http://www.pewresearch.org/fact-tank/2014/04/01/americans-disengaged-feeling-less-respected-but-still-see-u-s-as-worlds-military-superpower/

Pew Research Center. 2015. How Americans View the Top Energy and Environmental Issues. Online at: http://www.pewresearch.org/key-data-points/environment-energy-2/ (accessed March 29, 2015).

Philippides, Marios, ed. 2007. *Mehmed II the Conqueror and the Fall of the Franco-Byzantine Levant to the Ottoman Turks: Some Western Views and Testimonies (Medieval and Renaissance Texts and Studies)*. Amherst: University of Massachusetts Press.

Phuong, Catherine. 2010. *The International Protection of Internally Displaced Persons*. New York: Cambridge University Press.

Pielke, Roger. 2010. *The Climate Fix: What Scientists and Politicians Won't Tell You About Global Warming*. New York: Basic Books.

Pillar, Paul. 2001. *Terrorism and U.S. Foreign Policy*. Washington, D.C.: Brookings Institution Press.

Pin-Lin, Chong. 2010. Can China Become the World's Engine for Growth? Symposium contribution. *International Economy*, Winter: 10.

Plaut, Martin. 2010. Ethiopia Famine Aid "Spent on Weapons." *BBC News*. March 3. Online at http://news.bbc.co.uk/2/hi/8535189.stm (accessed September 25, 2012).

Plokhy, S. M. 2010. *Yalta: The Price of Peace*. New York: Viking Adult.

Pohlman, Edward. 2013. China's "One Child": Policy, Population, Pollution, Protest. Albany, New York: Planet Ethics Press.

Polman, Linda. 2010. *The Crisis Caravan: What's Wrong with Humanitarian Aid?* New York: Metropolitan Books.

Post, Jerrold. 1990. Explaining Saddam Hussein: a Psychological Profile. Presented to the House Armed Services Committee. December 1990. http://www.au.af.mil/au/awc/awcgate/iraq/saddam_post.htm

Post, Jerrold. 2004. *Leaders and Their Followers in a Dangerous World: The Psychology of Political Behavior* (Psychoanalysis and Social Theory). Ithaca, NY: Cornell University Press.

Post, Jerrold. 2005a. The New Face of Terrorism: Socio-Cultural Foundations of Contemporary Terrorism. *Behavioral Sciences and the Law* 23(4): 451–65.

Post, Jerrold. 2005b. When Hatred is Bred in the Bone: Psycho-Cultural Foundations of Contemporary Terrorism. *Journal of Political Psychology* 26 (4): 615–36.

Post, Jerrold. 2008. *The Mind of the Terrorist. The Psychology of Terrorism from the IRA to al-Qaeda*. New York: Palgrave Macmillan.

Power, Samantha. 2002. *A Problem from Hell: America and the Age of Genocide*. New York: Basic Books.

Prebisch, Raúl. 1989. *Antología del pensamiento político, social y económico de América Latina* (In Spanish). Buenos Aires: Ediciones de Cultura Hispánica.

Priest, Dana and William Arkin. 2010a. A Hidden World, Growing Beyond Control. *The Washington Post*. July 19, A7.

Priest, Dana and William Arkin. 2010b. National Security, Inc. *The Washington Post*, July 20, A1.

Priest, Dana and William Arkin. 2011. *Top Secret America: The Rise of the New American Security State*. Boston: Little, Brown, and Co.

Primakov, Evgeny. 2009. *Russia and the Arabs: Behind the Scenes in the Middle East from the Cold War to the Present*. New York: Basic Books.

Putnam, Robert. 1988. Diplomacy and Domestic Politics: The Logic of Two-Level Games, *International Organization* 42 (3): 427–60.

Queenan, Jeri. 2013. Global NGOs Spend More on Accounting Than Multinationals. *Harvard Business Review*. April 23, Online at: https://hbr.org/2013/04/the-efficiency-trap-of-global (accessed March 5, 2015).

Qutb, Sayyid. 2007. *Milestones*. Chicago, IL: Kazi Publications. Originally published in 1964.

Ramet, Sabrina. 2005. *Thinking about Yugoslavia: Scholarly Debates about the Yugoslav Breakup and the Wars in Bosnia and Kosovo*. New York: Cambridge University Press.

Rankin, Jennifer. 2010. Rules on Unusual Food Heading to Arbitration. *EuropeanVoice.com*. July 1. Online at http://www.europeanvoice.com/article/imported/rules-on-unusual-food-heading-to-arbitration/68372.aspx (accessed September 25, 2012).

Rapkin, David P. and Jonathan R. Strand. 2006. Reforming the IMF's Weighted Voting System. *The World Economy* 29 (3): 305–24.

Rapoport, David. 2004. The Four Waves of Terrorism. In *Attacking Terrorism*, eds. Audrey Cronin and James Ludes, Washington DC: Germantown University Press.

Rashid, Ahmed. 2008. *Descent into Chaos: The United States and the Failure of Nation Building in Pakistan, Afghanistan, and Central Asia*. New York: Viking Adult.

Reardon, Betty. 1985. *Sexism and the War System*. New York: Teachers College Press.

Rechkemmer, Andreas. 2004. *Postmodern Global Governance: The United Nations Convention to Combat Desertification*. Baden-Baden, Germany: Nomos Verlagsgesellschaft.

Reeves, Richard. 2001. *President Nixon: Alone in the White House*. New York: Simon & Schuster.

Renshon, Stanley. 2004. *In His Father's Shadow: The Transformations of George W. Bush*. New York: Palgrave Macmillan.

Renshon, Stanley. 2009. National Security in the Obama Administration: Reassessing the Bush Doctrine. New York: Routledge.

Renshon, Stanley. 2011. *Barack Obama and the Politics of Redemption*. New York: Routledge.

Reus-Smit, Christian. 2009. Constructivism. In *Theories of International Relations*, 4th edition, ed. Scott Burchill et al. New York: Palgrave Macmillan, 212–36.

Rey, Marie-Pierre. 2004. Europe Is Our Common Home. A Study of Gorbachev's Diplomatic Concept. *Cold War History* 4 (2): 33–65.

Rey, Marie-Pierre. 2008. The USSR and the Helsinki Process, 1969–75: Optimism, Doubt, or Defiance?

In *Origins of the European Security System. The Helsinki Process Revisited, 1965–1975*, eds. Andreas Wenger, Vojtech Mastny, and Christian Nuenlist. New York: Routledge Press.

Reynolds, John. 2012. *Deterring and Responding to Asymmetrical Threats*. BiblioScholar.

Rieff, David. 2006. *At the Point of a Gun: Democratic Dreams and Armed Intervention*. New York: Simon & Schuster.

Ritchie, Elspeth Cameron, Patricia Watson, and Mathew Friedman, eds. 2005. *Interventions Following Mass Violence and Disasters: Strategies for Mental Health Practice*. New York: The Guilford Press.

Roan, Sharon. 1989. *Ozone Crisis: The 15-Year Evolution of a Sudden Global Emergency*. Hoboken, NJ: Wiley.

Roberts, Adam. 2000. The So-Called "Right" of Humanitarian Intervention. *Yearbook of International Humanitarian Law* 3: 3–51.

Roberts, J. Timmons and Bradley Parks. 2006. *A Climate of Injustice: Global Inequality, North-South Politics, and Climate Policy*. Cambridge, MA: MIT Press.

Rogers, Peter, Kazi F. Jalal, and John Boyd. 2007. *An Introduction to Sustainable Development*. New York: Routledge.

Rogowski, Ronald. 1990. *Commerce and Coalitions: How Trade Affects Domestic Political Alignments*. Princeton, NJ: Princeton University Press.

Rooney, Ben. 2015. Best and Worst Countries for Women on Corporate Boards. *CNN Money*. Online at http://money.cnn.com/2015/01/13/news/companies/women-corporate-board-global/ (accessed April 17, 2015).

Rosenau, James, Ernst-Ulrich von Weizsäcker and Ulrich Petschow, eds. 2005. *Governance and Sustainability. Exploring the Roadmap to Sustainability after Johannesburg*. Sheffield: Greenleaf Publishing.

Rosenau, James. 1961. *Public Opinion and Foreign Policy: An Operational Formation*. New York: Random House.

Rosenau, James. 1999. Toward an Ontology for Global Governance. In *Approaches to Global Governance Theory*, eds. Martin Hewson and Timothy J. Sinclair. Albany: State University of New York.

Roth, John and Carol Rittner, ed. 2012. *Rape: Weapon of War and Genocide*. St. Paul, Minnesota: Paragon House.Ruggie, John. 2013. *Just Business: Multinational Corporations and Human Rights*. New York: Norton.

Royle, Trevor. 2004. *Crimea: The Great Crimean War, 1854–1856*. New York: Palgrave Macmillan.

Ruggie, John. 2013. *Just Business: Multinational Corporations and Human Rights*. New York: Norton.

Russet, Bruce and John Oneal. 2001. *Triangulating Peace: Democracy, Interdependence, and International Organizations*. New York: W.W. Norton.

Rynning, Sren and Jens Ringsmose. 2008. Why Are Revisionist States Revisionist? Reviving Classical Realism as an Approach to Understanding International Change. *International Politics* 45 (1): 19–39.

Sachs, Jeffrey. 2005. *The End of Poverty: Economic Possibilities for Our Time*. New York: Penguin Press.

Sachs, Jeffrey. 2015. *The Age of Sustainable Development*. New York: Columbia University Press.

Sageman, Marc. 2004. *Understanding Terror Networks*. Philadelphia: University of Pennsylvania Press.

Said, Edward. 1994. *Culture and Imperialism*. New York: Vintage.

Samuel, Katja. 2013. *The OIC, the UN, and Counter-Terrorism Law-Making: Conflicting or Cooperative Legal Orders?* Oxford, UK: Hart.

Sanford, George. 2009. *Katyn and the Soviet Massacre of 1940: Truth, Justice, and Memory*. New York: Routledge.

Sapolsky, Robert M. 2006. A Natural History of Peace. *Foreign Affairs* 85 (1) January/February: 104–120.

Saradzhyan, Simon. 2010. Chechnya: Divisions in the Ranks. *ISN: International Relations and Security Network*. August 11. Online at http://www.isn.ethz.ch/isn/Current-Affairs/Security-Watch/Detail/?lng=en&id=120017 (accessed September 20, 2012).

Sarkesian, Sam C., John Allen Williams, and Stephen J. Cimbala. 2007. *U.S. National Security: Policymakers, Processes and Politics*. 4th edition. Boulder, CO: Lynne Rienner.

Sarotte, Mary. 2009. *1989: The Struggle to Create Post-Cold War Europe*. Princeton, NJ: Princeton University Press.

Sathasivam, Kanishkan. 2005. *Uneasy Neighbors: India, Pakistan and U.S. Foreign Policy*. London: Ashgate.

Schein, Virginia E. 2002. A Global Look at Psychological Barriers to Women's Progress in Management. *Journal of Social Issues* 57 (4): 675–88.

Schellnhuber, Hans-Joachim, Gary Yohe, Wolfgang Cramer, Tom Wigley, Nebojsa Nakicenovic, eds. 2006. *Avoiding Dangerous Climate Change*. Cambridge, UK: Cambridge University Press.

Schlesinger, Stephen. 2003. *Act of Creation: The Founding of the United Nations: A Story of Superpowers,*

Secret Agents, Wartime Allies and Enemies and Their Quest for a Peaceful World. Boulder, CO: Westview Press.

Schmidt, Gustav, ed. 2001. *A History of NATO—The First Fifty Years: Three-Volume Set*. New York: Palgrave Macmillan.

Schulte, Constanze. 2005. *Compliance with Decisions of the International Court of Justice*. New York: Oxford University Press.

Schultz, Richard. 2004. Showstoppers: Nine Reasons Why We Never Sent Our Special Operation Forces after al Qaeda before 9/11. *Weekly Standard*, January 26, 25–33.

Schweller, Randall. 1997. New Realist Research on Alliances: Refining, Not Refuting, Waltz's Balancing Proposition. *American Political Science Review* 91 (4): 913–17.

Schweller, Randall. 2008. *Unanswered Threats: Political Constrains on the Balance of Power*. Princeton, NJ: Princeton University Press.

Scott, Bruce. 2001. The Great Divide in the Global Village. *Foreign Affairs* 80 (1) January/February: 160–77.

Scully, Eileen. 2001. *Bargaining with the State from Afar*. New York: Columbia University Press.

Sears, David, Leonie Huddy, and Robert Jervis, eds. 2003. *Oxford Handbook on Political Psychology*. New York: Oxford University Press.

Sen, Amartya. 1981. *Poverty and Famines: An Essay on Entitlement and Deprivation*. Oxford, UK: Oxford University Press.

Shah, Anup. 2014. Foreign Aid for Development Assistance. September 28. Online at http://www.globalissues.org/article/35/foreign-aid-development-assistance (accessed March 30, 2015).

Shahan, Cynthia. 2014. China Puts Billions Into Electric Cars & EV Charging Stations. *Clean Technica*, December 24. Online at http://cleantechnica.com/2014/12/24/china-puts-billions-electric-cars-ev-charging-stations (accessed March 30, 2015).

Shapiro, Judith. 2001. *Mao's War against Nature: Politics and the Environment in Revolutionary China*. New York: Cambridge University Press.

Sharp, Paul. 2009. *Diplomatic Theory of International Relations* (Cambridge Studies in International Relations Series). New York: Cambridge University Press.

Shelley, Louise. 2010. *Human Trafficking: A Global Perspective*. New York: Cambridge University Press.

Shepard, Todd. 2006. *The Invention of Decolonization*. Ithaca, NY: Cornell University Press.

Shiraev, Eric and David Levy. 2013. *Cross-Cultural Psychology: Critical Thinking and Contemporary Applications*. 5th edition. Boston: Allyn and Bacon.

Shiraev, Eric and Richard Sobel. 2006. *People and Their Opinions: Thinking Critically about Public Opinion*. New York: Longman.

Shiraev, Eric. 2013. *Russian Government and Politics*. 2nd edition. New York: Palgrave Macmillan.

Shirer, William. 1990. *The Rise and Fall of the Third Reich: A History of Nazi Germany*. New York: Simon & Schuster.

Shlapentokh, Vladimir, Eric Shiraev, and Eero Carroll. 2008. *The Soviet Union. Internal and External Perspectives on Soviet Society*. New York: Palgrave Macmillan.

Simon, Steven and Jeff Martini. 2004. Terrorism: Denying al Qaeda Its Popular Support. *The Washington Quarterly* 28 (1) Winter: 131–45.

Simons, Marlise. 2013. U.S. Grows More Helpful to International Criminal Court, a Body It First Scorned. *The New York Times*, April 2. Online at http://nyti.ms/1M8M9ww (accessed March 5, 2015).

Singer, Burt, Awash Teklehaimanot, Andrew Spielman, Al Schapira, and Yesim Tozan, eds., Jeffrey D. Sachs, series editor. 2005. *Coming to Grips with Malaria in the New Millennium*. London, UK: Earthscan.

Singer, Hans W. 1999. *Growth, Development and Trade: Selected Essays of Hans W. Singer*. Northhampton, MA: Edward Elgar Publishing.

Singh, Michael. 2010. Iran Re-Revolution: How the Green Movement Is Repeating Iranian History. *Foreign Affairs*. July 26. Online at http://fam.ag/aQJunk (accessed September 25, 2012). Registration is required. Another version is available online at http://bit.ly/1bwKeUK (accessed July 16, 2013).

Sjoberg, Laura, ed. 2009. *Gender and International Security: Feminist Perspectives*. New York: Routledge.

Sloan, Stanley. 2010. *Permanent Alliance?: NATO and the Transatlantic Bargain from Truman to Obama*. New York: Continuum.

Sloan, Stephen. 2006. *Terrorism: The Present Threat in Context*. London: Berg Publishers.

Smith, Adam. 1977. *An Inquiry into the Nature and Causes of the Wealth of Nations*. Chicago: University of Chicago Press.

Smith, Jeff. 2013. *Cold Peace: China-India Rivalry in the Twenty-First Century*. Plymouth, UK: Lexington Books.

Smith, Peter and Shalom Schwartz. 1997. Values. In *Handbook of Cross-Cultural Psychology*, vol. 3, eds. J. Berry, M. Segall, and C. Kagitcibasi. Boston, MA: Allyn & Bacon, 77–118.

Sniderman, Paul, Louk Hagendoorn, and Markus Prior. 2004. Predisposing Factors and Situational Triggers: Exclusionary Reactions to Immigrant Minorities. *American Political Science Review* 98 (1): 35–50.

Snyder, Jack. 2000. *From Voting to Violence. Democratization and Nationalist Violence.* New York: W. W. Norton.

Snyder, Jack. 2005. *Electing to Fight: Why Emerging Democracies Go to War.* Cambridge, MA: MIT Press.

Snyder-Hall, R. Claire. 2010. Third-Wave Feminism and the Defense of "Choice." *Perspectives on Politics* 8 (1): 255–61.

Sobek, David. 2008. *Causes of War.* Cambridge, UK: Polity.

Sobel, Richard and Eric Shiraev, eds. 2003. *International Public Opinion and the Bosnia Crisis.* Lanham, MD: Lexington Books.

Sobel, Richard. 2001. *The Impact of Public Opinion on U.S. Foreign Policy Since Vietnam.* New York: Oxford University Press.

Soetaert, Wim and Erik Vandamme, eds. 2009. *Biofuels.* West Sussex, UK: Wiley.

Soeters, Joseph. 2005. *Ethnic Conflict and Terrorism: The Origins and Dynamics of Civil Wars.* New York: Routledge.

Spector, Bertram, ed. 2005. *Fighting Corruption in Developing Countries: Strategies and Analysis.* Bloomfield, CT: Kumarian Press.

Spector, Stephen. 2008. *Evangelicals and Israel: The Story of American Christian Zionism.* New York: Oxford University Press.

Spivak, Gayatri Chakravorty. 1999. *A Critique of Post-Colonial Reason: Toward a History of the Vanishing Present.* Cambridge, MA: Harvard University |Press.

Steinbruner, John, D. 1974. *The Cybernetic Theory of Decision: New Dimensions of Political Analysis.* Princeton, NJ: Princeton University Press.

Stern, Jessica and J. M. Berger. 2015. *ISIS: The State of Terror.* New York: Ecco.

Stern, Jessica and J.M. Berger (2015). *ISIS: The State of Terror.* New york: Ecco.

Stern, Jessica. 2010. Mind over Martyr: How to De-radicalize Islamist Extremists. *Foreign Affairs* 89 (1) January/February: 95–108.

Stern, Nicholas. 2007. *The Economics of Climate Change: The Stern Review.* Cambridge, UK: Cambridge University Press.

Stewart, William. 2006. *How to Prepare for a Pandemic and Other Extended Disasters.* Charleston, SC: BookSurge Publishing.

Stiehm, Judith. 2009. Theses on the Military, Security, War and Women. In *Gender and International Security: Feminist Perspectives*, ed. Laura Sjoberg. New York: Routledge, 17–23.

Stiglitz, Joseph. 2002. *Globalization and Its Discontents.* New York: W. W. Norton & Company.

Stiglitz, Joseph. 2011. The Price of 9/11. *Economist's View.* September 1. Online at http://economistsview.typepad.com/economistsview/2011/09/stiglitz-the-price-of-911.html (accessed September 24, 2012).

Stoddard, Abby. 2006. *Humanitarian Alert: NGO Information and its Impact on U.S. Foreign Policy.* Bloomfield, CT: Kumarian Press.

Strand, Jonathan. 2013. *Regional Development Banks: Lending with a Regional Flavor* (Global Institutions). New York: Routledge.

Sweig, Julia. 2010. A New Global Player: Brazil's Far-Flung Agenda. *Foreign Affairs* 89 (6) November/December: 173–184.

Takiff, Michael. 2010. *A Complicated Man: The Life of Bill Clinton as Told by Those Who Know Him.* New Haven, CT: Yale University Press.

Taubman, William. 2004. *Khrushchev: The Man and His Era.* New York: W. W. Norton.

Tavares, Rodrigo. 2009. *Regional Security The Capacity of International Organizations.* New York: Routledge.

Tetlock, Philip, Richard Lebow, and Geoffrey Parker, eds. 2006. *Unmaking the West: "What If?" Scenarios That Rewrite History.* Ann Arbor: University of Michigan Press.

Tetlock, Philip. 2011. In an interview to the *Washington Post.* Online at http://wapo.st/1MEfbZI (accessed August 1, 2015).

Theiss-Morse, Elizabeth. 2009. *Who Counts as an American?: The Boundaries of National Identity.* New York: Cambridge University Press.

Thomas, Chris D., Alison Cameron, et al. 2004. Extinction Risk from Climate Change. *Nature* 427: 145–48.

Thomas, Daniel. 2001. *The Helsinki Effect: International Norms, Human Rights, and the Demise of Communism.* Princeton, NJ: Princeton University Press.

Thompson, Nicholas. 2009. *The Hawk and the Dove: Paul Nitze, George Kennan, and the History of the Cold War*. New York: Henry Holt.

Thucydides. 2003. *History of the Peloponnesian War*. Translated by Rex Warner. New York: Penguin Classics.

Thurow, Lester. 1992. *Head to Head: The Coming Battle among Japan, Europe, and America*. New York: William Morrow.

Tickner, Ann. 1992. *Gender in International Relations: Feminist Perspectives on Achieving Global Security*. New York: Columbia University Press.

Time to Call the Sweep? *The Economist*. November 18, 2010. Online at http://www.economist.com/node/17519770 (accessed September 25, 2012).

Tomaszewski, Fiona. 2002. *A Great Russia: Russia and the Triple Entente, 1905 to 1914*. Westport, CT: Praeger.

Tran, Mark. 2015. Phenomenal success for new film that criticises China's environmental policy. March 2. Online at http://bit.ly/1wKtjov (accessed May 7, 2015).

Tran, Mark. 2015. Phenomenal Success for New Film That Criticizes China's Environmental Policy. March 2. Online at http://bit.ly/1wKtjov (accessed May 7, 2015).

Trinitapoli, Jenny and Alexander Weinreb. 2012. *Religion and AIDS in Africa*. New York: Oxford University Press.

True, Jacqui. 2009. Feminism. In *Theories of International Relations*, ed. Scott Burchill et al. 4th edition. New York: Palgrave Macmillan, 237–59.

Tumulty, Karen. 2011. Will Obama Be Reelected? The Economy Could Hold the Answer. *The Washington Post*, August 5, A1.

U.S. Department of State. 2014. Trafficking in Persons Report. Online at http://www.state.gov/j/tip/rls/tiprpt/2014/index.htm (accessed January 29, 2015).

UN Documents. *Report of the World Commission on Environment and Development: Our Common Future*. 1987. Online at http://www.un-documents.net/wced-ocf.htm (accessed July 15, 2013).

UN High Commissioner for Refugees. 2012. Online at http://bit.ly/atXDsz (accessed July 15, 2013).

UN World Food Programme. 2015. Hunger Statistics. Online at https://www.wfp.org/hunger/stats (accessed March 31, 2015).

UNAIDS. 2015. Global AIDS Response Progress Reporting. Online at http://www.unaids.org/en/dataanalysis (accessed April 2, 2015).

UNEP, United Nations Environment Programme. 2010. *Annual Report*. New York: United Nations.

United Nations Information Service (UNIS) (2013). Press Releases. Online at http://www.unis.un-vienna.org/unis/en/pressrels/2013/unisinf488.html (accessed March 20, 2015).

United Nations Population Division. 2004. *World Population Prospects: The 2004 Revision*. New York: United Nations.

United Nations. 2004. A More Secure World: Our Shared Responsibility. Report of the High-Level Panel on Threats, Challenges and Change. http://www.un.org/en/peacebuilding/pdf/historical/hlp_more_secure_world.pdf (accessed August 1, 2015).

United Nations. 2006. Translating Principles into Practice: Humanitarian Policies. *Humanitarian Negotiations with Armed Groups: A Manual and Guidelines for Practitioners*. Online at https://docs.unocha.org/sites/dms/Documents/HumanitarianNegotiationswArmedGroupsManual.pdf (accessed March 23, 2015).

University Press.

Van Evera, Stephen. 2001. *Causes of War*. Ithaca, NY: Cornell University Press.

Van Evera, Stephen. 2001. *Causes of War: Power and the Roots of Conflict*. Ithaca, NY: Cornell University Press.

van Loon, Jeremy. 2011. Canada May Miss $6.7 Billion Carbon Offset Bill by Exiting Kyoto Protocol. *Bloomberg.com*. Online at http://bloom.bg/siU2bD (accessed July 16, 2013).

Vattel, Emerich de. 2001. *Law of Nations or Principles of the Law of Nature, Applied to the Conduct and Affairs of Nations and Sovereigns*. Holmes Beach, FL: Gaunt. Originally published in 1758.

Vernon, Raymond. 1971. *Sovereignty at Bay: The Multinational Spread of U.S. Enterprises*. New York: Basic Books.

Victor, David, Granger Morgan, Jay Apt, John Steinbruner, and Katharine Ricke. 2009. The Geoengineering Option: A Last Resort against Global Warming? *Foreign Affairs* 88 (2) March/April: 64–76.

Victor, David. 2006. Recovering Sustainable Development. *Foreign Affairs* 85 (1) January/February.

Volkan, Vamik and Norman Itzkowitz. 1984. *The Immortal Ataturk: A Psychobiography*. Chicago, IL: University of Chicago Press.

von Clausewitz, Carl. 1982. *On War*. New York: Penguin Books. Originally published in 1832.

Walker, Gordon. 2009. Globalizing Environmental Justice: The Geography and Politics of Frame

Contextualization and Evolution. *Global Social Policy* December (9): 355–82.

Walker, Gordon. 2012. *Environmental Justice: Concepts, Evidence and Politics*. New York: Routledge.

Wallechinsky, David. 2006. *Tyrants: The World's 20 Worst Living Dictators*. New York: Harper Paperbacks.

Wallerstein, Immanuel. 1979. *The Capitalist World-Economy*. Cambridge, UK: Cambridge University Press.

Wallerstein, Immanuel. 2004. *World-System Analysis: An Introduction*. Durham, NC: The Duke University Press.

Walley, Noah and Bradley Whitehead. 1994. It's Not Easy Being Green. *Harvard Business Review* 72 (3) May/June: 46–51.

Walt, Stephen. 1987. *The Origins of Alliances*. Ithaca, NY: Cornell University Press.

Walt, Stephen. 1991. The Renaissance of Security Studies. *International Studies Quarterly* 35 (2): 211–39.

Walt, Stephen. 1998. One World, Many Theories. *Foreign Policy* 110 (Spring): 29–46.

Walt, Stephen. 2005a. The Relationship between Theory and Policy in International Relations. *Annual Review of Political Science* 8: 23–48.

Walt, Stephen. 2005b. Taming American Power. *Foreign Affairs* 84 (5) September/October: 105–120.

Waltz, Kenneth. 2001. *Man, the State and War*. New York: Columbia University Press.

Waltz, Kenneth. 2010. *Theory of International Politics*. Long Grove, IL: Waveland Press.

Wapner, Paul. 2002. Paradise Lost? NGOs and Global Accountability. *Chicago Journal of International Law* 3 (155): 155.

Ward, Martin. 1999. Who Are the Many? *The Ottawa Citizen*. August 2, B6.

Waters, Tony. 2006. The Persistence of Subsistence Agriculture. Lanham, MD: Lexington Books.

Waylen, Georgina. 2010. A Comparative Politics of Gender: Limits and Possibilities. *Perspectives on Politics* 8 (1) March: 223–31.

Webb, James. 2014. *The Long Struggle against Malaria in Tropical Africa*. New York: Cambridge University Press.

Webb, Michael and Steven Krasner. 1989. Hegemonic Stability Theory: An Empirical Assessment. *Review of International Studies* 15 (2): 183–98.

Weinberg, Leonard and Ami Pedahzur. 2003. *Political Parties and Terrorist Groups*. New York: Routledge.

Weiss, Michael and Hassan Hassan. 2015. *ISIS: Inside the Army of Terror*. New York: Regan Arts.

Weiss, Thomas. 2004. The Sunset of Humanitarian Intervention? The Responsibility to Protect in a Unipolar Era. *Security Dialogue* 35 (2): 135–153.

Weiss, Thomas. 2007. *Humanitarian Intervention: Ideas in Action*. Cambridge, UK: Polity.

Weiss, Thomas. 2012. *Humanitarian Intervention: Ideas in Action*. Cambridge, UK: Polity.

Welsh, Jennifer M., ed. 2004. *Humanitarian Intervention and International Relations*. New York: Oxford University Press.

Wendt, Alexander. 1992. Anarchy Is What States Make of It: The Social Construction of Power Politics, *International Organization* 46 (2): 391–425.

Wendt, Alexander. 1999. *Social Theory of International Politics*. Cambridge, UK: Cambridge University Press.

Wendt, Alexander. 2003. Why a World State Is Inevitable. *European Journal of International Relations*, 9 (4): 491–542.

Westad, Odd Arne. 2007. *The Global Cold War: Third World Interventions and the Making of Our Times*. New York: Cambridge University Press.

Westad, Odd Arne. 2007. *The Global Cold War: Third World Interventions and the Making of Our Times*. New York: Cambridge University Press.

Whalley, John. 1997. Why Do Countries Seek Regional Trade Agreements? In *The Regionalization of the World Economy*, ed. Jeffrey Frankel. Chicago: University of Chicago Press, 63–86.

White, Brian. 2007. *Britain, Détente and Changing East-West Relations*. London and New York: Routledge.

Wibben, Annick. 2011. *Feminist Security Studies. A Narrative Approach*. New York: Routledge.

Wieviorka, Michel (2007). From Classical Terrorism to "Global" Terrorism. *International Journal of Conflict and Violence*, 1 (2): 92–104.

Wieviorka, Michel. 2007. From Classical Terrorism to "Global" Terrorism. *International Journal of Conflict and Violence* 1 (2): 92–104

Willets, Peter. 1983. *The Non-Aligned Movement: The Origins of a Third World Alliance*. London, UK: Pinter Publishing.

Williams, Michael. 2006. *Deforesting the Earth: From Prehistory to Global Crisis, an Abridgment*. Chicago: University of Chicago Press.

Williamson, David G. 1998. *Bismarck and Germany 1862–1890*. 2nd edition. Seminar Studies in History Series. New York: Longman.

Wittkopf, Eugene and James McCormick, eds. 2004. *The Domestic Sources of American Foreign Policy: Insights and Evidence*. Lanham, MD: Rowman & Littlefield.

Wittkopf, Eugene. 1990. *Faces of Internationalism: Public Opinion and American Foreign Policy*. Durham, NC: Duke University Press.

Wohlforth, William C. 1999. The Stability of a Unipolar World. *International Security* 24 (1): 5–41.

Wohlforth, William C., ed. 2003. *Cold War Endgame: Oral History, Analysis, Debates*. University Park: Pennsylvania State University Press.

Wolfe, Nathan. 2011. *The Viral Storm: The Dawn of a New Pandemic Age*. New York: Times Books.

Woodall, Pam. 2011. Hey Big Spenders. *The Economist*. Special Edition: The World in 2012, 140.

Woodall, Pam. 2011. Hey Big Spenders. *The Economist*. *Special Edition: The World in 2012*, 140.

Woods, Kevin, Palkki, David, and Stout, Mark, eds. 2011 *The Saddam Tapes: The Inner Workings of a Tyrant's Regime, 1978–2001*. New York, NY: Cambridge University Press.

Woods, Michael and Mary Woods. 2007. *Droughts (Disasters Up Close)*. Minneapolis, MN: Lerner Publications.

Woods, Ngaire. 2007. *The Globalizers: The IMF, the World Bank, and Their Borrowers*. Ithaca, NY: Cornell University Press.

Woodward, Bob. 2007. *State of Denial: Bush at War. Part III*. New York: Simon & Schuster.

World Bank. 2015. GDP (Gross Domestic Product) Online at http://data.worldbank.org/indicator/NY.GDP.MKTP.CD (accessed April 12, 2015).

World Health Organization. 2014. Malaria: Key Facts. Online at http://www.who.int/malaria/data/en/ (February 17, 2015).

World Resources Institute. 2015. Online at http://www.wri.org/

World Trade Organization. 2015. Online at http://bit.ly/a8VhKw (accessed April 18, 2015).

Wright, Lawrence. 2006. *The Looming Tower: Al Qaeda and the Road to 9/11*. New York: Vintage Books.

Wrong, Michela. 2002. *In the Footsteps of Mr. Kurtz: Living on the Brink of Disaster in Mobutu's Congo*. New York: Harper Perennial.

Wurzel, Rüdiger and Connelly, James. 2012. *The European Union as a Leader in International Climate Change Politics*. New York: Routledge.

WWF. 2015. Species Threatened by Climate Change. Online at http://wwf.panda.org/about_our_earth/aboutcc/problems/impacts/species/ (accessed March 29, 2015).

Yankelovich, Daniel. 2005. Poll Positions. *Foreign Affairs* 84 (5) September/October: 2–16.

Yergin, Daniel and Joseph Stanislaw. 1998. *The Commanding Heights: The Battle Between Government and the Marketplace That Is Remaking the Modern World*. New York: Free Press.

Young, Michael. 2010. Development at Gunpoint? Why Civilians Must Reclaim Stabilization Aid. *Foreign Affairs*. December 19. Online at http://fam.ag/hqPHpb (accessed July 18, 2013).

Zahariadis, Nikolaos. 2008. *State Subsidies in the Global Economy*. New York: Palgrave Macmillan.

Zakaria, Fareed. 2008. *The Post-American World*. New York: W. W. Norton.

Zaslavsky, Victor. 2004. *Class Cleansing: The Massacre at Katyn*. New York: Telos Press Publishing.

Zelikow, Philip and Condoleezza Rice. 1995. *Germany Unified and Europe Transformed: A Study in Statecraft*. Cambridge, MA: Harvard University Press.

Zellen, Barry S. 2009. *Arctic Doom, Arctic Boom: The Geopolitics of Climate Change in the Arctic*. Westport, CT: Praeger.

Ziegler, Jean. 1981. *Switzerland Exposed*. New York: Schocken Books.

Zinn, Howard. 2002. *The Power of Nonviolence: Writings by Advocates of Peace*. Boston, MA: Beacon Press.

Zizek, Slavoj. 2009. Berlusconi in Tehran. *London Review of Books*, 31 (14), July 23: 3–7.

Zoellick, Robert. 2012. *Robert Zoellick on China 2030 Report: Transcript of Media Questions and Answers*. Bejing, China, February 27. Online at http://bit.ly/zHjAiy (accessed July 19, 2013).

Zubok, Vladislav. 2007. *A Failed Empire: The Soviet Union in the Cold War from Stalin to Gorbachev* (The New Cold War History). Chapel Hill: University of North Carolina Press.

Zubok, Vladislav. 2014. With His Back Against the Wall: Gorbachev, Soviet Demise, and German Reunification. *Cold War History* 14 (4): 619–645.

Credits

Index